MODERN NEPAL

A Political History, 1769-1955
Volume 1: 1769-1885

MODERN NEPAL

A Political History, 1769-1955
Volume 1: 1769-1885

RISHIKESH SHAHA

MANOHAR
2023

First published 1990
Reprinted 1996
Reprinted in one Volume 2001, 2023

ISBN 978-81-7304-403-8

Published by
Ajay Kumar Jain *for*
Manohar Publishers & Distributors
4753/23 Ansari Road, Daryaganj
New Delhi 110 002

Printed at
Rajkamal Electric Press
B 35/9 G T Karnal Road Indl Area
Delhi 110 033

In fond memory of
my beloved wife Siddhanta,
known to her many friends and relatives as
Sanu Mana,
who was proud of being a Rana
but sacrificed her personal interests
and pleasures for my sake,
and to whom I owe everything in life.

Preface

This is a running account of political trends and developments in Nepal during a period of about two hundred years from the rise of King Prithvinarayan Shah (1769-1775), the founder of the present Shah dynasty till the end of the post-Tribhuvan revolutionary era. As it has run into nearly 650 pages, the publisher has decided to bring it out in two volumes in order to make it more convenient for the reader.

I have therefore chosen to close the first volume with the chapter on Maharaj Prime Minister Ranoddip Singh (1877-1885). His assasination by the sons of his youngest brother, Dhir Shamsher, ended the era of preeminence of seven brothers (Sat Bhai) including Jang Bahadur Kanwar Rana, the founder of the hereditary rule of Rana prime ministers who kept the kings as mere figureheads. Ranoddip's murder resulted in the removal of the descendants of Jang Bahadur and his five other brothers from the roll of succession to the prime ministership. The near-absolute power of the office thereafter became the monopoly of the members of the family of the youngest of seven brothers, Dhir Shamsher.

Following this historic transfer of power, the second volume opens with the chapter on Bir Shamsher who, as the eldest of Dhir Shamsher's seventeen sons, was the first of them to become the Maharaj Prime Minister. The volume deals with the administration of seven members of the Dhir Shamsher branch of the Rana family, which dominated Nepal for a period of sixty-five years. It also gives an account of the 1950-51 revolution, which brought the tentative beginnings of democracy and restored the king's traditional authority by putting an end to the 104 year old Rana rule. The last chapter in the book surveys the post revolutionary Tribhuvan era until 1955, the year in which King Tribhuvan the harbinger of democracy died.

I have four reasons for ending my history of modern Nepal in 1955: First, the 30 year rule which the Public Record Office and the India Office Library in London observe for opening their historical records to the public is, to my mind, a sound one because a fair interval of time will enable writers and researchers to take a detached and objective view of the events and present them in the right perspective. Second, the 30 year rule imposes on historians a practical constraint of a salutary nature in so far as they can hardly do justice to their subject without making use of the source materials available in these two archival centres. Third, as I have personally been involved deeply in Nepali politics during the last 30 years, I may be inclined to take a rather subjective view of the critical issues and events of the period. Last but not least, I have already published two books on the post-Tribhuvan period, and I humbly commend them to all those who may be interested in my interpretation of the more recent political past. These books are entitled *Nepali Politics – Retrospect and Prospect* (Delhi: Oxford University Press, second edition, 1978) and *Essays in the Practice of Government in Nepal* (Delhi: Manohar, 1982).

My fellowship from the Woodrow Wilson International Center for Scholars (1976-77) and the East-West Center, Honolulu (1984) has enabled me to write the first twelve chapters of this book. I should, therefore, like to take this opportunity to express my thanks to both the centres for their generous assistance.

I am most grateful to the British Council for its generous grant which paid for my travel to London and all my expenses during my three-month stay there. I spent most of my time reading the files of correspondence between the British envoys in Kathmandu and their government in India and London from 1929 through 1954 and also the contemporary records of notes and minutes by the officials of the British Foreign Office and the India Office in the files dealing with Nepal. I need hardly say that my perusal of all these records has immensely enriched my understanding of the Nepali history of the period.

For the earlier period, my task was greatly facilitated by the researches and published dissertations on specified periods of Anglo-Nepal relations by a number of Indian scholars over the last two decades, though their focus had been on Nepal's foreign relations rather than on internal politics. Let me take this opportunity to express my indebtedness to K.C. Chaudhuri, B.D. Sanwal, Satish Kumar, Ramakant, Asad Husain, M.S. Jain and Kanchanmoy Mojumdar, all of whose contributions in the field considerably lightened my own burden.

Among the more recent European and American authors from whose books I have most profited in writing this history are John Pemble, Leo E. Rose and John Whelpton. I owe a debt to all of them. Like others who have written on different aspects of the Nepali history, I have also drawn on the published works of William Kirkpatrick, Francis (Buchanan) Hamilton, Henry T. Prinsep, B.H. Hodgson, Orfeur Cavenagh, T. Smith, Laurence Oliphant, Daniel Wright, J.T. Wheeler, and H.A. Oldfield in the 19th century and those of Sylvain Levi, Perceval Landon, G.H.D. Gimlette, W.B. Northey, C.I. Morris and Francis Tuker in the 20th century.

I have also found useful the works of D.R. Regmi, Bhuwan Lal Joshi, Mahesh Chandra Regmi, L.F. Stiller and Krishna Kant Adhikari among the Nepali scholars who have written in English. My thanks are due to all of them.

My Nepali source is the *Bhasa Vamshavali* which is said to have been written and compiled by Subba Buddhi Man. I have also read with profit the historical publications in Nepali of Ambika Prasad Upadhyaya, Surya Bikram Jnawali, Baburam Acharya, Nayaraj Panta, Yogi Narahari Nath and Balchandra Sharma, to all of whom I record my gratitude. I have drawn copiously on the autobiographies of Kashi Nath Acharya Dikshit and of Balakrishna Sama, the well-known Nepali poet, painter, dramatist, critic and essayist, for information about contemporary events. I owe a special debt to both of them.

I realize that individuals do not always share the same perspective on historical trends and events, though every attempt must be made to reach a consensus on the date and sequence of events if history is at all to attain the level of scientific analysis and objectivity required of an academic discipline. However, the interpretation of historical issues and trends is always influenced by the writer's value system – I purposely want to avoid using the expression 'personal bias' because of its pejorative overtones. We must be clear in our minds that value-premises do influence the viewpoint from which reality is studied. But they do not in any way determine whether the factual data and relations among variables that are observed and analysed are correct: experience makes the determination. The fact remains that values and judgements are implied in our pursuit of truth as in all purposeful behaviour. A 'disinterested' social science has never existed nor can it ever exist unless we assume that analysts are capable of eliminating their own values.

From this standpoint my history of modern Nepal is apt to be different from somebody else's, and I strongly feel that everyone has his own view of historical trends and events. I had long planned to write my account of the nation's past according to my lights, and it took me quite a few years to do so.

Let me just add at the end that though I have greatly profited by frank discussions on different aspects of this history with several of my friends who have chosen to remain anonymous, the opinions and the conclusions in the book are my own. I shall, however, fail in my duty if I do not thank Father John Locke and Dr. Harka Gurung for reading my manuscript carefully and providing me with valuable insights into several issues dealt with in this study. My grateful thanks are due to Mr. and Mrs. Jharendra S.J.B. Rana who very kindly provided me with rare photographs of the Shah and Rana families for inclusion in this work. All the single photographs of kings and prime ministers of Nepal, however, belong to the private collection of Lieutenant General Indu S.J.B. Rana and his wife both of whom, had they been around, would have been very pleased to see them published in this form. Let me take this opportunity to record my profound indebtedness to them. I cannot of course forget to thank my friend, Meg Sheffield, for steadily encouraging and inspiring me to write this book as well as others in the past.

3 June 1989 RISHIKESH SHAHA

Contents

1

The Setting

Separated from the Tibetan region of China by the Himalayan Range and Tibetan border mountains on the north, and surrounded by Indian territory on the other three sides, Nepal is situated mostly on the southern slope of the Himalaya to the north-east of India. The Himalaya has proved to be a great physical and climatic barrier and, in a way, marks off Nepal and the South Asian region as a separate social and cultural unit from the rest of Central Asia. This does not, however, mean that there has been no physical contact or exchange of trade and culture between Nepal and Central and East Asia across the Himalaya. Several passes on the northern border of Nepal which cross the Himalaya into Tibetan territory have all along proved useful for purposes of local trade and transit. The Nepali Himalaya has twenty-one passes in general use, some of which are of considerable strategic significance. One of them is the Kuti pass in Tibetan territory, through which the Chinese-built Kathmandu-Lhasa highway (Arniko Raj Marga) runs. This is the first all-weather motorable road to cross the main Himalayan barrier and serves as a concrete example of how the revolutionary changes effected by modern technology in the global geostrategy has made it possible to overcome the topographical obstacle to some extent.

The Nepal-Tibet borderland has also been crossed, in the past, by Buddhist and Christian missionaries, highland traders and Nepali and Chinese-Tibetan armies, while several batches of immigrants have also trekked south across the Tibetan highlands to settle in the beautiful valleys enclosed in the great barrier of the Himalaya. Despite the imposing barrier of the Himalaya that separates South Asia from Central and East Asia, the difference between these two vast Asian regions in terms of ethnic, cultural and socio-psychological factors is not nearly as rigid and definite as is sometimes made out.

The Nepali territory that lies in the trans-Himalayan zone between the main Himalayan crest and the Tibetan border mountains is largely reminiscent of Tibetan landscape and culture. There are within Nepal several centuries-old subcultures of diverse origin with considerable influence over some sections of the present-day population. Those are related mostly to cultural patterns that have been traced back to Central Asia or the highland communities of South-East Asia. The Manjusri tradition, for example, is said to have come to Nepal from Central Asia where it is still alive. And some of the communities in Nepal are practitioners of Indo-Tibetan Buddhism. The intricate multifaceted nature of Nepal's cultural heritage has deeply influenced the Nepali world-view, which sometimes tends to regard the country as an intermediate and twilight zone between South and Central Asia, touching both regions and not exclusively attached to either.

The dominant cultural ethos in Nepal, however, derives its origin and influence from India. Nepal has been subject to the major tradition of Hinduism as well as its subsidiary traditions with their emphasis on the mother godlings and the clan deities. India's influence has been so dominant in all spheres of Nepali life that the Nepali people, by way of reaction, feel impelled to appear different from Indians at every possible opportunity. This is seen as almost essential for purposes of national identity in the context of the present-day political reality in the world. Nepal's fear of absorption into the Indian mother culture has been heightened by the tendency of some of the Indian leaders to over-emphasize their concept of 'greater India' in politico-cultural terms. In their zeal to counterbalance the tendency, Nepal's intellectuals are inclined to misrepresent the impact and nature of Nepal's relationship with China, which has been intermittent and never as close as its relationship with India.

For over a millennium, until the first decades of the present century, the Kathmandu Valley, also known as the Nepal Valley in the past, served as the principal entrepot for trans-Himalayan trade. A repository of culture from both Indian and Central Asian sources, it has been a conveyor of Nepali and Indian cultural products and influences across the Himalaya. Nepal's geographical frontiers have changed from time to time with the circumstances of its history and the shift in the centre of political gravity. The Kathmandu Valley because of its accessibility, temperate climate, and fertile soil has remained at the centre of the political stage. This, however, does not mean than it has always been the pivot of power. Unless we are prepared to take seriously the exaggerated and fictitious claims of panegyrists of some of the rulers about the extent of their territory, it is not possible to define the geopolitical boundaries of Nepal in ancient and medieval times.

During the Licchavi period (A.D. 400 to A.D. 879) the Kathmandu or Nepal Valley was under either a single king or dual rule at times but thereafter separate chieftaincies or fiefdoms sprung up within its confines. The process of disintegration seems to have set in with the rise and fall of chieftains with local influence in scattered pockets. The feudal overlords of Pharping, Nuwakot, Banepa and Patan considerably influenced the politics of the Nepal Valley during the medieval period. The Kathmandu Valley, having come under the sway of the Thakuri rulers of Nuwakot for two centuries after the Licchavi period, was ruled by early Mallas from the beginning of the 13th century, and by Jayasthiti Malla and his descendants from A.D. 1382. The valley had split into a number of political units after the rule of Yaksha Malla (A.D. 1428-1482). There were at least three independent kingdoms of Bhadgaun, Kathmandu and Patan by the end of the 15th century.

In 1955 Professor Giuseppe Tucci of the Ismeo Institute of Rome and a noted Nepali scholar-cum-ascetic, Yogi Naraharinath of the Kanphatta order of the Gorakhnath sect, discovered independently of each other the Dullu pillar and other inscriptions. This discovery brought to light the rule of the Malla kings in the Karnali region covering roughly the period from the 11th to 14th century. It has not only enabled us to locate the successive invasions of the Kathmandu Valley by King Jitari or Jayatari Malla from the Khas area of the Karnali region but has also made us realize for the first time that there existed contemporaneously other centres of power and civilization within the present day territory of Nepal. The Malla Kingdom reached the height of its power during the reign of Prithvi Malla, who ruled over a large area consisting of Guge, Purang, Kumaun and Garhwal. The kingdom extended as far as Dullu to the south-west, Mustang to the north-east, and Kapilavastu and Rupandehi to the south-east. Prithvi Malla's inscriptions indicate that he ruled between A.D. 1338 and A.D. 1358.

Prior to the unification of Nepal under the House of Gorkha which subsequently became the ruling Shah dynasty of modern Nepal, the present–day territory of Nepal was divided into several kingdoms or principalities. Besides the three kingdoms of Bhadgaun, Kathmandu and Patan, there existed in the west alone 46 principalities. These included

Chaubise, or Twenty-four Principalities, in the Gandaki region of central Nepal and the *Baise*, or Twenty-two Principalities, in the Karnali region of western Nepal. Beyond the Mahakali river, the present western boundary, were the kingdoms of Kumaun and Garhwal, and further to the west were the *Bahra Thakurai*, i.e., the Twelve Principalities and the *Athara Thakurai*, i.e., the Eighteen Principalities between the Tons and the Satlaj rivers.

In the south-east, the kingdoms of Makwanpur, Chaudandi and Vijayapur emerged under the rulership of the different branches of the Sen dynasty of Palpa. The last two had their capitals at Saptari and Morang in the tarai respectivly and also comprised the Kirati communities in the eastern hill districts of the present-day kingdom of Nepal. Although the above states nominally recognized the supremacy of several of the more powerful among them, they were virtually independent and engaged in continual warfare. The chaotic state of relations among these states prepared the way for the rise of the Gorkhalis, and, ultimately, for the formation of the modern state of Nepal. The present state of our knowledge does not enable us to write a comprehensive history of the entire area that comprises the modern state of Nepal. The information that we possess is limited mostly to the Kathmandu Valley, and many books have been published on the subject. As a matter of fact, so much has been written that the history of the Kathmandu Valley, which is after all a small part of the total area of today's kingdom of Nepal, has begun to pass for the medieval history of Nepal as a whole.

Under the circumstances it will only be fair and proper to assume that it was the Gorkhali conquest during the last quarter of the 18th century and the first decade of the 19th century that gave the entire territory comprising present-day Nepal a single name and a strong central government. Even the kingdoms of Kumaun and Garhwal to the west of the Mahakali river which marks Nepal's western boundary with India today, were incorporated in Nepal by 1794. The western Himachal comprising the Bahra Thakurai, that is, the Twelve Principalities, and the Athara Thakurai, that is, the Eighteen Principalities, were also annexed to the kingdom of Nepal by 1805 and ruled as part of it till the 1814-16 war with British India. In the beginning of the 19th century, Nepal's boundaries for a time extended as far as the Tista on the east and the Satlaj on the west.

After the 1814-16 war with British India, Nepal was reduced to its present frontiers between the Mechi river on the east and the Mahakali river on the west. Nepal does not have a well-defined and compact form in geographical terms. It has a rectangular shape with jagged borders. While its physical shape has been conditioned by its history, Nepal's spectacular geography has also deeply influenced the course of its history.

POLITICAL BOUNDARIES

Nepal extends across the southern slope of the Himalaya between longitudes 80°15′ and 88°10′ east and latitudes 26°20°′ and 30°10′ north. Its great length measures 804 km., and its breadth varies between 148 km. and 161 km., nowhere exceeding 225 km. With an area of 1,41,000 sq. km. and a population of 17 million Nepal is hardly a tiny country—70 per cent of the state members of the United Nations are smaller than Nepal in terms of population and over 40 per cent are smaller in terms of area. Yet she is dwarfed by her two giant neighbours, India and China. Approximately 804 km. of the 2,400 km. Himalayan Range lie in Nepal. Nepal's international boundary with China lies in the Himalaya, either along the crest or among lesser peaks beyond it, sometimes described as the marginal Tibetan mountains. The Himalayan range and the Tibetan border mountains in fact constitute a natural frontier in depth. Travel and commerce across the Nepal-Tibet border has been regulated by the Nepal-China agreements since 1956. In October 1961, the Nepal-China boundary treaty was signed, following the demarcation of the boundary line and the setting up of boundary pillars, wherever possible, along the northern frontier.

Nepal has a 804 km. long free and open border with India on the South. This boundary is demarcated by pillars set up at regular intervals, similar to the markers found along the United States-Canada border.

To the north-east, Nepal touches the Indian state of Sikkim, from which it is separated by Kanchenjunga and Singhalila ridge. South of the Sikkim line, the lesser foothills and the Mechi river demarcate Nepal's eastern border with the Darjeeling District of West Bengal in India. India's strategic land route to Assam, passing between Bangladesh on the south and Sikkim and the Buddhist Kingdom of Bhutan on the north touches the south-east corner of Nepal at this point. It is there that Nepal and Bangladesh are separated by less than twenty miles of Indian territory.

The Mahakali river marks Nepal's western boundary with India and drains only a narrow strip of westernmost Nepal. Beyond it is the

Kumaun Himalaya of India.

Only a few countries in the world, e.g., Mongolia, Botswana, Lesotho and Malawi, are as heavily dependent on one country alone for trade and transit facilities as Nepal. Nepal is completely landlocked: the nearest seaport is more than 402 km. away. Nepal has no viable outlet to the sea except across India, and must rely on that country for trade and transit facilities. Nepal's distance from the sea largely accounts for its backwardness in trade and development during the last century. Nepal's role, even in the profitable entrepot trade between India and the Tibetan region of China, suffered a decline ever since the beginning of the twentieth century as a result of the opening of the alternate trade route to Lhasa through Kalimpong and the Chumbi Valley in Tibet.

PHYSICAL DIVISIONS

The hilly region from Sikkim to Kumaun has four natural divisions, created by the mountain ridges of Kanchenjunga, Gosainthan, Dhaulagiri and Nanda Devi, running almost parallel to each other. Between these huge mountain ridges are large self-contained river basins named after the rivers by which they are drained: the Kosi region in the east, the Gandaki region in the centre, and the Karnali region in the west. The Mahakali basin is mainly in Kumaun. Each of the river systems includes one or two tributaries which rise in Tibet and enter Nepal through deep gorges. All of them slope towards the south and are fed by streams from the neighbouring mountain glaciers, some of which descend 20,000 feet before they reach the plains.

The parallel ranges of the main Himalaya, the Mahabharat and the Chure (Siwalik) alternate with characteristic landbelts popularly known as the *bhot*, or highlands, the *pahad*, or mid-montane region, the *bhitri madhesh*, or inner tarai and the *madhesh*, or the tarai lowlands. Each of these regions has its distinctive physical environment, population, agriculture and economy. The high *bhot* valleys are situated to the north of the main Himalayan range. Between the high Himalaya and the Mahabharat range lies the broad hill complex of the *pahad* country. Cramped for space, as it were, between the Mahabharat and the lower Chure hill chain, are the *bhitri madhesh* or inner tarai valleys which are called *duns* in India. To the south of the Chure hill chain lie the *madhesh* or the tarai lowlands.

ETHNIC COMPOSITION

From the very beginning, Nepal has been inhabited by diverse peoples with different racial, cultural and linguistic backgrounds. Because of the physical divisions of the country these peoples have developed in some degree of isolation from each other. Nepal's north-south river systems and rugged transverse ridges have hindered the development of east-west communications. If various areas of Nepal are not readily accessible to one another, even in our modern age, one can imagine how very much more difficult it must have been for people to move about in earlier days.

Yet they did move. Nepal was constantly subjected to pressures of immigration of peoples both from the north-east and from the south-west. It has offered shelter to waves of immigrants for at least two millenniums and perhaps longer than that. Within historical times, they have entered Nepal to escape from enemies or to seek economic and political security. The concept of 'racial purity' is nothing more than a myth in Nepal. The country is inhabited by a mixed race of people of both Mongoloid and Caucasoid stocks. There also exist to this day remnants of indigenous communities whose habitation predates the advent of the former two elements.

Elevation— that is to say, the type of agriculture conditioned by altitude—determines the ethnic character of Nepal's population which is nearly as diverse as its terrain. The Sherpas and Tamangs, who are most akin to the Tibetans, live in the northernmost region of Nepal. The Gurungs and Magars live in the mountain valleys in Central Nepal, the Gurungs preferring the slightly higher altitudes. The Rais and Limbus, collectively known as the Kiratis, live in the same belt in the eastern region of Nepal. The Khasas, Thakuris and Brahmins, whose original homes are said to be far-western Nepal, are scattered along the middle of the country together with the occupational castes like the Kamis, Damais and Sarkis. The Newars are concentrated in the Valley of Kathmandu. The Tharus live in the areas of the inner tarai and all along the tarai, we also find the Rajbamsis and Satars. Along the southernmost border next to India, we find people who pronouncedly resemble the Indians on the other side in every way. These are the Rajputs, Brahmins, Kayasthas, Yadavs and a number of occupational castes of the tarai. In addition, the Sunwars, Danwars, Murmis, Majhis, Dhimals, Chepangs, Kusundas, Rautyas, and Pohres are also important because of their more or less primitive ways of living and because of their interesting communal life and organization. Nepal's population also consists of a small section of Muslims and Christians both in the hills and in the plains.

The physical divisions of Nepal correspond roughly to the broad scheme of its well-marked racial and religious zones. The real high lands show the marked influence of Bon, or Shamanism, a primitive religion of Tibet prior to Buddhism, which in effect amounts to worship of spirits, animals and elements of Nature. The midlands or the hilly regions, consisting of the fertile mountain valleys, show the effect of the steady penetration of Hinduism from the south. But also included among the people in this area, as among the Newars of the Kathmandu Valley, are the Buddhist sub-groups who practise Mahayana or Tibetan Buddhism. The lowlands or the tarai are even more pronouncedly Hindu if we exclude the few aboriginal ethnic groups living there.

NEPAL'S RELIGIONS, CULTURE AND TRADITION

Pre-Aryan Cults

The worship of a Mother Goddess and a horned fertility god goes back to the Indus Valley civilization and Harappa culture of c. 2700-1700 B.C. This horned ithyphallic god, surrounded by animals, may well be the prototype of Shiva who, as the patron of reproduction in men, animals and plants, is known as Pashupati ("Lord of Beasts"). The oldest religion of the Kathmandu Valley seems to be related to the pre-Aryan Pashupat cult which at first merely consisted of the worship of a stone-missile (a stone weapon of war) but was later on assimilated into the doctrine of Shaivism. There are some indications that the Kirats — who are thought to be, historically speaking, the first rulers of Nepal to have had more than shadowy existence — practised a religion closely related to the Pashupat cult, but unfortunately the relics of the pre-Aryan period have not yet been unearthed, nor is there any reference to them in the inscriptions of the Licchavi period.

The Lingam-Yoni Symbol

The pre-Aryan cult of devotion encouraged the worship of images rather than abstract principles, and the first sculptural representation of specific deities was made either in anthropomorphic or in symbolic form. The main elements in the religion of Nepal are the adoration of the lingam, a short cylindrical pillar with a rounded top, and of the Cosmic Mother or Mother Goddess as the source of fertility and productivity. Shiva represents powers of destruction which are the bases of re-creation and was, and is, in its procreative aspect, worshipped in the form of Shivalinga which is both a phallic emblem, and, by symbolic inference, the tree and axis of the universe itself. The adoration of the lingam, along with the Yoni or the matrix, as the source of fertility and reproduction, lies at the root of the ancient religious cult of Nepal. The Yoni cannot stand without the *lingam* and the *lingam-yoni* symbol represents the union of the two resulting in the act of creation, that is, genesis. The sculptural representations of this union are found almost everywhere in the precincts of Nepali temples.

Various Hindu, Shaiva, and Shakta sects of Brahmanism or Hinduism and, after them, Mahayana Buddhism, also adopted and adapted the above two elements to their own needs and purposes in the process of religious evolution in Nepal. Shaivism was followed by Vaishnavism which probably sought to complete with Shaivism by popularizing ten incarnations of Vishnu.

Entry of Buddhism into Nepal

It is not precisely known when Buddhism actually entered into the Kathmandu Valley, but there can be no doubt that it did so from the south. Buddhism is said to have been introduced in Nepal by Ashoka and his daughter Charumati. However, little is known about its history except for the Ashokan pillars at Niglihava and Rupandehi in the Kapilavastu district of the Lumbini zone and the stupas at Patan and Kirtipur in the Kathmandu Valley.

While Buddhism was still engaged in its continuous and steady struggle with *Shamanism* or primitive animism across the Himalaya, Brahmanism in the Indian plains was gradually re-establishing its age-old authority in the wake of a religious revolution brought about by the comparatively new doctrine of Buddhism. As early as the 7th century A.D. Hsuan Tsang reported that Hinayana Buddhism had become extinct in most of India and was only flourishing in a few parts of western India. From about the first half of the 7th century A.D. religion in India became more and more associated with primitive ideas of sympathetic magic and sexual mysticism. Buddhism also could not escape this trend. A new vehicle, the Vehicle of the Thunderbolt, i.e., Vajrayana, had already spread throughout India by the 8th century and it grew rapidly under the Pala Kings of Bihar and Bengal (c. A.D. 760-1142)

Contact Between Nepal and Buddhist Centres of Learning in India

There had always been an exchange of students and teachers between Nepal and the Buddhist universities of Bihar and Bengal, such as Nalanda and Vikramashila. Great teachers of Buddhism, such as Shantarakshita and Padmasambhava, in the 8th century, and Atisha, in the 11th century, crossed the Himalaya on their way to Tibet and made a lasting contribution to Tibetan Buddhism. After the fall of the Pala dynasty (c. A.D. 760-1142) and the Sena dynasty (c. A.D. 1118-1199) in Bengal and of the Karnat dynasty (c. A.D. 1097-1346) in Tirhut, in Bihar, Tantric teachers from Bengal and Tirhut (Mithila) sought sanctuary in Nepal. And it was in Nepal that Tantricism had its heyday in the succeeding centuries.

Nepal as a Buddhist Cultural Link Between India and Tibet

Buddhism continued to flourish in the Kathmandu Valley stimulated by intellectuals, who were closely connected with the Buddhist universities and art schools of Bihar and Bengal. Nepal served as a relay-station for transmitting Buddhist religious and cultural products and influences across the Himalaya. For a long time, Nepal supplied teachers and artists to Tibet. Tibetan abbots and princes sent for Nepali artists, sculptors and craftsmen to beautify their temples with frescoes, or to cast statues, or to copy early Buddhist manuscripts. Tibetan monks learnt Sanskrit from Nepali teachers of Buddhism and translated into their own language the masterpieces of Buddhist ritualistic literature. Nepal has thus served as a channel for southern influences to penetrate to the north. As Professor Tucci, an authority on Indo-Tibetan cultural relations, says, "Nepal brought the task of mediation between Indian and Tibetan cultures to perfection."[1]

It was not until the 11th century that the Buddhists finally gave up their struggle in India. Thereafter, they either conformed to Hinduism or, especially after the waves of Muslim invasion had begun to assail India, sought sanctuary in Nepal and Bhutan. In the Kathmandu Valley and elsewhere in the hill regions of Nepal, however, Buddhism, in the long run, had to concede a good deal to the Brahmanic tradition, just as it had to make large concessions to the beliefs of the Bon and

Shamanist forms of animism in the northern hill areas. However, Buddhism in Nepal was re-absorbed by the Brahmanic tradition and was not destroyed or reconquered by it as in India — an important distinction.

Major Religious and Cultural Characteristics

Nepal's cultural process has been characterized by synthesis, flexibility and eclecticism. Nepali religious tradition has evolved along syncretic and symbiotic lines. The intricate texture of Nepali religious culture is woven from the main strands of Hinduism, Buddhism, Tantricism and Bon animism. The influence of these various religions are harmoniously blended in Nepali life and culture.

The similarity between the Buddhist and Hindu legends about the origin of the Kathmandu Valley emphasizes the essential harmony in religious outlook. These legends are based on the fact that the Kathmandu Valley was once a lake surrounded by mountains. According to Buddhist religious lore, a Buddha of a former aeon foresaw the future destiny of Nepal and made a pilgrimage to the lake to cast a lotus seed into its waters. A miraculous lotus blossomed in the middle of the lake, and a shaft of light, purer and more serene than the rays of the sun, issued forth from its centre. This is how the Adi-Buddha, the primordial Buddha, the Buddha from before all time, the self-existing one, the god of no-matter, was manifested directly in essence. According to John Brough's article "Legends of Khotan and Nepal", published in *Bulletin of the School of Oriental and African Studies* [vol. 12 (Part 2) (1948), p. 333-39], the lake legend was probably introduced by Tibetans who transferred to Nepal legends originally associated with Khotan (Chinese Turkestan).

Aeons passed and it became customary for the Buddha of each aeon to make a pilgrimage to the lake. Even the name of Sakyamuni occurs in legends before Gautam Buddha was actually born. It is said that Sakyamuni, in a previous incarnation as Mahasattva, performed a great act of self-immolation — letting a starving tiger feed on his own body. The Buddha of the third aeon prophesied that a Bodhisattva would appear and cause land to rise above the waters.

Bodhisattva Manjushri sensed that the deity had spontaneously manifested itself on the waters of the lake. Manjushri left his home behind seven walls in distant China. From the north-east he came through the mountains surrounding the lake. With a single stroke of his mighty sword, he cut the pass of Kotdwar through which the river Bagmati now flows out of the Valley. Thus did land appear, and the fair Valley of Kathmandu come into existence.

Even to this day once a year Nepali women of Kathmandu keep a vigil during a particular night in winter when Manjushri is supposed to return to Nepal. And on the following day both men and women pay their homage at a shrine, which contains footprints in stone, presumably of this first traveller from the north.

A Hindu version of this legend is also available in the *Puranas*. It does not change the character of the story relating to the origin of the Valley but it ascribes the feat of cutting the gorge and draining away the waters to Vishnu, in his Krishna manifestation.

The Nepalis have been able to fuse their divergent religious beliefs and practices in a remarkable way. Shiva came to be closely identified with Buddha in the gradual process of religious evolution. It may be appropriate to note in this connection that a Bodhisvatta's crown is placed on the *linga* of Pashupatinath on the eighth day of the bright half of the month of Kartik every year. Shiva is also combined with Vishnu in a syncretism such as Sankara-Narayana, Hari-Sankara or Hari-Hara.

Symbiotic

The process of religious fusion in Nepal has been clearly analysed by Dr. Stella Kramrisch thus:

> By their own myths the two great religions of Nepal (Hinduism and Buddhism) convey the same inner experience of reality. They have their own gods with their specific shapes to which India had given names and form. They came to Nepal readymade and Nepal infused them with the faith of its people so that the gods of Hinduism and Buddhism became identified with one another or assumed one another's qualities and attributes. Avalokiteshvara and Shiva coalesced in one image called Lokeshvara. To workship Buddha is to worship Shiva, says the Nepali Mahatmya, a text which guides the Brahmin pilgrim through Nepal.[2]

If the Nepal Mahatmya enjoins the Hindu pilgrim to worship Svayambhunath as Shiva, the Svayambhu Purana reciprocates the gesture by recommending the worship of Paṣhupati.

We find the images of Hindu gods in the environs of Buddhist shrines (Chaityas) and figures of Buddha in the precincts of Hindu temples. The Buddhist *Vihara* or monastery quadrangles and the Hindu temple compounds have attracted to them a myriad of shrines and images of the gods of the Hindu-Buddhist pantheon.

Hindu and Buddhist religious festivals are occasions for common rejoicing. The King of Nepal is a Hindu, but he presides over the big Buddhist festival, the *Samyak Puja*, which is held once every twelve years. The beliefs of Bon animism have also been considerably modified by contact with Hinduism and Buddhism, which, in their turn, have not remained wholly unaffected by the Bon faith. As the growth of the legend of *Bungadyo* or *Rato Matsyendra* clearly illustrates the processes of syncretism and symbiosis at work in the general evolution of the Nepali religious tradition and culture, it will be briefly examined here.

The Cult of Bungadyo or Rato Matsyendra

The worship of Bungadyo must have started as a local cult at Bungamati, a village with a population of about 3,000 people and about six kilometres to the south of Patan. It came to be related in due course to the Mahayana Buddhist tradition of Avalokiteshvara (Glancing Eye or the Lord who directs his gaze downward), Karunamaya (Compassionate), the Bodhisattva or the spiritual heir to the Dhyani (Meditational) or Tathagata (Thus-come, Thus-gone) Buddha, Amitabha (Boundless Light). Avalokiteshvara was well-known for his compassion for the suffering humanity and regarded as the giver of rain and fertility. The syncretic Nepali religious tradition subsequently associated Avalokiteshvara with Shiva as Lokeshvara who also possessed the same attributes as the aforementioned Bodhisattva. Over a period of centuries, the story of Avalokiteshvara as Lokeshvara, which could be a manifestation of either Shiva or Buddha, was so completely assimilated into the cult of the deified Natha Yogin Matsyendra that today the image of Avalokiteshvara is identified as Matsyendranath.

A quick look at the chronology of the cult itself will show the working of the processes of symbiosis and syncretism in actual practice. The oldest Nepali chronicle, the Gopalaraja Vamshavali, whose final redaction was completed during the reign of King Jayasthiti Malla (1381-1395) does not even mention Matsyendranath and merely states that King Narendradeva and his preceptor, the priest Bandhudãtta, were responsible for inaugurating the festival of Bugma Lokeshvara. One of the longer versions of the Svayambhu Purana which must have been composed after the beginning of Yaksha Malla's reign (1428-82), also does not mention Matsyendranath. The deity referred to is Lokeshvara or Avalokiteshvara and the reason given for bringing the deity to the Valley was a severe drought which lasted for twelve years. All the later accounts, whether in Nepali or in Newari, which belong to the 19th and the 20th centuries, show an interweaving of the standard legends of Matsyendranath and Gorakhnath from Bengal and other parts of India with the Buddhist tradition of the Valley.

The Story of Matsyendranath

It may also be appropriate to refer to the broad outline of the story of Matsyendranath which has obviously grown in telling. The subsequent Hindu and Buddhist rescensions, in spite of their differences in minor details and emphases, share the following features in common: (a) The advent of Avalokiteshvara Matsyendranath was preceded by a prolonged period of drought and famine brought about by Gorakhnath; (b) the deity was brought from Kamarupa (Assam or Mt. Kotpala); (c) the persons responsible for abducting the deity and bringing him to Nepal were King Narendradeva, Vajracharya Bandhudatta and a Jyapu or an ordinary farm hand named Ratna Cakra; (d) they had to surmount several obstacles before they could secure the deity for Nepal; and (e) there ensued differences about where the deity should be enshrined and his car festival held.[3]

Today both Hindus and Buddhists celebrate the *jatra* or the car festival of Matsyendranath and the exhibition of an upper garment or shirt, said to have belonged to him, is an annual event of public importance. The day on which the festival falls in the month of June is declared a public holiday and the King and all high ranking officers of the state are also present in person to watch the *bhoto jatra* or the showing of the shirt of Matsyendranath along with a mammoth gathering of people.

The Durga Cult

The Durga cult and its practices are inextricably mixed up or intertwined with the cults of other goddesses of diverse origins — the indigenous *mais* (mothers) and *ajimas* (grandmothers), the terrible aspects of the Buddhist Tara or Saviouress, the personification of the goddess of small-pox as Shitala-Hariti. Like them the collective Durga cult is also fused with the Bhairava cult. Some of the manifestations of the mother and grandmother goddess like Varahi, Guhyesvari and

Chhinnamasta are aspects of the collective Durga cult known as Astamatrika, Navadurga and Dashamahavidya whereas some others like Vajrayogini and Vajrabarahi appear to be distinct entities of the Vajrayanic Buddhist pantheon. Nepali culture is full of varied female divinities most of whom are syncretisms and are held in equally high esteem by both Hindus and Buddhists.

Thanks to the syncretic nature of Nepal's religious tradition and culture, only a few goddesses can be identified as Brahmanical, Buddhist and indigenous or folk in terms of their specific traits and attributes.

Let us take the example of Indrayani whose temple stands on the left bank of the River Vishnumati. She is worshipped by the common folk as Kankeshvari Ajima, an indigenous or local mother goddess. The Hindus worship her as Varahi and Dhumavati, manifestations of the two different collective Durga cults, Astamatrika and Dashamahavidya respectively, whereas the Buddhists worship the goddess as a form of Tara or Saviouress. Examples of this kind can be easily multiplied. The goddess with her shrine at Mahipi on the way to Balaju is popular among the common folk as the indigenous Mahipi Ajima. The Hindus worship her as Maheshvari, another Durga aspect, and the Buddhists as Jnaneshvari who is enshrined there with her consort Yogambara.

The Cult of Kumari or "Living Goddess"

According to Mary Slusser, there are at least two 13th century manuscripts concerned with choosing, ornamenting and worshipping Kumari but the Kumari institution in the Kathmandu Valley cannot be traced with certainty to a period before the 13th century. The cult of Kumari (Virgin) or 'the living goddess' who represents the virgin aspect of Durga, the Brahmanical goddess par excellence, may have come from Kangra or Bengal like other religious cults and survived in Nepal. But it is doubtful if in India the goddess was ever worshipped in the body of a Buddhist girl as in Nepal. Although there are lesser Kumaris, such as those of Kvabahal (Kathmandu), Haka-Bahal (Patan) and Chaturvarna Mahavihara (Bhaktapur), the principal Kumari or the Raj Kumari (the state or royal Kumari) is a goddess of considerable importance and resides in Rajalakshmikula-Vihara popularly known as Kumari Bahal in one of the principal buildings of the Kathmandu Darbar square. Except for the rich woodcarving which is full of the iconography of Mahisasuramardini, the slayer of the demon, and other related Durga manifestations and the Kumari's or the living goddess's personal living quarters on the third floor, the Kumari Bahal is typical of a three-storey vihara in which the groundfloor is assigned to the Five Dhyani (Meditational) Buddhas and the *agama*, the secret sanctum, is situated above it.

The office of the state or royal Kumari is always held by a Shakya girl belonging to a family associated with one of the Kathmandu viharas (bahals). Here is a clear case of a Buddhist girl embodying a Brahmanical divinity. When first chosen, the Kumari is normally a girl of 3 or 4, said to be without blemish and blessed with thirty-two special signs of her divinity.

One of the most important events respecting the principal Kumari is her annual procession, the Kumari chariot festival which coincides with Indra Jatra, the festival at the end of the rainy season (toward the end of September) to thank Indra, the rain god, for giving rains and making a good harvest possible. The Indra Jatra lasts much longer than the Kumari festival which is merely a three-day affair. On the last day of the Kumari festival or the Indra Jatra, His Majesty the King himself comes to Hanuman Dhoka to receive the Kumari's blessings for the ritualist or divine renewal of his mandate to rule. According to tradition, the Kumari's blessings were said to have been acquired by King Prithvinarayan Shah (1769-1775) when he invaded the town of Kathmandu during the combined celebration of the Indra and the Kumari Jatra on 26 September 1768. Each year after the consecration rite which consists of the King's receiving the *tika* from the Kumari's hand, the little 'living goddess' is put in her temple-like chariot. Her attendants, two Shakya boys representing Bhairava and Ganesha, are placed in smaller separate chariots and all the vehicles are drawn by the goddess's devotees along the prescribed route every day, each day visiting a particular quarter of Kathmandu where the Kumari is worshipped by the populace.[4]

Many legends are current about the institution of the Kumari but they vary in time, place and the cast of characters. The most popular tale is that during the reign of Jaya Prakash Malla (1735-1768) a virgin Shakya girl claimed to be possessed by Bhagavati. But Jayaprakash took her to be an impostor and banished her. But no sooner had the girl been expelled than the queen was seized with convulsions. Thereafter the King admitted his mistake and, to make amends for it, decreed that the girl be worshipped thence-forth as the goddess Durga she had professed to be. Another version of the story is that after a virgin Shakya girl died as a result of sexual molestation by Jayaprakash Malla, he established the cult of the Kumari or the virgin goddess to atone for his sin. According to the third version, Jayaprakash Malla was allowed to remain King of Kathmandu for another twelve years after he set up a temple devoted to Durga in her virgin aspect and introduced an annual chariot procession for her.

There is also a legend which credits Trailokya Malla (1561-1610) of Bhaktapur with the establishment of the institution of the Kumari. The story is that the cult of the Kumari came into being after Trailokya Malla, having lost his right to see Durga in person, was later granted permission to worship her in the body of a Buddhist girl.

The Bhairava Cult

The Bhairava cult has developed peculiar ramifications in Nepal and is related to both Brahmanical and Buddhist deities. Bhairava representing the terrible aspect of Shiva has caught the imagination of the Nepali people and acquired an important position in the art and culture of Nepal. Bhairava is also regarded as Hathudyo—a god to be feared and respected and appeased with blood and alcoholic drinks. His vahana or conveyance is a hideous dog whose favourite haunt is the cremation ground. Bhairava is associated with the mother goddesses whose cult pervades Nepali life and appears often in the viharas, temples and shrines of both Buddhist and Brahmanical deities. Among the sixty-four Bhairavas, grouped by eights with a leader, and each leader accompanying a terrifying female counterpart, a Yogini, the names of some of the textual Bhairavas popular in Nepal are Unmatta and Vatuka Bhairava. Nepali Bhairavas do not conform to the text in names or in kinds. Indigenous deities seem to have been assimilated into the Bhairava cult such as the guardian deity of the Licchavi Panchal whose members celebrated a collective feast in the name of their particular deity. In Nepal, Bhairava is worshipped in both iconic and aniconic forms and natural stones of unusual form and size are deified such as the huge boulder known as Tika Bhairava at a confluence near the Lele village. Bagha Bhairava (Vyagreshvara) of Kirtipur who is worshipped as the tongueless tiger also deserves mention in this connection.[5]

Mahakala is also one of Bhairava's epithets and assumed considerable importance as a cult in Malla Nepal. To Buddhists, he is one of the Eight Terrible ones, a defender of the law. In keeping with the syncretic religious tradition of Nepal the cults of Hindu Bhairava and Buddhist Mahakala were intertwined. Similarly, in recognition of the importance the female principle has assumed in Tantrism, a number of female deities were worshipped in the Vajrayanic style and their manifestations became tangled with those of Brahmanical Matrikas.

In the Kathmandu Valley, representations of Mahakala do not conform to the text and contain aspects of other divinities, such as, Samvara, Hevajra, Heruka. The Tundikhel Mahakala and Kala Bhairava of the Kathmandu Darbar resemble Bhairava as much as Samvara.

In the Nepali pantheon, Hindu and Buddhist gods and goddesses, partly because of the pervasive influence of Vajrayanic Tantricism, are found to interchange their names and even sex, but not their salient features and functions. Lhamo, who was, before conversion to Buddhism, a form of Kali and the twin sister and wife of Yama, the god of death, became the consort of Mahakala the "Great Black One", who was originally a terrible aspect of Shiva. Sarasvati, the Hindu goddess of speech and the consort and daughter of Brahma, sometimes also called Vagishvari, has been taken over by Buddhism as Manjushri whose other name is Vagishvara. The similarity of the sounds of the names Vagishvari and Vagishvara may have made this assimilation possible. But the Hindus cntinue to recognize her as one of the female goddesses of their own pantheon, and worship her at a temple which is on the same "cowtail hillock" as the great Buddhist chaitya, Svayambhunath. We find both Hindus and Buddhists worshipping the goddesses of small-pox, Sitala and Hariti, at Svayambhunath and Hadigaon with equal respects.

Prof. G.Tucci has made the following apt observation on the interrelation between these various religions and cults:

> Hinduişm has penetrated slowly from India, has prospered and has made itself at home. But it has been a superficial conquest only, in the sense that while it has assimilated native beliefs and given its own names to local cults, it has in fact adapted itself to a primitive religious world wherein the terror of men faithful to the cruel motherhood of the earth held away.[6]

Religion and Art

Religion has not only been the main source of inspiration and motifs of

Nepali art but has also imbued art with a spirit of synthesis. Stone pillars on which Vishnu is represented as sleeping on the Serpent of Eternity or seated on Garuda, the mythical sun-bird, are a common sight in the Kathmandu temples. These pieces of sculpture are not merely relics of old Vaishnavite culture but also symbolic representations of the story of the mythological origin of the Kathmandu Valley. In painting, the frontispieces of the Vamshavalis (chronicles) show the Buddhist shrine of Svaymbhunath by the side of a lotus in full bloom, followed by the image of Pashupatinath enclosed in a semi-circle of flowers with the rising sun on the right and the new moon on the left. It is said that the chaitya of Svayambhunath represents the god of no-matter which symbolized the original religion of Nepal; other symbols are indicative of the historical sequence in which Nepali religious culture developed. Most of the temples, both Hindu and Buddhist, are built in the Nepali style of construction, which represents a blend of the shikhar-cum-pagoda modes of temple architecture. Stone pillars of Vishnu atop on the back of Garuda, the pictures on the frontispieces of the Vamshavalis and the Nepali style in temple architecture emphasize the sum total of various influences on indigenous tradition and are emblems of the plurality of Nepali religious culture.

CONCLUSION

Situated between the two vast land belts of Asian civilization, India and China, Nepal has been a meeting-ground of influences from both these civilizations. While the Nepalis have retained physical features and other traits from the Mongoloid stock of the north, they have been influenced culturally much more from the south. When Muslim empires replaced the Hindu kingdoms in the wake of Muslim invasions of India in the ninth century and in the centuries following, Nepal became a political sanctuary for many fugitive Hindu chieftains. The Malla Dynasty which ruled the Nepal Valley from the thirteenth century until 1768-1769 and the present Shah Dynasty are said to have been founded by emigrant Hindu chiefs, keen on protecting their religious integrity from the inroads of Muslim power in India. Under such circumstances, it was no wonder that the rule of the Mallas and the Shahs led to a distinct Sanskritization of Nepali culture, at least at the official level, if not on a comprehensive popular scale.

The process of Sanskritization has been a dominant social phenomenon in Nepal for many centuries. From the Thakalis in remote central Nepal to the Magars, Gurungs, Rais, Limbus and Sunwars in the middle belt and further down to the Tharus at the base of Siwalik foothills, the people of Nepal have been gradually but steadily brought under the influence of this dynamic cultural force. As further evidence of the impact of this phenomenon, it may be pointed out that during the Rana period, some of the more pronounced Mongoloid ethnic groups like the Tamangs and Thakalis had applied to the government for initiation into Hindu religious tradition through acceptance of Brahmins as priests and restrictions on beef-eating.

The history of Nepal from the earliest times abounds in examples of indigenous tribes making false pretence to recent descent from some worthy Indian lineage. This is because of their natural desire to associate themselves with the culture and tradition of the socially and politically dominant groups.

The process of Sanskritization had been aided by enforced imposition of Brahmanic social systems and codes of behaviour by successive regimes in Nepal. It is interesting to note that the most important of these social codes were formalized during the administration of three of the outstanding men in Nepal's history—Jayasthiti Malla of Kathmandu (1382-1395), Rama Shah of Gorkha (1606-1633), and Jang Bahadur Rana, Prime Minister of Nepal (1846-1877). All of them were orthodox Hindus and sought to codify the structure of Nepali society, both Hindu and non-Hindu, within a basically orthodox Hindu framework.

The legal and social code introduced by Jayasthiti Malla under the guidance of five Indian Brahmins conformed to the rules of conduct laid down by Manu, the ancient lawgiver of the Hindus. The Newar population of the Kathmandu Valley was initially divided into sixty-four sub-groups purely on the basis of their occupations and crafts. In due course, the sub-groups acquired all the decadent features of the Hindu caste-system. At the time of Jayasthiti Malla, the Buddhist components of the Newari population were, as a rule, given the same social rank as their Hindu counterparts. The Buddhist clergy was put on an equal footing with the Brahmins or Kshatris, depending upon their status at birth. This social code governed Newari society not only during the Malla period, but operates to this day with a few modifications.

Rama Shah's code achieved the same results in consolidating the social system in Gorkha as did that of Jayasthiti Malla in Kathmandu.

A system of four castes (*varnas*) and thirty-six sub-castes (*jats*) was introduced in Gorkha. The latter figure is apt to be symbolic because the code does not seem to specify anywhere the actual number of sub-castes. However, the caste-Hindus, who found themselves in a minority, were forced to relax the rigid rules of their caste-system in order to accommodate the majority native population. A legal code based on Shastric injunctions, but modified with due respect for indigenous tradition, was introduced by Rama Shah. Rama Shah was also responsible for the standardization of weights and measures, fixation of pastures and rule for use of water for irrigation. His code covered a wide range of social and economic relations. As it was the first codified system in the hills, it produced a tremendous impact on the surrounding areas as well.

Both the codes introduced by Jayasthiti Malla and Rama Shah were limited in their scope and application. The unification of Nepal under the Shah Dynasty necessitated a comprehensive legal and social code applicable to the whole country. Initial measures in this respect were adopted during the reign of King Rana Bahadur Shah (1777-1799) and by Mukhtiyar Bhim Sen Thapa at the time of King Rajendra Bikram Shah (1816-1847). But the distinction of completing the task goes to Prime Minister Maharaj Jang Bahadur Rana during the reign of King Surendra Bikram Shah (1847-1881). *Mulki Ain* or the legal code under King Surendra Bikram was based on a few cardinal tenets of Brahmanic belief relating to inter-caste relations and caste-pollution. It does, however, allow each of the ethnic groups to follow its own tradition as long as it is not in direct conflict with the basic tenets of Hinduism. The Raj Guru or the Royal Preceptor, armed with the arbitrary power of dispensation and excommunication, i.e., authorizing people to dispense with the observance of religious rules, and punishing them for their non-observance, became a firm part of the establishment.

The pressing need for the modernization of Nepal seems to have checked the tendency towards Hindu orthodoxy. The most dynamic aspect of current cultural development is in the area of conflict between Sanskritizing and modernizing processes. Younger intellectuals tend to reject those traditional Hindu concepts and values which come into conflict with their distinctly 'modernist' orientation whereas the masses of the people are still steeped in their age-old mental stupor.

This situation is further aggravated by the ever-widening gulf of difference between a few thousand of the modern educated elite and the vast majority of the people in basic thinking and outlook on life and development, religion and morality. However, there is hope in the reflection that, throughout history, the Nepali tradition in religion, philosophy and culture, has, at its best, been characterized by an eclectic spirit of tolerance and understanding and that Nepal, in keeping with this tradition, will permit the logic and demonstration of science to correct the archaic, obsolete and superstitious aspects of religious and cultural life.

NOTES

1. Giuseppe Tucci, *Nepal—The Discovery of Malla* (London: George Allen and Unwin Ltd., 1962), p. 83.
2. Stella Kramrisch, *The Art of Nepal* (New York: The Asia Society, Inc., 1964), p. 15.
3. John K. Locke, S.J., *Karunamaya — The Cult of Avalokitesvara — Matsyendranath in the Valley of Nepal* (Kathmandu: Sahayogi Prakashan, 1980), pp. 293-98.
4. Michael Allen, *The Cult of Kumari — Virgin Worship in Nepal.* (Kathmandu: University Press, 1975) p. 8..
5. Mary Shepherd Slusser, *Nepal Mandala — A Cultural Study of the Kathmandu Valley* (Princeton, N.J.: Princeton University Press, 1983), pp. 235-39.
6. Giuseppe Tucci, op. cit., p. 51.
7. M.N. Srinivas, *Social Change in Modern India* (Berkeley, California: University of California, 1966), p. 6.

2

The Rise of King Prithvinarayan Shah (1769-1775) (Raja of Gorkha from 1743)

The Ruling House of Gorkha

The ruling houses of eight of the Chaubise or twenty-four principalities—Bhirkot, Garahun, Paiyun, Satahun, Nuwakot, Kaski, Dhor and Gorkha—came of the same stock as of the Khan family or their branches that had originally ruled from Bhirkot. The original family of the Khans split into sub-branches that later called themselves Shahs and Shahis. As the ruling house of Gorkha later became the ruling dynasty of Nepal, its links with the Rajput clan in Chitor, however tenuous, received a good deal of attention. However, the circumstances described in the chronicles do not always agree with the historical facts.

Some of the chronicles trace the ancestry of the ruling house of Gorkha to Bhupati Ranaji Rao of Chitor. According to these sources his son, Fateh Singh, refused to give his daughter in marriage to a Muslim Chief and invited his wrath. Fateh lost his life and kingdom in a fierce battle with the invading army. His two brothers, Udayambar and Manmath, continued to offer resistance to the Muslim usurper from Udaipur and Ujjain respectively. It was Manmath's son, Bhupal Ranaji, who entered the central Himalayan region and reached Ridi, near Palpa, in A.D. 1495.

Other chronicles trace the circumstances of the flight of Bhupati and Manmath to the conquest of Chitor by Ala-ud-din Khaljee (c. A.D. 1296-1316) in A.D. 1303. However, the chronicles generally agree that a descendant of Manmath, named Bhupal went to Palpa by way of Ridi from somewhere in India and settled in the village of Lasargha, situated on the Waigha Ridge on the left bank of the river Kali Gandaki.

Bhupal's son, Jain Khan, lived and died at Lasargha, but Surya Khan, Jain Khan's son, proceeded to Bhirkot and settled in a village called Khilung on the bank of the river Andhi-Khola. Of the two sons of Surya Khan, Khancha, the elder son, acquired control of Bhirkot, Garahun, Satahun and Dhor and became the king of that area. The younger son, Micha Khan, established his rule in Nuwakot and one of his descendants, named Kulmandan, adopted the title of Shah. Some of the later descendants of Micha Khan eventually seized control of Kaski and began to rule from there. While they were ruling in Kaski, Lamjung adopted as its king a prince of the family named Yasobrahma. Dravya Shah, who acquired the kingdom of Gorkha, was Yasobrahma's second son.

The credit for founding the ruling house of Gorkha belongs to Dravya Shah (1559-1570), who conquered the tribal kingdom of Gorkha and founded the Shah dynasty of that principality, which later became the ruling house of Nepal.

Long before Prithvinarayan Shah embarked upon his ambitious scheme for the incorporation of the Kathmandu Valley into his Gorkha kingdom, one of his predecessors, Rama Shah (c. 1606-1641), had already established a name and reputation for himself as a just and fair ruler not only among the Gorkhas but also in the entire midland region of Nepal. Rama Shah's name became a household word among the people in the mid-montane area because he introduced a legal code suited to the local customs and conditions of the time.

Prithvinarayan Shah (1769-1775), Raja of Gorkha from 1743, was the ninth generation descendant of Dravya Shah and the seventh generation descendant of Rama Shah. Prithvinarayan was the tenth in line of the Shah Kings of Gorkha. The military conquests and annexations of Prithvinarayan and his immediate successors were not so remarkable in themselves as for the manner in which they furthered the feeling of unity and patriotism among the people as a whole. The members of the diverse ethnic groups inhabiting Nepal joined the Gorkhali army that was ever triumphantly on the march and became partners in the great enterprise of building modern Nepal. It was thus that various races and tribes, speaking different dialects and observing different customs, were able to partake of an equal sense of pride in the name and tradition of Gorkha. It is noteworthy that even today anybody coming from anywhere in Nepal, irrespective of caste or religion, passes for a Gorkha outside Nepal; and so great is the sense of pride and respect felt by all Nepalis for the name and tradition of Gorkha that even social and political organizations of Nepalis domiciled in India and elsewhere are still called Gorkha.

The present kingdom of Nepal is in itself a concrete result of the breadth of vision and outlook of the Gorkha rulers, and is also a measure of their large-heartedness and generosity. Prithvinarayan Shah stands as a powerful force in the emergence of Nepali nationalism because he brought unity out of the prevailing chaos. In the course of his rule, Nepal made a distinct advance from a loose organization of tribal systems to a kingdom.

Up to the middle of the 18th century, the territory now contained within the present boundaries of Nepal was divided into a large number of small principalities which may be classified into four major groupings. In the eastern hills and tarai were the kingdoms of Makwanpur, Chaudandi and Vijayapur, the latter two of which also contained the semi-autonomous principalities of the Kirats. In the Kathmandu Valley were the three kingdoms ruled by the Mallas; to the west of the valley lay the fiefs of the Chaubise Rajas; and in the far west was a similar group of fiefs and thaneships, twenty-two in number and called the Baise Rajas. Although many of the principalities in these four categories owed nominal allegiance to the more powerful among them or, in the cases of the Baise and Chaubise Rajas, to the Mughal emperor in Delhi, they found themselves entirely free to engage in continual warfare among themselves.

The turbulent character of their relationships eventually led to the gradual ascendancy of the House of Gorkha, which was firmly set on forging a unified state of Nepal. The Shah kings of Nepal, originally belonging to the ruling House of Gorkha, played a very important part in bringing about the unification of Nepal. The role of Gorkha, a small hilly state ninety-one kilometres west of Kathmandu, is comparable, in this respect, to that of Sardinia-Piedmont in Italy and Castile in Spain.

The kingdom of Gorkha, as compared to some of the other kingdoms in Nepal at the time, was insignificant in size, population and resources. But Prithvinarayan's Gorkha was possessed by a new spirit and he had the foresight to recognize the need for unification of these small principalities as a condition of future survival. As his outlook on the future was well in accord with the trend of time and history, Prithvinarayan succeeded in accomplishing his mission of unifying several chieftaincies into a sizable kingdom.

As soon as he succeeded his father, Narabhupal Shah, as Raja of Gorkha in 1743, Prithvinarayan began to prepare for the conquest of Nuwakot towards the east. Prithvinarayan had learned useful lessons from the failure of his father's attempt to conquer Nuwakot; aware of Gorkha's limitations, he immediately made plans for enhancing its military strength. On his return from a pilgrimage to Varanasi in 1744, Prithvinarayan brought back with him a number of matchlock rifles and a few experts skilled in making traditional weapons of war. He increased the number of troops by giving military training to all male citizens and distributed to them weapons made in the workshops he established.

Having made these sound preparations, Prithvinarayan attacked Nuwakot and had no difficulty in annexing Nuwakot fort and Valley in 1744. The Valley of Nuwakot, irrigated by the Trisuli and the Tadi rivers, is very fertile, and its annexation increased Prithvinarayan's revenues.

As Prithvinarayan extended his kingdom to the east, the Rajas of the principalities to the west grew jealous of him. Some of the Chaubises launched attacks on Gorkha when Prithvinarayan was fighting in the east, thus forcing him to fight on two fronts. However, by his military prowess and diplomatic skill, Prithvinarayan prevented his enemies in the west from advancing. Prithvinarayan cultivated the more important of the twenty-two principalities, like Jajarkot and Salyan, to ensure their neutrality, if not direct support, in Gorkha's armed conflict with the twenty-four principalities. He repeatedly repulsed the attacks of these chieftains and eventually defeated and subjugated his adversaries to the east—the Sena Rajas of Chaudandi and Vijayapur along with their Kirati vassals in the hills—by mounting repeated offensives.

In the east the Malla kings of the Kathmandu Valley were not inferior to him in strength and resources. Their geographical position was a great asset to them, for their valley, surrounded by high mountains on all sides, was like a natural fortress. If the passes between the mountains were carefully guarded, no enemies could make their way into it. Thus, it was by no means an easy task to conquer the valley; and it took an outstanding warrior like Prithvinarayan Shah twenty-five years to accomplish the feat. Had there been cooperation among the three kingdoms of Kathmandu, Patan and Bhadgaun, it is doubtful whether Prithvinarayan Shah could have ever conquered the valley. Prithvinarayan spared no efforts to capitalize on the situation created by internal dissension among the Malla kings of the Kathmandu Valley.

After his conquest of Nuwakot, Prithvinarayan had the hills scaled and explored, and he set up outposts on the highest hill tops. In due course, he worked his way around to the east of Kathmandu Valley and acquired control of Sindhupalchok and Dolakha, which lie on the main trade route to Lhasa from Kathmandu through the Kuti pass. In 1746, Naldum, Sankhu and Changu inside the valley itself fell into the hands of the Gorkhas. In 1747, the Gorkhalis gained possession of Lamidanda from the Raja of Patan on the understanding that his people would be free to collect grass and firewood in the forest on the slope of the ridge.

The capture of Changu and Sankhu by the Gorkha military commander, Shivaram Singh Basnyat, posed a direct threat to the town of Kathmandu and seriously compromised Jayaprakash Malla's position as its ruler. Dati, an important official of his court, had previously been executed by Jayaprakash Malla (1736-1768). Dati's brother, Taudik for the purpose of avenging his brother's death, sought to exploit the situation caused by the loss of Changu to the Gorkhas. In mid-September 1746, Taudik, aided by Rajyaprakash Malla, Raja of Patan, and his troops, surprised the palace of Jayaprakash at midnight. This forced Jayaprakash Malla to abdicate in favour of his infant son, Jyotiprakash Malla, with his mother, Dayavati, acting as Regent, but after three and a half years, Jayaprakash returned to power in April 1750.

When Jayaprakash Malla had executed his brother, Kashiram Thapa, following his failure to recover Nuwakot from the Gorkhas, Parshuram Thapa had sided with Prithvinarayan Shah. Taudik's coup now neutralized Parshuram Thapa who did not go to the aid of Prithvinarayan's forces when they were attacked by Taudik's troops. As a consequence, the well-known Gorkha military commander, Shivaram Singh Basnyat, died fighting at the battle of Sangachok in order to save Naldum for the Gorkhas.

In 1755, Prithvinarayan Shah faced a combined attack on Gorkha itself by some of the Chaubises under the leadership of four Rajas, Mukunda Sen II (1756-1782), Raja of Palpa, Trivikram Sen (1749-1765), Raja of Tanahu, Biramardan Shah, Raja of Lamjung, and Shah Bam Malla, Raja of Parbat, who were also joined in this enterprise by their long-time enemy, Siddhinarayan Shah, Raja of Kaski. The combined Chaubise forces actually captured Siranchok inside Gorkha. It took Prithvinarayan a good deal of skill and effort to repulse them.

Following the battle of Siranchok in 1755, a truce was concluded between Gorkha and the Chaubises. Thereafter Prithvinarayan Shah lost no time in conquering Chitlang, Tistung, Palung and Pharping to the south-west of the Kathmandu Valley, and he was quick to exploit the circumstances surrounding the enthronement of Bishwajit Malla as Raja of Patan in the wake of the assassination of Kalidas, an important minister of the Patan court, by hirelings in the pay of Raja Jayaprakash Malla of Kathmandu. He annexed Kulekhani, Irpa, and Malta without difficulty in 1756. But in the following year his first attack on Kirtipur was repulsed.

The trade route to Lhasa by way of the Rasuwa pass, to the northwest of Kathmandu, had fallen into the hands of Gorkha after the conquest of Nuwakot. The route through the Kuti pass in the northeast was also controlled by the Gorkhas after they had taken possession of Sindhupalchok and Dolakha. For these reasons, Jayaprakash Malla, Raja of Kathmandu, was forced to conclude a pact with Gorkha in January 1757 to share the revenue from trade with Tibet, but this treaty remained ineffective from the beginning and was formally abrogated in 1759.

The Historic Struggle between Gorkha and Kathmandu to control the Trade Routes to Lhasa

The struggle between Gorkha and Kathmandu to control the trade routes to Lhasa dates back to the sixteenth century. The sixteenth and seventeenth centuries represented a critical phase in Nepal-Tibet relations. By 1600, Tibet was in a state of virtual anarchy, and the struggle between various Tibetan Buddhist sects was approaching a climax. The powerful fifth Dalai Lama, head of the Ge-lug-pa (Yellow-hat) sect, acquired temporal and spiritual authority over both Lhasa and Shigatse in the first half of the seventeenth century with the help of the Khoshote-Mongols. However, it was only in A.D. 1645 that the Sakya dynasty of Tsang, adherents of the Nying-ma-pa (Red-hat) sect, was completely overthrown and tenuous union of the two provinces was effected.

During these crucial years in the seventeenth century, Nepal had two strong and ambitious rulers in Rama Shah of Gorkha (c.1606-

1633) and Pratap Malla of Kathmandu (c.1624-1674). Both of them, after an initial preoccupation with their internal problems, turned their attention to developments across the Himalaya. Their motivation was the control of the main trade route between Nepal and Tibet for strategic as well as economic reasons. Although the two Nepali incursions into Tibet cannot be dated precisely, they took place around A.D. 1630. Probably the Gorkha conquests in Tibet under Rama Shah threatened one of those two important trade routes in Tibet. This necessitated immediate and bold action on the part of kings of the Kathmandu Valley to preserve their near monopoly on Nepal-Tibet trade.

Pratap Malla's Treaty with Tibet

According to Nepali sources, the Kathmandu Raja, Pratap Malla, sent an expedition to Tibet under his relative Kazi Bhim Malla, who overran Kuti and advanced some distance towards Shigatse. At that point the representatives of the Lamas met him and negotiated a peace settlement. The terms of this treaty may be summarized as follows:

1. Kathmandu was given joint authority with Tibet in the border towns of Kuti and Kerung.
2. Newari merchants of the Kathmandu Valley were permitted to establish thirty-two trading houses in Lhasa.
3. The Kathmandu Government was given the right to post a representative called Nayo at Lhasa.
4. Tibet agreed not to impose any charges or customs duties on Newar merchants who engaged in trade with Lhasa and other places in Tibet.
5. Tibet promised to pay one tola of Buki gold (valued at Rs.12), 13 mashas of silver (valued at Re.1 per masha) and three patties of silver per annum.
6. It was provided that Nepal would mint coins for Tibet though these coins would be struck in the name of the King of Nepal. Tibet would use these coins internally and would pay for having the coins minted in Nepal.
7. Tibet agreed that in all its trade with India, even that conducted by merchants other than the Newari merchants, the route through Kathmandu would be utilized in preference to the routes to the east (Sikkim and Bhutan or Tawang).[1]

This treaty contributed largely to the commercial prosperity of Kathmandu. Kathmandu played a very strong and profitable intermediarly role in trade between India and Tibet until early in the twentieth century, when the British opened the route to Lhasa through Sikkim and the Chumbi Valley following the Younghusband expedition of 1904. Thus the provision of the Pratap Malla treaty requiring all traders to use the route through Kathmandu for trade with Tibet was a great achievement for the Malla Raja, as a monopoly of this trade has always been a primary objective of any Nepal Government.

Apparently Nepal's control over Kuti lasted for less than 70 years. The Jesuit missionary, Father Grueber, who travelled from Tibet to India through Nepal in 1661, described Kuti as "one of the two chief cities of the Kingdom of Nekbal,"[2] indicating that Kathmandu controlled the city at that time. However, another Jesuit missionary, Father Ippolito Desideri, who resided in the same area for six months in 1721, indicated a change in the status of Kuti.[3] According to Chinese sources, it was the fifth Dalai Lama who regained the areas of Tibet seized by Pratap Malla. However, according to a Chinese source, entitled *Chin-ting-K'uo-er-k'a* (Summary account of the subjection of the Gorkhas), even after that date, the inhabitants of Kerung were required to pay an annual tribute to Kathmandu of several of the falcons and hawks that abound in that area.

In the first half of the eighteenth century Tibet became an area where indigenous religious sects and political factions, various Mongol tribes and China all vied for dominance. At first the Ch' ing dynasty was not too anxious to extend its military and political authority in Tibet despite the religious bond the Ch'ing dynasty emperors had with the yellow-hat sect in Tibet. The Ch'ing dynasty was, however, afraid that its main opponents—the Mongols on the borders of Tibet—might acquire ascendancy in Tibet. It was actually Mongol interference in Tibetan politics that led to the first Ch'ing military expedition into Tibet in 1718 and the subsequent expedition in 1720, which resulted in the first establishment of Chinese suzerainty in Tibet and the elimination of Mongolian influence.

In 1750, during a revolt organized by a number of Lhasa civil officials, the Chinese Resident as well as most of the Chinese officials and staff were assassinated. Even the Dalai Lama lost control of the situation as his orders were ignored by the rebels. Emperor Chi'ien-lung sent another military expedition to restore Chinese authority, avenge the murder of the Chinese officials, and help the Dalai Lama solve his problem with the civil officials at Lhasa and elsewhere. As a result of this expedition, a new administrative system was set up under which the Dalai Lama retained broad temporal powers that were to be exercised under the supervision of the Chinese Resident or the Amban. The day-to-day administration was to be run by a board of four officials known as Ka-lons under the general authority of the Dalai Lama.

If Nepal in the first half of the eighteenth century had enjoyed as strong and virile a leadership as the Gorkha dynasty was to provide in the first half of the nineteenth century, Nepal would probably have taken advantage of the chaotic situation in Tibet to promote its interests there. However, Nepal was going through a period of change and decline, and the Malla kingdoms in the Kathmandu Valley were busy with their own internal squabbles. The Gorkha kingdom's power was no doubt on the ascendancy, but whatever its attitude towards Tibet, the conquest of the Kathmandu Valley was considered a necessary prerequisite for any expansion to the north.

By 1757 the Gorkhas had entrenched themselves across both the major trade routes leading from Kathmandu to the Tibet border, and were actually in a position to cut off Kathmandu's trade with the north at their own discretion. That Gorkha under Prithvinarayan Shah did not do so but instead concluded a treaty with the Malla Raja of Kathmandu, Jayaprakash Malla, on a basis of equality, was probably due to the revenue it obtained through customs duties on this trade.

The agreement of 3 January 1757 between Kathmandu and Gorkha provides that:

1. Kathmandu and Gorkha were to exchange representatives.
2. Representatives of both Gorkha and Kathmandu were to be stationed in Tibet and all consignments of goods were to be opened jointly.
3. Both Kathmandu and Gorkha currency would be used by the Tibetan state and Gorkha and Kathmandu were to share equally in the coinage sent to Tibet.
4. All goods brought to Tibet without the consent of the Kathmandu and Gorkha representatives would be confiscated and the goods divided equally between the two states.
5. All gold, silver and currency brought either from Tibet or India would be shared between the two powers.
6. Any inhabitant of Kathmandu or Gorkha going to Tibet would be required to take the path through Nuwakot (controlled by the Gorkhas at that time).[4]

The Malla Raja of Kathmandu, Jayaprakash Malla, must have made these concessions to Gorkha only because of dire necessity. The treaty not only put Gorkha on an equal footing with Kathmandu but also gave the former a more effective control of the trade with Tibet. This treaty has been referred to even in the 1774 trade agreement between Nepal and Tibet.

Brief Occupancy of the Throne of Patan by Prithvinarayan's Brother

The rulers of the three kingdoms in the Valley had not been able to stop their internecine strife and conflict even in the face of the imminent and ever-present threat posed by Prithvinarayan's military and diplomatic manoeuvres over a protracted period of time. The kingdoms of Kathmandu and Bhadgaun were at cross-purposes with each other and the ministers or pradhans of the kingdom of Patan were engaged in their mischievous game of siding with one or the other of the two and changing their own kings according to their convenience and whims, thereby aggravating the situation of instability and uncertainty in the valley.

The Pradhans or Pramans (court-ministers) of Patan were very powerful and chose kings and got rid of them at will. They put Rajyaprakash Malla, brother of Jayaprakash Malla, on the throne of Patan, and then replaced him with Bishwajit Malla. In October 1760, they made Raja Jayaprakash Malla of Kathmandu also Raja of Patan. However, the Pramans of Patan substituted Ranajit Malla, Raja of Bhadgaun for Jayaprakash in 1762. In 1763, they requested Prithvinarayan himself to become Raja of Patan, but the latter sent his brother Dalamardan Shah to officiate for him in that capacity. Dalamardan Shah was forced by these court-ministers of Lalitpur to vacate his office in 1765. He was replaced by Tej Narsingh Malla (1765-1768), the last Malla Raja of Patan. Although Dalamardan's brief tenure as Raja of Patan was not in itself much of an asset to Gorkha's struggle for complete ascendancy in the Kathmandu Valley, it may be said to have prepared the people of the Valley psychologically for the eventual acceptance of the ruler of Gorkha by them as their own leader.

Prithvinarayan's objective was to force the Valley into economic isolation before making an all-out attempt at its conquest. Prithvinarayan was already in control of both the eastern and the western trade routes to Lhasa from the Kathmandu Valley. In 1762, he conquered Makwanpur, Timalkot, Sindhuli and Hariharpur on the Mahabharat range southwest of the Valley, thereby blocking the southern routes to India. He was thus successful in imposing an economic blockade on the Valley; but while carrying out his design, he clashed with two external forces: those of the Nawab of Bengal and those of the East India Company.

First, Ali Mir Kasim, the Nawab of Bengal, was instigated by the displaced ruler of Makwanpur, Digbandhan Sen (Prithvinarayan's first wife's brother), to attack the Gorkha stronghold in Makwanpur. Prithvinarayan checked the advance of troops led by Mir Kasim's general, Gurgin Khan, at Makwanpur, destroyed his army and forced him to retreat in 1763.

The Kinloch Expedition of 1767

The other external force Prithvinarayan clashed with was the growing strength of the British represented by the East India Company. By 1767, the Gorkha King had been laying siege for some time to the three ancient kingdoms of Kathmandu, Patan and Bhadgaun in the Kathmandu Valley. Emissaries of Jayaprakash Malla, the last Malla Raja of Kathmandu (1736-1768), requested the agents of the East India Company in Betiah and Patna for assistance against the Gorkhas.

This appeal was fully endorsed by the Capuchin missionaries who had been active in the Kathmandu Valley ever since their expulsion from Tibet by the Chinese about 1745. Kashmiri traders, sannyasis and gosains or merchant-pilgrims had always had their finger in the pie of the profitable trade between Tibet and Bengal that passed through Nepal. They were at the time keenly interested in reviving their declining trade with the Company's assistance. The economic blockade of the Kathmandu Valley by the Gorkhas had also led to a decline in the English Company's share of profit in the trade with Nepal and Tibet. It was the hope of reviving this gainful trade and of opening up the China trade through Nepali territory that led the Company to come to the assistance of Jayaprakash Malla.

In June 1767, the East India Company in Calcutta dispatched a military expedition to Nepal, on the request of Jayaprakash, to lift the siege laid by the Gorkhas on the Kathmandu Valley. This poorly organized and ill-timed expedition, led by G. Kinloch, never reached the Valley, partly due to the lack of provisions and personnel, and partly due to the commencement of the monsoon rains. The contingent of the

Company's forces under Kinloch had a short, sharp engagement with Prithvinarayan's forces at Sindhuli and were forced to withdraw into the districts of Bara, Parsa, and Rautahat in the low-lying tarai plains between the Kathmandu Valley and the northern border of the district of Betiah in the province of Bihar in India.

The failure of the Kinloch expedition and the reluctance of the East India Company to renew its attempt to rescue the beleaguered kings of the Kathmandu Valley frustrated the commercial aspirations of the Company at least for the time being. The conquest of the Kathmandu Valley by Prithvinarayan Shah in 1769 further dimmed the prospects for the East India Company's gains in Nepal, for Prithvinarayan Shah was fully conscious of the rapid rise of the Company from a commercial concern to a political power, and was only too familiar with the saying that had gained wide currency in the Indian plains at the time: "With the merchant comes the musket; and with the Bible comes the bayonet." His own experience with the Kinloch mission merely served to strengthen his strong suspicion of the motives of the European traders, represented by the East India Company, and those of the Christian missionaries. The fact that after two years the Company was still in control of tarai land, which was first occupied by the Company's forces during retreat from Sindhuli, proved to him a concrete manifestation of the Company's acquisitive nature.

Foreigners who had trade and other vested interests in the Kathmandu Valley were very much perturbed by the Gorkha conquest. The Capuchin missionaries, who were quite active during the Malla rule, took leave of Prithvinarayan on 4 February 1769 and withdrew from Nepal. The missionaries apprehended that Prithvinarayan's zeal to protect the Hindu religion might totally restrict the scope for their activities inside Nepal.

Like the missionaries, the Muslim owners of the Kashmiri trading houses in the Valley also feared persecution by Prithvinarayan on religious grounds and on suspicion of their past dealings and connections with the Malla rulers. The Kashmiri Muslims had had an important role to play in conducting trade between India and Tibet through Nepal. Prithvinarayan tried to persuade them to carry on their trade as before, but most of the Kashmiri trading houses closed down their business premises and their owners returned to India. In retaliation, Prithvinarayan wrote to the Dalai Lama and other high Tibetan officials at Lhasa, urging them to prohibit the import of foreign goods and to avoid any connection with the English or the Mughals in India.

Indirectly, the Kinloch expedition seems to have aroused British interest for the first time in the possibility of trade with Tibet and West China by way of Nepal. This is shown by the 1768 request of the Company's Board of Directors in London for intelligence regarding the scope for trade with the above-mentioned countries in cloth and other European commodities. Thus, in a limited sense, the Kinloch expedition may be regarded as the precursor of the Bogle and Turner missions to Tibet in 1784 and 1783. As Dr. Schuyler Camman has remarked in his book, *Trade Through the Himalayas*, "probably it was during the expedition into Nepal under Captain Kinloch, when the English first had a close view of the Himalayas, that aroused their interest in what might lie beyond the mountains."[5]

There was great resistance against the Gorkhas from inside the Kathmandu Valley itself. The small principality of Kirtipur, situated on a hillock three miles to the south-west of Kathmandu, fought fiercely against the Gorkhas in 1764, as they had done in 1757 when first attacked. It was only as a result of the third attack, in 1766, that the Gorkhas finally conquered Kirtipur. Kirtipur fell to the Gorkhas only because the three Valley kingdoms could not jointly come to its rescue as on the previous occasions of the Gorkhali attack on it owing to the machinations of the Pramans or the court ministers of Patan. The Gorkha conquerors avenged their past failures to take Kirtipur in a mean and vile manner by cutting off the ears and noses of a large number of the surviving people.

Eastward Expansion following the Setback in War with Chaubises

Having repulsed the attack by his external enemies and taken other precautionary measures to prevent British commercial penetration into the sub-Himalayan and the Tibetan regions, Prithvinarayan started his military offensive against the Kathmandu Valley. His economic blockade had weakened the kings and the people of the Valley, and they could now put up very little resistance against him. Jayaprakash Malla, the Raja of Kathmandu, had already fled from his palace when Prithvinarayan marched into Kathmandu on the day of Indrajatra or the chariot or car festival of Indra, the god of rains, in 1768 (26 September) and took his throne. Once Kathmandu had fallen into his hands, it did not take him long to take possession of Patan, and Bhadgaun was also incorporated in Prithvinarayan's kingdom by 1769 notwithstanding the last-ditch fight by the two displaced rulers of Kathmandu and

Patan in concert with the ruler of Bhadgaun, Raja Ranajit Malla.

After the conquest of the Kathmandu Valley, Prithvinarayan Shah found himself engaged in another war with the Chaubises in 1770. Although the Gorkhas had met with success in the initial phase of this war under the military leadership of Bamsharaj Pande, Keshar Singh Basnyat and Sardar Prabhu Malla, the Chaubises, under the leadership of Lamjung and Parbat, forced the Gorkhalis to retreat to the original boundary line of Gorkha, which was marked by the Marsyangdi river. In the east, the Gorkhali forces, led by Abhiman Singh Basnyat, along with Amar Singh Thapa and Ramkrishna Kanwar, acquired control of the kingdom of Chaudandi by 1773. Karna Sen, Raja of Chaudandi, and his minister, Ajit Rai, sought shelter with the East India Company's Government. Shortly after this, the Gorkha forces also conquered the kingdom of Vijayapur and Morang, which was being administered at the time by Minister Buddhakarna who had earlier displaced Raja Kamadatta Sen. After his defeat at the hands of the Gorkhas, Buddhakarna became a fugitive in the Purnea district of the East India Company's territory. Prithvinarayan extended his kingdom as far as Irsamalwa and Chyangthapu in the eastern hills and incorporated into Nepal what is today the Mechi Zone.

Prithvinarayan's rapid expansion towards the east can be explained in the light of two considerations. First, the acquisition of the kingdoms of Chaudandi and Vijayapur with sizable territory in the tarai would have yielded him revenue vitally needed for further territorial expansion. Prithvinarayan must have also felt that it would be much more difficult to conquer the principalities of the Chaubise Rajas, whose territory in the hills yielded much less revenue than the eastern kingdoms in the tarai.

Second, Prithvinarayan Shah was apprehensive of the possibility of the East India Company's opening a new route to Lhasa through the eastern hills. By 1770, the East India Company had no illusion about the possibility of resuming its normal trade with Tibet through Nepal on the traditional pattern. Prithvinarayan was fully aware of the importance of trade with Tibet and very much wanted to develop it, but not on the conditions under which it was carried on by the Malla rulers of the Kathmandu Valley. Prithvinarayan wanted to circulate his currency in Tibet but not on an equal rate of exchange with the debased coins of the displaced Rajas of Kathmandu and Bhadgaun, Jayaprakash Malla and Ranajit Malla, that were already in circulation there.

Further, Prithvinarayan wanted Kathmandu to acquire a monopoly of Tibetan trade by closing down trade routes to Tibet both in the east and in the west. Apprehensive of the British move to penetrate into Tibet, Bhutan had also acquired control of the outlets through the Himalaya by attacking Sikkim in 1770. That was the reason why Prithvinarayan had maintained the best of relationships with Desi Shidar, who had been Deb Raja of Bhutan since 1769. But Desi Shidar's sudden attack on Kuch Bihar in 1771 was met with a counter-attack by the East India Company Government which secured them a foothold in the sub-Himalayan area for trade with Tibet. Owing to Desi Shidar's lack of foresight, the East India Company's forces penetrated into the territory of Bhutan itself, and the new treaty with the Company was signed by a new Deb Raja. Prithvinarayan had earlier forewarned Desi Shidar of the probable consequences of his projected attack on Kuch Bihar, and once the British had moved, Prithvinarayan pleaded with the Panchen Lama at Tashilhunpo to offer mediation in the armed clash between Bhutan and the Company, but nothing substantial came out of these moves.

Prithvinarayan dispatched a large embassy to the Panchen Lama in Tashilhunpo with a letter advising the Lama to interpose his mediation between Bhutan and the British. The Panchen Lama, while admitting the wisdom of Prithvinarayan's suggestion, did not fail to point out that this disaster could have been averted had it not been for Nepal's obdurate stand on the question of trade through Kathmandu. Nepal's advice to the Panchen Lama for mediation boomeranged in a strange manner as it was the Tibetan offer for mediation that led to the preliminary contacts between Tibet and the British, resulting directly in Hastings' dispatch of the Bogle mission to Tibet in 1774. The principal object of the Bogle mission was to reopen the Nepal route or open some other trade route to Tibet.

Prithvinarayan, who had as real a concern for Tibetan trade as Hastings, though from a different point of view, reacted to the Bogle mission with great vigour in both the military and diplomatic spheres. An envoy was sent from Nepal to Tashilhunpo with letters for the Regent in Lhasa and for the Panchen Lama. According to the Panchen Lama's report to George Bogle, Prithvinarayan referred to his conquest of the Kirat Lands and Morang in eastern Nepal and thus indicated the closing of the trade route through that area. The following excerpt from Markham's report of the account given to Bogle by the sixth Panchen Lama throws some light on Prithvinarayan's plan.

> He (Prithvinarayan) did not wish to quarrel with this state, but if they had a mind for war, he let them know he was a Rajput; that he wanted to establish factories at Kuti, Kerant and another place, upon the borders of Tibet and Nepal, where the merchants of Tibet might purchase the commodities of his country and those of Bengal, and desired their concurrence; that he would allow the common articles of commerce to be transported through his kingdom, but no glasses or other curiosities, and desired them to prohibit the importation of them also; that he desired them further to have no connexion with the Fringies (English) or Moghuls, and not to admit them into the country, but to follow the ancient custom, which he was resolved likewise to do; that a Fringy had come to him upon some business, and was now in his country, but intended to send him back as soon as possible, and desired them to do the same with us; that he had also written about circulating his coin, and had sent 2,000 rupees for that purpose.[6]

System of Trans-Himalayan Trading

The Malla rulers of the Kathmandu Valley kingdoms had always profited from the entrepot trade between India and the Tibetan region of Central Asia that passed through Nepal. This trade was mainly conducted by Kashmiri Muslim trading houses with headquarters in Varanasi or Patna, and by Gosains (Hindu merchant-cum-pilgrim mendicants) in direct partnership with the Malla rulers themselves and also in collaboration with the Udaya traders of Kathmandu Valley. Both the Kashmiri Muslim trading houses and the Gosain merchants were strongly suspected by Prithvinarayan Shah of complicity with the Malla rulers in bringing about the unsuccessful Kinloch expedition against the Gorkhas in 1767. The Gosains were expelled from Nepal and restrictions were imposed on the trading activity of the Kashmiri merchant houses. By 1774 only two Kashmiri houses were left in Nepal. Two of the other merchant houses based in Nepal set up their business also in Bhutan, but their enterprise did not succeed because of the restrictions on trading in broad cloth and other commodities that were in demand.

However, Prithvinarayan Shah had good reasons to be interested in increasing revenue from trade, as the maintenance of his army in the field entailed a good deal of expenditure. Therefore, he sought to set up a new system of trading through the establishment of a trade mart at

Parsa Garhi, on the main route to India from Kathmandu, and at a few other points on the Tibetan border.

However, Tibet did not formally respond to the newly devised system of trade under which the Indian and Tibetan traders would bring merchandise to the established marts to be purchased by Nepali merchants and transported by them to India and Tibet as the case might be. By 1770, Tibet closed the trade routes to Nepal and Nepal-Tibet trade virtualy came to a standstill.

For a long time Nepal and Tibet had been in dispute over the circulation of Nepal-minted coins in Tibet. It had been customary for Nepal to seek to pocket a substantial part of the difference between the value of silver and gold and the face value of the coins while minting coins for Tibet. Tibet naturally wished the value of the metal it sent to Nepal to approximate the value of what it received in return, while Nepal sought to maximize its profit. As a deliberate means of financing the war against Prithvinarayan Shah, both Jayaprakash Malla and Ranajit Malla, the last Malla kings of Kathmandu and Bhadgaun, had excessively debased their coins by reducing the ratio of silver to other metals over a long period of time.

Prithvinarayan Shah was very much interested in the circulation of his coins in Tibet, and as soon as he conquered the Kathmandu Valley he sent a deputation to Tibet with newly minted coins of proper alloy struck in his name. However, Tibet refused to accept them for circulation until Prithvinarayan had undertaken to buy back at face value all the debased Malla coins. No agreement could be reached between Tibet and Nepal on the value of silver and that of coins to be minted in Nepal for Tibet in future, and on the exchange rate to be established between the new coins and the debased old coins of the Malla rulers. Prithvinarayan refused to accept responsibility for the coin sent by his enemies whereas Tibet insisted that as it had paid full value even for the debased coins, it was up to Nepal to take them back even at a loss.

The Gorkhas also intended to strengthen their bargaining position by engaging in military operations to annex new territory in the cis-Himalayan area. In 1774, the Gorkhas attacked Sikkim, and they carried their operations up to the borders of Bhutan when they seized Vijayapur the following year. Prithvinarayan was determined to close the Sikkim and Bhutan trade routes even if this meant a war with Tibet.

Toward the End of Prithvinarayan's Rule

Once the conquest of Kathmandu Valley was completed, relations between Prithvinarayan and his brothers became strained. The main cause of the brothers' dissatisfaction was that they were not adequately rewarded by Prithvinarayan for their part in extending the kingdom of Gorkha. However, Prithvinarayan's own concern for consolidation of the newly acquired territories into a powerful centralized kingdom did not allow him to satisfy the personal ambition of his brothers, who presumably each wished to be rewarded with a kingdom. Moreover, Prithvinarayan had reaped the benefit of the division of the Kathmandu Valley into three kingdoms and was fully aware of the consequences that a division of his own territory among his brothers might lead to. Although Prithvinarayan's powerful personality prevented his brothers from opposing him openly during his lifetime, they withdrew into inactivity or retirement. Even before Prithvinarayan's death his second brother, Mahoddam Kirti Shah, sought refuge in Tanahu, one of the Chaubise principalities.

Since Prithvinarayan Shah's energies were so largely engaged in expanding his kingdom, he had no time left to consolidate his newly acquired territories. In a message to his successors and future state officials, he described Nepal as a common garden for all castes of people and expressed his intention to make it a genuine piece of Hindusthan or the land of the Hindus uncontaminated by Muslims and Europeans. He also expressed his wish to introduce a legal and social code in keeping with the tradition of other illustrious kings of Nepal, like Jayasthiti Malla, Rama Shah and Mahendra Malla. But Prithvinarayan Shah did not live long enough to accomplish this end, for he died on 10-11 January 1775 at the age of 52.

By 1809 his successors had extended the kingdom from the Teesta in the east to the Satlaj in the west, and a portion of the tarai was also incorporated in it. Prithvinarayan had believed in making all the people of the conquered areas share a sense of a common stake in the future of the kingdom by extending to them equal justice and benevolence, but his successors lacked his foresight and were unable to consolidate their rule in the newly acquired territories because they failed to win the hearts and confidence of the people. Further, they neglected a valuable piece of advice left to them by Prithvinarayan Shah in his "Divine Counsel":

> The kingdom is like a yam between stones. Maintain friendly relations with the Emperor of China. Great friendship should also be maintained with the Emperor beyond the southern seas (i.e., the

British), but he is clever. He has kept India suppressed, and is entrenching himself on the plains. One day the army will come. Do not engage in offensive acts. Fighting should be conducted on defensive basis.[7]

The failure of Prithvinarayan's successors to heed this advice and warning led to their involvement in a war with China in 1792 and with the British in 1814-1816. Although the war with China did not cost Nepal much, its war with the British in India meant the loss of considerable territory to Nepal.

Prithvinarayan Shah's valour and statesmanship still inspire the people of Nepal with a sense of pride. As a result of his foresight and wisdom, a strong and viable state came into being, and the kingdom he created was to be for a long time the only independent Hindu state in the world.

NOTES

1. C.R.Nepali, "Nepal ra Tibet ko Sambandha" (Nepal-Tibet Relations), Pragati, Year II, Issue IV, NO. X.
2. Ashley, *A New General Collection of Voyages and Travels*, London, 1745-1747, Vol. IV, p. 653; quoted by Leo E. Rose, *Nepal: Strategy for Survival*, (Berkeley, University of California Press, 1971), p.14 ff.
3. Fillipo de Filippi, *An Account of Tibet, the Travels of Ippolito Desideri of Pistoia*, S.J. 1712-1727, (London, 1932), pp. 130-31.
4. C.R. Nepali, "Nepal ra Tibet ko Sambandha" (Nepal-Tibet Relations), *op. cit.*
5. Schuyler Camman, *Trade Through the Himalayas, The Early British Attempt to Open Tibet*, (Princeton: Princeton University Press, 1951), p. 25.
6. C.R. Markham, *Narratives of the Mission of George Bogle to Tibet and of the Journey of Thomas Manning to Lhasa*, (London: Trubner, 1879), p. 158.
7. Yogi Naraharinath and Baburam Acharya (ed.), *Shri Panch Bada Maharaja Prithvinarayan Shah ko Divya Upadesha* (Divine Counsel of King Prithvinarayan Shah the Great), (Kathmandu: Prithvi Jayanti Samaroha Samiti, 1951), pp. 15-16.

3

King Pratap Singh Shah (1775-1777) and Regency of Rajendralakshmi (1777-1785)

Following the death of Prithvinarayan Shah at Nuwakot, Swarup Singh Karki was sent there by the new ruler, Pratap Singh (1775-1777), with instructions to put his brother, Bahadur Shah, and his uncles, Dalamardan and Dalajit Shah, under house arrest for fear that they might create trouble in collusion with other Chaubise principalities. Dalajit Shah escaped arrest, but the last rites of his father were performed by Bahadur Shah while under detention. Prithvinarayan's full brother, Dalamardan Shah, also languished under house arrest.

The coronation of Prithvinarayan's eldest son, Pratap Singh, took place at Kathmandu on 25 January 1775. He was not of the same warlike temperament as his father but was a genial, warm-hearted person of a rather gentle nature. He loved music and poetry, and lived a life of ease and pleasure.

Early in life, he was initiated by his religious preceptor, Brajanath Pandit (Paudel), in the esoteric cult of Tantra. In keeping with the tradition of the Malla rulers of the Valley, from Pratap Malla (1624-1674) to Jayaprakash Malla (1735-1768), he practised Tantric worship of Guheshvari, a manifestation of the Hindu mother-goddess of power, Shakti. The performance of Tantric rites sometimes required participation of virgin girls in ritualistic orgies and, in his youth, Pratap Singh developed an infatuation for a Newari woman, Maiju Rani, who had been brought from Lalitpur as a child for ritualistic purposes.

During Prithvinarayan's lifetime, Pratap Singh had a son by Maiju Rani and named him Bidur Shahi. After some time, Pratap Singh's legally wedded wife, Rajendralakshmi, also bore him a son who was named Nagendra Shah. When Nagendra died a few months after his birth, the only heir left was Bidur Shahi, and Queen Rajendralakshmi began to regard this infant's mother as a thorn in her side.

With the rapid expansion of Gorkha, it became necessary to absorb into the central administration the elite families who had entrenched local influence in the newly acquired areas in addition to those families with an established tradition of service to the Shah dynasty within the original scope of Gorkhali rule. The association of non-Gorkha-based officers with the administration was viewed by the original Gorkha-based courtiers with suspicion at the beginning. Before he died, Prithvinarayan Shah himself warned his son of the growing influence of the non-Gorkha-based officers in his court. Pratap Singh's reign was characterized by the constant rivalry and conflict between Swarup Singh Karki, who was from the eastern hills, and Bamsharaj Pande, who belonged to the leading family of Pandes from Gorkha.

A brief reference to civil and military offices and the families who held them may not be out of place here. The role of Chautara was to officiate for the king at the routine meetings of the Council of State (Bhardari) and also to act as Regent during the minority of the king. The Chautara was shown due respect and courtesy as a royal relative, but he did not necessarily wield more power than other officers of state such as Kazis and Sardars who held high military and civil offices. The Bhardari, or the Council of State, was initially drawn from the leading Gorkha-based families such as Pande, Basnyat, Arjel, Khanal, Bohra, Pantha and Baniya. But with the expansion of the Gorkha kingdom, other families with influence in new areas had also to be accommodated in the Council of State.

After Pratap Singh's accession to the throne, even the functions and duties of a Chautara, normally discharged by a royal collateral, were temporarily assumed by Brajanath Pandit from Rising in the Syangja district. The position of Kazi, or minister, went to Swarup Singh Karki from eastern Nepal. Bidur Shahi's mother, Maiju Rani, continued to be the king's favourite consort. The king was thus in the hands of a clique drawn from outside Gorkha until Bamsharaj Pande, son of Kazi Kalu Pande, Prithvinarayan Shah's well-known minister, was made Kazi.

When Nepal's political agent in Varanasi, Gajaraj Mishra, grandson of Shriharsa Mishra, Prithivinarayan's relegious perceptor, visited Kathmandu to pay his respects to the new King, he pleaded for the release of Bahadur Shah and Dalamardan Shah, both of whom were under detention at the time. As a result of Gajaraj Mishra's intervention, both of them were released and allowed to live in India on state pensions.

Queen Rajendralakshmi gave birth to a second son, Rana Bahadur Shah, on 25 May 1775. Rana Bahadur Shah survived babyhood, and the influence of Maiju Rani in the palace began to decline.

Pratap Singh sought to improve his relation with both the British and the Tibetans. His interest in opening up trade with Tibet led to the conclusion of a treaty between Nepal and Tibet in 1775. The Panchen Lama expected improvement in the prospects for trade after the passing away of Prithvinarayan and almost immediately after his death the Panchen Lama wrote to King Pratap Singh Shah, the former's son and successor:

> I have heard of the death of your father, Prithi Narayan (sic). As this is the will of god you will not let your heart be cast down. You have now succeeded to the throne, and it is proper that you attend to the happiness of your people, and allow all merchants as Hindus, Mussulmans and the four castes to go and come and carry on their trade freely, which will lend to your advantage and to your good name. At present, they are afraid of you and no one will enter your country. Whatever has been the ancient custom let it be observed between you and me. It is improper that there should be more on your part, and it is improper that there should be more on mine.

The 1775 Treaty between Nepal and Tibet

The treaty of 1775 between Nepal and Tibet proved that the Panchen Lama's expectations were realistic. The main points of the treaty are as follows:

1. The rate of exchange between gold and silver would be fixed jointly by the two governments or else determined by the merchants who would settle their own rates and conduct their transactions.
2. The position of Newari *Mahajans* (merchants) and shopkeepers in Lhasa would remain unchanged.
3. The Eastern and Western Madhesh and Parbat (plains-mountain routes) would be closed even for Sanyasis (Gosains), Indians and merchants. Gorkha-Nepal would see to this on the Gorkha side. Lhasa would see to this on the Tibet side.

4. The Sikkim-Nepal boundary was fixed at the Kankai river and Nepal agreed to respect this boundary. (Tibet consented to pay Rs. 4,000 in compensation to Nepal for the death of four Brahmins who had been sent to the court of Sikkim as messengers.)

This treaty brought only a temporary relaxation of the prevailing tensions between Nepal and Tibet because it neither touched upon the main dispute with regard to Nepali currency in Tibet nor provided the type of trading structure preferred by the participants. As a matter of fact, the treaty stipulation regarding Sikkim was even violated during Pratap Singh's reign. Gorkha forces invaded Sikkim in late 1775 but did not succeed in changing the territorial limit fixed by the treaty because of a virtual stalemate in the fighting that took place along the boundary.

Pratap Singh's overtures to the British East India Company's Government resulted in the settlement of some of the issues that had arisen when the eastern tarai had been incorporated in the Gorkha kingdom during the reign of his father, Prithvinarayan Shah. He also sought to extend his kingdom towards the west and territorial gains were made between July and September 1777, at the cost of Tanahu, which lost Upardang Garhi, Chitwan and Someshwar Garhi.

Pratap Singh died on 17 November 1777 at the age of twenty-six.

Regency of Queen Rajendralakshmi (1777-1785)

Pratap Singh was succeeded as king by his infant son, Rana Bahadur Shah (1777-1799), with Queen Rajendralakshmi as Regent. The Regent Queen immediately sent for her husband's brother, Bahadur Shah, who was living in exile at Betiah on the Indian side of the border in the central tarai, and as soon as the formal mourning was over, Bahadur Shah took the reins of administration in his own hands.

Kazi Swarup Singh Karki fled to India on hearing that Bahadur Shah had left Betiah for Kathmandu. Brajanath Pandit was arrested, deprived of his caste and expelled to India on the charge of alleged complicity in an attempt on the life of King Rana Bahadur Shah. Parashuram Thapa was put in prison. Prithvinarayan's second half-brother, Mahoddam Kirti Shah, and his own brother, Dalamardan Shah, were asked to live in Varanasi for the rest of their lives, and an annual pension was fixed for them. Pratap Singh's mistress, Maiju Rani, who was pregnant at the time of her husband's death, was made to perform Sati (self-immolation) soon after she had given birth to her second son, Sher Bahadur Shahi.

Dalajit Shah, Prithvinarayan's youngest half-brother, was made Chautara. Two of Mahoddam Kirti Shah's sons, Balabhadra Shah and Shrikrishna Shah, were brought to Kathmandu and the former was made Kazi or minister. Sarbajit Rana, a Magar officer from the parental home area of the Regent Queen, was also appointed Kazi, and became the Regent Queen's right-hand man. Bamsharaj Pande, who retained his position as Kazi, was placed in charge of guarding the frontiers of Gorkha against the Chaubise rulers.

There was complete understanding between the Regent Queen and Bahadur Shah until a difference arose between them on the question of recruiting a larger force for the subjugation of Tanahu. As a result of this difference, Regent Queen Rajendralakshmi, with the help of Sarbajit Rana, interned Bahadur Shah until the latter was once again released on the request of Gajaraj Mishra. However, after his internment Bahadur Shah was not given any responsibility or work.

The reign of Prithvinarayan's immediate successors was characterized by intense rivalry for real power between the original Gorkha-based families, with a long-standing record of service to the Shah dynasty, and some of the newer families that had to be absorbed into the central administration because of their local influence in the newly acquired areas. This trend, which was already in evidence during the reign of Pratap Singh, became more pronounced during the regency of Queen Rajendralakshmi. Rajendralakshmi relied more on the officers drawn from these new families with influence outside the original jurisdiction of Gorkha, whereas the officers who belonged to the old Gorkha-based families naturally turned to Bahadur Shah for support and guidance.

Interregnum of Bahadur Shah's 10-Month Administration

Bahadur Shah, with the help of his uncle, Dalajit Shah, brought about the assassination of Sarbajit Rana, the Regent Queen's minister, and imprisoned the Queen herself in the palace on the alleged charge of having illicit relations with Sarbajit Rana. On 12 August 1778, Bahadur Shah gained control of the government for about ten months.

He had to postpone implementation of his plan for the conquest of Tanahu for four months. It was on 31 January 1779 that Bali Baniya, Bamsharaj Pande's colleague in charge of the garrison in Gorkha, captured Sura, the capital of Tanahu, without a battle. The Gorkhas were subsequently counterattacked and thrown back by Harakumaradatta Sen, Raja of Tanahu, with active assistance from Mukunda Sen II, Raja of Palpa. Bali Baniya and sixty-five other officers and men died fighting against their adversaries before Sura was ultimately abandoned on 10 March 1779.

Encouraged by the success of Tanahu, and also by dissension in Kathmandu, the Raja of Parbat hurriedly dispatched forces to Tanahu's assistance and their combined forces easily acquired control of Someshvar Garhi. When Bahadur Shah learnt of the loss of Someshwar Garhi, he rushed to Gorkha in person and dispatched an additional force to strengthen the Gorkha troops at Kabilasapur and Uparadang Garhi. These reinforced troops regained control of Someshvar Garhi on 22 April 1779, after inflicting a crushing defeat on the forces of Tanahu and Parbat.

While Bahadur Shah was in Gorkha directing war operations against the Chaubise Rajas, Regent Queen Rajendralakshmi, who was a spirited lady of firm purpose and high ambition, was not lying quietly as a prisoner in the palace. She secretly sent for Mahoddam Kirti Shah and Brajanath Pandit who were in India. Mahoddam Kirti Shah arrived at Kathmandu and disproved Bahadur Shah's allegation against the Regent Queen. She was not only set free by Mahoddam Kirti Shah's intervention, but was also able to regain her full powers as Regent on 20 June 1779.

Balabhadra Shah and Dalajit Shah, who even as Mahoddam Kirti's son and younger brother respectively, had been Bahadur Shah's partisans, were helpless against the action of their elder. Dalajit Shah not only made good his own escape but also warned Bahadur Shah, who was thus able to flee to safety in India. Shriharsa Pantha, who was held responsible for the conspiracy against the Regent Queen, had his face branded and was exiled to Tanahu. Gajaraj Mishra was deprived of his position as the Nepali agent in Varanasi, and Brajanath Pandit was appointed in his place.

As a result of an incident of a personal nature, which involved Lady Hastings, Dinanath Upadhyaya, Nepal's representative or Vakil in Calcutta, succeeded in securing the Governor-General's personal endorsement of Nepal's claim to the Rautahat district as against the appeal of Abdulla Beg, which was supported by the Company's lower-echelon officials. Regent Queen Rajendralakshmi sent prompt help to the Company's Government in response to Lady Hastings's appeal to

Nepal through its Vakil, Dinanath Upadhyaya, in July 1780, when Hastings was hard pressed to put down the rebellion of Raja Chait Singh in Varanasi.

Dinanath Upadhyaya, Nepal's Vakil or representative in Calcutta ever since the time of Prithvinarayan Shah, successfully negotiated with the Company's Government for the return to Nepal of portions of the territory of the erstwhile kingdoms of Chaudandi and Vijayapur, the possession of which had long been a matter of dispute.

Revival of British Interest in opening up Tibet as a Diplomatic Backdoor to China

Despite the failure of the Bogle mission in 1774, the British interest in opening up a route for trade with Tibet had not declined. Bogle had proposed that he himself should go to Peking at the time of the Panchen Lama's visit there. He hoped that diplomatic relations between Britain and China might be opened at Peking through the mediation of the Panchen Lama. It is quite clear that by April 1779, the use of Tibet as a diplomatic backdoor to China had become the goal of Hastings's Tibetan policy and had dwarfed considerations of frontier policy and local Indo-Tibetan trade. However, this plan also came to nought due to Bogle's death in India in 1779 and the Panchen Lama's death in Peking on 27 November 1780.

The 1783 Turner mission to Tibet was undertaken for the purpose of "extending British protection to that region for the better ascertaining of the nature of its production and of opening new sources of Commerce to our provinces." In 1784 Acting Governor-General Macpherson sent Purangir to Tibet on a similar mission.

Although these missions were obstensibly sent to convey the Calcutta Government's congratulations to the new Panchen Lama in 1783, and to attend his formal inauguration in 1784, they were motivated by the British interest in opening a new trade route to Tibet. However, nothing came of these missions except the expected piece of information about the readiness of the Tashilhunpo officials to maintain trade with Bengal on the prevailing conditions.

The Foxcraft Mission to the Government of Nepal mentioned in the proposed draft of Hastings's letter of 1 June 1784, which was intended to bring about improvement in the mutually advantageous trade between Nepal and Bengal, was merely planned on paper. The mission was probably never actually sent to Nepal; there is nothing on record about it except the draft of the letter proposed to be sent through Foxcraft.

With Lord Cornwallis's arrival in India in 1786 as the new Governor-General, trade between Bengal and Tibet suffered a great decline because he did not share Hastings's interest in it. No attempt was made to renew efforts to establish relations with Nepal until the exigencies of the Nepal-China War of 1792 forced the Governor-General to attend to developments in that area.

The passing of power into the hands of a woman naturally tempted the adversaries of the Gorkha kingdom both in the east and in the west to challenge it. The widow of Karna Sen, Raja of Vijayapur, sought to exploit the situation to her advantage by making a fresh bid for the recovery of her husband's territory of Vijayapur and Morang from the Gorkhas with the assistance of the British East India Company's Government. She also sought military assistance from Mukunda Sen II, Raja of Palpa, by offering to adopt one of his sons as her husband's heir. The Raja of Palpa did not give her any military help, but he sent his third son, Dhwajabir Sen, to be adopted by Karna Sen's widow as her husband's heir-apparent. Mukunda Sen II petitioned the Company's Government in Calcutta for its advocacy of Karna Sen's widow's case.

Mukunda Sen II also left no stone unturned to incite the Limbus of the Pallo Kirat and the Rajas of Sikkim and Bhutan against the Gorkhas. Help from the Company's Government was not forthcoming, nor were the Limbus of Pallo Kirat, with the backing of the Raja of Sikkim, eager to stir up a revolt against the Gorkhas. The leading Chaubise Rajas, whom Mukunda Sen II of Palpa had successfully mobilized against Gorkha, waited in vain for the news of unrest in the east. Their plan was to synchronize their attack on Gorkha with the start of a revolt in the east, which took place only after the Chaubises clashed with the Gorkhas. The Gorkhas, kept fully posted with information about developments in Calcutta and eastern Nepal, were also at the same time reinforcing their troops on their border with the Chaubise principalities in anticipation of an armed attack by them.

Regent Queen Rajendralakshmi depended primarily on her Magar officers for resistance against the Chaubise rulers, because she had reason to suspect the Gorkha-based officers of loyalty to Bahadur Shah. She sought to strengthen her position by appointing as Kazi Sarbajit Rana's elder brother, Bindu Rana, and Devadatta Thapa, both of whom were Magar officers of the court.

On 2 January 1782, the forces of Parbat, one of the leading Chaubise principalities, clashed with the Gorkha troops that had moved to a forward post within Tanahu to prevent an attack on Gorkha from there. The forces of Lamjung and Tanahu, led by Garud Dhwaj Pantha, launched an attack on Siranchok in Gorkha. The forces of Kaski were placed in the front line, but the ruler of Kaski, Siddhinarayan Shah, was persuaded by the Gorkha commander-in-chief, Kazi Balabhadra Shah, to abandon the struggle.

As this fight with the Chaubise rulers involved the question of the defence of Gorkha itself, all the leading army commanders took part in it along with Bindu Rana and Devadatta Thapa. Amar Singh Thapa played an important part in defeating the enemies and pushing them back to Lamjung whence they had come. The leading Chaubise Rajas fell out among themselves as a result of their reverses in the war. Kirti Bam Malla, Raja of Parbat, sought vengeance on Siddhinarayan Shah, the ruler of Kaski, for withdrawing his troops from the battle. When Kaski was attacked by the forces of Parbat, Raja Siddhinarayan Shah ran away from Kaski together with his son, and sought shelter in Gorkha.

Abhiman Singh Basnyat, who was in charge of the campaign in the east, was keeping a close watch on the situation there. He sensed that Gorkha's adversaries would not remain quiet until after the stronghold of Karna Sen's heirs was smashed. A company of troops was dispatched to Ghumgarh, which fell into the hands of the Gorkhas after an armed clash in which both Dhwajabir Sen, the heir-presumptive, and Karna Sen's illegitimate son, Ripu Mardan Sen, were killed, along with fifteen others. After this incident, the Pallo Kirat Limbus and the Sikkimese became quiet. Mukunda Sen II, the Raja of Palpa, reportedly died of grief caused by the death of his son, Dhwajabir Sen. Harakumaradatta Sen, Raja of Tanahu, sought shelter with Biramardan Shah, Raja of Lamjung.

Regent Queen Rajendralakshmi felt an obligation to rescue the Raja of Kaski, who had lost his principality to Parbat. She thought that it was not possible to restore Kaski to its original Raja without destroying Lamjung. She considered it expedient to enlist the service of the experienced old Gorkha-based commanders and Kazis like Bamsharaj Pande, who were living in exile. As soon as Pande received a royal summons in the name of King Rana Bahadur Shah, he left for Kathmandu. Once there, he successfully persuaded the Regent Queen to send for Dalamardan Shah, Prithvinarayan's brother, who was also living at Betiah. It is noteworthy that the war-cry against the Chaubise rulers helped the military leaders of the Gorkha Government to submerge their personal differences temporarily and to unite against the common foe.

As a result of the Gorkha military campaign, the rulers of Lamjung and Tanahu, Biramardan Shah and Harakumaradatta Sen, fled their territories. Siddhinarayan Shah, Raja of Kaski, was restored to his principality on the basis of a subsidiary alliance with the Gorkhas. After this, the leading Limbus of Pallo Kirat, who had been at Kathmandu, were sent back with arms and other concessions, and that area also became quiet. The only Chaubise principality which was unhurt by this campaign was that of Parbat, which was ruled by Kirti Bam Malla. However, this first campaign against the Chaubise principalities did not permanently subjugate them. The rulers of these principalities were merely left licking their wounds for a while.

Meanwhile, difference once again broke out among the ranking Gorkha officers. Kazi Bamsharaj Pande was unhappy at Regent Queen Rajendralakshmi's appointment of junior officers to important offices of state and the Queen had to exile him from Nepal on 26 December 1783. Swarup Singh Karki and Bhim Khawas, a junior officer, became her confidants.

Mukunda Sen II was succeeded by Maha Data Sen as ruler of Palpa and the new ruler became active against the Gorkhas. As the campaign in the east had come to a close, Abhiman Singh Basnyat, the officer in charge of the eastern campaign, was also sent for duties in the west. A plan was drawn up not only for an attack on Palpa but also for the subjugation of Parbat and all of the other twenty-four principalities. However, in the face of the resistance offered by Raja Kirti Bam Malla of Parbat, who had also made the Raja of Kaski denounce the subsidiary alliance with the Gorkhas, the plan remained unfulfilled. The Gorkha troops were withdrawn from their forward posts in the campaign against the Chaubise principalities.

Meanwhile, the Regent Queen developed symptoms of tuberculosis and sent for Prithvinarayan's brother Dalajit Shah, who had been in self-imposed exile in India. Rana Bahadur Shah's *bratabandha*, or the religious thread ceremony, was held on 19 January 1785. His uncle, Bahadur Shah, and his old associate Kazi Bamsharaj Pande were also invited to attend the ceremony presumably with a sinister purpose. This was proved by the execution of Bamsharaj Pande on 8 March 1785, in the palace garden and the subsequent imprisonment of Bahadur Shah on 2 July 1785. Probably the Regent Queen and her advisers felt that the young king's safety demanded the liquidation of these ranking officers of state who had suffered at the hands of the Regent Queen. Only twelve days after the imprisonment of Bahadur Shah, the Regent Queen herself died on 13 July 1785.

At the time of the Regent Queen's death, the campaign launched against the Chaubise principalities remained unaccomplished except for the absorption into the Gorkha kingdom of some of the smaller Chaubise principalities on the bank of the river Andhi-Khola. As her administration of the northern border area had not been satisfactory, trade with Tibet was in a state of decline. Deep-seated suspicions and rivalry still prevailed between the old Gorkha-based officers of the state and the officers from the eastern and western regions outside of Gorkha on whom the Regent Queen had relied. Her failure to remedy this state of affairs, because of her differences with Bahadur Shah, lay at the root of the failure of her administration to accomplish more in the way of expansion of the territory. However, it is evident that Regent Queen Rajendralakshmi was a strong personality whose determination and firmness as an administrator cannot be questioned.

4

Regency of Bahadur Shah (1785-1794) and the Wars with Tibet and China

There was naturally a considerable stir in palace circles following the death of Regent Queen Rajendralakshmi. Dalajit Shah, the Chautara, Abhiman Singh Basnyat, the leading Gorkha-based officer, and others who were away at the time of the Regent Queen's death, hurriedly assembled at Kathmandu. They held their counsel and reached the conclusion that nothing should be decided about the future without consulting Bahadur Shah, who was under detention.

Bahadur Shah was set free on the eleventh day of mourning. He immediately took over the administration as Naib or Regent, an office equal in status to that of Prime Minister, and his first act as Mukhtiyar was to have Swarup Singh Karki beheaded and Balabhadra Shah dismissed from the office of Kazi.

Bahadur Shah's administration was characterized by vigorous and rapid expansion of the Gorkha kingdom towards the west. Between 1786 and 1787, Parbat, Gulmi, Argha, Khanchi, Musikot, Galkot and Pyuthan were all incorporated in the Gorkha dominion. Dang was also conquered and was rendered a tributary vassal of Gorkha. Mahadatta Sen of Palpa and Angyal Dorjay of Mustang also received gifts from the King Rana Bahadur Shah. Gulmi, Argha and Khanchi were bestowed on Mahadatta Sen, Raja of Palpa, as a gift in recognition of his being a tributary vassal of the Gorkha King, and also because Mahadatta Sen was Bahadur Shah's father-in-law.

Dailekh, Dullu, Bajhang, Achham, and Doti were subsequently conquered, and by 1789 the Gorkhas gained control over the entire basin of the Karnali river. Kumaun was annexed to the Gorkha kingdom in 1790. The Gorkhas had acquired partial control of Garhwal as well by 1791.

But in 1791 China's intervention became imminent in the wake of the second Nepal-Tibet War of that year. This development led to the temporary suspension of the Gorkha military operations in the west. All the leading officers and most of the troops were withdrawn, to be deployed along the Tibetan border in anticipation of an attack by China.

Developments in the Trans-Himalayan Area

The power struggle in Tsang between the red-hat sect and the yellow-hat sect, represented by the Dalai Lama in Lhasa, afforded the Gorkhas an opportunity for an incursion into Tibetan politics. Their immediate objective was to consolidate the political position of the Tibetan red-hat faction that had, at least for the time being, allied with the Gorkhas. The yellow-hat Drungpa Trulku (Chumpa Hutuketu) was appointed regent by the Chinese for the new Panchen Lama, Bstan pa'i nyi ma (1781-1852). The red-hat Chosdup-Gyatse, the Ninth Karmapa Lama, the Shamar Trulku (Sva-dmar-pa Lama) was the Drungpa Trulku's younger brother. A serious fight ensued between the two brothers for power and influence in the Tsang region. The subsequent flight of the Shamar Trulku to Nepal, probably in 1786, in company of fifteen relatives and with a portion of the treasury of Tashilhunpo (Shigatse), was the catalyst that set in motion a whole chain of events that led to the war between Nepal and Tibet.

In 1788 the Gorkhas went to war with the Tibetans over the question of the circulation of Nepali currency in Tibet and the imposition of taxes on goods carried between India and Tibet through Nepal. But it should be realized that the Nepali invasions of Tibet were not undertaken solely in response to the preceding events, nor were they, as has been made out by some writers, merely stray raids aimed at the seizure of loot by the officers and soldiers before retiring into Nepali territory.

The First Nepal-Tibet War of 1788

In July 1788, the Gorkhas captured the border areas along the main passes into Tibet. Kuti and Kerung immediately fell into their hands, and Tingri was also occupied a little later. The Nepali army in the Kuti area advanced as far as the vicinity of Shekar Dzong, a short distance beyond Tingri on the road to Shigatse (Digarchi).

At the time when the main Gorkha forces were mounting the invasion of Tibet, two detachments of Gorkha troops, under Purna Ale and Johar Singh, were dispatched to seize Sikkim. They made their way into Sikkim through the Singhali La route and actually captured the Rajas's palace of Rabdentse (lit. peak of god), the capital of Sikkim, by October 1788. Raja Tenzing Namgyal (Chogyal) and his wife (Gyalmo) fled to Tibet. Purna Ale advanced as far as Reling, Karmi and Chyakhung, and Nepal's boundary was extended up to the Tista in the hills. As a result, the entire district of Darjeeling with the exception of Kalimpong became part of the kingdom of Nepal, and Sikkim was reduced to Gangtok and its confines situated between the two tributaries of the Tista River. Darjeeling, previously known as Nagri, was before 1782 the headquarters of the chief administrator of Sikkim and the site of a multistoried fort roofed with thatch. Nagri finds mention in historical literature since the 18th century and the Gorkha troops were stationed at Nagri as well. The local name for the place was Samdung and the Bengalis used to call it Nagrikot. Jayanta Khatri was the name of the Gorkha officer who had been in charge of the administration of the district which remained with Nepal till the end of the 1814-1816 war between Nepal and British India.

In this war, Sikkim joined hands with the British in wresting control of Darjeeling from the Gorkhas. As the treaty of Sugauli, concluded at the end of the war, required Nepal to return to the British all territory lying between the Mechi River and the Tista River both in the hills and in the tarai, Darjeeling remained with the British temporarily until 1817 when the treaty of Titaliya between British India and Sikkim transferred it to Sikkim again.

To turn to the Nepal-Tibet War of 1788, the Tibetans failed to receive assistance from the Calcutta Government and the Jumla Raja, to whom they had first appealed rather than to Lhasa and the Chinese Government, whose intervention might have had the effect of eliminating the already limited autonomy enjoyed by Tsang in its relations with Lhasa. Word finally reached Lhasa and the Chinese Government through its Resident there. To avert the consequences of the arrival of the Chinese army in Lhasa, both the Tasilhunpo and the Lhasa officials made strong efforts to negotiate a peace settlement with Nepal.

By May 1789, the officials designated to make the peace were assembled at Kerung. The Nepali side was represented by Chautara Bam Shah, Harihar Upadhyaya and Shamar Trulku, (Sva-dmar-pa Lama), and the Tibetan delegation consisted of Tenzin Paljor Doring (a nephew by marriage to the Shamar Trulku) and the Panchen Lama's father, along with the red-hat Sakya Lama.

The Nepal-Tibet Treaty of 1789

The terms finally agreed upon, according to various Nepali, Chinese and English sources, were:

1. Nepal agreed to withdraw from the border area of Tibet that it had seized during the war and to recognize the validity of the former boundary (though it retained the right to administer half of the town of Kuti granted to Raja Pratap Malla of Kathmandu 140 years earlier).
2. Nepal promised never to invade Tibet again.
3. Tibet promised to pay 300 ingots of silver each year (equivalent to 9,600 taels of Chinese silver or approximately 57,600 Nepali rupees as the rate prevalent at that time in Tibet was 6 rupees per tael. The figure usually quoted in Nepali and other sources is, however, 50,000 rupees).
4. Tibet agreed to accept and use Nepali coins, minted by the Nepal Government, and to exchange the Nepali currency at the rate of one new coin for one and one-half (1-1/2) old coins. (This was a compromise between the Nepali demand that the ratio be 1 new to 2 old coins and the Tibetan position that the exchange should be on a basis of equality.)
5. Nepal was granted the right to maintain a Gorkhali representative at Lhasa. (It would thus no longer have to depend upon the head of the Newari trading community at Lhasa to act as its representative.)
6. Trade between India and Tibet was to be channelled solely through Nepal and the alternate trade routes to the east and the west were to be closed.
7. A Tibetan Lama was to visit Kathmandu each year "to bless the temple."

An attempt was made to conceal the terms of this treaty from both the Chinese emperor and the Dalai Lama in Lhasa. The paramount aim of Tibetan delegate, Kalon Tenzin Paljor Doring, and the Chinese Resident, General Pa-chung, was to be able to report to the Chinese court that the Gorkhas had withdrawn from the Tibetan territory and had vowed never to attack it again.

The payment of tribute for the year 1789 was duly made to Nepal by Kalon Tenzin Paljor Doring, who raised 300 ingots of silver from various monasteries and individuals in Tsang by giving them the false impression that they would be repaid out of the Dalai Lama's treasury.

The Second Nepal-Tibet War of 1791

As the time for payment of the second tribute for 1790 approached, a rift began to appear in the treaty relations. The Lhasa officials could not keep the Dalai Lama in the dark about the terms of the treaty which involved financial expenditure from the treasury and this required the Dalai Lama's approval. Both the Dalai Lama and the Chinese Resident in Lhasa, Pao-tai, felt that the tribute was too high for Tibet to pay. Nepal naturally resented the Dalai Lama's unilateral abrogation of the treaty stipulation with regard to the tribute.

Negotiations initiated by Lhasa through Nijor Lama broke off, as the Lama had no authority to accept the Nepali demands. Apart from its unwillingness to respect the tribute provision of the treaty, Tibet also failed to stop the circulation of the old Malla coins, and it did not substitute for them at the ratio of one new for one-and-one-half old coins as stipulated in the 1789 treaty.

In the fall of 1790, a mission was sent from Nepal to Tibet asking for Tibet's compliance with the terms of the 1789 treaty and threatening the renewal of war in the event of non-compliance. The Chinese Resident was also asked, through this mission, to bestow customary land grants and subsidies on the King and the Regent, who had been invested by the Chinese Emperor with the titles of "Erdeni Wang" (Brilliant King) and "Kung" (Duke). The mission came back from Lhasa wholly dissatisfied.

However, the Dalai Lama averted Nepal's imminent military attack by sending a Khem-po Lama to the Nepal-Tibet frontier with silver amounting to one-half of the annual tribute stipulated in the treaty. The Khem-po Lama was also asked to drop a hint to the Gorkhas that Chinese assistance would be sought in case Nepal committed aggression against Tibet. The Khem po Lama's pleas were not entertained by the Nepali authorities, who expressed their unwillingness to discuss these matters with any Tibetan official other than Kalon Tenzin Paljor Doring or the Dalai Lama's uncle. Tibet made a last attempt at peaceful settlement by sending a 6-man delegation, headed by Tenzin Paljor Doring, with the full quantity of silver required for payment of the tribute for 1790.

In view of the fact that the Nepali and the Tibetan sources give contradictory versions, it is difficult to say what made the proposed negotiation take such a drastic turn and trigger the Gorkha attack on Kuti. On 6 August 1791, when Nepali troops, led by Bam Shah and Damodar Pande, crossed into Tibetan territory, the trade centre of Kuti at once fell into their hands. The Nepali army of 3,500 to 4,000 men advanced rapidly along the main trade route to Shigatse, captured Tingri, bypassed Shekar Dzong, and then occupied the important yellow-hat monastery and trade centre at Sakya. The "friendly" welcome they received there from the monks and the adherents of the red-hats is an indication of the sentiments of the red-hat sect towards the Gorkhas because of their association with the Shamar Trulku.

While the main Gorkha force proceeded along the Kuti trade route, an auxiliary force gained control of the Kerung pass and marched as far as Jhunga. It attacked the Tibetans there but was repulsed. Thus, the invading Gorkha forces were forced to withdraw to Kerung on this front. However, the main force, reinforced by a detachment that had invaded Tibet through the Hatia Pass, continued its march against feeble Tibetan opposition and, by 17 September 1791, reached Tashilunpo. The Tibetans were in a good position to offer resistance to the Gorkhas by virtue of the presence of 4,000 resident monks, many of whom were familiar with the use of arms. Despite this the Drungpa Trulku, Regent for the Panchen Lama, fled to Lhasa with most of the Tashilunpo treasury as soon as he heard of the approach of the Gorkha army. When the Gorkhas finally arrived at the gate of the monastery, they found only nine monks, including the Taitchong Lama, who was later executed by the Chinese.

The Gorkhas were hoping to realize the arrears of tribute for 1790 and 1791 and the expenditure of the campaign by acquiring possession of the Tashilunpo monastery. When they found the treasury almost empty, they sacked the monastery, stripping the walls and altars of a great quantity of gold, silver and precious stones which had been placed there over the centuries by devout Buddhists. The fact that the Gorkhas did not touch the treasury of the equally rich monastery of the red-hat sect, while pillaging the yellow-hat's Tashilunpo monastery, is another indication that the Gorkha army leaders were motivated by political consideration rather than by the sheer desire for loot.

The Nepal-China War of 1792

As soon as the Chinese Emperor, Ch'ien-lung (1736-1796), learned of the second Gorkha invasion of Tibet from the Dalai Lama and the Chinese Resident, Pao-tai, he commanded Ao-hiu, Governor of Szechuan, to proceed to Tibet to settle the matter. Ao-hiu did not go there himself but sent his commander, Cheng-teh, with a small force to make it know to the Gorkhas that they could not lightly get away with their invasion this time.

Pao-tai's leadership in repulsing the Gorkha invasion had already proved futile. He had proceeded to Shigatse at the head of about 1,000 troops, including some Chinese and Manchu troops. On the approach of the Gorkha army, he had beaten a retreat to Lhasa, taking with him the young Panchen Lama. Pao-tai felt so insecure that he sought permission from the Emperor to send both the Dalai Lama and the Panchen Lama to Peking. He could not obtain the Emperor's consent for this, and the Dalai Lama also refused to leave Lhasa under any circumstances.

The Chinese Resident repeated his pleas for accommodation with Nepal even as late as October 1791. Despite this, on 22 November 1791, Emperor Ch'ien-lung ordered his most trusted and renowned commander, Fu Kang-an, to Peking, indicating that he must be prepared to go to Tibet to command a Chinese army for an invasion of Nepal in the spring of 1792. The Emperor's main consideration in defending Tibet's interests was that the surrender of Tibet by the Chinese would adversely affect Chinese interests in Mongolia because Tibet was the land of the Dalai Lama, the religious head of the Mongols. Emperor Ch'ien-lung was bent on teaching the Gorkhas a lesson by inflicting military defeat on them.

The terms, laid down by the Emperor and communicated to the Gorkhas through Ao-hiu, required them to send Bahadur Shah or Shamar Trulku to the Chinese authorities in Tibet, and to reiterate their submission to China. The Emperor knew the Gorkhas would not accept these terms, but felt that this kind of overture would lull the Nepali authorities into thinking that the Chinese were, as in 1788-1789, contemplating a peaceful settlement. The Emperor hoped the Nepalis would, therefore, be taken by surprise when the Chinese army appeared across the Himalaya in the spring of 1792. But the Gorkhas, while reiterating their grievances to the Chinese Emperor and lodging a complaint with him against the Chinese Resident in Lhasa, Pao-tai, were intensifying their defensive preparations in anticipation of the Chinese attack.

The Gorkhali army, after a fruitless attempt to capture a fort within a day's march to the north of Tashilunpo, began a general retreat to the Nepal border on 4 October 1791. While retreating to Nepal by the more difficult Hatia pass, the forces suffered immense hardship and loss of life. Their strength was reduced to one half.

The Chinese authorities were meanwhile fully engaged in stepping up preparations for the invasion of Nepal by the following spring. As early as October 1791, the Tibetan and the Chinese forces had commenced joint operations to clear the Kuti and Kerung passes of Gorkha occupation. In November 1791, the Gorkha were pushed back from Tingri and, in 1792, the fort of Kuti fell into the hands of the Chinese after a month-long siege.

The Chinese also intensified diplomatic pressure and psychological and propaganda warfare against the Gorkhas; The British in India and the Rajas of other states bordering Nepal, including Jumla, were requested to assist in the Chinese war efforts against the Gorkhas. Some of the Newari merchants in Lhasa were recruited to act as fifth columnists behind the army lines, and others were sent in advance to Kathmandu where they were told to sow the seeds of dissension among the Newari population and rouse them against their erstwhile Gorkha conquerors.

Fu Kang-an had arrived in Tibet in January 1792, by the shorter route through Kokonor (Tsinghai) rather than Chamdo, thus saving a month's time on the journey. From here he wrote a note to the British in Calcutta.

Fu Kang-an's letter to the Governor-General at Calcutta, received in July 1792, called upon the "Philings (i.e., "Feringhi" or English) to do all they could to punish the Gorkhas. The letter deserves to be quoted at least in part because it reveals the gradiloquent character of Chinese diplomacy, based on an exaggerated sense of self-importance and a complete ignorance of the conditions outside the empire:

> All the Rajahas to the westward directing their attention to the good government of their own countries, and never deviating from their loyalty, have, under the protection of their most high emperor, remained content with the possession of their ancient dominions. . . . The original country of the Gurkha Raja is of very inconsiderable extent, but he has, by force, taken possession of the territories of the neighbouring princes. He has carried his depredations into Bhote (Tibet), and committed the most atrocious actions. As the country of Bhote and its inhabitants are subject to the em-

> peror of China, this incursion can be considered in no other light than a robbery. Nothing better in future is to be expected from this man. The benefits of His Imperial Majesty's protection and bounty are diffused over a thousand kingdoms. I shall certainly pursue to destruction all those persons who were concerned in this violent and unjust undertaking . . . I, the Chanchoo, have marched with a prodigious army, exceeding lacs and crores in numbers, with the intention of making war on him for the contempt he has shown to the imperial authority. . . . It behoves the Rajahas of all the adjacent countries to obey my commands. Any clemency towards the Gurkha Rajaha, after the crimes he has committed, would be universally condemned. The imperial army is now preparing to attack him, and as your dominions border on his, you should commence hostilities against him at the same time, and passing your own frontiers, carry the war into the enemy's country . . . Let the princes of all the neighbouring countries, cordially uniting on the same enterprise, use their utmost endeavour to destroy these robbers. Let them be put to death and let their eyes be plucked out and their hands, feet cut off and sent to me. Whoever has the merit of this action, I, the great Chanchoo, will reward him liberally, and when the intelligence of his success is reported to His Majesty he will confer on him the most honourable marks of his favour, and present him with a magnificent Khelaut. I desire you after due consideration of what I have written to pursue the proper measures for executing my wishes. I, the great Chanchoo, speak not in vain. Immediately on the receipt of this letter, I desire you to send me a distinct account of the time and place on which you commence your operations, and the route by which you advance.

Under Fu Kang-an's instructions, letters were also sent to the Governor-General by both the Dalai Lama and the Panchen Lama through the same messenger—the Gosain, Purangir.

The East India Company's Government had signed a treaty of commerce with Nepal on 1 March 1792, and was unlikely to respond to these overtures from the Chinese and the Tibetan authorities. Several months passed before a reply was sent by the Company's Government to the Chinese and Tibetan authorities.

Meanwhile, the Emperor in Peking, still desiring to lull the Nepalis into a false sense of security, expressed his displeasure with Fu Kang-an for writing to these "barbarian tribes" in this manner. He feared that the secret might be divulged by them.

Emperor Ch'ien-lung saw much advantage in deceiving the Gorkhas until the commencement of invasion. On 14 March 1792, he wrote that Fu Kang-an should ask King Rana Bahadur to come personally to the border so that he might feel assured about the Chinese desire for a peaceful settlement. Fu Kang-an, in accordance with the imperial orders, wrote twice to King Rana Bahadur and Regent Bahadur Shah in this vein but received no reply. Fu Kang-an had doubted that his communications would produce the intended effect on them, as the Gorkhas were already strengthening their fortification of the pass areas on their northern frontier.

As we have seen, Fu Kang-an sought to utilize the Newari traders in Lhasa to carry out his purposes. At his meeting with the head of the Newari community in Tibet, he had assured that the Newaris still held a deep "rancour" against the Gorkhas and were on the lookout for an opportunity to avenge themselves on their conquerors. The same Newari trader had told the general that all areas conquered by the Gorkhas were restless and not truly submissive to them, and the Chinese army would not encounter any resistance from the people. Fu Kang-an shared this appraisal by the Newari leader, and he employed seven Newari traders to act as guides inside Nepali territory and to penetrate behind the battle lines to arouse the Newars in the Kathmandu Valley against their Gorkha masters.

In January 1792, the General secretly sent a Newari trader, Nachi Nalang (in Chinese), to Kathmandu to establish contact with Balabhadra Shah and the Shamar Trulku and to renew submission to the Emperor of China. The Newari trader, while trying to cross into Nepal by a seldom-used pass, was arrested and sent to Kathmandu. When Bahadur Shah failed to get confirmation of his suspicions about this trader after close interrogation, he put him in strict isolation. After some time he was sent back to Lhasa as a courier with a petition to Fu Kang-an. The petition contained the old complaints about Tibet's failure to circulate the Nepali coins and to pay the tribute due to Nepal and requested Fu Kang-an to settle these matters.

In addition to this, Bahadur Shah put forward an interesting argument, which was to be used by the Nepali side on numerous occasions in the next sixty years, to impress upon the Chinese suzerainty in Tibet. Bahadur Shah informed the Chinese commander of the intentions of "the tribe of *Tilapacha*" of south "*Chakar*" (i.e. the British) to conquer Tibet and argued that Nepal, by acting as a barrier between India and

Tibet, had prevented the British from carrying out their designs. "If you grant more grace to us, we will continue to bar the way when *Tilapacha* makes trouble. If you do not, then we will let them occupy Tibet."

By May 1792, Fu Kang-an had been able to muster a sizeable force of 12,000 troops, mostly drawn from Szechuan and from the Kham tribes of eastern Tibet. Out of the total number 6,000 Tibetan troops were led by Kalon Horkhang. In addition, 3,000 men were kept in reserve on the Tibet-China border. Fu Kang-an thought that this was a good enough force to accomplish the task in hand and, in June 1792, stepped up the Chinese invasion of Nepal.

Fu Kang-an decided to open the battle on two fronts—Kerung and Kuti—to compel the Gorkhas to meet a dual threat. He intended to protect the rear of the main Chinese forces by preventing the Gorkhas from attacking its supply lines through the Kuti pass, situated between Kerung and Shigatse. With this end in view, the Chinese army was divided into two forces. The main force of 6,000 men led by Fu Kang-an himself was to enter Nepal by the Kerung pass, while a subsidiary force of 3,000 men under the command of Cheng-teh was to make its way into Nepal through the Kuti pass.

On 28 June 1792, Kerung fell to the Chinese, and hundreds of Nepali soldiers were taken prisoner or slain in battle. Five days later, the bridge on the Trishuli Gandaki near Rasuwa became the scene of another major engagement. Here again the Chinese were victorious. The Chinese army marched into Nepal to Syabru, where they came face-to-face with a strongly entrenched Nepali force under Sardar Prabal Rana, Rana Kishor Pande, Shankar Rana and Jugbal Shahi. Fu Kang-an divided his force into two units. One unit was sent through a bypass to the rear of the Nepalis. On 24-25 July 1792, both units of the Chinese army simultaneously launched an attack on the Gorkha force and completely routed it.

Dhunche and Deurali were the scene of the next major engagement. There, after three days of heavy fighting, August 19-21, the Chinese force outflanked the Nepali army, led by Damodar Pande, and forced it to retreat. The Chinese then set up a camp at Dhumche to recuperate from the fatigue of the previous battles.

Meanwhile, on the Kuti front, Cheng-teh had an encounter with a Nepali unit in Khasa and defeated it. The subsidiary Chinese force then advanced another eight miles to Listi. The Nepali troops, reinforced by newly arrived men from Kathmandu, were awaiting it. They withstood a strong Chinese assault on 28 July 1792, and forced the Chinese to retreat to Khasa. Thus, a stalemate was reached on this front, neither side being in a position to take the offensive.

The Chinese invasion of Nepal and the successive reverses suffered by Nepal had put Bahadur Shah's predominant political position in serious jeopardy. The death of the Shamar Trulku, Sva-dmar-pa Lama, Bahadur Shah's trusted adviser, on 3 July 1792, was the first reflection of a shift in the balance of power at Kathmandu. The official Nepali account of the Lama's death was that he contracted smallpox in March and died in July. Fu Kang-an observed that the date of the Lama's death coincided with the exact date of the start of the Chinese invasion. He assumed that the Lama must have been either put to death by the Gorkhas to prevent possible interrogation by the Chinese or that the Lama was hidden, and false stories of his death were being circulated by the Nepali Government. However, Tenzin Paljor Doring and two other Chinese officers were shown the body of the Shamar Trulku. The letter in the name of the King of Nepal, Rana Bahadur Shah, stated that on receiving the Chinese commander's letter which criticized the Lama's activities, the King summoned the Lama and informed him that he was going to be handed over to the Chinese. On hearing this, the Lama "turned pale" and requested the King to delay this act until he had recovered from his illness. The Lama died shortly afterwards and his body was cremated.

Nepali overtures to Fu Kang-an had begun when the Chinese army had scarcely crossed the Himalaya. In a letter dated 16 July 1792, sent through the Chinese officials mentioned above, Rana Bahadur analysed the causes of the dispute between Nepal and Tibet and blamed the Shamar Trulku for inciting the Gorkhas to violent action against the Tibetans. According to Rana Bahadur, he felt that the Lama had been unjustly treated in Tibet. He considered it his duty to help the Lama avenge himself on the Tibetan officials instrumental in ousting him from Tashilunpo. Rana Bahadur added that the Tibetans never apprised him of the machinations of the Lama, and it was only from Fu Kang-an that the Gorkhas learned what kind of man the Lama was. Fu Kang-an was requested to arbitrate the disputes between Nepal and Tibet and was assured that the Gorkhas would abide by his decision. Again, in a second letter dated 28 July 1792, Rana Bahadur put all the blame for what happened on the late Shamar Trulku. This letter was brought to the Chinese camp on 4 August by a Nepali official, accompanied by Tenzin Paljor Doring and Chinese and Tibetan soldiers.

In a letter dated 2 August, prepared before the receipt of King Rana Bahadur's second letter, Fu Kang-an disapproved of the sentiments expressed by Rana Bahadur. He also found fault with the manner in which the communication was delivered, that is, by Chinese soldiers instead of by Nepali officials in accordance with the proper procedure. However, by the grace of the Emperor, the Chinese were not going to annihilate the entire "Gorkha tribe" but would give them a chance to surrender. Fu Kang-an further pointed out that while the Shamar Trulku was no doubt guilty of plotting with foreigners "in order to destroy a Buddhist Land," the Gorkhas could not escape their share of the blame and King Rana Bahadur Shah and Regent Bahadur Shah should both confess their guilt. Fu Kang-an continued that if Bahadur Shah or Bam Shah were sent by the Nepal Government to his camp to beg formal apology, he would refer the matter to the Emperor and it would be up to the Emperor to forgive the Gorkhas. The Chinese general showed no interest in Tenzin Paljor Doring and dismissed the matter by merely saying that the Kalon's actions were faulty. For this reason, he had already been relieved of his post. In the end, Fu Kang-an disposed of the coinage issue by stating that Tibet was subject to China and as such Tibet was not under any obligation to circulate Nepali currency. As to the treaty of 1789, the general denounced its validity on the ground that it had been "privately" concluded by Tenzin Paljor Doring under duress.

The Chinese Commander's letter reached the Kathmandu Darbar on 4 August and a reply was sent to him by Rana Bahadur Shah on the following day. In this letter, Rana Bahadur Shah admitted his guilt for what had happened and expressed his desire to offer submission to the Chinese emperor. A delegation composed of four deputies—Bhutu Pande, Ranajit Pande, Narasingh Gurung and Bala Bahadur Khawas—was sent to arrange for a peace settlement, and Fu Kang-an was requested to favour them with an audience. Fu Kang-an had written that Bhutu Pande told him the Nepalis wanted to give him a written assurance not to cause trouble again. Fu Kang-an's reply was that this was not necessary because Gorkha's submission to the Chinese required no written engagement. However, according to the same Chinese sources, Rana Bahadur later denied having instructed Bhutu Pande to make such an offer and suggested the possibility of an error on the part of the interpreters.

In a letter dated 13 August, which was written in reply to Rana Bahadur's letter of 5 August, Fu Kang-an formally laid down the following conditions for the surrender of the Nepalis:

1. The remains of the Shamar Trulku should be sent to the Chinese camp for inspection and investigation.
2. The family, disciples and servants of the Shamar Trulku should be turned over to the Chinese for trial.
3. Nepal should restore all the treasure plundered in Tashilunpo.
4. The two copies of the 1789 treaty held by Nepal should be turned over to the Chinese.
5. The Gorkha army facing the Chinese should be withdrawn from their present position to enable the Chinese army to occupy a more suitable camp-site in order to receive the surrender of the Gorkhas.

Fu Kang-an conveyed the assurance that if Nepal complied with the above conditions, the Nepali people would be treated as part of the Chinese Empire. But he also warned that in the event of Nepal's refusal, the Chinese army would advance to Kathmandu. This letter was carried back to the Nepal Darbar by Ranajit Pande and Bala Bahadur Khawas, who had brought Rana Bahadur's letter of 5 August to the Chinese Emperor.

Having failed to receive a reply to his last letter of 19 August, Fu Kang-an ordered his army to start action against the Nepali forces entrenched on the heights above the Chinese camp. Thus ensued the most bloody three-day battle for Dhumche and Deurali. The outcome was a decisive victory for the Chinese, although the losses suffered by them were very heavy

This defeat caused great apprehension in the Nepal court. The court was more or less equally divided on the immediate policy to be pursued towards the Chinese, one section advocating immediate surrender and the other section wishing to continue the struggle to the bitter end. However, as a compromise, reinforcements were rushed to the front under the command of Shrikrishna Shah, an opponent of Bahadur Shah. Also a letter dated 26 August 1792 was dispatched to Fu Kang-an. In this letter Rana Bahadur Shah and Bahadur Shah once again confessed their guilt for all that had happened previously and stated their partial acceptance of the terms proposed by Fu Kang-an. Nepal agreed to turn over to the Chinese the remains of the Shamar Trulku, along with his family, disciples and servants, as well as the two Nepali texts of the controversial 1789 treaty. Rana Bahadur, while agreeing to the restoration of the loot from Tashilunpo, pleaded that an inventory would have to be made, as much of it had already been lost when the Nepali army sustained heavy losses while crossing the Himalaya on their return.

As to Fu Kang-an's suggestion that either Rana Bahadur Shah or Bahadur Shah should come in person to offer their submission to the Chinese Emperor, King Rana Bahadur Shah pleaded that both of them were afraid of facing the Chinese General after all that they had done in the past and begged not to be forced to come. The King, however, suggested that two leading Nepali court officials would be sent to Fu Kang-an's camp, and these men should be permitted to proceed to Peking to pay their respects to the Emperor. At the end, however, Rana Bahadur expressed his inability to accept the condition that the Gorkha army be withdrawn from their battle positions. He stated that, as the Gorkhas were "ants" in comparison to the Chinese, he hoped that the Chinese commander would pardon him and would not insist on this condition.

In accordance with the terms in the above letter, on 3 September 1792, the remains of the Shamar Trulku, as well as those of his confidential servant, Chi-lung (who had put himself to death on discovering that he would be turned over to the Chinese), were sent to Fu Kang-an's camp along with the Lama's personal belongings. Some of the loot from Tashilunpo was also restored, though Rana Bahadur Shah asked for more time to collect other valuables that had not been lost. Ten days later Daman Shah appeared at the Chinese camp with more of the plunder from Tashilunpo and with a letter from Rana Bahadur which said that Nepal was preparing a mission of tribute to China, but as the Gorkhas were a "small, barbarous people," they would like to know what would be proper to send. However, despite the acceptance of most of his terms by the Gorkhas in Rana Bahadur's letter of 26 August, Fu Kang-an did not accept the Gorkha offer since Bahadur Shah had not come in person to offer surrender. In his report to the Chinese Emperor, he stated that he saw no point in giving the Gorkhas further instructions and would merely wait to see to what they would do next.

Despite their unbroken line of successes in battle after battle, the position of the Chinese army had become almost untenable. The Chinese army was far removed from its bases of supply in Tibet and Szechuan. Moreover, winter was approaching and the passes for crossing into Tibet were going to be blocked after the first snowfalls around mid-October. Heavy losses sustained by the Chinese army in successive battles were not easily reparable. A virulent form of malaria prevalent in these areas had also taken a heavy toll of lives. Reinforcements were hard to get and supplies could be brought in only with great difficulty. The Chinese army was faced with an imminent serious shortage of both men and supplies. The only alternatives left for Fu Kang-an now were either to accept the Nepali terms or to advance to Kathmandu, where supplies could be obtained.

Undaunted by circumstances, in the second week of September, Fu Kang-an ordered his army to mount an offensive, with Dhaibung as the immediate target. A fierce battle raged as the Chinese army tried to cross the Betravati river. The Gorkhas, in a last-ditch fight, succeeded in repulsing the advance of the Chinese army, forcing it to retreat to the previous camp-ground. The success of the Gorkhas in this battle must have boosted their morale to an extent and must have also made the Chinese feel that the advance to Kathmandu would not be as easy as they had thought. Cut off completely from their bases of supply in Tibet and Szechuan, the Chinese soldiers must have also begun to feel the strains of the war. In these unfamiliar surroundings and inclement weather, the General himself, though a veteran of many campaigns in the past, must have grown a little war-weary, and his enthusiasm for marching to Kathmandu proved to be short-lived. He must have felt a sense of relief when he finally received the Chinese Emperor's order to return home soon before the snowfall started, even if his mission were not accomplished.

In accordance with the imperial instructions, and in view of the difficulty of marching to Kathmandu and the possibility of having to retreat back into Tibet, Fu Kang-an finally decided to accept the Nepali Government's request for peace on the very terms which he had first rejected. However, Fu Kang-an made one more effort to bring Bahadur Shah personally to his camp by making Bhotu Pande and Narasingh Gurung, who were still in Chinese custody, write to Rana Bahadur and Bahadur Shah on this subject. But this final effort, too, proved unsuccessful.

In his reply to the Chinese letter dated 22 September, Rana Bahadur pleaded that he was too young to go to Peking and Bahadur Shah had his hands full with state affairs, but that Devadatta Thapa, the leading Kazi of the Nepal Court, would be sent as the leader of the Nepali mission to Peking. Devadatta Thapa and three other officials turned up at Fu Kang-an's camp on 23 September, prostrated themselves before Fu Kang-an and made a solemn vow that the Gorkhas would now consider themselves as subject to the Chinese Emperor. Devadatta Thapa mentioned that Nepal would like to send a mission, with presents, every five years under the leadership of an outstanding Kazi. Fu Kang-an agreed to act on their request to forward a petition to the Emperor at Peking and also informed the envoys that, in view of their statement, he would "temporarily" withdraw all Chinese forces from Nepal.

It should be noted here that according to both Nepali and Chinese primary sources, at the conclusion of this war, there was no treaty in the form of a single written document signed by both parties. Five days later, a letter dated 27 September 1792 was received by Fu Kang-an from Rana Bahadur endorsing what Devadatta had told him orally. In this letter, Rana Bahadur promised to send periodic missions to China as prescribed by the Emperor and also vowed never again to mention the 1789 treaty with Tibet. Rana Bahadur commented that Nepal had customarily received a "tribute" of falcons and horses from Kerung, but he would not demand this treatment in the future as Fu Kang-an had been kind enough to pardon the Gorkhas. He also agreed to surrender to Tibet the "Chamu" area on the frontier which had long been the object of contention between the Nepalis and the Tibetans.

As to the currency issue, Rana Bahadur conceded that the Nepali demand for an exchange ratio of 1 new coin for 2 old coins had been unfair to Tibet and promised to drop it. He stated that hereafter in trading with Tibet, a fair exchange rate based on the value of silver would be maintained. In reply to the letter expressing Rana Bahadur's willingness to change the exchange rate in favour of Tibet, Fu Kang-an made a formal acceptance of the terms offered by the Gorkhas and said again that his army would "temporarily" withdraw from Nepal. However, he warned that if Nepal did not continue to respect the imperial decrees, another Chinese army would again invade Nepal and Rana Bahadur could not expect to obtain pardon the second time. The Chinese army began its withdrawal on 6 October 1792, and on 15 October crossed the Jeso bridge into the Tibetan area of Kerung.

Thus, by the end of 1792, peace was restored between Nepal and China on terms which, if somewhat humiliating, were far from disastrous for Nepal. The Nepali Government's neglect of Prithvinarayan's sound counsel on the necessity of maintaining close friendship with China had almost brought the Gorkha dynasty to the brink of ruin. As events turned out, however, the war had little or no influence on Nepal's political structure or its military strength, although it did have a long-term effect on Nepal's foreign policy.

The Nepali Government quickly reverted to the fundamentals of its foreign policy laid down by Prithvinarayan, the founder of modern Nepal. Close relations were sought with China, while contacts with the British were reduced to a minimum. Unfortunately for Nepal, however, this war proved to be instrumental in shaping Peking's trans-Himalyan policy in a manner restricting Nepal's future opportunities to gain advantage through the pursuit of a policy of balance of power between China and British India. Although the Gorkha skill in diplomacy and on the battlefield made a lasting impression upon the Chinese, this war engendered in the minds of the Chinese officials in Tibet a sustained basic distrust of Nepali intentions. This kind of attitude, developed by the Chinese officials as a result of the war of 1792, proved to be the rock on which every attempt by the Nepalis to involve the Chinese in countering British expansion in India foundered. Again, as Leo Rose has pointed out, "the vast expenditure required for the campaign in Tibet and Nepal and the absence of positive results in the form of territorial acquisitions apparently convinced the Chinese of the inadvisability of extending Chinese interest into the trans-Himalayan area." As a result, in the decades subsequent to the 1792 war, Nepal was playing a losing game in its efforts to balance the Chinese against the British. It is interesting to note that it took the British several decades to realize the real character of Chinese interest in this area and to infer that the British could formulate their policy in the cis-Himalayan region without much apprehension of possible Chinese reaction.

Lord Cornwallis, who assumed the office of Governor-General in September 1786, concerned himself more with the consolidation of the Company's existing territories than with adventurous military projects for expansion. That was why he merely set himself the task of settling boundaries with Nepal and turned a deaf ear to all proposals from the hill Rajas for military action against it. There were still many scions of the overthrown Rajas who cherished hopes of being restored to their dominions with the Company's assistance. The Gorkha expansion westward, in the direction of the Gogra or Karnali, had also produced in the minds of other hill Rajas a sense of fear about their own future. It is not surprising that Cornwallis received concrete proposals from Raja Kirti Bam Malla of Malebam and the Raja of Jumla for action against the Gorkha King of Nepal. Their requests for joint military action against the Gorkhas were not heeded by the Company, but the petitions of the hill Rajas had the effect of creating a feeling of distrust between the Company and the Nepal Government. This manifested itself in the exchange of letters of complaint and counter-complaint.

By 1791 the Gorkhas had extended their kingdom as far as Garhwal to the west, and as far north as Digarchi (Shigatse), the seat of Tashilunpo. We have already looked into the circumstances of Nepal's war with Tibet and China (1788-1792). It has also been noted that when the Governor-General was approached by the Panchen Lama for help at the time of the first attack on his territory by the Gorkhas, the Company's Government had told him that although it was not in a position to render military assistance to the Lama, it would certainly not help the Gorkhas. Suffice it to note here that the East India Company had also been earlier requested by the Gorkhas not to lend assistance to the Lama. Chinese intervention in the war had inclined the Gorkhas to look to the Company for assistance. About the same time, the Gorkhas also made representations to the Rohilla Sardar, Nawab Faizullah Khan, for 2,000 soldiers and to the Company for two battalions of Europeans, one of native soldiers (sepoys) with military stores and a suitable number of guns. This was in addition to ten pieces of cannon and ten European sergeants, which the Gorkhas had requested previously.

The 1792 Treaty of Commerce between Nepal and the East India Company

The Nepali Government favoured a commercial treaty with the Company at the time of the war with China in the hope that it would bring them much needed military assistance from the Company. The treaty was a result of the joint efforts of Ali Ibrahim Khan, Judge at Varanasi, and Gajaraj Mishra, the royal preceptor of Nepal. But the proposal for the treaty, even after its acceptance by Jonathan Duncan, Resident in Varanasi, was not at first enthusiastically received by the Government of Nepal. Abdul Kadir Khan, Munsif of the Dewani Adalat of the city of Varanasi, was sent to Nepal by Duncan, with gifts for the King in order to obtain his seal on the treaty. At the time, King Rana Bahadur Shah was a minor and Bahadur Shah, his uncle, was the Regent and *de facto* ruler of Nepal. It took a great deal of patience and tact on the part of Abdul Kadir Khan to obtain the consent to the treaty which was signed on 1 March 1792.

This treaty consisted of seven articles. The first article provided for a duty of $2^1/_2$ per cent on imports from either country at their market price. The second article stated that once the duty was paid at the opposite stations and the proper receipt *(rowannah)* obtained, no further duty should be charged. The third article provided for the exemplary punishment of officers by the governments concerned, should the former be found to exact duty in excess of the amount agreed upon. Article 4 required the proprietors of the spot where theft or robbery might occur, to compensate the merchant for the loss of his goods. Article 5 of the treaty enjoined both governments to extend protection to the merchants against oppression or violence. Article 6 provided that the merchants should be free to take the commodities that were not sold to countries beyond the frontiers of the contracting countries without payment of any duty. The last article stated that this treaty would immediately come into force and should be binding upon the successors of the present rulers of the two countries and that it should be the basis for the growth of concord and friendship between the two states.

The treaty, however, did not bring any military assistance to Nepal from the Company. Cornwallis adhered to the Company's policy of non-intervention in the affairs of the hill Rajas and took into account the adverse effect military assistance to Nepal would have upon the Company's own relations with the Chinese Government. Therefore, he came forward belatedly with an offer of mediation between Nepal and the Chinese Government through the dispatch of a mission led by Captain William Kirkpatrick. Shortly after Kirkpatrick reached Patna on his proposed mission to Nepal, the need for his mediation disappeared with the conclusion of peace between Nepal and China in September 1792. The King of Nepal, in a letter to Jonathan Duncan conveyed the information that as an understanding was reached and peace concluded between Nepal and China, Kirkpatrick should not be sent to Nepal.

This clearly shows that even after the signing of the treaty of commerce, there was no change in the attitude of the Nepali Government towards the English. They continued to look upon them with the same suspicion and fear as before. To the Nepal Government, the commercial treaty of 1792 was nothing more than an act of despair; it had outlived its utility the moment of compelling circumstance of war with China vanished. Difficulties were already being experienced with regard to implementation of the commercial treaty. This is clear from one of the complaints of Mr. Pangan, a white settler in the Morang-Purnea border area. to Duncan against the insistence of Nepali officials on the exaction of former dues.

The Company's Government was still anxious that Kirkpatrick should proceed to Nepal on a fact-finding mission and should be accompanied by Abdul Kadir Khan, who might be of help to him in negotiating better terms for trade on the basis of the existing commercial treaty. Captain Kirkpatrick wrote directly to the King of Nepal for permission to visit the country with a view to advancing the cause of friendship between the Company and the Nepal Government. Before Kirkpatrick was granted permission to visit Nepal, he was met by Bam Shah and Dinanath Upadhyaya at Patna. On their advice, subsequently supported by Gajaraj Mishra, the King finally agreed to Kirkpatrick's visit in a letter to the Governor-General on 2 January 1793.

The Kirkpatrick Mission of 1793

Since the original purpose of Kirkpatrick's mission had changed, Cornwallis sent him fresh instructions which covered a wide range of interests. Kirkpatrick was asked to ascertain the "real cause" of war between Nepal and China, with a view to assessing the possibility of the Company's mediation in the event of another war between the two. He was also instructed to assure the King of the Company's friendly intentions toward him and to persuade the Nepali Government to abide by the terms of the commercial treaty. A final settlement of the outstanding boundary dispute was also included in his terms of reference. In addition, Kirkpatrick was asked to investigate the extent of Nepal's trade with Tibet and Tartary and assess the prospects for British exports in this market. He was also asked to make general observations on the form and nature of the government, on the religion, manners and customs of the people of Nepal, and to collect as much information as possible about the roads, geography, etc., of Nepal and the neighbouring countries. Abdul Kadir Khan accompanied Kirkpatrick to advise him on commercial negotiations.

It was the eagerness of the Kirkpatrick mission to find roads to Nepal that seems to have roused Nepali suspicions against possible future designs of the British against Nepal. The proposal of having Lieutenant Wilfred, the Company's military surveyor, accompany Kirkpatrick was dropped because of the King's specific objection to it. Kirkpatrick himself, accompanied by Lt. W.O. Knox, was not taken to the Kathmandu Valley directly but was first taken to Nuwakot by a more difficult and circuitous way and then brought into the Valley.

Kirkpatrick's mission failed to achieve anything concrete in the improvement of commercial relations between the two countries or in the settlement of the outstanding boundary disputes between them. Yet its success as a fact-finding mission must be admitted inasmuch as it made Nepal better known to the East India Company through Kirkpatrick's accounts, based on his firsthand observations and on information supplied by Gajaraj Mishra and Abdul Kadir Khan. These observations were later published in the form of a book called *An Account of the Kingdom of Nepal* (London: William Miller, Albemarle Street, 1811). This, incidentally, was the first book on Nepal to be published in the west.

By 1794, King Rana Bahadur Shah, Bahadur Shah's nephew, had come of age. Bahadur Shah's predominant role in the administration during the years of the King's minority had not only aroused a feeling of suspicion and jealousy in the mind of the young King, but had also created many enemies for him in the ranks of the officers and courtiers and among the near relatives of the King. The outcome of the war with China also posed a serious threat to Bahadur Shah's unchallenged position at the Kathmandu Court.

His adversaries were not able to have Bahadur Shah removed from office at once, because he continued to have considerable support from various elements in the Court of Nepal whose personal interests were linked with his own. Regent Bahadur Shah's group consisted of the royal collaterals and relatives, like Bam Shah and Rana Bahadur Shah's half brothers, Bidur Shahi and Sher Bahadur Shahi, both of whom had regal ambitions of their own. He also enjoyed the support of the *Kala* (Black) Pande section, led by Damodar Pande, a section of the Brahmin royal priests and preceptors, headed by Gajaraj Mishra, and the Palpa royal family of the Sens (into which Bahadur Shah had married), whose position as the almost autonomous vassal of the Shah dynasty of Nepal gave the Raja of Palpa an important say in the affairs of administration. Finally, a multitude of civil and military officials who were appointed to their offices by the Regent upheld their patron.

Among Bahadur Shah's opponents, who favoured his removal as Regent and the royal takeover of the administration, were members of the royal family such as Shrikrishna Shah and Balabhadra Shah, first cousins of Bahadur Shah and uncles of Rana Bahadur Shah; the Thapa family, whose most well-known member at the time was Amarsingh Thapa; the "Gora" (White) Pande section led by Dalabhanjan Pande; an influential group of Brahmins headed by Dinanath Upadhyaya, which was later joined by Ranganath Pandit. Ranganath was son of Brajanath Pandit, King Pratap Singh's religious preceptor, who had been expelled by Bahadur Shah to Varanasi. And a host of ambitious and self-seeking Nepalis who had lost their official position or had been refused any post by the Regent were anxious for a new regime.

Rana Bahadur's unwillingness to renew Bahadur Shah's appointment as Chautara (First Minister) at the Pajani or the annual renewal of service ceremony in July 1792 was the first indication of a decline in Bahadur Shah's position. However, Bahadur Shah continued to exercise his overall authority as Regent. For about two years the groups for and against Bahadur Shah were eventually balanced in power. But as the King's attitude towards Bahadur Shah grew worse instead of improving, the Regent's position became more and more difficult until he was dismissed from all offices and Rana Bahadur Shah assumed full powers in May 1794.

For the first time a Nepali political group sought Chinese intervention on its behalf in Nepal's internal politics. Bahadur Shah, sometime after his dismissal, requested the Chinese Amban in Lhasa by letter to forward an enclosed petition from him to the Emperor in Peking. The Amban did not comply with Bahadur Shah's request and wrote to both Rana Bahadur and Bahadur Shah suggesting that they should remain in harmony and friendship. The Amban dismissed the question of the ex-Regent's dismissal as a domestic affair about which he had nothing to say. But the Amban's attitude did not seem to discourage Bahadur Shah and he sought permission to go to Peking to see the Emperor. At this, the Amban inquired of King Rana Bahadur Shah whether he approved of Bahadur Shah's proposed visit to Peking.

It was only natural for Rana Bahadur Shah to be perturbed by this inquiry. He immediately sent the officer in charge of Tibetan relations to Lhasa with a long list of charges and allegations against the ex-Regent. One of the allegations was that Bahadur Shah was entirely responsible for the war with Tibet and China. Bahadur Shah was imprisoned after this and died in confinement on 9 July 1797, under highly suspicious circumstances

5

The Rana Bahadur Era (1794-1806)

Rana Bahadur Shah's Personal Rule

King Rana Bahadur Shah (1777-1799) began to exercise absolute power at the age of twenty, and at first he showed great skill and vigour in the conduct of both internal administration and foreign policy. There was initially keen rivalry among his immediate relatives for the position of Chautara. Rana Bahadur wanted his half-brothers, Bidur Shahi and Sher Bahadur Shahi, to share this position. Balabhadra Shah, his cousin one generation removed, was put in charge of the outlying districts. Abhimansingh Basnyat and Damodar Pande were retained as Kazis or ministers.

The Abdul Kadir Khan Mission of 1795

Even after the failure of the Kirkpatrick mission and removal of Bahadur Shah, who had favoured the improvement of relations with the Company's Government, the East India Company persisted in its attempt to explore the possibility of starting trade with Nepal on the basis of the 1792 treaty of commerce. With this end in view, the Company decided to send another mission to the Court of Nepal to be led by Abdul Kadir Khan. King Rana Bahadur Shah was initially cool to the proposal for this "commercial" mission but with some difficulty Gajaraj Mishra finally succeeded in persuading the King to agree to it.

The leader selected for this mission was Maulvi Abdul Kadir Khan, who came of a good family and had connections with high British Indian officials. He had already gained considerable experience in dealing with the Nepalis at the time of the signing of the commercial treaty of 1792, and also during the Kirkpatrick mission of 1793, and it was thought that since he was not a European, he might be better able to overcome the Nepali distrust of the Company's agents in general, and the Europeans in particular.

Sir John Shore, the Company's Governor-General, further made it a condition that Abdul Kadir Khan should regard himself "as a merchant" and not as an agent of Government, although he was given credentials to prove to the satisfaction of the Nepali authorities that his visit was intended "merely for the purpose of cementing the friendship between the states and forwarding and improving their commercial intercourse".[1] Abdul Kadir Khan was asked to impress upon the King and his ministers the urgency of the need to promote trade, friendship and understanding between the two states. He was even authorized to give compliance to any proposal from the Raja, subject to the approval of the Company, and was pointedly asked to find out which of the King's ministers were hostile to the trade proposals and which of them were in support. In addition, Abdul Kadir Khan was charged with the task of raising the question of settling the boundary disputes between Morang and Purnea and of securing the cooperation of the Nepal Government in meeting the menace of the raids and outrages perpetrated by the *faquirs* and *sannyasis* from Morang on the people of the Company's provinces. From Abdul Kadir Khan's instructions and terms of reference it is clear that his mission was official and had both a political and commercial character.

Maulvi Abdul Kadir Khan could not proceed to Nepal without encountering the same initial difficulties as Kirkpatrick. King Rana Bahadur Shah sought to discourage the mission by saying that since the war with China had laid waste a large area of Tibet, there was no possibility of trade with that country and the articles of trade from India could not be disposed of. His final suggestion was that Jonathan Duncan, Resident in Varanasi, should suspend the Abdul Kadir mission.[2] To the other point mentioned by the Governor-General in his letter suggesting Abdul Kadir Khan's mission, King Rana Bahadur replied that he had already dispatched two companies of soldiers to deal with the *faquirs*, and complained of the raids from the Company's territory by robbers led by Gudjaree Roy.[3] The King also wrote to Maulvi Abdul Khan directly asking him not to bring any merchandise along as there was no scope for its sale, and the King's reputation would suffer in case loss was sustained by the Company as a result of the considerable expenditure involved in transporting the articles.

However, these were not the real reasons why Rana Bahadur discouraged the mission, as Gajaraj Mishra pointed out in a letter to Maulvi Abdul Kadir Khan. By refusing permission to the mission, Rana Bahadur wanted to draw the attention of the Company to the adjustment of boundaries between Morang and Bengal and to Nepal's claims to Kashipur and Rudrapur, the two districts in the south-west. Again, Nepal's diplomatic agent in India, Dinanath Upadhyaya, who enjoyed a monopoly on Nepal's trade with Bengal, was also suspected of having prejudiced the Raja against acceptance of the proposal for the Abdul Kadir mission.

Gajaraj Mishra, the royal preceptor of Nepal, who was living in Varanasi, had to pay a visit to Kathmandu to persuade the King to let the Moulvi in. He went armed with a letter from the Resident to the King wherein the King was clearly told that "importation (sic) of acting contrary to engagement among rulers high in place were very disgraceful". In the same letter, the Resident thus explained the objectives of the Abdul Kadir mission:

> First, for him to pay respects to you. Secondly, to transmit the presents intended for you. Thirdly, to transmit the *Khellaut* and letters from the Nawab vizier. Fourthly, to communicate with you in respect to settling the boundary between Morang and Pŭrnea which you are so desirous of. Fifthly, to converse with you on the subject of Cashipoor and Rudrapoor (sic) for which you formerly made application in the manner the Governor-General had authorized and on the endeavours which out of consideration for your attachment are made for that purpose and as the Khan had with him some specimens of goods which he proposed to trade with on his own account and as in friendship and candor (sic) it was necessary to inform you of this application also made by the Khan to the Governor-General for a recommendation on that account, the Governor-General out of consideration for the union subsisting between the two states may have written to you by way of recommending him.[4]

The deliberate attempt of the Company to conceal the real character of the Abdul Kadir mission is clear from the concluding section of the above quotation. The mission was obviously designed to meet Nepal's objection to trading. Again, references to the settlement of boundaries between Morang and Bengal and to the possibility of examining Nepali claims to Kashipur and Rudrapur, with the co-operation of the Nawab vizier, were dangled merely as baits to make the King swallow the Abdul Kadir mission.

At last, Rana Bahadur agreed to welcome the mission and wrote to Duncan saying that he had never had any objection to the mission as such, but his solicitude for the interests of the Company had made him request the postponement of the Abdul Kadir mission.[5] In order to get over the feeling of self-embarrassment caused by inconsistency in his own attitude towards the mission, Rana Bahadur made his minister, Damodar Pande, also write to the Resident in Varanasi, "Do not suspect, Sir, that any other motive influenced the Rajah."[6]

The embassy of Maulvi Abdul Kadir arrived in Kathmandu sometime in June or July of 1795, and was received with the courtesy due to any foreign mission. Abdul Kadir Khan was forced by circumstances beyond his control to visit Nepal during the monsoon and malarial season, and he became sick in Kathmandu.

In his reply to the Governor-General's letter, carried by Abdul Kadir Khan, King Rana Bahadur acknowledged the letter and the gifts with thanks, and assured the Company of his utmost co-operation in punishing the Sannyasi raiders by expressing his friendliness towards the Company in these terms: "I reckon any person who plunders or otherwise infests the Company's territory as an absolute enemy to my own country and, please God, I will continue to chastise such riotous persons."[7]

The King further agreed to forward to the Governor-General the papers relating to the boundary dispute between Morang and Purnea. He also expressed his hope since the days of the Kirkpatrick mission of gaining, as a recognition of services by the Gorkhas in the Rohilla war (1774), the districts of Kashipur and Rudrapur from the Nawab vizier through the good offices of the Governor-General.

Abdul Kadir pressed Duncan, Resident in Varanasi, to use his influence with the Governor-General to have the King's request granted. However, the outcome of all these efforts was that the Governor-General ordered adjustments of the Morang boundary dispute in accordance with the King's wishes,[8] but expressed his inability to do anything about the transfer of Rudrapur and Kashipur to Nepal from the Nawab vizier's territory.[9]

Abdul Kadir's political achievement was minor but he rendered a more useful service to the Company from the commercial point of view. He had brought with him merchandise worth Rs. 15,000 consisting of broadcloth of various shades of colour, large corals, white Kash-

mabad cloth and Mirzapur chints. The sale of this merchandise, as stated by K.C. Chaudhuri, "was the first practical experiment in trade with Nepal for assessing the actual value and potentialities of the Indo-Nepalese trade."[10] This commercial prospecting proved to be of a limited value. The small gross profit from the sale of the merchandise would not have proved encouraging if the transportation and handling charges were to be added to its price. However, it should be noted that this was not a commercial venture in the usual sense, as the Maulvi used the goods also as gifts and not wholly as commodities for sale. Abdul Kadir estimated the total value of exports from the Company's territory to Nepal could be Rs. 400,000 to Rs. 500,000 per year.

In view of the great demand for broadcloth in all these hilly countries he suggested that if it and other articles of European manufacture could be introduced there with the consent of the Rajas, their hands would soon be forced by the rising popular demand for these goods, and they would be required to remove all obstacles to trade with the Company.[11] He also furnished the Company with a list of trade goods which should be exported.

An assessment of the comparative rate of profit made by Abdul Kadir Khan on the sale of the above articles would show that there was a much higher percentage of profit in trade with Tibet than with Nepal. Broadcloth, coral, pearls, cotton cloth, conch shells, Bengal raw silk, woollen carpets (small size), looking glasses, knives and scissors, brass scales and weights, nutmeg, cardamoms, asafoetida, sandalwood, googool, alum, chohara, Varanasi Kumtchab, silk and cotton piece goods, cotton staples, Murshidabad and Sylhet-made shields, tobacco, Varanasi sugar, kuff of diamonds (ferrous sulphate), indigo, *kurua* (unbleached) cloth, are the articles mentioned in Abdul Kadir Khan's list.

Although Nepal itself produced few articles for export to Tibet, Abdul Kadir Khan paid tribute to the commercial skill of the Nepali traders who had a large share of profit in the entrepot trade between Tibet and India. Khan's prejudice against the Hindu Gosains, who were excellent traders, was apparent when he suggested that the physical and climatic conditions and terrain in Tibet did not suit the comfort-loving Hindu traders, as the rules of their religion and caste would require them to live on a strict diet which could not be had in those conditions. His advice was that the Nepalis must be conciliated so that they would consent to play a prominent role in this trade with Tibet and Central Asia.[12]

He made a concrete suggestion with regard to the opening of warehouses in the following five places where the Tibetans could come to purchase the articles they needed: (1) near the border of Buxar district of Kuch Bihar; (2) in Sirkar Champaran; (3) in the Nawab vizier's dominion adjoining Butwal; (4) near Kumaun in the Nawab vizier's dominion; and (5) at the westernmost boundary of the Nawab vizier's dominion towards Srinagar (Garhwal). According to him, these warehouses, being close to Nepal, could also cater to its needs and particularly to the needs of the Tibetans and the Chinese who were likely to visit these factories in the cold weather once they knew they could buy the things they wanted there. These suggestions were made to circumvent Kathmandu, since to reach all of these outposts, except (2) and (3), it was not necessary to go through the territory controlled by the Gorkhas, and even to reach the two exceptions it was not essential to use the trail through Kathmandu. The opening up of trade with Tibet and Western China by way of Nepal being of interest to the Company's Government, Abdul Kadir Khan's assessment of prospects for such trade must have been of great value to it.

Abdul Kadir made three observations on internal politics in Nepal which, by their nature, had a direct bearing on the commercial relations between Nepal and the Company. The first observation related to the attitude of various ministers towards the question of trade with the Company. He was of the opinion that, with the exception of Dinanath Upadhyaya, all the high officials of the Court were in favour of this trade. Because of Khan's friendship with Gajaraj Mishra, between whose family and the Upadhyaya family traditional rivalry existed, Khan's attitude toward Dinanath Upadhyaya may have been prejudiced.

Further, according to Abdul Kadir, Bahadur Shah's reinstatement was suggested to the King by the Chinese Emperor. The King explained that he had removed his uncle from office for his share of blame for the Sino-Nepalese war. Abdul Kadir Khan also hinted to the Company's Government that if Bahadur Shah could be brought back to power by some means, the prospects for commerce and friendship between Nepal and the company would increase as Rana Bahadur Shah, being a young and inexperienced man, was not much devoted to the interests of the people.[13] The third observation related to an interesting piece of information about the presence of three "Firinghees" or Europeans who were in charge of artillery. One of them was a Frenchman, with great professional skill in casting cannons, who was paid a salary of Rs. 500 a year. When his pay was stopped after he had cast 200 cannons, and after the Nepalis themselves had acquired the skill, he complained of the bad faith of the Government and wanted to resign and leave the country but was refused permission to do so. After two attempts to escape had failed, he was put in fetters and imprisoned and, according to Abdul Kadir, he was probably dead by the time the Maulvi was there.[14]

Sir John Shore, the Company's Governor-General at this time, realistically assessed the value of Abdul Kadir's mission in the following words:

> Of the results of the mercantile transactions entrusted to the conduct of M. Kadir, we are not yet qualified to form a judgement . . . but considering the commercial as well as political information derived from his deputation it cannot be deemed useless and unimportant. This communication has enabled us to open some judgement of the character of the Raja and his principal officers and to ascertain their disposition towards this government. . . . This political impediment resulting from the character and conduct of the Raja are of more consequence and whilst these exist, the commerce must remain in a feeble state. We ought to look forward to a period of better administration in Nepal and intermediately to promote our connection with the Raja.[15]

The Wazir Ali Incident

Even if the Abdul Kadir mission failed to bring about any visible improvement in the relations between Nepal and the Company, it certainly had not done anything to worsen it. This was proved by the readiness on the part of Rana Bahadur to offer assistance to the Company's Government by initiating a vigorous search for Wazir Ali.

Wazir Ali long harboured a design against the Company because it was responsible for his suppression, by his uncle Sa'adat Ali, as the Nawab of Oudh following Nawab vizier Asaf-ud-dulah's death in 1797. Apprehensive of Wazir Ali's design, the Company had asked Cherry, Resident of Varanasi, to escort him to Calcutta where he was to be confined. Wazir Ali made good his escape after murdering Cherry and several other Englishmen. Ali was reported to have been hiding in the tarai forests of central Nepal near Butwal along with twenty-five horsemen.

In response to King Rana Bahadur's offer of help, the Governor-General requested Rana Bahadur to alert his officers and men everywhere in the country so that Wazir Ali might not be able to escape.[16] The Governor-General also requested Rana Bahadur to pass to the Nawab of Oudh any information he might have about the activities of Wazir Ali and his party.[17] The Company's Government offered a reward of Rs. 40,000 for the arrest of Wazir Ali and the Nawab of Oudh also announced a large grant of land for the same purpose.

The Nepal Government also sent a body of soldiers under an officer to apprehend Wazir Ali. When he was informed of the approach of the Nepali soldiers, he returned to the Company's territory where he was arrested in 1799 by Raja Pratap Singh and handed over to the English, who kept him in confinement until his death in 1817.

The Wazir Ali incident gave the Gorkhas a chance to place the Company's Government under an obligation to them by informing the Governor-General of Wazir Ali's presence in Butwal and by joining in efforts to apprehend him. Commenting on this point, Chaudhuri writes: "Well might the government of Nepal claim, as they actually did at a later date, that they had not been 'wanting in good offices towards the English and will not be so hereafter.'[18] However, one must not forget to note that the readiness of the Gorkhas to act in this case was inspired less by any inclination to help the Company than by their hatred of Muslims dating back to Mir Kasim's attack on the Gorkhas on 1763.

Internal Disorder and Rana Bahadur's Exit from Nepal

No sooner had the Wazir Ali affair ended than King Rana Bahadur Shah informed the Governor-General that he was abdicating in favour of his infant son, Girvana Yuddha, then eighteen months old, and that he planned to devote the rest of his life to the worship of God. In the same letter, Rana Bahadur also requested the Governor-General to extend to his son the same consideration which he had always received during his own rule. Governor-General Wellesley assured him of the Company's highest consideration in order to "connect and strengthen the bonds of amity and unity."[19] The abdication of Rana Bahadur and the accession of his son, Girvana Yuddha, took place on 23 March 1799.

The reasons for Rana Bahadur's abdication, however, were not as simple as those mentioned above; his exit from Nepal was brought about by circumstances beyond his control. A sidelight on this most critical period in Nepal's history will be in order here. It will also help to place our appreciation and understanding of Nepal's relations with the Company in proper perspective.

Young Rana Bahadur had a difficult task stepping into the shoes of his uncle, the former Regent, Bahadur Shah, who had steered the ship of state clear of many a shoal during the most difficult and exciting phase of the kingdom's physical expansion. Nevertheless, when Rana Bahadur took full control of the government, he temporarily surpassed even the most optimistic expectations. He was full of youthful dash and daring, though something of a profligate. But soon he lapsed into his old life of dissipation. The excesses of vice and pleasure had begun to tell on his frail constitution and mind.

Meanwhile he had developed an infatuation for a young Maithili Brahmin widow of bewitching beauty, Kantavati. She had succeeded in extracting a promise from him that if she bore him a son, he would succeed to the throne after his father. Kantavati did give birth to a male child in 1797, though she herself fell ill after the child's birth. Her condition grew worse from day to day, and it appeared as though her days were numbered. Rana Bahadur neglected his duties of state and spent all his time attending her. At about the same time, Rana Bahadur was told by an astrologer that he also was going to die very soon; and he became all the more anxious about his infant son's future. He wanted to do everything possible to make good his promise to Kantavati while both of them were still alive.

Though Rana Bahadur had no son by his first wife, Rajarajeshvari, he had two sons by his second wife, Suvarnaprabha. The elder of the two, Ranodyot Shah, had to be superseded to clear the way for the succession of Rana Bahadur's infant son by Kantavati. Rana Bahadur declared Ranodyot illegitimate and deprived him of his claims to the throne. Rana Bahadur anticipated the Court's opposition to his infant son's succession since the child had undeniably been born out of wedlock. Hence he put his infant son on the throne during his own lifetime and made all the high officials of the kingdom swear allegiance to him. For all this, he probably had the consent of his eldest Queen, Rajarajeshvari, who was childless and had always feared the possibility of Queen Suvarnaprabha's ascendancy over her as mother of the heir to the throne. Queen Rajarajeshvari seemed to prefer Kantavati's son to Suvarnaprabha's son.

Rana Bahadur was not content even with this, and wanted to make sure that Kantavati's son, King Girvana Yuddha (1799-1816), would

King Prithvinarayan Shah Dev (1769-1775), the founder of the ruling Shah dynasty of Nepal

King Pratap Singh Shah Dev (1775-1777)

Commander-in-Chief of the Gorkhali Army Kazi Bamsharaj Pande (1777-1779)

King Rana Bahadur Shah Dev (1777-1799); assassinated in April 1806 as Regent for his son, King Girvana Yuddha Bikram Shah Dev

Kazi Damodar Pande (1785-1804), one of the leading Commanders of the Gorkhali army and Prime Minister (1802-1804)

King Girvan Yuddha Shah Dev (1799-1816)

Prime Minister General Bhimsen Thapa (1806-1837)

King Rajendra Bikram Shah Dev (1816-1847) deposed when his son was placed on the throne by Jang Bahadur on 12 May 1847

Prime Minister Ranganath Pandit (Poudyal) (December 1837 - August 1838)

Prime Minister Rana Jang Pande (6 February - 1 November 1840)

Prime Minister General Mathbar Singh Thapa (December 1843 - May 1845)

Prime Minister Fatte Jang Shah (November 1840 - March 1843 and September 1845 - September 1846)

Jang Bahadur Kanwar Rana, the strong man of Nepal (15 September 1846 - 25 February 1877)

Maharaj Jang Bahadur with his senior Maharani, Hiranyagarbha Kumari, whose daughter became the mother of King Prithvi Bir Bikram Shah Dev

King Surendra Bikram Shah Dev (12 May 1847 - 19 May 1881)

Crown Prince Trailokya Bikram Shah (born 30 November 1847, died 30 March 1878) father of King Prithvi Bir Bikram Shah Dev

Prime Minister Bam Bahadur Kanwar Rana (6 August 1856 - 25 May 1857)

General Badri Narsing Kanwar Rana (1846-1851 when he was expelled to India)

C.-in-C. Krishna Bahadur Kanwar Rana from 1857 till 1863 (also Acting Prime Minister for sometime in May-June 1857)

A hunting party in far Western Nepal Tarai in 1876: Maharaj Prime Minister Jang Bahadur, wearing a 'sombrero' is seated to the left of the Prince of Wales (later King Edward VII)

Maharaj Prime Minister Ranoddip Singh Kanwar Rana (1877-1885) with his first wife Bada Maharani Haripriya Devi)

Maharaj Prime Minister Ranoddip Singh with the infant king, Prithvi Bir Bikram Shah Dev (1883)

Commander-in-Chief Dhir Shamsher (1879-1884), who died without becoming the Maharaj Prime Minister himself but several of his sons and grandsons held the highest political office in the land

Senior Commanding General Jagat Jang (1879-1882), who should have inherited the most powerful office of the Maharaj of Kaski and Lamjung according to Jang Bahadur's dispensation, but was deprived of it as a result of the machinations of Jang's surviving brothers

Senior Commanding General Jagat Jang's eldest son, General Juddhe Pratap Jang who was also killed like his father on the morrow of the assassination of Ranoddip Singh by Dhir Shamsher's sons.

Senior Commanding General Jit Jang (1882-1885), Jang Bahadur's second son, who lost his position following the *coup d' etat* by Dhir Shamsher's sons on 22 November 1885

Maharaj Ranoddip Singh with Earl de Grey in their hunting camp in the Tarai in 1883

have no rival claimants to the throne in the future. Rana Bahadur had his cousin, Chautara Kuldip Shah, Dalamardan Shah's son, blinded in the left eye, thus depriving him of any chance of claiming the throne in the future. By convention, the throne could not pass to someone who was maimed or otherwise defective. Since the death in prison of Bahadur Shah, Kuldip was the only legitimate surviving descendant of Prithvinarayan Shah.

Despite all the care and attention bestowed on her, and despite everything poor Rana Bahadur did to fulfil her wishes, Kantavati succumbed to her illness and passed away in early 1799. 1,20,000 rupees had been paid to Brahmin priests to pray for her recovery. Her death gave Rana Bahadur such a shock that he was thrown completely off balance, and, in a paroxysm of grief, he began to indulge in mad orgies of mutilating Brahmins and desecrating the temples. The ministers of the Court had an anxious time and, in consultation with the senior Regent Queen, Rajarajeshvari, they had the infant King removed to Nawakot for his own safety. At one stage, Rana Bahadur even wanted to take back all his powers as King. Courtiers led by Kirtiman Singh Basnyat and Damodar Pande resisted his demand and told him firmly that he was no longer the King as he himself had made over his power to his son whom it had now become their duty to protect. Rana Bahadur sought to gain the support of some army officers, but the army and the population generally were sorely tired of his antics. When Rana Bahadur's repeated appeals failed to produce the desired effects, he withdrew to Varanasi on 27 May 1799, accompanied by his senior Queen Rajarajeshvari, Balabhadra Shah and a party of his followers. Among them happened to be Bhimsen Thapa, the future Prime Minister of Nepal.[20]

Regency of Queen Suvarnaprabha (April 1800 to February 1803)

After Rana Bahadur withdrew to Varanasi, Kirtiman Singh Basnyat headed the administration of Nepal for about thirteen months with Rana Bahadur's second wife, Queen Suvarnaprabha, as Regent.

Circumstances Leading to the Conclusion of the Treaty of 1801

As soon as Governor-General Wellesley heard of Rana Bahadur's arrival in Varanasi, he lost no time in appointing an officer by the name of Captain W.O. Knox to attend upon the ex-King regularly.[21] Knox had accompanied Kirkpatrick on his 1793 mission to Nepal. We have already seen how keenly interested the Company was in opening up a regular channel of trade between Nepal and the Company's Government. So far, scant progress had been made in this direction, even after the signing of the commercial treaty of 1792 and the subsequent missions of Captain William Kirkpatrick in 1793 and of Maulvi Abdul Kadir Khan in 1795. The presence of Rana Bahadur in Varanasi presented the Company with a golden opportunity to pressure the Nepali Government to secure concessions in matters of trade and treaty relations. Wellesley would have been the last person to let such an opportunity go unexploited.

As soon as Rana Bahadur arrived in Varanasi, he wrote to the Governor-General asking for assistance in recovering the throne.[22] The Governor-General's reply was delivered to Rana Bahadur by Captain Knox, and it assured him of the Company's friendly disposition towards him. Gajaraj Mishra, his religious preceptor, who also had taken up residence in Varanasi, appealed to the Governor-General to assist Rana Bahadur.

Captain Knox was given detailed instructions on how to deal with Rana Bahadur and the Government of Nepal in order to promote the Company's political and commercial interests. On the plea that the Company could not remain indifferent to developments of such magnitude in a state bordering on its territories, Captain Knox was asked to obtain detailed information about the circumstances that led to the exit of Rana Bahadur.[23] Knox was pointedly asked not to give Rana Bahadur the slightest impression that the Company would restore "his authority by force" until he was ordered to do so. As the Governor-General was primarily interested in promoting the Company's interest in Nepal by acting as mediator between the *de facto* Government of Nepal and Rana Bahadur Shah, Knox was authorized to entertain proposals from Rana Bahadur, and to find out from the Nepali Government whether it was willing to readmit Rana Bahadur "under the guarantee of the British Government."

That the Governor-General-in-Council was not interested in military intervention on behalf of Rana Bahadur is clear from the following instructions to Knox.

> The primary object of the Governor-General-in-Council is to be instrumental, by his mediation, in the re-establishment of the Rajah's authority and by this service to conciliate the gratitude of the prince

> and to obtain from him in return such concessions as should be effectively calculated to improve and secure its commercial intercourse of the two countries.[24]

It must be said to the credit of Rana Bahadur Shah that even as a supplicant at the Company's door, he did not want the Company to intervene directly except perhaps as a last resort. He merely sought to use the Company to frighten the Nepali Government into accepting his restoration. To enhance the threat, he used to talk openly "of returning to Nepal with a British army."[25] Yet he was fully aware of the conditions that prevented British armed intervention. The contents of Knox's letter, dated 23 February 1801, reveal Rana Bahadur's perception of the prevailing situation. "They (the English) will not resort to violence, for the country (Nepal) being entirely mountainous; they are at war with Vizier Ali, the Sikhs, the French, and the Deccanese. The French have lately captured six of their ships, and a son of Mr. Graham, the first member of the Board of Revenue, was killed on one of them."[26]

As an outward gesture of his eagerness to reassert his authority in Nepal and wreak vengeance on the men whom he held responsible for his exile, Rana Bahadur even put forward an outrageous proposal that if the Company restored him to his throne, he would pay it $37^1/_2$ per cent and 50 per cent of the land taxes from the hill and tarai areas of Nepal respectively. Rana Bahadur even went to the extent of suggesting that if at any time none of his descendants survived, "the whole of the country of Nepal shall devolve to the administration and control of the Company."[27] Rana Bahadur knew full well that the British could never accept this proposal because its acceptance would oblige the British to ensure the rule of his dynasty on a permanent basis for a concession no Government in Nepal would be prepared to make except under duress. Moreover, Rana Bahadur rightly guessed that the ministers of the Kathmandu Court would not be able to anticipate the British rejection of his proposal and he, therefore, made it a point to leak its contents deliberately, with a view to misleading his political rivals in Nepal.

Rana Bahadur sought financial assistance from the British through Hakeem Antony, a disreputable adventurer of mixed Indian and Portuguese origin. This aroused the fear and suspicion of the British. Rana Bahadur wanted to borrow money from the Company on his assurance of repayment upon his return to power and wanted to be left alone thereafter to persist in his intrigues. As is clear from Knox's reports, Rana Bahadur wanted merely to solicit the Company's friendship without disclosing his plans. The Governor-General asked Knox to make it clear to Rana Bahadur that he could not withdraw himself from the surveillance of the Company's Government without its consent.[28] However, without the Company's knowledge, Rana Bahadur sent Gajaraj Mishra to Nepal to negotiate terms with the *de facto* Government. For a while, this led the Company to suspect Gajaraj of double-dealing.[29] On the other hand, Rana Bahadur told Knox that Gajaraj did not enjoy his confidence because of his complicity in Bahadur Shah's conspiracy on his life.[30] Knox did not know whom to believe until Gajaraj's continued loyalty to the British cleared him of suspicion.

Knox did not take long to find out that Rana Bahadur was not dependable from the British point of view. So he opened negotiations directly with the high officials of the *de facto* Nepal Government for a direct settlement. The settlement visualized by the Company's Government entailed a provision in the shape of a *jagir*, or land-grant, for the ex-King, Rana Bahadur. Because of Gajaraj's past experience and record in the conduct of negotiations between the two Governments, and also because of the fact that he enjoyed the confidence of both parties at the time, Knox employed him for the purpose of negotiating a settlement. But from the beginning, Rana Bahadur's actions made the task of the negotiator difficult and complicated.

While Rana Bahadur was making constant pleas to the Company for immediate armed intervention in Nepal, he was simultaneously writing to the Nepali officials warning them against the plausible designs of the Company and against signing any treaties with it. When he knew that Gajaraj Mishra was employed by the Company for negotiations with the *de facto* Government of Nepal, Rana Bahadur did not hesitate to brand him, as "interested in the prosperity of the English."[31]

Despite the excesses of his youth, Rana Bahadur possessed a sharp intellect. The moment he knew that Knox had decided not to take up the question of his reinstatement, his attitude changed completely. His contradictory letters to the British Government and the Nepal Government and the sudden change in his attitude towards Gajaraj Mishra can only be explained by this perception. Rana Bahadur was sufficiently intelligent to realize that his claim to power was being bypassed in the negotiations, and the best he could do in his own interest was to prevent successful negotiations, thereby leaving the way open for him to regain power.

Gajaraj Mishra had a hard time convincing the court in Nepal that an understanding with the Company was of lasting interest to Nepal.

The Nepali Court's deep-rooted suspicion of the Company's designs and its faith in its traditional policy of isolation made the court shift grounds in negotiations so often that Gajaraj Mishra himself was misunderstood by the Company. Again, Rana Bahadur, even from Varanasi, was constantly playing on the Nepali court's natural distrust of the British. The ministers of the court were faced with a serious dilemma: whether to accept a treaty with the Company and the Residency it would impose on Nepal, and thus prevent Rana Bahadur from staging a comeback with the Company's support, or whether to leave themselves open to the manoeuvres of the Company through Rana Bahadur. As a result of Gajaraj Mishra's persistent assurances about the Company's good intentions, the ministers finally decided to sign a treaty, mainly in order to frustrate Rana Bahadur's efforts to return to power. As we shall see later, this treaty gave Rana Bahadur a handle to rally the anti-British sentiment. He did this so successfully that the army officers forgot his earlier excesses and sided with him.

The Treaty of 1801

The treaty between Nepal and the East India Company's government concluded on 26 October 1801 also laid down the terms and conditions of the *jageer* or land grant for ex-King Rana Bahadur. The treaty itself consisted of thirteen articles. The first referred to the desire and need for improvement in the existing friendship between the two parties. The second article provided that "the incendiary and turbulent representations of the disaffected, (who were) the disturbers of our mutual friendship, " would not be attended to without investigation and proof. The reference was obviously to the designs and activities of Rana Bahadur Shah in Varanasi.

The third article must have been introduced to allay the fears and suspicions of the officials of the Nepal Government and also to afford a sense of protection to the Company against possible moves and designs of Nepal, in concert with other rulers in India, against its interests. This third article went much further than the second article and stated that "the principals and officers of both Governments" would "cordially consider the friends and enemies of either state to be the friends and enemies of the other." Article four obliged the Nepal Government and the Company's Government to inform each other, through the *vakeels*, or diplomatic representatives of the respective Governments, of "any attempts by any one of the neighbouring powers of either state" to "commence any altercation or dispute, and design, without provocation, unjustly to possess himself of the territories of either country" or "entertain hostile intentions with the view of taking that country."

The fifth article provided for the settlement of the boundary disputes generally "through (their) respective *vakeels* or other officers according to the principles of justice and right." The sixth article stipulated that disputes that might arise with regard to "such places as are upon the frontiers of the dominions of the Nawab Vizier and of Nepaul would be settled by the mediation of the *vakeel* on the part of the Company, in the presence of one from the Nepal Government, and one from his Excellency the Vizier."

Article seven abolished Nepal's payment of tribute (in elephants) to the Company on behalf of Muckanacinpoor (Makwanpur). The eighth article provided that each of the Governments would apprehend and extradite fugitive dacoits, who were a constant major problem in the border area. Article nine settled a grant of land or *jageer* on Rana Bahadur Shah, the former King in exile, referred to as Samee Jeo (*Swamijee*), the title he chose for himself upon his abdication in favour of his infant son. Vijayapur was settled upon Rana Bahadur as his *jageer*, and he was given the alternative of either going there and managing the farmland himself or staying within the Company's territory and receiving income from the said Land by instalments.

Article ten provided for the appointment of deputation of a confidential person to each other as *vakeel* (diplomatic representative), who, by remaining in attendance upon their respective Governments, might "effect the objects above specified, and promote whatever may tend to the daily improvement of friendship subsisting between the two states." Article eleven clearly stated that the *vakeels* thus appointed should enjoy the "regard and respect," the rank, privilege and protection due to an accredited representative "by the laws of nations." Article twelve, in order to allay the Nepali suspicion of the Company's interference in Nepal's internal affairs, clearly laid down that the *vakeels* of both states should hold no intercourse whatever with any of the subjects or inhabitants of the country, excepting with the officers of government, without the permission of those officers." The final article emphasized the fact that both sides should "abide by the spirit of this treaty" and invoked the punishment of God on any person "who might transgress against it."[32]

The treaty was not ratified by Nepal until October 1802, although the Company itself had ratified it on 30 October 1801. The Nepalis' one-year delay shows their considerable hesitation in accepting the agreement. Indeed the conclusion of the treaty created a split among the ranking ministers of the court, each faction contending for control of the minor King.

Both the groups were opposed to the acceptance of a British Residency in Nepal. To them, the acceptance of Residency meant the Company's penetration into the internal affairs of Nepal, a step towards Nepal's loss of independence. In view of the record of Residents in the state of India, their fears cannot be said to have been ill-founded. This was the reason the Nepali officials deliberately omitted any reference to an exchange of *vakeels*, or diplomatic representatives, in their own draft of the treaty.

The Nepali draft had amounted to nothing but a profession of pious friendly intentions and had not conceded real advantage of any sort to the English Company but, on the other hand, had sought to ensure the Company Government's protection and help for Nepal against China by having both the Governments consider friends and enemies of one state to be the friends and enemies of the other. The text of the treaty proposed by the Nepali side is as follows:

> That as a treaty was formerly entered into between the two states since it is the mutual wish of both governments to draw more closely the relations of amity, it is agreed that the Amlahs and Nobles of both the states shall, forever from generation to generation, keep up a friendly intercourse with each other, and considering each other's state as their own and without any difference or disunity of interest shall endeavour agreeably to their respective tenets and religion to promote the prosperity, success and welfare of both states and all territories appertaining to them, and that they shall consider from their hearts the friends and enemies of one state the friends and enemies of the other.[33]

Exchange of Resident Representative between Nepal and the Company's Government

In accordance with the treaty of 1801 (26 October), Captain W.O. Knox was appointed the first British representative in Kathmandu, and he took up his official duties in April 1802, months before Nepal had formally ratified it. Before Knox left for Kathmandu, three young men, all close relatives of important officials of the Nepali court, Lakshman Shah, son of a royal collateral, Chautara Bam Shah, Karbir Singh Pande, son of Damodar Pande, and Kesharjang Singh, son of Indra Bir Singh, had arrived at Patna to represent Nepal in the Company's dominions. It was so manipulated that they should stay at Patna until the beginning of the following winter, thus allowing the Company plenty of time to assess the Nepali attitude towards Knox's residency. Despite the treaty, so great was the mutual suspicion that the three Nepali representatives were treated as hostages to ensure Knox's safety inside Nepal. K.C. Chaudhury has rightly pointed out that though "these young men were not avowedly dispatched as hostages, yet such they were in reality."[34] Because of his past experience in dealing with Nepali officials and their delay in ratifying the treaty, wisely took along as his escort Bam Shah, a deputy Kathmandu, and he Knox anticipated difficulties upon his arrival at originally sent by the Nepali Government to negotiate the treaty on their behalf.

Objectives and Purpose of the Knox Mission

The Company's instructions to Captain Knox covered a wide range of political, military, and commercial subjects. Knox was asked to investigate Nepal's treaty relations and alliances with other countries, especially with China.[35] He was told to suggest the means of ensuring Nepal's cooperation in extraditing criminals from Nepali territory and in settling boundary problems on the frontiers of Purnea and Tirhut. The Company sought to impress on Knox, in the following words, the need to cultivate close relations with Nepal:

> Independently of those considerations which suggest the general policy of forming a close connection with neighbouring and contiguous states, the local situation of the territories of Nepaul, skirting considerable part of the northern frontier of Bengal and Bihar and nearly the whole North Eastern limit of the Province of Oude, renders an intimate alliance with the State an object of peculiar importance to the political interests of the Company.[36]

At one stage in the treaty negotiations, Knox had suggested to the Governor-General that Damodar Pande and Bam Shah be paid some kind of pension by the Company and that "an annual sum of twenty-four thousand rupees, divided between Daundhar Bum Shah and Gudjeraja Misser (sic), would purchase the entire command to their service and consequently the accomplishment of every point that the government may be desirous of carrying."[37] The British Government was so interested in securing a foothold in Nepal that it was even prepared to follow this dubious method of securing its influence in Nepal's administration. However, Wellesley, while accepting the suggestion, was careful to point out that this should not be taken to imply an obligation on the part of the Company to support Damodar Pande and Bam Shah against their rivals for power because "such an obligation" would be "inconsistent with the dignity of the British Government and would militate against the fundamental principles of alliance."[38] Wellesley further made it clear to Knox that once relations with Nepal were put on a secure basis, the British Government should endeavour to support the legal government by whatever means possible.

On the military and strategic side, Captain Knox was asked to collect data about the strength of the Nepali army and the state of the country's internal and external defences. Regarding commercial activities, the Company's commercial interests in Nepal had remained more or less the same since the time of Warren Hastings's first overtures in 1784. Knox was asked to secure implementation of the commercial treaty of 1792, which had theretofore remained a dead letter. He Company's border in exchange for an equivalent one of the produce and forest resources and to assess their commercial value. Knox was told to explore the possibility of using Nepal as an overland trade route to Tibet and to assess the prospect for the sale of the Company's European manufactured goods in Nepal and Tibet. The Company also had an eye on the timber trade as the supply of sal, fir and pine from Nepal would considerably reduce their cost for the Company. At the time timber was imported from distant Pegu and Eastern Islands.

Captain Knox was further asked to explore the possibility of cession by the Nepal Government of a belt of forest lands on the Company's border in exchange for an equivalent one of the Company's territory, or for its price in cash. He was specifically asked to find out if the Nepal Government would be willing to cede this belt of forest land in exchange for the transfer of the Districts of Kashipur and Rudrapur to Nepal by arrangement with the Nawab Vizier. Knox was instructed to study carefully the causes of Nepali suspicion and hostility towards the Company and to suggest remedies.

On his way to Nepal, Captain Knox received several deputations from the Rajas of the neighbouring hill states, and met several times with the Vakeel of the Raja of Palpa and Butwal. They wanted to be taken under the Company's protection and offered ready-made plans for military action against Nepal with the Company's assistance. Captain Knox pleaded with his Government that if Butwal were to receive the Company's protection, this could always be used as a means of putting pressure on the Nepali administration to gain any objects the Company might desire. Knox also pointed out to the Company the obvious strategic and commercial advantages of Palpa and Butwal as an outlet for trade with the northern areas and as an alternative route for mounting a military offensive against Nepal, should the need ever arise. All the same, Knox was careful to point out that any alliance with Palpa and Butwal would completely destroy the prospects for Nepali cooperation in the implementation of the recently concluded treaty. At the very beginning, the Governor-General expressed himself against any hostile measures for the enforcement of the treaty and made it clear to Knox that "even under the dissolution of our engagement with the state of Nepal the same consideration would render it the duty of the British Government to restrain the Rajah of Butwal as a dependent of the Company from the execution of his vindictive projects, without the express sanction of the government."[39]

Knox viewed the treaty of 1801 merely as "an offspring of fear", and he was absolutely right in thinking that it had not even slightly changed Nepali suspicions of the Company's designs. Knox guessed correctly that the treaty would remain in force only as long as Rana Bahadur was kept in Varanasi under the protection of the Company. When Knox advocated the Company's alliance with the Raja of Palpa and Butwal, he was thinking of the time when, in the event of Rana Bahadur's return to Nepal, the Company would need another means of putting pressure on the Nepali authorities. Subsequent events proved Knox's prognostication correct. When Rana Bahadur returned to Nepal and successfully asserted his authority there, he took immediate action to oust the Raja of Palpa and Butwal on the plea that the Raja had always remained a tributary of Nepal.

To add to the state of instability, and to further complicate Knox's task, Rajàrajeshvari left Varanasi apparently as a protest against being maltreated by her husband, who reportedly had a liaison with a Varanasi prostitute at the time. However, there are also indications that the above story of his affair with a lowly girl was put out to hoodwink both the Kathmandu authorities and British officials about the Queen's real intentions.

Rajarajeshvari, accompanied by Balabhadra Shah and ten of her maidservants, first proceeded to Ramnagar in Betiah. She stayed there for some time with the displaced Raja of Tanahu, Harakumaradatta Sen, with whom she had spent her childhood.

The Kathmandu courtiers who were on the side of Senior Queen Rajarajeshvari had naturally been jealous of Kirtiman Singh Basnyat's position as Chief Officer of the Court or *Mul Kazi.* One night, towards the close of the year 1801, Kirtiman Singh, while returning home from the Royal Palace, was brutally murdered. His body was thrown inside the compound walls which enclosed the shed for royal elephants. The Regent Queen and Sher Bahadur Shahi, Rana Bahadur's half brother, held a court of inquiry and eighty officers were put under arrest. Sher Bahadur Shahi helped his elder brother, Bidur Shahi, flee from Kathmandu by informing him about the proposed court of inquiry. Damodar Pande was dismissed from his post, but was not imprisoned because he made a solemn vow that he would not run away from the country. His son, Rana Kishore Pande, was put in fetters, while Ranajit Pande escaped to the tarai. Because of the widely talked-about rivalry between Kirtiman Singh Basnyat and Damodar Pande during Regent Queen Suvarnaprabha's regency, Damodar Pande and his relatives were suspected of having something to do with the assasination of Kirtiman Singh Basnyat. Pratiman Rana, Garbu Khwas and other officers were executed on the charge of spreading false rumours about inimacy between the Regent Queen and the late Kirtiman Singh Basnyat. Kirtiman Singh's brother, Bakhtawar Singh Basnyat, succeeded him as *Mul Kazi.*

On receiving news of the assassination of the Chief Officer of the Court, Kirtiman Singh Basnyat, in Kathmandu, she moved to a village called Katarban in the Rautahat district of Nepal. Before Knox had started for Kathmandu, she was there, biding her time awaiting the opportunity to return to Kathmandu and take over the Regency herself with the help of sympathetic officers. The real man behind Kirtiman Singh's assassination had been Shrikrishna Shah, Rana Bahadur's cousin one generation removed. Having been expelled from Nepal on the charge of complicity in the assassination plot, Shrikrishna Shah spent some time in Patna and then joined Queen Rajarajeshvari at the village in Rautahat.

Although Bakhtawar Singh Basnyat was nominally the Mul Kazi, the chief adviser to Regent Queen Suvarnaprabha in Kathmandu was Subuddhi Khadga. In March 1802, in Jhanchura just inside Nepal, Knox was met by a high-powered delegation from the Court of Nepal. It included Damodar Pande, Chantara Bam Shah and Tribhuvan Singh, Kazi Dhanwat's son. Damodar Pande and Tribhuvan Singh-Pradhan discussed a proposal for the settlement of an adequate land grant on Senior Queen Rajarajeshvari, thus enabling her to live inside Nepal. Bam Shah favoured the idea of having the King and the Senior Queen reside in the Company's territory. His view was supported by Gajaraj Mishra who thought that the Senior Queen's entry into Nepal would pave the way for the return of Rana Bahadur to power. Tribhuvan Singh objected to the inclusion of armed soldiers in Knox's mission, but he dropped his objection after Gajaraj Mishra explained to him that it was the normal practice of the Company's Government to have armed guards accompany the Resident.

Once Knox was at Kathmandu, he was courteously received and treated in a manner befitting the position of a foreign Government's representative, but before long the attitude of the Court toward Knox and the members of his party underwent a change and they began to be subjected to pinpricks of every sort. However, internal conditions forced Regent Queen Suvarnaprabha in the end to cultivate the British Resident. Opposition against her was mounting, and the return of Senior Queen Rajarajeshvari posed a serious threat to her. The Regent Queen was aware that her position was slipping fast and she requested Knox to intervene on her behalf and work out a settlement with Queen Rajarajeshvari by offering her a handsome allowance.

In response to the Regent Queen's request, Knox sent his agent, Mirza Mehdi, to the village of Katarban in Rautahat where Rajarajeshvari was camping. Scarcely had Mehdi reached there when the Senior Queen left for Kathmandu. Marching triumphantly at the head of the very same army sent by the Regent Queen to resist her, Rajarajeshvari appeared at Thankot, a village about eight miles to the west of Kathmandu. This caused a great sensation in the town, but the drama was over when the incumbent Regent Queen, with the infant King, sought sanctuary in the temple of Pashupatinath. Queen Rajarajeshvari had no difficulty in taking over the regency. She appointed Damodar Pande as Mul Kazi, or Chief Minister, notwithstanding the fact that he was sent by the incumbent Regent Queen to intercede with Rajarajeshvari at Thankot.

Regency of Queen Rajarajeshvari (February 1803 to March 1804)

The relations between the new regency and Knox started well, because Regent Queen Rajarajeshvari undertook to abide by the terms of the treaty of 1801 and ordered immediate reimbursement of arrears due to the Company with respect to Rana Bahadur's pension. But soon differences arose over two issues. The first point related to the Nepali Government's reluctance to issue two officials of the Residency with visas to visit Nepal. The second issue was the transfer of the two districts of Vijayapur and Morang to Gajaraj Mishra so that he might obtain farm revenue from them and make payment of allowances to Rana Bahadur in Varanasi.[40]

After several unsuccessful attempts to have these matters settled, Captain Knox threatened to withdraw into the Company's territory unless they were resolved by 12 March 1803. His ultimatum brought only verbal assurances from the Court of Regent Queen Rajarajeshvari and he publicly notified the Nepal Government of his decision to leave Kathmandu on 18 March 1803. At the last minute, pressure was apparently put on Knox to change his decision, but he thought that any late change in his decision would compromise the honour of his Government and he left Kathmandu on the announced date.

It Knox's account is to be believed, he was earnestly requested to return to Kathmandu even after he had started on his journey to India. Kazi Ranadhir Singh met him at Pharping, a village within a day's march from Kathmandu, and brought the personal regrets of the infant King and the Regent. He appealed to Knox to change his mind. In doing so the messenger went to the extent of describing the high Government officials of the day as "greedy unprincipled men who had shown their disregard for all obligations,"[41] and assured Knox that the Regent Queen was willing to punish these people if "she had the continued friendship and support of the British Government."

Another delegation of officials also met him. The plan suggested by them to end the state of instability in Nepal was the restoration of Rana Bahadur "at the head of the administration to be formed with the concurrence of the British Government (and this condition should be made indispensable in future removals and appointments)."[42]

Still another message, which was supposedly conveyed to him by a Nepali officer on behalf of the Raja of Butwal, said that "affairs in Nepal were in that state of hopeless disorder that nothing excepting the interposition of the British Government would remedy."[43] The Raja of

Butwal, according to Knox, was of the opinion that all the Rajas dispossessed of their lands by the Gorkhas would support the Company's armed intervention in the hope of regaining their lost possessions. Knox's own conclusion is summed up in the following quote: "Nepaul presents to its inhabitants no other change of escaping the miseries of anarchy than by submission to foreign control."[44]

Knox's account of the circumstances of his withdrawal from Kathmandu and his report on his interviews with different persons in the course of his journey to India appear to have been so designed as to put his own action in a favourable light with his superiors and to pave the way for the Company's armed intervention. This becomes all the more apparent when we examine Knox's anxiety to remove his Government's suspicion of Chinese reaction to British armed intervention in Nepal. Knox gave his opinion on this aspect of the question in the following words:

> With respect of their (Nepal Government's) right consistent with their relation to China, . . . that the people of Nepaul were perfectly independent of the court, that no application for its assistance against the dangers that at one time apprehended from us, nor for composing the internecine feuds, has even been thought of. Had China possessed a right or felt a wish to interfere with the affairs of Nepaul, it would scarcely have passed unnoticed the many important changes that have agitated that country, nor my reception there as the acknowledged minister of a foreign power.[45]

Captain Knox was not merely content with this explanation, but went to the extent of suggesting that the only way to enforce payment of allowances to Rana Bahadur would be physical occupation of a portion of the tarai, preferably Almora.[46] This could be achieved by putting forward the plea that Rana Bahadur should be restored to power.

But Knox's arguments did not seem to have any effect upon his superiors. They, too, must have asked the questions which we are inclined to ask now: Why did Knox withdraw at all from Kathmandu if the Government, however belatedly, had been willing to meet his demands, and especially if there had been a popular demand for the British intervention in Nepal? According to Knox, even after he had withdrawn to the Company's territory, the Regent Queen herself requested his return to Kathmandu through her uncle, Harakumaradatta Sen.[47]

The situation, although not hopeless from the Nepali point of view, was fluid. The new Regent Queen had released Amarsingh Thapa and sent him on a military expedition to conquer Garhwal. Knox's report was coloured by the feeling of those who were thinking of securing personal gains through the Company's intervention, or those who might have stood to lose directly as a result of the British withdrawal. Knox and Gajaraj themselves belonged to one or both of the above categories. Knox's insistence on the transfer of Vijayapur and Morang to Gajaraj Mishra for the regular enforcement of the payment of allowance to Rana Bahadur Shah cannot be explained except as a personal favour for his friend or, let us say, for a friend of the Company. The readiness of the Nepali Government to make reimbursements to the Company, at regular intervals of time, for payments to Rana Bahadur exposes Knox's intention. As Regent Queen Rajarajeshvari had already reimbursed the Company, Knox does not seem to have any reason to doubt her *bona fides* in this respect.

The Governor-General ignored Knox's suggestions for restoring Rana Bahadur to power by deciding "to abstain from the conclusion of any engagements whatever with that prince."[48] Rana Bahadur was left free to return to Nepal if he so desired. The Governor-General discovered, however belatedly, that there was no genuine desire on the part of the Nepal Government to cultivate friendship with Britain or to implement the provisions of the treaty of 1801. He also realized that the Nepal Government's profession of goodwill towards Britain was conditioned merely by its fear of British support for Rana Bahadur. He, therefore, gave formal notice to the King of Nepal that the treaty would be regarded as null and void, effective 24 January 1804.[49] Thus Knox's mission ended on an unpropitious note.

Such was the end of the Knox mission. Surprisingly enough, Chaudhury, in his appraisal of the mission, blames its failures on Nepal's not being used to a Residency at its court and on what he describes as the "unsteady nature of a woman's rule."[50] From this, he jumps to the following conclusion: "But it must be said to the credit of Captain Knox that he had done his job admirably well and quite in keeping with the prestige of the government."[51] Since Chaudhury refers to Knox's presence in Kathmandu as the residency of Knox, it must be pointed out that Knox's position in Kathmandu was very different from that of Residents in other large Indian states of the time, i.e., Oudh and

Hyderabad, where they were responsible for the maintenance of internal law and order and also for the protection of the princes against their subjects.

The Knox mission failed in its professed objective to gain commercial advantages for the Company. The growing criticism in the British Parliament of Wellesley's policy of acquiring greater responsibility for the Company in the internal administration of the territories might also have made him react unfavourably to Knox's suggestions. This consideration, coupled with the Company's preoccupation with the Marathas in 1803-1805 and the Napoleonic wars in Europe, prevented British intervention despite Knox's best efforts to bring it about. Again, consideration of the Chinese reaction to Britain's interference in Nepal must also have dominated the thinking of the Company's policy-makers.

Had it not been for the above considerations, the so-called "forward policy" of Wellesley (1801-1805) would probably have been extended to Nepal and it too would have been brought under the Subsidiary Alliance of the Company. Knox perhaps thought that his report would influence the Governor-General to pursue the same kind of policy towards Nepal as Wellesley had followed towards Mysore and Hyderabad in the Indian subcontinent.

Rana Bahadur's Return to Nepal

Rana Bahadur Shah returned to Nepal early in 1804, claiming full credit for the dissolution of the treaty. While in Varanasi, he had been busy rallying the anti-British feeling of the Nepalis behind him. His foresight in this respect paid him a rich dividend. Public memory is proverbially short, and people had already forgiven or forgotten his past excesses. Rana Bahadur's return to Nepal was characterized by an upsurge of popular enthusiasm for him, and he eventually succeeded in acquiring control of the Government. He himself became *Muktiyar* or Prime Minister.

Within thirteen days of his return to Kathmandu, Rana Bahadur ordered the execution of Damodar Pande and banished his Senior Queen Rajarajeshvari to Helambu, north of Kathmandu, declaring both of them guilty of permitting the British mission to enter Nepal. He invited Prithvipal Sen, Raja of Palpa, to Kathmandu on the pretext of having the Raja personally give away his grand-daughter in marriage to Rana Bahadur. But after the Raja of Palpa arrived in Kathmandu, he was imprisoned as punishment for his attempt to plot with the Company's Government against Nepal. Rana Bahadur encouraged military expeditions towards the west under the able leadership of Amarsingh Thapa.

It took Rana Bahadur about a year to consolidate his position in Nepal even after the elimination of Damodar Pande and his principal supporters in 1804 because factional rivalries were rampant and intense. Even Rana Bahadur had to manreuvre a good deal to acquire the position of Mukhtiar-cum-Regent and gain full powers to rule in his son's name and appoint Bhimsen Thapa as Kazi. As a matter of fact, his efforts to use the Regent's authority against his adversaries resulted in his assassination in April 1806.

The period of Rana Bahadur's second administration after his return to Nepal from Varanasi was characterized by frantic efforts to prepare for what now appeared inevitable to him, the war with the East India Company's Government. He turned his attention, with great energy, to the problem of providing the finance required to step up military preparations. As a means of finding new sources of revenue, the legal basis and the terms on which rent-free land grants (*Kus Birta*) had been given to Brahmins by the predecessors of the Gorkha Kings were examined and, in the cases where irregularities were detected, the lands were either taken over by the state or else subjected to normal land taxes.

The period of Rana Bahadur's second administration was short-lived, as he was assassinated by his younger half brother, Sher Bahadur Shahi, at an open court that was being held to re-inquire into the accusations against him (Sher Bahadur Shahi) and other ranking officers during the period of the regency of the two queens. Thus came to an end an era characterized in large part by weakness, opportunism and treachery. However, notwithstanding the prolonged state of internal strife and instability during the Rana Bahadur era, Nepal's able military leaders such as Bahadur Shah, Damodar Pande, Amarsingh Thapa, Abhiman Singh Basnyat, Bam Shah, Hasti Dal Shah, Sardar Bhakti Thapa, Pratiman Ale and Angad Gurung had had considerable successes. By the time of Rana Bahadur's death Nepal's boundaries extended from the Tista on the east to the Satlaj on the west.

The war with Tibet and China between 1788 and 1792 followed by a period of internal strife and instability leading to King Rana Bahadur's exile to Varanasi in 1799 and his subsequent return to Nepal in 1804 and continuance in power till his assassination in 1806 proved to be an obstacle to Gorkhali expansion in the west. Yet in 1803 itself,

Amarsingh Thapa was sent by Regent Queen Rajarajeshvari to accomplish his conquest of Garhwal and territories further to the west. Amarsingh, though advanced in age, retained intact his youthful dream of pushing the frontiers of the Gorkhali kingdom as far as Kashmir, and he welcomed this opportunity to add lustre to his well-established reputation in the battlefield. The Gorkhali commander would have gone a long way towards achieving his end, had he only been more discriminating and not acted in haste to acquire fresh conquests without consolidating his position in the newly acquired principalities. Pressed by the urgency of his desire to fulfil his ambition quickly in view of his age, he allowed his emotions to get the better of his judgement and discretion. He fell a victim to the guiles of one Shiva Datta Rai, who laid a claim to oracular prophecies and kept on fuelling the Gorkhali ambition of conquest. Towards the end Amarsingh Thapa began to play into the hands of this man completely and rely on his advice even in conducting the administration of the conquered fiefdoms.

Even before the advancing Gorkha troops in the west returned to Kathmandu in 1791 at the prospect of war with China, Chautara Bahadur Shah, Kazi Jagjit Pande and Sardar Amarsingh Thapa had already captured Almora, the capital of Kumaun, by defeating its ruler, Raja Mahendra Singh, and his uncle Lal Singh in a battle in early 1790. Although the Gorkhas had not been able to advance beyond Langur Garh in their attempt to conquer Garhwal at the beginning in 1791, Raja Pradyumna Shah, the ruler of Garhwal, chose to buy peace and friendship with Nepal by agreeing to pay an annual tribute of twenty-five thousand rupees to the Nepal Government. It must be said to the credit of the Raja of Garhwal that he remained faithful to Nepal and refused to lend his support to Harak Dev Joshi's scheme for a coalition against the Gorkhas. But all these peaceful gestures of faith and goodwill could not avert ultimate disaster for him.

In 1801 Dehra Dun was plundered by the Marathas from Saharanpur and in 1803 a terrible earthquake devastated Srinagar, the capital of Garhwal. Later in the same year, the Gorkhali commander, Kazi Amarsingh Thapa, led a large army and invaded Garhwal, and the Raja fled to Dehra Dun. The Gorkhas followed him there and defeated him. But this apparently weak and nervous Raja showed great courage at the time of adversity. He raised a force of mercenaries in the plains and went back to challenge the Gorkha invaders in January 1804. It proved to be a futile gesture in the end. The Raja himself died fighting against the Gorkhas and his sons sought refuge in the territory of the East India

Company.

When Amarsingh Thapa occupied Garhwal it was in a state of devastation, but the Gorkhali conqueror did little or nothing to restore order and harmony in the life of its people. In his haste to conquer new territories, Amarsingh Thapa neglected the task of providing constructive administration to Garhwal. The land taxes were raised so high that it was beyond the capacity of the cultivators to pay them. The occupation troops showed no hesitation in realizing them from the people by force, and popular resistance against this forcible extortion often met with brutal retaliation. However, the conquest of Garhwal temporarily extended the boundary of Nepal as far as the Jamna river on the west.

The tract between the Jamna and the Satlaj rivers, comprising roughly an area of five and half thousand square miles, was at the beginning of the nineteenth century divided into as many as thirty states or principalities. The inaccessibility of the hill areas and the unwillingness of the Mughals to bring them under their direct rule had made them an ideal sanctuary for political and religious refugees from the plains. Following the great exodus from north India in the thirteenth and fourteenth centuries in the wake of successive waves of Muslim invasion, many emigrant Rajput chiefs had carved out kingdoms for themselves in this area just as they had done in the rest of the hilly region of western Nepal. Thus, in their strongholds in the hills, they had pursued their age-old feudal way of life undisturbed.

However, by 1803, a pattern had begun to emerge from the initial amorphous multiplicity. Four states – Sirmur, Bilaspur, Hindur, and Basahar–had grown in strength and size at the cost of others. Garhwal adjoined Sirmur on the east and Bilaspur, Hindur and Basahar lay to its west, south and north respectively. These four principalities along with the remaining fourteen scattered over the basins of the Tons, Pabar and Giri rivers were sometimes called Athara Thakurai or the Eighteen Chiefdoms. The other fourteen principalities as listed by Ross are as follows: Jubal, Kotgarh, Balsan, Kanatu, Karankulu, Detailu, Thioka, Pandur, Kiund, Utraj, Sarani, Sangri, Barauli, and Darkoti.

Another cluster of principalities known as Bara Thakurai or Twelve Chiefdoms lay between Bilaspur and Basahar. Ross names them as follows: Kionthal, Baghat, Baghal, Kothar, Kumahrsin, Bhajji, Mailag, Dhami, Koti, Kiari, Kunhiar, and Mangal. All these states were nominally vassals of the Emperor in Delhi but actually had the power to extort levies and ransoms from the relatively weaker ones ostensibly in the name of the Emperor. As the practice of making military service available in lieu of pecuniary contribution was widely prevalent, these small states maintained armies which were disproportionate to their size and resources. But these armies were undisciplined rabbles who lacked weapons and organization.

Hindur and Bilaspur were ruled by dynasties related to each other by blood who had lived together in peace as good neighbours throughout the centuries. Lately, however, Hindur had a strong and ambitious raja in Ram Saran Sen who had succeeded in aggrandizing himself at the cost of his relative of Bilaspur by exploiting mutual jealousy among the local rajas. Driven by his ambition to emerge as the master of the entire tract between the Satlaj and the Jamna rivers, Hindur had actually usurped Bilaspur's suzerainty over the Twelve Chiefdoms and also acquired possession of its cis-Satlaj territory. In 1804 Hindur was also interfering in the internal affairs of the Raja of Sirmur, Karman Prakash, by inciting a group of rebels who did not like him.

Faced with the risk of losing his throne, Karman Prakash of Sirmur sought the armed assistance of the Gorkha commander, Kazi Amarsingh Thapa, who had just acquired possession of Garhwal. In May 1804, a detachment of seven hundred soldiers sent by Amarsingh Thapa to quell the internal revolt against the Raja of Sirmur was encircled by the troops of Raja Ram Saran Sen of Hindur and forced to retreat in defeat. Meanwhile even the easy-going and slothful Raja of Bilaspur, Maha Chand, was feeling very restless and angry because he had lost the richest areas of his kingdom as a result of the encroachments of his own cousin, Raja Ram Saran Sen of Hindur, in concert with the Raja of Katoch across the Satlaj river.

Now the Gorkha Kazi, Amarsingh Thapa, under the influence of his soothsayer, Shiva Datta Rai, who was a native of Bilaspur, came forward to extend his support and patronage to this weak and undependable Raja of Bilaspur. Thus, in October 1804, Kazi Amarsingh Thapa himself crossed the Jamna river and set his foot in the territory which a decade later proved to be the site of his life-and-death struggle against the British. He engaged the troops of Raja Ram Saran Sen of Hindur in a battle at Ajmaigarh and stormed the forts of Ramgarh and Nalagarh. As his troops surrendered under the influence of bribes, Raja Ram Saran Sen fled south to the fort of Palasi. Karman Prakash, the Raja of Sirmur who was earlier ousted by a group of his adversaries with the backing of Raja Ram Saran Sen of Hindur, was also restored to his throne as a Gorkha vassal and all the territory he had lost to the Hindu Raja, including the Twelve Chiefdoms, was restored to Raja Maha

Chand of Bilaspur under the arrangement that in future he was to be guided by Siva Datta Rai as an agent of Kazi Amarsingh Thapa in conducting the affairs of the state.

Even before Amarsingh Thapa had had time to consolidate his power in the newly acquired territory between the Jamna and Satlaj rivers, Siva Datta Rai urged Amarsingh Thapa to launch an attack on the Raja of Katoch who had despoiled Bilaspur of its territorial possessions on the west bank of the Satlaj. Even Kazi Amarsingh Thapa, the seasoned Gorkha commander and a veteran of many wars, made the foolish mistake of grossly underestimating the strength of the Raja of Katoch, Sansar Chand, who had restored to his kingdom from the Mughals the redoubtable fortress in the Himalaya known as Quilla Kangra. We shall turn to the account of the Kazi's unsuccessful siege on the fort of Kangra in the next chapter.

NOTES

1. *Political Consultations*, 10 November 1794, No. 29.
2. *Political Consultations*, 20 March 1795, Nos. 22, 23.
3. *Ibid.*
4. *Political Consultations*, 1 May 1795, No. 12.
5. *Political Consultations*, 11 May 1795, No. 14.
6. *Political Consultations*, 10 November 1794, Nos. 29-30.
7. *Political Consultations*, 21 September 1795, No. 25.
8. *Political Consultations*, 21 September 1795, No. 26.
9. *Political Consultations*, 7 March 1796, No. 9.
10. K.C. Chaudhuri, *Anglo-Nepal Relations*, Calcutta, 1960, p. 87.
11. *Political Consultations*, 7 March 1796, No. 4.
12. *Political Consultations*, 7 March 1796, No. 3.
13. *Political Consultations*, 7 March 1792, No. 9
14. *Political Consultations*, 7 March 1796, No. 9.
15. *Political Consultations*, 7 March 1796, No. 23.
16. *Political Consultations*, 1 March 1799, No. 7.
17. *Political Consultations*, 11 March 1799, No. 23.
18. K.C. Chaudhuri, *Anglo-Nepalese Relations*, Calcutta, 1960, pp. 100-1.
19. *Political Consultations*, 3 September 1799, No. 7.
20. *Secret Consultations*, 30 June 1802, No. 42.
21. *Secret Consultations*, 26 June 1800, No. 85.
22. *Secret Consultations*, 26 June 1800, No. 85.
23. *Secret Consultations*, 26 June 1800, No. 86.
24. *Secret Consultations*, 26 June 1800, No. 86.
25. *Secret Consultations*, 21 August 1800, No. 62.
26. *Secret Consultations*, 16 April 1801, No. 130.

27 *Secret Proceedings*, 30 June 1802; Consultation No. 15; "Paper of Propositions from Rana Bahadur to Wellesley," November 6, 1801.
28. *Secret Consultations*, 9 March 1801, No. 84.
29. *Secret Consultations*, 18 April 1802, No. 1.
30. *Secret Consultations*, 21 August 1800, No. 2.
31. *Secret Consultations*, 16 April 1801, No. 130.
32. C.V. Aitchison, *A Collection of Treaties, Engagements, and Sunnuds relating to India and Neighbouring Countries*, Vol. II, Calcutta, 1863, p. 103.
33. *Secret Consultations*, No. 130, dated 16 April 1801; *Secret Proceedings*, June 30, 1802; Anson Campbell, *Supplementary Narrative on Nepal, British Relations*, unpublished manuscript in Brian Hodgson collection (I.O.L.).
34. K.C. Chaudhury, *Anglo-Nepal Relations*, Calcutta, 1960, p. 119.
35. *Secret Consultations*, 30 June 1802, No. 2.
36. *Secret Consultations*, 30 June 1802, No. 11, para. 19.
37. *Secret Consultations*, 30 June 1802, No. 2.
38. *Secret Consultations*, 30 June 1802, No. 11.
39. *Secret Consultations*, 30 June 1802, No. 56.
40. *Secret Consultations*, 7 July 1803, No. 28.
41. *Secret Consultations*, 2 May 1805, No. 350.
42. *Secret Consultations*, 2 May 1805, No. 350, para. 3.
43. *Op. cit.*
44. *Secret Consultations*, 2 May 1805, No. 350, para. 5.
45. *Secret Consultations*, 2 May 1805, No. 350, para. 12.
46. *Op. cit.*
47. *Secret Consultations*, 2 May 1805, No. 350, para. 11.
48. *Secret Consultations*, 26 April 1804, No. 297.
49. *Op. cit.*
50. K.C. Chaudhury, *Anglo-Nepalese Relations*, Calcutta, 1960, p. 139.
51. *Op. cit.*

6

The Rise and Fall of Bhimsen Thapa: East India Company at War with Nepal

Regency of Tripurasundari (April 1806 to April 1832)

The assassination of Rana Bahadur Shah resulted in the establishment of a new regency under one of his younger wives, Tripurasundari who had become a widow at the age of twelve. There is no doubt that she became regent with the backing of Bhimsen Thapa (April 1806 to July 1837) who took office as *Mukhtiyar* at the same time as she became Regent Queen.

Thapa used the opportunity provided by the assassination of Rana Bahadur to liquidate all his potential rivals among court officials by implicating them, on trumped-up charges, in the plot against Rana Bahadur's life. He now contrived to bring about the *sati*, or ritualistic cremation, of Rajarajeshvari, Rana Bahadur's eldest queen, along with fifteen other wives, mistresses, and maidservants, and thus made it possible for his own candidate, Tripurasundari, to become Regent Queen.

Furthermore, Rana Bahadur's elder half-brother, Bidur Shahi, together with other relatives of the royal family such as Prithvipal Sen, Raja of Palpa, and his brother, Rana Bahadur Sen, were all executed in the wake of the assassination of Rana Bahadur Shah. Bhimsen Thapa thus removed the possibility of any interference with his administration on the part of the royal family.

Two high ranking officials of the court, Tribhuvan Pradhan and Narsingh Gurung, were beheaded at the same time, and eighteen bodyguards of the Raja of Palpa and thirteen others were also executed. In all, 93 persons – 16 women and 77 men – lost their lives as a result of the plot engineered by Bhimsen Thapa following Rana Bahadur's death.

Bhimsen Thapa also exercised strict vigilance over the life of the child monarch. He deliberately excluded the King from contact with people other than trusted members of the Thapa family.

After Bhimsen whose family was Gorkha-based, came to power, he also continued with great vigour the military efforts that had commenced since the Regency of Queen Rajarajeshvari (1803-1804) to expand the kingdom towards the west. He had an ulterior motive for doing so: to keep away from the capital, the centre of power, such stalwarts of the Gorkha Darbar as Kazi Amar Singh Thapa (Bada), and the royal collaterals, Chautara Bam Shah and Rudra Bir Shah, who were Bhimsen's adversaries and potential rivals to power. Bhimsen thought that it would be easier for him to strengthen and consolidate his hold on the central government if the leading officers of the Court were away in distant theatres of war.

It was in the name of the Regent Queen, Tripurasundari, who remained a teenager for the first six years of her regency, that Bhimsen sought to lay the foundation for his future power. But in the process he incurred the deep hatred and animosity of the Chautaras and members of the Gorkha-based Pande family, who had enjoyed the well-established tradition of providing *Kazis* or ministers to the Gorkhali kings since the days of King Prithvinarayan Shah. The execution of Kazi Damodar Pande and the virtual expulsion of Chautara Bam Shah to distant Doti as governor following the return of Rana Bahadur Shah to Nepal in 1804 were also attributed to Bhimsen Thapa's advice to him. As soon as Bhimsen became all in all, he assumed the title of General and also gave the same rank to his own father (Amar or) Ambar Singh Thapa (who is to be distinguished from the aforementioned Gorkhali commander and hero, Kazi Amar Singh Thapa of an altogether different Thapa family). It was for two reasons that Bhimsen appointed his father Governor of Palpa, the most important seat of authority outside Kathmandu: first, because he wanted his father to keep a constant watch over the activities of his rivals in court politics, who were then engaged in administering newly-acquired territory on the west and further extending it, and second, because Bhimsen wanted to appropriate to his family the income from the tarai *zamindaris* or landed estates of Butwal and Syuraj originally leased by the Nawab of Oudh to Raja Prithvipal Sen of Palpa as his vassal.

It was the issue of sovereignty over these two territories that proved to be the immediate cause of the war between Nepal and British India in 1814-1816.

The Siege of Kangra

Military expeditions towards the west under the able leadership of Amar Singh Thapa were in progress. For three long years from April 1806, the siege of Kangra continued, and, in the end, proved futile. When Sansar Chand, Raja of Kangra himself was approached by Amar Singh for a truce or compromise, the overture was turned down by the haughty Rajput, who refused to have anything to do with a lowly Khas Chhetri, Thapa or his agent, and insisted on dealing with Rudrabir Shah, brother of Bam Shah, whom the Kangra ruler considered his equal in caste and status. As a matter of fact, Sansar Chand had even forwarded his terms of agreement direct to the King of Nepal through Rudrabir Shah. Amar Singh, who had a high sense of self-respect, was so piqued by this incident that he not only dissuaded Kathmandu from accepting Sansar Chand's terms but never forgave the lesser Shah brother for this humiliation. Consequently, Rudrabir Shah was relieved of his command with the field army and Hastidal Shah lost his Governorship of Garhwal and was transferred to Doti. Bam Shah alone remained Governor of Kumaun after the incident.[1]

Sansar Chand had earlier rejected Maharaja Ranjit Singh's terms for help, preferring to make peace with Nepal. In the absence of any response from the Nepali side to his gesture, Sansar Chand turned to Ranjit Singh again. However, Sansar Chand was meanwhile humouring the Gorkhas with a view to embroiling them in a conflict with the Sikhs. Ranjit Singh also prevaricated for some time and continued his talks with Amar Singh. In this game of intrigues both Amar Singh and Sansar Chand were outfoxed by Ranjit Singh of the Punjab, who was a past master in the art of scheming. In the end, complaining and grumbling that he was cheated by the Sikhs, Amar Singh retreated across the Satlaj and set about consolidating his position in the area between the Jamna and the Satlaj. Ranjit Singh occupied Kangra and kept it for himself.[2]

After Amar Singh retreated across the Satlaj, he set himself to the task of punishing the Rajas in the cis-Satlaj area for their acts of betrayal. Karman Prakash of Sirmur was removed from the office of Raja, and several of the Twelve Chiefdom rulers were forced to run for their lives. It was only with considerable difficulty that the Gorkhas could subdue some of them. The chief of Balsan gallantly defended his fort, Nagana, and, with the help of several of his neighbours including the Raja of Basahar, who supplied 10,000 men, the chief put up a stubborn resistance against the Gorkhas, successfully repulsing their attack three times.

In May 1811, Amar Singh Thapa himself marched on Nagana from Sabathu with a large number of troops and captured the fort. He then proceeded to occupy Rampur, the capital of Basahar, which was situated in the mid-Satlaj Valley known for its scenic beauty and fertility. He happened to invade the capital at a time when a state of confusion prevailed there as a result of the ruler's recent death and the succession of an infant to the throne.[3] As soon as the news of the Gorkhali attack reached the court, it moved itself across the Satlaj and, after considerable delay, reached an agreement with the Gorkhas by means of which the infant Raja enjoyed possession of his territory in the trans-Satlaj area as a Gorkha vassal.

Thus, on the eve of the war with the British, the dominion of the Gorkhas extended from the Tista river in the east to the Satlaj river in the west. As John Pemble has rightly pointed out, "In the space of half a century, the Gorkhas had unified, for the first time in history, a belt of territory which was the most beautiful, the most inaccessible and traditionally the most politically fragmented in Asia."[4]

Relative Strength and Weakness of the Gorkha and the British Army

The credit for pushing out the frontiers of the kingdom of Nepal entirely belongs to the Gorkhali army. None of the other Himalayan states with the possible exception of the Sikhs under Ranjit Singh had an army that could rival that of the Gorkhalis, and the Sikh ruler had his eye on Kashmir rather than on Nepali territories. The Gorkhali army was largely composed of Chhetris, Thakuris, Magars and Gurungs who were to prove their worth as fighting men in their battles with the British. Though short in stature, the Gorkhali soldiers were sturdy in build and had a keen sense of loyalty and discipline. Unlike the British army's soldiers from the Indian plains, they were not strict in observing caste rules and restrictions on eating and drinking.

It was for these reasons that the British decided to recruit Gorkhas into their own army, even before the 1814-1816 War between Nepal and British India was over. The first Gorkha battalion, called the Nausiri Battalion, was formed out of the remnants of Kazi Amar Singh Thapa's force after it was disbanded following its defeat at the hands of Major-General Ochterlony at Malaun in 1815. This was before the second and decisive phase of the war had hardly begun. Governor-

General Hastings promised employment to all Gorkha deserters, and three battalions were subsequently raised and were designated the 1st and 2nd Nausiri Battalions and the Sirmur Battalion, each consisting of 960 privates.

The peacetime strength of the Gorkhali army was between eight and ten thousand. But thanks to the practice of keeping troops in reserve by rotation and without pay, their potential strength could be easily doubled at the time of need.

The officers and soldiers of the Nepali army were not paid in cash but were given land for the duration of their service in the army. The tenants of the land had to pay these soldiers and officers in kind on terms agreed upon between them. In the event of the non-fulfilment of the terms by the cultivating tenant, he would forfeit his tenancy right, and the military personnel concerned would be free to transfer the right to a new tenant of his choice. The actual ownership of the land always remained vested in the ruler or the state.

The conquest of new territories proved an attraction not only to the state but also to the entire military personnel because of the prospect it held for immediate gain for them as well. It was the hope of this gain that provided a lasting incentive to both the governing military elites and the most active elements in the population to engage in this profitable yet dangerous enterprise of war.

For about half a century or so, the entire apparatus of the Government and the economy of the whole country were geared to this war policy. The army was supplied by the *Jhara* system under which porters and carriers had to be provided by the districts through which the troops passed. In every district a portion of land was settled on the cultivators to secure fulfilment of the above conditions of service, but *begar* or forced labour was also employed when the necessity arose.

A district had to provide from among its inhabitants porters to carry mail and other supplies for the army up to its ultimate boundary, where they would be relieved by their counterparts from the next adjoining district. This system of supplying the needs of the army by relays of porters proved quite effective in solving the logistical problems increasingly faced by the Gorkha army as it advanced farther and farther towards the west.

The civil-cum-military administrators of the strategic districts were called *umraos*, and it was their duty not only to raise recruits needed for the army but also to ensure steady supply of war materials such as good quality iron, copper, zinc, and sulphur for the manufacture of arms, weapons, and ammunition and also cotton, wool and leather needed for making uniforms, boots and belts for the army. A sizable tract of land was placed at the disposal of the District Governor who used the produce and returns from it to subsidize the people involved in working the mines and tanning leather. This shows how the entire administrative machinery was geared to the task of mobilizing the total efforts of the people for the war.

The Gorkhali army was being modelled after the East India Company's Bengal army long before the 1814-1816 war, and it was the general opinion of the East India Company's British officers that the Gorkha battalions did not compare unfavourably with their own battalions in fitness and training. Although initially organized in companies, the Nepali army began to be regrouped into battalions after King Rana Bahadur Shah's return from Varanasi in 1804. English words of command were actually mimicked while trying to imitate British army drill. Uniforms and ranks such as captains, colonels and generals were copied from the British army.

It may be pointed out here in passing that since the days of King Prithvinarayan Shah, the founder of the present ruling house of Nepal, the Gorkhas acquired not only weapons but also methods and tactics of warfare from every available source. King Prithvinarayan Shah initially imported European muskets from Calcutta but soon with the help of French deserters established factories in Nepal for the production of musket-loading rifles. Three Frenchmen were associated with artillery in Nepal till the 1790s, and even in 1814 there were two British deserters named Byrnes and Bell who were helping the Nepalis cast cannons. Byrnes was also employed as a teacher of English for the Nepali officers, and Bell was made an officer of artillery.

Except for the flints which had to be imported from India to make its firearms work properly, Nepal produced everything else needed for its armaments such as high quality steel for muskets, swords and khukris (curved Gorkha knives); copper and zinc for brass cannons; lead for ammunition; and sulphur for gunpowder. The Gorkhas had learnt from the Chinese who invaded Nepal in 1792 how to use portable light leather guns that could fire one-pound shot three or four times before bursting. At the time of war with British India, Nepal must have had a total of four or five hundred guns of all kinds.

On the British Indian side, the East India Company's Bengal army was made up of:

Corps	*Total all ranks*
Engineers	31 *
Horse artillery	312
3 battalions of foot artillery	1,761
1 regiment of European infantry	1,103
Total European contingent	3,207
1 battalion of native foot artillery (Golandaz)	952
54 companies of gun lascars	2,975
8 regiments of native cavalry	4,512
27 regiments of native infantry (including the marine regiment)	52,880 *
Pioneers	728
Miners	131
Ordnance drivers	2,860 *
Total Native Army	65,038
Grand Total	68,245

According to John Pemble from whose book the above figures are taken, the asterisk-marked figures appear to be an underestimate.

In addition to the above army of the Company, there were in 1814, 7,000 officers and soldiers in two cavalry and six infantry regiments of the King's Army in Bengal alone. This brought the ratio of the European force to one-sixth of the native.

The morale and quality of the European contingents in the Company's army were not so good as those of the King's Army. There was considerable jealousy between the European officers of the King's Army and those of the Company's army although a local king's beret was granted to all company officers in 1788. The officers of the King's Army enjoyed the higher prestige of belonging to the British army as well as many other tangible advantages and privileges. For example, promotion was very slow in the Company's army and its elderly officers often had to serve under the command of much younger officers of the King's Army. Filling of vacancies in the Company's army took many months because of the delay and the cost involved in their recruitment, transportation and maintenance. It was the exorbitant cost of maintaining the European component of its army that made the East

India Company in due course accept Crown regiments in increasing numbers, even though the royal troops had to be paid higher salaries than the salaries of its own contingents.

European officers and soldiers in general found conditions of service in India very hard. The heat of India was intense and oppressive, and the climate was malarial and inhospitable. A high percentage of men and officers became ill and many died of disease. There were no clubs or libraries, and in the absence of any other form of organized recreation for the military personnel, they generally took to cheap local liquors and native concubines. It gradually became the practice of the King's troops not to let anyone above the age of thirty serve in India.

Many did not even live to be thirty: the annual mortality rate among British troops during the first half of the nineteenth century was one in fourteen. More deaths resulted from dipsomania disease and suicide than from action in battle. Hence the constant need for bringing in replacements from the home country.

Background to the 1814-1816 war with the East India Company

The eighteenth century was characterized by the gradual decline and decay of the Mughal empire in India. The previous governors or agents of the emperor in Delhi such as the Nawabs of Bengal and Oudh in the north and the Nizam of Hyderabad in the south had already begun to assert their independence while successive waves of invasion by the rulers of Persia and Afghanistan such as Nadir Shah and Ahmed Shah Abdali had already shaken the foundation of Mughal imperial authority. The main contenders for the Mughal legacy were the Hindus and the Europeans.

It was natural that there should have been an upsurge of Hindu irredentism. The Mughal rulers, because of their origin and religion were never wholly accepted by the subject races. Furthermore, Hindu culture has a militant aspect of its own. This has been blurred in a large measure by the great emphasis that leaders of the twentieth century Indian nationalist movement such as Mahatma Gandhi laid on peace, non-violence and secularism to secure Muslim support in their struggle against the British. The rise of the Gorkhas, Sikhs, Marathas, all of whom were basically Hindus, represented the growth of the Hindu irridentist movement.

The European powers aspiring to the Mughal heritage were the British and the French. The lack of understanding and unity among the

Hindu irridentist elements and the superiority of the British in arms and organization ultimately decided the issue in their favour. But even until the beginning of the nineteenth century the spectre of joint military action by the Hindu irridentist elements seemed to haunt the British Governors-General. In correspondence with his Government in London, the Marquess of Hastings offered it as a plea in support of his proposal for military action against Nepal.

If we take into consideration the fact that at the time of the war with Nepal, there was no possibility of the British troops in India being reinforced by fresh supply from Britain because of the renewal of the stir in Europe caused by Napoleon's escape from St. Helena, Hastings's plea cannot be dismissed lightly. The Bengal army, as we shall see, proved utterly inadequate to the task of defeating Nepal in the first phase of the war and therefore troops had to be brought from other frontiers in the subcontinent and also from other colonies to reinforce it. Even then the war against Nepal strained the resources of the English East India Company's Government in Calcutta to the utmost. If the Sikhs and the Marathas, or either, had joined hands with the Gorkhas, it is entirely possible that the British would not have been able to retain their foothold in northern India.

By the beginning of the 19th century the expansion of the Gorkhas in the hills was running parallel to that of the British in the northern and eastern parts of India, and they had evolved a common land frontier extending along a distance, of at least 700 miles. Nowhere else in Asia the frontiers had ever been demarcated and the problem of frontiers was at its worst in India during those uncertain times when the British advances from Bengal were creating a stir in the entire region.

The Gorkhali kingdom throughout its whole length adjoined territories either administered or protected by the East India Company's Government. The Gorkha expansion towards the west synchronized with the extension of its northern frontiers by the British company.

Both the Gorkhas and the British soon realized that they had inherited old boundary disputes when they acquired new dominions. These disputes became all the more complicated when the hill states' new rulers, including the East India Company itself, came into possession of lands by merely acting as tax collectors on behalf of the Mughal emperor or the Nawabs of Oudh and Bengal. In certain cases, private individuals living in the dominion of one Government were found to own land in that of another, and as a result one Government became unwittingly involved in a private individual's dispute with another Government.

Between 1808 and 1814 several disputes arose between Nepal and British India all along their common border–on the frontier of Purnea in the east, on those of the frontiers of Gorakhpur and Saran to the south of central Nepal and on the frontiers of Bareilly in the west.[5] But the most serious differences were those regarding the borders of Gorakhpur and Saran where the Butwal and Syuraj incidents and the Gorkhas' capture of 22 Saran villages triggered the war of 1814-1816 between Nepal and British India.

The basic cause of the war goes much further and deeper than that. During the period of the Napoleonic wars in Europe from 1805 to 1814, the East India Company had been very careful to avoid war with Nepal. Its policy had concentrated on retaining territories already in British possession and avoiding new military ventures as far as possible.

However, by 1814 Napoleon had been exiled to St. Helena and now a sizable British army, trained in battle, was available for use elsewhere. The territorial disputes involving Butwal and Syuraj and 22 villages in Saran were no longer to be settled in the same manner as similar disputes in the past, for now came a sudden and abrupt change in the Company's manner of handling border problems. The Gorkhas had not increased their aggressiveness: Lord Moira, later Marquess of Hastings (1813-1823) had arrived as Governor-General in 1813 determined to make an end of the fiction of the Mughal Government and to replace it by executive British rule. Furthermore, the Charter of the East India Company had recently been renewed in such a way as to leave no doubt about the British Government's sovereignty over the lands in India controlled by the East India Company.

Much as the Gorkhas prized every inch of the land in the tarai, they also dreaded the military strength of the English, who had by now emerged triumphant over other European powers in their race for supremacy in India and had, by that time, shown themselves to be the only European power with a potential for the military conquest and subjugation of the whole of India.

The Nepali Government had been willing to hand over to the British the control of the 22 villages of the frontiers of Saran pending the outcome of a joint inquiry and investigation on the spot

In the case of Butwal and Syuraj, Major Paris Bradshaw, the British representative on the Joint Inquiry Commission, unilaterally concluded the proceedings of inquiry and informed his Government that the investigation had fully established the right of the Company's Government to those districts under dispute. In May 1814, the Company's Government was actually the first to use force. Its men captured Butwal and Syuraj.

Nepali forces retook those two villages on 29 May, following the death of a British Indian police officer in battle,[6] and, as a result of this conflict, the Marquess of Hastings. wrote a letter to the King of Nepal on 14 June 1814, asking him to compare the moderation of the British with what the Governor-General alleged was "the evasion and deceit" on the part of the Nepali Government. Hastings wanted the King to punish the officers responsible for what was described as "the outrage and bloodshed." The same letter also contained a strong threat that if the King did not act in accordance with the Governor-General's suggestion, the Company would resort to direct action, a war, which would surely destroy the kingdom of Nepal.

In reply, the King of Nepal could have drawn the attention of the Governor-General to the murder of a Nepali Government official, Lakshman Giri, in the incident on the border of Saran, in which case the British Government had protected the perpetrators. But the King did nothing of the kind. He instead sent a letter which was very mild in tone but firm in its demand for restitution of the 22 villages which had earlier been handed over to the Company's custody pending the outcome of the investigation. The King also took the opportunity to condemn in strong terms acts of highhandedness and violence on the part of the Company's officers and agents.

The Kathmandu Government, even in the face of the Governor-General's provocation, did not make any hostile moves but instead asked for the advice of its experienced military officers and Governors in the west of Nepal on the question of going to war with the British. Bam Shah, Governor of Kumaun, Hastidal Shah, Governor of Doti, and Amar Singh Thapa, Governor of the entire far west were unanimously of the opinion that it was not the proper time for Nepal to fight the British, that peace must be secured with them at all costs–if necessary, by again handing over the disputed areas of Butwal and Syuraj.

Two major considerations influenced their thinking. They were well aware that they had not, so far, been able to consolidate their position in the newly acquired territories in the west. In addition, they felt that the British, having made peace with the Marathas and the Sikhs, were in a particularly strong position to mount a fresh military undertaking.[7]

Preparing for War

It was after considerable thought and planning that the Marquess of Hastings declared war against Nepal on 1 November 1814. Before doing so he had collected information from various sources regarding the economic and military resources of Nepal, and he took particular care to examine Nepal's relations with other countries. His main concern was with the topography of the country--its natural line of defence being so formidable--and with the right kind of equipment to ensure the comfort and efficiency of the Company's troops in Nepal's climate and altitude.

For these purposes he drew mainly on the following sources of information:

A. The accounts of Nepal given by Captain Kinloch in 1767, by Lieutenant-Colonel William Kirkpatrick in 1793 and by Captain W.O. Knox in 1804.
B. "Routes in the Nepal Country" by Colonel Crawford.
C. Topographical and geographical information about Nepal with a sketch map of the country and notes on camping equipment, supplies, provisions, and artillery required, etc., by Hyder Young Hearsey dated Bareily, 9 September 1814, and a letter from him to the Secretary to the government dated Bareily, 24 August 1814.[8]

The Governor-General also turned to letters from the Company's civilian and military officers stationed on duty all along the border for information about the people and the road features of Nepal.

Hastings himself has thus summed up the considerations that guided him in planning the war campaign against Nepal:

> The extent of the Nepalese frontier, the exposed conditions of our own, offering no natural or artificial obstacles to an invading army, the singular construction of the Gorkha Empire composed of the territories of a variety of petty states, subdued at periods more or less remote by his arms, and reduced to a greater or less degree of subjection, the uncommonest strength of the country, the character of the people and the novelty of the service to our troops, accustomed to an entirely different species of warfare from that which was now to be undertaken, all conspired to render the information of the plan of the war, a subject of most serious and anxious deliberation.[9]

Hastings drew up the actual plan of operations. The Company's forces were to launch a five-pronged attack on Nepal from Rupar, Saharanpur, Gorakhpur, Saran and Purnea. The first division was placed under the command of Colonel David Ochterlony and consisted of 7,000 men and 22 cannons together with 4,500 irregulars, to which was later added a battalion of soldiers recruited in Nepal itself, bringing the total number of soldiers under his command to 11,500. This division was to attack the westernmost part of Nepal and advance by the Rupar Road. The second division, under Major-General Robert Rollo Gillespie and encamped at Saharanpur, was to invade Garhwal. It at first consisted of 10,000 men and had about 20 cannons, but eventually, 6,500 irregulars were added to this division. The third division, consisting of 5,000 regular soldiers and about 1,000 irregulars, was placed under Major-General John Sullivan Wood who was encamped at Gorakhpur and had 15 cannons. The fourth division, which was to make a direct advance on Kathmandu by way of Makwanpur, was under Major-General Bennet Marley. It consisted of 8,000 soldiers and 26 cannons. The fifth division of about 2,700 men under Captain Barre Latter was to guard the frontier between the Kosi and Tista rivers and to launch expeditions into eastern Nepal whenever possible. In all, nearly 45,000 soldiers and 85 cannons were brought into action against Nepal.

The first division, organized under Ochterlony at Rupar, was charged with the responsibility of attacking Amar Singh Thapa; the second division, which was concentrated at Saharanpur was assigned the task of capturing Dehra Dun and other valleys in Garhwal, and controlling the passage through which the Ganga and the Jamna rivers flowed into the plains. By this strategy it was hoped that Amar Singh's forces would be cut off from their main line of supply and communication with the rest of Nepal. It was also felt that this division might be employed to mount an offensive against Kumaun if the prospects for its occupation looked good. The third division at Gorakhpur was entrusted with the task of occupying the hills of Palpa in addition to acquiring the territories of Butwal and Syuraj. It was rightly thought that if Palpa could be controlled by the Company's forces, the main line of communication between Kathmandu and the western territories could be effectively intercepted. However, the main concentration of troops was in Saran, and their chief objective was to reach Kathmandu.

The Military operations were reinforced by political and psychological warfare. Special political assistants were attached to each of the five divisions. Their duty was to instigate rebellion amongst the local inhabitants by holding out promises of emancipation from Gorkha rule. The rulers of those principalities which had recently been conquered by the Gorkhas naturally had good reason to oppose their conquerors and the company gave these chieftains false hopes of being reinstated as rulers once the Gorkhas were defeated in war. This was done to ensure the active support of the ousted rulers.

Ochterlony's political assistant was W. Fraser who made efforts to collect every kind of information about the deposed Raja of Srinagar (Garhwal) and examined the possibility of putting up some other candidate as Raja of Kumaun. Lal Singh, a scion of the old ruling family of Kumaun, was not considered a suitable candidate by the Governor-General. In the Gorakhpur area Major-General John Sullivan Wood had political duties assigned to him, in addition to his military charges, and was directed to contact the family of the Raja of Palpa, living in exile in Gorakhpur. Ratna Sen, the exiled Raja of Palpa was to be told that if success attended British arms, his territories, with the exception of the plains of Butwal, would be restored in return for his assistance in raising a force that could be used in war against the Gorkhas. This force was to be financed by the Company.[10]

Major Paris Bradshaw acted as the political agent of the 4th Division under Major-General Marley. Bradshaw's instructions were to inform all the rulers in the 4th Division area who had been deposed by the Gorkhas that the tarai would be permanently incorporated into the Company's dominions, but that their principalities in the foothills would be restored to them in the event of the Company's success in war. By this means Udaya Pratap Sen, the aspirant to the principality of Makwanpur, was persuaded to offer his services to the Company, and Raja Tej Pratap Sen of Ramnagar was encouraged to renew his ancestral claim to the hill district of Tanahu. Major Bradshaw was also asked to maintain contact with the brother and nephew of the late Nepali Prime Minister, Damodar Pande, and to find out whether the services of these men could be profitably used during the campaign.

In the far east, David Scott, the magistrate of Rangpur, was asked to open correspondence with the Raja of Sikkim, the Deb Raja of Bhutan and the Government of Lhasa. Scott sought the cooperation of the Raja of Sikkim by tempting him with a proposal for the recovery of the territory he had lost to the Gorkhas. Scott also informed the Governments of Lhasa and Bhutan of his correspondence with Sikkim because of their interest in Sikkim's affairs. Captain Latter, who was to work as Scott's political assistant, had instructions to incite the Kiratis against the Gorkhas in every possible way.[11]

In addition to making elaborate preparations for political and psychological warfare, the Company took precautions to neutralize China and the Sikh kingdom of Maharaja Ranjit Singh, both of which were powerful sovereign states with interests in the Central Himalaya. Colonel Ochterlony was asked to ensure the cooperation of Raja Sansar Chand against the Gorkhas without raising Ranjit Singh's suspicion that the British were using Sansar Chand against him. Ochterlony was especially asked to allay Ranjit Singh's suspicions before his troops advanced from Ludhiana. This extreme precaution was taken despite the fact that the chances of collusion between the Gorkhas and the Sikhs was almost non-existent because of the clash between the two that had earlier taken place in Kangra. Nor did it appear likely that Ranjit Singh would use the opportunity provided by the withdrawal of British troops from Ludhiana to encroach on the eastern bank of the Satlaj River.

The Company was aware that Nepal's relations with China were governed by an understanding reached between the two countries in 1792. Hastings deemed it wise to find out from the Company's officials in Canton what the Chinese reaction would be in the event of British attack on Nepal. The Company's officer in Canton replied that the Chinese officials in Canton would not know about it, and, even if they came to know about it, they would not be willing to talk about the matter unless they were instructed by Peking to do so. The Company's officials in Canton did not believe that the Anglo-Nepalese war would adversely affect the Company's trade interest in China.

It is interesting to note that the Nepalis used the bogey of Chinese armed intervention as a psychological arm of their struggle against the British. This is illustrated by Amarsingh Thapa's declaration in May 1815: "The Gorkhas will fight for every inch of ground from the Satlaj to the Tista. If they are turned out, they will go to China."

The Battle of Nalapani (Kalanga)

Although war was formally declared by the British only on 1 November 1814, the first military campaign had opened with the capture of Timli pass by Lieutenant-Colonel Carpenter on 2 October 1814. This paved the way for the occupation of Dehra Dun by Lieutenant-Colonel Sebright Mawby on 22 October. Major-General Robert Rollo Gillespie, in charge of the overall command in the area, then advanced to Dehra Dun on 24 October and took possession of the ferry ghats on the Jamna.

At a distance of five miles from Dehra Dun, the fort of Kalanga was situated on a hill 500 or 600 feet high. It was not well fortified, having only one small cannon, and Balabhadra Kanwar, the ranking Nepali officer, had under his command only 600 defenders, including women and children. He was still improving his fortifications when Major-General Gillespie appeared at Dehra Dun.

On the basis of intelligence received earlier that the fort had been abandoned by the Gorkhas, Colonel Morris was sent with a small detachment to occupy it while Gillespie would proceed to the town of Nahan. But when he was informed by Colonel Morris of the signs of the repairs made on the fort, the Major-General turned his attention to Kalanga.

The British force of three thousand men was divided into five detachments: four detachments were to attack the fort from different directions, while the fifth was to be kept in reserve. The Kalanga hill, atop which the Gorkha fortification stood, was about half a mile long. Gillespie had a cannon mounted on the hill at a distance hardly 600 yards from the wall of the fort, and four columns of British soldiers would attack as soon as the bugle sounded the signal.

The following day artillery fire commenced at dawn, and a portion of the wall immediately gave way. The general was so encouraged by the sight of the falling ramparts that he ordered a full-scale attack an hour earlier than scheduled. As a result, only two of the detachments heard the signal and launched their attack on the fort. The other two detachments were still waiting to hear the signal as originally planned.

Balabhadra had purposely left the small door in the main entrance open by wedging two beams across it from inside, and he had placed a small cannon in such a way that it actually projected out through the opening. The Gorkha soldiers sat quietly under cover, with their rifles laid across the wall, and allowed the British soldiers to come right up to the wall. When the British started scaling the wall, the Gorkhas opened fire with the cannon.

Constant firing from the gun created confusion in the British ranks. On finding a small door open, the British soldiers, tried to force their way through it into the fort. But the two heavy beams of teakwood that had been laid across it from inside, stopped them. Under incessant fire from inside the fort, the attacking British soldiers lost courage and turned back.

At this point, Gillespie himself advanced with his fifth European infantry regiment. The general, who seems to have had a greater share of courage than discretion, pushed on with a number of his select Dragoon soldiers, but by the time his small force reached the fort, the general himself and 54 of his men had been killed.

On that day the total British casualties were: one general, four officers, and 18 soldiers dead, and 15 officers and 213 men wounded. It reflects credit on the Gorkhas that these heavy casualties were brought about by such a small group pitted against a well equipped section of the British Indian army. It appears that Balabhadra had accurately anticipated the manner in which he would be attacked by the British and had planned his defence strategy skilfully.

After Gillespie died in battle, Lieutenant-Colonel Sebright Mawby took over as commanding officer and returned to Dehra Dun for reinforcements. The next assault on the fort of Kalanga started only a month later. This time the British changed their strategy slightly and had their guns placed at a distance of only 300 yards from the fort. From this short distance, the walls of the fort were subjected to incessant pounding. By 27 November, a considerable portion of the walls surrounding the fort had been brought down and a breach opened.

But once again the Gorkhas frustrated the attempt of the English to make their way into the fort. A number of Grenadiers managed to get as far as the wall but suffered heavy casualties in the process. A gun was dragged, with great difficulty, to the opening in the wall. The purpose was to enable the British soldiers to march into the fort under the cover of shells and smoke afforded by the firing of the gun.

It was expected that the Gorkhas would naturally retreat under the pressure of gunfire, but they stood firm; although many were killed, others continued to fight. In the end, the British officer gave way, and this was enough to frighten the Indian soldiers on the British side and they gave up the attack. Some of the British soldiers, who had actually proceeded as far as the breach, returned with the report that it was impossible to enter the fort that way, as one had to jump to the ground from a high wall and sharp bamboo stakes were planted upright in the ground. The British soldiers were then ordered to retreat, and they fell back.

In that day's battle, the British lost four officers, 15 English soldiers, and 18 native Indian soldiers. Fifteen officers, 215 English soldiers, and 211 native Indian soldiers were wounded during the two-day engagement, making the British casualties much higher than those of the Gorkhas.

On the third day, the British continued their heavy bombardment of the battered fort. Inside the fort there was no underground shelter for protection against the bombardment, and at the start of the siege, the British had blocked the flow of drinking water into the fort. The outcome was inevitable: of the 600 Gorkha men, women and children, all but 70 died of thirst or wounds. The survivors, led by their brave commander, Balabhadra, left the fort during the night of 30 November. After a brief exchange of fire, they broke through the British lines and disappeared into the neighbouring hills.

The Battle of Jaithak

Major-General Gabriel Martindell was appointed to take Gillespie's place, and he arrived in Nahan on 19 December 1814. The Gorkhas withdrew from Nahan and assembled under Colonel Keshari Singh in the fort of Jaithak. After occupying the fort of Kalanga Nalapani on 24 December 1814, General Martindell sent two battalions to Jaithak from two different sides.

The fort of Jaithak stood at a height of about 3,600 feet above the plains, and was situated on the highest spot at the centre of a plateau at which two ranges of hills met. One of the forces sent by Martindell consisted of 1,000 men and the other of 730 men. They were commanded by Major Ludlow and Major William Richards and had light guns and cannons suited to mountain warfare with elephants to carry them.

On the approach of the Company's forces, the Gorkhas gave up two of their positions without battle, but they stood firm elsewhere. Major Richards reached his destination on one side of Jaithak on the morning of 27 December and began his attack on the Gorkhas as planned. But Major Ludlow's column failed to move up on time. Major Ludlow's detachment had been attacked by the Gorkhas and his progress was held up, and this hindered Richards's effectiveness. At this point Major-General Martindell, discouraged by the failure of Ludlow to reach the destination at the appointed time, sent orders to Major Richards to return to camp.

Major Richards had held his position on one side of Jaithak by repelling, throughout the day, the repeated and vigorous assaults of the Gorkhas.[12] At sundown, as Richards and his men were preparing to retreat in compliance with the General's orders, the Gorkhas, who had just defeated Ludlow, regrouped and attacked the detachment led by Richards. Richards, his ammunition exhausted, retired with extreme difficulty. The Gorkhas, not realizing that the British forces were retreating under orders, jumped to the conclusion that they were retiring due to the fatigue of battle. The Gorkhas hotly pursued them and inflicted heavy casualties. Had it not been for the cover offered to the British forces by a gallant charge of the light company fo the First Battalion of the 26th Regiment, the losses would have been heavier.

After suffering this reverse, Martindell decided to embark on no further operations against the Gorkhas until reinforcements had arrived. The Governor-General was very disappointed with the conduct of operations by Martindell and sent orders to Ochterlony that he should proceed to Nahan and take over command of the forces there. The Governor-General's orders were based on the expectation that Malaun, under Amar Singh Thapa, would collapse, but this hope was not immediately fulfilled.

The Battle of Jitgarh

In the Gorakhpur area Major-General John Sullivan Wood apparently relied on a piece of intelligence supplied by one Kanakanidhi Tiwari that the main body of Nepali soldiers had fled from Butwal and that the small fort of Jitgarh was defended by only a handful of Nepali soldiers. The same person also told Major-General Wood that the capture of Jitgarh would enable him to launch an assault on the major Nepali fort of Nayakot. This man, Kanakanidhi, led a detachment of British forces to within 50 yards of the fort; but contrary to his previous intelligence, the entire side of the hill on which the fort stood was well covered and protected by Gorkha soldiers.

On noticing this, Kanakanidhi led the British soldiers to the top of a neighbouring hill from which he thought the British would be able to open fire on the Gorkhas with long-range guns. However, this hill proved to be lower than the hill on which the Gorkha fortification was situated. The British soldiers opened fire on Jitgarh and valiantly withstood the onslaught of Gorkha fire from the higher nearby hill. In the end, the British attack proved abortive, as the Gorkhas had the tactical advantage. The failure of his men to take the fort of Jitgarh seemed to dishearten Major-General Wood so much that he did not engage his men in further battle until 15 April 1815.[13]

The Battle of Parsa and Samanpur

Major-General Bennet Marley, who was charged with the task of mounting an offensive directly on Kathmandu, had occupied a few posts in the tarai. He deployed a section of his forces under Captain Silby at Parsa and posted another force at Samanpur under Captain Blackney. The Nepali troops at Makwanpur were under the command of Colonel Ranadhir Singh. He divided his forces and attacked both Parsa and Samanpur simultaneously while leaving only a small garrison at Makwanpur. The British were caught napping. Captains Silby and Blackney and their men were completely routed by the surprise attack of the smaller Gorkha units.

Had General Marley decided to attack the Gorkha stronghold of Makwanpur at the that time, he could easily have stormed it as there were no more than 200 defenders,[14] but the initial success of the Gorkhas apparently made Marley hesitate. He seems to have been convinced by Gorkha propaganda that there were more than 18,000 soldiers available to meet his attacks, and he delayed his move against Makwanpur so long that 7,300 porters, hired to carry the British army's supplies into the hills, had to be discharged as they were costing the Company about Rs. 70,000 per month. In the end, the Company's Government found Marley incompetent and asked Major-General George Wood to take over his command.

Under Major-General Wood, the Company's force of some 13,400 men in this sector did little better. Even the temporary success of Lieutenant Joshua Pickersgill in defeating 500 Gorkha soldiers on one occasion did not encourage the General to be more active. When the magistrate of Gorakhpur asked for Wood's assistance in preventing the Gorkhas from creating disturbances on the border, he did nothing. He did not believe in tampering with the strength of his main forces by sending them away in sizable numbers to deal with such disturbances. The reason given by the General for his inaction was the approach of the fever season.

The Battle of Katalgarh

At the commencement of hostilities, Edward Gardner was put in charge of political negotiations in Kumaun. He informed the Governor-General that Kumaun was poorly garrisoned by the Gorkhas and some of the local landlords were enthusiastic about action against them. On learning this, Lord Moira decided to open a new front in that area with the help of irregular troops raised by Captain Hyder Hearsey and Lieutenant-Colonel William Gardner for service in Kumaun.

In deciding on this course of action, Lord Moira was guided by the consideration that this would create a useful diversion in the area of Garhwal, forcing the Gorkhas to meet a new attack when they were already engaged on several other fronts. Furthermore, it was thought that the success of the expedition against Kumaun would have the effect of isolating Amar Singh Thapa from the rest of the Nepali territories towards the east. This would, at the same time, make it difficult for Amar Singh Thapa to retreat if he should need to do so.

It was not until 15 February 1815 that the Company's forces entered the Kumaun hills. As Lieutenant-Colonel Gardner occupied the Chilkia pass and advanced along the river bed, the Gorkhas withdrew towards Almora. Gardner took his position on the hill at Kampur, and found himself face to face with Gorkhas who had been in retreat.[15]

The Gorkhas had been reinforced by soldiers from Almora, so Gardner decided to avoid a frontal clash and wait for the arrival of an additional force of 1,000 irregulars from the plains before undertaking a manoeuvre to outflank the Gorkhas. Gardner carried out this manoeuvring successfully, and the Gorkhas were forced to leave their stockade. They withdrew to Katarmal and finally to the main ridge of Almora.

As Gardner advanced towards Almora, another small detachment of British soldiers was working its way up the Burohne pass, thus creating a diversion for the Gorkhas. Captain Hearsey, who had occupied the Timla pass, advanced up the Kali river and occupied Champawat, the capital of Kali (East Kumaun), and laid siege to the Gorkha fortress of Katalgarh. Thus, Kumaun was virtually caught in a pincer movement by these two detachments. But Hearsey, instead of concentrating his efforts and attention on guarding the ghats across the Kali river, proceeded to capture the forts in the interior as well. His troops were now so thinly and widely scattered that they proved to be inadequate for either purpose.

About this time, Hastidal Shah, the Nepali Governor of Doti, crossed the Kali at a point in the mountains above Captain Hearsey's detachment. Faced with the danger of being attacked by Hastidal Shah from a vantage point, Captain Hearsey decided that attack was the best defence under the circumstances. He moved his men forward to attack Hastidal Shah's position, leaving behind only a part of his force to maintain the siege on Katalgarh.

Captain Hearsey marched the night with 270 men and reached the scene of action the following morning. But Hastidal Shah, taking advantage of Hearsey's preoccupation with crossing the river below the actual spot of encounter, was waiting to give him a battle at Khilpati about 5 miles northwest of Champawat.

The fight that took place was fierce. Hearsey's men were already exhausted, thirsty and short of ammunition, and they fled when the captain himself fell wounded in the thigh. It is said that Captain Hearsey's life was spared because of his acquaintance with Hastidal Shah dating back to an official meeting between the two men.

Thus, in the first phase of the war of 1814-16, covering a period of about six months from October 1814 through March 1815, the British met with reverses on almost every front along a 700-mile frontier. The Nepali forces showed remarkable valour and an intelligent use of tactics, but it was the incompetence and slothfulness of the British Generals that was largely responsible for the Company's poor showing.

In the second phase of the campaign, British arms proved much more successful. The reverses suffered by the Company's forces in Gorakhpur and Saran, along with the operation in Kumaun, had temporarily relieved the Gorkhas of the threat of an attack on their capital and left them in a better position to send reinforcements to their troops stationed in the western area. On the other hand, the Company's forces made additional efforts to prevent reinforcements from reaching Amar Singh Thapa.[16]

The Battle of Almora

Operations in Kumaun were renewed on 8 April 1815, and Lieutenant-Colonel Jasper Nicolls, a King's officer of the 14th Foot, was put in command of about 2,000 regular troops in addition to a force of irregulars he already commanded. Intelligence had reached Nicolls about the presence of a body of Gorkha troops in the Gananath area under Hastidal Shah, and a detachment under Major Patton was sent to Gananath, a mountain ridge situated to the southwest of Almora. In the fierce battle that ensued, Hastidal Shah was fatally wounded, and there were many other casualties among the Gorkha officers.

The Gorkhas were very disheartened by this defeat and by the loss of their able commander. Colonel Nicolls took advantage of the situation and launched an attack on Almora on 25 April. He himself led the first battalion towards the Gorkhas' main fortification, situated on the north end of the Sitoli ridge. The assault on the ridge was a success and was followed by the capture of the fortification leading to Kalmatia and the Raja's palace. Thus, the Gorkha forces within the main fort of Almora were not only completely isolated, but were also deprived of every avenue of retreat. The northern British post was temporarily retaken by the Gorkhas the same night, but was soon recovered by the British despite vigorous efforts made by the Gorkhas to regain its possession. The encounters resulted in heavy losses on both sides. The Gorkha troops inside the fort actually moved out to repulse the attack of the advanced section of the British forces but were compelled to retreat. The fighting continued through the night, and the British brought mortars along and laid them in front of the fort.

Next morning the advanced columns marched to within 70 yards of the fort. The Gorkha garrison was forced to remain inactive and in hiding under the firing of several eight-inch mortar shells. At this time, a large number of Gorkha soldiers pretended to leave the fort in order to confuse the enemy. When a party of British soldiers advanced to occupy it in the expectation that it had been abandoned, they were subjected to heavy fire by the Gorkha garrison that had reassembled. Thus, the British were compelled to retreat.

It was only at 9.00 p.m. on 20 April 1815 that a proposal for a truce came to Colonel Nicolls in the form of a white flag and a letter from Bam Shah, the Gorkha Governor of Kumaun, and from Captain Hearsey, who was then a prisoner in the hands of the Gorkhas. Nicolls accepted the truce proposal. This brought the fighting to an end, and the Gorkhas withdrew to the east of the Kali river.

The Battles of Deuthal and Malaun[17]

Colonel (afterwards Major-General) David Ochterlony, who proved to be the ablest of the British Generals, prepared his strategy against the Gorkhas carefully from the beginning. He was pitted against the ablest Gorkha general, Amar Singh Thapa, on the westernmost area of Nepal. Ochterlony, unlike other British Generals, never underestimated the strength of his opponents, and nowhere did he launch a frontal attack on any Gorkha stronghold. He was the only General who took maximum advantage of his superior artillery. Wherever artillery could be used, he never resorted to a bayonet charge or rifle fire. Furthermore, he employed the same tactics against the Gorkhas which the latter had used successfully against the British in other sectors.

Ochterlony had about 7,000 men under him at the start of hostilities, whereas Amar Singh Thapa, the Gorkha General, had hardly 3,000 soldiers. Despite this numerical superiority, Ochterlony did not initiate any major action against the Gorkhas until 15 April 1815, although he had actually entered the Himalayan foothills as early as 5 November 1814. For about five months or so, Ochterlony was content to manoeuvre his soldiers either in the rear or on the flank of the enemy, thereby forcing the small advance posts of the Gorkhas to abandon their stockades. Nalagarh was the first fort which Ochterlony captured in November 1814. He garrisoned it with a small party of British soldiers and used it as a centre of communication with the plains.

At one stage, Ochterlony had thought that Amar Singh Thapa would not be interested in defending the area and would withdraw towards the Kali river on the east because the areas on the far west were not easily defensible against the long-range British guns. However, Amar Singh Thapa resolved to make a stand. He moved his forces from his headquarters at Arki and took up a defensive position on a high, difficult ridge of mountains, with the fort of Ramgarh on his right and a high and fortified range of hills on his left. The ridge on which he established his position extended to the right beyond Ramgarh, and the entire ridge was fortified with stockades. At the back of this range, and running almost parallel to it, was another high range of mountains on which the forts of Malaun, Ratanpur, and Surajgarh were situated. The Gambar rivers flows between these ridges and joins the Satlaj near Bilaspur. Behind the Malaun ridge, and close to its base, passes the Gamrola river.

Amar Singh had very good relations with the Raja of Bilaspur, on whose territory the Gorkhas depended for many supplies. He also received supplies from his former headquarters in Arki, which was now maintained as a communications link with other positions on that side. Bilaspur and Arki were both important because of the lines of communication and supply between Amar Singh's new position and other Gorkha stockades passed through these places.

As Amar Singh's position could not be frontally assailed, Ochterlony attacked and attempted to turn the enemy's left flank by capturing the peak of Kot. From this hill, which had not been fortified by the

Gorkhas, Ochterlony could mount an offensive on the rest of the ridge.

Lieutenant Colonel Thompson failed to occupy the village of Kahanani, in spite of the fact that a road was constructed to enable the elephants and porters to carry up two six pounders, two mortars, and two howitzers. After the guns, ammunition, and other supplies were taken to a place in the vicinity and the battery opened fire, it was found that the post of the Gorkhas was too far off to be affected by gun fire. On the other hand, the Gorkhas attacked the British party with great vigour and forced it to retreat with heavy losses.

Ochterlony had learnt useful lessons from the reverses suffered at Kalanga and Jaithak. He concentrated on improvising gun positions and on the recruitment of local troops. The first thing Ochterlony did on that night was to cut off the line of supply between Bilaspur and the Gorkha position in Malaun by placing the British forces between them. He won the local Raja's support and, with the latter's help, constructed a road from Kadri to Nahan.

Amar Singh countered these tactics by abandoning all the posts on the range to the left of Ramgarh and making the rear his front. On 16 January 1815, Ochterlony marched on with his reserve forces, crossed the Gambar river and held a position on the road to Arki. Lieutenant-Colonel Cooper was left with his artillery battalion at the former post of Nori near the southern end of the Malaun range. Colonel Arnold was asked to open his assault with the rest of the armed men in Bilaspur, Malaun or Mangu-Ka-Dhar, as the circumstances permitted. Amar Singh foresaw this plan and withdrew to Malaun, leaving only small parties of soldiers in Ramgarh and other posts on that range. Colonel Arnold, in spite of the hazards of the climate and the difficult nature of the terrain, occupied the stockades evacuated by the Gorkhas and finally established a post for himself and his men in Ratanpur, which lay between Malaun and Bilaspur. Thus, Arnold not only succeeded in turning the enemy's flank, but he found himself in a position to intercept their line of supply.

About the same time, Lieutenant-Colonel Cooper left Nori and climbed the Ramgarh ridge. Eighteen pounders had been brought up with great hardship, and Ramgarh soon collapsed under heavy fire from these guns. The success of this well-planned move by Ochterlony was proved by the fact that the small but well-guarded stone forts of Jorjoru, Taragarh, and Chamba fell one after another, and British forces took up their assigned position before Malaun on 1 April 1815.

Ochterlony had relied on Field Engineer Lieutenant Peter Lawtie of the Engineers for information and guidance in laying out the battle-plan. At that time, the forts of Malaun and Surajgarh were protecting the flanks of the Gorkha Army. The Gorkhas had most of the hilltops in the neighbourhood garrisoned and fortified with fences and stockades. Only two hills, Raila and Deuthal, remained unprotected.

General Ochterlony was quick to discover this. He attacked and captured the hillock of Raila. The Gorkhas had left it rather unprotected, thinking that the British would not bother to capture it because of the difficulty in transporting big guns there. On 15 April, the first day of the attack, Raila fell without much opposition to a grenadier battalion led by Major Innes.

The Capture of Deuthal

Ochterlony was aware of the fact that the control of Deuthal by his forces would endanger the entire Gorkha line of defence, so he took Deuthal by a surprise action. On the day of attack, he assembled his forces and pretended to attack the main Gorkha forces in Malaun from the northwest and the northeast, although his immediate objective was Deuthal. Detachments under Captain Showers, sent forward to make the pretence of attacking the Gorkha rear, suffered heavy losses at the hands of the Gorkhas, and the captain himself lost his life. Another detachment, under Captain Bowyer, which approached another flank of the Gorkhas, also had a sharp encounter with them, but there was not much loss on either side after the day's fighting. However, these moves, planned by Ochterlony only to divert the Gorkhas from concentrating on the defence of Deuthal, proved very successful, inasmuch as they enabled Ochterlony to acquire control of Deuthal without any resistance.

Bhakti Thapa's Valiant Attempt to Regain Deuthal

The importance of Deuthal to the Gorkhas is proved by the fact that they made a heroic attempt to recapture it. Ochterlony lost no time in garrisoning Deuthal and having it fortified with long-range guns. The Gorkhas had no chance of recapturing it, and Amar Singh knew this better than anybody else. But Sardar Bhakti Thapa, a veteran of many wars, insisted on being allowed an opportunity to make the attempt. Amar Singh tried to dissuade, him but Bhakti told Amar Singh that he could not choose a better way to die in his old age than attempting to recapture this vital link in the Gorkha line of defence. Bhakti probably knew he was going to die on the day of the attack because he had asked his two wives to be prepared to burn themselves with his body on the following day. Although the recapture of Deuthal would reverse the advantage held by Ochterlony, the odds were heavily against the Gorkhas.

Bhakti Thapa launched his attack with 2,000 troops. The British forces were already on the height of Deuthal, and they had fortified it with heavy guns and mortars, whereas the Gorkhas' uphill attack had no artillery for support. Despite these handicaps, they began their first attack with such vigour that it proved difficult for the British forces to stop them. A number of Gorkhas, who had got as far as the British line on top of the hill, were killed by a bayonet charge. They made several attempts to break through the fence protecting the hilltop, but all their efforts proved unavailing.

Time and again Bhakti led his men up the steep hillside in a desperate attempt to capture the peak. All through the attacks, Amar Singh and his son stood in the open near their colours and within musket range, inspiring their men to greater efforts. Fighting continued throughout the day. Towards the evening, Bhakti Thapa died a hero's death on the battlefield. Later, when the Gorkhas asked for his body, Ochterlony had the corpse covered with a white sheet of linen and returned it with military rites and honours. The British were deeply moved by the sacrifice and courage of this man.

Even after the battle of Deuthal, Amar Singh hesitated to surrender, despite the fact that his force was reduced to less than five hundred men. At last he gave in, but only after he received news of the fall of Kumaun. The Gorkhas had thrown all their available forces into the counterattack on Deuthal and were not in a position to reinforce them. Ochterlony, in recognition of their valour, permitted Amar Singh and his son Ranajor Singh to return to Kathmandu with all the honours of war.

Peace Negotiations

The withdrawal of the Gorkhas from Malaun sealed their fate in the war and broke their power of resistance against the British. Nepal started negotiations for peace in May 1815, at different places. While Gajaraj Mishra and Chandrashekhar Upadhyaya were negotiating with Major Paris Bradshaw on the frontiers of Saran, in Kumaun, frequent meetings took place between Bam Shah and Rudrabir Shah on the Nepali side and Edward Gardner on the British side.[18] However, these negotiations broke down when the British insisted that Nepal should part with all lands in the plains in addition to the territories to the west of River Kali. Actually, a proposal for the treaty including cession of the tarai land to the British was sent to the Government at Kathmandu for its final approval, but under the influence of Amar Singh Thapa, the King of Nepal refused to accept the proposal without substantial changes. Amar Singh's line of argument was the same as he had put forward in his letter to the King of Nepal, sent from Rajpur, dated 2 March 1815:

> When our power is once reduced, we shall have another Knox's mission, under pretence of concluding a treaty of alliance and friendship and founding commercial establishments. If we decline receiving their mission, they will insist; and if we are unable to oppose forces, and desire them to come unaccompanied with troops, they will not comply. They will begin by introducing a company, a battalion will soon after follow, and at length an army will be assembled for the subjugation of Nepal.

Amar Singh's main opposition to the draft treaty centred on the article that made provision for payment of cash pensions to Nepali officials in exchange for tarai territory ceded to the East India Company. He felt that this article would have the effect of making high officers of the Nepali Government paid agents of a foreign power. For this reason, the Government of Nepal was unwilling to approve the draft treaty.

Ochterlony (who had since been knighted) was now vested with full military and political powers to initiate a new campaign against the Gorkhas. The main purpose of the resumed military operations was to compel the Nepali Government to accept the proposed draft of the treaty, and Ochterlony was asked to step up military operations if the treaty was not ratified at an early stage. Ochterlony's instructions were "to advance on the Makwanpur Valley, with a view to its occupation, the reduction of its forts and the complete establishment of the British troops on the northern heights of Makwanpur, and in the entire tract of the valley by the Rapti and Bagmati, before any attempt was made to cross into the valley of Nepal proper."[19]

The Final Phase of the War

Considerable hesitation and delay were shown by the Government of Nepal in ratifying the treaty of peace even after its representatives had initialled it at Sugauli on 2 December 1815. This prompted Hastings to proceed with his plans to overwhelm the Gorkhas with a massive attack through the foothills below the Kathmandu Valley culminating in the swift occupation of the three forts of Hetaura, Makwanpur and Hariharpur within the first range of hills. And even after that if the Government of Nepal did not give in and accept the treaty, the army had orders to march into the Kathmandu Valley itself and occupy the capital by force. It was planned to complete the military operations against Nepal before the onset of the rainy season and as the actual campaign of war did not start till the second week of January 1816, all concerned with its planning and execution felt hard pressed for time.

Hastings sought to compensate for the shortage of time by providing Ochterlony with four brigades totalling almost 20,000 men and no fewer than eighty-three pieces of ordnance. As no troops were sent from England in response to the Hastings's request, troops who had arrived in Calcutta from Mauritius in August 1815 came in handy for the Governor-General's purpose. H.M. 87th, the Prince's Own Irish Regiment of Foot (later 87th Royal Irish Fusiliers) was amongst those sent to the frontier to join Ochterlony's army. In addition, Ochterlony's invading army was made up of two other King's regiments: the 24th Foot that had seen action in the eastern front the previous year and the 66th Foot (later the Royal Berkshire Regiment) along with its three companies that had just arrived from Ceylon.

Hastings's plan was not merely to mount an increased offensive against the Kathmandu Valley. He had a far more elaborate plan of military action against Nepal during this second phase of war as well.

At the extreme eastern end of the line of operation, Barre Latter was once again authorized to take up command at Titalia and he actually succeeded in inciting the Sikkimese to lay siege on Nagri (modern Darjeeling) once again.

In the centre Hastings had put Major-General John Wood in charge of a 5,000 strong division and assigned him the task of completing the occupation of the tarai north of Gorakhpur and marching, if possible, to Palpa and other hill districts immediately to the west of Kathmandu.

Further to the west, Lieutenant Colonel Jasper Nicolls was given the responsibility of advancing into Doti with 6,500 men and 0 pieces of ordnance. Edward Gardner was asked to accompany Nicolls and find out if the Shah brothers, Bam Shah and Rudrabir Shah, could be won over to the British side by promising them independent sovereignty over the territories they were administering at the time. Nicolls's assault on Doti was to be facilitated by an armed attack under Lieutenant Colonel Adams from Kumaun on the flank of the Nepali positions. But Ochterlony's advance to Makwanpur was so swift and decisive that the separate divisions under Wood, Nicolls and Adams had not even started making their moves at the time of Nepal's acceptance of the treaty of Sugauli, which brought to an end the second and final phase of the 1814-1816 war between Nepal and British India.

The Battle of Makwanpur

Upon Nepal's refusal to accept the draft of the treaty proposed at Sugauli, Ochterlony was directed to launch a new military campaign against the Gorkhas and to compel the Nepal Government to accept the proposed treaty. In February 1816, Major-General David Ochterlony advanced on Makwanpur with a force of about 20,000 men. He stationed a section of his forces at Bhullowee, a village on the Saran border, about 6 miles from the tarai forests, and set out to gather information about the hills and routes leading to Makwanpur.

The immediate objective of Ochterlony's military expedition was to occupy the three forts of Hetaura, Makwanpur, and Hariharpur within the first range of hills, but, if this failed to bring the Gorkhas to submission, Ochterlony had instructions to advance into the Kathmandu Valley and strike at the capital itself. Ochterlony planned that his troops should cross the foothills at three points. He was to head the central column of about 9,500 men in all and force his way through the Bhichakhori (Amlekhganj) pass and proceed on to take Hetaura and Makwanpur. Thirty miles to the west, Lieutenant-Colonel Nicolls with 5,000 troops of all ranks was to enter the Rapti Valley through Mahajogi and proceed eastward to join Ochterlony. Major Kelly, with about 7,000 troops under his command, was to march up the ravine of Lakanda, an eastern tributary of the Bagmati, and capture Hariharpur.

Ochterlony, at the head of his troops, reached Bhichakhori by way of Simra. He was at Bhichakhori for five days and, according to the information of the scouts and spies, the pass was impregnable. But on the morning of 4 February 1816, Ochterlony had a piece of good luck. An informer conveyed to him the information that there was a pass on the

Chure range which was not garrisoned and was accessible, though difficult.

The same evening, Ochterlony ordered a brigade under Colonel Miller to parade before the camp after dark in order to deceive the prying Gorkhas into thinking that the brigade would be in camp that night. This brigade had orders to leave Bhichakhori the same night, but to leave all tents standing. Colonel Burnet, who was to remain in the camp, was asked to have his men occupy these tents as far as their number would permit. This was done to conceal from the Gorkhas any change in the camp.

The brigade under Colonel Miller marched all night and reached its destination at the base of the hill at 8:00 a.m. on 15 February 1816. The same day Colonel Burnet advanced with his brigade towards the main Chure pass, which was deserted by the Gorkhas after being outflanked by the forces under Colonel Miller.

With his men in control of the pass, Ochterlony marched towards the township and the fortified heights of Makwanpur. There he found that the Gorkhas were entrenched in their positions on a steep hill opposite his left flank and in another position to the right on the same ridge. Early on the morning of 28 February, the first of these positions– called Sikhar Khatri (Sikharkoti) was abandoned by the Gorkhas and occupied by the British. When the Gorkhas realized their mistake and attempted to recover it, it was already too late. At noon the Gorkhas launched a vigorous attack on the post and renewed their assaults on it several times in the course of the day. However, the charge by a British infantry battalion finally compelled them to disperse in confusion.

On 29 February 1816, a fierce battle raged all day between the British troops, advancing under Major Kelly from the Bagmati side towards Bhagwanpur, and the Nepali contingents placed in charge of the fort of Hariharpur and the adjoining outposts. As the British forces received reinforcements, the Nepali contingents first retired into their fortification at Hariharpur and then withdrew from there the next day. Thus, the fort of Hariharpur also fell into British hands.

The treaty of Sugauli was finally accepted by Nepal only after Ochterlony's successes posed a direct threat to the capital. The ratification of the treaty was submitted by Kazi Bakhtawar Singh Thapa, Bhimsen Thapa's brother, to Ochterlony on 4 March 1816.

The Peace of Sugauli

The Government of Nepal was eager to patch up a peace with the Company's Government from the time of the first occurrence of the border incidents and even during the progress of the campaign following the formal declaration of war by the Company's Government against Nepal. But Chandrashekhar Upadhyaya, representative of the King of Nepal, was prevented from proceeding to Calcutta on his diplomatic mission. Major Bradshaw first told him that he could not let Upadhyaya go to Calcutta unless the Governor-General gave his consent. Later on, Upadhyaya was informed by the Governor-General, through Bradshaw, that no Nepali agent would be admitted into British territory unless he had full powers to settle all outstanding differences between the two Governments on a permanent and satisfactory basis. Chandrashekhar was asked to return to Kathmandu. Chandrashekhar then tried to obtain a travel permit from the Magistrate of Tirhut, but his efforts were of no avail. He was finally captured in Barharwa, a Nepali Government office close to the British Indian border in Tirhut, when Major Bradshaw occupied the post by force in November 1814: when he was taken prisoner all his papers fell into British hands.

With Major Bradshaw's permission, and probably under duress, Chandrashekhar wrote a letter to the King of Nepal describing the circumstances of the capture of the post and urging that Bhimsen Thapa, the Prime Minister, should himself meet Major Bradshaw and negotiate peace to save the state from final destruction. It is interesting to note that the Nepali Government protested against the violation of the person and papers of the Vàkeel, who was a diplomatic representative, and condemned this act of the Company's Government as "contrary to the practice and usages of nations and to the observances of courtesy usual between Governments even in a state of war."

Lord Moira's argument, however, was that Chandrashekhar lost his diplomatic status and character the moment the British refused him admittance into the Company's territory. He further pointed out that Chandrashekhar deliberately sought arrest by remaining at the frontier post unitl its capture by British forces under Bradshaw. In reply to Chandrashekhar's letter, the King of Nepal expressed his desire for peace and asked Upadhyaya to conduct negotiations with the English in keeping with Nepal's peaceful intentions. The King confessed that he had not thought the British would start a war over petty frontier disputes and suggested that even General Bhimsen Thapa, his Prime Minister, would be prepared to meet the British officials and negotiate peace with them.

It had, however, become clear by then that peace could not be had merely on the basis of the settlement of disputes relating to the tarai lands, because the British had reached the conclusion "that the end of the extension of the Gorkha power west of the Kali was an indispensable condition of pacification." The British concern was one "of effecting a material reduction in the strength and resources of the enemy – the Gorkhas."

This was the reason why nothing had come of several attempts by the Government of Nepal to negotiate peace with the British through Brook, the Company's agent in Varanasi, or through Amar Singh Thapa, or through Bam Shah, at different places and times. Even the services of Gajaraj Mishra, who had always had the reputation of being pro-British since the days of the Knox mission, were employed by the Government of Nepal to seek peace with the Company's Government.

As a matter of fact, Gajaraj Mishra and Chandrashekhar met Major Bradshaw on 20 May 1815 with proper credentials from the King, authorizing them to discuss all matters in dispute between the two Governments. Bradshaw, under instructions from the Governor-General, put the following proposals before them:

First, restoration of peaceful relations;
Second, abandonment by the Gorkhas of all disputed lands;
Third, surrender of the low lands of the tarai from the Kali to the Tista;
Fourth cession of Nagri and Nagarkot to the Raja of Sikkim;
Fifth, renunciation of all claim to a connection with the territories west of the Kali;
Sixth, recognition of any treaties which the British Government might make with chiefs, tribes, or subjects of Nepal;
Seventh, concrete assurances for the security of the land of the Raja of Sikkim;
Eighth, exclusion of the subjects of European and American states from the services of the Government of Nepal;
Ninth, exchange of resident ministers between the two Governments; and
Last, the revival of the commercial treaty of 1792.

The terms proposed by Bradshaw and subsequently incorporated in the Treaty of Sugauli were found entirely unacceptable, and Gajaraj Mishra made it clear to Bradshaw that he had no "authority to comply with such extensive demands, and that sacrifices of such magnitude were not contemplated by any party at Kathmandu, as justly resulting from the events or actual state of the war. At this point, Bradshaw informed Gajaraj that if it were so, he could not continue discussions with him.

Proposals containing more or less the same terms were offered through Bam Shah by Edward Gardner in Kumaun, and their talks also borke down on the question of cession of the tarai lands. When Rudrabir Shah, brother of Bam Shah, pointed out that he had no authority to discuss the matter, the Governor-General offered an alternative proposal that the Company would compensate through pensions or grants the chiefs of Nepal whose interests would be affected as a result of cession of the tarai lands. Even this alternative did not prove acceptable to the Nepali authorities.

On 22 July 1815, the Governor-General, in a letter to the King of Nepal, regretted that Gajaraj Mishra and Bam Shah did not have full powers for negotiations and pointed out that the British Government did not insist on demands which it did not mean to pursue to the very end. He also warned the King of the consequences of his rejection of the "just terms" offered by the British Government and threatened that any delay on the part of the King in accepting those terms would force the British Government to take stronger measures against him. Thus, discussions so far had broken down on the question of cession of the tarai land.

In August 1815, Colonel Bradshaw informed his Government that Gajaraj Mishra and Chandrashekhar were then granted full powers to negotiate any matter with the representative of the Company's Government. The Nepali Government seemed to have given up their earlier stand on the question of cession of the tarai, as shown by its instruction to Gajaraj Mishra: "With regard to the conquests by the British Government of the country towards Kumaun in the west and the Tarai, whatever may be the result of negotiations will be approved by *me*. Do not entertain any doubt on that head." From the above instructions it is clear that Gajaraj had the authority to negotiate peace with the British, even on the condition of cession of the tarai.

The Governor-General also slightly modified his demand for the cession of the entire tarai by suggesting to Colonel Bradshaw that he should discuss the alternative proposal of granting the Company's pension to Nepali chiefs in lieu of the tarai land to be ceded by Nepal. Lord Moira authorized Bradshaw even to reduce the original demand for cession of the entire tarai and settle merely for that section of the tarai which had actually been occupied by the British troops. When the originally proposed terms were offered to Gajaraj Mishra on 12 September 1815, with the above slight amendment as to cession of the tarai land, Gajaraj put off the talks until 16 September. He informed Bradshaw that he had no authority to agree to unconditional surrender of these lands since Nepal, according to Mishra, drew its sustenance from the tarai land and could not survive without it.

This was what Gajaraj said to Bradshaw, as reported by the letter "He had always felt that the Tarai, however, contended for would be relinquished to the Raja. He knew that aversion with which every person in Nepal, of the Gorkha dynasty, who was of consequence sufficient to have any weight in the general voice, regarded the cession of territory, and was aware of the odium which would be incurred by him who should be the instrument of it."[20] After this, it became clear to the agents of both sides that there was no use pursuing discussion of the draft proposal.

Gajaraj Mishra forwarded the draft to Kathmandu and Colonel Bradshaw set an ultimatum of twenty-one days for receipt of the King's reply to Gajaraj's letter. At this point, the Governor-General also intervened to make it clear to the Nepali Government that the draft treaty represented the minimum that was acceptable to the British and no changes therein would be acceptable to them. The Government of Nepal, in reply to the Governor-General's letter, merely requested the mitigation of the conditions of peace in Nepal's favour and said that it had authorized Gajaraj Mishra to sign the peace treaty on that condition.

However, Amar Singh Thapa's opposition to the treaty provision for payment of cash grants or pensions by the Company to the Nepali officials resulted in non-acceptance of this treaty by the Nepali Government. At this point Bhimsen Thapa seems to have made an alternative proposal to Colonel Bradshaw, through a confidential agent named Umakanta, that cash payment should be substituted for cession of the tarai. Colonel Bradshaw told Bhimsen Thapa's agent that the Governor-General would consider this amendment favourably in case the proposed draft treaty was ratified by the Government of Nepal but insisted on a prior acceptance by the Nepali Government of the draft treaty as it was.

When the Government of Nepal refused to accept the draft, Ochterlony was authorized to step up the military campaign against Kathmandu itself in February 1816. It was only after Ochterlony had captured Makwanpur and posed a direct threat to the capital that Nepal's formal acceptance of this draft proposal was submitted to Ochterlony by Kazi Bakhtawar Singh Thapa, Prime Minister Bhimsen Thapa's brother, at Makwanpur, on 4 March 1816. Thus, the draft of the peace treaty which was done at Sugauli on 2 December 1815 was accepted as a treaty only on 4 March 1816. The Treaty of Sugauli was subsequently modified by the Memorandum presented to the Government of Nepal by the Company's Government on 8 December 1816. The Memorandum permitted Nepal to retain possession of the land in the tarai on the east and cancelled the arrangement for payment by the Company's Government to the Nepali officials through the King of Nepal, as envisaged in the original treaty of Sugauli.

From the above account of the negotiations and war between the Gorkhas and the British, it is clear that the British attitude towards the Gorkhas had gone through a remarkable change since 1813. The Company's Government was determined to reduce the strength and territories of the Gorkhas after the Company's charter was renewed in that year. Once the war started, the British were not content with less than Nepal's acceptance of a dictated peace. The British insistence of cession of the tarai by the Gorkhas to the Company's Government was also motivated by its desire to reduce the military potential of the Gorkhas, because most of the Gorkha officers depended on land grants in the tarai for their own maintenance and for the maintenance of the body of soldiers under them.

Nepal's International Status following the Treaty of Sugauli

If the alternaive British proposal for the grant of cash pensions to the Nepali officers, through their King, had been impelemented, it would have adversely affected the morale of the Nepali officers and might even have led to the absorption of Nepal into the Company's system of protectorates and subsidiary alliances. Nepal proved very lucky to have this arrangement changed in December 1816, even after accepting it in the form of a treaty stipulation in March of the same year. Considered from this point of view, the Memorandum of 8 December 1816 has special significance.

However, Atricle 4 of the Treaty of Sugauli, which provided for the indemnification of the chiefs and officers of Nepal by the Company's Government, through pensions in the aggregate amount of 200,000 rupees per year, is not similar to Article 5 of the Treaty that the Company's Government had had with the Nizam in 1798. This article of the Company's Treaty with the Nizam runs as follows:

> The said subsidiary force will at all times be ready to execute services of importance, such as the protection of the person of His Highness, his heirs and successors, from race to race, and overawing and chastising all rebels or exciters of disturbances in the dominions of this state; but it is not to be employed in trifling occasions, nor like *sebundy*, to be stationed in the country to collect the revenue thereof.

Article 2 of the Subsidiary Treaty with the Raja of Mysore (1799) is also similar in content and states:

> The Honourable Maharaja Mysore Krishna Raja Oodiaver Bahadur agrees to receive, a military force for the defence and security of His Highness's dominions; in consideration of which protection, His Highness engages to pay the annual sum of seven lakhs of Star Pagodas to the said East India Company, the said sum to be paid in twelve equal monthly instalments, commencing from the 1st of July Anno Domini 1799, and His Highness further agrees that the disposal of the said sum, together with the arrangement and employment of the troops to be maintained by it, shall be entirely left to the Company.

The above stipulations clearly show that these two states had accepted a subsidiary position in relation to the Company, and the signing of the treaties was prompted by the Company's interest in strengthening its position in India by taking direct responsibility for establishing stability and peace in these states. Its net effect was that the poor peasants and the tax collectors in those states began to look up to the Company's Government as the repository of the ultimate power and prestige which, for the last 200 years, had been vested in the Mughul Emperor in Delhi. To them the Company became the *Sarkar* or the mighty government and the Company *Bahadur*, or the all-powerful Company. The resident representative of the Company's Government in these member states of the Subsidiary Alliance became more powerful than the ruler of the state himself. In the case of Nepal, however, the acceptance of a British representative in Kathmandu, under the terms of the treaty of Sugauli, did not imply any power or responsibility for him in the internal administration of the country.

The treaty between the British and Nepal resembled more the treaties they had had with the frontier states beyond India, such as Afghanistan and Iran, which also contained provisions for the presence of British representatives, but did not in any way make them responsible for internal administration in these countries. Article 2 of the British treaty with Iran (1841) and Article 4 of the Company's treaty with Amir Yakub Khan of Afghanistan (26 May 1879), given below, merit comparison with Article 8 of the Treaty of Sugauli with Nepal which states that "in order to secure and improve the relations of amity and peace hereby established between two states, it is agreed that accredited Ministers from each will reside at the court of the other."

Article 2 of the British treaty with Iran (1841) runs as follows :

> As it is necessary, for the purpose of attending to the affairs of the merchants of the two parties, respectively, that from both governments commercial agents should be appointed to reside in stated places, it is therefore arranged that two commercial agents on the part of the British Government shall reside, one in the capital and one in Tabrez, and in those places only, and on this condition, that he who shall reside at Tabrez and he alone shall be honoured with the privileges of Council General; and as for a series of years a Resident of the British Government has resided at Bushire, the Persian government grants permission that the said resident shall reside there as heretofore; and in like manner two commercial agents shall reside on the part of the Persian government one in the capital of London and one in the port of Bombay, and shall enjoy the same rank and privilege which the commercial agents of the British government shall enjoy in Persia.

Article 4 of the above-mentioned British Treaty with Afghanistan states:

> With a view to the maintenance of the direct and intimate relations now established between the British Government and his Highness the Amir of Afghanistan, and for the better protection of the frontiers of His Highness's dominions, it is agreed that a British repre-

> sentative shall reside at Kabul, with a suitable escort in a place of residence appropriate to his rank and dignity. It is also agreed that the British Government shall have the right to depute British Agents with suitable escorts to the Afghanistan frontiers, whensover this may be considered necessary by the British Government in the interests of both states. On the occurrence of any important external fact, His Highness the Amir of Afghanistan may on his part depute an agent to reside at the Court of His Excellency the Viceroy and Governor-General of India, and at such other places in British India as may be similarly agreed upon.

Comparison of these articles with similar articles in the Treaty of Sugauli shows that the treaty with Nepal, like the treaties with the above-mentioned states neighbouring India, were more like agreements between two sovereign countries than subsidiary treaties. Different states in India actually accepted a subsidiary relationship with the East India Company, which by that time had proved itself the paramount power in India; the relationship between these states and the Company's Government was one between a paramount military power and its weaker neighbours and supporters. But the same cannot be said about the agreements and treaties concluded between the East India Company and the frontier states of Afghanistan and Iran. These treaties were actually necessitated by the rivalry between the two sovereign European powers, Russia and Britain, in extending their influence in the area.

The Company's treaty with Nepal falls into the same category as its treaty with Afghanistan and Iran. But in Nepal's case, this factor of rivalry between two sovereign powers was not as pronounced. Russia and Nepal did not have a common frontier but were separated from each other by Tibet. Further, China at that time was not in a position to influence developments in Tibet or Nepal because of the physical distance between China and those countries and also because China did not at the time possess the requisite military strength.

It is interesting to note that in the case of Afghanistan and Iran, the Company's Government wanted its representative to reside not at the capitals of these states, Kabul and Teheran, but at Herat and Tabrez, the centres where Russians were said to be active. In the case of Nepal, however, the British representative resided at the capital and not in one of the frontier outposts. It was all quiet on the northern frontier of Nepal, and Tibet, with a population of hardly one million and no standing army, was not a power to reckon with.

Although all these treaties were not uniform in character, it is interesting to note that they had so much in common. If Nepal had not had a very weak neighbour to the north, the British administration in India would have shown much greater interest in controlling Nepal's frontier relations, as it had done in the case of Kashmir, which adjoined Sinkiang, and in the case of western Tibet and Baluchistan, which bordered Iran. In other words, if Nepal had been as important as Afghanistan and Iran in the game of international power politics played in the 18th and 19th centuries, it would probably have been absorbed into the British Empire in some way or other and would not have been used merely as a pawn like Afghanistan and Iran.

Effects of the Peace of Sugauli

The total results of the peace of Sugauli can be summed up as follows: First, it removed the danger to the Company of a possible, but not a probable, Hindu coalition of the Marathas, the Sikhs and the Gorkhas, who had at various times threatened the northern and the western frontiers of the Company's territories during the first half of the 19th century. Second, it put a decisive check on Gorkhali expansion towards the west and restricted the Gorkhas to the hills east of the Mahakali river. Third, the Company annexed the districts of Kumaun, Garhwal and Himachal Pradesh, where health resorts and sanatoria were built for European officers and also the western tarai between the River Rapti and the River Mahakali. Lastly, the presence of the Company's representative in Kathmandu enabled the Company's Government to keep a constant and close watch over the machinations of the Gorkhas against the Company's Government. The Company continued to suspect that Nepal might be in league with other powers, such as the Sikhs and the Marathas who, at that time, had not been entirely subjugated.

The 1816 Treaty of Sugauli deprived Nepal of one-third of its territory, mainly on the west and on the south. A British envoy, with a small escort of Indian sepoys, thereafter lived in Nepal's capital. The Government of Nepal relinquished its right–enjoyed by every other independent state–to choose advisers from any country it liked and was deprived of all "claim to or connection with the countries lying to the west of River Kali." The treaty forced Nepal to accept British arbitration in the event of any dispute with Sikkim.

Chinese Reaction to Nepal's War with British India

When Nepal found itself at war with British India in 1814, it had appealed to China for military assistance against the British. The Chinese response was slow and not encouraging, but finally a detachment of Chinese troops did show up on the Nepali frontier after the war was already over.

The Government of Nepal did its best to exploit the situation created by the appearance of Chinese troops on the border but to no avail. The British representative was told by Nepal that the Chinese were greatly disturbed by his presence in Kathmandu and also by the discontinuation of the Nepali quinquennial missions to China. At the same time, the Nepali Government subtly suggested to the Chinese officer that Nepal might have occasion to look to the British for protection in case the Chinese exerted too much pressure; but British mediation was never formally sought.

On the whole the Chnese were satisfied with the peace treaty concluded between Nepal and British India, though they continued to chide Nepali officers for committing aggression against foreign territories and soliciting the Chinese Emperor's aid after signing the treaty. On Nepal's insistence, a Chinese officer wrote to Marquess of Hastings: "This is a matter of no consequence; (but) if you would out of kindness towards us and in consideration of his friendship, withdraw your Vakeel from there, it would be better, and we would be expressly grateful".[21]

It is clear from the records of the confidential deliberations of the Company's Government that, if the Chinese had seriously objected to the British presence in Nepal, the Resident would have been withdrawn, because the Company's Government was in no mood to endanger the long-term interests of Anglo-Chinese maritime trade by giving offence. But the Chinese did not press the matter, and this Nepali ploy had no effect.

King Girvana Yuddha Bikram passed away on 20 November 1816 even before the Memorandum giving effect to Marquess of Hastings's gift to him of the tarai land from the western limits of the district of Gorakhpur to the Kosi River initially ceded to the British by Nepal in accordance with the Treaty of Sugauli had materialized. His death at an early age of 19 and the accession to the throne of his one-and-a-half year old infant son, Rajendra Bikram Shah, served to prolong the regency of Queen Tripurasundari and thereby further strengthened the hands of Bhimsen Thapa as the administrator of the country with near-absolute powers. Although no convincing proof of the allegation that Bhimsen had a hand in bringing about the death of King Girvana Yuddha has been available, yet in view of the prevailing atmosphere of suspicion, conspiracy and murders in the court, Bhimsen's complicity cannot be completely ruled out.

Even after the formal ratification of the Treaty of Sugauli by Nepal and its subsequent modification by the Memorandum of 8 December 1816, the Nepali Government headed by Mukhtiyar General Bhimsen Thapa did not, without a hitch and delay, surrender to the British that section of the western tarai which was to be restored to the Nawab of Oudh. The Nepali side's contention was that since the treaty stipulation referred only to the tarai land between the Rapti river and the Mahakali river, Nepal was not obliged by the treaty to part with the land beyond the Rapti river and the western limits of the district of Gorakhpur. This tract of land was not handed over by the Gorkhas to the British for return to the Nawab of Oudh until the tract of land between the Narayani or Gandak river and the Tinau river was given to Nepal in compensation.

Again, the difference of opinion between the two Governments on the implication of the treaty stipulation with regard to "all the low lands included between the ridges and projecting from the first range of hills towards the plains" almost led to an armed clash between them. The Gorkhas vacated their occupation of the lands claimed by the British on the basis of their interpretation of the above reference in the treaty only after a showdown by Marquess of Hastings who threatened to withdraw the British Resident from Kathmandu unless the Gorkhas respected the British claim in this respect. It was only on 23 July 1817 that the tarai from the Rapti river to the Mahakali river was handed over to the Nawab of Oudh. The delimitation of the the frontier between Nepal and the English East India Company's territory in this sector was not finalized until Bhimsen Thapa accepted on 23 July 1819 the frontier as delimited by Lieutenant Grant and two Nepali Commissioners, Chautara Bam Shah and Rudrabir Shah.

Bhimsen Thapa considered the Shah brothers his rivals and antagonists in Nepali court politics and had deliberately wanted to involve them directly in implementing the provision of the Treaty especially in the light of its open denunciation by Kazi Amar Singh Thapa (Bada), the highly respected veteran Gorkha commander. It was only in the winter of 1819-20 that the boundary was actually demarcated on the ground.

The delimitation and demarcation of the frontier between Nepal and the English East India Company's territory on the eastern side, i.e., from the western limits of the district of Gorakhpur to the Kosi river presented difficulties firstly because the tarai land in this sector was intended as a gift from the Company's Government to the Raja of Nepal and, secondly and more importantly, because unlike in the west no concrete basis or formula was provided on the basis of which the frontier could readily be defined. The principles on which the frontier was sought to be defined on the east were in themselves extremely vague and general insofar as the only guidelines provided were to avoid difficulties that may hinder the drawing up of the exact boundary line in future and the maintenance of the permanent tranquility of the frontier. Further, it was suggested that the boundary was to be kept straight as far as possible even by means of the exchange of lands for the purpose. The Company's Government came forward to undertake the entire expenditure involved in the survey and demarcation of the frontier and the boundary line.

By 27 March 1817, the demarcation of the frontier along Butwal and Syuraj was concluded by Lieutenant-Colonel Paris Bradshaw. It was indeed strange that both Butwal and Syuraj, conflicting claims and armed clashes over which had triggered off the 1814-1816 war, were left in possession of Nepal even after its defeat. This was evidence of the fact that the British had used this incident merely as a pretext for waging war against Nepal about which they had already made up their mind.

The demarcation of the frontier adjoining the Saran district was completed by 30 April 1817 and that along the districts of Gkorakhpur and Tirhut by March and May 1817 respectively.

There were also differences with regard to the settlement of land between the Orriah river and the Narayani or the Gandak river. The boundary there was demarcated by the British unilaterally in December 1817 and the Nepali side sought to register its protest by absenting itself from the spot at the time.

The English East India Company's preoccupation with the suppression of the Pindaris and the Marathas in Central India in the years immediately following the conclusion of the Treaty of Sugauli with Nepal prevented the Company's Government from insisting on the strict implementation of the terms of the treaty. This emboldened Nepal to make diplomatic overtures to the Sikh Maharaja Ranjit Singh in

Lahore and also to the Emperor of China, Chia-Ch'ing. Apart from that, Nepal sent Padmapani as its emissary to the court of Peshwa Baji Rao II in Poona and that of Daulat Rao Sindhia in Gwalior in order to explore the possibility of forming a military alliance with them against the British.

A Peep into Contemporary Maratha History

It may be appropriate here to take a quick look at the Maratha history of the time. Unfortunately for the Marathas, their great leaders of yesteryears such as Mahadaji Sindhia, Malhar Rao Holkar and Tukoji Holkar were no longer alive. With the death of the shrewd old Maratha statesman, Nana Fadnavis, at Poona on 13 March 1800 no Maratha leader of ability and standing was left to deal with the British. Peshwa Baji Rao II, who was weak-minded and given to intrigues, turned to the British after his army along with that of Daulat Rao Sindhia was defeated by Jaswant Rao Holkar at Poona and Vinayak Rao was installed in his place on the Peshwa's throne or masnad. After Baji Rao II acceded to the Subsidiary Alliance and signed the Treaty of Bassein on 31 December 1802 sacrificing "his independence as the price of protection," a British force under Arthur Wellesley (later the Duke of Wellington) conducted him to Poona and restored him to his throne on 13 May 1803.

But the Peshwa repented his action and shortly afterwards sent secret messages encouraging other Maratha leaders to organize joint resistance against the British. Daulat Rao Sindhia and Raghuji Bhonsle II of Berar joined hands and also made efforts to get Jaswant Rao Holkar on their side. But the Holkar preferred to stand by and watch events, and the Gaikwar, Anand Rao, remained neutral. By the end of 1803, both Daulat Rao and Raghuji were decisively defeated by the British and were forced to sign treaties ceding considerable territory and accepting British Residents at their courts. After this the Nizam of Hyderabad, Mir Akbar Ali Khan Sikandar Jah, and Peshwa Baji Rao II came all the more under British influence and the British had only Jaswant Rao Holkar left to deal with.

No sooner had peace been made with the Sindhia and the Bhonsle than the hostilities between the Holkar and the British commenced. Although the Holkar was prevented by the British Resident Ochterlony from occupying Delhi and was also personally defeated by General Lake at Dig on 13 November 1804, the English suffered a serious loss of reputation as a result of Lake's failure to capture the fortress of Bharatpur early in 1805. However, the Raja of Bharatpur concluded a treaty with the British on 10 April 1805 putting the Holkar in a precarious position. It was only Wellesley's sudden recall that saved the situation for the Holkar at the time. Subsequently, the Holkar was pursued by Lord Lake up to Amritsar and he finally signed peace with the British on 7 January 1806 after the Sikhs under Ranjit Singh failed to respond to his call for help. Jaswant Rao Holkar died on 20 October 1811 after secretly assassinating his brother and his nephew. Power fell into the hands of his mistress, Tulsi Bai, who even with the support of her minister, Balaram Seth, and Amir Khan, the Pathan leader of Central India, miserably failed in the task of administering the state.

However, it was only after another trial of strength with the British that the Marathas finally succumbed. Their mutual jealousy and distrust notwithstanding all the Maratha chiefs including Peshwa Baji Rao II, who had been restored to his throne with British help, nurtured in their hearts a burning hatred of the British and it appeared as though the year 1817 would provide them a favourable opportunity to rise jointly against the British.

Peshwa Baji Rao II had not given up his old dream of organizing a confederacy of Maratha chiefs against the British. In 1814 the Gaikwar sent his pro-English Chief Minister Gangadhar Shastri to the Peshwa, who conducted him to Nasik. Here he was murdered at the instigation of the Peshwa's unscrupulous favourite, Trimbakji Danglia. Peshwa Baji Rao II, after considerable hesitation and delay, surrendered Trimbakji to the British Resident at Poona, Mountstuart Elphinstone, who imprisoned him in the fortress of Thana. A year later Trimbakji escaped from the fortress allegedly with the connivance of the Peshwa.

Matters came to a head in 1817 when the Peshwa made serious attempts to organize against the English a confederacy of the Maratha chiefs by opening negotiations with them as well as with the Pathan chief, Amir Khan, and the Pindaris. But by 13 June 1817 the Marquess of Hastings succeeded in forcing the Peshwa to sign the Treaty of Poona by which he renounced the headship of the Maratha Confederacy. The Sindhia of Gwalior, Daulat Rao, was also compelled to sign the Treaty of Gwalior on 5 November 1817 which bound him to cooperate with the English in crushing the Pindaris and authorized the Company to enter freely into engagements with the Rajput states beyond Chambal whom the English had always wanted to befriend. Raghuji Bhonsle of Berar died on 22 March 1816 and was succeeded by his imbecile son Parsoji, who had as his regent his able but ambitious cousin, Appa Saheb. The English won over Appa Saheb by recognizing his regency on his signing the Treaty of Subsidiary Alliance on 27 May 1816.

These Treaties of Poona, Gwalior and Nagpur ought to have added immensely to the influence of the English over them, but none of the Maratha chiefs were yet reconciled to the loss of their independence. On the very day Daulat Rao Sindhia signed the Treaty with the English, 5 November 1817, Peshwa Baji Rao II plundered and burnt the British Residency in Poona and launched an attack with 27,000 men on a small British army of 2,800 under Colonel Burr at Khirki. But the Peshwa was badly defeated.

Appa Saheb of Nagpur and Malhar Rao Holkar II, son of Jaswant Rao Holkar, also took up arms against the English. But the Holkar's forces were trounced by Hislop at Mahidpur on 21 December 1817 after the Nagpur troops had already been defeated at Sitabaldi on 27 November 1817. Appa Saheb fled to the Punjab and then to Jodhpur, where he died in 1840. The British took away the districts lying to the north of the Narmada river, placed a minor grandson of Raghuji Bhonsle II on the throne and made the Holkar sign the Treaty of Mandasar on 6 January 1818. By this treaty, the Holkar renounced his claims on the Rajput states, undertook to maintain a subsidiary force within his territory and submit his foreign relations to the arbitration of the British.

The Peshwa, even after his defeat at Khirki, fought two more battles with the English at Korega on 1 January 1818 and at Ashti on 20 February 1818. He was worsted in both and lost his able General Gokhale in the second battle. It was not until 3 June 1818 that Baji Rao II surrendered to the British. The Peshwaship, which had served as a symbol of collective leadership and unity among the Marathas, was abolished and Baji Rao II was allowed to live in retirement at Bithur near Kanpur on a pension of Rs. 800,000 a year while Trimbakji was condemned to lifelong imprisonment in the fort of Chunar.

Padmapani, who was sent as Nepal's emissary to the Peshwa and the Sindhia, was arrested by the British in the Company's territory and his papers also fell into their hands. The Nepali Government was thus forced to save its face by telling the English Company's Government that its emissary, Padmapani, had exceeded the limits of authority given him in his dealings with the Maratha chiefs. Luckily for Nepal, this happened immediately after the British signed the treaty with

Daulat Rao Sindhia of Gwalior on 5 November 1817. The Nepali Government seized the opportunity to disavow the real intentions of its overtures to Poona, Gwalior and China, and the British Indian Government was apparently satisfied with this disavowal. By March 1818, Bhimsen was fully convinced of the turn of tide in favour of the British in their war with the Maratha rulers and went so far as to offer to the Company's Government the services of Gorkha troops as a token of Nepal's cordial and sincere friendship.[22] But this did not mean that there was any change in Nepal's attitude towards the resident British Minister. He was viewed with the same suspicion as before and the restrictions on his movements and on his contacts with the people were by no means relaxed. A company of soldiers was posted round the clock near the British Residency compound in order to prevent anyone from trying to see the British Minister. He himself was not allowed to travel freely in the valley of Kathmandu itself. Even the customary diplomatic immunities were denied him, and his supplies of food and personal baggage from India were invariably searched on entering Nepal.

Even after the decisive victory of the British over all the Maratha chiefs and Peshwa Baji Rao II himself in 1818, Edward Gardner, the British Minister at the Court of Nepal, wrote to his superiors in India that "my intercourse with the court is confined to the mere courtesies and attentions incidental to my public situation here."[23] Sir H. Maddock, who succeeded Gardner in February 1832, also stated that contact between the Nepal Darbar and the Residency was limited to two visits by the Minister to the King, one on the occasion of the Holi festival and the other on that of Dasai, and two formal visits by the Mukhtiyar or Prime Minister to the Minister in the Residency.

Further, the Nepali Government's success in enforcing its policy of isolation and exclusion of foreigners is attested by the following words in which Maddock describes the Resident Minister's position in his time: "While the jealousy of the Nepal government and its original aversion to the establishment of our mission here are still undiminished, the narrow bounds within which it strives to limit its intercourse with the Resident and the strict interdict placed upon its subjects who might otherwise seek our society, have conduced to render our situation more isolated, with reference both to the court and to the people of the country, than is the case anywhere else."

Even private visits by Europeans were viewed with great suspicion. No European visitor could enter Nepal without obtaining an invitation from the Nepal Darbar and clearance from the Company's Government. White women were not initially permitted and it was not until 1844 that Mrs. Hanoria Lawrence, wife of Resident Minister Henry Lawrence (1843-1845), became the first European woman ever to enter Nepal. It had probably been the sheer strain and hardship of living alone for a period of 13 years from 1829 till 1843, first as Acting and then as full-fledged Resident Minister, that made even a serious person with scholarly interests like Brian Houghton Hodgson take a local mistress and have children by her.

The Gorkhalis were highly suspicious of both European missionaries and traders. They literally believed in the adage that "with the Bible comes the bayonet, with the merchant comes the musket." Nepal's fear of foreign traders was based on the awareness deep down in its heart of how the British who came to India initially as traders had already ended up being political masters of a vast area of the Indian subcontinent. Nepal's own experience of dealing with the British since 1792, culminating in the 1814-1816 war and the Treaty of Sugauli, also served to deepen its distrust of the British and made even normal trade relations with them suspect irrespective of consideration of economic, commercial or any other gain for Nepal.

Hastings thought that he had broken the military power of Nepal in 1816, but he had not entirely done so. The Nepali army actually increased its numbers and efficiency to a point unknown before the war. What Bhimsen had done was merely to change the tactics of "open obstruction" to "covert frustration." With Nepal's policy of skilful hindrance, the mercantile arrangements between Nepal and India became a dead letter. So in a country without trade outlets war was the natural and eventual occupation of the people. Military service alone offered a scope and outlet for the energy of the classes above the ordinary peasants working on the land. Regent Queen Tripurasundari (1806-1832), and Prime Minister Bhimsen Thapa (1806-1837), knew that their tenure of office depended in the long run on their success in providing a career of arms for chiefs and the higher class of people in Nepal.

It is interesting to note that Hodgson, the most well known of all the British Residents in Nepal, clearly saw this problem and suggested to his Government plans for the commercial development of Nepal and also for the British enlistment of Gorkhas, with a view to providing an outlet for the surplus energy of the people of Nepal. We shall see in due course how his ideas for the improvement of Nepal's commerce was rejected by his Government even after its acceptance by the Nepali government with some reluctance and delay. Both the Nepali and the British Governments were cool to his plan for the enlistment of Gorkhas into the British army, but it was nonetheless put into practice in due course.

Hodgson even conceived a plan of negotiating with Nepal for the service of a portion of its organized troops. When this suggestion was first made by Hodgson, it was thought by the British Government that the employment of separate bodies of foreign mercenaries would not be consistent with the military policy of the British Government in India, and nothing was done about implementing Hodgson's proposal. It was not until 1850 and 1856 that Dalhousie recognized the Indian Gorkha batallions into regiments and urged the increase of this force as essential to the security of the British in India.

Long-standing boundary disputes in the western and the eastern tarai were not settled until 1830-1833. The British Resident continued to be kept in isolation, and Hodgson's repeated pleas for a direct audience with the king were always turned down. As late as 1833 Hodgson reported the arrival of a Russian agent in Kathmandu and the dispatch of a Nepali agent to Lahore and Teheran.

Bhimsen Thapa remained in full control of the administration until 1832, when Regent Quen Tripurasundari died. Thereafter he found his position gradually slipping. King Rajendra Bikram Shah (1816-1847) at the age of one and a half years had succeeded his father, King Girvana Yuddha, and had already attained his majority in 1832 during Regent Queen Tripurasundari's lifetime. King Rajendra Bikram Shah now began increasingly to assert his position over the Prime Minister, encouraged by Bhimsen Thapa's enemies at the court led by Rana Jang Pande, son of Damodar Pande. The year after Regent Queen Tripurasundari died, King Rajendra Bikram temporarily held up the *Pajani* or annual routine confirmation of the Prime Minister in his office, although Bhimsen Thapa was later confirmed. Yet the very delay in the routine confirmation proved portentous for Bhimsen. Despite ruthless persecution by Bhimsen Thapa in the past years, the Pande family had enjoyed the support of Senior Queen Samrajyalakshmi and had regained its influence in the court with her support in the aftermath of the war of 1814-1816.

The death of Regent Queen Tripurasundari on 6 April 1832 at the relatively young age of 38 and the attainment of majority by King Rajendra Bikram about the same time boded ill for Bhimsen Thapa.

Her death was followed by "evil omens" in succession. A strong earth tremor was felt in the Kathmandu Valley on 18 September 1833 and the following year a thunderbolt struck the powder magazine on 19 June. A fortnight later there was another devastating earthquake which was followed within months by unprecedented floods in the Bagmati river. And from December 1834 commenced the determined move against Bhimsen Thapa by the Kala Pandes witht the open backing of King Rajendra Bikram's senior queen, Samrajyalakshmi Devi.

Bhimsen was able to read the signs of the time and sought to arrest the decline in his power with the Darbar of King Rajendra by acquiring influence with the English East India Company's Government through its Resident Minister. But Hodgson who had served as Acting Resident Minister in Nepal in 1829, was fully aware of Bhimsen's game and refused to cooperate with him in his time of need except on his own terms: the removal of restrictions on his movement and action and direct access for himself to the King as the Head of State. Bhimsen was not prepared to let Hodgson have free and direct access to the King for fear that the Resident might influence the King against the Prime Minister himself.

After Hodgson's initial failure to revive the Treaty of 1792, the very existence of which was denied by Bhimsen Thapa in August 1834, the Resident proposed a draft for a more favourable new treaty fixing the duty to be levied on Nepal's exports to India at 4 per cent ad valorem and on Indian exports to Nepal at 5 per cent ad valorem. When this treaty was referred to the Governor-General for his approval after it had obtained the consent of the Government of Nepal, the Company's Board of Customs, Salt and Opium considered the duty on Nepal's exports too low and advised rejection of the draft. However, in June 1836, the Company's Government exempted all Nepali goods from customs duties and expressed the hope that the Government of Nepal would also reciprocate the gesture in order to ensure a free and smooth flow of trade between the two countries. The British Government's action was welcomed by Nepal but it was not prepared to exempt Indian exports from Nepali duties.

Bhimsen's acceptance of the draft of the treaty proposed by Hodgson was a calculated gesture in itself to cultivate Hodgson and through him the English East India Company's Government. Another move by Bhimsen in the same direction was to send his nephew Mathbar Singh Thapa to London as Nepal's Ambassador. But Hodgson was not cooperative at all, and Mathbar came back disappointed from Calcutta when he was told by the officials of the Company's Government that he would not be treated as an Ambassador in London but he might go there as a private person if he wished.

The more Bhimsen sought to lean on Hodgson to safeguard his fast declining power, the more Hodgson was inclined to exploit Bhimsen's plight to secure direct access to the King and thus to increase his own and the Company's direct influence with the Head of State himself. Bhimsen, having failed to gain the British support for himself, once again tried to join the anti-British war cry which was already being raised by courtiers of the rival Pande family. But even this failed to save him.

Bhimsen's policy of caution towards the British had always been under fire from another section of the courtiers led by Rana Jang Pande and his group who ousted Bhimsen Thapa from the Prime Ministership in 1837 with the backing of the Senior Queen Samrajyalakshmi. Bhimsen Thapa was dismissed on the charge that one of the royal children by the Senior Queen had died of poison administered by a native apothecary at Bhimsen's instigation. The charges against Bhimsen could not be proved and he was released briefly, only to be rearrested in 1839 on the same charge and on the additional charge of having poisoned the King's father, King Girvana Yuddha Bikram Shah (c. 1799-1816). Again he was put in prison, where he was reported to have committed suicide. It is said that the members of the Pande family regarded Bhimsen's presence, even in prison, as a continued threat to their own position and power. They saw to it that Bhimsen was deliberately informed by some of his men that his wife had been subjected to the indignity of being marched naked through the streets of Kathmandu. This shame proved too much for the old general and he put an end to his life with a stroke of his *khukri*.

NOTES

1. John Pemble, *The Invasion of Nepal* (Oxford: Clarendon Press, 1971), p. 24.
2. John Pemble, *op. cit.*, p. 25.
3. John Pemble, *op. cit.*, p. 25.
4. John Pemble, *op. cit.*, p. 25.
5. B.D. Sanwal, *Nepal and the East India Company* (Bombay: Asia Publishing House, 1965), pp. 116-17.
6. Letter from Major P. Bradshaw to the Political Secretary dated 8 April 1814, Bengal Consultations cited in B.D. Sanwal, *op. cit.*, pp. 140-42.

7. Henry T. Prinsep, *History of the Political and Military Transaction in India during the Administration of Marquess of Hastings*, 1813-1823, (London, 1825), pp. 459-61, Surya Bikram Jnawali (translated by Lalji Sahay), *Amar Singh Thapa* (Hindi), (Darjeeling: Himachal Hindi Bhawan), pp. 78-79.
8. *Narrative of the War*, Secret letter from Lord Moira dated 2 August 1815, cited in *ibid.*, pp. 144-145.
9. *Narrative of the War*, Secret letter from Lord Moira, 2 October 1815.
10. B.D. Sanwal. *op. cit.*, p. 149.
11. B.D. Sanwal, *op. cit.*, p. 151.
12. B.D. Sanwal, *op. cit.*, p. 161.
13 B.D. Sanwal, *op. cit.*, p. 178.
14. B.D. Sanwal, *op. cit.*, p. 179.
15. B.D. Sanwal, *op. cit.*, pp. 174-75.
16. B.D. Sanwal, *op. cit.*, p. 175.
17. B.D. Sanwal, pp. 162-67.
18. B.D. Sanwal, *op. cit.*, p. 203.
19. B.d. Sanwal, *op. cit.*, pp. 183-85.
20. Quoted in B.D. Sanwal, *op. cit.*, p. 205.
21. Foreign Secret Consultations, 11 January 1817, No. 7.
22. Foreign Political Consultation, 27 March 1818, No. 31, cited in Ramakant, *op. cit.*, p. 175.
23. Ramakant, *op. cit.*, p. 80.

7

Towards the Kot Massacre

The young King Rajendra Bikram Shah may be said to have shown initially a fair measure of skill and self-confidence in cutting down to size Bhimsen Thapa–a minister who had, in Hodgson's words, "grown so great by virtue of two minorities (with but a short interval between them) and 30 years of almost uninterrupted sovereign sway."[1] But once Bhimsen was removed from the scene, the King failed to rise to the occasion. He thereby missed forever the opportunity he had to consolidate royal power once again in his own hands and to exercise it to his own advantage and that of his dynasty and his nation. It was unfortunate that at the most crucial period of its history Nepal had a weak, intriguing, suspicious and vacillating person as a king, a man who was neither capable of using power himself nor of trusting others to exercise it on his behalf.

Rajendra's emergence on the political scene served to aggravate rather than to ease the divisive tendencies prevailing in the court. Following the removal of Bhimsen, competition for power among the leading families revived in full vigour.

Among the foremost contenders were the original Gorkha-based Pande family to which Nepal's outstanding military commanders and administrators such as Kazi Kalu Pande, Kazi Bamsharaj Pande and Kazi Damodar Pande belonged. During the rule of King Prithvinarayan Shah and his immediate successors they had played a vital role in forging the state of Nepal, but ever since the rise of Bhimsen Thapa to power, leading members of this family had suffered ruthless persecution at the hands of the newly-emerged Thapa family.

Members of the particular branch of the old Pande family descended from Kazi Kalu Pande, and were sometimes referred to as "Kala (Black) Pandes", as distinguished from "Gora (White) Pandes" who were members of another branch of the same family headed by Kalu Pande's brother, Kazi Tula Ram Pande, and did not undergo suffering and humiliation at the hands of Mukhtiyar General Bhimsen Thapa (1806-1837) and Prime Minister and General Mathbar Singh Thapa (1843-1845). Mathbar himself is credited with making his distinction between members of the same family as "Gora" and "Kala" Pandes from the point of view of the newly emerged Thapa family. The Thapas looked upon Kala Pandes as their formidable foes whereas they were able to conciliate the "Gora" Pandes by matrimonial alliance or by other means.

Throughout Bhimsen Thapa's ascendancy, the "Kala Pandes" had been biding their time, waiting for an opportunity to take revenge on the Thapas. To the surviving members of the family of Kalu Pande, apart from considerations of personal and interfamily rivalry and jealousy, it was simply unbearable that Bhimsen, without any outstanding record of service to the state and even without so much as taking part in a single battle, had risen to the position of Mukhtiyar and given himself the title of General. The "Kala Pandes" had all along held Bhimsen Thapa responsible for the loss of one-third of Nepal's previously existing territory in the 1814-1816 war.

The prevailing view also held that Bhimsen Thapa's precipitate action to recover Butwal and Syuraj gave the British a ready-made excuse to start a war against Nepal. The Kala Pandes further accused Bhimsen Thapa of taking this action in utter disregard of the advice and warning of outstanding military commanders in the field. Kazi Amar Singh Thapa Bada (to whose name the epithet 'Bada' is added in order to distinguish him and his branch of the Thapa family from that of Bhimsen Thapa's father who was also of the same name). Chautara Bam Shah, Sardar Hasti Dal Shah and others had petitioned the King that under no circumstances should His Majesty allow the country to be dragged into war as the odds were heavily stacked against Nepal at the time.

The caustic reference to Bhimsen Thapa in Kazi Amar Singh Thapa Bada's letter to the King on the eve of the war is worth recollecting. The veteran commander, Amar Singh Thapa Bada, had warned King Girvana Yuddha Bikram against acting on the advice of a man who would boast of bringing death and destruction to the British empire in India, without so much as having ever seen a battlefield in his entire life.[2]

Rise of Rana Jang Pande

From July 1837 through November 1840, Rana Jang Pande played an important part in Nepali court politics with Queen Samrajyalakshmi's active support, notwithstanding frequent changes in the Mukhtiyarship which was almost equivalent to prime ministership. Guru Ranganath Pandit who belonged to the family of royal preceptors became Mukhtiyar for about nine months from December 1837 till August 1838 and during his administration Bhimsen was temporarily acquitted only to be tried again in 1839 and condemned to imprisonment. The Brahmin Mukhtiyar, in spite of his well-meaning efforts, was unable to hold the balance between the two antagonistic forces at work in the politics of the Nepal Darbar but merely succeeded in preventing the emerging forces represented by Senior Queen Samrajyalakshmi and the Pandes from overwhelming their opponents in the Darbar all at once.

After Ranganath Pandit voluntarily quitted the office of Mukhtiyar, a joint ministry or a diumvirate of Puskar Shah and Rana Jang Pande shouldered the burden of administration from October 1838 to end of 1839. By April 1839 Puskar Shah had become subordinate to Rana Jang Pande and, on 6 February 1840, Rana Jang was appointed Mukhtiyar and held that position till he was removed from office in November under pressure from the British Government.

Following the rise of Rana Jang Pande to power, the hostility of Nepal towards the British Government assumed a more open form, and preparations for war were stepped up after news reached Nepal that the British had suffered a setback in Afghanistan in 1840. As a precaution against Nepal's designs, the British had, however, in the winter of 1838-39 strengthened their forces all along the frontier extending from the Gandak river to the Kosi river, and laid plans for their rapid deployment under General Oglander should this prove necessary.

Developments in Afghanistan

It may not be out of place here to refer briefly to the developments in Afghanistan at the time. Herat, which was regarded by the British as the key to India, had been put under siege by Mohammed Shah of Persia in November 1837 with the support of the Russians. This led the British to think that Persia was fast coming under complete domination by the Russian Government. The British sought to counter the growing

Russian influence by concluding alliances with the rulers of Herat, Kabul and Kandahar. In 1837 Dost Mohammed, the ruler of Kabul, initially welcomed the British mission under Captain (later Sir) Alexander Burnes in the hope that the British might help Kabul recover Peshawar. However, Burnes would not give the assurance Dost Mohammed had sought from him. Meanwhile, after a Russian agent arrived in Kabul, the British mission abruptly ended talks and left the city.

In the wake of the failure of Burnes's mission, the Governor-General of India, Lord Auckland, launched an invasion of Afghanistan with a view to restoring Shah Shuja to the throne. In April 1839, after experiencing immense hardships and guerrilla attack on the way, a British force finally made its way to Kandahar and Shah Shuja was crowned king in the mosque situated next to the mausoleum of Ahmad Shah. Ghazni and Kabul also fell into British hands by July 1839 and thereupon Shah Shuja was again crowned in Kabul. Dost Mohammed had made good his escape first to Balkh, then to Bukhara, only to be finally arrested and imprisoned by the British there.

However, Dost Mohammed eventually escaped from prison and returned to Kabul to lead his supporters who had already started the fight against the British. On 2 November 1840, Dost Mohammed had the better of the British in a battle at Parwandarah but he surrendered to them in Kabul the very next day. He was treated well by the British but they took him to India with most of his family. After his deportation, insurrections became widespread in the country and the advent of winter rendered the British position in Kabul all the more untenable. The dilatory tactic adopted by Sir William Hay Machaghten as a bargaining counter in negotiating terms of withdrawal with Akbar Khan, Dost Mohammed's son, had disastrous consequences. Machaghten himself died at the hands of Akbar Khan. On 6 March 1842 about 4,500 British and Indian troops with 12,000 camp followers were forced by circumstances to pull out of Kabul. Scattered bands of Afghan guerrillas had a field day and the retreat turned into a total holocaust leaving only a few survivors.

British Involvement in the "Opium" War

Let us now briefly inquire into the cause and circumstances of the "Opium War" in China. The cause of the Opium War in China may be traced back to a late 18th century British attempt to meet the unfavourable balance of trade with China by exporting Indian opium to it. In 1779 the East India Company acquired the monopoly of the opium trade, and by 1819, the company had commenced shipping large quantities of opium to China. This caused a ceaseless drain of Chinese silver creating serious economic and social problems for the country. The imperial court of China banned the import of opium, but the ban never came into effect because of rampant corruption among the officials and soldiers responsible for enforcing the ban.

Thus by the beginning of the nineteenth century an illicit opium trade had become the sole business of private Indian traders who were authorized to handle the inter-Asian trade only under the Company's licence. These private businessmen created the opium market in China in defiance of the opium ban, and as time passed they grew callous towards Chinese law and order in general.

In 1834 the British Parliament finally revoked the East India Company's monopoly. In 1834, William John Napier, who was appointed Chief Superintendent of British Trade in China, tried but failed to negotiate a settlement with the Canton authorities.

In Peking itself a proposal to relax restraint on opium trade received support from several quarters, but it came to naught when the Ch'ing Emperor, Hsuan-tsung, appointed a patriotic officer, Lin Tse-hau, as Imperial Commissioner for the anti-opium campaign. Lin seized 20,000 chests of illegal opium and destroyed them in March 1839, and by September that year sporadic armed clashes between the British and the Chinese had already commenced.

In February 1840 the British Government decided to launch a full-scale military expedition. Sixteen British warships, having assembled in Hong Kong by June, proceeded northward to the mouth of the Pei Ho to force China to yield to British demands. But the Chinese authorities remained adamant. In May 1841 the walled city of Canton itself was, without warning, subjected to heavy shelling by long-range guns, and a ransom of U.S. $ 6,000,000 was extorted from the Cantonese. This marked the beginning of a continuing conflict between the British and the Cantonese.

The Ch'ing Emperor had no effective defence against the powerful British navy guns. The British also took advantage of the prevailing distance between the Government and the people in China by professing that they were not against the Chinese people but against the Chinese Government officials and soldiers who oppressed them. This also mitigated the chances of popular resistance against the British.

A new British Commissioner, Henry Pottinger, arrived at Macau in August 1841 and led a northward expedition. With reinforcements from India, Pottinger resumed action in May 1842. As a result, Nanking surrendered in August 1842 and hostilities came to an end with the conclusion of the Treaty of Nanking.

Effect of Developments in Afghanistan and China on the Policy of the Nepal Darbar

Reports of the failure and success of British military adventures in Afghanistan and China during the 1830-1842 period, as received and interpreted by the Kathmandu Darbar, affected the efforts and activities of the anti-British section of the court, consisting of the Senior Queen of King Rajendra Bikram, Samrajyalakshmi Devi, her son, Crown Prince Surendra Bikram Shah, and the Kala Pandes such as Mukhtiyar Rana Jang Pande, Kul Bir Pande, Kul Bahadur Pande, the royal preceptor, Mishra Guru and others. As Resident B.H. Hodgson (1832-43) described it, "The barometer of the Nepalese hostility against us rises and falls with each rumour of our being in trouble with other states." Until 1841 the Nepali Government, albeit in a haphazard manner, persisted in its attempt to forge an anti-British multinational bloc in order to stem the tide of the aggressiveness of the East India Company's Government. With that end in view, it not only sought contacts with a number of Indian princes, such as those of Udaipur, Jodhpur, Gwalior, Hyderabad, and the Mahratta and Sikh rulers, but also opened communications with China, Afghanistan, Persia, and the Court of Ava (Burma). The missions sent out to the different states in the Indian subcontinent, even in the face of British opposition, on the pretext of looking for a suitable bride for the Crown Prince were, in fact, intended to explore the possibility of concerted diplomatic and military action against the Company's Government of India.

Armed Incursion into Ramnagar

The news of difficulties and hardships encountered by the British in the initial stage of the Afghan campaign and the British involvement in the Opium War may have tempted Rana Jang Pande to launch an incursion into Ramnagar on 12 April 1840. An armed force of about 100 men led by Fauzdar Jas Bir Rana crossed the Someshwar range on its southern side and forced its way to Ramnagar which was situated in the Bettiah district of northern Bihar, 8 miles south of this range, which formed the boundary between Nepal and British India. The Nepali troops captured 91 villages on a rather tendentious plea that they had in the past been given in dowry to a Nepali princess who was married to a local chief and should now be returned to Nepal because the Nepali princess's husband had died without leaving any heirs. Upon investigation, the Company's Government discovered that not only Ramnagar but the southern flank of the Someshwar ridge also belonged to it and the ridge was of considerable strategic value in any plan for military action against Nepal.

Hodgson remonstrated with the Nepali Government for committing aggression and demanded immediate withdrawal of Gorkha soldiers to the northern side of the Someshwar range and the immediate return of forcibly occupied Indian territory. Despite the Resident's threatening attitude, Nepal played for time first by giving oral assurances, and then, only after repeated protests, pretending to issue written orders for the arrest of Fauzdar Jas Bir Rana and the withdrawal of troops. No formal explanation was, however, offered for the act nor was the territory itself actually vacated unitl after considerable time. The British also were not in a position to do anything more about it at the time because of their military preoccupations in Afghanistan.

Meanwhile, a mutiny of 6,000 soldiers were orchestrated in Kathmandu on 21 June 1840, the men airing their grievances over reduced pay and uncertainty of employment. Rana Jang Pande and Senior Queen Samrajyalakshmi deliberately and wilfully made themselves unavailable for immediate consultation by King Rajendra. The Senior Queen left for Thankot and Rana Jang Pande absented himself from work on that day on the plea of illness. The rebellious soldiers gathered in front of the British Residency voicing their demands as if the Residency itself had been responsible for reduction in their salary. The sentiments of the mutineers are summed up in what is reported as their slogans in Hodgson's dispatch of 3 July 1840 to his Government:

> Woe to those who live in luxury themselves while they advise the starving and poor soldiers! Down with the chiefs! Down with the Firingies! We will be chiefs ourselves. We will have back our old territories. We will conquer the Ganges![3]

The following entry in Hodgson's private notebook about the happenings on the night of 21 June 1840 may be of interest to the reader as it reveals a deeply laid conspiracy to which the Senior Queen and the Kala Pandes were party:

> I was called to the Darbar ostensibly for a mere formal visit. I went as usual with the gentleman of Residency at 7 p.m. At 10 o'clock, I rose to go but the Raja begged me to stay awhile and so again at 11 o'clock and again at midnight. Still something was always urged by the court to keep us, and though no adequate cause was assigned, I assented in order, if possible, to discover the real cause of our detention. I felt there was some cause and possibly a serious one, as I whispered to Dr. Campbell (The Residency Surgeon and Honorary Assistant Resident).
>
> Soon after midnight, at a sign from one of the Raja's attendants, His Highness asked me to go to Queen's apartment. I went, Her Highness received me with scant civility, and presently grew angry and offensive, with reference to business. I replied at first seriously and then passed to compliments ending in a jest. This made her laugh and under the cover of momentary good humour Raja carried me off, apparently only too happy to have thus easily got me through an interview demanded by his virago wife, who was the prime mover in all mischief then brewing. It was daylight when I and the gentlemen left the palace and shortly after came rumours of an uproar in the Nepal Cantonments. It was reported to me that the troops at the capital were in a mutinous state, and were threatening mischief to the Residency, they having been told that the Resident had been all night insisting on a reduction of the Gorkha army by instruction from his government.[4]

Having withdrawn themselves from the precincts of the Residency without causing any material damage, the troops on 21 and 22 June 1840, apparently in a state of mutiny, looted the houses of Ranganath Pandit, Puskar Shah, Kulraj Pande and Karbir Pande. The British Residency was left unprotected on 22 June in violation of the established code of international behaviour. King Rajendra, accompanied by the entire body of troops, proceeded to Thankot to fetch the Senior Queen. By the evening the Senior Queen was persuaded to return to Kathmandu and the demands of the mutineers were apparently also conceded.

But on the morning of 24 June the soldiers were mischievously informed that as the King needed money badly to fight the British, the soldiers should continue to accept lower pay for a few years and the soldiers understandably refused to agree to this proposal. The soldiers replied to King Rajendra's pleas with them for restraint and moderation in the following terms as given in Hodgson's dispatch to his Government: "True the English Government is great, but care the wild dogs of Nepal how large is the herd they attack. They are sure to get their bellies filled. We want no money for making war; for war shall support itself. We will plunder Lucknow and Patna. But we must get rid of the Resident who sees and forestalls all. . . . Give the word we shall destroy the Resident and we shall soon make the Ganges your boundary or if English, as they say, are your friends and want peace, why do they keep possession of half your dominions? Let them restore Kumaon and Sikkim. Those are yours, demand them both. If they refuse drive out the Resident and let us have war."[5] The mutiny was obviously engineered to harass the King and the Resident with a view to securing, if possible, plenipotentiary powers for the Senior Queen. But the purpose of the so-called mutiny was not achieved.

On the other hand, both the Ramnagar incursion and the mutiny of 21-22 June 1840 led the British Government to demand explanations from King Rajendra, who vacillated under the influence of the Senior Queen and the Kala Pandes and kept on giving evasive replies until faced with a British ultimatum. On 27 August 1840, Lord Auckland, the Governor-General of India, addressed a very strong letter to King Rajendra, listing his demands and also at the same time asked the Commander-in-Chief of India to prepare for military action against Nepal in case the British demands were not conceded. The British Indian Governor-General's demands were as follows: (1) The immediate withdrawal of the Gorkhas from Ramnagar; (2) the redress of grievances of Indian traders regarding the inordinate delay in the disposal of their cases, and the censure of Mishra Guru for his denial of justice to them; (3) the cessation of the Nepal Darbar's intrigues with Indian States including the Punjab; (4) an explanation for leaving the Residency unprotected during the soldiers' mutiny on 21 and 22 June 1840; and (5) the formal disavowal by the King of the anti-British sentiments and slogans aired on that occasion.

On 1 September 1840, Hodgson put forward the British demands with a clear note of warning that "if compliance (was) not yielded within 10 days from this date, His Lordship (the Governor-General) will be compelled at the expiration of the period at once to add to the amount of pecuniary reparation now required, the whole cost of such military reparation."[6]

This move on the part of the Government of India produced the desired effect on the King. On 3 September 1840, a sum of five thousand rupees was deposited with the British Residency as compensation in advance for the damage that might have been done as a result of the Ramnagar incursion. By 20 September 1840, the Gorkha troops had been withdrawn from Ramnagar and a confession obtained from the Mishra Guru about the deliberate denial of justice by him to Indian traders. The officers said to be responsible for the Ramnagar incursion were punished, and two out of the four cases involving Indian traders were settled. The Residency was convinced by October 1840 that the non-complicity of the British in the move to reduce the soldiers' salary had been made known to the soldiers through their officers. Even an unexpected gesture of surrendering Indian dacoits to the British was made and cooperation in the matter of extradition in future was also promised.

In a communication addressed to King Rajendra on 26 October 1840, Lord Auckland stated that mere verbal compliance by the King with the British demands was no longer going to satisfy the Company's Government. While insisting that all the demands put forward by the Company's Government be fulfilled without delay, the Governor-General categorically called for the immediate dismissal of all such Nepali officers as had been responsible for anti-British action in the past on the pain of Nepal's suffering the consequences of military action contemplated by the British.

Referring to the apprehension in Varanasi of a secret Nepali mission under Captain Karbir Khatri on its way to the court of Maharaja Ranjit Singh in Lahore and the discovery of certain incriminating documents in its possession, Lord Auckland sent another communication to the King even after the dismissal of Mukhtiyar Rana Jang Pande, who had proved unacceptable to the British. The actual words are reproduced below to acquaint the reader with a classic example of the circumlocutory manner of expression so typical of British diplomacy in the heyday of imperialism.

> I now send the letters and papers alluded to through Mr. Hodgson to you – you will not be surprised that, after the detection of such malpractices at a time when Your Highness has been professing new repentance and making engagements to refrain from all intrigue, *the British Government must wholly withdraw its con-*

> *fidence from the Darbar of Nepal, while it shall be guided by its present evil counsellors, and must look to the employment of force, and to no further hollw negotiations, wherever its rights may appear to be in the least degree exposed to injury*. Your Highness can in no other way show your abhorrence of these proceedings, the tendency of which must be ruinous to the good name of Nepal amongst all states, than by instantly removing from power and favour the parties who have so signally abused the confidence you have reposed in them.[7]

The appointment as minister of Nepal on 1 November 1840 of pro-British Chautara Fatte Jang Shah in place of Mukhtiyar Rana Jang Pande was not enough to satisfy the British. Hodgson felt that this was no proof of real change in the character of the Government and its policies. Hodgson on behalf of the British Government persisted in putting pressure on King Rajendra Bikram Shah as if no change at all had taken place in the Nepali administration. He went to the extent of subtly insinuating that if the King did not change the entire personnel of his Government and his policy with regard to British India, Nepal might even have to de deprived of the tarai which, according to Hodgson, was given to Nepal only on the promise of and as an earnest of its further good behaviour. This was not, in fact, true as the tarai had been returned to Nepal unconditionally and forever in December 1816 and boundary surveyed and demarcated in 1817. But Hodgson's insinuation had its effect: it seriously perturbed the King and his advisers and made them listen to him.

However, following a meeting with Mishra Guru, Senior Queen Samrajyalakshmi Devi Shah left suddenly for Nuwakot along with the Crown Prince on 28 December 1840 and thus created a last minute hitch in the King's plan for the removal of all her Kala Pande and Brahmin (Guru) supporters from the Government. On the following day, the King proceeded to Nuwakot against the advice of Prime Minister Fatte Jang Shah and his colleagues. Inflammatory placards inciting the soldiers to rise against Fatte Jang and the British went up on the city walls shortly afterwards. Whenever the King took any conciliatory step to appease or mollify the British, the Senior Queen sought to block it by refusig to see anyone or by threatening to quit the palace. Her frowns and minatory gestures would at once throw the King off balance and paralyse the court. This time the Pandes also resorted to the novel tactic of displaying anti-Fatte Jang and anti-Resident placards and spreading rumours that they were negotiating the country's sell-out to the East India Company's Government.

The newly appointed Prime Minister, Chautara Fatte Jang Shah, and Guru Krishna Ram Pandit (Paudel) pleaded with Resident Hodgson that he also should proceed to Nuwakot to help the King make up his mind about concluding the final deal with the British Government notwithstanding the Queen's opposition. Hodgson met Prime Minister Fatte Jang Shah and Guru Krishna Ram Pandit who informed him officially that four other supporters of the Kala Pandes, whose inclusion in the new Government was opposed by Hodgson, had been dropped and four more signatures were obtained for the joint declaration of good faith in a policy of friendship towards the British, signed by 92 officers of the court in all. This seemed to satisfy Hodgson and the Company's Government at least for the time being.

The British action had substantially undermined the control of the administration of Nepal which Senior Queen Samrajyalakshmi and a section of the Pande family had been steadily acquiring throughout a greater part of 1840. With the full backing of Governor-General Auckland, Hodgson had, as we have seen, succeeded in replacing Rana Jang Pande by Fatte Jang Shah as Mukhtiyar. But the Senior Queen and the Pandes still retained considerable control over the King and would not let him transfer full authority to the new Premier. Hodgson had consequently gone ahead, with the tacit if not the express consent of Lord Auckland, to cultivate a number of Nepali courtiers and encourage them to form a 'party' of their own to counteract the pressure of the Senior Queen and the Pandes with the result that the East India Company's Government had become directly involved in the politics of the Nepal Darbar.

The 'peace party' thus created in 1840 consisted of the Junior Queen, Rajyalakshmi, the Chautaras under Fatte Jang Shah and his brother, Guru Prasad Shah, and a section of the royal priests and preceptors under Guru Ranganath Pandit (Paudel) and Guru Krishna Ram Pandit (Paudel). Ranged against them in the so-called 'war party' were, in addition to the Senior Queen and members of the Kala Pande family under Rana Jang Pande and Karbir Pande, another section of the royal priests and preceptors under Mishra Guru (Krishna Ram Mishra).

The 'peace party', which was under the overall leadrship of Chautara Fatte Jang Shah, was fortified by the belief that it could rely on the protection of the East India Company's Government, and retention of an 'observation force' on the frontier under Colonel Oliver, which was, in fact, partly intended to sustain Fatte's new ministry. But the Senior Queen in one way or another continued to create difficulties in the implementation of a pro-British policy till the very end of her life.

In compliance with the King's earlier promise to the Company's Government Mishra Guru (Guru Krishna Ram Mishra), the royal preceptor, was asked to leave for Varanasi. Senior Queen Samrajyalakshmi could not easily reconcile hereself to this move to expel the Guru, who was a pillar of the anti-British faction in the court. On 20 February 1841, accompanied by King Rajendra, Crown Prince Surendra and three ministers including the Prime Minister and his brother, she left for Hetauda. Her departure perturbed the Resident as it was declared that she would also proceed to Varanasi with a view to performing the marriage ceremony of her second son somewhere in the Indian plains. Hodgson sent his assistant, G.W. William, to Hetauda to remain in attendance on the royal party and especially to be on hand to observe and, if possible, check the anti-British moves of the Queen.

At 11 a.m. on 27 February 1841 the King, followed by the Crown Prince, suddenly started back for Kathmandu, on the plea of having to perform some religious ceremony there. He asked the Assistant Resident to accompany him but the latter expressed his inability to do so as long as the Queen was at Hetauda. The Senior Queen actually did not return to Kathmandu till 14 Mar 1841. Leading members of the Kala Pande family and their supporters, altogether five in number, some of whom where only recently dismissed from Government service, also joined the royal entourage in Hetauda and were in constant touch with the Senior Queen. They were Kulraj Pande, Jagat Bam Pande, the sons of Karbir and Rana Jang Pande and their supporter, Kul Chand Shah.

During her stay at Hetauda the Senior Queen threatened to go to Makwanpur but could not do so because of the opposition of the ministers and the Assistant British Resident. Finally, on 6 March 1841, the royal party left for Kathmandu, but when they reached Chisapani the Senior Queen refused to proceed further and, instead, thought of going directly to Makwanpur. Hodgson had already taken the necessary steps to dissuade the Senior Queen from crossing the frontier. Had she decided to do so without proper authorization, the Queen would have been allowed to cross into India only on condition of travelling alone without her entourage. In the end the Queen returned to Kathmandu quietly on 14 March 1841 and made her presence known by angry denuciations of the ministers and of a large unmber of courtiers and also by summoning ex-minister Rana Jang to attend on her.

As long as she lived, Queen Samrajyalakshmi persisted in following her anti-British policy with the same vigour even after Hodgson had succeeded in rallying against her all political elements including the King himself and excepting only members of the Kala Pande and the Mishra Guru families. The translation of a poster displayed on the Tundikhel (the Parade Ground) on 22 July 1841 is reproduced below in full to serve as a sample of the kind of propaganda carried on by the interested parties among the people – and among the soldiers in particular – against the policy of the pro-British Government of Nepal and that of the Company's Government.

> Ranganath Pandit, Dalbhanjan Pande, Singh Bir Pande, Fatteh Jung Shah, Guru Prasad Shah, Ranjore Thapa, Rangambir Pandey, Bir Kishore Pande, Dal Kesar Pandey, Prasad Singh Basnyat, Bal Narsingh Kunwar, Kazi Kalu Shahi, Badri Bam Shahi, Kirti Bir Karki, Captain Gagan Singh, Kazi Abhiman Rana, Balmardan Thapa, in all 17 persons have agreed to surrender the Tarai to the *Feringhis* and presently to pay them 9 lakhs of rupees with other smaller gratuities, on condition that the *Feringhis* confirm them in their power for 5 years and to that end prevent the Raja and Rani from coming together, or Ranjung Pandey from approaching either of them. All nominations to office in the past year were made at the will of the *Feringhis* (Resident) who were then assured of the absolute control of the kingdom in all the reign of the present Raja.
>
> Those who did so last year to obtain office are now humbling themselves to the *Feringhis* again to obtain office for the coming year. They have enlisted Jyapus, Bhotias, Par Gharties, in the *Kampu*, in order that such vile wretches may be the instruments of their will. The traitors who act thus must be speedily decapitated, or the kingdom is lost, for by enchantment and spells they have gained over and subdued the Raja. We will again sack the house of Rangnath Pandit. If anyone presume to destroy or remove this paper before the Raja and Maharani have seen it, may Pashupati, Guhyeswari, Bhat Bhateni, the Bhim Sen of Dolakha, the Devi of Nuwakot, Mankamana, and Kala Bhairav make him a leper and may the sin of killing 7 cows and 7 Brahmans be his. Let this *arzi* be taken directly to the Raja and senior Rani and let the Raja and Rani be assured that if they destroy not the 17 traitors named above without delay, all is lost, for was not Rangnath's wife lately sent to

the Maharani to practice with spells on her affections and health, so that they (the present ministers) might then obtain office for the coming year. We, 8,000 men of the *Kampu* (or Cantonment), desire that Ranjung Pandey should be premier, and the kingdom in general desires the same thing. Let this be, and the rascally *Feringhi* (Resident) will be glad to be off his own accord. Let your Highnesses (Raja and Rani) bestir yourselves. Deep frauds are designed. Your treasures are going to the English. Let Rangnath Pandit be shaved and expatriated and let all the rest (of the ministers) be decapitated. The kingdom is Your Highnesses'. What we (the soldiery) have seen and heard and know to be true, we have spoken. To consider its tenor is your business and duty. Whatever thereafter you may command us to do, we are prepared to accomplish for you. Be not afraid or perplexed. When the 17 traitors we have denounced are disposed of, you will be yourself again. Be bold and rely on us, but beware of delay.[8]

(True Translation – B.H. Hodgson)

By August 1841, Nepal under King Rajendra Bikram seemed to be returning to the anti-British policy advocated by the Senior Queen and members of the Kala Pande family. Besides the continued British entanglement in China and Afghanistan, there was the consideration of the fact that the conquest of some parts of Tibet by the Sikh General, Zorawar Singh, had made the boundaries of Nepal and the Panjab contiguous to each other. This might have aroused hope and expectation of a new alliance between the Panjab and Nepal. The Governor of Jumla was ordered to meet Zorawar Singh in person and explore the possibility of alliance with him to make a joint incursion into Tibet in order to seize a gold mine which was said to be located in the vicinity of the Nepal border. But the news of the crushing defeat of Zorawar Singh by the Tibetans in the second half of September dashed Nepal's hopes for military ventures in this quarter.

The Senior Queen had already been ill for quite some time when she vented her rage on 20 September 1841 following a heated discussion with the King and the notables on the policy to be followed towards the Company's Government. Thereafter, her condition worsened and by October she was showing signs of extreme fatigue and exhaustion. She perhaps realised that her days were numbered and therefore made a frantic attempt to frighten the King into placing her son, Crown Prince Surendra, on the throne. With this end in view, she held another stormy discussion with the King and the nobility before she died on 6 October 1841.

Even the passing away of Samrajyalakshmi Devi, who had dominated the proceedings of the court of Nepal ever since the downfall of Bhimsen Thapa in 1837 and was regarded as the main inspiration behind, if not the main architect of, the anti-British policy, did not produce any change in the vacillating attitude of her weak, suspicious, timid and irresolute husband, King Rajendra Bikhram Shah. The King now tended to lean more and more on Crown Prince Surendra Bikram Shah for the exercise of power and the conduct of the Government, pulling strings from behind and using him as a cover to evade responsibility, just as he had previously used his Senior Queen, Samrajyalakshmi, and the Pandes by making them take the blame for the anti-British policies to which he himself was as much a party as they were. King Rajendra Bikram was ambitious but was afraid of facing the consequence of his actions. His duplicity and cunning did not enable him to hide the fact that he was henpecked, weak and fickle-minded.

Soon after Samrajyalakshmi's death, King Rajendra sought to play his old game with the ministers by putting Crown Prince Surendra Bikram in the deceased Queen's role. He started spoiling the Prince by letting him satisfy his wildest fancies and indulge in excesses as he liked. He would fondly call Surendra Bikram even 'Maharajadhiraj' (a title exclusively reserved for the King) and bid others do the same. The King even tried to persuade the Resident to treat the Crown Prince as the King's equal.

For a while the King proved cooperative and the ministers were confirmed in their position on 9 November 1841, but within a week of their reappointment, the King and the Crown Prince went off to Hetauda with 2,500 troops for no apparent reason, returning to Kathmandu five days later. He then sent a communication to Lord Auckland through Hodgson asking the Governor-General to withdraw the observation corps of troops stationed at the frontiers. The Resident refused to accept the communication until the King accounted for his contacts with the Sikhs and his recent visit to Hetauda. The King explained that the contact with the Sikhs was necessitated by the fact that their conquest of Ladakh had made the boundaries of their land contiguous to those of Nepal, and he sought to attribute his journey to Hetauda to the "sudden caprice of a child", by thus putting the blame for it on the Crown Prince.

When news of the British disaster in Afghanistan reached Kathmandu in early 1842, Nepal did not at first show any sign of hostility towards the Company's Government, and accordingly Hodgson asked in February for the 'observation force' to be moved back from the frontier. Thereafter, Rajendra's attitude rapidly changed again as the following example shows.

Furore over a Newspaper Report

Shortly after the removal of the British forces, the King was airing sentiments not quite consistent with his earlier professions of peace. The publication in an English language Indian newspaper of a report that the Senior Queen, Samrajyalakshmi Devi Shah, had died by poison had greatly upset the King and he at once sent for the Resident. Hardly had Resident Hodgson reached the Residency gate on his way to the palace when he saw the King and the Crown Prince standing on the road, along with several leading officers of the court. The King asked the Resident whether he had informed the Governor-General of the Queen's death. The Resident answered him in the affirmative and also conveyed to the King the Governor-General's assurance that everything possible would be done to apprehend the miscreant responsible for the poisoning allegation. Upon hearing this King Rajendra Bikram flew into a rage and exploded: "Tell the Governor-General he must and shall give him up. I will have him and flay him alive, and rub him with salt and lemon until he dies. Further, tell the Governor-General that if this infamous calumniator is not delivered up, there shall be war between us." The heir apparent then started abusing his father whom he struck repeatedly. The scene was enacted once again in a Guru's garden where the King and the Crown Prince with their entourage including Hodgson had gone from the street. However, for those undignified and highly offensive expressions used by the King on the occasion, a full apology was subsequently made to the British Government.[9]

The Kasinath Incident

On 23 April 1842, King Rajendra once again publicly indulged in a fit of violent and erratic behaviour in connection with the lawsuit in which an Indian trader named Kasinath was involved. This gave rise to an incident which had far-reaching repercussions on the domestic and external affairs of Nepal. It is all the more strange because the case was not particularly important and the sum of money involved was not substantial. Eventually the issue was settled in accordance with the terms of the Treaty of 1839 in the courts of Varanasi (Banaras) where it was first brought up.

Kasinath Mull and Gosain Shiva Baks Puri were both British Indian subjects. Their families had long been engaged in trade in both India and Nepal. There was a lawsuit relating to the settlement of mutual debts pending in the court in Varanasi.

While in Kathmandu on some other business, Kasinath was seized by the Government of Nepal and brought to the court in connection with his alleged debt to Shiva Baks Puri. Kasinath was made to deposit with the Nepali court the full amount claimed by Shiva Baks, 36,400 rupees, out of which he eventually had to forfeit 16,800 rupees (representing the sum owed by Shiva Baks to Nepal's exchequer) as well as paying a fine. Kasinath's appeal to the Resident in this matter bore fruit and upon Hodgson's protests the council of chiefs or Bhardari set aside the decision on the ground that the judge's taking a deposit from one side only had been unlawful and that as Shiva Baks had left Nepal no further investigation could now take place.[10]

However, late in February 1842, Shiva Baks returned to Kathmandu and the case reopened. On 6 and 8 April 1842, the Darbar's *munshi* came to fetch Kasinath, who had for some time been living in the Residency both for medical treatment and for protection. Hodgson refused to hand him over to the *Munshi* and requested an interview with the King, but instead of granting this request King Rajendra himself, accompanied by a large number of chiefs and about 2,000 troops, came to the Residency on 23 April 1842. He demanded the surrender of Kasinath and wanted to know if the Resident had any reasons for non-compliance.

Hodgson explained that Kasinath was a British subject and his "case was not one of disputed jurisdiction but of strong-handed interference with all legal proceedings." Hodgson further added that the merchant was in the Residency for medical treatment and was being held up, because he had not as yet been given back his cash deposit without which he could not go to the plains. Meanwhile, Kasinath himself came out and pleaded that he had no intention of opposing or embrrassing the King, and merely solicited justice from him. Despite Kasinath's humble pleas, the King ordered that Kasinath be arrested or seized forcibly. Upon this, Hodgson told the King that if the King insisted on arresting him, he would lay himself to the charge of using force or coercion against the envoy and his "duties as an ambassador would come to an end." Then the heir apparent came forward and urged his father to have Kasinath dragged away. The King himself rushed on the merchant in an attempt to "bear him off." The sequel is described by Hodgson as follows:

> I threw my arms around the merchant and said sternly to the Raja "you take both of us or neither".. This was more than Raja could screw up his resolution. . . . Seizing the moment, I made an appeal to his better feelings and thus at length cast the balance against the mischief makers.[11]

Once again the King and the Prince attempted to seize Kasinath, but the Resident frustrated their moves with caution and resoluteness. At last the King retired and sent his principal officers to negotiate with the Resident. On their request, Hodgson allowed Kasinath to go to the Darbar on the express guarantee from the ministers that his life and property would be safe.

Meanwhile, a far-reaching change had already taken place in the British Indian administration. Lord Auckland' term of office had been unceremoniously terminated by the British Government on 28 February 1842 at the height of the Afghan disaster. Lord Ellenborough, who succeeded Lord Auckland in March, gave the impression in his conversation that "he believed his mission to be a reversal of his predecessor's measures and suppression of his predecessor's men."[12]

The new Governor-General disapproved of Hodgson's move to influence the trends of court politics by supporting one section of courtiers. On 5 June 1842 Hodgson was warned against getting himself and the British Government mixed up in the politics of a foreign country and instructed to take immediate steps to disengage himself from the political process in Nepal. Lord Ellenborough also failed to understand the real nature of the dispute between the Resident and the King over Kasinath, telling Hodgson he also should have shown more caution and respect in dealing with the Head of State and should not have allowed himself to be drawn into taking sides with Kasinath. Above all, the new Governor-General was angered by Hodgson's suppressing his letter of reprimand of 8 May 1842 to the Nepali Minister and substituting for it his own version on the plea that the communication of the Governor-General's instructions in the original form would have harmed the interest of the Company's Government by making the minister lose face in the Darbar. In his letter of 8 July 1842 to the East India Company's secret committee in London, Ellenborough stated that had it not been for Hodgson's indifferent health, he would have immediately removed him from Nepal because it would be difficult for Hodgson, having been involved so deeply with particular individuals and with internal political developments in Nepal, to follow a new policy of disengagement.

The Governor-General had actually sent Hodgson a letter of recall on 21 June 1842 but he relented immediately; and even before Hodgson had a chance to put in his plea in defence of his action, he wrote again on 22 June cancelling the dismissal.[13]

After receiving from Hodgson a detailed account of the policy so far pursued vis-˜-vis Nepal, Ellenborough's attitude towards him softened further though he still stuck to his original view that a new policy should better be carried out by a new man rather than by Hodgson who was "so mixed up with a party in Nepal."[14] But later it was Hodgson himself who was asked to initiate the policy of disengagement and to implement it till his departure from Kathmandu on 5 December 1843.

The Governor-General's change of heart was seen in his dispatch of 8 August 1842 which struck a more conciliatory tone vis-˜-vis the Resident. While still insisting on the necessity to end as early as possible the existing relationship between the Resident and the ministers, which was clearly of a protective and paternalistic nature, the Governor-general left it to the discretion of the Resident to decide in what manner he should conduct himself so as to withdraw the Indian Government gradually from the position of involvement in the court politics "without injury to persons who may rely upon its protection."[15]

The worsening of the internal situation in Nepal towards the end of 1842 is sometimes regarded as a result of the disengagement of the British Government from Nepali politics. Hodgson's critics tend to view the crisis as a culmination of Hodgson's past actions and policies, while some of them even go so far as to contend that the critical situation was deliberately brought about by Hodgson to put his men in power before he finally withdrew from Nepal. Whatever the reason, tension ran high in the court of Nepal throughout the better part of 1842.

The policy advocated by Ellenborough was certainly more becoming of the dignity of a great power and was in the long run apt to evoke enduring admiration and respect for his Government from the host country itself. But in defence of Hodgson's policy it may be pleaded that what might have been possible during the period from the second half of 1842 till 1844 might have proved disastrous earlier. However, Hodgson endeavoured hard to implement the new policy of non-interference as conscientiously as possible. He told the ministers that in the past the East India Company's Government supported them to keep the hostile factions at bay; but now that the times had changed, he would neither openly support them nor remonstrate with the Pandes or the Crown Prince. Hodgson did not want to make a complete break with his past policy until the developments in Afghanistan and China had grown favourable to the British. In Hodgson's own words, he followed a policy "rather to let change of ministry come if it must than to precipitate it; while watching and prepared to avail (himself) yet further of the course of events."[16]

The change in the attitude of the Resident was reflected in an increase in outrageous behaviour by the Crown Prince and the related cases of evasion of responsibility by the King. The King continued to pester the Company's Governor-General with petty matters even after the British victory in Afghanistan and China. For example, the King would insist on a reply to his letter requesting the Governor-General to find out the mischief-monger responsible for the publication of the news item in the Anglo-Indian newspaper about the poisoning of the Senior Queen. The King kept on asking the Resident to address the Crown Prince as Maharajadhiraj, but the Resident firmly refused to do so until the King abdicated in favour of his son. The Pandes were also still active and were inciting the Crown Prince to assert his authority in every possible way.

The Crown Prince, under the influence of the Pandes, went to the extent of demanding the throne from his father. In September 1842, the Crown Prince went to Hetauda with a large body of soldiers, letting it be known that if the King did not abdicate in his favour, he would proceed to Gaya without the resident's permission. The King also followed the Crown prince to Hetauda but did nothing else, as he was also interested in keeping the situation confused.

The trump-card of the Resident's power to grant or withhold permits to travel to India always came in handy for the purpose of restraining the undesired activities of the royal actors on Nepal's political stage. The Indian Government asked the Resident not to allow anyone in the Prince's party to enter India territory without due authorization and also warned the King that if the Crown Prince crossed the frontier with more than 300 soldiers, it would be regarded as an act of hostility. The Crown Prince, to the relief of all concerned, returned to Kathmandu on 9 November 1842, but the son's struggle with the father for the throne continued.

The Pande family had until then managed to retain a degree of influence. Their tactics included playing on the ambition of the Crown Prince by spreading the idea that he was an incarnation born to extirpate the Feringhees (meaning the English). They used to stage mock battles in which this theme was enacted. Developments abroad and at home, however, weakened their position: by October 1842 the British had won decisive victories both in Afghanistan and in China and as a result King Rajendra's attitude towards the East India Company also changed.

Again, ever since the death of the Senior Queen, the Junior Queen, Rajyalakshmi, had been doing her best to free the King from Pande influence so as to increase her own power in the Darbar. Then in November 1842 some important members of the Kala Pande family were found guilty of defaming the King. A handout was found in which the Pandes had falsely and maliciously alleged that the late Senior Queen had died of poisoning. This was enough to turn the King against the family. Prominent members of the Pande family such as Kul Raj Pande, Rana Jang Pande, and Karbir Pande were put on trial. Kul Raj was found guilty of incriminating the King. His right hand was cut off, he was expelled from the country and his property was confiscated.

Crown Prince Surendra Bikram Shah took a sadistic pleasure in subjecting innocent people to inhuman cruelties and King Rajendra, instead of restraining him, seemed to encourage his spoiled son in perpetrating all kinds of excesses. The frequent recurrence of these incidents of barbaric cruelty created a general feeling of discontent among the people and even the ministers found it impossible to carry on the day-to-day administration of the country because of the unrestrained attitude and actions of the Crown Prince. Fatte Jang Shah actually laid down the burden of office professing that it was not possible for him to serve two masters and would not resume his office until the King controlled the Crown Prince.

The King not only evaded responsibility for all the murders and mayhem, beatings and indignities committed at the behest of the Crown Prince, but was also at times helpless against his son's punishing people for obeying the father's own commands.

Petition of Rights of 7 December 1842 and Delegation of the Hukum to the Junior Queen

The general discontent took the form of a popular movement. At a meeting of 675 ranking civil and military officers presided over by Prime Minister Fatte Jang Shah that had the apparent backing of 8,000 troops, a petition for due protection of the legitimate rights of the people was drawn up. It demanded an immediate end to the state of uncertainty which had been created by the dual rule of the King and the Crown Prince and the establishment of a stable administration strong enough to secure the rights and privileges of both the nobles and the general public.

This petition was presented to King Rajendra on 7 December 1842, and in a move to defuse the tense situation, the King acceded to its term. He formally delegated the *hukum*, the sovereign power to rule by peremptory command, to Junior Queen Rajyalakshmi Devi on 1 January 1843:

However, neither King Rajendra nor Crown Prince Surendra was actually prepared to accept, even temporarily, any real concentration of power in the hands of the Junior Queen, and the state of uncertainty continued as before. A new arrangement was improvised according to which the Government was to be run by the King in consultation with the Junior Queen and the Crown Prince. This meant in actual practice no real abdication or delegation of power, but it did make the Junior Queen a force to be reckoned with henceforth in Darbar politics.

Crown Prince Surendra continued to grow more and more wayward and it became increasingly difficult to manage him. The policy of the British Government was to ignore the Crown Prince and restrict itself to dealing with the King alone. Ever since June 1842 Crown Prince Surendra had started visiting the Residency and even at times requested the Resident to bring pressure to bear on the King to resign, but the Resident had standing instructions not to have anything to do with him without the "open approval" of the King.

The withdrawal of British support from the Chautaras and the ascendancy of Junior Queen Rajyalakshmi in the Darbar affairs had set off new trends of development in Nepali politics. Just as Senior Queen Samrajyalakshmi had been anxious to see her son Surendra as King of Nepal before she died, so also Junior Queen Rajyalakshmi had long cherished the desire to have her own son, Prince Ranendra, replace Crown Prince Surendra as heir apparent and eventually succeed King

Rajendra on the throne. While Senior Queen Samrajyalakshmi was alive, the two queens were in constant competition with each other not only to acquire the status of the King's favourite wife but also to realize their mutually exclusive political ends; the rivalry between the two Queens engendered by their respective concern for the future of their sons had always been at the root of their manoeuvres in the Darbar politics.

After the removal of Senior Queen Samrajyalakshmi Devi from the scene, Crown Prince Surendra and the Junior Queen, each in their own way, sought to manipulate political developments. The weak and vacillating King sided sometimes with one and sometimes with the other.

After the Kasinath case, the Chautara had completely forfeited the goodwill of the King who had begun to look elsewhere for someone to assist him in running the administration. The Pandes had also fallen into the King's disfavour after the discovery of incriminating evidence against them which led to their trial culminating in mutilation and expulsion of one of them from the country. The Junior Queen, Rajyalakshmi Devi, also felt that the Chautaras and the Pandes would never serve her purpose of having her son replace the Crown Prince. Under the circumstances, she was inclined to look to the Thapas for support.

The Return of Mathbar Singh Thapa and the Departure of Brian Hodgson

King Rajendra, in consultation with the Junior Queen invited Mathbar Singh Thapa to come back to the country and help him run the Government. Mathbar, the leading member of the Thapa family, had escaped punishment at the hands of the Kala Pandes by slipping out of the country in 1838 in the nick of time before he could be caught up in the next round of adverse events leading to the reopening of the case against Bhimsen Thapa and Bhimsen's suicide in prison. Mathbar had been living on a British pension of one thousand rupees a month ever since his return from the Panjab to British territory.

Fully aware of the fact that the King was fickle-minded and unreliable, Mathbar took his own time to return to Kathmandu. He spent some time in the frontier collecting information about the latest developments in Nepal and before he reached Kathmandu on 17 April 1843, he had made sure that Hodgson was not wholly for the

Chautaras.

Resident B.H. Hodgson who was, in the words of Cecil Bendall, a pioneer in research on Nepal and "the greatest and least thanked" of all British Residents in the country, left Nepal on 5 December 1843 after more than twenty-two years' service, first as acting Resident from 1820 till 1832 and then from January 1833 onward as Resident. Despite his own repeated entreaties to the Governor-General to have his tenure of office in Nepal extended by at least another year, entreaties which were backed up by an unprecedented request from the Sovereign of Nepal himself for the extension of his term, Governor-General Ellenborough remained adamant in his stand on the principle that Hodgson could not be allowed to serve at the same post for an inordinately long period of time. It may be pointed out here that Ellenborough, having once recalled Hodgson in a huff in July 1842 for suppressing the contents of the Governor-General's letter to the Minister and substituting his own version, had afterwards cancelled his order for recall and even had it removed from the file. In addition, Ellenborough had also allowed Hodgson to extend his stay by a year till the winter of 1843 upon his request on the grounds of health. Under the circumstances, Ellenborough did not find it proper to give in to pressure for a further extension of Hodgson's tour of duty in Nepal.

Hodgson had a most touching farewell which many an envoy who had been active for such a long time on a highly controversial and sensitive mission on foreign soil would have reason to envy. A formal public Darbar or reception attended by all important Nepali notables was held to say goodbye to Hodgson. The King of Nepal, Rajendra Bikram Shah, with whom Hodgson had been involved in many an ugly and unpleasant incident in the past, "burst into tears, and referring to the exertions by which Hodgson had so often averted a war, called him 'the saviour of Nepal.'"[17]

Hodgson's concern for the growth of trans-Himalayan trade through Nepal, and for employment of Gorkhas as soldiers for use by the British Government in its time of need, showed his foresight and grasp of the real problems of Nepal. His scholarly contributions on various aspects of Nepali life, on botany and zoology along with the literature, religion and culture of Nepal, deserve special mention. His writings covered a wide range of subjects such as the flora and fauna of the country, the ethnological, anthropological and linguistic backgrounds of a number of Nepal's diverse tribes and ethnic groups, and also the mystical intricacies and subtleties of the Vajrayana, the cult of the thunderbolt or the so-called Tibetan Buddhism with its emphasis on metaphysical dialectics and psycho-experimental methods of meditation. He made generous gifts of innumerable valuable manuscripts, works of art and artifacts he had collected in Nepal to institutes of higher learning and research, libraries and museums all over Europe.

Hodgson's critics among his own countrymen and others tend to blame him for what they call his interference in the internal affairs of Nepal that prevented the situation there from reaching its own logical culmination and arriving at its own solution to the problem. His supporters and admirers, of whom there is no dearth among both Nepalis and Europeans, are of the opinion that by preventing war between Nepal and British at an inopportune time through his skilled diplomacy and even through questionable methods of promising protection and help to Nepali officials in his attempt to cultivate and manipulate them, Hodgson served not only his own Government but also the host country and its Government. War might have spelt the end of Nepal's independence. By postponing the explosion of the crisis which was fast building up in Nepal until such time as the country found itself better prepared to cope with it, he also served Nepal's interests.

All told, the last paragraph of the document King Rajendra presented to Hodgson with the Red Seal(Lal Mohar), dated 1 December 1843, is a human and touching expression of sincere appreciation of the outgoing Resident's qualities and services, which had endeared him to all concerned notwithstanding his active involvement in the most taxing and vexatious public engagements:

> But from being many years here and entirely owing to your kindness, wisdom, and forbearance, you caused the Governor-General's anger to be abated and instilled wisdom into me, and by God's blessing and your kindness, friendship was once more established between the two governments–and for your kindness I shall ever be grateful and wherever you may go and whatever you do, may God bless and prosper it, and to hear of such will give me pleasure.[18]

Assumption of Office by Mathbar

Mathbar had already been eight months in Kathmandu before he finally took over the administration as Prime Minister on 26 December 1843. Before he formally assumed the office of Mukhtiyar, Mathbar had requested King Rajendra and Queen Rajyalakshmi to vindicate the honour of his family whose members had been, without any valid reason or evidence, maligned and persecuted in the past. The King and the Queen took the necessary steps to arraign the Kala Pandes for convicting Bhimsen Thapa on the basis of trumped-up charges and forcing him to commit suicide in utter despair. The Pandes were eventually declared guilty of wilfully framing Bhimsen Thapa.

As punishment for their involvement in the denial of justice to Bhimsen Thapa and his family, Karbir Pande and Kul Bir Pande were promptly executed. As the former Mukhtiyar, Rana Jang Pande, was seriously ill and already on his deathbed, he was not actually executed, but he died almost immediately upon his return to his house after having been subjected to public humiliation and indignity. The property of all of them was confiscated. Dittha Kanak Singh Mahat who had acted as a prosecutor in the trial of Bhimsen Thapa and was said to have drawn up charges against Bhimsen Thapa under King Rajendra's own instructions, was also decapitated. Even two members of the Thapa family itself, Ram Bir Thapa and Indra Bir Thapa, were executed as accomplices of the Kala Pandes. Buddhiman Karki had his nose and lips cut off and Bamsharaj Basnyat was deprived of his nose.

Before Mathbar took over the prime ministership formally, Hodgson had already retired and Major Henry Lawrence had taken charge of the Residency. The politics of the Nepal Darbar were in complete disarray. Royal authority was in practice shared by King Rajendra Bikram Shah, Junior Queen Rajyalakshmi Devi and Crown Prince Surendra Bikram Shah and they were at cross purposes with each other. Crown Prince Surendra wanted the King to adbicate in his favour. Junior Queen Rajyalakshmi Devi desired the throne for her son, Ranendra Bikram Shah. King Rajendra Bikram wanted to continue as King and retain ultimate authority, while at the same time keeping both the Junior queen and the Crown Prince in good humour by pretending to give them an effective say in the country's administration.

As pointed out sarcastically by Resident Lawrence, the royal authority in Nepal at the time was shared by "Mr. Nepal, Master Nepal and Mrs. Nepal." The new Prime Minister and Commander-in-Chief, Mathbar Singh Thapa, initially experienced difficulties becuase of the division of royal authority between the King and the Crown Prince although on the face of it he should have had no difficulty. The King himself had appeared anxious to secure for the Crown Prince a status equal to his own, and had granted the Crown Prince the right to be addressed as Maharajadhiraj on all occasions to enable the Prince to exercise authority over ministers, notables and civil and army personnel and even to take precedence over the King himself. King Rajendra had even asked Lawrence to make available to the Crown Prince a copy of his official statement on arrival at Kathmandu.

Hence Mathbar, when pressing for the King's abdication in favour of the Crown Prince, felt that he was but asking King Rajendra to follow his action to its logical conclusion. Mathbar sought Resident Lawrence's assistance in obtaining the King's abdication, but Lawrence altogether refused to give him any advice in the matter pleading that it would be against the policy of his Government to do so. Lawrence was instructed by Calcutta to turn a deaf ear if Mathbar ever threatened to take action against the reigning monarch or dynasty.

Under the circumstances, the relationship between the Darbar and the new Resident became cold and formal. Lawrence was afraid that this might be wrongly interpreted by the Nepalis as the decline of British influence at the court, but Ellenborough asked him to maintain a correct posture of decorum vis-˜-vis the Darbar whatever the result might be.

Mathbar could not function effectively because of the constant tussle for power between the King and the Crown Prince. The King would neither abdicate in favour of the Crown Prince nor was he able to prevent the Crown Prince's unwarranted interference in the administration.

Mathbar even orchestrated a mutiny of soldiers in order to bring pressure on the King to abdicate the throne. On 22 January 1844, the palace was surrounded by mutineers who demanded that there should be only one ruler in the country. King Rajendra was able to pacify them only by offering to abdicate the throne on the following day. On 23 January 1844, a meeting of notables or Bhardari was held, but Mathbar did not attend it on the plea that the troops would not let him out of the house until the King had resigned from office. The King was once again reluctant to abdicate. He procrastinated as usual and several alternative methods of regulating authority in future were discussed but the situation remained unchanged. Finding it difficult to carry on the administration, Mathbar dramatically resigned from the prime ministership in the summer of 1844 in order to reassess his strength and support among the soldiers, and the situation deteriorated all the more. The Crown Prince's excesses increased in their frequency and brutality: he took sadistic pleasure in inflicting pain and punishment on human beings and animals, and even Brahmins and cows were not spared physical torture. It was commonly believed that the Crown Prince's apparent tantrums and intemperate behaviour were designed to bring pressure on his feeble-minded and doting father to abdicate the throne in his favour once and for all.

On 18 October 1844, Mathbar resumed the prime ministership after the King declared that in future there would be only one ruler, he the King. But this declaration could not come into force because the Crown Prince reacted to it very sharply and reduced the King to the state of "virtually a prisoner" by "driving away anyone who came near his father."[19]

In November 1844 a large number of members of the Pande family who had been languishing in prison ever since Mathbar's return were expelled from the country.

On 4 December 1844, events once again took a dramatic turn when the Crown Prince accompanied by the King, Junior Queen Rajyalakshmi Devi, Prime Minister Mathbar Singh Thapa and other notables went to Hetauda apparently on a Hatti-Kheda (a wild elephant-catching expedition) in the inner tarai. Actually the excursion was part of a well-contrived plan to compel the King to abdicate in favour of the Crown Prince. It was public knowledge that the Crown Prince had ordered the officers and soldiers to follow the royal party and had also strongly warned the King that he would go to Varanasi if the King hesitated to abdicate the throne in his favour. The King, however, did not seem to realize the gravity of the situation.

As usual, the Resident protested on behalf of the Company's government that there would be serious consequences if the Crown Prince approached the Indian border at the head of the army. The party stayed at Hetauda for two days and thereafter the Crown Prince with Mathbar Singh Thapa at the head of a large body of troops advanced up to Dhukuwabas at the Chure pass and threatened to proceed to Varanasi if the King did not resign his office forthwith.

This was a clever move by the Crown Prince and Mathbar to involve the British Residency in their design to compel the King's abdication by creating a situation in which the Residency had to remonstrate with the King to prevent the Crown Prince from approaching the frontier. The plan succeeded, albeit temporarily, as King Rajendra ordered his troops to accept the Prince as King on 10 December 1844.

Crown Prince Surendra, in an extremely cruel and vulgar

demonstration of his newly acquired authority, thereupon commanded that sixteen minor officers be decapitated and three others be deprived of their caste and expelled from the country for their alleged disobedience to General Mathbar Singh Thapa.

On 13 December 1844, Mathbar returned to Kathmandu to organize a royal reception for the Crown Prince and Surendra himself arrived in the capital the next day. The King had by then responded to his son's demand, and had authorized the Crown Prince "to issue all orders and share the *gaddi* (throne) with him," and on 18 December 1844, this arrangement was given a formal shape when King Rajendra stated in clear terms that "except *gaddi*, the mint, the direction of Chinese and foreign affairs", which the King reserved for himself, all authority was transferred to the Crown Prince.[20]

However, within a few more days the King undoubtedly realized that the new arrangement would give the Crown Prince and Mathbar almost supreme powers, and he annulled it on 23 December 1844. He sought to modify it by declaring that there had been reconciliation between father and son, that"he (King Rajendra Bikram) was to remain as before and that he would issue orders through the Crown Prince."[21]

The son put his own construction on this and claimed that he was to issue orders in nominal consultation with the King, his father.

The Resident, in his turn, had nothing to do with all these attempts to tamper with royal authority as it had hitherto existed. He refused to join the triumphal procession held to celebrate the Crown Prince's return as 'Maharajadhiraj'. Although he found the Crown Prince sitting on the throne when he called on the King on 18 December 1844 by appointment, both Resident Lawrence and the Company's Government refused to accept the new arrangement by 28 December 1945.

> As pointed out in contemporary British records, Prime Minister Mathbar Singh Thapa (1843-45) considered he was "impelled in four different directions by the Raja (Rajendra Bikram Shah), Prince (Heir Apparent Surendra Bikram Shah) and Ranee (Junior Queen Rajyalakshmi) and the British government, that if he acted against the Maharaja (King Rajendra), it would be called ingratitude, and if against the Prince, it would draw his wrath, from which the Raja would not protect him, that the Ranee was anxious for herself and children and that he (Mathbar) did not know what the British government might say at the revolution."[22]

Resident Major Lawrence had described Mathbar as "an intelligent man, particularly expert in military matters but though young in years, particularly versed in intrigues."[23] But Mathbar had fallen an easy victim to the plot hatched against him by King Rajendra and Queen Rajyalakshmi in complicity with Gagan Singh and Jang Bahadur. Well-known for his military expertise, Mathbar was a man of extraordinary physical strength and was proud of his reputation and popularity among the military personnel to the point of being arrogant. He was full of drive and his personality was characterized by a domineering spirit. His tendency to underestimate his rivals and adversaries in court politics proved to be his undoing in the end. He was also a man of ambition and had in fact a much wider political outlook than most of his contemporaries as he had had first-hand experience in dealing with Indian rulers and British officials during his self-imposed exile in India. He was the first head of government to be formally designated Prime Minister of Nepal and also the first Nepali to pay an official visit to the Governor-General of India as a full-fledged representative of its Government in 1835.

People with an unusual driving force and overconfidence have a blindspot, and fail to see even clear danger signals posed by the moves of their scheming adversaries. Mathbar seemed to feel that the King and the Queen were no match for him in statecraft and he certainly stood head and shoulders above other officers of the court at the time. He failed to see that the lavish showering of honours on him by the King was merely a ruse contrived to induce a false sense of security.

In the spring of 1845 he raised three new regiments of troops and thereby aroused the King's suspicions of him all the more. Furthermore, he did not realize that the troops, who had looked upon him as their hero and benefactor, would feel humiliated and disappointed with him when he made them pull down their old barracks and carry the building materials like ordinary porters to the site for the construction of new barracks adjacent to his own residence. Mathbar was so confident of the unassailability of his position that he did not heed Resident Lawrence's timely warning to him against incurring the displeasure of the King and the troops by these actions, and, despite this, Lawrence still described Mathbar in a letter to Governor-General Auckland as a dynamic person of considerable vigour and ability fit to be referred to as a hero compared with other Gorkha chiefs and stated that "it would be difficult to find such a man in Nepal."[24]

Politial Conditions on the Eve of the Emergence of Jang Bahadur

Before describing the assassination of Prime Minister Mathbar Singh and the rise of Jang Bahadur to pre-eminence it may not be out of place to review the political situation in Nepal which had been brought about by King Rajendra's failure to fill the vacuum created by the fall of Bhimsen Thapa. Weak and ineffective, yet also extremely suspicious and jealous of others' usurping his power, the King leant heavily on members of his immediate family (Senior Queen Samrajyalakshmi until her death, then Junior Queen Rajyalakshmi and Heir Apparent Surendra Bikram Shah), but at the same time he continuously tried to play them off against each other. It was not surprising that the various factions among the nobility sought to exploit the antagonisms within the royal family by joining, abandoning or rejoining one side or another on considerations of sheer expediency.

Throughout the period 1837-1838 the chief identifiable interest groups at the court were the Chautaras (royal collaterals), the Gurus or priestly class, and, last but not least, the three leading families of the time, the Thapas, the Pandes and the Basnyats. Despite the frequently shifting allegiances there was an element of continuity in the line followed by certain of the factions. The Kala Pandes, until their elimination as an effective political force, had supported Senior Queen Samrajyalakshmi, through whom they had regained their influence at court, and after her death they were on the side of her son, Crown Prince Surendra. The *Chautaras* and the *Gurus* were, on the whole, for the King and also for the heir apparent out of their respect for the principle of primogeniture, if for nothing else. But King Rajendra Bikram Shah himself made it difficult for them to support him at all times, by remaining utterly helpless initially against the wild and thoughtless actions of the Senior Queen and, later on, against the excesses of the Crown Prince.

Although politics in Nepal had a pronounced familial basis, this did not mean that the leading families always remained united. It is well known that Bhimsen Thapa was allegedly betrayed by his own brother, Rana Bir Singh Thapa, and among those who were dismissed along with the Kala Pandes as their associates in January 1841 were Indra Bir Thapa and Rana Bam Thapa. The Pande family was divided between the Kala Pandes and the Gora Pandes, the latter escaping the persecution which the former had to suffer at the hands of ex-King Rana Bahadur as Regent and Bhimsen Thapa as Mukhtiyar. The priestly class of the *Gurus* was also divided, with the descendants of Brajanath Pandit, Ranganath Pandit, Krishna Ram Pandit and others on the one side and the Royal Preceptor or the *Raj Guru*, Mishra Guru (Krishna Ram Mishra), the brother of the famous Gajaraj Mishra who had acted as a mediator between the British and the Nepal Governments at critical moments in the past, on the other side. Further, intermarriage among members of the three leading families, the Pandes, the Basnyats and the Thapas, also affected alignment and realignment of the forces at work in court politics. Therefore, the theory of exclusive group rivalry between the leading families is an oversimplification.

However, the result of all this intrafamilial and interfamilial feuding was a state of utter chaos in the upper echelons of the Government with an ever-growing sense of fear, suspicion and insecurity among the people in general. The atmosphere of the court was thick with conspiracy. Intrigues had become the order of the day, as manoeuvres and counter-manoeuvres proceeded apace and Prime Minister succeeded Prime Minister in quick succession. In the nine years that intervened between the dismissal of Bhimsen Thapa in 1837 and the rise of Jang Bahadur in 1846, there were as many as eight major changes in the Government, and none of the Prime Ministers, with the exception of the Brahmin, Ranganath Pandit, died a natural death. The danger of total disintegration stared the country in the face, and the situation was further aggravated by the fact that the British, having accomplished their object in the Indian subcontinent, were in no mood to tolerate for very long a volatile and unstable situation on their northeastern frontier.

Jang's Entry into Court Politics

Jang Bahadur belonged to one of the Gorkha-based Kanwar families and one of his ancestors, Sardar Ram Krishna Kanwar, had fought with Prithvinarayan Shah in many a battle. He was the second son of Kazi Bal Narsingh Kanwar who came into prominence in 1806 by slaying Sher Bahadur Shah at an open court almost immediately after the latter had assassinated ex-King Rana Bahadur Shah. Bal Narsingh had only one son by his first marriage, but by his second wife he had seven sons and two daughters. Jang Bahadur was the eldest of these nine children and was born on 18 June 1817.

Jang Bahadur's mother, Ganesh Kumari, was the daughter of Nain Singh Thapa, father of Prime Minister and Commander-in-Chief Mathbar Singh Thapa (December 1843 to May 1845) and brother of Mukhtiyar General Bhimsen Thapa (1806-1837). Because of his matrimonial ties with the Thapa family, Jang Bahadur's father was appointed District Governor during the administration of Bhimsen Thapa. As Bal Narsingh took his son along wherever he was posted, Jang had a chance to see, as a growing boy, people in different kinds of circumstances and environments. Jang eventually became a subaltern in the army under the command of his father, who was the Governor of a northwestern hill district when Bhimsen was removed from office.

In the aftermath of the fall of Bhimsen Thapa in 1837, most members and dependents of the Thapa family lost their jobs and influence, and some of them were even subjected to ruthless persecution by Prime Minister Rana Jang Pande. The Pande family itself, after having gone through hardships and suffering in the hey-day of the Thapas, had just gained ascendancy in the court. Bal Narsingh lost his job as a District Governor, and at about the same time Jang left the army. Jang's father had already found it difficult to control his brash young son even as a subordinate officer under his own military command. Intolerant and contemptuous of the authority of his superiors, Jang Bahadur paid little or no heed to discipline in military duties, but he had shown a knack of ingratiating himself with the rank and file of the army by being ever ready to voice their grievances and plead for their redress.

Jang Bahadur had re-established himself in the palace as early as 1840 by pleasing King Rajendra with his exploits during an elephant hunt, but he began to play a prominent role in court politics only when Mathbar returned from India in 1843. Although the maternal uncle and nephew fell foul of each other soon enough, yet Jang Bahadur had at first looked upon his uncle as his protector and guide. As a matter of fact, Jang's own attitude toward Mathbar was based on a sort of love-hate relationship. Jang admired and envied not only Mathbar's rank and position but also his physical valour, fitness and stamina, and above all his personal charm and dynamism. Jang also had personal reasons to be fond and proud of the uncle who had initially taken such a great fancy to him as to give him the name of Jang Bahadur (literally brave in war) after he had been named Bir Narsingh as a baby. But Jang also began to hate Mathbar for the manner in which he had of late started throwing his weight around and imposing himself on everyone including his own nephew.

Jang was shrewder and no less ambitious than his maternal uncle and quickly sensed that he had to be always on the winning side in the game of court politics in order to get to the top. He also realized soon enough that in the prevailing circumstances in the court, it was not possible for him to fulfil his high ambition through Mathbar, whose arrogance had created powerful enemies in high places who were bound to destroy him. Jang therefore started cultivating General Gagan Singh Bhandari as a temporary ally to gain the confidence of the Junior Queen, Rajyalakshmi Devi, and to promote his own position in the court. Gagan Singh, a comely and courtly person with an imposing figure and the reputation of being a lady's man, had risen to his present high position in the court primarily as Junior Queen Rajyalakshmi Devi's favourite.

Assassination of Prime Minister Mathbar

What had happened at Hetauda in December 1844 and Mathbar's role in those events had aroused the suspicion of King Rajendra against the Prime Minister. But Mathbar's dynamic personality and his hold on a large section of the army combined with the support of the Crown Prince, made him a formidable foe whom the King and the Junior Queen did not dare to challenge openly. The King sought to hoodwink Mathbar about his real intentions by appointing him Prime Minister for life on 20 January 1845. Then King Rajendra Bikram Shah, in collusion with Junior Queen Rajyalakshmi Devi, who had also by then turned against Mathbar, laid a plot to take Mathbar's life with Gagan Singh and Jang Bahadur Kanwar as their instruments.

The Junior Queen had come to the conclusion that Mathbar had completely gone over to the side of the heir apparent and would be a formidable obstacle rather than a help to the fulfilment of her design to put her own eldest son on the throne. Jang Bahadur, the future Prime Minister and Maharaj of Nepal, may have viewed cooperation in their matter as the first necessary step to realize his own ultimate ambition.

Jang's liaison with one of Queen Rajyalakshmi's trusted maids of honour, who was also flirting with Gagan Singh at the same time, initially helped Jang Bahadur to gain the confidence of the court. The following quotation from General Padma Jang Bahadur Rana's biography of Maharaj Jang Bahadur throws a flood of light on the political role and influence of innumerable maids of honour who were attached to the Queen's household:

> The queen's court had become a hotbed of vice and villainy. Every

> form of wickedness, from a stolen kiss to the foulest murder, was daily practised as a very necessity of existence. Every inmate of the court, from the Queen-Regent down to the humblest maid, was inextricably involved in love intrigues of one description or another. In fact, chastity seemed to be an unknown entity both among the men and the women connected with the court. . . . The court dames were all young and goodlooking, and there were nearly one thousand of them, who attended for fifteen days in the month by turns. The fortnight leisure that each of them enjoyed in the month, was spent in the company of lovers and paramours, in the choice of whom no restriction was recognized as to number, as these girls were not only powerful engines of immorality but the mighty engines of political preferment; so that the amount of influence a maid possessed over the Regent was generally the measure of her capacity to elicit love and admiration of her paramours; and their number was also in proportion to their influence.[25]

On 17 May 1845, Prime Minister Mathbar Singh Thapa was summoned to the palace through Kulman Singh Thapa on the pretext that Junior Queen Rajyalakshmi Devi had suddently fallen ill. Mathbar's son, Ranojjal Singh Thapa suspected a trap and asked his father to take a few bodyguards along. But Mathbar did not listen to him, saying in jest that he could account for seven men singlehanded if the need arose.

When Mathbar reached the palace, he was made to wait in the courtyard for some time before he was accosted by a maidservant with a broad grin and led upstairs to the room where King Rajendra was lying on a bedstead with Queen Rajyalakshmi seated at his feet. No sooner had Mathbar entered the room than the King and Queen made the prearranged signal to Mathbar's own sister's son, Jang Bahadur Kanwar, who was waiting behind the door with a loaded gun in the ready position. General Gagan Singh was standing by Jang's side to back him up with a second shot if necessary.

Mathbar was struck by a bullet in his head and by "two or more small balls and some small shot" in other parts of the body. Before he breathed his last, he staggered forward in the agony of death only to invoke the King's mercy on his mother and children. Meanwhile he was struck from behind, and when he fell to the ground with his hands stretched out as though in supplication to the King, one of the armed guards nearly severed his wrists from his arms with a sword

King Rajendra was so angry with Mathbar that after making sure he was dead, the King started kicking his head and abusing him. By King Rajendra's command Mathbar's mangled body was bundled up in a sheet of cloth and let down into the street from a window of the royal palace by a rope. Before daylight it was carried by a party of soldiers to the river by the Pashupatinath temple to be cremated. Religious-minded passersby on their way to the temple before day-break were said to have noticed stains cuased by blood dripping from Mathbar's wounds all along the 3-kilometre road to Pashupatinath.[26]

Who killed Mathbar?

On 18 May 1845, the King informed the Resident that he had himself shot Mathbar to death and he also informed the Governor-General of India that he had found his Prime Minister guilty of treason and insubordination and "therefore I put the traitor Thapa to death with my own hands, killing him with gun and sword."[27]

But nobody seemed to believe his story. Only a few days after the incident, Crown Prince Surendra is reported to have challenged the King's statement in open court and said to the King: "You killed Mathbar Singh, indeed. You could not kill a rat.[28] Resident Henry Lawrence's reaction to the role claimed by the King and the Resident's own version of the tragic incident are recorded in the following excerpt from his dispatch to his Government.

> Gagan Singh and four or five others killed the Minister. The Maharaja may have mangled the corpse; but I must doubt His Highness having courage to fire a gun, much more to face his late Minister.[29]

After he was deposed, King Rajendra wrote to the Governor-General of India, Hardinge (1844-47), on 15 August 1847:

> On General Marthbar (sic) Singh's misbehaving himself, I sent for Jang Bahadur, and ordered him to kill Marthbar Singh threatening him with death if he refused to obey.[30]

Jang Bahadur himself had owed to Mathbar his position in the army and much else in life. Jang, therefore, could never overcome his sense of remorse for having killed his maternal uncle. Years after the event, while showing one of his European guests around his Thapathali residence, Jang is said to have drawn his visitor's attention to the picture of the man with piercing eyes and a prominent forehead and to have said fondly:

That is my uncle, Mathbar Singh, whom I shot; it is very like him.[31]

After the death of Mathbar Singh Thapa the pace of events slowed down for a while, for nobody was willing to shoulder the responsibility of running the administration. Kind Rajendra and Junior Queen Rajyalakshmi Devi were temporarily reconciled and Heir Apparent Surendra also quieted down considerably. They carried on the government as a triumvirate for about six months, issuing orders in military matters through Jang Bahadur and in all affairs of civil administration through Gagan Singh. Gagan Singh had become the most influential man in the court as a strong partisan of the interests of Junior Queen Rajyalakshmi Devi.

Coalition Government under the Nominal Leadership of Fatte Jang Shah

When Mathbar had returned to Nepal in 1843, Fatte Jang Shah who had headed the pro-British cabinet from November 1840 till March 1843 as Mukhtiyar, abruptly left the country for Gaya in India, for fear of being victimized by Mathbar Singh Thapa as the new Prime Minister. Mathbar, in his turn, had Fatte Jang's property confiscated for absenting himself from the country without the prior knowledge and consent of the Prime Minister. Mathbar apprehended trouble from the Chautara acting in league with the members of the Kala Pande family who had gone into exile in India. It was only in response to a royal summons after the assassination of Mathbar Singh Thapa that Chautara Fatte Jang Shah returned to Kathmandu on 14 August 1845.

King Rajendra Bikram Shah had considerable difficulty in persuading Fatte Jang Shah to accept on 25 September 1845 the nominal leadership of a kind of coalition government of which the other members were to be Gagan Singh Bhandari, Abhiman Singh Rana Magar and Kazi Dalabhanjan Gora Pande. Fatte Jang Shah was given command of only three regiments, while Gagan Singh was given charge of seven regiments with the rank of General and Abhiman Singh Rana Magar that of two regiments with a similar title. Fatte Jang Shah's family was put in charge of administration of all territory from Palpa westwards and he himself, as Mukhtiyar, was entrusted with the responsibility of conducting relation with Great Britain and China. General Abhiman Singh Rana Magar was put in charge of the administration of all territory east of Palpa. Gagan Singh was to look after all the Darbar affairs and army supplies, and the regiments under his command were deployed in protection of the palace and its surroundings. Kazi Dalabhanjan Gora Pande, who was extremely old and had been a contemporary and minor colleague of Bhimsen Thapa, was also included in the cabinet just for cosmetic purposes. He was given charge of only one regiment and was supposed to advise the other three ministers as and when necessary.

It was apparent that Junior Queen Rajyalakshmi Devi had a major say in the shaping of this coalition ministry and in effecting the division of work and authority among its members. General Gagan Singh held all real power in his hands and "was the actual premier in all except name." Jang Bahadur was not included in the cabinet at first except as a "military member" becuase it was suspected that Jang Bahadur, like his uncle, Mathbar, supported the interests of the heir apparent. Both the King and the Junior Queen, however, were anxious not to incur the enmity of a man of Jang Bahadur's "energy, talent and daring" and he was therefore allowed to retain the rank of General with the command of the three regiments already entrusted to him.

The quality of military officers and the standard of conduct in the court and life of Nepal had reached an all-time low at the time of Mathbar's assassination. The following excerpt from Resident Henry Lawrence's letter of 25 May 1845 to Governor-General Hardinge (1844-47), bears testimony to the above fact:

> There is not a soldier in Nepal; scarcely a single man that has seen a shot fired, and not one that could lead the army. The chiefs are a very poor set, effeminate debauched creatures, wanting in all respectable qualities.[32]

There is yet another letter which throws light on the contemporary state of affairs in Nepal. In January 1846, Lawrence's wife Honoria sent a letter from Sugauli, a village to the south of Indo-Nepal frontier, to George Clerk, her husband's early friend and adviser and a member of the Council of India in London. The letter was intended to convey her husband's views about developments in Nepal since the appointment of Chautara Fatte Jang Shah as Prime Minister following the assassination of Mathbar Singh Thapa. As it gives a picture of the state of affairs in the court on the eve of the most critical event in modern Nepali history and furnishes valuable clues to the motivations of the principal participants, it deserves special attention. The relevant extracts from the letter are reproduced below:

Mrs. Lawrence to George Clerk, Esq.

Segowlee, January 1846

My dear Mr. Clerk,

I would not venture to obtrude my feminine politics on any public man but yourself, but I think you will do me the justice to believe that I only wish to transmit to you my husband's views—to say for him what he now has no leisure to say for himself.

I forget when my husband last wrote to you, not I think, since the appointment of Fatte Jang Chountra (sic) as minister. He is a timid, nervous creature, who seems to live with a drawn sword, in every point a contrast to poor Matabur (sic).

The Chountra affects great simplicity and even poverty in his dress, &c; has a small sawaree, and very few soldiers and hangers-on about his gates. He always gets *a pain in his stomach* when he is summoned to Durbar and feels afraid to go.

The man with real influence is Guggur Sing[33] (sic), now a general originally a slave. He is in appearance, like Matabur, and seems to have some of his *pluck*. According to report, he and the Maharanee carry everything their own way, the Chountra being afraid to act, and young *Absalom* of a prince being very quiet for some months past, occasionally telling his papa that if he is not placed on the Guddee he will go and turn Fakeer at Kassee (sic), and now and then putting an officer, who had been too obsequious to Guggur Sing, to stand all day in a pond.

Jung Bahadur (sic), Mathur's nephew, is likewise a general and called commander-in-chief. He takes no very prominent part just and now, and seems to spend his energies in devising new uniforms. But he is active and intelligent, and if (perhaps it would be more correct to say, *when*) there is another slaughter in the Durbar, the struggle will probably be between Jung Bahadur and Guggur Sing.

The Maharajah goes on the same inexplicable way, apparently afraid of his son, yet putting him forward, and at the same time seeming to allow the Maharanee and Guggur Sing to be the virtual rulers of the country. Possibly he has heard of the Kilkenny cats. The Rajah never was so civil to Lawrence as for the last two or three months, when they met on the road, getting out of his palkee and walking with him–almost apologizing for Matabur's murder, saying he had warned the general and expostulated in vain, and that it was plain *both* could not live. When we left Nepaul last month we were allowed to come down Phirfung (sic) road, which no European ever before traversed and is mentioned, I think, even by Kirkpatrick, as jealously guarded. For travellers it is a much better road than our old one by Chitlang (sic), being admirably laid out, and as good as the road from Sabathoo to Simla. But it is full ten miles longer than the Chitlang road, by which, Lawrence says he would prefer leading a force. . .[34]

Assassination of Gagan Singh

General Gagan Singh, favourite of Queen Rajyalakshmi, fell to an assassin's bullet on 14 September 1846, and the Queen herself, who was of a fiery temperament, exploded in uncontrollable rage on hearing the news. King Rajendra Bikram Shah had vested full powers in her in 1843 and she chose to assert these broadly to seek out and punish whoever might have been responsible for the assassination.

To this day it is not known for certain who the real culprit was. Gagan Singh had attracted general hostility because he had risen to the post of Commander-in-Chief from that of a mere macebearer by virtue of being the Queen's favourite, and many people would thus have had a motive for the crime. King Rajendra himself and Crown Prince Surendra, however, had a particular reason to be displeased with Gagan because of the near-public scandal about Junior Queen Rajyalakshmi's liaison with him. It was therefore probable that the King and the Crown Prince themselves had something to do with the assassination.

Some sources state that a Maithili Brahmin by the name of Lal Jha was hired for the purpose and confessed his guilt when he was later arrested in Kathmandu, where he had been sent by Jagat Bam Pande from Bettiah on a mission to murder Jang Bahadur. According to Dr. H. Ambrose Oldfield, British Residency surgeon at the time, Fatte Jang Shah, General Abhiman Singh Rana Magar, Kazi Dalabhanjan Pande and Bir Kishor Gora Pande, as well as the King and his two sons by his Senior Queen, were aware of the plot to murder Gagan Singh.[35] However, these sources seem to rely merely on rumours spread by the perpetrators of the deed to cover up their own part in it. According to the last words of a dying man, General Abhiman Singh Rana Magar, who was one of the ministers of the court, Jang Bahadur himself murdered General Gagan Singh.[36] But on the basis of reliable information handed down by word of mouth from generation to generation in the family of the seven Jang Bahadur brothers, the author is inclined to believe that it was Jang Bahadur's brother, Badri Narsingh, who, under his elder brother's instructions, actually shot Gagan Singh. As Badri Narsingh was engaged in a love affair with Gagan Singh's daughter he had easy access to the General's house.[37]

Whoever may have murdered Gagan Singh, his assassination triggered off the infamous event known in the history of Nepal as the Kot Massacre. It paved the way for the rise of a strong man as demanded by the chaos in the country. Further, it sealed the fate of the monarchy for more than a hundred years, as the strong man who emerged subsequently established the Rana system of hereditary Prime Ministers, who ruled Nepal until 1951 under a succession of Kings who were mere figureheads.

NOTES

1. Foreign Secret Consultation, 5 March 1833, No. 24.
2. Henry T. Prinsep, *History of the Political and Military Transactions in India during the Administration of Marquess of Hastings*, 1813-1823, (London), pp. 459-61; (Surya Bikram Jnawali (translated by Lalji Shahay), *Amarsingh Thapa* (Hindi), Darjeeling: Himachal Hindi Bhawan), pp. 78-79.
3. Secret Consultation, 20 July 1840, No. 59, published (in edited form) in L. Stiller, *The Kot Massacre*, (Kathmandu, CNAS), 1981.
4. Quoted in W.W. Hunter, *Life of Brian Houghton Hodgson*, (London 1896), pp. 184-85.
5. Secret Consultation, 20 July 1840, No. 59.
6. Secret Consultation, September 21, 1840, No. 151, cited in Ramakant, *Indo-Nepalese Relations, 1816-1877* (Delhi: S. Chand and Co., 1968), p. 179.
7. Secret Consultation, 2 November 1840, No. 122, published in Stiller, *op. cit.*, p. 47.
8. Secret Consultation, 16 August 1841, No. 115, as published in *op. cit.*, pp. 113-14.
9. Narrative of Political Events in Nepal, 1840-1851 (Political Consultation, 11 November 1853, November 22-24).
10. The Darbar never accepted the British argument that the case was outside their jurisdiction. L Stiller, *op. cit.*, pp. 138-39.

11. Secret Consultation, 3 August 1842, No. 66, cited in Ramakant, Indo-Nepalese Relations, *op. cit.*, p. 203.
12. Hunter. *op. cit.*, p. 204.
13. Secretary to the Indian Government with the Governor-General to the Resident in Nepal dated June 22, 1842, cited in Hunter, p. 217.
14. Government to Hodgson, dated 6 July 1842, cited in Hunter, *op. cit.*, p. 220.
15. Secret Consultation, 19 October 1842, No. 64, cited in Ramakant, *op. cit.*, p. 211.
16. Secret Consultation, 5 October 1842, No. 148, cited in Ramakant, *op. cit.*, p. 214.
17. Hunter, *op. cit.*, p. 231.
18. Secret Consultation, 27 January 1844, No. 49, published in L. Stiller, *The Kot Massacre*, (Kathmandu CNAS, 1981), p. 208.
19. Secret Consultation, 23 November 1844, No. 113, cited in Ramakant, *op. cit.*, p. 225.
20. Secret Consultation, 24 January 1845, No. 116, Ramakant, *op. cit.*, p. 225.
21. Secret Consultation, 25 January 1845, No. 118, cited in Ramakant, *op. cit.*, pp. 243-44.
22. Resident Lawrence to Government, 24 December 1844, published in Stiller, *op. cit.*, pp. 243-44.
23. Daniel Wright, *History of Nepal* (Cambridge University Press, 1879), p. 33.
24. Letter from H. Lawrence to Lord Auckland dated 25 May 1845, cited in H.B. Edwards and H. Merivale, *Life of Sir Henry Lawrence* (London: Smith, Elder and Co., 1872) No.64, Vol. 1, p. 8, and Diary of Events in Nepal, 18 May 1845.
25. General Pudma Jung Bahadur, *Life of Maharaja Sir Jung Bahadur, G.C.B., G.C.S.I., of Nepal*, (Allahabad, Pioneer Press, 1909), pp. 46-47.
26. H. Ambrose Oldfield, *Sketches from Nepal* (London: W.H. Allen and Co., 1880), Vol. 1, p. 346.
27. Foreign Secret Consultation, 13 June 1845, No. 15.
28. Quoted by Edwards and Merivale in *Life of Sir Henry Lawrence*, p. 336.
29. Quoted by Edwards and Merivale, (London: Smith, Elder, and Company, 1872), Vol. 1, *op. cit.*, p. 336.
30. King Rajendra's *Khareeta* to Governor General dated 20 Sravan 1904 Vikram Samvat (15 August 1847), Foreign Secret Consultation, 25 September 1847, No. 173.
31. Lawrence Oliphant, *A Journey to Nepal with the Camp of Jung Bahadur* (New York: Appleton & Co., 1852), p. 166.
32. H.B. Edwards and H. Merivale, *Life of Henry Lawrence* (London: Smith, Elder and Co., 1872), Vol. II, pp. 8-9.
33. Gagan Singh was in fact a Bhandari Chhetri by caste and thus could not have been a slave. He belonged to one of the Gorkha-based elite Chhetri families.
34. H.B. Edwards and H. Merivale, *op. cit.*, pp. 39-41.
35. H. Ambrose Oldfield, *op. cit.*, Vol. I, p. 121.
36. General Pudma Jung Bahadur Rana, *op. cit.*, p. 72; P. Landon, *Nepal* (London: Constable & Co., 1928), Vol. I, p. 123; Pratiman Thapa, *Maharaj Jang Bahadur Ko Jivan Charitra*, Calcutta, 1908.
37. Baburam Acharya, *Baburam Acharya Ra Uhanka Kriti* (Kathmandu; Institute of Nepal and Asian Studies, 1973), p. 35. Baburam Acharya agreed with the interviewer that Badri Narsingh shot Gagan, but denied he was involved with Gagan's daughter.

8

An Overview of the Shah Kings' Politics and Statecraft

An Historical Overview

We have already examined the historic role played by King Prithvinarayn Shah (c.1769-1775, Raja of Gorkha for c.1743) in laying down the foundation of the modern kingdom of Nepal. The conquest of the Kathmandu Valley kingdoms took him about twenty-five years and was accomplished by 1769. Before he died in 1775, Prithvinarayan had annexed almost all of today's eastern Nepal including the districts of Makwanpur, Rautahat and Bara Parsa to the southeast of the Valley. The task of expanding the kingdom to the west was completed by his successors.

Prithvinarayan's eldest son and successor, King Pratap Singh (c.1775-1777) died after a brief reign of hardly two years, and it was unfortunate for the Shah dynasty that the throne was occupied thereafter by minors until 1832 except for a brief chaotic interlude in the last decade of the eighteenth century. This led to the isolation of the King from the political process and to the concentration of power in the hands of regents and officials.

Regent Queen Rajendralakshmi, mother of King Rana Bahadur (c.1777-1799), ran the administration from 1777 to 1785 except for a brief period of inactivity during her imprisonment in the palace by her husband's brother, Bahadur Shah; Naib or Regent Bahadur Shah dominated the scene from 1785 to 1794. Then the Basnyat and Pande families were pre-eminent under the leadership of Kazi Kirtiman Singh Basnyat and Kazi Damodar Pande from 1799 to 1804, during the regencies of Queen Subarnaprabha (April 1800 to February 1803) and Queen Rajarajeshvari (February 1803 to March 1804). The Thapa family, led by Mukhtiyar General Bhimsen Thapa from 1806 to 1837, was dominant during the Regency of Queen Tripurasundari (1806-1832).

The decade following the fall of Bhimsen Thapa in 1837 was characterized by desperate and spasmodic efforts on the part of King Rajendra Bikram Shah (1816-1847) to assert his own power and that of the royal family. The removal of Mukhtiyar General Bhimsen Thapa, the strong man of Nepal for thirty years, afforded King Rajendra Bikram Shah an opportunity to establish his royal authority: this was a situation in which he could have effectively exercised his sovereign power. But he proved to be too weak to manage the administration on his own. He constantly turned for advice from one or the other of his two Queens and soon felt that he could not do without a Prime Minister (Mukhtiyar).

Rana Jang Pande was the key factor in Nepali court politics with senior Queen Samrajyalakshmi's support, from July 1837 through November 1840, notwithstanding frequent changes in the prime ministership. Ranganath Pandit became Mukhtiyar for about nine months from December 1837 till August 1838 Following his resignation, a joint ministry of Pushkar Shah and Rana Jang Pande carried on the administration from October 1838 to the end of 1839. By April 1839 Pushkar Shah had become subordinate to Rana Jang Pande, and in February 1840 Rana Jang Pande once again became Mukhtiyar and remained in that position till November of the same year, when a coalition under the Mukhtiyarship of Chautara Fatte Jang Shah (1840-1843) came into power with the backing of the British Resident and continued in office till December 1843, when Mathbar Singh Thapa became and Commander-in-Chief.

General Mathbar Singh Thapa (December 1843 to 1845) was murdered on 17 May 1845 at the behest of King Rajendra Bikram Shah and Junior Queen Rajyalakshmi. It took King Rajendra four months to persuade Chautara Fatte Jang Shah (September 1845 to September 1846) to be the nominal head of an ill-fated coalition government. The cabinet consisted of the Junior Queen's favourite, General Gagan Singh, who was "Prime Minister except in name," General Abhiman Singh Rana and Kazi Dalabhanjan Gora Pande. All of them were killed on the night of 14 September 1846, in the wake of the efficiently conducted massacre at the Kot which paved the way for the emergence of a real strong man, Jang Bahadur Rana.

Before the notorious Kot bloodletting, an atmosphere of fear, suspicion and uncertainty had prevailed in Nepal, the result of perpetual strife between the two leading families of the time, the Pandes and the Thapas. The situation was made worse by the attempt of a weak and vacillating King to set one family against the other in the hope of maintaining his own supremacy while the immediate members of his family–his two Queens, Samrajyalakshmi and Rajyalakshmi, and his eldest son and heir apparent, Prince Surendra Bikram Shah–were at cross-purposes with one another and sided with one faction of the courtiers or the other, depending on the exigencies of the situation. By refusing to control the actions of the royal antagonists, King Rajendra maintained a technique of playing off his two Queens against each other and, after the death of Senior Queen Samrajyalakshmi, pitted Heir Apparent Surendra against Junior Queen Rajyalakshmi. Thus, as a result of King Rajendra's misguided policy, the process of "waning kingship," which had already started during Bhimsen's long term of office, attained its culmination when Jang Bahadur had consolidated his own power and that of his family.

The Gorkhali System.

In the principality of Gorkha in the eighteenth century a system of government was developed which was later applied to all of Nepal with suitable modifications conditioned by local needs and customs. The King carried on the administration of the country with the help of his advisers called Kazis, whom he could appoint or dismiss at his pleasure. Among the officers of the state were one Chautara, four Kazis, four Sardars, two Khardars, one Kapardar and one Khazanchi.

The Chautara, who did not necessarily possess the authority of Chief among the Kazis, was nominally considered above other councillors just because he was the King's blood relation. As the Government was of a military type, the Kazis and Sardars performed both civil and military functions of the highest level. The Khardars were lower in rank and functioned as office supervisors. The Kapardar was the controller of the King's household and was in charge of the King's wardrobe, jewellery and kitchen. The Khazanchi was the treasurer of the Government.

The other officials in order of importance were Takshali, Dharmadhikar, Dittha, Bichari, Jetha Budha, Subba and Umrao. The Takshali was the master of the mint. The Mir Umrao and Umrao were like the lords of the manor in medieval Europe whose duty it was to administer not only a fort but also the territory around it with a view to providing well-equipped and trained soldiers when needed and also the material goods and services needed in war. The Subba and the Jetha Budha were local Government officials responsible for the maintenance of law and order, collecting land taxes and administering other local affairs.

The Bhardari or the Council of Notables

Upon ex-King Rana Bahadur Shah's return to Nepal in 1804 from exile in Varanasi, he functioned as Mukhtiyar to his minor son, King Girvana Yuddha Bikram Shah (c. 1799-1816). The traditional role of the Chautaras, the King's collaterals, and the Kazis also underwent a change after this. All of them became part of the Bhardari, the enlarged Council of notables. It became their duty to perform certain specific functions under the King's direct supervision. Such authority as the members of the Bhardari nominally enjoyed was derived from the King.

The Court System

The highest court of the country consisted of the Dharmadhikar who was usually a learned Brahman knowledgeable in the *Dharma Shastra* or religio-legal codes, on which penalties for criminal offences of a serious nature were based, and who had a paramount say in cases relating to them; four Bicharis, whose function was to investigate and report on all civil cases including disputes over land and other property, and who under certain circumstances enjoyed authority higher than that of the Dharmadhikar himself in matters within their exclusive jurisdiction; the Dittha, the Chief Constable and Public Prosecutor, who assisted the Bicharis in investigating cases; and the Jetha Budha (meaning the elder) who, in an honorary capacity and on a voluntary basis, offered whatever assistance he could in dispensing justice.

In the outlying areas, one of the ranking local officers convened a court of elders or panchayat to hear disputes, but an appeal over the panchayat's ruling lay in the court presided over by the Bichari. Certain cases considered serious enough by the Bichari, as well as appeals over the Bichari's decisions, were referred to the Kazi or the Sardar, one of the top officials, who in is turn might submit the matter to the

King's personal attention if necessary.

At times the King himself referred cases he considered important to the Bhardari or the Council of Notables.[1] However, in every case the King was the final court of appeal and held the power to endorse or reverse the decision of the highest officials.

The 1806 trial of Sher Bahadur Shah, who was Chautara during the regency of Queen Subarnaprabha (April 1800 to February 1803), the trial of Tribhuvan Pradhan, who was in charge of the Treasury during the same period, after ex-King Rana Bahadur Shah's return to Kathmandu as Mukhtiyar in 1804; the trial of Bhimsen Thapa in 1837 and 1839, after the return to power of Rana Jang Pande; and that of Rana Jang Pande and Karbir Pande after the restoration of Mathbar Singh Thapa to power in 1843 are examples of trial by the Council of Notables.

These trials had one feature in common: they were of a political nature. They were conducted by a particular section of the courtiers or by members of a particular elite family to legitimize their political triumph over the vanquished side, rather than to administer justice to the accused.

Land Revenue Settlement and Reclamation influenced by Considerations of War

War afforded an opportunity to acquire new land to be distributed as grants among the officers and soldiers. The burden of war, however, had to be shouldered mainly by the peasantry, who had to work on the land and produce enough not only to ensure the supply of food, arms, and ammunition to the officers and soldiers engaged in fighting but also to meet the normal expenditure of the Government. The feudal military elite, very small in number compared to the total population, prized war as an all-purpose enterprise.

In Nepal, land was regarded as the property of the state or of the ruler who represented that state. In the early days of Gorkha rule it was believed that all land belonged to the King. King Prithvinarayan Shah was very conscious of the need for increasing agricultural production, as is clear from his following directive:

> Even if there are houses on land fit to be turned into terrace farms, shift the houses elsewhere, dig water channels for irrigation and cultivate the field.[2]

As war had to be financed with the help of agricultural surplus, land settlement and reclamation were encouraged as a means of stepping up agricultural production. Because of the local shortage of labour, owing to the low density of population, administrators were asked to bring in settlers from India so that vacant land might be turned over to them for cultivation.

As a particular society's political outlook influences its land policy and also its attitude towards property in land, Nepal's belief in conducting military operations as a means of acquiring new land affected the system of land tenure and revenue in the country. The retainers of land, such as Birtawars and Jagirdars, were obliged to supply military requirements such as arrows and saltpetre for the manufacture of gunpowder. In the 1814-1816 war against the British, they were forced to fulfil this obligation on pain of confiscation of their land.[3]

It is also remarkable that his war campaign was conducted by Nepal largely with the help of *Jhara*, unpaid or forced labour. *Jhara* provided the basis for the growth of the *Hulak* system of organizing relays of porters along designated routes for the quick dispatch of military supplies and mail. The people engaged in performing *Hulak* services were, however, given compensatory benefits and concessions as cultivators.

Again, the *Jagir* land granted to the employees of the state in lieu of cash payment was, as an inducement to men and officers engaged in war, brought under the *Kut* system, which enabled the holders of this kind of land to levy rents in kind or cash on their own terms rather than on the basis of the *Adhiya* system, which entitled them to only one-half of the main paddy crop.

In addition, the Birtawars and Jagirdars were entitled to revenues from other sources, such as litigation fees and local levies on commercial goods in transit, and also enjoyed the privilege of dispensing justice and exacting for private purpose *Jhara*, unpaid or forced labour of both kinds–*Beth* and *Begar*. *Beth* implied unpaid labour for work in the farms and *Begar* meant unpaid use of labour for other purposes such as carrying loads, building roads, digging water channels, planting trees and repairing public buildings.

Difference from the Feudal System in Medieval Europe

The Birtawars and Jagirdars derived their authority from the ruler and from the use and possession of land granted by that ruler. It must be noted here that, unlike the European feudal lords in medieval times, who had taken advantage of the breakdown of the central power in asserting their independent authority based on the ownership of land, the feudal retainers of all categories in Nepal enjoyed their right to hold land at the pleasure and discretion of the ruler at the centre. As a result, there were constant changes not only in the ownership of the land but also in the composition of the nobility. This actually hindered the growth in Nepal of a powerful feudal class strong enough to challenge the absolute authority of the King, the sort of class that did develop in European countries, notably in England and Germany.

The peasantry had to suffer excessive burden of the feudal tenure system irrespective of the changes in the composition of the feudal class. Generally in the 17th and the 18th centuries, and particularly during the period after 1804, vast areas of cultivated land were converted from *Birta*, *Raikar* and *Kipat* to *Jagir*, as dictated by the overwhelming needs of protracted military campaigns.[4] Even *Guthi*, land granted for religious purposes, was not spared.

It is worth noting here that just as the Nepali feudal vassals and nobles, as compared with their European counterparts in medieval times, were weaker against the absolute power of the King, so also the religious establishment in Nepal was much less powerful than the church in West vis-a-vis the ruler. Religion in Nepal was always used as a handmaid of politics. There was no Nepali counterpart of Cardinal Richelieu or even a Thomas Becket. Even the apparently powerful institution of the royal preceptor, equipped with the arbitrary power of dispensation and excommunication, i.e., authorizing people to dispense with observance of religious rules and punishing them for non-observance, was always used in Nepal to legitimize the acts of the powers-that-be.

An Overall Picture

The Government's function mainly consisted in collecting fixed revenue and mobilizing additional resources to meet the growing expenditure of administration and military operations. Even the concept of the country as one single customs area was not immediately realized in practice, as transit duties were levied on river and highway traffic, persons and goods, as in the days before the conquest. Territorial expansion, under the Shah dynasty of Nepal, merely created a skeletal form of the basic political framework for eventual national integration.

Mere subjugation of different regions inhabited by polyglot ethnic groups, with diverse religious and cultural backgrounds, could not possibly have imbued the entire population all at once with a sense of communal harmony and belonging together. Territorial expansion under the Shah Kings, however, has given the country a single name and a strong central government.

The King at the Apex --- Power and Constraints

By virtue of its long-established sovereign position in the country since 1769, when King Prithvinarayan founded modern Nepal, the Shah dynasty secured the allegiance of the key elite families and the ultimate loyalty of the army. The King could always exercise his authority over the administration through the time-honoured practice of *pajani*, the annual renewal of service, a screening of both civil and military government officials from the lowest to the highest rank, after which they were either confirmed in their posts for another year or dismissed. Even the mere postponement of *pajani* served as a prelude to the downfall of Regent Bahadur Shah (1785-1794) and Mukhtiyar Bhimsen Thapa (1806-1837), both of whom were strong men in their own right.

The principle of primogeniture which was followed in regulating succession to the throne, reduced the status of the King's brothers, cousins and uncles to that of dependent relations who had royal status without power. A member of this group of royal relatives could enjoy real power only as Naib or Regent for a minor King or as a Chautara, and not all of them could be accommodated as Chautaras.

Once the conquest of the Kathmandu Valley was completed in 1769 the relations between King Prithvinarayan Shah and his brothers became strained. The main cause of the brothers' dissatisfaction was that they were not adequately rewarded by King Prithvinarayan for their part in expanding the Kingdom of Gorkha. However, King Prithvinarayan's own concern for the consolidation of the newly acquired territories into a powerful kingdom did not allow him to satisfy the personal ambition of his brothers who presumably wished to be rewarded with a kingdom each. Moreover, Prithvinarayan who had reaped the benefit of the division of the Malla Kingdom of the Kathmandu Valley into three Kingdoms after 1481, was fully aware of the consequences which the division of his territory among his brothers might lead to.

Although Prithvinarayan's powerful personality prevented his brothers from opposing him openly during his lifetime, they had withdrawn into forced retirement. Even before Prithvinarayan's death, one of his half-brothers, Mahoddam Kirti Shah, sought refuge in Tanahu, one of the Chaubise or twenty-four principalities.

At the beginning, the conquest and consolidation of new territories led to the strengthening of the Shah monarchy. The rule of King Prithvinarayan's immediate successors was characterized by intense rivalry between the original Gorkha-based families with a long and outstanding record of service to the Shah dynasty and some of the newer families, who had to be absorbed into the central administration because of their local influence in the newly acquired areas. This trend, which was already in evidence during the reign of King Pratap Singh (1775-1777), became more pronounced during the regency of Queen Rajendralakshmi (1777-1785). Swarup Singh Karki, probably from the eastern hills, seems to have grown influential during the rule of King Pratap Singh and was actually entrusted with the task of imprisoning the new King's brothers and uncles at Nuwakot. Regent Queen Rajendralakshmi relied more on the officers drawn from those new families with influence outside the original jurisdiction of Gorkha, whereas the officers who belonged to the old Gorkha-based families naturally turned to Bahadur Shah, King Prithvinarayan's second son, for support and guidance. Regent Queen Rajendralakshmi's right hand man was Sarbajit Rana, a Magar Officer from her parents's home district of Gulmi in west Nepal.

Political Behaviour and Stratagem

The principal actors on the Nepali political stage were generally guided by the essence of Machiavelli's teaching to European princes that in politics the end always justifies the means and whether an action is good or evil can only be decided in the light of what it is intended to accomplish and whether it successfully accomplishes it:

> The fact is that a man who wants to act virtuously in every way comes to grief among so many who are not virtuous. Therefore, if a prince wants to maintain his rule, he must learn how not to be virtuous, and to make use of this or not according to need.[5]

Gorkhali tradition did not reject unscrupulous methods to secure personal ends. Apart from the habitual use of deceit and treachery to gain selfish political ends, astrology, assassination, poisoning and tantric worship were also employed for the purpose. King Prithvinarayan Shah, the founder of modern Nepal, practised deceit in dealing with his political opponents such as the Raja of Tanahu, Tribikram Sen, whom he betrayed and arrested at Jyamir Ghat on the Marsyangdi river.[6] King Prithvinarayan practised the following Machiavellian maxim and its Kautilyan parallels from time to time with great skill:

> So it follows that a prudent ruler cannot and should not honour his word when it places him at a disadvantage and when the reasons for which he made his promise no longer exist. If all men were good, this precept would not be good; but because men are wretched creatures who would not keep their word to you, you need not keep your word to them. And a prince will never lack good excuses to colour his bad faith.[7]

King Prithvinarayan also hired assassins to get rid of persons whom he suspected to be in league with his enemies. He himself recorded an instance of how he made use of a person by the name of Jhagal Gurung to assassinate Parashuram Thapa's brother, who was suspected of having been sent by Parashuram to plot against Gorkha in complicity with the Chaubise or the twenty-four principalities.[8]

Professional astrologers were used to set the auspicious time and date for the performance of state functions and duties of importance.[9] King Prithvinarayan Shah always attacked a new territory on a day considered auspicious by his court astrologers. Tantric and other forms of worship were habitually practised to aid political and military efforts. King Pratap Singh Shah (c. 1775-1777), King Prithvinarayan's son and successor, was himself initiated by his religious preceptor in the practice of the esoteric tantric cult.

Poisoning was also used at times as a means of eliminating politically undesirable persons. It was suspected that Mukhtiyar Bhimsen Thapa poisoned King Girvana Yuddha Shah as he approached the age of majority. In fact, Bhimsen Thapa was tried in 1837 and 1839 on the charge of poisoning one of the royal children as well as King Girvana Yuddha. Politically controversial and key persons died very frequently of smallpox, both in Nepal and Tibet. As late as 1878, Crown Prince Trailokya Bikram Shah died of smallpox under suspicious circumstances.

Relation between the Royal Family and the Notable Families

Theoretically, the royal family held the centre of the stage with the other important families contending for positions of power and influence under the royal shadow. There was such a long-established tradition of rivalry among the most important families that no one family could enhance its political influence except at the cost of another. The zero-sum principle in game theory applied literally to the prevailing situation of competition among them. Until the rise of the Rana family, members of the ruling elite came from the three prominent Chhetri families who were called noble families. The Shahs were the royal family; the leading families were the Pandes, the Basnyats and the Thapas. The political authority of the Shah ruler in the country was above question, but the effectiveness of his rule was circumscribed. Internal conflicts and tensions within the royal family compelled important officials to adjust their political tactics for the sake of their own survival. The rulers were as much guided by the spirit of personal gain and familial advancement as were the noble families. However, the members of the elite families were not always losers in the process, as the throne allowed its own rights and privileges to be encroached upon from time to time. Whenever an opportunity presented itself, the courtier families did not fail to enhance their own position at the cost of royal power.

The Process of "Waning Kingship"

The succession of two minors on the throne, combined with the favours he received from Regent Queen Tripurasundari, enabled Bhimsen Thapa to acquire powers never before exercised by a minister. Brian Hodgson, the British Resident of the time in Kathmandu, has thus described the growing power of Mukhtiyar General Bhimsen Thapa in his confidential letter dated 18 February 1833:

> . . . The minister . . . has grown so great by virtue of two minorities (with but a short interval between them) and 30 years of almost uninterrupted sovereign sway that he cannot now subside into a subject, and is determined to keep the Raja a cypher, as in his nonage, both with respect to power, and to observance as far as possible. Almost every post and office is filled by Bhimsen's creatures.[10]

During the period between 1806 and 1837 the position of kingship reached its lowest ebb of the pre-Rana period. Hodgson thus recorded his impression of the King's plight during Bhimsen's prime ministership:

> The Raja is hemmed into his palace beyond which he cannot stir unaccompanied by the minister (the Mukhtiyar) and then only to the extent of a short ride or drive. Even within the walls of his palace, the minister and his brother both reside, the latter in the special capacity of a 'dry nurse' to His Highness.
>
> Last year, the Raja desired to make an excursion into the lower hills to shoot. He was prevented. . . . Of power, he has not a particle, nor seems to wish it. Of patronage, he has not a fraction, and is naturally galled at this, as well as at being sentinelled all round by Bhim Sen's creatures even within his own abode, at being debarred from almost all liberty of locomotion, and of intercourse with the Sirdars and gentry of the country. The Raja has been purposely so trained as to possess little energy of body or mind. . . . [11]

The existence of the King's illegitimate sons, who were sometimes appointed Chautaras, led to the further fragmentation of the Shah family, and this provided a tempting opportunity to the courtiers for self-aggrandizement by setting the members of the royal family against one another, as exemplified by the rivalry among King Rana Bahadur's half-brothers and cousins for the office of Chautara prior to his choice of his half-brothers Bidur Shah and Sher Bahadur Shah[12] as Chautaras, and by the assassination of Rana Bahadur Shah as Mukhtiyar by his natural half-brother, Sher Bahadur Shah.

The traditional practice of the Shah Kings to have two queens also had significant repercussions on the balance of political forces. This practice may have been motivated by the desire to ensure uninterrupted succession to the throne, but it led to a situation in which the queens, apart from competing for the status of favourite wife, were involved in the struggle for political power. At times the struggle was aimed not at personal rule but at securing succession rights for their respective children. The prolonged power struggle between the two Queens of King Rajendra Bikram Shah, Samrajyalakshmi and Rajyalakshmi, which was later joined by Crown Prince Surendra Bikram Shah himself, is a case in point.

The King had the final say in the appointment of the Mukhtiyar and in all matters pertaining to the Government, but the exigencies of politics at times compelled him to delegate his supreme power of Hukum, or peremptory command, to the Queen or the Crown Prince. King Rajendra, for example, bestowed the prerogative of Hukum on Junior Queen Rajyalakshmi in January 1843 and on Crown Prince Surendra Bikram Shah in December 1844, with Prime Minister Mathbar Singh Thapa strongly insisting on the King's abdication following a revolt of soldiers in January 1844. At times, the Mukhtiyar was chosen through a consensus among the members of the royal family and the nobility. The appointment of General Mathbar Singh Thapa as Prime Minister in December 1843 came very close to being the result of collective decision of the various parties concerned.

The rise to power of one family was accomplished by wholesale purging of the others from the administration and the actual liquidation of the leading members of the rival families. The inhuman treatment meted out by Mukhtiyar General Bhimsen Thapa and Prime Minister and Commander-in-Chief Mathbar Singh Thapa to members of the Pande family including Kazi Damodar Pande and his sons, and the persecution of the members of the Thapa family by Rana Jang Pande as Mukhtiyar are apt examples. This also applies to the Basnyat family whose members, although prominent in the royal court and the army, sought to play a behind-the-scene role rather than aspiring to the top position. Even the matrimonial alliance between the Basnyat and the Pande families did not prevent the latter from working against the Basnyats when they were in power. Nor did the Basnyats escape the fate of the Pande and Thapas: the powerful Kazi Kirtiman Singh Basnyat (1790-1801) died by the assassin's dagger.

Irrespective of who was in power, or which family dominated the scene, the aims and methods of political behaviour remained unchanged. The paramount consideration was the enhancement of the material and political fortune of the concerned individual and that of his family. Self-advancement and family loyalty were the only motivations that led men to contemplate joint political action. Political alliances outside the family were not considered reliable or enduring in the prevailing atmosphere of mutual suspicion and jealousy, and cases of betrayal even by family members were frequent. The wholesale elimination of hostile groups or potential threats to power was considered the only guarantee of security for the group in power. Small wonder, then, that the political process was characterized by intrigue, bloodshed and violence.

Politics provided a fertile field for an immense variety of manoeuvres and countermanoeuvres, to which members of the royal family and the King himself were often a party. From the death of Prithvinarayan Shah in 1775 until 1846 there hardly existed any conditions for the maintenance of equilibrium among the contending forces. None of the Mukhtiyars with the exception of a Brahman Mukhtiyar died a natural death during the period between 1776 and 1846.

According to H. Ambrose Oldfield, the uncertain political situation was a result of the "imbecility of the king . . . the ambitious intrigues of the Maharani and the violent and extravagant conduct of the heir apparent.[13] However, he does not record that the unsettled political situation during the period between the appointment of Rana Jang Pande as Prime Minister in 1837 and the Kot Massacre in 1846 was in some measure also a result of the subsequent British support in the early eighteen-forties of the so-called 'peace party' consisting of Junior Queen Rajyalakshmi, Ranganath Pandit, the Thapas, the Gurus and the Chautaras, with a view to countering the actions and policies of the "war party" led by Rana Jang Pande, Karbir Pande, Kulbir Pande, Kulraj Pande and Mishra Guru Krishna Ram. The intrusion of British influence into the political process of the Nepal Darbar at times of instability had by now become common. It had begun with the establishment of the Knox mission in 1803 and continued to exist until the departure of the British from India in 1947.

NOTES

1. In view of the non-existence of long established families of standing and influence of their own as a result of the circumstances peculiar to the patrimonial system prevailing in Nepal, the present writer would prefer to describe Nepali courtiers as notables rather than nobles.
2. Yogi Narahari Nath, and Baburam Acharya (eds.), *Rastrapita Shree 5 Bada Maharaj Prithvinarayan Shah Dev Ko Divya Upadesh* (Divine Counsel of the Great King Prithvinarayan Shah Dev, Father of the Nation), (Kathmandu: Prithvi Jayanti Samaroha Samiti, V.S. 2010 (1953), second revised edition), p. 26.
3. Mahesh Chandra Regmi, *A Study in Nepali Economic History* (1768-1846) (New Delhi: Manjusri Publishing House, 1971), p. 41. The Birtawars were the recipients of the Birta land in the case of which the historic rent generally accruing to the state was appropriated by the beneficiaries of this kind of land-grant and the Jagirdars were the recipients of the *Jagir* land granted to the employees of the state in lieu of cash payment for their services.
4. *Ibid*, page 45. Raikar is the state-owned land from which taxes are realized directly from the individual owners and *Kipat* is a form of communal land-ownership in vogue among the *Kiratis* and other Mongoloid ethnic groups.

5. Niccolo Machiavelli, *The Prince* (London: Penguin, 1973), p. 99.
6. Baburam Acharya, *Prithvinarayan Shah Ko Samkshipta Jivani* (Trans. A Short Biography of Prithvinarayan Shah) (Kathmandu: H.M. the King's Secretariat, Royal Palace, 1967), Vol. II, p. 295.
7. Niccolo Machiavelli, *The Prince* (London: Penguin Books, 1973), pp. 99-100.
8. Gautam, Vajracharya (ed.), *Shri Panch Prithvinarayan Shah Ko Upadesh* (Counsel of Shri Five Prithvinarayan Shah) (Lalitpur: Jagadamba Press Prakashan, date of publication, n.a), p. 391.
9. Baburam, Acharya, *op. cit.*, p. 226.
10. Foreign Secret Consultation, 5 March 1833, No. 24.
11. Cited in W.W. Hunter, *Life of Brian Houghton Hodgson* (London: John Murray, 1896), Chapter I, p. 132.
12. Bidur and Sher Bahadur are ofter referred to as *Shahi* and not *Shah* in Nepali writings probably just to indicate that they were born out of wedlock. However, the Shahs and the Shahis are equally respectable subdivisions of the Thakuri clan.
13. Ambrose Oldfield, *Sketches from Nepal* (London: W.H. Allen & Co., 1880), Vol. I, p. 326.

9

The Kot Massacre: The Emergence of Jang Bahadur as the Strong Man of Nepal

The Kot Massacre

The news of the murder of General Gagan Singh Bhandari while at prayer at 10 p.m. on 14 September 1846 was immediately brought by the General's son, Captain Wazir Singh, to Queen Rajyalakshmi at her palace at Hanuman Dhoka. On receiving this tragic piece of news, the Queen was overwhelmed by sorrow and wailed bitterly. Then she reportedly went to the late General's house on foot taking along with her a vessel of water from the Ganga, basil (tulsi) leaves and a nugget of gold. There she asked Gagan Singh's widows not to perform Sati and tried to console the General's three sons, Captain Wazir Singh, Sher Singh, and Khadga Bir Singh. She asked them to attend to the last rites of their father and she ordered a state funeral for the late general.[1]

The Queen, her hair dishevelled and tears trickling down her cheeks, snatched the drawn sword of state from the hands of her Kotha Mache (the chief female attendant whose duty it was to carry the Queen's sword and shield) and holding the sword in her hand, proceeded to the quadrangle of the Kot (armoury), a consecrated place where regimental flags and ceremonial weapons of war were stored and worshipped. In this quadrangle stood several *maulas* or wooden pegs to which animals were tied for slaughter in sacrificial rites on special religious occasions.

On this occasion the quadrangle was to present a gruesome spectacle of human carnage. General Abhiman Singh Rana Magar, who lived close by, was sent for. The bugles were sounded to collect the troops, and messengers despatched post-haste to summon the high-ranking civil and military officers to an emergency state council.

Jang Bahadur and his brothers were the first to arrive at the head of their regiments. The Queen was seated on the floor of a hall in the second storey of the armoury building and was heard to state loudly that she would neither taste food nor take water until the man who had murdered so faithful a minister was duly apprehended and executed. On the ground that the King had already conferred full powers on Queen Rajyalakshmi,[2] Jang Bahadur advised her to order, on her own authority, a prompt and strict investigation into all the circumstances surrounding the murder of General Gagan Singh Bhandari and to punish severely those found guilty.

While Jang was advising the Queen, General Abhiman Singh Rana had gone to the palace and brought the King to the Kot, where a large number of functionaries of state had already assembled. Most of them came unarmed as commanded by the Queen. Only Prime Minister Chautara Fatte Jang Shah and his relatives had not yet arrived, and Jang Bahadur's brother, Bam Bahadur, was sent to call them at once.

Queen Rajyalakshmi ordered General Abhiman Singh to put Kapardar Bir Kishor Gora Pande in fetters, as she suspected his hand in the murder of Gagan Singh. General Abhiman immediately complied with the royal command. The prisoner was then questioned as to who had assassinated General Gagan Singh and whether he himself had not abetted the murder. When the Queen found that it was not possible to extort a confession from Bir Kishor Gora Pande, she handed her naked sword to General Abhiman Singh and ordered him to cut off Bir Kishor Pande's head. General Abhiman dramatically referred the Queen's command to the King in the open court. As the King refused to sanction the execution without a trial or the confession of the prisoner, General Abhiman returned to the Queen, laid the sword at her feet and left the Queen's presence after pleading his inability to carry out her order under the circumstances.

After being told by Jang Bahadur that Bam Bahadur had not yet brought the Chautaras, the Queen wanted to start the inquiry into the murder immediately. But the King objected to it and pleaded that no investigation could be formal and legal, and therefore safe and complete, except in the presence of the Prime Minister. He then rode off to the Prime Minister's house, accompanied by Jang Bahadur's brother, Badri Narsingh.

After deliberating with Fatte Jang Shah for some time, the King sent the Prime Minister to the Kot along with his son, Khadga Bikram Shah, his two brothers, Sardar Birbahu Shah and Captain Rana Sher Shah, and some other members of the family, as well as with Bam Bahadur and Badri Narsingh. Meanwhile, the King also informed Captain Ottley, the officer-in-charge of the British Residency, of the murder of Gagan Singh but could not meet him as it was past midnight.[3] On his way back to the Kot, it is said, the King saw the gutter in the street crimson with blood and, on the advice of the bystanders, retired to the safety of his Hanuman Dhoka palace.

To return to the scene in the quadrangle of the Kot. Jang Bahadur, who was acting as the Queen's agent, met Fatte Jang and his party upon their arrival at the Kot, and suggested that if the plenipotentiary queen were to be pacified, both Kapardar Bir Kishor Gora Pande and General Abhiman Singh had to be executed in compliance with her command. Jang was also said to have made the suggestion that, in the event of their being executed in accordance with the Queen's wish, Fatte Jang would continue as Prime Minister and Jang Bahadur as Commander-in-Chief acting under his instructions. Fatte Jang, however, did not approve of this plan.

Prime Minister Chautara Fatte Jang Shah went to the northern side of the quadrangle of the Kot where General Abhiman Singh was sitting and told him everything he had learned from Jang Bahadur. This explains why General Abhiman Singh had alerted the officers of his regiments to have the soldiers load their rifles and keep them at the ready. Meanwhile Jang Bahadur, who had gone upstairs to see the Queen, must have seen from there that Abhiman's soldiers were loading their muskets with balls and cartridges and tipped the Queen off.

Suddenly, in a fit of passion, Queen Rajyalakshmi, sword in hand, descended the stairs and went to the large open space in front of the western section of the armoury building. Calling out to Chautara Prime Minister Fatte Jang Shah, Chautara Narahari Bikram Shah, General Abhiman Singh Rana Magar and Kazi Dalabhanjan Gora Pande, the Queen asked them to name the person who had killed Gagan Singh. When nobody answered her question and Fatte Jang counselled patience, the Queen, sword in hand, rushed at Bir Kishor Gora Pande. The Prime Minister and others prevented her from actually attacking Bir Kishor.

Thereafter, a heated exchange of words took place between the Queen and the courtiers. Fatte Jang pleaded that it was their duty to find out the guilty and not to punish the innocent. According to him,

General Abhiman was justified in refusing to carry out the Queen's orders. The Queen mounted the staircase in the dark and the three officers were slowly walking behind her when rifle shots rent the air and Chautara Fatte Jang Shah and Kazi Dalabhanjan Gora Pande dropped dead and General Abhiman Singh Rana was wounded. According to Oldfield, one of Jang's brothers might have given the order for the firing, thinking that either Jang or they themselves were endangered. It is also probable that Jang after his interview in the courtyard with Fatte and before rejoining the Queen, might have asked them to be specially watchful. General Abhiman Rana Magar, while rushing to the main gate of the Kot compound so that he might invoke the aid of soldiers under his command, exclaimed in a loud voice that it was Jang Bahadur who had killed Gagan Singh. But before General Abhiman could reach the gate, Krishna Bahadur Kanwar, one of Jang Bahadur's brothers, at one stroke of his sword, cut him in two and the general fell dead.

Prime Minister Fatte Jang's eldest son, Chautara Khadga Bikram, and Sardar Birbahu Shah, a younger brother of Fatte Jang, were also present on the spot with many other chautaras, kazis, sardars, captains and kumedans.[4] Upon learning of the death of his own father and seeing Krishna Bahadur cut down Abhiman Rana Magar, Khadga Bikram looked around for Subba Bishnu Das who always carried Fatte Jang's sword. As Bishnu Das could not be spotted, Khadga Bikram, before he was himself shot to death either by Jang or his youngest brother, Dhir Shamsher, used his orderly's small Khukri in wounding Bam Bahadur, Krishna Bahadur, and another person.

Meanwhile, a sword-battle broke out among the high officials assembled in the quadrangle. Most of the notables gathered there were taken unawares and found themselves unprepared to meet the situation. But Jang Bahadur had prepared himself for any eventuality by stationing his battalions at hand. In the flurry of action that preceded and followed the shooting of Prime Minister Fatte Jang Shah and others, reportedly by Jang Bahadur's men, members of the leading families were caught in a melee which lasted until Jang Bahadur's crack personal guards armed with double-barrel guns arrived upon the scene from outside.

Most of the officers were shot or cut down. Only a very few were saved by Jang Bahadur's brothers who held them by the hand and let them slip out of the quadrangle through a small doorway at the back. According to General Padma Jung, "the names of fifty-five of the slain, along with those of their slayers, have come down to us",[5] but the number must have been many times greater than this as the list does not mention the names of any but very important men.[6] Six thousand persons left the country as refugees in the aftermath of the event.[7]

Events Immediately Following the Kot Massacre

A conversation is said to have taken place between King Rajendra and Jang Bahadur on the morrow of the Kot Massacre. According to Captain Ottley's report to his Government, it went as follows: The King said to Jang, "By whose command have so many nobles been killed?" Jang's instant reply: By the command of the Queen to whom you yourself had made over sovereign power." The King then proceeded to the Queen's apartment and was told by the Queen that there would be greater bloodshed in the country if her son was not declared heir apparent.[8]

For the first eight or nine months immediately following the Kot Massacre, Jang Bahadur controlled the royal antagonists by playing them off against one another and also by seeking one's sanction for action against the other as it suited the occasion and his own immediate purpose. This was, in a way, the same game which King Rajendra himself had tried to play before the Kot Massacre with such disastrous consequences. However, Jang Bahadur played his cards with such consummate skill that he eventually succeeded not only in acquiring power for himself but also in paving the way for the concentration of power in his own family for upwards of a century.

After he was named Prime Minister on the very morrow of the Kot Massacre, Jang Bahadur made it known that he was authorized by all the three sovereigns, King Rajendra, Junior Queen Rajyalakshmi and Heir Apparent Surendra to announce his appointment. We have already seen how Jang had sought shelter behind the Queen's peremptory command to tell off the King when he demanded an explanation for the notorious bloodletting on the night of 14-15 September 1846. But we shall presently see how Jang pretended to seek the sanction of the King to take action against the Queen and expel her to Varanasi with her two sons. Later on, Jang also employed the official sanction of Heir Apparent Surendra, after having, of course, duly put him on the throne, to arrest King Rajendra and bring him to Kathmandu as a royal prisoner.

For some time in the wake of the Kot Massacre, Jang Bahadur was apparently acting by command of the plenipotentiary Queen on the plea that King Rajendra had already delegated his sovereign power of peremptory command to Queen Rajyalakshmi. Jang Bahadur also knew full well that it was dangerous to invite her wrath by challenging her or going against her will without fully consolidating his own position.

Queen Rajyalakshmi was a veritable termagant hell-bent on having her own way at all costs. The Queen was mad with rage at the King, at this time not so much because of her suspicion of the King's hand in bringing about the assassination of General Gagan Singh as because of the King's opposition to her proposal of replacing Prince Surendra by her own son, Prince Ranendra, as heir apparent.

She used her power to murder in cold blood a faithful servant of the King, Bhawani Singh, while he was seated on elephant-back behind King Rajendra.[9] The Queen must have done that deliberately to put pressure on the weak King so that he would accede to her proposal of making her own son heir apparent. Ever since King Rana Bahadur (1777-1799) and his Maithili Brahmin Queen, Kantavati, had successfully manipulated the court to put their favourite child, King Girvana Yuddha (1799-1816), on the throne by superseding the first-born, Prince Ranodyot Shah, in violation of the principle of primogeniture, the Queens of the Shah Kings had felt tempted to compete between themselves not only to be the favourite of their husbands but also to gain the throne for their own sons.

On 23 September 1846, Jang publicly announced that all those in hiding must leave the country within 10 days, threatening them with dire consequence should they fail to do so. The property of all the notables who died in the Kot Massacre or fled the country in its aftermath was confiscated.

Jang then took advantage of the differences between King Rajendra and Junior Queen Rajyalakshmi to fill the resulting vacancies with his own men at the *Pajani*, the routine annual renewal of service, held after the Kot Massacre.[10] Jang professed to act under the authority of the Queen, while at the same time retaining the positions of the King and the heir apparent intact for use when needed to counter her moves against the newly appointed Prime Minister himself. Jang's purpose in doing so was ultimately to gather all powers in his own hands.[11]

Meanwhile, Junior Queen Rajyalakshmi persisted in pressing Jang to comply with her demand that Heir Apparent Surendra and his brother, Prince Upendra, be put to death and her own eldest son, Ranendra, be declared heir apparent. Jang Bahadur at first made all kinds of excuses for delay in fulfilling the Queen's desire, but once he had taken the necessary precautions to consolidate his position, he openly defied the Queen's authority. He not only refused to carry out her command but also threatened to take appropriate action against her, should she persist in her murderous designs. Jang Bahadur reportedly wrote her a letter which contained a piece of stern admonition to Queen Rajyalakshmi herself:

> My duty to the state bids me to submit that, should Your Majesty ever repeat this order, you shall be prosecuted for attempt at murder by the law of the land.[12]

The Basnyat Conspiracy[13]

Queen Rajyalakshmi was not a person to take anyone's challenge meekly. She immediately hatched a plot to have Jang assassinated, but Jang proved to be more than a match for her. On the night of 31 October 1846, Jang was summoned to the palace where a regiment under the command of Captain Wazir Singh, General Gagan Singh's son, was waiting to destroy Jang Bahadur upon his arrival. On that fateful evening Kazi Birdhwaj Basnyat was, as planned, sent to call Jang Bahadur to the palace. As soon as the Kazi had delivered the Queen's message to the Prime Minister, he was shot at a signal from Jang.[14] A senior religious functionary, then Dharmadhikar, Vijaya Raj Pande and one of the Queen's maids in love with Jang who subsequently married her as Putali Maharani, had already revealed to Jang the secret of the Basnyat conspiracy.

After having got rid of the conspirator, Jang Bahadur went straight to King Rajendra. As a gesture of relinquishing his office, Jang placed his official headgear or *pagaree* at the King's feet and begged that either he be relieved of his duties or given full authority to deal with the enemies of the heir apparent. The King was said to have embraced Jang Bahadur and told him that the enemies of his beloved son were his enemies. Jang was given the power he asked for, and before it was night, 4 prominent Basnyats and 4 other officers as well as two subedars and two sepoys were executed and Queen Rajyalakshmi and her two sons moved to the house of Krishna Ram Pandit where they were kept under strict watch prior to their expulsion from the country.[15]

On 22 November 1846, Queen Rajyalakshmi and her two sons, Prince Ranendra and Prince Birendra, voluntarily accompanied by

King Rajendra himself, left Nepal for the Indian city of Varanasi.

In 1847, only a few months after his self-imposed exile in Varanasi, King Rajendra sought to regain power by plotting against Jang Bahadur's life. Several attempts were made on Jang's life. In 1847 Sanak Singh, one of the plotters, was killed by troops in Kathmandu and another plot hatched in complicity with Sher Mardan and Dambar Singh was also foiled.[16]

The Alau Incident

On 23 February 1847, King Rajendra set out on his return journey to Kathmandu from Varanasi, and arrived at Sugauli on 25 March 1847. A large number of political refugees and the discontented gathered at the royal camp on the border and persuaded the King to disregard repeated appeals to him from Crown Prince Surendra and Prince Upendra and Prime Minister Jang Bahadur to return to the capital. The refugees seem to have prevailed on him to proceed to Alau in Nepali territory and set up his camp in its vicinity. He assembled a small force of 1,500 to 1,600 riffraff and placed it under the command of Chautara Guru Prasad Shah, the late Prime Minister Fatte Jang Shah's brother, and Jagat Bam Pande, a grandson of Kazi Damodar Pande.

Jang had hesitantly expressed his desire to depose King Rajendra as early as April 1847 and the discovery of the plot on 12 May 1847 clinched the issue. Prince Surendra ascended the throne at 8 p.m. on 12 May 1847.[17]

Jang Bahadur had kept a strict watch over the King's activities from the beginning. The troops Jang sent under the command of his brother-in-law Sanak Singh Tandan had no trouble dealing with the armed men on the King's side, fifty or sixty of whom lost their lives in scattered encounters. Chautara Guru Prasad Shah and Jagat Bam Pande escaped to safety in Indian territory.[18] Rajendra Bikram himself was taken prisoner on 28 July 1847 and brought to Kathmandu in silver fetters and kept under strict surveillance.

It may be noted here that Jang Bahadur employed the traditional source of royal sanction against King Rajendra Bikram Shah and had him technically arrested by the command of his son, Surendra Bikram Shah, now on the throne. During the last century until the transfer of total power to the Rana family no act of state was legitimized except with some sort of royal sanction. When Kirtiman Singh Basnyat and Damodar Pande forced King Rana Bahadur Shah (1777-99) to go into exile in Varanasi in May 1800, they also acted under the sanction of royal authority said to have been given them by Rana Bahadur's infant son, Girvana Yuddha Bikram Shah (c. 1799-1816), who was then on the throne. However, unlike Rana Bahadur Shah who staged a successful comeback to power, Rajendra Bikram Shah (c. 1816-1847) failed miserably in his attempt to regain authority in Nepal.

Compensation for Confiscated Guthi and Birta Lands

Political considerations led Jang Bahadur to introduce new measures to regularize *Birta* and *Guthi* land entitlements. He sought to create a sense of security among members of the landed and religious establishments as a first step to consolidate his newly acquired authority. With this end in view, he made a gesture of compensating those who had had their *Birta* and *Guthi* lands confiscated in 1805-1806 under the policy of ex-King Rana Bahadur and Bhimsen Thapa.[19] It was not practicable to return their confiscated land to the original owners as it had already changed hands several times during the previous 30 years. Therefore, the original land holders were given new land acquired from the families of the notables who were the victims of the Kot Massacre.

If Jang thus found a means of endearing himself to the quiescent vested interests in land and in the religious establishment, he had also contrived a legal stratagem to acquire land for distribution among his supporters. The continuous possession of land for 16 years was set as a condition for the revalidation of one's title to the *Birta* and *Guthi* land. This enabled Jang to rescrutinize the titles to ownership of land acquired between July 1837, after the fall of Bhimsen, and January 1854, when the new law relating to the scrutiny of the *Birta* entitlements was codified.

The 'Hunting Expedition of 1848

Jang's 'hunting expedition' to the tarai in December 1848 with King Surendra Bikram Shah, numerous high ranking civil and military officers and about 7,000 troops seems to have caused a good deal of misgiving in the English East India Company's Government at the time. The timing and circumstances of the expedition were responsible for this: the fact that it took place immediately after the British had refused Nepal's military assistance for action in the Panjab for the second time aroused British suspicion. But the expedition ended in January 1849 when an epidemic broke out.[20]

Actually it had been a cover for dealing firmly with the activities of unreconciled elements who had been at large in the tarai in the wake of the Kot Massacre. In addition, it resulted in the institution of a system of land administration and settlement to ensure timely collection of land taxes. Jang set up an office for supervising the collection of land taxes, with a land-revenue office initially at Katarban (Rautahat) and finally at Makwanpur.[21]

Jang's Visit to Britain and France

After he had quickly consolidated his position inside the country, Jang turned his attention outwards. Highly pragmatic as he was, he soon reached the conclusion that British power had come to stay in India, and the best course of action for him and for his country would be to remain on friendly terms with the British. He therefore arranged for a formal visit to England in 1850 as an Ambassador, the representative of his sovereign. (It is worth noting here that Mathbar Singh Thapa had cancelled his own plan to visit Britain in 1835 on account of the British Government's reluctance to accept him as the Nepali King's Ambassador).

Jang's Entourage

Jang's entourage on this historic journey to Britain and more briefly to France consisted of fifteen men in all. The highest ranking members of the group were Jang's two younger brothers, Colonel Jagat Shamsher and Colonel Dhir Shamsher. Dhir seemed to have made a greater impression on Britons than his elder brother, Jagat. Both remained loyal to Jang till the end of his life and died after becoming Commanders-in-Chief in succession to each other in the early 1880s.

The third ranking member of the group was Jang's old crony Bada (Senior) Captain Rana Mehar Adhikari who had stood by Jang's side and protected his master and friend in many a bloody encounter. It was Rana Mehar who had slain Kazi Birdhwaj Basnyat at the critical moment of the Basnyat conspiracy in 1846.

The next in rank was Kazi Karbir Khatri who had acquired a good deal of diplomatic experience from his missions to Peking and India and was, according to Hodgson, "informed on Indian affairs, shrewd, prudent, and intelligent." In 1840 he was arrested by the British Indian authorities in Varanasi while on a mission to deliver secret letters to the Sikh ruler in Lahore. After the Kot Massacre, he was posted by Jang in Varanasi to keep watch on the activities of King Rajendra and Queen Rajyalakshmi. But he was suspected of misappropriating royal funds and was included in Jang's entourage only because Jang wanted to exercise surveillance over him. No wonder that Karbir upon his return to Nepal joined Jang's brothers in their conspiracy against Jang. Lawrence Oliphant described him as "poor old Kur Beer Khutrie (sic). . . a venerable looking man bigoted to an excess and full of disgust at the land of beefeaters."

Kazi Hem Dal Thapa was Jang's kinsman and confidant whose son was married to Jang's daughter. The other Kazi Dilli Singh Basnyat, was the officer in charge of the Government's agency for conducting operations for catching elephants.

Subba Siddhi Man Rajbhandari also enjoyed Jang's full confidence and was deputed to Varanasi along with Kazi Karbir Khatri and Kazi Hemdal Thapa to keep watch on Jang's behalf on King Rajendra and Queen Rajyalakshmi. He was an officer in the department of finance and was also placed in charge of administration of the tarai districts. He was appointed Colonel after he successfully conducted the survey of Naya Muluk (lit. new territory) comprising the westernmost tarai districts restored to Nepal by the British in return for assistance during the Indian mutiny. Even while in charge of the administration of the eastern tarai districts, Colonel Siddhi Man Rajbhandari later accompanied Jang Bahadur on his visit to Calcutta in 1871.

Among the junior officers, Lieutenant Lal Singh Khatri and Lieutenant Karbir Khatri deserve special mention. Both of them knew English. Lal Singh had once belonged to the contingent of Nepali guards attached to the British Residency and was taught English by Brian Hodgson at that time. His letter on the subject of the Nepal-Tibet border was published in the *Illustrated London News*. He was also trained as a surveyor and jointly with the British officers conducted a survey of Nepal's border with the British Indian districts of Purnea and Saran in Bihar. He was appointed the Nepali Government's agent in Calcutta in 1859 with the title of Lieutenant-Colonel. Lieutenant Karbir Khatri might be the same person who had asked Resident Henry Lawrence the meaning of the word 'prime minister' just two months before the political assassination of General Mathbar Singh Thapa, to whom the King and the Queen had sought to give a false sense of security by bestowing on him all kinds of titles including that of Prime Minister for life.

Khardar Prithvidhar Padhya might have been a cook with the title of a junior civilian official and Subedar Dalamardan Thapa might have been Jang's personal attendant or orderly with the title of a non-commissioned military officer. The remaining two members of Jang's entourage were the traditional type physician or Vaidya, Chakra Pani, and the artist, Bhajuman, some of whose paintings are prized to this day.

Problems with British Customs Authorities

As soon as Jang Bahadur arrived in Southampton on 25 May 1850, he had trouble with the local customs authorities who insisted on opening his baggage. Jang felt so insulted that he threatened to take the next steamer back to Alexandria if they would not clear his baggage unopened. He had to spend a day or two in the Peninsular Shipping Company's Southampton offices before the local customs authorities obtained instructions from London to clear his baggage unchecked.

The incident shows that Jang was very sensitive to the question of the honour of his country and of his own prestige as its Ambassador and would not compromise under any circumstances. On relatively unimportant matters, however, he did not mind yielding at times even to the reprimands of Captain Orfeur Cavenagh, the British officer in attendance on him.

Contact with British Officials

Jang Bahadur had to wait for about three weeks before he could have an audience with Queen Victoria because of her accouchement. Meanwhile he met Sir John Hobhouse, President of the Board of Control for Indian Affairs, Captain Shepherd, Chairman of the Court of Directors of the East India Company, other directors and also the Duke of Wellington, for whom Jang had the highest admiration as the man who had defeated the great Napoleon. The two military leaders were said to have become fond of each other.

Examples of Jang's Diplomacy

Jang Bahadur's reply to the toast proposed to his sovereign and himself at the banquet given by the Court of Directors of the East India Company on 15 June 1850 at the London Tavern is a frank and forthright expression of his appraisal of the power of the British Government at the time. According to Cavenagh's translation of Jang Bahadur's speech as reported in the *Atlas for India* of 24 June 1850, Jang "was convinced that the destiny of the English was great, more specially since he had witnessed the conquests achieved in India during the reign of her present Majesty, the wisdom of her senators and the bravery of her soldiers, which dazzled the eyes of mankind. Seeing the wisdom of this country and knowing its victories, it had given him great satisfaction to visit a land and see a queen who ruled over so wise and so gallant a nation."

Jang also took the opportunity to pledge his support to the British in future by assuring his audience that "his army, his munitions of war, and his own life would be devoted hereafter to the service of the great British nation." His reply seemed to produce the desired effect, as the editorial in *The Times* of 21 June 1850 reported that "his speech demonstrated a sincere anxiety to preserve concord between the two states by that cordial alliance of sentiment and strength which he promised for his sovereign and himself."

The British speeches were also full of rhetoric and voiced similar sentiments of friendship and understanding between the two countries. But the British speakers did not fail to take notice of Nepal's position between India and China. Sir John Hobhouse expressed his belief that Nepal would side with his country in the event of a war between Britain and China. Lord Brougham told the distinguished Nepali visitor that he could rest assured that Britain would never take even an inch of Nepali territory.

Confusion about Jang's Ambassadorial Status

It seemed as though the British Government itself was unsure what Jang Bahadur's status as an Ambassador of the King of Nepal ought to entail. At this time no emissaries from Indian states, not even from the Emperor in Delhi, were recognized by the British as full-fledged ambassadors. But Jang Bahadur was officially recognized as an Ambassador and had to be treated as such. This seemed to present a problem to the British Government, which they tried to solve in an improvised manner.

Jang Bahadur was not presented to Queen Victoria by the British

Foreign Secretary, Lord Palmerston, as a foreign Ambassador would have normally been. Although even a usually well-informed newspaper such as *The Times* had reported on 3 June 1850 that Lord Palmerston would undertake the task in due course of time, yet it was Sir John Hobhouse, another member of the cabinet and President of the Board of Control for Indian Affairs, who actually presented Jang Bahadur to the Queen on 19 June 1850. The European press and public, however, always took Jang Bahadur in the same light as they would look at the Ambassadors of such oriental countries as Turkey and Persia.

The Ceremony of a Drawing Room

If the Nepali visitors had reasons to be careful about their official reception, appearances and utterances in public, the English press and public also seemed to be concerned in their own way about making the right kind of impression upon the Nepali visitors. The following comment of *The Times* of 21 June 1850 on the casual manner in which the British Prime Minister, Lord John Russell, was dressed on the occasion when Jang Bahadur was received by Queen Victoria on 19 June 1850 at the ceremony of a drawing room' bears testimony to the above fact: "The court of a constitutional monarchy would, perhaps be hardly more intelligible to an Oriental Prince than Hyde Park review to the Autocrat of all the Russians. Except by a powerful effort of the imagination certain of the household uniform can hardly be thought to communicate an idea of dignity or grace, nor can we conclude that his Excellency's impression of the grandeur of England was likely to be heightened by the holiday costume of the Prime Minister." What a striking contrast there must have been between the casual holiday clothes of the British Prime Minister and the ornate glittering dress of the distinguished Nepali guest and other members of his entourage!

Press Opinion of Jang and his Entourage

However, thanks to its correspondents in India the British press seemed to be fully informed of Jang Bahadur's political background and position in his own country. After expressing the fear that the reference to Jang Bahadur's bloodstained career might have made him appear to readers in an unfavourable light, the author of the letter from Calcutta which was published in *The Times* of 10 August 1850 states his opinion of Jang's standing in his own country in these words:

> ... his manners, his ability, his tact and energy have alike confirmed him in the goodwill of the Nepalese army and people; and I look upon his visit to England as one of the many gradual but sure measures and steps by which the Almighty is paving Asia with civilization. His power as minister is unbounded (over life and death), and is, indeed, greater than that of his sovereign, and I suspect that like Macbeth, "he shall be King hereafter".

Except for its foreboding about Jang Bahadur being the King in future like Macbeth, which did not of course come true literally, this assessment of Jang's position in his country was quite valid.

Jang Bahadur and his brothers, dressed in magnificent costumes of Chinese silk and brocade embroidered with threads of gold and silver, and sporting their picturesque headgear inlaid with glittering gems and precious stones and peaked with the white bird of paradise plumes, must have indeed proved a rare and romantic sight to the general public in England and France. The press coverage as a rule overemphasized the exotic and the unfamiliar aspects of the appearance of the Nepali visitors. This was what *The Atlas* of 24 July 1850 wrote after the Nepali visitors had been in England for a couple of months:

> They came, they were seen and forthwith they conquered. To look at the lustre of their retinue, to count the diamonds which sparkled in their brown skins, to mark the gemmed turbans, the jewelled aigrets, the white bird of Paradise plumes -- who would not have been forgiven for believing that the whole party might be an incarnation from 'the Arabian night' whisked thither from Baghdad or a city of Cathay, attended by the fiery Pari Banou, with Solomon's seal in the carpet bags and journeying with passports covered with hieroglyphics and stars, the genuine autographs of the King of Genii?

Meetings with Queen Victoria

Jang was formally presented to the Queen for the first time on 19 June. After this, Jang met the Queen three times before his departure from Britain. On 22 June he was invited to the christening party for her son, Prince Albert, and it was on that occasion that he was also introduced to Queen Victoria's son-in-law, Crown Prince Kaiser Wilhelm of Germany. Jang had a chance to see the Queen once again when he was invited to attend the state ball on 26 June 1850.

The Lion of the London Social Season

Jang seemed to enjoy the company of ladies at the ball as he had done previously at a party given by Viscount and Viscountess Palmerston and also at Her Majesty's Theatre to which the Nepali visitors were invited by its manager, Benjamin Lumley. Jang's remark on the female artistes of Her Majesty's Theatre may be cited as an example of his habitually flattering compliments to English ladies: "There are singers and dancers in my own country, but these are spirits and angels." Although Jang did not fail to impress the polite company of high society ladies with his wit and courtesy, which never seemed to desert him, he did not quite approve of the Queen's dancing with her subordinates.

Jang's dress and headgear in themselves proved a mighty attraction for the ladies who were no less interested in the stirring stories of his adventures and escapades. Although language proved to be a barrier to effective communication between Jang and these ladies, he did not fail to cast his charm on them. On all accounts, Jang Bahadur had become the lion of the London social season in 1850.

Highly exaggerated and false reports of Jang's wealth and riches were in circulation. According to one report, perhaps based on just hearsay, Jang was said to have paid one hundred and fifty thousand pounds for spending a night with London's most prominent prostitute of the time, Laura Bell; but India Office records indicate the total sum of the English money Jang had available during his trip was just thirty thousand pounds sterling. Jang's generous gifts to some of the lady artistes and performers and the keen personal interest shown by him in meeting them might have provided additional grounds for romanticized accounts in the newspapers.

The Indian News of 1 August 1850 wrote thus about the manner in which the Nepali visitors were received by London society and about the impression the guests from Nepal had left on it:

> Our Nepali guests have abundantly partaken of the national hospitality, they have been lionised in private and public, armies have been paraded before them and royalty itself has been their *cicerone*.[22] No evening party having the slightest pretension to the aristocracy of either rank, wealth or talent is held to be complete without them. And this as it should be. They visited our shores

dona ferentes,[23] they have spent their money among us with a liberality amounting to profusion, and they have received our hospitalities with a full appreciation of the spirit in which they have been offered.

Visit to Mining and Manufacturing Districts

The British Government decided to show the Nepali visitors some mining and manufacturing districts of the country as well as the shipyards and warships in which Jang Bahadur had shown special interest. The Nepali party was taken to Plymouth, where they saw shipbuilding at the Devonport Dockyard, and also to Birmingham and Edinburgh by train. The Nepalis were not a little thrilled to find that this new mode of transportation greatly reduced distance with its great speed.

This tour was organized to create a favourable impression of Britain's industrial strength and naval might upon the minds of the Nepali visitors specially in view of Jang's insistence on pursuing his plan to visit France. After Jang returned to London from his tour of Scotland, he took his leave of Queen Victoria in his final audience with her on 14 August. After having spent 87 days in the United Kingdom, he left for France on 20 August 1850.

Visit to France

Jang Bahadur arrived in Paris with his party on 21 August 1850 and had to wait till 30 August before he could be received by the French President, Prince Louis Napoleon, who was away on a tour of the provinces.

The Nepali visitors, even while in France, seemed to be under the strict surveillance of the British officers, Captain Cavenagh and Captain James. They must have purposely put up Jang and his party at the Hotel Sinet on Rue Faubourg Saint Honore since it was near the British Embassy. Jang Bahadur understandably wanted to avoid giving the French the impression that he was a British vassal, but the British officers attached to his entourage saw to it that he could not maintain communication with the French authorities except through the British.

A Problem with Protocol

As soon as Jang arrived in France, there was a protocol hitch. Should

Jang call on the British Ambassador to France, Lord Normanby, first, or should the Briton make the first call? Jang Bahadur was not just an Ambassador but the Prime Minister of his country, but Cavenagh insisted that as Jang Bahadur was newly arrived in France, it was obligatory on him to call on the British Ambassador first. Jang Bahadur, on the other hand, felt that it was up to Lord Normanby to call on him first because of his prime ministership. The problem was resolved when Jang Bahadur called on Lord Normanby first after the latter had offered to make the first call himself.

Attempts to make Direct Contact with the French Government

When Jang Bahadur sought to have direct contact with the French Government independently of the British embassy or Captain Cavenagh, the French authorities wanted him to come through the British embassy. Apart from their consideration for British feelings, the French probably did not think it proper to deal directly with the Nepali visitors since Nepal and France did not have direct diplomatic relations with each other.

Jang Bahadur was, however, given a good deal of diplomatic attention when he was in Paris. The French Minister for Foreign Affairs paid a visit to Jang Bahadur, and General Nicolas Changarnier in command of the national Guard and his suite also called on him, and so did the Turkish Ambassador to France.

Jang Bahadur may have actually feigned illness to prolong his stay in France, which was originally planned to be only a week but lasted 48 days. He managed to see all that was worth seeing in Paris, he visited other places of interest in the immediate neighbourhood such as Compiegne, Fontainebleau, Versailles, and Saint Cloud, and he travelled south to Marseilles for four days before sailing for Alexandria.

Meeting with the French President

Jang Bahadur was very much interested in meeting Prince Louis Napoleon primarily because he was the nephew of Napoleon Bonaparte, and Jang greatly admired the great emperor's military career and heroic deeds. His appreciation of Napoleon perhaps derived from the fact that Napoleon had also, like himself, risen from a humble position in the army to be the Emperor of France. Expressing his anxiety to see Louis Napoleon, Jang was reported to have said to a correspondent, " . . . my nation and myself have a great veneration for the name of the Emperor."

M. Bacchiochi, aide-de-camp to the President, escorted Jang Bahadur in the presidential carriage to the Elysee Palace where he was received by Louis Napoleon on 30 August 1850. Jang held a long conversation with the President with Captains Cavenagh and James acting as interpreters. When the President suggested that French dress was less impressive and gorgeous than Nepali dress, Jang replied with his usual tact and resourcefulness in this manner: "It is true that in our country they serve to distinguish the different ranks and classes from one another. But if France is not conspicuous for the splendour of her dress, she is the foremost nation of the world through the splendour of her science, the prestige of her civilization and the excellent organization of her administration and government."

According to *La Constitutionel* of 1 September 1850, which reported this conversation, one of the interpreters interrupted the Prime Minister's brilliant reply and pointed out that France was a republic. Cavenagh complained to a French official about this report and denied that either he or Captain James had done anything of the kind.

Jang embarrassed his host, the President himself, by asking to see a parade of 100,000 soldiers. The exigencies of internal politics made it most unwise to amass such a large number of troops in one place and only a few thousand troops were paraded before Jang Bahadur at Sartary on 24 September 1850.

Jang paid a visit to the tomb of Emperor Napoleon Bonarparte as a mark of respect to his military prowess and was not a little delighted to receive as a gift from Prince Louis Napoleon the great Napoleon's own sword, which is still preserved in the Kathmandu museum.

An Odd Incident in the French Academy

French academicians, while seeking to impress their guest from Nepal with their familiarity with oriental languages and culture, made a *faux pas* by pronouncing his name in an odd and peculiar manner. As Jang entered the hall, the only Persian expert in the Academy apparently pronounced Jang's name as 'Bahag-Thaumor' and the rest of the members of the audience responded to him by repeating 'Braquemor, Blaganor'. Jang did not understand what was going on and at first was so shocked and insulted that he almost left immediately without attending the reception. But after the permanent secretary of the Academy explained to him that it was meant as a gesture of respect and goodwill towards him, Jang stayed on and had a conversation with the academicians. (It may have happened that the Persian scholar pronounced the name correctly but journalists and other members of the Academy misheard it and responded to it in an awkward manner.)

French Press Not Informed about the Nepali Visitors

The French press seemed to be unaware of the real national and religious identity of the Nepali visitors who were sometimes referred to as Indians, sometimes as Hindus and at other times as Muslim Nawabs. It carried exaggerated reports about the munificence and wealth of Jang Bahadur and his party. Soon after his arrival in France, Jang and other members of his entourage were overwhelmed by invitations from ladies of high society to all kinds of parties; at first the Nepali guests politely declined them on the ground of headache or some other minor illness, but later they became sociable.

Fondness for the French Ballet

Jang apparently took a real fancy to the French ballet and started going to the Opera whenever he had a chance. He was so much impressed by the performance of the celebrated French ballerina Mme Fanny Cerito in 'Le Violon du Diable' that he sent for her after the performance was over and presented her with a pair of diamond bracelets which he was wearing himself.

Jang Bahadur seemed to win the heart of fashionable Parisian society by making this generous gesture. After this, Jang Bahadur went to see "Stella" and several other performances at the Opera. No matter whether he was in the balcony or the wings, he attracted so much notice that all the glinting opera glasses moved alternately from the dancer to the distinguished Nepali visitor and back again.

Jang very much wanted to see a ballet in rehearsal. No sooner had M. Nestor Roqueplan, the director of the Opera, heard it than he arranged for the Nepali visitors to see a full-dress rehearsal commanded by the ballet-master M. Saint-Leon like a commander-in-chief, with the best pupils in front. Two acts of L'Enfant Prodigue' were performed for the entertainment and pleasure of the Nepali guests.

After the performance was over, Jang Bahadur paid a moving

tribute to the participants at the rehearsal. This was what he had said to them, according to the *L'Evenement* of 26 September 1850.

> I shall be leaving soon, but I shall take to my own country the memory of everything I have seen at the greatest theatre in the world. My thoughts will often leave the court of Nepal to return to you and I shall repeat there what I am fortunate enough to be able to say to you today. *Never have I seen such grace, such talent and above all, such youth and beauty* (italics supplied). I should be glad if you too, could sometimes think of the stranger you welcomed so warmly. However, as I cannot give each of you individually something to remember me by, I am asking the director to act as an intermediary between me and his gracious company.

After this he gave one hundred gold sovereign (equivalent to 2,500 francs) to the director for distribution among the performers.

Lola Montez

During his stay in France, Jang also found a female companion in Mm Marie Cibert whose stage name was 'Lola Montez'. She was different from other women Jang Bahadur might have met in Europe because she spoke the Hindustani language in which Jang could hold a direct conversation with her. To Jang, who had been completely starved of association with women with whom he could talk without interpreters, 'Lola Montez' must have proved to be a rare find. She had grown up in India and had also gone back there as the wife of a military officer who was her first husband. She had subsequently married another man. Meanwhile, she had started a career as a dancer and had also had an affair with King Ludwig of Bavaria, who had made her the Countess of Lansfeld. No wonder that a woman with such a background had enticed Jang Bahadur as well. In a moment of weakness Jang Bahadur might have promised to take her to India and Nepal, but he found a handy excuse for not actually being able to do so: he said the British officers cited the clause of the Anglo-Nepal treaty of 1815 which required Nepal to obtain the prior consent of the British Government in order to employ any European in its service. All that 'Lola Montez' received from Jang was a gown of gold as a farewell present.

Jang's Personal Traits and Temperament

When it came to dealing with officials at an equal or lesser level, Jang Bahadur was always careful about retaining his dignity. Although he was almost obsequious in paying his respects to the Queen of Great Britain and to the President of France, when he was presented to them, Jang never lost his wit and composure in their presence. He was, as always, full of aplomb and savoir-faire. Once when Queen Victoria was said to have asked Jang in the midst of an opera as to what had made him applaud even when he did not understand what was being sung, Jang's instant reply was: "Nor do I understand what the nightingales sing."

Because of Hindu caste dietary restrictions, Jang would not eat at official banquets. When Queen Victoria once asked him at a banquet as to why he was not eating anything, Jang was said to have replied at once that it was not the custom in his country to eat in the presence of one's superior.

Jang could, however, be quick-tempered and impulsive at times. This explains his exchange of blows with an ordinary tradesman in his hotel in Paris on 4 October 1850, the day on which he departed for Marseilles. Jang had lost his temper on discovering that his party was cheated by the tradesman in a particular business transaction. When the shopkeeper threatened to prevent the Prime Minister's party from leaving the hotel without settling his bills, Jang struck the tradesman, who hit back. This created a highly embarrassing situation for all concerned, and it was with some difficulty that his British companion managed to get Jang into his carriage and safely away.

Jang was at times quite capable of telling people what they wanted to hear. If Jang had complained to the British captain, Cavenagh, at Versailles about the loose formation and indiscipline of the French army, he was, at the same time, according to the *La Constitutionel* of 10 October 1850, full of praises to the French--themselves for the fine quality of their army, its speed of manoeuvre and the precision of its drill.

However, this did not mean that Jang Bahadur was not capable of a balanced judgement on more serious matters. When a newspaper correspondent asked Jang's opinion of the French and the English as he had found them in the course of his visit, Jang's reply was both perceptive and diplomatic. This was what he was reported to have told *La Constitutionel*:

I have a high opinion of the English but if I had to make my home in Europe I would come to live among the French. I prefer their warmth and amiability to the formality natural to the English.

Desire to Stay in Europe

It was only in the fitness of things that life in Europe should have held a great attraction for Jang Bahadur, who was hardly 32 years old and always in search of new thrills and challenges. While in England, Jang mentioned to Cavenagh that he would have lived there as a residential ambassador if he had only had the financial means to do so. Cavenagh, as expected, told Jang that his presence was badly needed in his own country at that time. Some other Europeans and at least one American interpreted Jang's desire to be away from his own country as a concrete manifestation of his longing for personal safety and security in Europe in preference to the grim prospects of bloodshed, violence and revenge at home.

Jang once even seriously suggested to his brothers and other members of his entourage in France that all of them should return home and let Jang Bahadur live in Europe on his own for a few years. When they opposed his suggestion, Jang was so angry with them for a few days that he did not permit them to accompany him to the Opera. Later, his brothers had to go to the extent of seeking Cavenagh's help in persuading Jang to go back to Nepal along with the rest of the party.

European Curiosity about the Personal Habits of the Nepali Visitors

Let us now turn to the lighter aspects of Jang's visit in Europe. The Nepali visitors were under the constant watch of the press and public wherever they went in Great Britain and France. Personal habits of the Nepalis, particularly their practice of bathing in the open with a loin cloth tied with a string round their waist, attracted public notice and comments in the newspapers. So, too, did the Nepalis' refusal to eat cooked food of any kind at the functions they were invited to or to eat at the same table with any Europeans. After joining the others at the table for a few minutes before dinner was served, the Nepali guests would then withdraw to a separate room to partake all by themselves of different kinds of fruits especially provided for them and rejoin other guests only after they had finished eating their dinner.

Outside of London, wherever the Nepalis had to put up at a private home as somebody's guests or in a hotel, they insisted on making their own separate arrangements for cooking, because their caste rules did not permit them to eat cooked food touched by Europeans or to have drinks including water served by them. The Nepalis wanted to make sure that even milk for their use was not touched by Europeans and therefore they had a cow brought to their place of residence every morning so that it could be milked by the Nepali servants accompanying the party. When the French press noticed that a cow was being taken everyday to where the Nepalis were staying, the newspapers made an altogether wrong guess that the cattle must have been taken there to be killed for meat. Little did they seem to realize that there was such a strong religious taboo on beef-eating among the Nepalis that the punishment for killing a cow in Nepal itself was death.

Meat-eating Leads to Attempted Revolt

The Nepalis had a problem finding the kind of meat they could eat. They had had difficulty in this regard even while aboard the ship on their way to England. They seem to have, however, tried to solve their problem by eating meat of the long tailed sheep, which they were not as a rule supposed to eat. But one of the members of Jang's entourage, Kazi Karbir Khatri, who was on a vegetarian diet at the time, prevented them from doing so during the voyage. After arrival in Britain they may well have eaten the forbidden meat, since there is a popular story in Nepal that after their return to Nepal Karbir Khatri accused them of doing this. Whether in fact the accusation concerned this particular taboo, Karbir certainly did allege that his companions had violated caste rules while in Europe. This actually triggered off an unsuccessful conspiracy joined by Kazi Karbir Khatri and some of Jang's own brothers to remove him from office.

As soon as Jang Bahadur returned to Kathmandu from his journey to Europe, he had to deal with a conspiracy to remove him from power. In February-March 1851 Jang Bahadur's third brother Badri Narsingh, who was left in charge of the administration along with Bam Bahadur, the officiating Prime Minister during Jang's absence in Europe, was expelled to Chunar in India along with the King's second brother, Prince Upendra and Jaya Bahadur. Badri Narsingh was charged with plotting Jang's assassination and usurping the prime ministership by putting the King's brother on the throne. Reportedly both of Jang's brothers, Bam Bahadur and Badri Narsingh, were equally involved in the plot but Bam Bahadur lost his nerve at the last minute and confessed everything to Maharaj Jang to save his skin. It was also alleged that the clique had been responsible for spreading malicious rumours that Jang Bahadur had lost his caste by crossing the ocean. However, prior to his return to Nepal, Jang Bahadur had taken the precaution of making a pilgrimage to Rameshwaram at the tip of the Indian peninsula, where he underwent a religious ceremony of purification. In 1852, there was another conspiracy by Bhotu Singh Basnyat to kill Jang Bahadur and his brothers, and this also failed.

Successful Trip

Despite the difference not only in habits of food and dress, but also in language, religion and culture, and despite their complete lack of previous exposure to European life and surroundings, manners and speech, Jang and his party seemed to acquit themselves quite creditably on the whole in their private as well as public dealings with the Europeans.

Importance of Jang Bahadur's Visit to Europe

From the viewpoint of the apparently never-ending discussion on how free Nepal was in the different periods of its history or whether at this time or that time Nepal was regarded as more independent or less independent by the great powers of the day, Jang Bahadur's visit to Europe has an importance of its own. Neither General Mathbar Singh Thapa before Jang, nor Maharaja-cum-Prime Minister Chandra Shamsher after him, was able to visit Great Britain in the official capacity of the Ambassador of his King and country as Jang did. General Mathbar Singh Thapa had actually cancelled his proposed visit to England in 1835 precisely because the British Government was unwilling to treat him as the Ambassador of his country. After Jang, Maharaja Bir Shamsher gave up the idea of visiting England more or less for the same reasons, and when Maharaja Chandra Shamsher visited England in 1908, the British Government avoided the situation of having to recognize him as an ambassador of an independent country by extending to him the same kind of welcome as Britain would offer one of the ruling princes or Maharajas of the 'A' class Indian native states. Chandra's only special treatment was to be received with a 19- rather than a 17-gun salute.

For yet another reason Jang Bahadur's journey to Europe proved to be of special interest not only to the European countries but also to Nepal's own immediate neighbours. No other prince or potentate from this part of the world had, before Jang Bahadur, ventured to acquire the religious stigma of crossing the ocean even for the very good reason of finding out the real nature and strength of the European power which had already ended the independent political existence of most states in the South Asian region. It was true that Raja Rammohan Roy and Dwarka Nath Tagore from Bengal in India had visited Europe previously, but neither of them had enjoyed recognition as an official ambassador in the host country.

Thus Jang Bahadur's visit to Britain and France provided for the first time an opportunity for face-to-face contact in the midst of European surroundings between the governing elites of two European countries and those of Nepal. The excerpts from English and French news coverage on Jang Bahadur's visit to Europe, which are reproduced above, cast an interesting sidelight on various aspects of the direct encounter at both official and unofficial levels between two sets of governing elites with very different cultural backgrounds.

Again, Jang Bahadur's journey to Britain and France, even if we are to ignore its immediate impact on contemporary public opinion in both Europe and South Asia, proved to be an event of immense historical significance for Nepal itself with enduring consequences for policy initiatives and decisions in future on both internal and external issues critically important to the state. Friendship with Britain, or rather with the British power in India, henceforth became the cornerstone of Nepal's foreign policy, while Nepal at the same time persisted in continuing its traditional policy of isolation and exclusion of foreigners and of maintaining minimal contact with them at the official level only. Jang Bahadur's visit to Europe set the pattern for this policy which was rigidly and conscientiously followed by Jang and his successors for a century with real success in achieving the desired objective. This objective of course had been the maintenance of the independence and territorial integrity of Nepal in the face of the fierce wind of change that was blowing strongly across the entire region and had brought very nearly all of the Indian subcontinent under foreign domination.

It was the self-same policy that made Nepal aid the British in the 1857 Indian Mutiny and the 1903 Younghusband expedition to Tibet, and also to fight on the British side in the first and the second world wars. These concrete policy measures adopted by Nepal in the past may not be in consonance with the present-day spirit of Nepali nationalism, but the fact remains that if Nepal had not resorted to such a course of action at the time, it might not have been able to retain intact its independence and territorial integrity. In essence, it was their unqualified support of Britain in its foreign policy that ensured a relatively wide measure of freedom for Nepal's governing elite in the management of the internal affairs of the country during the days of the British raj.

After Jang's return from Britain, Nepal was convinced of the overwhelming nature of British power, as is clear from what Jang is reported to have told Captain Cavenagh, the British officer in attendance of Jang Bahadur, during his visit in Europe:

> A cat would fly at an elephant if it were forced into a corner, but it must be a very small corner into which the Nepalese would be forced before they would fly at the British or cease to be their faithful ally.[24]

Jang Bahadur also took a few concrete steps to draw Nepal closer to Britain. Since 24 May 1850, a salute of 21 guns was fired in Kathmandu as a gesture of rejoicing on the occasion of the British sovereign's birthday. The Duke of Wellington, whom Jang had met in London, had caught the Nepali leader's imagination as the man who had defeated the great Napoleon at Waterloo. When the Duke passed away, a gun salute of 83 minutes was given on 5 November 1852.

Jang's visit to Europe also had its effect on Nepal's domestic policy. The visit must certainly have inspired Jang Bahadur to propound the legal code called *Mulki Ain* in January 1854, with the help of a body of counsellors known as Kaushal, for he had been impressed by the concept of the rule of law he had become familiar with in Europe. The preamble to the 1854 Legal Code contains the King's categorical statement: "We have given the *hukum* (peremptory command) that all–from us to subjects–shall abide by this law." At least in theory, the code was regarded as equally binding on the King, members of the royal family, the Prime Minister and the rest of the people–a standard which Nepal is still endeavouring to approximate in practice.

Following Jang's return from Europe mutilation was abolished and so was capital punishment except for a certain category of offences. Jang also partially abolished *Sati*, the practice of widows burning themselves with the bodies of their dead husbands.

Significant as were these legal and social consequences of the visit, the exposure of Jang and his party to modern science and technology was of even greater importance. The strength of the impact made can be gauged from many passages of the *Belait-yatra*, an account in Nepali of Jang's visit to Europe written by one of the members of his entourage.

Matrimonial Alliance with the Royal Family

Now, to turn to domestic matters, Jang Bahadur sought to raise the social status of his family in the hope that if he and his family were held in greater esteem in Nepal and India, this would lend force to his pretensions to royal authority. On 5 May 1848, Jang had already received a *Lal Mohar*, a royal edict bearing the Red Seal, which entitled him and his brothers and descendants to call themselves Ranas.[25] The social status of Kanwars, who had thus been given the more distinguished title and sub-caste of Rana, became greatly enhanced compared to that of other Nepali Chhetri families. Even more important, the Ranas now found themselves in a position to contract matrimonial alliances with the Shah dynasty of Nepal and with Indian Rajput families, who would normally have disdained relations with mere Kanwar Chhetris.

The royal edict of 5 May 1849 had, however, expressly barred Jang Bahadur and his descendants from entering into matrimonial alliances with those Rajput families in the hills and the tarai, who had such relations with the royal family. But after a few years, Jang Bahadur himself married into the family of the King's collaterals, some of whose members had turned against Jang after the Kot Massacre. Fatte Jang Shah's sister, Hiranyagarbha Kumari Devi, was married to Jang Bahadur in 1853. In 1854, his eldest son, General Jagat Jang, married King Surendra's second daughter.[26] In 1856, Jang gave his daughter, Tara Kumari, in marriage to the heir apparent, Trailokya Bikram Shah, and in 1860, the heir apparent also married Lalit Rajyalakshmi, Jang's daughter by Hiranyagarbha Kumari Devi,[27] who became the mother of King Prithvi Bir Bikram Shah Dev (1818-1911). Jang thus strengthened his position and that of his family through matrimonial alliances with the royal family.

War with Tibet

Jang Bahadur's time was not entirely taken up with these domestic matters. Nepal's quinquennial "tributary" mission of 1852-54 to Peking returned to Kathmandu belatedly because it was harassed by the Tibetan authorities for unauthorized possession of opium. Jang Bahadur made this harassment an excuse to go to war against Tibet. He took advantage of Chinese preoccupation with the T'aiping Rebellion (1850-1864) and British involvement in the Crimean War of 1854, to attack Tibet with a view to acquiring territorial and commercial advantages from it.

In the fall of 1854, an ultimatum was served on Tibet. It stated that if a large sum of money was not paid by Tibet for the wrongs done to Nepal in the past, and if the Nepali residents in Tibet were not guaranteed justice in future, Tibet(Xizang) would be invaded and the border area would be annexed by Nepal in the following spring. When Tibet sent its representatives to Kathmandu to discuss the Nepali demands, the Government of Nepal insisted on payment of ten million rupees by Tibet and cession of the Kerung and Kuti passes to Nepal.

Tibet did not accept these demands, and Nepal's army marched north. The first phase of the war, in 1855, was inconclusive. Nepali troops occupied the fortress of Jhunga and the passes of Kuti and Kerung with considerable difficulty. In July 1855, a Chinese official paid a visit to Kathmandu to take up negotiations on behalf of Tibet. But upon the breakdown of negotiations as a result of Jang Bahadur's insistence on Tibet's compliance with his original demands, hostilities were resumed. Tibet temporarily succeeded in recovering the lost territory, but Nepal regained it in due course, and a treaty of ten articles was signed on 24 March 1856, putting an end to the war.

Indeed, until 1952 this agreement regulated the commercial relations between the two countries in a way that resembled the old relations between China and Russia via *Kiakhta*. Fairs would be held every spring at Kuti and Kerung, where Tibetans could come to exchange, under official control, tea and salt for the merchandise of Nepal. In fact Nepal, by virtue of its traditional rights, held in Lhasa a grant administered by a Nepali agent under the protection of a Nepali army post. The Tibetan Government pledged to pay Nepal an annual tribute of ten thousand rupees and it was further provided that of the children born of marriages between Nepalis and Tibetans, the sons would have Nepali citizenship and the daughters would be Tibetan. Legal disputes in which Nepalis were involved would be decided only in the presence of the Nepali representative in Lhasa.[28]

The Lal Panja (Red Palm Print) of 1856

Jang Bahadur temporarily resigned the prime ministership on 1 August 1856, in favour of his brother, Bam Bahadur (August 1856 to May 1857), but this was only a step towards his becoming even more powerful. Not long after his resignation, Jang Bahadur turned down the offer of kingship made to him in a public ceremony conducted by Vijaya Raj Pande, a Brahmin functionary who, after the Kot Massacre, had risen from the position of a *Dharmadhikar* to that of Royal preceptor.[29]

During the period of his voluntary retirement from office, Jang Bahadur not only received the title of Maharaj from King Surendra and the sovereignty of two districts, Kaski and Lamjung, but also acquired power over the King himself through an edict bearing the King's red seal and dated 6 August 1856. The document stated:

I am pleased with you for the following reasons:

1. You secured to me the throne of Nepal by killing those persons who were aiding the efforts of the Junior Queen of Rajendra Bikram Shah (who had earlier given her sovereign powers) to put her own son on the throne, and deprive me of my rights;
2. You promoted friendship with the Queen of England by paying a visit to that country;
3. You won the war with Tibet, and made it pay an annual tribute to Nepal in cash;
4. You treated with respect and kindness my father, ex-king Rajendra Bikram Shah, in the face of his conspiracies against your life;
5. You did not inflict the death sentence on my younger brother, Upendra Bikram Shah, who had conspired against you. Instead, you were lenient to him and interned him only for five years with due regard for his status;
6. During your prime ministership, you have satisfied the nobility, the soldiery and peasantry of Nepal, rendered them justice, and promoted peace and prosperity;
7. You have increased the military force of Nepal, observed economy, and added to the state exchequer.

After receiving such loyal service from you, I swore to abdicate the throne if you should resign the viziership. But when you came to relinquish your charges as vizier, I forgot my promise. I could not consult the queen and other *Umraos*, and since you had requested the prime ministership for your brother, I granted it. If I keep you out of service (lit. empty) and continue to sit on the throne, I would be guilty of perjury. The subjects would begin to say that I have not duly recognised the services of such a loyal vizier. So, for this reason, I give you the title of Sri Maharaj of Kaski and Lamjung. As the Maharaj of these lands, you should restrain me at any time, with the assistance of the *Umraos*, the people, and the army if I try to injure the friendship with the Queen-Empress of England and the Emperor of China. If, in your attempts to do so, I apply force, then my *Umraos* and army should support you. Whenever Prime Minister Bam Bahadur commits any mistakes in his responsibility for conducting the civil and military affairs of the state, *Pajani* and friendly relations with the Emperor of China and England, you should advise him. If he persists and refuses to accept your advice, then my *Mir Umrao* and the army will carry out any orders given by you. Keep your kingdom happy. In matters of justice we have given you the authority to inflict capital punishment. Live happily with your title of Sri Maharaj of your kingdom. If any subjects of my country try to plot against your kingdom and your life, we have authorized you to kill such persons if necessary. These rights will be inheritable by your children. Along with your brothers, according to the roll of succession we have established for the office of Mukhtiyar, your son Jagat Jang Bahadur Kanwar Rana will be the Mukhtiyar after the completion of the roll with Dhir Shamsher Jang Kanwar Ranajee.[30]

The Significance of this Historic Document

This amazing document wrested power from the helpless reigning monarch, King Surendra, and led to the institutionalization of the position of the Rana family within the political structure. It was this innovation which distinguished the character of the Rana regime from that of earlier and otherwise similar family administrations. It provided a legal basis for the Rana regime which lasted for more than a century. It bestowed in perpetuity on Jang and his successors absolute authority in civil and military administration, justice and foreign relations, including the right to supersede the King if it were found necessary in the national interest. The royal family was thus deprived of all of its sovereign powers and was confined within the limits of the palace grounds, although the exalted title of Maharajadhiraj (king of kings) was reserved for the King.

The roll of succession mentioned in the decree was an attempt to secure a permanent position for the Rana family within the political structure of Nepal. Jang Bahadur drew up a roll of succession on which all the male descendants of the Rana family were enrolled in chronological order of their dates of birth. It was laid down that the eldest agnate of the family would succeed to the prime ministership upon the incumbent's death. Other male members of the family, upon attaining majority, would hold the key civil and military posts. After the first generation of brothers, in the second and subsequent generations seniority still prevailed among the eligible candidates for offices. However, in practice, a younger uncle would take precedence over an older nephew in respect of succession to the office of Prime Minister.

All of those placed on the roll would hold the military rank of Lieutenant-Colonel or above. This elaborate arrangement was probably made to ensure that every aspirant to the office of Prime Minister acquired the necessary experience for the high office by holding various ranks in the hierarchy during the earlier stages of his career. The Prime Minister, however, could make changes in the roll of succession for disciplinary and other reasons. Non-members of the Rana family could not aspire to any rank higher than that of a commanding colonel in the army and that of a *bada kazi* in the civil service.

The subsequent *lal mohars* or official documents relating to the roll of succession to the office of the Mukhtiyar or the Prime Minister were issued in 1860 and 1867. The documents were deliberately silent on the question of succession to the office of the Maharaj of Kaski and Lamjung which the 1856 *lal mohar* had expressly made inheritable by Jang Bahadur's children alone. The *lal mohars* of 1860 and 1867 placed Jang Bahadur's sons and grandsons, who were younger than his brothers' children, higher in rank and on the roll of succession without any regard for the principle of seniority in relationship or age. This seemed to disregard the very principle which formed the basis of roll of succession as laid down in 1856. Rolls of succession which were subsequently drawn up must have caused anxiety and dismay to Jang Bahadur's brothers and their sons, but there was nothing they could do about it as long as Jang Bahadur was alive.

The Office of the Maharaj of Kaski and Lamjung

From the viewpoint of political development, the creation of the office of Maharaj of Kaski and Lamjung was of special significance, since the 1856 document vested absolute authority in this office. It is extremely doubtful whether the roll of succession as contained in the above-mentioned document applied to the office of Maharaj, for the document is so phrased as to make one believe that Jang Bahadur was interested in establishing primogeniture as the basis of succession to the office. Such an arrangement would have enabled his eldest son, Jagat Jang, to inherit the title of Maharaj with full powers and would have deprived the Prime Minister's office of supreme powers. But after Jang Bahadur died, his brothers compelled the King to appoint the eldest surviving brother, Ranoddip Singh (1877-1885), as both Prime Minister and Maharaj of Kaski and Lamjung. Thus, a precedent was created that was maintained throughout the Rana period.

Subsequent division of the Rana family on the caste and sub-branch lines seriously affected the working of the succession system. In 1856 only the so-called pure members of the family, i.e., the sons of a Rana by a wife of equal caste, were included on the roll of succession. Jang Bahadur himself violated the rule during his own lifetime, and his example was followed by his successors, Maharaj Bir Shamsher and Maharaj Bhim Shamsher.

Maharaj Chandra Shamsher sought to divide the Rana family into 'a', 'b' and 'c' classes without, however, tampering with the roll of succession established by Bir Shamsher. According to Perceval Landon, in whose book on Nepal the three classes of Rana were mentioned for the first time, "those born of lawful marriage and in equal caste with their parents" were to be regarded as 'a', "those born lawful but unequal marriage" 'b', and "those born illegitimate" 'c'.[31] Maharaj Bhim Shamsher (1929-1932) ignored Chandra Shamsher's rules and also altered the roll of succession. But Juddha Shamsher (1932-1946) decided to revise the roll in accordance with the caste principles propounded by Chandra Shamsher, and this finally destroyed the solidarity of the Rana family, with the consequence that a number of wealthy and powerful 'c' class Ranas joined hands with non-Rana discontented elements in bringing about the overthrow of the Rana family rule in 1951.

It may be recalled here that Jang Bahadur had earlier resigned from the prime ministership on the ground of undue physical strain to his health and also on the plea that his gesture of resignation, in favour of his brothers, would make them show favour and consideration to his sons after his death. Once Jang Bahadur had resigned from the office of Prime Minister, the British Resident began to transact official business only with Prime Minister Bam Bahadur. Although Jang Bahadur, through the royal edict of 1856, had obtained powers of control even over the King and the Prime Minister, the British Resident, Major George Ramsay (1852-1864), under instructions from his Government, did not conduct any official business through Jang Bahadur.[32]

This was something which Jang Bahadur could not understand. He sought to interfere from time to time in dealings between the Prime Minister and the British Resident with a view to making the British feel the impact of his authority. Jang once sought to embarrass the British Resident by creating difficulties with regard to the privileges and status of British traders. But the British were set on ignoring Jang Bahadur's newly acquired higher-than-royal status.

Arrangements were made to send a special envoy to Ramsay to inform the British Resident officially of Jang's elevation to the position of Maharaj, because Jang Bahadur felt that his title of Maharaj would have no meaning unless it was externally recognized. But the British Governor-General of India, Lord Dalhousie (1848-1856), thought that the recognition of two Maharajs within a country could create all kinds of difficulties. Furthermore, the British Government had very good reasons to suspect that Jang Bahadur was seeking to usurp the throne for himself and his descendants. Two of Jang Bahadur's sons were already married to the King's daughters, and it was declared that the daughters would inherit the throne in the absence of direct male heirs. (It was only later that Jang's daughters were married to King Surendra's sons).

The British fear was that their recognition of Jang's new status might encourage Jang Bahadur to usurp kingship even at the risk of a civil war. This largely accounts for the British hesitation to recognize any authority in place of the traditional Maharaj of Nepal who, at the time, was King Surendra Bikram Shah. Thus, Jang Bahadur, after having got himself appointed to the higher office of Maharaj, found himself not only being ignored by the British but also unable to succeed to the prime ministership without violating the self-same royal decree which had elevated him to the position of Maharaj, and which had also set up for his brothers, sons and nephews a roll of succession to the prime ministership.

After Bam Bahadur's death on 25 May 1857, Krishna Bahadur, the next brother in order of seniority, carried on the functions of the Prime Minister. Meanwhile, news of the outbreak of the Indian Mutiny reached Kathmandu. On 31 May 1857, the Acting Prime Minister, Krishna Bahadur, made an offer of military help to the British, and Jang Bahadur repeated the same offer on 1 June 1857. Ramsay ignored Jang's help but accepted Krishna Bahadur's offer of assistance subject to the Governor-General's approval.

Jang Bahadur felt very uneasy and wanted to go to Calcutta immediately in order to sort out some of these internal matters with the Governor-General himself. Discouraged by Ramsay from going to Calcutta until word was received from the Governor-General, Jang Bahadur resumed the prime ministership as soon as the British Government's formal request for help was received on 26 June 1857.

Jang Bahadur's Role in the Indian Mutiny

Jang Bahadur's decision to help the British quell the Indian Mutiny of 1857 was not popular among all sections of the court and the army. The second Basnyat plot of 1857 and disaffection within the Gurung regiment indicate opposition to Jang's move to offer assistance to the British.

On 2 June 1857, about 1,750 men of a Gurung regiment were going to be annihilated for their refusal to carry out the death sentence on a *jamadar* who was convicted for complicity in a conspiracy to assassinate Jang. But the British Residency prevailed on the Prime Minister to change his plan and avoid mass bloodshed.[33]

The Indian Mutiny, which began with the revolt of sepoys at Meerut on 10 May 1857, had spread all over the North-Western Province and Oudh by the end of June. Even in the midst of such pressing circumstances, Lord Canning (1856-62) initially turned down the offer of Nepali troops, but within a fortnight of rejecting the offer he had to ask for the services of three thousand Gorkha troops. By July 1857, the Nepali troops were assembled at Sugauli.

The British at Lucknow collapsed with the death of Sir Henry Lawrence on 4 July 1857. The troops from Nepal rushed to recover from the rebels Jaunpur and also Azamgarh, an outpost of Varanasi that commanded the direct route from Oudh to Ghazipur and eastward. On 10 December 1857, Jang Bahadur himself left Kathmandu at the head of 9,000 troops. His farewell speech on the eve of his departure from Kathmandu deserves notice inasmuch as it plainly sets forth his reasons for allying himself with the British:

> I have three motives for acting as I am now doing. First to show that Gorkhas possess fidelity and will pour out their blood in defence of those who treat them with honour and repose confidence in them. Second, that I knew the power of (the) British government and were I to take part against (it), although I might have temporary success for a time, my country would afterward have been ruined and (the) Gorkha dynasty annihilated. Third, that I know that upon the success of British arms and re-establishment of British power in India, its government will be stronger than ever, and that I and my brother and my country will all then benefit by our alliance with you (the British) as your (the British) remembrance of our past sacrifices will render our present friendship lasting and will prevent you (the British) even molesting us.[34]

Jang Bahadur occupied Gorakhpur in January 1858, and met with little resistance. Leaving behind a regiment to guard Gorakhpur, he then moved to restore British authority over Lucknow by dispersing the rebels under the self-styled Nizam Muhammad Hossain of Gorakhpur. On 11 March, Jang Bahadur's troops along with those of Col. Pahalman Singh Basnyat, were employed in lifting the siege of Lucknow. By 13 March, the whole of Lucknow was freed from the rebels.

The Nepali troops also played a part in the capture of Begum Kothi, Alambagh, Tara Kothi, Kaisergarh and Musa Bagh in Lucknow. Jang's role in suppressing the Mutiny, though considered crucial by some writers, was not as significant and vital from the military point of view as it was made out. However, it probably had the effect of boosting the morale of the British by dampening the enthusiasm and courage of the rebels.[35]

On 17 May 1858, Lord Canning (1856-62) informed the King through Jang Bahadur of the British Government's intention to restore to Nepal the whole of Nepal's former territory below the hills, extending from the River Ghagra (Karnali) on the west to the British territory of Gorakhpur on the east, and bounded on the south by Khairagarh and the district of Bahraich and on the north by the hills.[36]

The expenditure involved in employing the Nepali troops in India and training them was borne by the British Indian Government. It amounted to Rs.230,615. An additional sum of Rs. 450,000 was paid as cash gifts to all those men and officers who had taken part in suppressing the Mutiny, as gratuities in lieu of pension and compensation to the families of officers and soldiers who had lost their lives in action.[37] On 23 March 1858, Jang Bahadur went to Allahabad to meet Lord Canning and requested the Governor-General to replace Resident Ramsay with some other officer.[38] Ramsay was called to Calcutta in April 1858 and an inquiry was held into Jang Bahadur's complaints against him. They were of a ridiculous and frivolous character such as Ramsay's failure to pay wages to porters and the Resident's carriage having crossed a bridge against the rules. Lord Canning found Ramsay innocent and sent him back to Nepal on 23 February 1859.

Jang Bahadur's complaint against Ramsay had been designed to serve two ends. The first was to make the officers of the Nepali court think that Jang Bahadur had moved against a Resident who had not been helpful in securing the return to Nepal of all the land in the west, which it had ceded to the Company as a result of the Treaty of Sugauli in 1816.

Jang's Designs on the Throne

Jang's second motive, which the British did not understand, or, at any rate, pretended not to understand at the time, was to show his resentment against apparent British coolness to his suggestion of becoming king. As early as 26 August 1854, Lord Dalhousie had reasons to suspect that Jang coveted the throne for himself and noted that Jang Bahadur "will infallibly try to subvert that dynasty (the Shah dynasty) some day, and it is the toss-up of a rupee whether he will be Rajah or have his throat cut."[39] Discouraged by the British lack of enthusiasm about his design on the throne, Jang was finding fault with Ramsay, who had conveyed to Jang Bahadur the British Government's viewpoint on the question.

Jang Bahadur spared no effort to convince the British that he had become indispensable to Nepal. He would probably have usurped the throne had he felt confident of the enthusiastic support of the British Government. He sought the assurance of British patronage on several occasions both immediately before and after the Indian Mutiny.

After the offer of Jang's help to the British to quell the Mutiny, the British Government was constantly reminded by the Nepali side of the reward Maharaja Gulab Singh of Kashmir had received for the the assistance he had rendered to the British during the Sikh war. Jang's orderly officer, Karbir Khatri, had made the implication clear by stating that Jang expected from the British either recognition as an independent sovereign in Nepal or the grant of some other territory as a reward.[40] Even as late as 9 June 1863 the English language newspaper, *Friend of India*, published from Calcutta, wrote editorially under the caption, The Maharaja Jung Bahadur, G.C.B., and Our Relations with Nepal" about Jang's designs on the throne of Nepal.[41]

But the British Government in India took a neutral position on the matter and simply pointed out that any change in the form of government was Nepal's internal affair. If Jang had ever harboured a design to supplant the monarch, he gave it up, partly because of the British lack of enthusiasm for it and partly because he anticipated a cool if not a hostile reaction from his own brothers against such a move. The alternative he chose under the circumstances was to found a dynasty of hereditary Prime Ministers which would initially satisfy the brothers, institutionalize power in the family through the roll of succession and maintain the monarchy in form only.

He took the British Resident, George Ramsay, into confidence about the alleged misconduct of King Surendra Bikram Shah.[42] According to Jang, the King's Maharanis or wives complained to him as the Prime Minister-cum-Maharaja that the King was having homosexual relations with three stable attendants and should therefore be declared as an outcaste according to the law of the land. Upon receiving the complaint, Jang prevented the three grooms from going to the King's living quarters. At this the King attempted to commit suicide twice in one day and declared his desire to abdicate the throne. Jang thus placed his dilemma before Ramsay and sought his advice on how best he could deal with the situations. Ramsay at once sensed what Jang was up to and replied to him:

> . . . that the matter was of a purely domestic nature concerning the Gorkhas only, and having no direct political bearing upon the relations between the two States, and that I believed my Government would object to my offering any more definite advice than I was about to give him. I said that I believe His Excellency the Viceroy

> would disapprove taking upon myself a responsibility of this nature, and giving advice which might or might not lead to measures of coercion against the sovereign, which I had no right to suggest. I told him that, with reference to the abominable to which he had referred, I thought that not only the members in general of the king's family, but the Sirdars and the people would approve of his taking such steps as would prevent its occurrence; *but that he should remember that although he is the minister of Nepal, he is also a subject, and that he ought to be careful not to interfere with his sovereign's authority more than is absolutely called for by the peculiar circumstances of the case*[43] (emphasis added).

Jang seems to have given up the idea of supplanting monarchy after 1868, when he drew up the revised role of succession to the office of Majaraj and Prime Minister with the apparent consent of the King. However, towards the end of his life, he even started showing signs of extreme obsequiousness to the King in public as a gesture to gain the royal favour for himself and for his descendants after his death. Before he left Kathmandu for the last time on a hunting excursion in the tarai, in the presence of all the notables in an open court Jang obtained permission from the 48-year old King Surendra, whose daughters were married to his sons, and carried his sovereign himself pickaback up and down the stairs of the palace to the open quadrangle. After performing this spectacular feat at the age of 60, Jang took the King's leave by begging his mercy on himself and his children should anything untoward happen to him.

Again Jang's decision to move his statue, which had been erected in his own lifetime, to a new site inside the compound of the religious temple of Jagannath built by him on the bank of the Vishnumati river in Kathmandu seems to have been inspired by his fear that his own public monument might be desecrated or destroyed by the adversaries in the same way as Bhimsen Thapa's Bhim Mukhteshvar unless it was associated with the name of God and the King. The temple of Jagannath with Jang's statue in its compound has survived intact to this day as a testimony to Jang's sound common sense and practical shrewdness.

Although Jang Bahadur had acquired the *de facto* powers of the supreme ruler in Nepal even though he was only the Maharaj of Kaski and Lamjung, yet he showed signs of uneasiness from time to time about the continuance of the King or Maharajadhiraj even as a nominal ruler for ceremonial purposes. Even as late as 1864 he had not given up feeling out the British in his own way on the prospect of supplanting monarchy in Nepal.

The Aftermath of the 1857 Indian Mutiny

The last two months of 1859 saw vigorous joint action by British and Nepali troops against the Indian rebels who had made their way to the tarai. Jang Bahadur repeatedly complained against the crossing of Nepali territory by British troops, and serious misunderstandings initially arose out of this as well as out of Jang Bahadur's attitude towards the refugees after the Mutiny.[44]

Jang finally requested the British Government to prohibit its troops from crossing India's frontiers into Nepal. This request represented the final culmination of Jang's frequent complaints to the Resident about maltreatment of Nepalis and plunder of Nepali villages by British Indian troops. Jang may have done this as an excuse to initiate on his own a large-scale mop-up against the rebels and then claim the cost of the expedition from the British. By the end of the year 1859, Jang Bahadur completed this task under his own direct command but in collaboration with the British Indian troops. By 10 January 1860, the British troops were ordered to leave Nepal and return to Indian territory.

Jang Bahadur actually granted asylum to some mutiny leaders such as Peshwa Nana Sahib, Dhondu Pant and his brother, Bala Rao, Hazrat Mahal, the Begum of Oudh and her son, Birjis Qadar, Devi Bux, Beni Madho, Jwala Prasad, Devi Din of the Nassarbad Brigade and Khan Bahadur Khan of Bareilly. However, he persisted in telling the British that the most wanted among the refugees such as Nana Sahib were not traceable. About this time, distinguished refugees such as the ladies of Nana Sahib and his brother, with about 13 attendants, arrived at Kathmandu. They were followed by Begum Hazrat Mahal and her son, Birjis Qadar, with 28 attendants.

It cannot be ruled out that, humanitarian considerations apart, Jang was allured by the prospect of acquiring a share in the wealth that the more distinguished of these refugees were reported to have brought along.[45] Hazrat Mahal, the Begum of Oudh, died in Nepal, unlike Chand Kaur, Maharaja Ranjit Singh's Maharani Jhindan. Chand Kaur who had lived in exile in Nepal (following her escape from imprisonment in the Chunar fort in 1849 till her departure from Nepal) found it difficult to put up with Jang Bahadur's taxing demands and left Nepal after coming to terms with the British Indian Government. Hazrat Mahal's son Birjis Qadar also returned to India after coming to terms with the British after his mother's death.

Unfulfilled Plans for Visit to Great Britain

In 1862, Jang Bahadur proposed a second visit to Europe: to England, France, and Austria. He had three goals in mind. Firstly, he wanted to introduce his brothers and sons to Queen Victoria's favourable notice, request her protection for them and make arrangements for their education in England under a suitable guardian. The children should be educated by European teachers in the presence of a Nepali officer to ensure observance of the rules of caste. He could seek a more adequate reward for his services to Britain in 1857. And he could try to secure an engagement under the queen's signature guaranteeing non-interference in the affairs of Nepal by any Governor-General as long as Nepal maintained friendship and peace with the British.[46]

In 1865, the proposal for the visit was revived, and the Queen was requested to take under her protection Jang Bahadur's eldest son, Jagat Jang, as the son-in-law of the Maharajadhiraj. But the idea was abandoned when it did not meet with the approval of the Resident.[47]

But ten years later the British agreed to receive him: by now no personal motives remained and no wish was expressed to visit other countries in Europe.

Jang Bahadur left Kathmandu on 19 December 1874 to take a ship to England from Bombay in the first week of February 1875. But he fell from horseback and was injured while riding in Bombay, and the visit was abandoned.[48]

Closing Years of Jang's Life

Let us take a cursory look at the events of the closing years in the life of this dynamic personality. They were dull and routine compared to those of his earlier days, which had been packed with drama.

In 1871, Jang Bahadur was awarded by the Chinese Emperor the title, "Thong Ling Pinma-Ko Kang-Wang-Syang", the Highly Honoured Commander and Controller of Military and Political Affairs, the Augmenter and Instructor (disciplinarian) of the Army, the Aggrandizer of the Country and the Satisfier of the Low and High by Increasing the Reputation and Revenue of the Country. Jang Bahadur was also made Knight Grand Commander of the Exalted Order of the Star of India.

A severe famine struck Nepal in June 1874, and the British Indian Government supplied a stock of 24,233 maunds or 891 tons of rice at the cost of Rs. 80,777 to mitigate the suffering of the Nepali people.[49]

In 1876, the Prince of Wales (later Edward VII) visited the western tarai for a hunt from 16 February to 5 March on the invitation of Maharaj Jang. The Prince of Wales and his suite shot altogether 23 tigers, one leopard and one bear. The record bag for a day consisted of seven tigers. But not a single rhinoceros was shot during the hunt as it had become extinct in the area by that time. Before the Prince of Wales, Queen Victoria's second son, the Duke in Edinburgh, had also hunted in the same area from 23 February to 28 February 1870.[50]

A revolt of a novel kind was started against Jang Bahadur's authority at Gorkha in 1876 by Ram Lakhan Thapa, who claimed to be a reincarnation of a traditional hero in Magar folklore. Ram Lakhan professed himself to be a messenger and agent of the goddess Manakamana of Gorkha, who had commanded him to kill Jang Bahadur. The significant aspect of this revolt was that it acquired a popular character as a section of common people openly defied Jang Bahadur's authority at Gorkha. Jang, however, ruthlessly suppressed the followers of Ram Lakhan Thapa who was himself publicly executed.[51]

Jang Bahadur passed away on 25 February 1877, at Patharghatta in the tarai on the bank of the River Bagmati. He was succeeded to the office of Maharaj and Prime Minister by his brother, Ranoddip Singh (1877-85). Crown Prince Trailokya Bikram Shah and Jang Bahadur's eldest son and the King's son-in-law, Jagat Jang, seem to have been deliberately sent away from Kathmandu on the pretext that Jang Bahadur was seriously ill at his hunting camp in the tarai. In the absence of his son and son-in-law, King Surendra was easily prevailed upon to make Ranoddip both Maharaj and Prime Minister.

State of the Country's Economy, Population, Revenue and Army

Nepali authorities generally estimated the population of Nepal to be 5,200,000 or 5,600,000, in 1856, but according to British sources it was then 1,950,000 and this figure was probably more accurate than the figures given by the Nepalis, who tended to exaggerate their numbers for the satisfaction of their self-pride. For example, in the course of a conversation with the British Resident, Jang Bahadur is said to have once insisted that Kathmandu had 300,000 inhabitants, whereas its population was in fact 30,000 or 35,000.

The Nepalis, as a rule, exaggerated the figures of the country's population and revenue with a view to impressing foreigners. Jang Bahadur told the British Resident that Nepal's annual revenue was about 7 to 8 million rupees in the mid-1850s whereas Resident Hodgson estimated it at Rs. 4,350,000 in 1837. The standing army of Nepal was about 17,000 men, but its strength could easily be trebled in the event of a war. The system of *Pajani* or the annual renewal of army service enabled the Government to remove about 5% of the total military strength, thereby creating an unpaid reserve of trained soldiers who could at once be called upon to take up arms.[52]

Like his predecessors, Jang Bahadur strongly apprehended that free and unrestricted commercial intercourse might result in economic and political subjugation. The question of the revival of free trade between Nepal and India received top priority in British policy towards Nepal after 1767. It was revived in Jang Bahadur's time with an eye to the development of trade relations with Tibet and Central Asia through Nepal, for it was thought by the British that the opening up of Tibet, Bhutan, Sikkim, and Nepal would provide scope not only for an increased flow of trade but also for investment of British capital in tea gardens, orchards, woollen mills, saw mills, and similar industries. But Nepal's traditional apprehension about the motives of foreign traders proved to be an insurmountable obstacle to the growth of free trade from British India.

Jang Bahadur's attitude towards trade also reflected his desire to monopolize lucrative trade with India and his extreme opposition to commercial intercourse with the British Government in India.

The sale of timber and customs duties were the main sources of state revenue. Jang Bahadur established a Government monopoly over edible oil, tobacco, sugar, grains of all kinds, cotton, salt, clarified butter (ghee) and other necessaries of life to the great distress of the common people and to the detriment of foreign trade. All senior civil and military officers of the realm, all of Jang Bahadur's brothers and close kin, were engaged in this monopolistic trade. Monopoly rights were sold to favoured merchants, who remitted a share of their huge profits to Jang Bahadur. Marts that were set up on the Indo-Nepal border were given to his closest relatives and confidants.[53]

Land Administration and Settlement

Before Jang came to power, the tarai land was leased to the highest bidder for the purpose of collecting taxes on the basis of a periodic contract, for five years in the first instance, and on certain other specific conditions. The Government's share in the taxes realized from the cultivators amounted to one-eighth of the total yield from the land.[54] Jang Bahadur was keenly interested in raising land taxes and ensuring their timely and systematic collection in order to meet the increased expenditure of the Government and also to enrich himself.

Although there were *jimdars* in the tarai before Jang Bahadur's time, they had not performed the function of collecting taxes. Now, as part of Jang Bahadur's reforms in land administration and settlement, a select few of them at the village level alongside were assigned this responsibility, which they shared with the existing Chaudharis or collectors of revenue at the Pargana or divisional level. As an inducement to reclaim virgin forest lands for cultivation, the *jimdars* were given tax-exemption for 10 years, one-tenth of the total reclaimed land as Birta and any kind of wasteland for which no settlers and cultivators were available as *jirayat*. The *jimdars* legally enjoyed the privilege of using unpaid forced labour in clutivating the *jirayat* land.

The policy of land administration and settlement introduced by Jang Bahadur resulted in the reclamation of large areas of land in the tarai over the subsequent decade.[55] The changes that he made also strengthened government control by leaving less to the discretion of the *jimdars*.

Role of Jang Bahadur in Creating the Apparatus of the Government

Jang Bahadur laid down the basis for the Rana administrative system, both civil and military. Just as he had established an elaborate roll of succession among the members of his own and his brothers' families to the office of Prime Minister with a view to enforcing harmony and order in the political life, so also he set up *Mulki Adda* under a *Mulki Subba*, that is, a sort of central office or Secretariat of the Government under a permanent secretary-general for carrying on the general administration of the country.

As the Rana Government was an oligarchy of a military type, *Jangi Adda*, or the office of the army, was also started after Jang Bahadur's return from London to modernize the army on the basis of an elaborate manual drawn up by Jang himself. *Ain Khana* and *Kausal* were established by Jang Bahadur to draft new laws and codify the existing ones.

Jang Bahadur's famous legal code or *Mulki Ain* was the handiwork of a *Kausal* or Council, consisting of 232 members, which was created in 1851.

Moth Tahavil was created for the administration of all revenue and *Kathmahal* as the forest office. An office for the exchange of Nepali and East India Company rupees was set up and called *Saraf Khana*. A public works department to look after roads, bridges and public buildings was placed directly under the Prime Minister. The office for registering the names of all civil and military employees, called *Kitab Khana*, was opened in 1848. The Government Treasury or *Mulki Khana* was also Jang Bahadur's creation. He, however, retained the existing *Tosha Khana* as the disbursement office. *Munshi Khana* or the Foreign Office, as started by Mukhtiyar General Bhimsen Thapa (1806-1837), was retained and so was *Kumari Chowk*, the audit and accounts office established by King Prithvinarayan Shah (1769-1775). It is clear from the above that the credit for creating a machinery for running the Government of Nepal in a modern sense largely belongs to Jang Bahadur.

Jang Bahadur's Foreign Policy

With the decline of Chinese power in the latter half of the nineteenth century, Nepal was not in a position to pursue a balance of power between China and British India. The policy of Maharaj-cum-Prime Minister Jang Bahadur Rana toward British India was motivated by fear and distrust as well as by a healthy respect for the superior strength and intelligence of the British in India. The founder of the Rana system of government, whose foreign policy guidelines were followed for over a century till the very end of the Rana regime in 1951, believed that the best guarantee of Nepal's independence lay in maintaining formal and friendly relations with the British Indian Government, while at the same time keeping Nepal closed as far as possible to outside influences.

The *raison d'etre* of the policy of the Rana Government is frankly and succinctly stated in the following excerpt from the record of a conversation between Jang Bahadur and the British Resident on the subject of permitting a British merchant to carry on private trade in Nepal:

> You say we are independent; the British Government tells us that it has no desire to interfere . . . with our internal affairs and not even

> to advise us respecting them. We know you are the stronger power, you are lion, we are like a cat; but the lion would soon kill the cat. You can force us to change our policy, you can take our country if it pleases you to do so; but we will make no change in that policy, by the strict observance of which we have preserved our independence as a nation to the present time, unless you compel us to do so. We shall not allow Mr. Cameron to come into the country, except as a private gentleman and your guest and upon your assurance that he will not attempt to engage in trade or make any inquiries into the resources of the country.[56]

A strong case is also made for the policy of isolation and the exclusion of foreigners in the following statement, which was recorded as Jang Bahadur's spontaneous reaction to the British account of how the detention by the Raja of Sikkim of Dr. Campbell and Dr. Hooker, who were engaged in biological research in Sikkim, had compelled the British to occupy the kingdom of Sikkim in 1849-50.

> Well; but if they had not gone to gather rhododendrons that would not have happened and the Raja of Sikkim would not have lost his country. How do I know that some of our officials through ignorance, or perhaps, through enmity to myself, might not ill-treat some of the British subjects and then you would take half, if not the whole, of the country. All other native states have either fallen entirely under your rule, or you interfere with the management.[57]

The most important reason why Nepal was not brought under British rule at this time was that, after the mid-nineteenth century, the British got everything they wanted from Nepal without having to exert themselves further. The Rana rulers of Nepal were convinced that Nepal could not hope to match the British in a trial of strength and hence made themselves, as rulers of an independent country, so useful to Britain that there never arose any real need for the British to bring Nepal under direct rule.

It may be noted here that free trade with Nepal and the recruitment of Gorkhas, which had begun surreptitiously in 1815, were the two major objectives the British had sought to achieve in Nepal. Neither objective was fully achieved in the time of Jang Bahadur. Nepal subsequently proved to be a source of British military strength in Asia, and the British Empire found the services of Gorkha troops invaluable in times of crisis. For upwards of a century, Nepal had diplomatic relations only with Britain, China, and Tibet and, in 1934, London became the only capital in the world where Nepal maintained a permanent diplomatic representation.

Adventurous Life

Early in his life, Jang Bahadur picked up the habit of gambling and remained an inveterate gambler all his life, prone to take high risks in all his undertakings. As a young man, he had at one time seriously thought of catching elephants in the tarai forests to pay off his gambling debts. This plan of his actually came to nothing, but was revealing in the sense that it gave an idea of the kind of man Jang Bahadur was. He was resolute at heart and full of daring. Although he might have failed in his venture to catch elephants single-handed, yet with his single-minded purpose and determination he subsequently proved himself capable of winning far greater successes in the more serious enterprises of his life.

It was in pursuit of his plan to catch elephants that Jang stayed for some time in the Tharu villages on the outskirts of forests. He lived there, like Tharu villagers, sharing their everyday joys and sorrow and taking part in their fun and frolicks, pastimes and adventures, especially those of the hunt. Jang figures prominently in Tharu folklore which fondly enshrines many incidents and experiences of that time in Jang's life. The most familiar episode is one of a king cobra standing half erect and spreading its hood over Jang's head as a protective umbrella when Jang himself, tired and exhaused after hard work involving excessive physical strain, was one day lying fast asleep on the open village ground adjoining a forest. No wonder that after he came into power, Jang appointed many Tharus to official positions and also gifted lands to them.

The first-hand information he had gathered about the ways of big game including wild elephants, and particularly the skill and experience he had acquired in tackling them in the wild, stood him in good stead ever afterwards. In 1840 Jang Bahadur was said to have rehabilitated himself in military services as a captain of the artillery by impressing King Rajendra Bikram by his feat in lassoing a wild elephant in the course of a royal hunt. Fighting the wild tuskers with trained elephants, with himself monoeuvring them in the fight, remained one of Jang Bahadur's favourite pastimes till the end of his life.

Hunting was Jang's greatest interest outside his political life. He was a first-rate shot and impressed his Western guests by knocking down a fleeing wild boar clean dead at two hundred yards after a fusilade from a party of his guests had failed to stop it. At archery and horsemanship, he was second to none. He was a fine wrestler and enjoyed fights between animals

Jang Bahadur Already a Legend among his People

Many stories were already in circulation about Jang's personal courage and skill in facing difficult situations and dangers even before he went to Europe. The great daring displayed by Jang Bahadur in rescuing a hapless mother and a daughter from a house on fire formed the burden of one of those tales. Another story was related to Jang Bahadur's boldness and sagacity in leaping from a roof onto the neck of an elephant in rut, which had broken loose and was on the rampage in the congested narrow streets of Kathmandu. His leap on horseback into the Trishuli river from a height of eighty feet and his jumping down a dark deep unexplored well allegedly at the behest of Crown Prince Surendra were his two other widely known escapades.

After being compelled to leap on horseback from a narrow suspension bridge into the swift currents of the flooded Trishuli river while turning back sharply in compliance with the Crown Prince's command, Jang disappeared from sight for quite some time. His friends finally discovered that he had swum to safety a fair distance downstream.

His second adventure consisted of jumping by the mandatory command of the Crown Prince into a well that had not been cleaned for twelve years and was partly filled with buffalo bones. He survived this experience by clinging to the brickwork until he was rescued by his friends after an hour or so.

According to yet another story, Jang was once ordered by the selfsame Crown Prince, on pain of death, to jump from the top of Dharahara, Kathmandu's tallest structure at that time. Jang is said to have performed this feat successfully with the aid of a pair of parasols.

If these popular tales of Jang Bahadur's stirring adventures in folklore serve to project his image as a man of exceptional courage, strength and sagacity, they at the same time invariably tend to cast Crown Prince Surendra in an adverse light as a cruel and capricious individual. After Captain Cavenagh's *Rough Notes on Nepal* was published, Jang himself told Resident George Ramsay that some of the stories he had told Cavenagh were entirely fabricated But it may be that there is "a core of truth to the anecdotes" as claimed by John Whelpton, a perceptive research scholar of the life and times of Jang Bahadur. Even if these episodes were concocted merely to project Jang Bahadur's image in a favourable light, they reveal a rare gift and high quality of political salesmanship or public relations on the part of whoever might have been responsible for them. One wonders to this day how far these anecdotes were true and how far they were deliberately spread to raise Jang Bahadur to the status of a hero or superhuman figure in the eyes of the common folk. Whatever might have been the truth, the tales of Jang's feats were widely believed and actually served the purpose of making Jang a legendary figure among the common people of Nepal for a long time even after his death.

Habit and Temperament

Jang Bahadur did not keep regular hours and would get up in the morning at any time between five and ten o'clock. He lost his temper easily and towards the end of his life became even more irritable. But he was always ready to hear the other side of a case even when it was presented by a poor unknown person, and he would admit it, if the other side was right. Despite his sporadic efforts, he found it impossible to learn English. He was in fact semi-literate but had Indian and English newspapers read and explained to him.

To the end of his life, Jang Bahadur remained intractable even to those who were close to him. He perhaps realized that some people would never forgive him or forget the manner in which he rose to power. Therefore, he was extremely wary and took no chances. Whenever he went out, be it on a hunting expedition or his morning ride across the Tundikhel, the parade ground at the heart of Kathmandu, he was accompanied by a strong armed escort. Even when he was in the house, he had his bodyguard either with him or within instant call. Nobody knew in which room or where he was spending the night. Because of his early experiences, he never trusted human nature. However much one may condemn the method by which he climbed to power, there seems to be something about this lonely and terrible autocrat that evokes the same feeling of awe and admiration as a hero in a Greek tragedy. Even people who do not seem to us to be admirable have in fact served Nepal well, as we realize when we examine their accomplishments.

Evaluation and Conclusion

Jang Bahadur stands head and shoulders above all other Nepali political leaders of the nineteenth century, no matter who they were or what their official designations–King, Mukhtiyar, Prime Minister or Maharaj. If there is anyone who merits comparison with Jang, it is Mukhtiyar General Bhimsen Thapa, who was prominent on the Nepali scene for about 31 years from 1806 till 1837.

Jang Bahadur's reputation has suffered a decline as a result of the anti-Rana sentiments–even hatred–deliberately and wilfully fostered by the democratic movement in the years immediately before and after the 1951 political change. At the same time, Bhimsen has been grossly overrated for the sole reason that he was a non-Rana. He has even been raised to the status of a national hero, notwithstanding his role in destroying the traditional practice of *Bhara-Pancha*, an indigenous mode of popular participation in government.

It is interesting to compare Bhimsen's record and achievements with those of Maharaj Jang Bahadur with a view to enabling the reader to form his own estimate of the relative importance and greatness of these two historical figures.

First, Jang was able to add to Nepal's land area during his administration, whereas Bhimsen was responsible for the loss of a sizable portion of the existing territory in his time. Bhimsen could not escape the blame for the 1814-1816 war, as a result of which Nepal lost one-third of its territory and might even have lost its independence. Jang deserves credit for putting an end to a state of instability within the country and preventing foreign intervention, for the British Indian Government might not have tolerated much longer a mercurial situation on its north-eastern frontier.

Further, Jang won back a portion of the territory that Bhimsen had lost as a result of his lack of foresight in ignoring the sound advice of experienced military generals against provoking the war. According to the noted Nepali historian, Baburam Acharya, the fact that Bhimsen's father, Amar or Ambar Singh Thapa was the direct beneficiary of the income from landholdings which had previously belonged to the Raja of Palpa, was instrumental in influencing Bhimsen's decision to use force to recover Butwal and Syuraj from the Company's Government, thus precipitating war with the British.

Second, a comparison of the methods by which Bhimsen and Jang actually acquired power, although very similar, places the latter in a more favourable light. Bhimsen Thapa became Mukhtiyar with Tripurasundari as Regent Queen. He used the opportunity provided by the assassination of King Rana Bahadur Shah to liquidate all his potential rivals among the court officials by implicating them in trumped-up charges in the plot against Rana Bahadur's life. Even their innocent retinues and maidservants were not spared. Ironically, he did not realize that the same tactics would be employed against him by his enemies at a future date.

Jang Bahadur also came to power as a result of the slaying of a number of important officers and notables of the court. However, the risk involved was far greater for Jang than for Bhimsen, because even if the Kot Massacre is regarded as having been stage-managed by Jang himself, it still laid him and his brothers open to danger in a free-for-all which lasted for hours.

Third, if we compare the two as administrators, again it was Jang who codified the *Mulki Ain*, Nepal's Legal Code, along the lines of the Napoleonic code, introduced far-reaching reforms in land settlement and revenue collection in the tarai, and finally created a national army under a unified command in place of regiments committed to the personal charge and command of individual officers.

Fourth, both Bhimsen and Jang exercised strict vigilance over the life and activity of the monarch. They deliberately excluded the King from contact with people other than trusted members of their own family and men enjoying their highest confidence. Both of them followed the policy of preventing other notables and courtiers from having direct contact with the palace and the British Residency--but with one vital difference. Jang made a success of it in the end by effectively controlling the actions of the royal antagonists themselves under the most trying circumstances, whereas in Bhimsen's hands the same policy proved to be a dismal failure, eventually leading to his suicide in captivity.

On the whole, if Jang Bahadur was a dynamic and forward-looking personality whose action was mostly characterized by a sense of drama and suspense, Bhimsen proved to be a creature of the court, the first leader in Nepal to adopt the Western title and uniform of a General without ever having seen a battlefield or having any first-hand military experience. Initially successful in court intrigues essentially as a manipulator and operator behind the scenes, Bhimsen never grew out of his limited concept of how to govern a country. He lived and died playing the age-old game of court politics with its established rules and without ever cherishing the slightest hope of changing them, even to his own advantage or to that of his family.

Jang Bahadur, on the other hand, proved to be an innovator who masterminded schemes and who succeeded in smashing once and for all the feuding factions in court politics. He established a stable basis for law and order in the country by concentrating power in himself and his family.

Jang Bahadur thus deserves to be recognized as one of the three outstanding figures who have dominated the history of modern Nepal so far. The other two were King Prithvinarayan Shah Deva (1769-1775) and King Mahendra Bir Bikram Shah Deva (1955-1972). The truth is that they not only fashioned strategies best suited to the needs of their time, but also carried them out with consummate skill. In doing so, they gained power for themselves and their families and also safeguarded the independence and security of Nepal.

Whether they were able to promote the well-being of the people is a different question. Indeed it is not relevant to the traditional Nepali political culture, in which the governing elite did not envisage a constituency of the masses, and the organs of Government were used largely for personal gain while the masses were exploited rather than benefited.

NOTES

1. Citing someone alive at the time of the event, Balachandra Sharma states that the Queen did not go to Gagan Singh's residence after the murder. Balachandra Sharma, *Nepal Ko Aitihasik Rooprekha* (Varanasi, 2022 V.S.), pp. 307-8.
2. Translation of a Lal Mohar granted by the King to the Queen dated Poush Sudi 1, 1899 Bikram Samvat (1 January 1843); Foreign Secret Consultation, 22 February 1843, No. 73.
3. Two versions of the incident are available in the British records. The first version, furnished by Captain Ottley, the Assistant Resident, is as follows: The King approached the British Residency and through the Subedar in attendance there informed it of the murder of Gagan Singh and the convening of an emergency meeting of the Council of Notables which was already in progress in the Kot to inquire into the grave situation that had arisen. Ottley felt that the King expected a visit from him and therefore sent the Mir Munshi to the King as Ottley himself was suffering from rheumatism (Foreign Secret Consultation, 31 October 1846).

   The second version of the same incident, given by Resident Thorsby after five months, is as follows: King Rajendra requested an interview with Captain Ottley through Subedar Munno Singh to discuss the matter relating to the murder of Gagan Singh. But as it was midnight, Ottley sent the Mir Munshi to the King (Foreign Secret Consultation, 27 March 1847).

4. A military rank of the time slightly lower than that of captain and equivalent to that of a lieutenant.
5. General Padma Jung Bahadur, *op. cit.*, p. 76; however, according to Ottley's report on 24 September 1846 only 31 men were killed (including Gagan Singh). Foreign Secret Consultation, 31 October 1846, No. 161.
6. What was described by the Darbar Munshi as an imperfect and tentative list of those killed in the affray of 14-15 September 1846 was submitted to George O.B. Ottley, Acting Officiating Resident-in-charge who forwarded it to his government on 24 September 1846. 31 names, including those of Gagan Singh and Bhawani Singh that the list contains, are as follows: (1) Chautara Fatte Jang Shah, (2) Chautara Narahari Bikram Shah, (3) Chautara Khadga Bikram Shah, (4) Kazi Dala Bhanjan Pande, (5) Kazi Ranagambhir Pande, (6) Kazi Ranajore Thapa, (7) Kazi Narsingh Thapa, (8) Kazi Go Prasad Shah, (9) Kazi Dal Bahadur Shah, (10) Kazi Bakhtawar Bhandari, (11) General Gagan Singh, (12) General Abhiman Singh Rana, (13) Sardar Bhawani Singh, (14) Sardar Ras Singh, (15) Samar Bahadur Shah, (16) Sardar Gun Prakash, (17) Sardar Shatru Bhanjan Shah, (18) Sardar Juddharanjan Shahi, (19) Sardar Arjun Thapa, (20) Captain Mohan Bir Shahi, (21) Captain (a son of Mohan Bir Shahi), (22) Captain Bir Bahadur Shah, (23) A son of Badriban Shahi, (24) Dada Dand Keshar, (25) Dware Jag Raj, (26) Kumedan Gainda Mal, (27) Kapardar Bir Kishor Pande, (28) Kirti Dhoj Pande, (29) Jamadar Katru, (30) Havaldar Kalu Khawas, (31) Orderly Indra Bir Raut. (Foreign Secret Consultation, 31 Oct. 1846, No. 160).
7. Foreign Secret Consultation, 26 December 1846, No. 144
8. Foreign Secret Consultation, 27 March 1847, No. 113.
9. Landon, *op. cit.*, p. 126.
10. Foreign Secret Consultation, 28 December 1846, No. 144.
11. Hardinge's Memo on Nepal Affairs dated 23 July 1847, Foreign Secret Consultation, 31 July 1847, No. 203.
12. Landon, *op. cit.*, Vol. 1, p. 126.
13. Oldfield, *op. cit.*, Vol. 1, p. 371.
14. According to Pudma Jung B. Rana the Kazi was cut to pieces by Capt. Ram Mehar Adhikari. P. Jung, *op. cit.*, pp. 87-88.
15. Oldfield, *op. cit.*, Vol. 1, p. 371. According to Padma Jung, 23 persons were killed in all. Padma Jung Bahadur Rana, *op. cit.*, p. 88.
16. Foreign Secret Consultation, 26 June 1847, Nos. 182, 183 and 187.
17. Foreign Secret Consultation, 26 June 1847, Nos. 177, 183 and 187.
18. *Ibid.*
19. Before King Rajendra left for Varanasi in November 1846, he proclaimed this through a royal edict with Red Seal (Lal Mohar) *Sandhipatra Sangraha*, p. 74; cited in M.S. Jain, *The Emergence of a New Aristocracy in Nepal* (Agra: Sri Ram & Co., 1972), p. 122.
20. Foreign Secret Consultation, 25 November 1849, Nos. 251-52.
21. Jain, *op. cit.*, fn., pp. 100-1.
22. Guide.
23. Bearing gifts.
24. O. Cavenagh, *op. cit.*, p. 141
25. Satish Kumar, *Rana Polity in Nepal* (Bombay: Asia Publishing House, 1967), Appendix 3.
26. Oldfield, *op. cit.*, Vol. I, p. 408; *Ibid.*, Vol. II, p. 2; Vol. II, p. 20.

27. Landon, Vol. I, *op. cit.*, p. 408; *Events at the Court of Nepal*, III, 1852-61, Foreign Deptartment Political, B. Nos. 145-64, March 1875 (I).
28. Brief Memorandum of the Political Relations between Her Majesty's Indian Government and the State of Nepal from 1854-1867 (Prepared by Resident Col. G. Ramsay for Pol. B. March 1875, Nos. 145-64).
29. Landon, *op. cit.*, p. 146.
30. Abstract translation of the Lal Mohar granted by King Surendra Bikram Shah of Nepal to Jang Bahadur conferring on him the sovereignty of Kaski and Lamjung and the title of Maharaj, dated 1913 V.S.; Sravan Sudi 6, Corresponding to August 6, 1856 (manuscript of Buddhi Man Singh, *Bhasa Vamshavali*, Nepali genealogy in the Berkeley Collection, which was subsequently made over to His Majesty's Government's National Archives in Kathmandu.)
31. Genealogical Tree of the Rana family of Nepal, Landon, *op. cit.*, Vol. II.
32. Foreign Secret Consultation, 29 August 1856, No. 63.
33. See under the year 1857 in *Events at the Court of Nepal*, III-1852-61, (Foreign Department Political, B. No. 145-64, March 1875 (I).
34. Foreign Secret Consultation, 29 January 1853, No. 377.
35. Ramakant, *Indo-Nepal Relations (1816-1877)*, (Delhi: S. Chand & Co., 1968), p. 289.
36. Foreign Secret Consultation, 30 July 1858, No. 121.
37. Foreign Secret Consultation, 27 August 1858, No. 92.
38. Melleson, *Indian Mutiny*, Vol. III, p. 226.
39. G.A. Baird (ed.), *Private Letters of the Marquess of Dalhousie*, (London, 1911); cited in Ramakant, *op. cit.*, p. 275.
40. Foreign Secret Consultation, 27 November 1857, No. 423.
41. Foreign Political A., August 1863, No. 73.
42. 'Alleged misconduct of the Maharajah Dheeraj', Ramsay to Colonel H.M. Durand, Foreign Secretary, Government of India (No. 34 dated 1 November 1864). Foreign Department Political, November 1864 (Nos. 52-8) (N.A.I.).
43. *Ibid.*, Ramsay to Durand, No. 34, dated 1 November 1864, cited in Asad Husain, *op. cit.*, pp. 101-2.
44. Foreign Political Consultation, 22 July 1859, No. 200.
45. Foreign Political Consultation, 22 April 1859, Nos. 197 and 30, December 1850, Nos. 541, 544, 546, and 548.
46. Foreign Political A., May 1862, No. 24.
47. Foreign Political A., October 1865, No. 80.
48. Foreign Political B., March 1875, Nos. 145 and 155.
49. Foreign General B., October 1874, Nos. 156-57.
50. The dates and the details of the hunt are reproduced from his late Field Marshal Kaiser Shamsher J.B. Rana's account of big game hunting in Nepal.
51. General Padma Jung Bahadur Rana, *op. cit.*, p. 303.
52. See under the year 1861 in *Events at the Court of Nepal, III-1852-61*. Foreign Department Political, B. Nos.145-64, March 1875 (1).
53. Foreign Political, A., August 1864.
54. Foreign Political Consultation, 8 July 1831, Nos. 13-14.
55. Mahesh C. Regmi, *Landownership in Nepal* (Berkeley: University of California Press, 1976), p. 108.
56. Foreign Political Proceedings, A Category, August 1864, No. 51.
57. *Ibid.*

10

Ranoddip Singh(1877-1885): The End of the Era of Seven Brothers' (Satbhai) Pre-eminence

Jang Bahadur Kanwar Ranaji (K.R.) had formally initiated the rule of the seven brothers by including their names in the roll of succession to the prime ministership on the basis of the agnatic principle. Jang Bahadur K.R.'s second and fourth brothers, Minister Bam Bahadur K.R. and Commander-in-Chief Krishna Bahadur K.R. had predeceased Jang Bahadur and his third brother, Badri Narsingh K.R., who was removed from the roll of succession in 1851 for his complicity in the plot against Jang Bahadur, had also died in A.D. 1874. At the time of Jang's death, Commander-in-Chief Ranoddip Singh K.R. was thus the eldest of the surviving brothers on the latest roll of succession as drawn up by Jang Bahadur on 3 February 1868 with the approval of King Surendra Bikram Shah Dev (1847-81). The remaining two brothers were Senior Commanding General Jagat Shamsher K.R., and Eastern Commanding General Dhir Shamsher K.R., both of whom enjoyed precedence in the line of succession to the prime ministership over Jang Bahadur's two eldest sons–Southern Commanding General Jagat Jang Bahadur K.R. and Northern Commanding General Jit Jang Bahadur K.R.

Jang Bahadur, as we have seen earlier, had sought to accommodate all male descendants of his six brothers and his own in the roll of succession at least to prime ministership if not to that of the office of Maharaj, initially excluding those who were born out of wedlock. However, on 3 February 1868, Jang revised the previous roll of succession in such a manner as not only to include some of his favourite natural sons but also to place some of his own sons and grandsons above his brothers' sons in disregard of the principle of seniority in age and agnatic relationship.

The roll of succession as revised and drawn up by Jang Bahadur in 1868 was as follows:

1. Shri Tin Maharaj Jang Bahadur Kanwar Ranaji, Prime Minister Supreme Commander-in-Chief.
2. Commander-in-Chief General. Ranoddip Singh K.R. (Jang's brother)
3. Senior Commanding General Jagat Shamsher Jang K.R. Western Command) (Jang's brother).
4. Commanding General Dhir Shamsher K.R. (Eastern Command) (Jang's brother)
5. Commanding General Jagat Jang Bahadur K.R. (Southern Command) (Jang's son).
6. Commanding General Jit Jang Bahadur K.R (Northern Command) (Jang's son).
7. General Padma Jang Bahadur (Jang's son).
8. Any other legitimate son of Jang Bahadur if born.
9. Lieutenant-General Babar Jang Bahadur K.R. (born of his favourite wife, Putali Maharani).
10. Lieutenant-General Rana Bir Jang K.R. (born of his married wife's sister, who had been previously married to somebody else).
11. Major-General Yuddha Pratap Jang Bahadur K.R. (Jang's grandson born of the royal princess married to his eldest son).
12. Any son, if born to General Jagat Jang and his wife who was also a royal princess.

Only the positions after the twelfth went to the sons of Jang's brothers and his nephews:

13. Major-General Kedar Narsingh K.R. (Badri Narsingh's son).
14. Major-General Bam Bikram Bahadur K.R.(Bam Bahadur's son).
15. Major-General Buddhi Bikram Bahadur K.R. (Krishna Bahadur's son)
16. Lieutenant-Colonel Bir Shamsher Jang K.R. (Dhir's son).
17. Lieutenant-Colonel Ambar Jang K.R. (Jagat Shamsher's son).
18. Lietenant-Colonel Dhoj Narsingh K.R. (Badri Narsingh's son).

19. Major-General Ram Krishna K.R. (Krishna Bahadur's son).
20. Lieutenant-Colonel Khadga Shamsher K.R. (Dhir's son).
21. Lieutenant-Colonel Bhupendra Jang K.R. (Jagat Shamsher's son).
22. Lieutenant-Colonel Rana Shamsher Jang K.R. (Dhir's son).
23. Lieutenant-Colonel Dev Shamsher Jang K.R. (Dhir's son)
24. Lieutenant-Colonel Chandra Shamsher Jang K.R. (Dhir's son)
25. Lieutenant-Colonel Bir Bikram Jang K.R. (Bam Bahadur's son).
26. Lieutenant-Colonel Bhim Shamsher Jang K.R. (Dhir's son).
27. Lieutenant-Colonel Fatte Shamsher Jang K.R. (Dhir's son).
28. Lalit Shamsher Jang K.R. (Dhir's son).

The positions after this were reserved for the sons born of married wives of Jang Bahadur and his remaining three brothers. Meanwhile, however, the positions were assigned to:

29. Lieutanant-Colonel Bhairav Narsingh K.R. (Badri Narsingh's son).
30. Colonel Yaksha Bikram Bahadur K.R. (Bam Bahadur's son).

It was the above revised roll of succession that had caused a good deal of dissension and heart-burning among the members of Jang Bahadur's own family and also between Jang Bahadur and his surviving brothers as has been indicated earlier in this book. Ever since Jang Bahadur's death, his brothers and nephews were on the look out for changing the roll of succession, but his brothers did not go beyond making the roll of succession apply also to the office of Maharaj which should have, according to Jang Bahadur's dispensation, gone to his eldest son, General Jagat Jang, after his death.

Succession of Ranoddip Singh to the Prime Ministership

Jang Bahadur's brothers seemed to have deliberately suppressed the news of his death for some time. His youngest brother, Dhir Shamsher, left Kathmandu with a party consisting of Jang Bahadur's son-in-law, Crown Prince Trailokya Bikram Shah, and his wife and several of Jang's sons including the eldest one, Southern Commanding General Jagat Jang Bahadur K.R. All of them were given the false impression that Maharaj Jang Bahadur was lying seriously ill at his hunting camp in the tarai. Crown Prince Trailokya, his wife and General Jagat Jang returned to Kathmandu from Chitlang when they finally learnt of Jang's death. But during their brief absence from Kathmandu, Jang's brothers were easily able to manipulate King Surendra and prevail on him to confer both the prime ministership and the office of the Maharaj of Kaski and Lamjung on Ranoddip Singh K. R. (1877-1885).

Ranoddip Singh, the fifth brother of Jang Bahadur, was the sixth son of Kazi Bal Narsingh Kanwar, whose eldest son by his first marriage, General Bhakta Bir Kanwar, though older than Jang Bahadur himself, was not included in the roll of succession. Following the death of Commander-in-Chief Krishna Bahadur K.R. in 1863, Ranoddip Singh had succeeded him and remained in that office until he became Maharaj and Prime Minister on 25 February 1877.

Estrangement of Jang Bahadur's Sons

The appropriation of the title of the Maharaj of Kaski and Lamjung by Ranoddip Singh understandably caused dismay amongst Jang Bahadur's sons and their adherents and particularly to Jang's eldest son Jagat Jang, who should have succeeded to that office in accordance with the Lal Mohar granted by King Surendra to Jang Bahadur on 6 August 1856. According to this document, the office of the Maharaj of Kaski and Lamjung was inheritable by Jang's direct descendants alone. C.E.R. Girdlestone, the British Resident at that time, was also of the opinion that Jagat Jang's claim to the office of the Maharaj of Kaski and Lamjung was rightful. Girdlestone wrote to A.C. Lyall, the foreign secretary in India, that "the original parbatiya copy is before me now, and the expression is 'santan dar santan samma rajai bhog garo' – that is, literally, enjoy the kingdom up to offspring upon offspring."[1]

Even the new Maharaj sensed that Jagat Jang was not the only one to be dissatisfied at being deprived of his legitimate claim to the title and benefice of the Maharaj of Kaski and Lamjung. There was a general feeling among officials and also among the common people that Jang's sons were not being treated fairly by their uncles. This is clear from the passionate pleas for unity and discipline Maharaj Ranoddip Singh K.R. made in his speech to the principal officers of the state at a banquet specially held for them on 26 November 1877.

Circumstances following Ranoddip's Installation as the Maharaj

Everyone including the representatives of the British Indian Government in Nepal had felt that Jang Bahadur's death would be followed by a sharp struggle for power between his sons and his brothers. Jang Bahadur's sons were in a position to cash in on their father's reputation, their own following among a section of the army and members of the Rana family, and also on their matrimonial alliance with the royal family. However, Senior Commanding General Jagat Jang, the leader of Jang Bahadur's family and its supporters, proved to be less than a match for his uncle, Dhir Shamsher, who was Jang's youngest brother. Jagat Jang was certainly ambitious and intriguing but proved to be rather incautious and imprudent on the whole.

The situation in Nepal remained very tense for quite some time after Jang Bahadur's death. Officiating Resident Henvey expected Jang's sons to challenge their uncle and reported to the British Government that "the common saying is . . . Jang Bahadur's turban is too big for Ranoddip Singh; tenure of power by the latter is not to be looked for."[2] Daniel Wright, the Residency Surgeon, also had predicted that there would be "a succession of struggles for power, accompanied with much bloodshed, amongst his relatives."[3] Richard Temple, the Lientenant-Governor of Bengal, who had visited Kathmandu less than a year before Jang's death, thought that Dhir might seize power by killing Ranoddip.[4]

Crown Prince Trailokya Bikram Shah, who had been born on 30 November 1847, died on 30 March 1878 under suspicious circumstances although the cause was officially given as smallpox. It had been said that he was only biding his time to restore the power of the monarchy. Now that he was dead, the devolution of his royal rights upon his infant son, Prithvi Bir Bikram Shah, by Jang Bahadur's daughter, Lalit Rajyalakshmi, created an opening for intrigues.

The younger generation of the Thapas who were keen on avenging the death of Prime Minister Mathbar Singh Thapa and the relatives of some of the notables who were killed in the Kot Massacre, were engaged in a conspiracy against both the Jang Ranas and the Shamsher Ranas. Commander-in-Chief Jagat Shamsher had handled the situation with considerable tact and firmness and succeeded in holding the conspiracy in check, but he himself died in 1879.

Commander-in-Chief Jagat Shamsher had been the next in line of succession. His brother Dhir Shamsher was at first unwilling to relinquish his direct command of the army as Senior Commanding General to succeed Jagat Shamsher and he was even prepared to let Eastern Commanding General Jagat Jang become Commander-in-Chief because the latter post under the Rana regime involved responsibility for general civil administration rather than military duties. But Jagat Jang would not agree to accept the rank of Commander-in-Chief unless Dhir was prepared to give up his prior right of succession to the prime ministership as well. While Jagat Jang's attitude on this made Dhir all the more suspicious of Jagat Jang's future designs, Jagat Jang was for the time being allowed to become Senior Commanding General and take over supervision of the army.

King Surendra Bikram Shah Dev (1847-1881) passed away on 19 May 1881, about three years after his eldest son, Crown Prince Trailokya had died. King Surendra's grandson, Prithvi Bir Bikram Shah Dev (1881-1910), now ascended the throne at the age of six. Ranoddip and Dhir lost no time in enthroning King Prithvi because his great grandfather, ex-King Rajendra, who was still alive, had not given up his claim to the throne. The Maharaj and the Commander-in-Chief also feared that Jang Bahadur's sons might support a bid for the throne by Prince Narendra Bikram Shah, King Surendra's second son, if there was any delay in British recognition of the new King, and so sought to obtain this as soon as possible.

Ex-King Rajendra died on 12 July 1881, before the British reply had been received. Though he had not been on the throne since 1847, ex-King Rajendra had survived both his son and grandson and reached the age of 68, thus living longer than any other Shah King in history.

Two Plots in the offing Side by Side

The death within less than four years of direct hereditary successors of three generations of the royal line apparently removed the possibility of any direct threat to the Rana rule from the royal family. However, with a minor on the throne and with a weak and vacillating Prime Minister, conspiratorial politics were again in full swing. Two conspiracies with different objectives were under way about the same time, and if either of the plots had succeeded, Dhir and his sons would have been total losers in the political game.

Senior Commanding General Jagat Jang, Jang's eldest son, had won over to his side his sister, Tara Kumari, the first wife of the deceased Crown Prince Trailokya Bikram Shah, by promising the throne to her daughter in the event of the success of Jagat Jang's conspiracy. He had also enlisted the support of Maharaj-cum-Prime Minister Ranoddip's seniormost wife, Bada Maharani Haripriya Devi, in his move to divest Dhir and his sons of their power by setting the Maharaj against them. Jagat Jang was thus actively engaged in capturing real power for himself.

Prince Narendra Bikram Shah, brother of Crown Prince Trailokya Bikram Shah and uncle of the six-year-old King, was on the grounds of legitimacy based on superior caste vis-˜-vis King Prithvi who was born of a Kanwar's daughter, plotting to gain the throne for himself by getting rid of Maharaj Ranoddip Singh, Dhir Shamsher and his sons along with Jang's sons and other nephews on the roll of succession. Fully aware of the activities of Prince Narendra Bikram Shah's men, Senior Commanding General Jagat Jang was biding his time to jump into the fray at its decisive stage only after the conspirators had physically liquidated Maharaj Ranoddip Singh, Commander-in-Chief Dhir and his sons. If Prince Narendra Bikram Shah enjoyed the support of members of the Thapa, Basnyat and Bista families who were angry at the total usurpation of power by the Rana family, Jagat Jang had succeeded in enlisting the support of the sons of Bam Bahadur and Badri Narsingh who were also jealous of the dominant position of Dhir Shamsher and the growing influence of his sons.

Prince Narendra Bikram's associates had originally planned to execute their plot during Maharaj Ranoddip's visit to India on pilgrimage in 1880, but were unable to put their plans into action. After his return from India the Maharaj went to the tarai on a hunting excursion in December 1881. Jagat Jang also happened to be in India on pilgrimage at that time. Thus, Prince Narendra Bikram Shah and his associates had another chance to act and they actually set 6 January 1882 as the date for striking the decisive blow.

In the nick of time, General Gagan Singh Bhandari's son, Colonel Uttar Dhoj Bhandari, out of his family's traditional hostility against the Thapas, revealed the plans of Prince Narendra Bikram and his associates to Commander-in-Chief Dhir Shamsher. Dhir was already aware of the attitude and moves of both Narendra Bikram's and Jagat Jang's parties and was merely waiting for a suitable pretext to take action against both. Once in possession of concrete and tangible evidence of the Narendra Bikram faction's actual plan of action, Dhir Shamsher decided to lump together Prince Narendra's accomplices with Jagat Jang and his associates for the sake of convenience and strike against members of both the conspiratorial groups at one and the same time.

Suppression of the Plots by Dhir

Dhir did not lose time in using this opportunity to implicate all the enemies and adversaries of the Shamsher Ranas in the plot despite the fact that Jagat Jang himself was away in India and it was most unlikely that his associates would have gone into action without awaiting the final outcome of the efforts of Prince Narendra Bikram's group. Dhir and his sons by their prompt and resolute action effectively forestalled any move by Jagat Jang and his associates, who had to pay dearly in the end for their indecisiveness.

Maharaj Ranoddip Singh returned post-haste to the capital upon receipt of the news of an abortive coup and the arrests of high-ranking officers connected with it. Commander-in-Chief Dhir Shamsher convinced the Maharaj of the complicity of Senior Commanding General Jagat Jang, General Padma Jang and Major-General Bam Bikram Bahadur in a plot to kill the Maharaj, the Commander-in-Chief and his sons in collusion with certain members of the Thapa, Basnyat and Bista families, and some other conspirators were also held guilty of plotting to place Prince Narendra Bikram Shah on the throne. A summary trial was first held at the *dalan*, the official meeting hall at the Commander-in-Chief's residence, where coercive methods were said to have been freely employed in extorting confessions from the alleged conspirators implicating General Jagat Jang, Padma Jang and Bam Bikram Bahadur besides Prince Narendra Bikram Shah in the plot. Its preliminary findings were fully confirmed at the final trial held at the *baithak*, the official meeting hall at the Prime Minister's residence.

Although Dhir's efforts to have Jagat Jang extradited to Nepal were of no avail, the latter was removed from the roll of succession and Jit Jang, his younger brother, was appointed Senior Commanding General in his place. General Padma Jang Bahadur escaped punishment as a result of the intervention of the dowager Queen Mother, who was his half-sister. Prince Narendra Bikram Shah and Major-General Bam Bikram Bahadur were expelled from Nepal to be kept as state prisoners at Chunar in the United Provinces India, under the surveillance of the British Indian Government.

As an aftermath of the suppression of the plot in 1882, out of fifty persons who were arrested in all, ten Brahmins including Subba Tanka Nath and Subba Hom Nath Khatwida were spared their lives by reason of their caste. They were, however, formally rendered outcastes, which involved having their cheeks branded with a red-hot iron and their heads shaven crosswise before they were sent around the city with piglets hanging from their necks and accompanied by drummers who proclaimed to passers-by the nature of the penalty that was being inflicted on them. Colonel Bikram Singh Thapa and Colonel Amar Singh Thapa, who were former Prime Minister Mathbar Singh Thapa's sons, Colonel Indra Singh Shripali Tandon, who was Jang Bahadur's brother-in-law Colonel Sanak Singh Tandon's son, Dhir Man Singh Basnyat, Kul Man Singh Basnyat, Colonel Chandra Singh Pande, Major Sangram Shoor Bista and Khazanchi Shiv Prasad were among those convicted, and twenty of them were executed. Thus Dhir Shamsher dealt with the conspiracy with an iron hand and succeeded in partially clearing the way for the eventual rise of his sons to power in Nepal.

Dhir Shamsher's Predominance

After the ruthless suppression of the conspiracy, real power was exercised by Dhir Shamsher as the strong man while Ranoddip remained the Maharaj only in name. Dhir Shamsher had always been a favourite with Jang Bahadur as his youngest brother, and his long apprenticeship to his famous brother in the administration of both civil and military affairs of state stood him in good stead ever afterwards. He had accompanied Jang Bahadur to Europe in 1850 and also assisted his brother in his campaign against the mutineers in India and ably commanded the Nepali troops there after his brother's return to Nepal. Even before that, Dhir Shamsher had given a very good account of himself as a military commander in Nepal's war with Tibet in 1855-56. His initial occupation of the Kuti pass without the loss of a single life, his superb tactics in capturing Suna-Gompa (the Golden Monastery) on the road between Shigatse and Nepal and the boldness and determination with which he recaptured Kuti after it had been recovered by the Tibetans, earned him well-deserved praise as the hero of that campaign.

Dhir also had experience in conducting Nepal's foreign relations. Immediately before Jang died, Dhir Shamsher had represented the King of Nepal as his Ambassador in the Imperial Darbar held in Delhi in January 1877. He did not sit there with Indian ruling princes but took his seat in a special section reserved for foreign ambassadors.

Among Dhir's contributions in the sphere of Nepal's domestic affairs were the arrangements he made to provide free board and lodging to Brahmin students at the capital and the construction of the road to

Bhimphedi from Chure.

Laurence Oliphant, who met Jang and Dhir in Ceylon on their return journey from Europe in 1851 and accompanied them to Nepal, has recorded his impression of Dhir in the following words:

> My especial favourite of them all was Colonel Dhere Shum Shere (sic) whose thoroughly frank and amiable disposition endeared him to everyone, while his courage and daring commanded universal respect. I know of no one I would rather have by my side in a row than the young colonel, and his brother Jang evidently thought so too when he chose him to assist the capture of the conspirators in the attempt on his life.[5]

Dhir Shamsher had a large family of seventeen sons, and their economic condition was far from satisfactory. They were, therefore, jealous of the position and wealth that Jang Bahadur's sons had had. Furthermore, Dhir's sons had been uncertain about their future, because they felt that after the death of Ranoddip Singh and their own father, absolute authority would devolve on Jagat Jang, Jang Bahadur's eldest son, King Surendra Bikram Shah Dev's son-in-law and Crown Prince Trailokya Bikram Shah's double brother-in-law whose relations with Dhir had always been uneasy.

Prophecy about Ranoddip's Downfall

Sometime before Dhir Shamsher died, Resident Girdlestone had reported to his Government:

> It is not likely that Ranauddip (sic) will outlive him (Dhir) for he may die at any moment. But should he survive, his chance of dying a natural death would be lessened. Except his brother, Dhir Shamsher and the priests whose creature he is, he has not a friend. By neglect of his duties he has alienated the people . . . he has incurred the animosity of every important *sardar* in the country . . . with the strong hand of Dhir Shamsher on his side, he lives in no small dread about his safety. Without his brother's protection, his enemies might be too much for him.[6]

That these words had a prophetic ring about them was proved by subsequent events.

Circumstances following Dhir's Death

Dhir Shamsher died on 14 October 1884 leaving behind him seventeen sons in all. Ten of them, namely, Bir Shamsher, Khadga Shamsher, Rana Shamsher, Dev Shamsher, Chandra Shamsher, Bhim Shamsher, Fatte Shamsher, Lalit Shamsher, Jit Shamsher and Juddha Shamsher were on the roll of succession – of whom, five were destined to become Prime Minister-cum-Maharaj of Nepal in their turn. The remaining seven, namely Dambar Shamsher, Purna Shamsher, Yadu Shamsher, Khamba Shamsher, Durga Shamsher, Sher Shamsher and Harkha Shamsher were not included in the roll on the ground that they were born out of wedlock.

Hardly had five months passed after Dhir's death when General Jagat Jang returned to Kathmandu in April 1885 in the hope of being reinstated on the roll of succession. After the death of Dhir Shamsher, the rivalry between the two factions represented by Jang Bahadur's sons and Dhir Shamsher's sons, known as the Jang Ranas and Shamsher Ranas respectively, became all the more intense, because Ranoddip, always indolent and easy-going, had prematurely shown signs of age and senility and had begun to play more and more into the hands of his seniormost wife, Bada Maharani Haripriya Devi. She was foolish, vain and highly susceptible to flattery, She was known to nag her weak and doting husband habitually, and she embarrassed him by asking him to make her a sort of coronet like his own in public recognition of her active role in conducting the affairs of state. Jagat Jang had ingratiated himself with her by playing on her weaknesses and he now hoped to regain power with her assistance.

Power Struggle between the Jang Ranas and the Shamsher Ranas

After Dhir Shamsher's death, the Kathmandu Valley began to buzz with rumours that Maharaj Ranoddip Singh was not only going to reinstate Jagat Jang on the roll of succession to the prime ministership but was also planning to abdicate in his favour. To Dhir Shamsher's sons, the signs of rapprochement between Ranoddip Singh and Jagat Jang posed a direct threat to their political survival. However, unlike Jang Bahadur's sons who had come under the corruptive and debilitating influence of inherited wealth and position, Dhir Shamsher's seventeen sons were united among themselves and firm in their resolve to meet the threat to their political existence collectively. They had all along nurtured a grievance against Jang Bahadur and his sons on the ground that the Lal Mohars of 1860 and 1867 had placed Jang Bahadur's own sons and grandsons, who were younger than Jang's brothers' sons, higher on the roll of succession without any regard for the principle of seniority in age and agnatic relationship.

Jang Bahadur's sons were divided among themselves and did not seem to fully realize the gravity of the situation they faced. The marriage of the sister of their half-brother Ranabir Jang to Crown Prince Trailokya's first cousin, Dhirendra Bikram Shah, who was Prince Upendra's son, proved to be a source of dissatisfaction to the eldest-born sons of Jang Bahadur, Jagat Jang and Jit Jang, who were born of Colonel Sanak Singh Shripali Tandon's sister. In the caste-ridden atmosphere of Nepali society at the time the fact that the uterine sister of Jagat Jang and Jit Jang was married to just another member of the Khas Chhetri caste, Gajaraj Singh Thapa, son of Kazi Hem Dal Thapa, whereas Ranabir Singh's sister, like Jang's daughters born of wives of the higher Thakuri and Chhetri caste, were married to members of the royal family, caused friction and misunderstanding between Jang's children by his first wife and those by some others.

The marriage of their half-brother General Ranabir Jang's sister to the Crown Prince's first cousin, Dhirendra Bikram Shah, in violation of the formal restriction imposed by the Lal Mohar of 3 May 1849 on the Kanwar Ranajis to marry into families having matrimonial relations with the ruling Shah family, had not pleased the legitimate sons of Jang Bahadur, Jagat Jang and Jit Jang, despite the fact that they themselves, like their father, had earlier married into the Shah family in disregard of the very same legal stipulation. Although their marriage to the members of the Shah family had on the whole helped them move upward in caste and society, yet its immediate effect was one of causing rancour and dissension among Jang Bahadur's sons and daughters because these marriages had also had an unsettling effect on the existing power structure as evidenced by the subsequent changes in the roll of succession. The important role of hypogamous and hypergamous marriages (marriages with a person of lower and higher social class or position respectively) in influencing the political and social power structure in Nepal deserves special notice, although the purity or the superiority of the caste alone did not always determine political succession and preferment.

The younger children born of Jang Bahadur's favourite wives were given precedence in the roll of succession over elder children born of wives other than the mother of Jagat Jang and Jit Jang and the higher caste Thakuri wives belonging to the Chautara family.

On her marriage to Jang Bahadur the Chautaria lady, Hiranya Garbha Kumari Devi, was elevated to the status of Senior or Bada Maharani over the wives he had married earlier. This must have also caused heart-burnings among Jang's other wives and their children. General Padma Jang born of Vishnu Kumari, a daughter of Bada Maharani Hiranya Garbha Kumari's brother, Rana Sher Shah, was placed in the roll of succession above Jang's sons senior to him in age. This must have given offence to Ranabir Jang and also to Jagat Jang's sister, Jethi Maharani Tara Kumari, Crown Prince Trailokya Bikram's first wife, who sided with her brother General Jagat Jang in the ensuing power struggle between the Shamsher Ranas and the Jang Ranas. But General Ranabir Jang's full sister, Khadga Kumari alias Chirbire Maiyan, found herself on the side of the Shamsher brothers probably because of her marriage to Dhirendra Bikram Shah, who had also subsequently married Dip Kumari alias Kanchhi Maiyan, the full sister of the mother of King Prithvi Bir Bikram Shah Dev.

Jang Bahadur, by also including in the roll of succession some other sons of his, born out of wedlock, sought to mollify them and eliminate the dissension among his sons and daughters which chiefly centered on the question of rank and legitimate birth based on caste. Yet the exception made in the case of Jagat Jang's son Yuddha Pratap Jang alias Mukhiya General, by making him a General from the day of his birth as the Royal Princess's son and by granting him precedence over some of his uncles and their sons, caused dissatisfaction among Jang's other children. Notwithstanding Jang's half-hearted and ad hoc measures to harmonize relationship among his own sons on the one hand and between them and his brother's sons on the other, a state of uneasiness and tension existed among Jang Bahadur's sons.

No wonder that this state of affairs gave edge to the Shamsher brothers in their struggle for power with the Jang Ranas. Jagat Jang was doing his best to enlist the support of his cousins other than Dhir Shamsher's sons by using his wealth and prestige as Jang's eldest son and husband of the King's eldest daughter to entice them. But Jagat Jang could not even get the backing of his own full brother at the most critical time.

Jit Jang had become Commander-in-Chief and the next man in line of succession to the prime ministership after the death of Dhir Shamsher, because Jagat Jang, his elder brother, had been removed from the roll of succession as a penalty for his involvement in the 1882 conspiracy. Dissatisfied with the growing rapprochement between Maharaj Ranoddip and General Jagat Jang through the mediation of the Maharaj's senior wife, Haripriya Devi, and fearful of the prospect of having to concede his number two position in the roll of succession to his brother, Commander-in-Chief Jit Jang left for India, soon after his elder brother's return to Kathmandu, on the pretext of having medical treatment. However, Jit Jang continued to plead with his uncle, the Maharaj, from India that he should not tamper with the roll of succession under any circumstances. In his letter to Maharaj Ranoddip, Jit Jang drew his attention to Jang Bahadur's explicit instruction that none shall change the order of succession after it has been established even though it might have been ordained that goats be tied to the posts meant for tying elephants.

Assassination of Maharaj Ranoddip by Dhir Shamsher's Sons

Dhir Shamsher's sons had always felt that there would be no chance for their political survival once Jagat Jang succeeded to Ranoddip Singh as the Maharaj and Prime Minister of Nepal. Even before Jagat Jang was implicated in the plot and removed from the roll of succession during Dhir's lifetime, Ranoddip had himself in a document addressed to Dhir Shamsher levelled the following charges against Jagat Jang: that Jagat (1) called himself His Royal Highness Prince Jagat Jang, (2) named his residence Manohara Palace, (3) called his son also Prince,(4) embossed the documents with his seal modelled after that of the Prime Minister and the Commander-in-Chief, (5) flew a flag at his house and also from his carriage, and (6) did not pay any respect to the Prime Minister and the Commander-in-Chief. Ranoddip had also enacted formal rules and regulations forbidding such actions by Jagat.

But ever since Jagat Jang was called back to Kathmandu by Maharaj Ranoddip under constant prodding by his senior wife, Bada Maharani Haripriya Devi, there had been rumours for months on end not only that Jagat Jang would be reinstated on the roll of succession but even that Ranoddip would resign as Maharaj in favour of Jagat Jang. It was only natural for Dhir's sons to be disturbed by the persistence of these rumours which in fact stimulated them to act before it was too late.

Dhir's sons had taken full advantage of the differences among Jang Bahadur's sons and daughters and had actually won over to their side

Queen Mother Lalit Rajyalakshmi Devi Shah herself, her own sister Dip Kumari Shah known as the Second Princess of Bagh, and their half-sister Khadga Kamari Shah alias Chirbire Maiyan - all of whom were Jang Bahadur's daughters. The fact that Bir Shamsher was raised as a child in Jang Bahadur's house and also that Bir Shamsher was married to the daughter of Prince Upendra whose son was married to Dip Kumari and Khadga Kumari afforded him the opportunity for personal contact with them. If Bir was said to have intimate relations with the Queen Mother, Lalit Rajyalakshmi, Khadga was said to be in love with her full sister, Dip Kumari Shah, wife of Sahebjyu Dhirendra Bikram Shah.

Another lady who played an important part in the court politics of the time was another Khadga Kumari alias Kahili Maiyan, Dhir Shamsher's widow daughter who, although married to the old Raja of Sallyan as a small girl, was childless and had lived with her father and brothers ever since her husband's death. Kahili Maiyan was very close to her first cousin and Jang's daughter, Dip Kumari, who had actually invited Kahili Maiyan to live with her in her house and to take care of her infant son, Bhupatindra, who was sickly.

The Shamsher brothers seem to have exploited to their maximum political advantage the mutual rivalry and jealousy between King Prithvi's mother, Lalit Rajyalakshmi, and her half-sister Tara Kumari, both of whom were married to Crown Prince Trailokya Bikram Shah. Jagat Jang's full sister, Tara Kumari, although the first and the eldest wife of the Crown Prince, had only a daughter and no son of her own whereas Lalit Rajyalakshmi, who was her co-wife, had already seen her son placed on the throne. This partly explains why Tara Kumari found herself on the side of General Jagat Jang while the the King's mother and her full sister, the Second Princess of Bagh, found themselves on the side of Bir Shamsher and Khadga Shamsher.

The power struggle between the Jang Ranas and the Shamsher Ranas that had steadily grown in its intensity since the passing away of Commander-in-Chief Dhir Shamsher reached its climax in November 1885. At that time Bir Shamsher, Dhir's eldest son, was put in charge of four regiments which were being sent to take part in a military parade in India and the Shamsher brothers did not fail to exploit the opportunity presented by Bir Shamsher finding himself in sole and direct command of these four regiments.

On the night of 22 November 1885, the Shamsher brothers went to Ranoddip Singh's Narayan Hiti residence to accomplish their design on the life of the Maharaj and thus to permanently deprive Jang's sons of power and take over complete power for themselves. In a move to ingratiate himself with the royal family, Ranoddip Singh had brought the young King and his mother to Ranoddip's Narayan Hiti residence and had set up permanent living quarters for them there. The conspirators' plan was to assassinate Maharaj Ranoddip and take the King away to his great-uncle's house apparently for his safety and there have him formally appoint Bir Shamsher as the Maharaj and Prime Minister.

On the fateful night of 22 November 1885, Bir Shamsher and his father-in-law, Prince Upendra, who was the 10-year-old King's grand uncle, were waiting downstairs at the main entrance to Maharaj Ranodipp's place at Narayan Hiti (situated at the site of present royal palace in Kathmandu) while four of Bir's half-brothers, Dambar Shamsher, Khadga Shamsher, Chandra Shamsher and Bhim Shamsher, forced their way upstairs by breaking open the lock on the door over the stairs leading to the living quarters of the Maharaj.

There is an eyewitness account of what followed. Gunkeshari, the governess of Balakrishna Sama, the eminent Nepali litterateur, was fourteen years old at the time of Maharaj Ranoddip's assassination and was actually present on the spot. Her description of the event as recorded in Sama's autobiography and regarded as authentic by competent Nepali authorities is as follows:

> In a room locked from inside, the Maharaj was having his back massaged with oil while lying prone and writing the name 'Rama' repeatedly on the pipal leaf before him. The Maharani, his wife, was seated on the floor at some distance from him and I was holding hookah and preparing to offer the pipe to him. An old man was reading aloud from the newspaper and I later on came to learn that Kazi Bal Man was the person. One of the Maharaj's grandnephews by one of his nieces, Chautara Rana Bikram Shah, was heard to repeat in haste in fear, 'Grandpa, please open the door, I am here.' Even after the Maharaj responded by saying that he was having oil applied over his body and therefore the boy should wait outside for a while, the Chautara, whose pet name was Sanu Chautara, continued to knock on the door almost in fright repeating that his maternal uncles were there to talk with the Maharaj. Notwithstanding the Maharaj's instruction to wait for some time, it appeared as though some grown-up men were trying to force the door open by

> kicking hard against it from outside. Everyone inside the room was startled and had eyes fixed on the door. The Maharaj also stopped writing 'Rama' and called out in rage as to who they were. The door came unbolted by itself as a result of the pressure applied from the outside. The men in long black coats looking like messengers of Yama, the Hindu god of death, stampeded into the room. I recognized them later on as Khadga Shamsher, Chandra Shamsher, Bhim Shamsher and your own grandfather, Dambar Shamsher. Dambar was the first to kneel in front of the Maharaj stuttering all along that such will be the fate of one who seeks shelter under the petticoat of one's wife. But your grandfather was breathing so hard that he could hardly hold his handgun's aim firm. Meanwhile Khadga Shamsher rested his hand on Dambar's shoulder and fired a bullet which grazed through the upper crust of the Maharaj's head and shattered the glass of an almirah in the room. The Maharaj holding his head in both of his hands slumped over the pipal leaf shouting 'The sinner has got me!' All of us screamed and stood on our feet. At that very moment, your grandfather, Dambar fired another fatal shot causing the Maharaj's jaws to fall apart — Bada Maharani (the Maharaj's wife) and all of us maidservants started throwing vases, picture frames and other articles, at those messengers of the god of death who, regardless of everything, dragged the Maharaj's body by the feet. Bhim Shamsher fired another bullet at the Maharaj's thighs as if to frighten us and pulled the dead body along the ladder letting the Maharaja's head strike against its every rung. They tried to take away the Maharaj's wife but could not do so.[7]

Captain Fauda Singh Khatri Chhetri had been posted at the lane leading to the bungalow of General Dhor Narsingh, the adopted son and aide-de-camp of Maharaj Ranoddip, with strict instructions to shoot the General if he came that way after hearing the conspirator' gunfire upstairs in the Maharaj's palace. When Fauda Singh proceeded to the General's bungalow sometime after he had himself heard the fire of the revolvers, General Dhor Narsingh came staggering towards him dead drunk and the captain saw no reason to take his life for nothing. The murdered Maharaj's wife was heard to shout from one of the windows that Dhir Shamsher's sons had murdered the Maharaj. But the security guards were no longer there and Subba Bal Man and others had also run for their lives.

This dreadful event, the cold-blooded murder of a childless aged uncle by his own nephews, marked the transition from the rule of Jang Bahadur's seven brothers (Satbhai) to that of Dhir Shamsher's seventeen sons (Satrabhai) in the political history of Nepal.

After killing Maharaj Ranoddip, Khadga and others made their way to the royal living quarters in the Maharaj's residence and escorted the 10-year-old King along with his mother Lalit Rajyalakshmi and her sister, Dip Kumari, to the main gate where Bir was waiting for them with his father-in-law.

They immediately put the King and the ladies of the royal household in a waiting horse-drawn carriage and set out for the residence of the King's great-uncle, Upendra. When the head of the murdered Prime Minister's security force, Narabir Basnyat, turned up with his men at that juncture, he was told that it appeared as though there had been an attempt on life of the Maharaj and his men should follow the carriage to protect the King and other members of the royal family. The officer and men of the security force carried out the instruction without demur.

As soon as the royal party accompanied by some of Dhir Shamsher's sons arrived at the King's great-uncle's residence, Bir was proclaimed Maharaj by the King. The residence known as Bagh Darbar was already guarded by the four regiments of soldiers placed under Bir's command for being sent to the Rawalpindi march past in India.

Jagat Jang, Jang Bahadur's eldest son, was the other target of the 1885 coup d'etat, and his physical elimination, too, had been preplanned. Lalit Man Singh, Bir Shamsher's maternal uncle, was assigned the task of killing Jagat Jang. Lalit Man Singh reportedly surrounded his Manohara residence with troops and shot him dead as he came down the stairs in response to a call from Lalit Man Singh.

Harka Jang, one of Jang Bahadur's natural sons, who had unwittingly gone to the central parade ground in response to the bugle's call early in the morning, reportedly made his way to their Thapathali residence and informed his half-brothers of the coup before troops loyal to Bir Shamsher had had time to lay a siege on the palace. Three of Jang's descendants, two sons and one grandson, all of whom were on the roll of succession, General Padma Jang, General Ranabir Jang and General Juddha Pratap Jang who was Jang's grandson by the royal princess married to Jagat Jang, had thus been able to escape from the Thapathali Palace to seek asylum in the British Residency.

On their way to the British Residency, two sons of Jang Bahadur started discussing what valuables they had been able to bring along with them such as gold, gold coins, and jewels. On overhearing their conversation, their nephew Juddha Pratap Jang decided to go back back to the palace so that he might carry away some of his own jewellery and valuables. But this decision cost him his life. The palace was surrounded by Bir Shamsher's troops by the time he was ready to leave it again and while trying to get out of the palace compound, Juddha Pratap Jang was shot dead by a sentry in the field. Thus, by the morning of 23 November 1885, not only Maharaj Ranoddip but two other important personages had lost their lives: the eldest son and a grandson of Maharaj Jang Bahadur.

Among those who sought asylum in the British Residency were not only Jang's sons, General Padma Jang and General Ranabir Jang, but also Jang's third brother Badri Narsingh's sons, General Kedar Narsingh and his younger brother, General Dhor Narsingh who was the adopted son and aide-de-camp of the murdered Maharaj along with the King's uncle, Narendra Bikram Shah. The King's stepmother, the eldest dowager Maharani, Tara Kumari, and the murdered Prime Minister's first wife, Haripriya Devi, were the two ladies of high rank who fled to the British Residency for their safety.

Bir's second half-brother Khadga Shamsher went to the British Residency and, with Acting Resident Colonel Berkeley's permission, met all of the refugees and tried to persuade them to return to their homes. He succeeded in persuading four of them to leave; the King's stepmother, the King's uncle, General Padma Jang and General Kedar Narsingh. All of them except Narendra Bikram Shah, the King's uncle, made their way to India in due course, and those who refused to leave the Residency under Khadga's persuasion were safely conducted to India with their personal assets intact by the British Residency under its own care and protection.

Brief Assessment of Ranoddip's Prime Ministership

Ranoddip continued the policy of friendship with the British in India more or less on the same terms as Jang Bahadur. When a British Resident was murdered in Kabul in 1880, Ranoddip not only sympathized with the British verbally but also made an offer of military assistance to the British, should the necessity arise, in the same way as his eldest brother Jang had done in 1857, and he did not also fail to congratulate the British on their victory in Egypt in 1882.

However, the British Government in India thought of him essentially as a weak and headstrong Prime Minister. They regarded his friendly gestures merely as an easy method of demonstrating loyalty to the British cause with a view to obtaining titles and other concessions from the British so that he might be able to strengthen his own position in Nepal.

The question of the removal of restrictions on the movement of the Resident and the recruitment of Nepali men as soldiers in the British army appeared to be the main concerns of the British Residents in Nepal. Left to themselves, they would have liked to use British recognition of every change in, or succession to, the office of head of state or head of government as a political leverage to secure the removal of the above-mentioned restrictions. But the British Government in India always seemed to stop them from putting too much pressure on the Nepali authorities to gain these ends.

Though Jang Bahadur's immediate successors, both Ranoddip and Bir, did not allow greater freedom of movement and access to the British Residents, they did tend to relax gradually their opposition to the recruitment of Nepali soldiers for the British army. This change occurred after the British had dangled before them the prospect of their being able to purchase rifles, guns, and ammunition in direct proportion to the number of men the British were allowed to recruit.

When the question of British recognition of King Surendra's successor arose in 1881, both Resident Girdlestone and Acting Resident Colonel Impey seemed to have at one stage thought of exploiting the internal situation by withholding recognition of the 6-year-old King Prithvi Bir Bikram Shah Dev in order to press Maharaj Ranoddip for the removal of restrictions on the British Resident and on the entry of private British citizens into Nepal. But Governor-General Dufferin, on the advice of Foreign Secretary Lyall, asked the Resident not to put "authoritative pressure on the Nepali Government" for these matters. The Foreign Secretary had made the Government of India's stand on the question very clear by noting on the margin of the file for the Governor-General that

> I am not sure that our own security demands an alteration of the Resident's position, and failing, it is open to question whether we have the right to exact from an independent state concessions to which its rules, and perhaps its peoples, are strongly opposed – the Durbar is not bound, being independent, and outside the recognized

circle of our Indian feudatories, to give him the right of free communication with its subjects.[8]

Trade had all along proved to be another vexing problem between Nepal and British India. Nepal was opposed to the entry of private British merchants into the country. Trade was carried on with Nepal by British Indian merchants. Improved transport would have facilitated the growth of trade, but the Nepali authorities felt rightly or wrongly till the end of the last century that any change in the antiquated system of roads would increase Nepal's vulnerability to invasion by the British; it was Nepal's concern for its basic security that prevented it from cooperating with the British in modernizing transport.

It was not that the Nepali authorities were not interested in raising their revenues from trade. Trade marts were specially set up at several points on the border with India so that Indian merchants might buy and sell goods freely there upon payment of customs and other charges to the Nepali authorities. But difficulties and differences with regard to the tariff policy of the two countries also hindered the free flow of trade.

Like his predecessor, Jang Bahadur, Maharaj Ranoddip also once lodged a complaint with the Governor-General against the Resident. But the difference was that Ranoddip was afraid of even incurring the displeasure of Resident Girdlestone and asked Dufferin not to let his complaints against him spoil his relations with Girdlestone, whereas Jang Bahadur had demanded the removal of Resident Ramsay in his note to Governor-General Canning. Ranoddip's letter of complaint was taken to be "a treacherous attack on the Viceroy's representative" and returned to the Maharaj without its having been placed before Dufferin, but the Resident was asked not to seek an explanation from the Prime Minister for fear of "a diplomatic rupture".[9] This incident sheds some light on how diplomacy was conducted between Nepal and India in actual practice at the time. Ranoddip's attempt to continue Jang Bahadur's basic policy vis-a-vis the British in India might not have satisfied the British, but it must be said to the credit of Ranoddip that on the whole his policy prevented the British in India from exploiting his weak position inside his own country.

NOTES

1. Girdlestone to Lyall—Foreign Department Political—A Proceedings, 10 September 1879, Nos. 386, 90 K.W. No. 1 (N.A.I), cited in Asad Husain, *British India's*

Relations with the Kingdom of Nepal (London: George Allen & Unwin, Ltd., 1970), p. 112.

2. Foreign Department Political—A Proceedings, 22 March 1877—Nos. 1,7,11 K.W. No. 55 (N.A.I), cited in Kanchanmoy Mojumdar, *Political Relations Between India and Nepal (1877-1923)* (Delhi: Munshiram Manoharlal Publishers Private Ltd., 1973), p. 20.
3. Daniel Wright, *History of Nepal* (Cambridge: Cambridge University Press, 1877), p. 68.
4. Richard Temple, ed., *Journals Kept in Hyderabad, Kashmir, Sikkim and Nepal*, 2 Vols (London, 1887), pp. 249-62.
5. Laurence Oliphant, *A Journey to Kathmandu* (London: John Murray, 1852), p. 165.
6. Girdlestone to Lyall—Foreign Department Political—A Proceedings, 30 April 1881—No. 285 (N.A.I.) cited in Kanchanmoy Mojumdar, *Political Relations between India and Nepal (1877-1923)* (Delhi: Munshiram Manoharlal Publishers Private Ltd., 1973), p. 40.
7. Balakrishna Sama, *Mero Kavita ko Aradhana* (lit. *My Devotion to Poetry)* (Kathmandu, Royal Nepal Academy, 2023 (V.S.) (A.D. 1966)), Vol. 1, pp. 27-28.
8. Report of the Under Secretary, Foreign Political—A, February 1882, Nos. 283-304 (NAI) cited in Asad Husain, *op. cit.*, p. 118.
9. Asad Husain, *op. cit.*, pp. 128-29.

Chronology

1769-1775	- Reign of King Prithvinarayan Shah.
1768 (26 September)	- King Prithvinarayan marched into Kathmandu and sat on its throne. Patan also fell into his hands.
1769	- King Prithvinarayan also took possession of Bhadgaun.
1770	- The Gorkhali forces defeated in a war with the Chaubise, or the Twenty-four Principality rulers.
1773	- Prithvinarayan's troops acquired control of Chaudandi.
1775	- Vijayapur and Morang conquered.
1770-1775	- Restrictions on trade with Tibet and dispute over the circulation of Nepal-minted coins in Tibet.
1774	- The Gorkhas attacked Sikkim and carried their operations to the borders of Bhutan in a move to close the Sikkim and Bhutan trade routes.
1775 (11 January)	- Death of King Prithvinarayan Shah and accession of his eldest son Pratap Singh Shah to throne at the age of 23.
1775-1777	- Reign of King Pratap Singh Shah.
1775	- Treaty between Nepal and Tibet.
1777	- Upardang Garhi, Chitwan and Someshwar Garhi annexed.
(July-September)	
1777 (November)	- Death of King Pratap Singh Shah and acces-

	sion of his 2½ year-old infant son Rana Bahadur Shah to the throne with Dowager Queen Rajendralakshmi as Regent.
1777-1799	- Reign of King Rana Bahadur Shah.
1777-1785	- Regency of Dowager Queen Rajendralakshmi (except for an interregnum of her brother-in-law Bahadur Shah's ten-month administration between August 1778 and June 1779).
1779-1785	- Her campaign against the Chaubise remained unaccomplished except for the absorption into the Gorkhali Kingdom of some of the smaller Chaubise principalities on the bank of the river Andhi Khola.
1785 (July)	- Death of Regent Queen Rajendralakshmi.
1785-1794	- Regency of Naib Bahadur Shah.
1786-1787	- Parbat, Gulmi Argha Khanchi, Musikot, Galkot and Pyuthan incorporated in the Gorkhali Kingdom.
1788	- First Nepal-Tibet War.
1789	- Control over the entire Karnali basin following the annexation of Dailekh, Dullu, Bajhang, Achham and Doti.
1789	- Nepal-Tibet Treaty.
1790	- Annexation of Kumaun.
1791	- Partial Control of Garhwal.
1791	- Second Nepal Tibet War.
1792 (March)	- Treaty of Commerce between Nepal and the East India Company's Government.
1792	- The Nepal-China War, which ended in late September.
1793	- The Kirkpatrick Mission to Kathmandu.
1794 (May)	- Dismissal of Regent Bahadur Shah and assumption of full powers by King Rana Bahadur Shah.
1795	- The Abdul Kadir Khan Mission.
1797 (July)	- Death of Bahadur Shah in confinement.
1797-1799	- The Wazir Ali Incident.
1799 (23 March)	- Abdication of King Rana Bahadur Shah and accession of his infant son, King Girvana Yuddha Shah Dev, aged 1½ years. Regency

	of Queen Rajarajeshvari and joint Council (March 1799 - May 1799).
1799-1816	- Reign of King Girvana Yuddha Bikram Shah.
1799 (27 May)	- Rana Bahadur's withdrawal to Varanasi accompanied by his Senior Queen Rajarajeshvari, Balabhadra Shah and Bhimsen Thapa.
1800-1803	- Regency of Queen Suvarnaprabha.
1801 (26 October)	- The Treaty of 1801 with the East-India Company's Government-
1802 (April)	- W.O. Knox took up his residence in Kathmandu as the first British representative.
1803 (February)	- Regency of Queen Suvarnaprabha ended.
1803 (February)– 1804 (March)	- Regency of Queen Rajarajeshvari.
1803 (March)	- Withdrawal of the Knox Mission from Kathmandu.
1803	- Nepal's expansion towards the west resumed under the leadership of Amar Singh Thapa.
1804	- The Treaty of 1801 regarded as null and avoid, effective 24 January 1804.
1804	- Return of ex-King Rana Bahadur Shah to Kathmandu.
1804	- Expulsion of Queen Rajarajeshvari to Helambu and execution of her Minister, Kazi Damodar Pande.
1806 (April)	- Regent (ex-King) Rana Bahadur Shah assassinated.
	- The Gorkha Kingdom extended westward as far as the Satlaj River.
1806 (April) 1832 (April)	- Regency of Queen Tripurasundari with Bhimsen Thapa as Mukhtiyar General.
1814-1816	- War with the East India Company's Government.
1815 (2 December)	- Treaty of Sugauli initialled.
1816 (4 March)	- Treaty of Sugauli ratified by Nepal at Makwanpur after more fighting.
1816 (20 November)	- Death of King Girvana Yuddha Bikram Shah Dev and accession of King Rajendra Bikram Shah Dev, aged 21 years.
1816-1847	- Reign of King Rajendra Bikram Shah.

1832 (6 April)	- Death of Regent Queen Tripurasundari (1806-1832).
1837 (July)	- Dismissal of Mukhtiyar General Bhimsen Thapa and Rise of Rana Jang Pande as Mukhtiyar.
1837 (December)	- Replacement of Rana Jang Pande by Guru Ranga Nath Pandit as Mukhtiyar.
1838 (August)	- Joint Mukhtiyarship of Chautara Pushkar Shah and Rana Jang Pande.
1839 (April)	- Pushkar Shah had become subordinate to Rana Jang Pande.
1839	- Rearrest and suicide of Bhimsen Thapa.
1840 (6 February)	- Appointment of Rana Jang Pande as Mukhtiyar.
1840 (13 April)	- Ramnagar Incursion.
1840 (21-22 June)	- A mutiny of 6,000 soldiers orchestrated by Mukhtiyar Rana Jang Pande and Senior Queen Samrajyalakhsmi.
1840 (September)	- Withdrawal of Gorkha troops from Ramnagar, India and payment of Rs 5,000 as compensation.
1840 (1 November	- Replacement of Rana Jang Pande by Chautara Fatte Jang
to March 1843)	Shah as Mukhtiyar or Prime Minister.
1840 (6 October)	- Death of Senior Queen Samrajyalakhsmi Devi.
1842 (7 December)	- Public demands presented to King Rajendra by court officials.
1843 (1 January)	- Delegation of the *hukum*, the sovereign power to rule by peremptory command, to Junior Queen Rajyalakshmi Devi.
1843 (17 April)	- Return of Mathbar Singh Thapa to Kathmandu.
1843 (30 November)	- Arrival of Major Henry Lawrence as new Resident.
1843 (5 December)	- Departure of Resident Hodgson from Kathmandu after more than 22 years' service, first as Acting Resident from 1820 till 1832 and then from January 1833 onward as Resident.
1843 (26 December)	- Assumption of prime ministership by General Mathbar Singh Thapa.

1844 (22 January)	- Unsuccessful mutiny of soldiers orchestrated by General Mathbar Singh Thapa demanding only one ruler of the country.
1844 (May)	- Abrupt resignation of General Mathbar.
1844 (18 October)	- Mathbar resumed the prime ministership after King Rajendra declared that there would be only one ruler.
1844 (10 December)	- The Dhukuwabas incident forced King Rajendra to order his troops to accept the Heir Apparent as King.
1844 (13 December)	- Mathbar Singh returned to Kathmandu.
1844 (14 December)	- "Maharajadhiraj" Surendra returned to Kathmandu.
1844 (18 December)	- King Rajendra handed over partial authority to the Crown Prince.
1844 (23 December)	- Cancellation of the order of 10 December by King.
1845 (20 January)	- Mathbar appointed Prime Minister for life.
1845 (17 May)	- Assassination of Prime Minister Mathbar Singh Thapa by Jang Bahadur Rana in league with General Gagan Singh Bhandari.
1845 (18 May)	- Jang Bahadur appointed General.
1845 (14 August)	- Fatte Jang returned to Kathmandu.
1845 (22 September)	- A coalition Government consisting of General Gagan Singh Bhandari, General Abhiman Singh Rana Magar and Kazi Dalabhanjan Pande, with General Jang Bahadur Rana as its "military member" was formed under the nominal leadership of Chautara Fatte Jang Shah.
1846 (14-15 September)	- Assassination of General Gagan Singh and the Kot Massacre.
1846-1877	- Rule of Prime Minister Jang Bahadur Rana.
1846 (31 October)	- The Basnyat conspiracy foiled by Jang Bahadur Rana.
1846 (22 November)	- Junior Queen Rajyalakshmi and her two sons, Princes Rajendra and Birendra, voluntarily accompanied by King Rajendra left for Varanasi.

1847 (March-April)	- King Rajendra returned to Alau and with the support of Chautara Guru Prasad Shah and Jagat Bam Pande made an unsuccessful bid for power in Kathmandu.
1847 (12 May at 8.00 p.m.)	- Crown Prince Surendra Bikram Shah was crowned King in place of King Rajendra Bikram Shah.
1847 (30 November)	- Crown Prince Trailokya Bikram born.
1847-1881	- Reign of King Surendra Bikram Shah.
1847 (28 July)	- Ex-King Rajendra Bikram Shah brought to Kathmandu in fetters and kept under strict surveillance till his death in July 1881.
1848 (December)	- The royal "Hunting Expedition" in the tarai accompanied by Jang Bahadur and Nepali troops in considerable strength.
1850 (25 May to 20 August)	- Jang Bahadur's visit to Great Britain.
1850 (2 August to 10 October)	- Jang Bahadur's visit to France.
1854	- Promulgation of the Mulki Ain, and legal code.
1854 (8 May)	- Marriage of Jang Bahadur's eldest son General Jagat Jang to King Surendra's second daughter.
1854	A few days after his son's marriage Jang Bahadur married 23 year-old Hiranyagarbha Kumari, sister of Chautara Prime Minister Fatte Jang Shah, who was killed in the Kot Massacre.
1855-1856	- The Nepal-Tibet War and the 1856 Nepal-Tibet Treaty of 24 March 1856.
1856 (6 August)	- Jang Bahadur made Maharaj of Kaski and Lamjung with absolute authority over the King and the Prime Minister.
1856	- Marriage of Jang Bahadur's eldest daughter Tara Kumari to Heir Apparent Trailokya Bikram Shah.
1857 (10 December)	- Departure of Jang Bahadur from Kathmandu with 9,0000 troops to assist the East India Company's Government suppress the Indian Mutiny.

1858	- Jang Bahadur occupied Gorakhpur in January 1858 and took part in lifting the siege on Lucknow on 13 March.
1859	- Retrocession to Nepal a portion of territory it had ceded to the Nawab of Oudh following the 1814-1816 war with the East India Company's Government.
1860	- Marriage of Heir Apparent Trailokya Bikram Shah to Lalit Rajyalakshmi, Jang Bahadur's daughter by Hiranyagarbha Kumari, who became the mother of King Prithvi Bir Bikram Shah Dev (1881-1911).
1877 (25 February)	- Death of Jang Bahadur who was succeeded to the office of Maharaj and Prime Minister by his eldest surviving brother Ranoddip Singh.
1877-1885	- Rule of Maharaj Ranoddip Singh.
1878	- Death of Crown Prince Trailokya Bikram Shah and the devolution of his royal rights on his infant son Pritivi Bir Bikram Shah.
1879	- Death of Commander-in-Chief Jagat Shamsher.
1881 (19 May)	- Death of King Surendra Bikram Shah Dev and accession of his 6 year-old grandson King Pritivi Bir Bikram Shah Dev.
1881-1911	- Reign of Pritivi Bir Bikram Shah Dev.
1881 (12 July)	- Death of ex-King Rajendra Bikram Shah Dev.
1882	- Suppression by C.-in-C. Dhir Shamsher of two plots that had been in the offing since 1878.
1884 (14 October)	- Death of C.-in-C. Dhir Shamsher.
1885 (22 November)	- Assassination of Maharaj Prime Minister Ranoddip Singh; Bir Shamsher proclaimed Maharaj Prime Minister.
1885-1901	- Rule of Maharaj Bir Shamsher.
1885 (23 November)	- By the morning of 23 November two other important personages had lost their lives the eldest son and grandson of Maharaj Jang Bahadur, General Jagat Jang and General Yuddha Pratap Jang.

1885 Some of the surviving sons of Jang Bahadur and Badri Narsingh along with the King's uncle, Narendra Bikram Shah and the two ladies of high rank, the King's stepmother, the eldest dowager Maharani Tara Kumari and the murdered Prime Minister's first wife, Haripriya Devi, fled to the British Residency for their safety. All of them except the King's uncle, Narendra Bikram Shah, made their way to India.

Bibliography

Western Languages

Adhikari, Krishna Kant. *Nepal under Jang Bahadur 1846-1877*, Vol. 1. Kathmandu: 'Buku', 1984.

Agarwal, Hem Narayan. *The Administrative System of Nepal. From Tradition to Modernity*. Delhi: Vikash, 1976.

Aitchison, C.U. *A Collection of Treaties, Engagements, and Sunnuds Relating to India and Neighbouring Countires*. Vols. I (1862), II (1863), V (1864) and XIV (1929), Calcutta.

Allen, Michael. *The Cult of Kumari–Virgin Worship in Nepal*. Kathmandu: University Press, 1975.

Ballantine, Henry. *On India's Frontier or Nepal. The Gurkhas' Mysterious Land*. London: Redway, 1896.

Berreman, Gerald. *Hindus of the Himalayas*. Berkeley: University of California Press, 1963.

Bhasin, A.S. *Documents on Nepal's Relations with India and China (1946-66)*. Bombay: Academic Books, 1970.

Bhattacharjee, G.P. *India and the Politics of Modern Nepal*. Calcutta: Minerva Associates, 1970.

Bista, Dor Bahadur. *The People of Nepal*. Kathmandu: Department of Publicity, 1967.

Cammann, Schuyler. *Trade Through the Himalayas: The Early British Attempts to Open Tibet*. Princeton, N.J.: Princeton University Press, 1951.

Caplan. Lionel, *Land and Social Change in East Nepal: A Study of Hindu Tribal Relations*. London: Routledge and Kegan Paul, 1970.

Chatterji, Bhola. *A Study of Recent Nepalese Politics*. Calcutta: World Press, 1967.

Chaudhuri, K.C. *Anglo-Nepalese Relations*. Calcutta: Modern Book Agency, 1960.

Chauhan, R.S. *Political Development in Nepal, 1950-70*. New Delhi: Associated Publishing House, 1970.

Davis, Hassoldt. *Nepal, Land of Mystery*. London: Robert Hale, 1942.

Digby, William, 1857. *A Friend in Need: 1887, Friendship Forgotten: An Episode in Indian Foreign Office Administration*. London: Indian Political Agency, 1890.

Edwardes, Sir Herbert Benjamin and Merivale, Herman. *Life of Sir Henry Lawrence*, Vols. I and II, London: Smith, Elder and Co. 1872.

Egerton, Francis. *Journal of a Winter's Tour in India: With a Visit to the Court of Nepal*. London: John Murray, 1852, 2 Vols.

Gaige, Frederick H. *Regionalism and National Unity in Nepal*. Berkeley, Los Angeles, London: University of California Press, 1975.

Furer-Haimendorf, Christoph von. *The Sherpas of Nepal: Buddhist Highlanders*. Berkeley: University of California Press, 1964.

———, *Himalayan Traders*. London: John Murray, 1976.

Goodall, Merill, R. 'Administrative Changes in Nepal', Chapter 10 in Braibanti (ed.), *Asian Bureaucratic Systems Emergent from the British Imperial Tradition*. Durban, N.C.: Duke University Press, 1966, pp. 605-42.

Goyal, Narendra. *The King and His Constitution: Observation and Commentary on the Constitution of the Kingdom of Nepal*. New Delhi: Nepal Trading Corporation, 1959.

———, *Political History of Himalayan States–India's Relations with Himalayan States Since 1947*. New Delhi: Cambridge Book and Stationery Stores, 1964. (2nd edition).

Gupta, A. *Politics in Nepal: A Study of Post-Rana Political Developments and Party Politics*. Bombay: Allied Publishers, 1964.

Hagen, Toni. *Nepal, the Kingdom in the Himalayas*. Berne: Kummerly and Frey, Geographical Publishers, 1961.

Hamilton, Francis (Buchanan). *An Account of the Kingdom of Nepal and of the Territories Annexed to this Dominion by the House of Gurkha*. Edinburgh: Archibald Constable and Co., 1819.

Harris, George L., *et al.* U.S. *Army Areas Handbook for Nepal (With Sikkim and Bhutan)*. Washington: Government Printing Offce, 1964.

Hasrat, Bikrama Jit, ed. *History of Nepal as Told by its Own and Contemporary Chroniclers*. Hoshiarpur: V.V. Research Institute Press, 1970.

Hitchcock, John T. *The Magars of Banyan Hill*, New York: Hold, Rinehart and Winston, 1966.

Hodgson, Brian Houghton. *Essays on the Languages, Litrature, and Religion of Nepal and Tibet, Together with Further Papers on the Geography, Ethnology, and Commerce of Those Countries*, London: Trubner, 1874.

Hunter, William Wilson. *Life of Brian Houghton Hodgson: British Resident at the Court of Nepal*. London: John Murray, 1896.

Husain, Asad. *British India's Relations with the Kingdom of Nepal*, London: George Allen and Unwin, 1970.

Jain, M.S. *Emergence of a New Aristocracy in Nepal (1837-58)*. Agra: Sri Ram Mehta and Co., 1972.

Joshi, Bhuwan Lal and Leo E. Rose. *Democratic Innovations in Nepal: A Case Study of Political Acculturation*. Berkeley: University of California Press, 1966.

Kirkpatrick, W. *An Account of the Kingdom of Nepal (being the substance of observations made during a mission to the country in the year 1793)*, London. William Miller, 1811.

Kramrisch, Stella. *The Art of Nepal*. New York: The Asia Society, Inc., 1964.

Krishnamurti, Y.G. *His Majesty King Mahendra Bir Bikram Shaha Deva: An Analytical Biography*. Bombay: The Nityanand Society, no date.

Kumar, Satish, *Rana Polity in Nepal: Origin and Growth*. Bombay: Asia Publishing House, 1967.

Landon, Perceval, *Nepal*. London: Constable and Co., 1928, 2 Vols.

Levi, Sylvain. *Le Nepal: Etude Historique d'un Royaume Hindion*. Paris: Ernest Leroux, 1905, 1908. Annales du Musee Guimet; Bibliotheque d'etudes, Tomes XVII, XVIII, and XIX.

Locke, John K., *Karunamaya – The Cult of Avalokitesvara – Matsyendranath in the Valley of Nepal*. Kathmandu: University Press, 1975.

——— *Buddhist Monasteries of Nepal*. Kathmandu, Sahayogi Press, 1985.

Manandhar, Tri Ratna. *Some Aspects of Rana Rule in Nepal*. Kathmandu: Purna Devi Manandhar, 1983.

Markham. Clements R. *Narratives of the Mission of George Bogle to Tibet and of the Journey of Thomas Manning to Lhasa*. London: Trubner, 1879.

Mihaly, Eugene Bramer. *Foreign Aid and Politics in Nepal: A Case Study*. London: Oxford University Press, 1965.

Mojumdar, Kanchanmoy. *Political Relations between India and Nepal (1877-1923)*. Delhi: Munshiram Manoharlal, 1973.

———. *Anglo-Napalese Relations in the Nineteenth Century*. Calcutta: Firma K.L. Mukhopadhyay, 1973.

———. *Nepal and the Indian Nationalist Movement*. Calcutta: Firma K.L . Mukhopadhyay, 1975.

Muni, S.D. *Foreign Policy of Nepal*. Delhi: National Publishing House, 1973.

Northey, W. Brook, and Morris, C.J. *The Gurkhas, their Manners, Customs and Country*. London: John Lane, 1928.

Oldfield, H.A. *Sketches from Nepal*. London: W.H. Allen and Co., 1880, 2 Vols.

Pemble, John. *The Invasion of Nepal: John Company at War*. Oxford: Clarendon Press 1971.

Petech, Luciano. *Medieval History of Nepal (c. 750-1490)*. Rome: Institute Italiano Per II Medio Estremo Oriente, 1958.

Prasad, Ishwari. *The Life and Times of Maharaja Juddha Shumsher Jung Bahadur Rana of Nepal*. New Delhi: Asia Publishing House, 1975.

Prinsep, Henry T. *A Narrative of the Political and Military Transactions of British India, Under the Administration of the Marquess of Hastings (1813-1818)*, Chapters II and V. London: John Murray, 1820.

Ramakant. *Indo-Napalese Relations 1868-1877*. Delhi: S. Chand and Co., 1968.

Rana, Pramode Shumshere. *Rana Nepal An Insider's View* (with a foreword by Professor M.R. Allen, University of Sydney, Australia). Kathmandu: Sahayogi Press, 1978.

Rana, Pudma Jung Bahadur (ed. A.C. Mukherji). *Life of Maharaja Sir Jung Bahadur of Nepal*. Allahabad: Pioneer Press, 1909.

Reed, Horace, B. and Marry I. Reed. *Nepal in Transition: Educational Innovation*. University of Pittsburgh Press, 1968.

Regmi, Dilli Raman. *A Century of Family Autocracy in Nepal*. Banaras: *Nepali National Congress*, 1950.

———. *Modern Nepal*. Calcutta:Firma K.L. Mukhopadhyay, 1961.

———. *Modern Nepal: Rise and Growth in the Eighteenth Century.* Vol. I, Calcutta: Firma K.L. Mukhopadhyay, 1975.

———. *Modern Nepal.* Vol. II, Calcutta : Firma K.L. Mukhopadhyay, 1975.

Regmi, Mahesh C. *Land Tenure and Taxation in Nepal.* Berkeley: Institute of International Studies, Univesity of California, 1963-68, 4 Vols.

———. *A Study in Nepali Economic History (1768-1846).* New Delhi: Manjusri Publishing House, 1971.

———. *Landownership in Nepal.* Berkeley, Los Angeles, London: University of California Press, 1976.

———. *Thatched Huts and Stucco Palaces: Peasant and Landlord in the Nineteenth Century Nepal.* New Delhi: Vikas, 1979.

Rose, Leo, E. 'Communism under High Atmospheric Conditions: The Party in Nepal', in Scalapino (ed.), *Comparative Communism in Asia.* New York: Prentice-Hall, 1965.

———. *Nepal—Strategy for Survival.* Berkeley: University of California Press, 1971.

———. *Nepal: Government and Politics.* New Haven: Human Relations Area Files, 1956.

Rose, Leo, E. and Margaret W. Fisher, *The Politics of Nepal: Persistence and Change in an Asian Monarchy.* Ithaca: Cornell University Press, 1970.

———. *England, India, Nepal, Tibet, China, 1765-1958.* Berkeley: University of California Press, June 1959.

Sanwal, B.D. *Nepal and the East India Company.* Bombay: Asia Publishing House, 1965.

Shaha, Rishikesh, *Nepal and the World,* 3rd edition. Kathmandu: Naya Nepal Prakashan, 1962.

———. *Heroes and Builders of Nepal,* 5th reprint. Calcutta: Oxford University Press, 1970.

———. *Nepali Politics: Retrospect and Prospect,* 2nd edition. Delhi: Oxford University Press, 1978.

———. *An Introduction to Nepal.* Kathmandu: Ratna Pustak Bhandar, 1975.

———. *Essays in the Practice of Government in Nepal.* Delhi: Manohar, 1982.

Slusser, Mary Shepherd. *Nepal Mandala – A Cultural Study of the Kathmandu Valley.* Princeton, N.J.: Princeton University Press, 1983.

Snellgrove, David. *Buddhist Himalaya: Travels and Studies in Quest of the Origins and Nature of Tibetan Religion*. New York: Philosophical Library, 1958.

———. *Indo-Tibetan Buddhism*, Indian Buddhists and their Tibetan Successors, 2 vols. Boston: Shambhala, 1987.

———. *Himalayan Pilgrimage: A Study of Tibetan Religion*. Oxford Bruno Cassirer, 1961.

Stiller, L.F. *Prithwinarayan Shah in the Light of Dibya Upadesh*. Ranchi: The Catholic Press, 1968.

———. *The Rise of the House of Gorkha: A Study in the Unification of Nepal*. New Delhi: Manjusri Publishing House, 1973.

———. *The Silent Cry: The People of Nepal (1816-1839)*. Kathmandu: Sahayogi Press, 1976.

———. (ed.) *Letters from Kathmandu: The Kot Massacre*. Kirtipur, Kathmandu: Research Centre for Nepal and Asian Studies, 1981.

Tucci, Giuseppe, *Nepal: The Discovery of the Malla*. London: George Allen and Unwin, 1962.

Tuker, Francis. *Gorkha, the Story of the Gurkhas of Nepal*. London: Constable and Co., 1957.

———. *While Memory Serves*, App. VIII, pp. 624-46. London, Cassel, 1950.

Uprety, Prem R. *Nepal: A Small Nation in the Vortex of International Conflicts, 1900-1950*. Kathmandu: Pugo Mi, no date.

Whelpton, John. *Jang Bahadur in Europe*. (with an introduction by Rishikesh Shaha), Kathmandu: Sahayogi Press, 1983.

Wright, Daniel, *History of Nepal*. Cambridge University Press, 1879.

Nepali Language: Unless Otherwise Specified

Acharya, Baburam. "Rana Sahi ra Shadyantra" (Rana Rule and Conspiracy), *Sharada*, XXI:5, V.E. 2013 (1957 A.D.), 1-8.

———. "Aitihasik Patra" (Historical Letter), *Purushartha*, I:1, Pous 2006 V.E. (December 1949-January 1950 A.D.), 11-13.

———. "Bhimsen Thapa ko Patan" (The Downfall of Bhimsen Thapa), *Pragati*, II:4 (1957), 115-123.

———. *China ra Tibet Sita Nepal ko Sambandha* (Nepal's Relations with China and Tibet). Kathmandu: Jorganesh Press, 1958. 35 pp.

———. "Sri Sri Jaya Prakash Malla", *Pragati*, 3, No. 1 (1958), 35-85.

———. "Bhimsen Thapa ko Utthan" (The Rise of Bhimsen Thapa), *Rup-Rekha*, V.E. 2017 (January-February, 1961), 5 pp.

———. "Janaral Bhim Sen Thapa ko Parakram ra Unle Samarjang Kampani lai Diyeko Danda" (Gen. Bhimsen Thapa's Prowess and the Punishment Meted Out by Him to the Samar Jang Company), *Arti*, Baisakh, (V.E.) 2024 (April 1967), 3-11.

———. *Nepal ko Samkshipta Vritanta* (A Brief Account of Nepal). Kathmandu: Pramod Shamsher and Nir Bikram Pyasi, 1964. 152 pp.

———. *Prithvinarayan Shah ko Sankshipta Jivani* (A short Biography of Prithvinarayan Shah), 4 Vols. Kathmandu: Royal Press Secretariat, 1967-1968. 843 pp.

———. *Baburam Acharya ra Uhanka Kirti*. Kathmandu: Institute of Nepal and Asian Studies, 1973. 148 pp.

Acharya Dikshit, Kashinath. *Bhayeko Kura* (Actual Facts), edited and published by his son, Narendra Mani Acharya Dikshit, Kathmandu, 1974 (V.S.2031), 364 pp.

Acharya Dixit. Keshar Mani. "Girvana Yuddha Bir Bikram Lai Bharat Bata Nepali Vakil ko Patra" (Letter from the Nepali Vakil in India to Girvana Yuddha Bir Bikram), *Sanskrit Sandesh*, I:9, 38-43.

Agrawal, Basudev Sharan. "Himalaya, Ganga ra Nepal" (Himalayas, the Ganges and Nepal), *Sanskritik Parishad Patra*, I:1 (1952), 17-20.

Bajracharya, Dhanabajra *et al.* (eds.). *Aitihasik Patra Sangraha* (A Collection of Historical Letters), Part I. Kathmandu: Nepal Samskritik Parishad, 1957. 110 pp.

———. "Girvan Yuddha Bir Bikram Shah Lai Amar Singh Thapa ko Patra" (Amar Singh Thapa's Letter to Girvana Yuddha Bir Bikram Shah) *Sanskrit Sandesh*, I:7, pp. 22-26, I:8, 35-38: and I:9, 31-34).

———. *Triratna Saundarya Gatha* (An Account of the Beauty of the Three Jewels). Kathmandu: Nepal Cultural Council, 1963. 317 pp.

Bhandari, Dhundiraj. *Nepal ko Aitihasik Vivechana* (Historical Analysis of Nepal), Banaras: Krishna Kumari, 1958. 368 pp.

Bisht, Som Dhwaj, *Shahi Sainik Itihas* (History of the Royal Army). Kathmandu: G.N.J. Shah and N.M.S. Basnyat, V.E. 2020 (1963 A.D.)

Dixit, Kamal (ed.). *Jang Bahadur ko Bilayet Yatra* (Jang Bahadur's Trip to England). Kathmandu: Madan Library, V.E. 2014 (1957 A.D.). 57 pp.

———. *Janga Gita* (Song of Jang). Lalitpur: Jagadamba Prakashan, 1983. 162 pp.

———. *Chandra Jyoti* (Light of Chandra), Lalitpur: Jagadamba Prakashan, 1984. 208 pp.

Giri, Tulsi. "Bharat-Birodhi Kaun, Nepal-Prem Kya" (who is Anti-India, What does Love for Nepal mean?) *Nepal Sandesh* (Hindi), Poush 17, 2023) (January 1, 1967)

Gorkha Vamsavali (The Chronicles of the Gorkha Kings). Banaras: Yoga Pracharini, V.E. 2009 (1952 A.D.). 144 pp.

Itihas Prakash (Lights on History). Kathmandu: Nepal Press, 1955-56, 4 Vols., paged separately.

Itihas-Samsodhan (History Corrections). A valuable series pamphlets published by various Nepali historians and Sanskrit Scholars. Contributors included Dhanabajra Bajracharya, Gautam Bajra Bajracharya, Akrur Kuwinkel, Babu Ram Nepal, Jnan Mani Nepal, Mahesh Raj Pant, Bhola Nath Poudel, Naya Nath Poudel, Mohan Nath Pandey, Shyam Raj Pokhrel, Laxman Satyal, Aishwarya Dhar Sharma, Kumar Dhar Sharma, Ghana Shyam Subedi and Maheshwar Raj Subedi, 1955-58.

Jnawali, Surya Bikram. *Amar Singh Thapa* (Hindi). Darjeeling: Ratnakar Press, 1951, 230 pp.

———. *Nepali Birharu* (Nepali Heroes). Darjeeling: Nepali Sahitya Sammelan, 1951. 87 pp.

———. *Rama Shah ko Jivan Charitra* (A Biography of Rama Shah). Darjeeling, 1933. 25 pp.

———. *Nepal Upatyakako Madhya Kalin Itihas* (Medieval History of the Nepal Valley). Kathmandu: Royal Nepal Academy, V.E. 2019 (1962 A.D.). 338 pp.

———. *Nepal Vijeta Shri Panch Prithvi Narayan Shah ko Jivani* (Life of King Prithvi Narayan Shah, the Conqueror of Nepal). Darjeeling. 1935.

Joshi, Satya Mohan. "Chini Nepali Samskritik Sambandha" (Sino-Napalese Cultural Relations), *Gorkhapatra*, September 23, 1960.

Lal, Manik. "Rana Haruko Nijamati Prashasan Pranali" (The Civil Administration System of the Ranas). Unpublished. Ms. 23 pp.

Lal, Shyam Bihari. "Nepal ko Baideshik Byapar ma Ek Adhyayan" (A Study in Nepal's Foreign Trade), *Byapar Patrika*, Vol. 2, No.7, Kartik, V.E. 2021 (October-November 1964).

Naraharinath, Yogi. *Gorkhaliharu ko Sainik Itihas* (Military History of the Gorkhas). Kathmandu: Annapurna Press, 1954. 24 pp.

———. *Itihas Prakash ma Sandhi Patra Sangraha* (A Collection of Treaties in the Illumination of History), Kathmandu, V.E. 2022 (1966). Published on the occasion of the Spiritual Conference convened at Dang. 786 pp.

———, and Baburam Acharya. *Sri Panch Bada Maharaj Prithvi Narayan Shah ko Divya Upadesh* (Divine Counsel of King Prithivi Narayan Shah the Great). Kathmandu: Shri Bagiswar Press, 1953. 38 pp.

Nepal-China Friendship Association. *Miteri Gantho* (Ties of Friendship). (A Collection of Articles on Nepal-China Friendship). Kathmandu, 1963. 41 pp.

Nepali, Chitta Ranjan. "Chautariya Bahadur Shah ko Nayabi Kal" (The Period of the Nayabship of Chautaria Bahadur Shah), *Sharada*, XXII:1, V.E. 2014 (1957 A.D.), 21-29.

———. *Janaral Bhimsen Thapa ra Tatkalin Nepal* (General Bhim Sen Thapa and the Nepal of His Day). Kathmandu: Jorganesh Press, 1957, 334 pp.

———. "Vartaman Nepal ko Nirmanma Sri Panch Prithvi Narayan Shah" (King Prithvi Narayan Shah's Role in the Building of Modern Nepal). *Pragati*, Year 3, Issue 2 (n.d.), 78-110.

———. "Nepal-Chin Yuddha", (Nepal-China War), *Sharada*, XXI:1, V.E. 2013 (1956 A.D.), 202-16.

———. "Nepal ra British Gorkha Rifles" (Nepal and the British Gorkha Rifles), *Rup-Rekha*, V:4, Bhadra, V.E. 2021 (August-September, 1964), 9-16.

———. "Nepal Ra British Samrajya" (Nepal and the British Empire), *Sharada*, XXI:3, V.E. 2013 (1956 A.D.), 11-12.

———. "Nepal ra Tibet ko Sambandha" (Nepal-Tibet Relations), *Pragati*, Year II, IV:10 (n.d.), 103-15.

———. *Shri Panch Rana Bahadur Shah*. Kathmandu: Shrimati Mary Rajbhandari, 1964. 154 pp.

———. "Trayi Shashan" (Triumvirate), *Sharada*, Year 24, Issue 3, Poush, V.E. 2016 (December 1959-January 1960), 1-14.

Pande, Bhim Bahdur (Sardar), *Tyas Bakhat ko Nepal* (Nepal of That Time), vol.II: Kathmandu: Centre for Nepal and Asian Studies, 1982 (V.S 2039), 477 pp.

Pande Kshatri, Bhim Bahadur (Sardar), *Rastra Bhakti ko Jhalak* (Glimpse of Loyalty to the Nation). Kathmandu, Ratna Pustak Bhandar, 1977 (V.S 2034), 247 pp.

Pande, Totra Raj and Naya Raj Pant. *Nepal ko Sankshipta Itihas* (An Abridged History of Nepal). Banaras: V.E. 2004 (1947 A.D.).

Pant, Maheshraj, "Nepal-Angrej Yudda ko Tayari" (Preparations for Anglo-Nepali War), *Purnima*, I:2, Shravan Sankranti, V.E. 2021 (July 16, 1964).

———. "The Second Stage of Anglo-Nepal War", *Purnima*, 8, Magh 1, V.E. 2022 (January 14, 1966), 41-49.

Pant, Naya Raj. "Damodar Pande Lai Ran Bahadur ko Patra" (Letter from Ran Bahadur to Damodar Pande), *Sanskrit Sandesh*, I:5, 36-43.

———. "Shree Tin Maharaj Padma Shamsher ko kura" (An Account of the History of the Rana Period as Narrated by Shree Three Maharaj Padma Shamsher in Verse), *Purnima*, No. 40, Vol.10, No.4, no date, 123 pp.

———. *et al. Shree Panch Prithvinarayan Shah ko Upadesh* (Counsel of Shri Five Prithvinarayan Shah), 4 Vols. Lalitpur: Jagadamba Prakashan, no date. 800 pp.

Poudyal, Bholanath and Dhanabajra Bajracharya (eds.). *Galli ma Fyakiyeko Kasingar–Pandit Bhavani Datta Pande le Gare ko Muddrarakshasa Haru ka Nepali Anubad* (Letters Thrown in the Street . . . Renderings in Nepali of the Mudrarakshasa Drama and other Sanskrit Works . . .). Kathmandu: Jagdamba Prakashan, 1961. 269 pp.

Sama Balakrishna, *Mero Kavita Ko Aradhana* (My Devotion to Poetry) vol. I. Kathmandu: Royal Nepal Academy, 1966 (V.S. 2033), 318 pp.

______. *Mero Kavita Ko Aradhana* (My Devotion to Poetry) vol. II. Kathmandu: Sajha Prakashan, 1974 (V.S. 2031), 246 pp.

Sharma, Balchandra. *Nepalko Aitihasik Rup Rekha* (An Outline of the History of Nepal). Banaras: Madav Prasad Sharma, 1951. 440 pp.

Shrestha, Baburam. "Hamro Byapar Sthiti" (Our Commercial Situation), *Gorkhapatra*, Kartik 16, V.E. 2021 (November 1, 1964).

Shrestha, K.N. "Hamro Vyapar Bastusthiti ra Vikash Path" (Facts About Our Trade and Ways of its Development), *Gorkhapatra*, Poush 11, V.E. 2021 (December 25, 1964).

Singh, Iman. *Kirat Itihas* (Kirat History). Gangtok, Sikkim, 1952. 72 pp.

Tiwari, Ramji. *et al. (eds.). Abhilekh Sangraha* (A Collection of Inscriptions). Kathmandu: Samshodhan Mandal, 1961-63, Volumes 1-9, 11, paged separately.

———. *et al. (eds.). Aitihasik Patra Sangraha (Dosro Bhag)* (Collection of Historical Documents, Part II), Kathmandu: Nepal Samskritik Parishad, V.E. 2021 (A.D. 1964). 126 pp.

———, "Vikram Samvat 1843 ma Bhayeko Kehi Mukhya Ghatana" (Some Important Events of 1786), *Purnima*, 1:2, Shravan Sankranti, V.E. 2021 (July 16, 1964).

Upadhyaya, Ramji. *Nepal ko Itihas* (History of Nepal). Banaras: Subha Hom Nath Kedar Nath, 1950.

———. *Nepal Digdarshan* (A survey of Nepali History). Banaras: Gopal Press, 1950. 486 pp.

"Vyas", "Nepal-Bharat Vyapar Sambandha, Duwai Rashtra ko Arthik Hit ko Paripati" (Nepal-India Trade Relations, A Means for the Economic Benefit of Both Nations), *Gorkhapatra*, Jestha 30, V.E. 2024 (June 13, 1967), 4-5.

Index

MODERN NEPAL

A Political History, 1769-1955
Volume 2: 1885-1955

MODERN NEPAL

A Political History, 1769-1955
Volume 2: 1885-1955

RISHIKESH SHAHA

MANOHAR
2023

First published 1990
Reprinted 1996
Reprinted in one Volume 2001, 2023

ISBN 978-81-7304-403-8

Published by
Ajay Kumar Jain *for*
Manohar Publishers & Distributors
4753/23 Ansari Road, Daryaganj
New Delhi 110 002

Printed at
Rajkamal Electric Press
B 35/9 G T Karnal Road Indl Area
Delhi 110 033

In fond memory of
my beloved wife Siddhanta,
known to her many friends and relatives as
Sanu Mana,
who was proud of being a Rana
but sacrificed her personal interests
and pleasures for my sake,
and to whom I owe everything in life.

Preface

This is a running account of political trends and developments in Nepal during a period of about two hundred years from the rise of King Prithvinarayan Shah (1769-1775), the founder of the present Shah dynasty till the end of the post-Tribhuvan revolutionary era. As it has run into nearly 650 pages, the publisher has decided to bring it out in two volumes in order to make it more convenient for the reader.

I have therefore chosen to close the first volume with the chapter on Maharaj Prime Minister Ranoddip Singh (1877-1885). His assasination by the sons of his youngest brother, Dhir Shamsher, ended the era of preeminence of seven brothers (Sat Bhai) including Jang Bahadur Kanwar Rana, the founder of the hereditary rule of Rana prime ministers who kept the kings as mere figureheads. Ranoddip's murder resulted in the removal of the descendants of Jang Bahadur and his five other brothers from the roll of succession to the prime ministership. The near-absolute power of the office thereafter became the monopoly of the members of the family of the youngest of seven brothers, Dhir Shamsher.

Following this historic transfer of power, the second volume opens with the chapter on Bir Shamsher who, as the eldest of Dhir Shamsher's seventeen sons, was the first of them to become the Maharaj Prime Minister. The volume deals with the administration of seven members of the Dhir Shamsher branch of the Rana family, which dominated Nepal for a period of sixty-five years. It also gives an account of the 1950-51 revolution, which brought the tentative beginnings of democracy and restored the king's traditional authority by putting an end to the 104 year old Rana rule. The last chapter in the book surveys the post revolutionary Tribhuvan era until 1955, the year in which King Tribhuvan the harbinger of democracy died.

I have four reasons for ending my history of modern Nepal in 1955: First, the 30 year rule which the Public Record Office and the India Office Library in London observe for opening their historical records to the public is, to my mind, a sound one because a fair interval of time will enable writers and researchers to take a detached and objective view of the events and present them in the right perspective. Second, the 30 year rule imposes on historians a practical constraint of a salutary nature in so far as they can hardly do justice to their subject without making use of the source materials available in these two archival centres. Third, as I have personally been involved deeply in Nepali politics during the last 30 years, I may be inclined to take a rather subjective view of the critical issues and events of the period. Last but not least, I have already published two books on the post-Tribhuvan period, and I humbly commend them to all those who may be interested in my interpretation of the more recent political past. These books are entitled *Nepali Politics – Retrospect and Prospect* (Delhi: Oxford University Press, second edition, 1978) and *Essays in the Practice of Government in Nepal* (Delhi: Manohar, 1982).

My fellowship from the Woodrow Wilson International Center for Scholars (1976-77) and the East-West Center, Honolulu (1984) has enabled me to write the first twelve chapters of this book. I should, therefore, like to take this opportunity to express my thanks to both the centres for their generous assistance.

I am most grateful to the British Council for its generous grant which paid for my travel to London and all my expenses during my three-month stay there. I spent most of my time reading the files of correspondence between the British envoys in Kathmandu and their government in India and London from 1929 through 1954 and also the contemporary records of notes and minutes by the officials of the British Foreign Office and the India Office in the files dealing with Nepal. I need hardly say that my perusal of all these records has immensely enriched my understanding of the Nepali history of the period.

For the earlier period, my task was greatly facilitated by the researches and published dissertations on specified periods of Anglo-Nepal relations by a number of Indian scholars over the last two decades, though their focus had been on Nepal's foreign relations rather than on internal politics. Let me take this opportunity to express my indebtedness to K.C. Chaudhuri, B.D. Sanwal, Satish Kumar, Ramakant, Asad Husain, M.S. Jain and Kanchanmoy Mojumdar, all of whose contributions in the field considerably lightened my own burden.

Among the more recent European and American authors from whose books I have most profited in writing this history are John Pemble, Leo E. Rose and John Whelpton. I owe a debt to all of them. Like others who have written on different aspects of the Nepali history, I have also drawn on the published works of William Kirkpatrick, Francis (Buchanan) Hamilton, Henry T. Prinsep, B.H. Hodgson, Orfeur Cavenagh, T. Smith, Laurence Oliphant, Daniel Wright, J.T. Wheeler, and H.A. Oldfield in the 19th century and those of Sylvain Levi, Perceval Landon, G.H.D. Gimlette, W.B. Northey, C.I. Morris and Francis Tuker in the 20th century.

I have also found useful the works of D.R. Regmi, Bhuwan Lal Joshi, Mahesh Chandra Regmi, L.F. Stiller and Krishna Kant Adhikari among the Nepali scholars who have written in English. My thanks are due to all of them.

My Nepali source is the *Bhasa Vamshavali* which is said to have been written and compiled by Subba Buddhi Man. I have also read with profit the historical publications in Nepali of Ambika Prasad Upadhyaya, Surya Bikram Jnawali, Baburam Acharya, Nayaraj Panta, Yogi Narahari Nath and Balchandra Sharma, to all of whom I record my gratitude. I have drawn copiously on the autobiographies of Kashi Nath Acharya Dikshit and of Balakrishna Sama, the well-known Nepali poet, painter, dramatist, critic and essayist, for information about contemporary events. I owe a special debt to both of them.

I realize that individuals do not always share the same perspective on historical trends and events, though every attempt must be made to reach a consensus on the date and sequence of events if history is at all to attain the level of scientific analysis and objectivity required of an academic discipline. However, the interpretation of historical issues and trends is always influenced by the writer's value system – I purposely want to avoid using the expression 'personal bias' because of its pejorative overtones. We must be clear in our minds that value-premises do influence the viewpoint from which reality is studied. But they do not in any way determine whether the factual data and relations among variables that are observed and analysed are correct: experience makes the determination. The fact remains that values and judgements are implied in our pursuit of truth as in all purposeful behaviour. A 'disinterested' social science has never existed nor can it ever exist if we assume that analysts are capable of eliminating their own values.

From this standpoint my history of modern Nepal is apt to be different from somebody else's, and I strongly feel that everyone has his own view of historical trends and events. I had long planned to write my account of the nation's past according to my lights, and it took me quite a few years to do so.

Let me just add at the end that though I have greatly profited by frank discussions on different aspects of this history with several of my friends who have chosen to remain anonymous, the opinions and the conclusions in the book are my own. I shall, however, fail in my duty if I do not thank Father John Locke and Dr. Harka Gurung for reading my manuscript carefully and providing me with valuable insights into several issues dealt with in this study. My grateful thanks are due to Mr. and Mrs. Jharendra S.J.B. Rana who very kindly provided me with rare photographs of the Shah and Rana families for inclusion in this work. All the single photographs of kings and prime ministers of Nepal, however, belong to the private collection of Lieutenant General Indu S.J.B. Rana and his wife both of whom, had they been around, would have been very pleased to see them published in this form. Let me take this opportunity to record my profound indebtedness to them. I cannot of course forget to thank my friend, Meg Sheffield, for steadily encouraging and inspiring me to write this book as well as others in the past.

3 June 1989 RISHIKESH SHAHA

Contents

11

Maharaj Bir Shamsher (1885-1901): Dawn of Seventeen Brothers' (Satrabhai) Dominance

We have seen in the previous chapter how Bir Shamsher was proclaimed Maharaj by the 10-year-old boy King, Prithvi Bir Bikram Shah Dev, under dramatic circumstances following the assassination of Maharaj Ranoddip Singh. According to the roll of succession to the Office of the Maharaj and Prime Minister in effect at the time of Maharaj Ranoddip Singh, Bir Shamsher would have had to wait for at least six of his predecessors to die before he could himself have become Maharaj and Prime Minister. Commanding General Yuddha Pratap Jang, Maharaj Jang Bahadur's grandson, who preceded Bir on the roll of succession, was much younger than he.

The roll of succession in effect at the time of the assassination of Ranoddip was as follows:

1. Maharaj Ranoddip Kanwar Ranaji, Prime Minister and Supreme Commander-in-Chief.
2. Commander-in-Chief General Jit Jang Bahadur K.R.
3. Senior Commanding General Padma Jang Bahadur K.R. (Western Command).
4. Commanding General Rana Bir Jang Bahadur K.R. (Eastern Command).
5. Commanding General Yuddha Pratap Jang Bahadur K.R. (Southern Command).
6. Commanding General Kedar Narsingh K.R. (Northern Command).
7. General Bir Shamsher Jang K.R.

8. General Ambar Jang K.R.
9. General Dhoj Narsingh K.R.
10. General Khadga Shamsher K.R.
11. General Bhupendra Jang K.R.
12. General Rana Shamsher Jang K.R.
13. General Dev Shamsher Jang K.R.
14. Colonel Chandra Shamsher Jang K.R.
15. Colonel Bhim Shamsher Jang K.R.
16. Colonel Fatte Shamsher Jang K.R.
17. Colonel Lalit Shamsher Jang K.R.
18. Colonel Jit Shamsher Jang K.R.
19. Colonel Juddha Shamsher Jang K.R.
20. General Bhairav Narsingh K.R.
21. General Yaksha Bikram K.R.

When Bir Shamsher became Maharaj and Prime Minister at the age of thirty-three as a result of the successful coup d'etat, he acted very boldly and appropriated solely to the Shamsher brothers the roll of succession or the agnatic system of hereditary Prime Ministers set up by Maharaj Jang Bahadur Rana in 1856. The names of the descendants of Maharaj Jang Bahadur and of his other five brothers were removed from the roll of succession for good. Bir Shamsher's action posed a direct and determined challenge not only to Jang Bahadur's sons and grandsons but also to the descendants of all of his other five brothers and their retinues. The revision of the roll of succession by Bir Shamsher meant promotion and higher ranks for all of his half-brothers already on the roll of succession. Bir's other half-brothers born out of wedlock were also given higher military ranks and, as members of the family of seventeen brothers or Dhir Shamsher's seventeen sons, were treated as a class distinct from the Rana descendants of Dhir's six brothers.

The roll of succession drawn up by Bir Shamsher after he became Prime Minister was as follows:

1. Shri Tin Maharaj Bir Shamsher Jang Rana Bahadur, Prime Minister and Supreme Commander-in-Chief.
2. Commander-in-Chief General Khadga Shamsher J.R.B.
3. Senior Commanding General Rana Shamsher J.R.B. (Western Command) (Bir's half-brother).

4. Commanding General Dev Shamsher J.R.B (Eastern Command) (Khadga's brother).
5. Commanding General Chandra Shamsher J.R.B. (Southern Command) (Khadga's brother).
6. Commanding General Bhim Shamsher J.R.B. (Northern Command) (Khadga's brother)
7. General Fatte Shamsher J.R.B. (Bir's half-brother).
8. General Lalit Shamsher J.R.B. (Fatte's brother).
9. General Jit Shamsher J.R.B. (Fatte's brother).
10. Colonel Juddha Shamsher J.R.B. (Bir's half-brother).
11. Colonel Gehendra Shamsher J.R.B. (Bir's eldest son).
12. Colonel Dharma Shamsher J.R.B. (Bir's second son).
13. Colonel Padma Shamsher J.R.B. (Bhim's eldest son).
14. Colonel Punya Shamsher J.R.B. (Khadga's eldest son).
15. Colonel Bikram Shamsher J.R.B. (Khadga's second son).

Bir Shamsher was not content with removing others from the roll of succession; he also decided to expel them from the country at least temporarily so that he might gain time to consolidate his own position and that of his brothers in the changed political setup. Perceval Landon has pointed out perceptively that "with a constitution such as that which prevails in Nepal, there is no other course open to the autocrat who establishes himself by violence but to secure his position by the absence of those whom he had indeed expelled from power, but whose resentment and intrigues would entail a wearisome and probably ineffectual surveillance were they permitted to remain in the country".

Bir actually went even a step further than that in confiscating the house and landed property of some of them and distributing them among his Shamsher half-brothers. The Shamsher brothers, before the 1885 coup d'etat, had been so poor that seventeen of them had to share Dhir Shamsher's old residence in common. Now Commander-in-Chief Jit Jang's house went to Khadga Shamsher and General Padma Jang's house was shared by Dev Shamsher and Bhim Shamsher, and Chandra Shamsher was given General Juddha Pratap Jang's house at Thapathali. To Fatte Shamsher's share fell the residence of General Ranabir Jang, and Lalit Shamsher and Jit Shamsher received General Babar Jang's and General Kedar Narsingh's house respectively. Rana Shamsher was given a house in Dilli Bazar.[2]

It took Bir considerable time and effort to consolidate his own position as the new Maharaj and Prime Minister and that of the Shamsher

Ranas as a whole in the political hierarchy of Nepal. Jang's sons, in their bid to recapture power, understandably sought to mobilize the combined efforts of all those opposed to the Shamsher Ranas both inside and outside Nepal. Commander-in-Chief General Jit Jang Bahadur Rana who had been living in India ever since his eldest brother Jagat Jang had returned to Nepal, apparently in the hope of being reinstated by Maharaj Ranoddip in the roll of succession, proved to be the main hope for all those against Bir Shamsher's assumption of power in Nepal.

Jang Bahadur's sons believed they would receive substantial help and support from the British Government in staging a comeback to power in Nepal. Little did they realize that the policy of states is seldom determined by subjective considerations of services and personal friendship in the past.

The British Indian Government was approached by the Nepali exiles in India for help or even for its direct intervention in ousting Bir Shamsher's regime in Nepal. As the British Government had had very good reasons to regard Jang Bahadur as its friend in need and deed, its agents and representatives in India were very helpful to members of Jang Bahadur's family, but purely at a personal level. The British Residency in Kathmandu ensured the safe conduct of the refugees to India with their personal assets intact under its protection, and the British Indian Government sought to help its protection, and the British Indian Government sought to help some of the members of Jang's family who were in India by providing allowances on its own and also by using its influence with the new regime in Nepal to obtain financial grants for the ranking political Nepali refugees in India.

In 1890 William Digby published his book entitled *1857, A Friend in Need: 1887, Friendship Forgotten: An Episode in Indian Foreign Office Administration.* A case was made out by him in a highly partisan manner for what he saw as the neglect and betrayal of Jang Bahadur's sons by the British administration in India. Digby was not at all fair in accusing Acting Resident Colonel Berkeley on page 96 of his book of "making Bir Shamsher's treachery and ferocity respectable by ensuring its success". Colonel Berkeley's assessment of the actual political situation as reflected in the following excerpt from his communication to his Government is quite objective and balanced:

> My view is that there is little to choose between the 'ins' and 'outs'; and that, though the value of Jang Bahadur's services to us

> was great, it is possible to exaggerate it. When all is said, we cannot forget that Jang Bahadur was steeped in blood. And no one in Nepal doubts that if Juggut Jang had come to power there would have been a terrible reckoning with his enemies. The present minister and his family are as bad as they can be; but they have already rendered us service and it is conceivable that they might be able to do as much for us as Jang Bahadur did.[3]

The ranking political refugees from Nepal were granted interviews by the highest officials of the British Government in India. The former Commander-in-Chief of Nepal, General Jit Jang Bahadur Rana, was received by the Viceroy, Lord Dufferin, himself on 20 January 1886. At this interview, Lord Dufferin, while making known his "warmest feelings of friendship for the sons of so distinguished a father and reminding General Jit Jang of the role of the Resident in ensuring the protection and safe conduct of the political refugees to India, also added, "but his personal feelings must not be confused with the wider political considerations which were associated with his office."[4]

Lady Dufferin also received Jang Bahadur's daughter and Jit Jang's sister, Dowager Maharani Tara Kumari, wife of Crown Prince Trailokya Bikram Shah and stepmother of King Prithvi Bir Bikram Shah Dev, on 1 February 1886. As the Dowager Queen did not speak English, she put in the following plea to the Vicerein in writing:

> It is entirely owing to the kindness of His Excellency Lord Dufferin that I have been rescued from the clutches of the rebels, and I consider myself fortunate so far that I have got this opportunity of seeing your Ladyship.

While stating their willingness to do everything they could for the distinguished refugees from Nepal in the way of making their stay in India safe and reasonably comfortable, the British authorities clearly expressed their inability to help them regain their position or power in Nepal.

The Foreign Secretary of the British Government in India received General Kedar Narsingh and General Dhoj Narsingh and heard their grievances in person. However, the British Government's policy with regard to the descendants of Jang Bahadur and their adherents did not go in essence beyond reiterating what was stated in Acting Resident Berkeley's following communication to his Government:

> In regard to his claims upon the government, no doubt they were great, for Jang Bahadur was a loyal and valuable ally; but his services were amply recognized in his lifetime; and the protection and support afforded to his family on the occasion of the late revolution were no small matters.[5]

The persistent attempt of the political refugees in India to persuade the British Government not to recognize Bir Shamsher as the *de jure* prime minister of Nepal did not bear fruit. About a month after General Jit Jang's interview with the Viceroy and five months after the assassination of Maharaj Ranoddip Singh, the British Government in India extended its formal recognition to the new regime in Nepal in March 1886.

The fact of the matter was that Bir Shamsher was himself very anxious to win the favour and goodwill of the British Government in India and the Viceroy, Lord Dufferin, also refused to exploit the initial difficulties of the new regime in utter disregard of the advice of his senior advisers such as Commander-in-Chief Sir Frederick Roberts, Foreign Secretary Mortimer Durand and Resident Charles Girdlestone, none of whom were in favour of accepting the murderer as Minister. Even Roberts, who became Bir Shamsher's friend and admirer after his formal visit to Nepal in 1892, was at the beginning an advocate of strong action against Bir in order to set up a recruiting depot at Kathmandu itself in view of the possibilities of a war with Russia in the immediate future.[6] Mortimer Durand was in favour of supporting the Jang Ranas as against the Shamsher Ranas. Resident Girdlestone, on the evidence of Dr.G.H.D. Gimlette whom he had sent on deputation in September 1886 to persuade the Viceroy to put firm pressure on Bir for recruitment facilities, was full of sympathy for the Jang Ranas and had a strong prejudice against the Shamsher brothers. Girdlestone's representation through Gimlette was rejected by Lord Dufferin who reprimanded the Resident for pressing him "to wards Nepal" when his hands were full with the Burmese affair. Dufferin was so much dissatisfied with Girldestone that he was removed from Nepal in early 1888 before Bir's visit to India. Lord Dufferin reprimanded Bir for the murder and asked him to rule "peacefully and humanely."

However, the British Government's attitude did not deter General Jit Jang from persisting in his efforts to destabilize Bir Shamsher's regime in every possible way. General Jit Jang also seemed to change his tactics vis-a-vis the British Government and now sought its intervention merely to secure his personal claim, as Jang Bahadur's eldest surviving son, to the land in the tarai which was restored to Nepal by the British Government in return for Jang Bahadur's services to it in the 1857 Mutiny in India. It was in this connection that Jit Jang had cast his net far and wide to enlist the support of other allies of his cause to bring pressure to bear on the British Government. He actually succeeded in persuading Raja Sheoraj Singh of Kashipur to write a letter to the British Government suggesting that it should at least help General Jit Jang regain possession of the tarai land even if it found itself unable to secure him the prime ministership of Nepal.

This change in tactics did not help General Jit Jang with the British nor did the letter of a petty Indian Raja on the Nepali border have any effect on the British Government. On the other hand, his claim for the reclamation of land for himself as his father's property made his political intentions suspect not only among those civilians and military officers in Nepal whose support he had sought to unleash against Bir Shamsher but also proved to be the cause of dissension between him on the one hand and his sister, the Dowager Queen and his half-brothers on the other. Bir Shamsher later on tried to placate General Jit Jang's sons and his half-brothers by distributing part of the same land among them.

General Jit Jang's efforts to destablize Bir's regime inside Nepal did not go very far. Mathbar Singh, one of General Jit Jang's supporters, had collected some people with a view to launching an attack on the easternmost district of Ilam in Nepal from the British Indian district of Darjeeling. Nothing happened after Mathbar Singh was arrested by the British authorities on the request of the Nepali district administration. Bir Shamsher's administration issued a public notice to all concerned that nothing would happen to them even if they had unwittingly supported Mathbar Singh if they returned to their respective areas in Nepal. But this notice warned them that if they did not do so, they would be arrested by the British Government on Nepal's request.[7] This was the end of General Jit Jang's direct and personal involvement in efforts to oust Bir Shamsher although he did extend financial and moral support to his younger half-brother, General Rana Bir Jang, and authorized him to use his name in subsequent attempts to create disturbances in Nepal in 1889 and 1893.

Like his uncle, Maharaj Jang Bahadur, Bir Shamsher was called upon to deal with an alleged conspiracy against him by his own half-brother, Commander-in-Chief General Khadga Shamsher, who was next in line of succession to the office of the Maharaj and Prime Minister. It is also alleged that it was Khadga's full brother, Chandra Shamsher, who, having initially hatched a plot with Khadga, revealed it to Bir Shamsher to secure his own position and promotion much in the same way as Bam Bahadur had betrayed Badri Narsingh by revealing to Maharaj Jang Bahadur the conspiracy against him to which both the brothers had been a party to begin with.

Two incidents reportedly seemed to indicate Bir's gradual decline of faith in and growing displeasure with Khadga. The first occurred when Maharaj Bir suddenly came to Khadga's house and started hearing the case against Colonel Siddhi Man Rajbhandari's son, Major Samar Bahadur. The Maharaj in a fit of rage had Samar Bahadur whipped in the presence of the officers of the court. Everyone inferred from it that Bir was dissatisfied with Commander-in-Chief Khadga's handling of the case.

Again, towards the end of 1886, Bir once suddenly showed up at Khadga's Thapathali house at about 10 a.m. and asked the Commander-in-Chief to dismiss all those who did not regularly attend the Salam, the reveille or the morning's gathering at the Prime Minister's residence. When Khadga intervened on their behalf by saying that the Prime Minister had earlier asked the officers of the court to attend to their work and not to come to his house except on business, Bir insisted that all of them should have come to his house and ordered the instant dismissal of seventeen of them including top ranking administrative officers such as Sardar Bhakta Bir and Sardar Hari Bhakta. Bir Shamsher's gesture was clearly intended to cut Commander-in-Chief General Khadga down to size. Khadga, too, was quick to receive the message and pretended to have lost all interest in his work.

While all of those who were at the time on the roll of succession to the office of the Maharaj and Prime Minister were Dhir Shamsher's sons or grandsons, some of them were born of the same mother and were full brothers. Among them were Khadga, Deva, Chandra and Bhim, and the other two, Fatte and Jit were also full brothers and sons of the full sister of the mother of the previous four. Although Bir was the Prime Minister by virtue of his being the eldest born of all the half-brothers, he had very good reason to be on his guard against conspiracy by some of them in the prevailing atmosphere of Nepali court politics. Every brother had his own personal retinues and followers, though everyone including the number-two man or Commander-in-

Chief was taken to be subservient to the Maharaj. The Maharaj was supposed to rule in exercise of his right to hukum or peremptory command accruing to him from the *lal panja*, the legal document with the King's palm print, first obtained by Maharaj Jang Bahadur Kanwar Ranaji from King Surendra Bikram Shah Dev on 6 August 1856. This document remained the legal basis of Rana rule in Nepal in principle for 104 years until the roll of succession to the office of the Maharaj and Prime Minister was abolished on 18 February 1951. The system of Rana rule was never seriously challenged by the people in general until the mid-twentieth century, but this did not mean that the politics of the nineteenth century were not subject to built-in pressures and tensions.

That Bir had already grown highly suspicious of his half-brother's designs against him is also clear from yet another incident recorded in the autobiography of one of the Brahmin functionaries in Dhir Shamsher's household, Kashinath Acharya Dikshit, who had had personal dealings with each of Dhir's sons and was particularly close to Chandra and Khadga.[8] When Khadga invited Bir to attend a dinner in celebration of the sacred thread ceremony of one of Dhir's younger sons, Sher Shamsher, Bir sat in a place reserved for Khadga and not meant for himself despite Khadga's protestation. Among those present were Bir's confidants such as Colonel Fauda Singh, Colonel Kirti Man and Major Majhi and Commander-in-Chief Khadga's trusted men such as Colonel Jit Bahadur and Major Tej Bahdur Malla. All of them looked disturbed but there was nothing anyone could do.

Incidents such as those referred to above and the dubious roles of informers among the close adherents and partisans of the two half-brothers themselves must have been instrumental in heightening the tension and deepening the suspicion between them. But the culmination was reached when Bir Shamsher sent for Commander-in-Chief General Khadga one fine day in March 1887 and told him that he was henceforth dismissed from his post, was removed from the roll of succession and was at once going to be expelled to Thada, a village close to the headquarters of the Palpa district, as punishment for hatching a plot against the Maharaj's life.

According to Dikshit's autobiography, Khadga already had a premonition that something untoward might happen to him after he was asked by Maharaj Bir to come to his palace for a piece of business on that fateful Sunday. When General Fatte, Bir's aide-de-camp, called at Khadga's house that morning, Khadga subtly hinting at the probability of his own removal from the roll of succession, had told his younger half-brother in joke that he might find himself promoted that day to a higher rank on the roll of succession. Fatte had just smiled in response before he took leave of the Commander-in-Chief. Khadga's two other Brahmin retainers, Pandit Jiv Nath and Pandit Hari Nath, had informed him that very morning that Maharaj Bir had asked them how good Khadga's stars or signs of luck were when they had gone to the Maharaj to perform the ritual of holding the new month on its first day (Samkranti). As there was a rice-feeding ceremony for Khadga's children that day at 12 noon, some of his other brothers and half-brothers including Chandra, Fatte, and Purna happened to be at Khadga's place before Khadga left for Bir's house. Chandra did not want to go along with them on the plea that he had to attend a parade. According to Dikshit, who accompanied Chandra to his house from Khadga's place that day, Chandra was in a state of unease until Lieutenant Naval Singh came from the Prime Minister's Narayan Hiti palace with a letter. After reading the letter, Chandra was visibly moved and hurriedly left his house.[9]

Even Dikshit's autobiography, published by one of his sons about one hundred years after the above event had taken place, is not clear about the extent of Chandra's involvement in the plot against Khadga. Records of these plots and counterplots are hardly available except for Landon's references to them in his book, and this work was commissioned by Chandra Shamsher when he himself was the Maharaj of Nepal and was based entirely on the partisan views and materials made available to the author by Chandra. Hence, an attempt has been made here to draw on the autobiographies of contemporaries of the main actors on the stage and on the prevailing hearsay among the members of their families, but these too cannot be entirely free from bias. On the other hand, the records of these events available in the British and Indian archives, however meagre, have always been treated as more authentic.

General Khadga was, on all accounts, full of daring and dynamism and had played a more important role than others in the 1885 coup d'etat. According to reliable accounts, Khadga was a colourful person and basically an extrovert who believed in acting with a flair at all times. Bir, his eldest half-brother, was just the opposite, an introvert full of reserve and reticence and slightly inclined towards indolence. Chandra, Khadga's full brother and Bir's half-brother, although at the time the fifth in line of succession to the highest executive office, was regarded by his brothers as the most cautious and the ablest of them all despite his poor health. He was certainly the most educated of the seventeen brothers, as he was the first and the only one among Dhir Shamsher's sons and the only Rana Prime Minister to pass the entrance examination of Calcutta University at which his elder brother, Khadga, reportedly had failed. Bir had also attended Devton College in Calcutta and was able to converse in English, though haltingly, and knew a bit of Urdu and Persian.

Although the reputation of Chandra Shamsher for cunning and craftiness began to grow more and more as the regime of the Shamsher brothers advanced in time, yet it would be difficult to find any tangible evidence of Chandra's direct complicity at the time of the unearthing of the alleged plot against Bir and also against the young King. According to Landon, others who were implicated in the alleged plot against the Maharaj as Khadga's accomplices were his maternal uncle Keshar Singh Thapa who was interned at Salyan; and the two ranking ladies, Dip Kumari Shah, wife of Sahebjyu Dhirendra Bikram Shah, the King's uncle, but alleged to be secretly in love with Khadga, and her friend, Khadga Kumari Shah alias Kahili Maiyan, wife of the late Raja of Salyan, and Khadga's widow sister, who were also expelled to the eastern hill districts.[10]

Action against the Sijapati Family as the Aftermath of His Brothers' Conspiracy against Bir

After the dismissal and removal of C-in-C Khadga Shamsher from the roll of succession, General Rana Shamsher, the next in succession, had become Commander-in-Chief. He died in 1887 and was succeeded by Dev Shamsher, and Chandra Shamsher took Dev's place as senior Commanding General (Western Command).

Even after Khadga Shamsher's expulsion to Palpa, his full brothers Dev, Chandra and Bhim along with Bir's aide-de-camp, General Fatte, seem to have laid a conspiracy against Bir. The plot was to invite Bir to Dev's house on the occasion of a religious festival on 3 August 1888 and get him drunk before killing him.[11] Colonel Rana Singh Sijapati, his son Captain Indra Bahadur Sijapati, and his brother Lal Singh and Lal Singh's sons were parties to the plot.

Captain Bikram Bahadur was promoted by Bir to the rank of Colonel and was asked to go to the tarai with a body of 1,000 men to assist in the administration of certain districts. But then Bir Shamsher dismissed him and other members of his family on 3 August 1888 on the ground that they had disobeyed him by delaying their departure to the tarai. According to the British Resident, the actual fact was that the conspirators had tried to arm these 1,000 men with guns and ammunition so that they might be able to lend support to the Maharaj's four half-brothers after they had killed the Maharaj.

Lal Singh and Dugal Singh betrayed the secret to the Maharaj at the last minute and the conspiring brothers also came to learn of the betrayal of their plot almost at the same time. Dev and Chandra initially sought to save themselves by apparently coming forward to suppress the plotters and manipulating the evidence in such a way to leave even the names of their brothers, Bhim and Fatte, intact in the incriminating document after having their own names snipped off. In the opinion of the present author, Dev and Chandra might have done so thinking that Bhim and Fatte would be eventually spared punishment by Bir as they were among his most favourite half-brothers.

The end result was that old Colonel Rana Singh Sijapati and his son, Captain Indra Bahadur were sent into exile in Varanasi and others, such as Colonels Bambu Bahadur and Bikram Bahadur and Captains Noor Bahadur, Shamsher Bahadur, Khamba Singh, Kanchha Bahadur and Bhagat, were expelled to different districts in the eastern and the western hills.[12] It may be pointed out here in passing that not only Kashinath Dikshit who was, on his own admission, Chandra Shamsher's lifelong confidant and loyal servant, but also Perceval Landon, clearly sought to suppress the complicity of the brothers in the above plot against Bir. Landon mentions the affair obliquely in a passing reference to Vansittart in a footnote on p. 76 of the second volume of his book published in 1928. The footnote runs as follows:

> Captain Vansittart states that another plot was discovered early in 1888, and that after its failure the conspirators were put to death. But this is denied by the present Maharaj, and may perhaps be a misreading of notes connected with Ranbir's rising.

General Ranabir Jang, one of Maharaj Jang's sons in exile, launched a poorly organized military expedition into the central tarai from India in the name of his elder brother, former Commander-in-Chief General Jit Jang, and in his own name. General Ranabir was counting on Jit Jang's son in Palpa to incite the garrison there to mutiny, but the former Commander-in-Chief's son was promptly arrested and brought to Kathmandu along with fifty-four of his accomplices.

Five among them were executed and a few Brahmins were subjected to defilement and expulsion from their caste and sentenced to lifelong imprisonment in lieu of death sentence, since Brahmins were exempt from capital punishment on religious grounds. All the rest were incarcerated for various lengths of time. General Ranabir Jang himself was temporarily detained by the British authorities before he could cross the frontier and his men suffered a crushing defeat at Butwal at the hands of the soldiers loyal to Bir. After that, nothing was heard of General Ranabir Jang's activities until 1893, when some of his apparent supporters made a pretense of raiding a few offices in the eastern tarai districts but readily surrendered, without a fight, to the Government soldiers on duty.

The year 1888 proved to be a crucial year for Bir in more ways than one. He paid an official visit to Lord Dufferin in Calcutta, where he was received with full honours, and he assured the Viceroy of regular supply of army recruits from Nepal in the future. After he returned from Calcutta, he married off two of his daughters, Kirti Divyeshvari alias Shri Panch Sahila Bada Maharani and Durga Divyeshvari alias Shri Panch Kanchha Bada Maharani to King Prithvi Bir Bikram Shah Dev, who had been married for the first time in 1887 to two other Rajput brides from India, Revatiraman Rajyalakshmi and Lakshmi Divyeshvari alias Shri Panch Mahila Bada Maharani, the mother of King Tribhuvan.

The Dowager Maharani, Tarakumari, the eldest wife of Crown Prince Trailokya and the King's stepmother, had earlier protested to the Viceroy that the intended brides were born of Bir Shamsher's low-caste wife and were not socially and religiously eligible for being married to a higher caste person, not to speak of one belonging to the royal family. But her protest had proved to be of no avail as Lord Duffiren refused to intervene in the affair.

It was true that Bir Shamsher's two daughters married to the King were born of a Newari Shrestha girl who had first come to Bir Shamsher's house as his first wife's maid, Khanjan.[13] As this girl's mother had chosen to cohabit with a kau or blacksmith after she had already had this daughter by her Shrestha husband, it had become customary for Bir's detractors to vilify this girl herself as a "kauni" or blacksmith girl, thereby implying that she herself was also someone from whose hands you could not even take water. If their allegation was true, this girl could not possibly have been employed as a maidservant in the King's uncle's house.

Khanjan was a charming girl of bewitching beauty and Bir's father-in-law, Prince Upendra, had reportedly warned his daughter against taking this girl to her husband's house as her favourite housemaid. After Bir started having a liaison with the girl, his wife, in utter despair, had once sought to blind her by pouring arsenic into her eyes when she was fast asleep. Her eyes were luckily saved, but the acid burn left a permanent scar on her beautiful face as a constant reminder of what she had had to go through to attain to rank and power in later life.

Bir's first wife's vengeful act of jealousy cost her dearly in terms of her intimacy with him for he would have nothing to do with her after that. But the intended victim had everything to gain by it, because, apart from remaining her husband's favourite concubine, she later became a formally recognized wife of equal status as Kanchha Bada Maharani Toph Rajyalakshmi, all of her sons were included in the roll of succession and both of her daughters married to the King.

Common women could and did at that time attain social position and political influence only through the medium of the bedroom. It was actually after the marriage of her daughters to the King that Bir promoted her to the rank of Kanchha Bada Maharani and included his sons by her in the roll of succession. Thus, Bir Shamsher, like Jang Bahadur before him, felt compelled to revise the roll of succession in order to accommodate his sons by his favourite wife.

The roll of succession as revised by Bir in 1888 was as follows:

1. Bir Shamsher, Prime Minister-cum-Maharaj and Supreme Commander-in-Chief.
2. Dev Shamsher, Commander-in-Chief.
3. Chandra Shamsher, Senior Commanding General (Western Command).
4. Bhim Shamsher, Commanding General (Eastern Command).
5. Fatte Shamsher, Commanding General (Southern Command).
6. Lalit Shamsher, Commanding General (Northern Command).
7. General Jit Shamsher.
8. General Juddha Shamsher.
9. General Gehendra Shamsher.
10. Colonel Dharma Shamsher.
11. Colonel Chakra Shamsher (Bir's son).
12. Colonel Rudra Shamsher.
13. Colonel Padma Shamsher.

14. Colonel Punya Shamsher.
15. Colonel Bikram Shamsher.
16. Colonel Tej Shamsher (Bir's son).
17. Colonel Mohan Shamsher.
18. Colonel Pratap Shamsher (Bir's son).
19. Colonel Jang Shamsher (Dev's son).

Bir and Jang, as we have seen, followed the same policy in respect of matrimonial alliances with the royal family and also with regard to the revision of the roll of succession, although in both cases, their specially favoured sons were unable to gain politically by their royal connections. But Jang Bahadur proved more fortunate than Bir in one respect. His maternal grandson was able to sit on the throne of Nepal whereas Bir's dream to see his daughter's son on the throne remained unfulfilled in spite of his best efforts.

Bir Shamsher, through the King's mother and servants in the palace, reportedly saw to it that the young King, who was hardly twelve or thirteen when he was married, spent most of his time with Bir's favourite elder daughter, who was known as Shri Panch Sahila Bada Maharani. The King was discouraged from keeping company with his other queens including Bir's own second daughter. But Bir's favourite daughter remained childless whereas his youngest daughter bore a son who died as an infant, and had several miscarriages. During Bir's lifetime the King had no male heir born to him. It was five years after Bir's death that the King's second queen from India, Shri Panch Mahila Bada Maharani Lakshmi Divyeshvari Devi, gave birth to King Tribhuvan.

Let us now turn to Maharaj Bir's administration, for under a patriarchal system of rule the ruler's personal style of functioning is most important. Bir had come to power as a result of the cold-blooded assassination of the incumbent Maharaj and Prime Minister, and he had not failed to learn from the experience of his predecessor. His first priority was to ensure his own personal safety. He, therefore, organized a special force of personal bodyguards and stationed it in the compound of his own residence. A company of these guards was on 24-hour standby with instructions to rush to the Prime Minister's presence should they sense any danger to his life. No one wearing an overcoat was to be permitted to enter the Prime Minister's house; an abiding lesson had been learnt from the murder of Ranoddip by the Shamsher brothers who were wearing their military overcoats at the time they killed their uncle. Also the guards had strict orders not to let anyone in without the prior approval of the Aid-de-Camp General, who was called Hazuria General.

The first person chosen to be appointed to the post of the Aide-de-Camp General was no less a person than Bir's own eldest half-brother, Dambar Shamsher. He had played the leading role in shooting Maharaj Ranoddip to death, and he reportedly refused to be included in the roll of succession. He had, therefore, been given a higher salary and other privileges.

Every morning at the appointed hour, the Maharaj displayed himself on the balcony of his residence and received the salute by the army band. Then, after being heralded in a typical Persian mode of expression (*Naquib Boli*) by two red turbanned mace-bearers dressed in white, who would shower panegyrics and benedictions on him, the Maharaj would proceed to hear popular grievances in keeping with the grand manner of great Mughal emperors dispensing direct justice to their people. No one under any circumstances could be barred from attendance at this open court called Salam or reveille held as though to signal the start of the business of the state. Simple cases of dispute were decided right on the spot, but parties to more complicated cases were asked to present themselves at the Maharaj's official court, which was held in the main hall of his residence in the late afternoon on working days.

Although attendance was not officially compulsory at this open afternoon court, everyone of importance made it a point to be present for fear of being victimized or persecuted, because it was known that the Maharaj's informers carefully noted who were there. Even the lowest employees of the Government made it a point to appear before the Maharaj after their office hours, when he would display himself from the balcony of his residence as he had done in the morning. Regular attendance in the evening was sometimes treated as a criterion for promotion or rewards.

The Maharaj enjoyed sovereign authority in every matter; nothing was beyond his jurisdiction. He not only had powers of life and death over the King's subjects but also had the authority in writing to control and discipline the King himself as and when he deemed it necessary to do so. The document imparting supreme authority to the Maharaj and Prime Minister stated unequivocally that it was the bounden duty of the army and all other officers of the state to obey the Maharaj under all circumstances, even if the King himself personally ever asked them to do otherwise. The Maharaj was thus not only the chief executive of the Government and supreme commander-in-chief of the army but also the final court of appeal in matters of justice.

At his court in the main hall of his residence, called Lal Darbar, every day late in the afternoon, decisions would be handed out in complicated cases involving judicial appeal in consultation in public with high-ranking civilian and judicial officers known as Kazis and Sardars. The Maharaj also received reports from the District Governors known as Talukwalas and Bada Hakims on the state of administration in their respective areas and would seek assistance of some of his brothers in investigating those reports with a view to helping him issue final administrative orders.

It was rather strange that the person next in line of succession to the supreme office of the Maharaj and Prime Minister even as the Commander-in-Chief, had little or nothing to do with the army but was placed in charge of general civilian administration. Like the Maharaj himself, he did not have to attend any office and held his own court in the groundfloor hall of his residence where all matters within his jurisdiction were formally disposed of. The number-three man, who was officially designated as Senior Commanding General in charge of the west was actually in charge of the entire army and was virtually the army chief. But neither the Commander-in-Chief nor the Senior Commanding General could make any appointments or dismissals on their own without the approval of the Maharaj and Prime Minister himself. The Commander-in-Chief and the Senior Commanding General would recruit the lowest level clerical staff and the soldiers respectively, but even these appointments were subject to the subsequent approval of the Maharaj, who retained the authority to reject them if he so wished.

During the administration of Maharaj Ranoddip, his youngest brother and Commander-in-Chief Dhir Shamsher had established two sections in the office or agency for general administration (Mulki Adda): an office for the management of the hills (Pahad Bandobasta) and an office for the management of the plains or the tarai (Madhesh Bandobasta). The tarai district headquarters were called *goswaras* and the hill district headquarters were known as *tahsils*. Dhir had also been responsible for improving the arrangements for the realization of land taxes and for the audit of governmental accounts, and he had also brought in English engineers from India to conduct feasibility surveys for installation of hydroelectric projects and ropeways.

The *Munshi Khana* and *Jaishi Kotha* constituted the foreign office and handled relations with India and China including Tibet. Until very nearly the end of the Rana regime the foreign office remained in charge of a single Newari family, that acquired the appellation of the *Munshi Khalak*. The family had been associated with the foreign office since the time of Bhimsen Thapa. A member of this family, Balman, headed the foreign office during the administration of both Maharaj Ranoddip and Maharaj Bir. Balman was probably the first Nepali to pass the entrance examination of Calcutta University.

Dhir's eldest son, Bir Shamsher, also introduced reforms at all levels of the central and district governments as well as in the administration of revenue, law and justice. His training under his able father, his experience as the Governor of Palpa and his posting as the Representative of his country in Calcutta – all stood Bir in good stead after he became the Prime Minister. He strengthened the administration and training of the militia battalions. He was the first to establish the Haziri Goswara, the office for taking attendance of all Government servants and preparing reports on the quality and progress of their work and the Sahar Safai or Sanitation Office to look after the sanitation of Kathmandu.

In 1895, Nepal was divided into 35 administrative units called *zillas* in the tarai and *tahsils* in the hills. There were 12 zillas and 23 tahsils at the time. During the latter part of the period of Bir Shamsher's administration the tarai units were brought together under four circles, each under a bada hakim. The bada hakims were assisted by the zamindar and the patwari in the collection of land taxes. Bir left the system of Chaudharis intact.

Bir introduced judicial reforms in 1897 and 1901. A number of law courts of the first instance were set up in the hill districts and appellate courts were set up for groups of districts in the Kathmandu Valley as well as outside it. A high court of appeal or *bhardari* under a General on the roll of succession was established in Kathmandu. Above this *bhardari* court was, of course, the Maharaj himself as the final court of appeal and justice.

The project for supplying piped drinking water to Kathmandu and Bhadgaun was initiated by Bir in 1888, and piped water was first available to the inhabitants of Kathmandu in 1889 and to those of Bhadgaun three years later. It was during Bir's administration that Kathmandu saw sewerage and drainage on a limited scale. The only hospital in Kathmandu had been the British Residency hospital; now Bir opened the first public hospital. The old school house that had been built by

Maharaj Ranoddip to the north of Ranipokhari was turned into barracks for Bir's personal bodyguards and a new building for Darbar High School was constructed by him. The suspension bridge at Kulekhani and the clock tower to the east of Ranipokhari were also built in Bir's time.

But Bir spent much more on the palatial buildings for himself and his sons than on the projects for public welfare. He initially employed Indian architects and engineers in designing and building two well-known palaces, the Seto Darbar (the White Palace) and the Lal Darbar (the Red Palace) along the lines of Graeco-Roman architecture. Thus Nepal's rich tradition of art and architecture gave way to imitations of western models. Seto Darbar was modelled after Calcutta's famous Government House known as Belvedere Palace. The main hall of Seto Darbar known as *Thulo Baithak* displayed crystal chandeliers, life-size mirrors, and Bohemian glassware imported from London, Rome, and Venice along with valuable paintings. Its floor was paved with Italian marble slabs and covered from wall to wall with beautiful and costly Persian and Belgian rugs. All these were lost when the palace accidentally caught fire in 1934, and its main hall with everything in it was literally burnt to ashes. The best efforts of the Rana Government and the army could not save it because there was no fire brigade in Nepal at the time. Some sections of Bir's palaces were later designed and built by Nepali engineers, Colonels Kishor Narsingh and Kumar Narsingh, who were General Badri Narsingh's sons and Bir's nephews. Bir also renovated Maharaj Ranoddip's old residence at Narayan Hiti and turned it into a permanent royal palace primarily because its site was close to his own residence.

As regards music, while he was fond of western musical instruments, as pointed out by Commander-in-Chief Roberts, and engaged the services of an English bandmaster, Bir showed a more discerning interest and equally patronized traditional Indian classical music, drama and dances. Some of the leading Muslim maestros such as Tej Khan and Dhundi Khan, belonging to the classiest *Gharanas* or families of the practitioners of traditional Indian classical music, were employed by Bir on the most generous terms to teach music to his children and to the members of Nach-Talim Khana, the permanent performing troupe of female singers, dancers and actresses maintained by Bir in a special annexe to his palace in keeping with the Mughal tradition of a harem. Some of these girls were also taught how to play piano, guitar, and drums because Bir was as fond of western musical instruments as he was of *tanpura, sitar and tabla*. They staged dances, dramas and musical performances for the entertainment of the Maharaj and his family and guests in a special auditorium in Lal Darbar where formal shows were held to the delight of all present.

Bir did much to boost the cause of traditional classical music in both Nepal and India. He held something like an international music conference in the winter of 1900 at an obscure place in the Nepal tarai Bagadi Jalsa, which became well known both in Nepal and India because all of the leading maestros and virtuosos who counted had taken part in it. The only Indian nationalist English language daily newspaper of the time, the *Amrita Bazar Patrika*, on 7 February 1900 gave the conference a highly favourable write-up. The paper said that it had gone a long way in reviving and promoting interest in classical music, which had suffered a real decline as a result of competition from emerging patterns of Indian popular music, dance, and drama based on rather poor imitations of western musical tunes and dramatic techniques.

While Bir fully deserved Perceval Landon's compliment as a great builder and no mean musician, he was fond of other good things of life as well. He was as good a connoisseur of food as that of music; he was a real gourmet with a special taste for Mughalai dishes which were specially prepared for him by Nepali cooks in observance of caste rules but under the strict guidance of trained Muslim chefs who would tell them or show them from a distance what was to be done without actually touching the spices, condiments or other ingredients.

Bir's Foreign Policy

Bir Shamsher's relations with British Residents Girdlestone (1883-1888) and Durand (1888-1891) were far from satisfactory, but both the Viceroys, Lord Dufferin (1884-1888) and Lord Lansdowne (1888-1894), refused to put pressure on Bir along the lines suggested by their representatives in Nepal. Then, with the appointment of Colonel H.Wylie (1891-1898) as Resident in April 1891, there was a marked improvement in the relations between Maharaj Bir and the Resident. Colonel Wylie gave favourable reports to his Government on Bir's domestic and foreign policies from 1891 to 1895. He expressed satisfaction with Nepal's cooperation with British authorities in demarcating the boundary between their two countries and also in suppressing crime in the border areas by handing over even criminals who were not actually covered by the treaty of extradition.

Bir Shamsher's cooperation in ensuring the supply of Gorkha recruits and in preventing the escape of Chogyal Thutob Namgyal, the ruler of Sikkim, to Tibet through eastern Nepal in 1892 were specially mentioned. Though Bir Shamsher had sought to dissuade the British from sending the Macaulay mission to Tibet in 1886, the Tibetan attempt to push themselves into Sikkim in 1888 led Bir to believe that Tibet was overplaying its hand. When Lhasa sent an emissary to Kathmandu in the spring of 1888 seeking help in accordance with the terms of the 1856 treaty, Bir offered mediation but did not come forward to help the Tibetans against the British.

According to Wylie's report, there had been an increase in the volume of trade between the two countries:

Year	Export (Rupees)	Dollars (millions)	Imports (Rupees)	Dollars (million)
1895-1896	1,83,36,959	2 1/4	1,36,23,888	2 1/4
1896-1897	1,89,30,554	2 1/3	1,53,67,519	2 1/4
1897-1898	2,05,65,292	4	1,82,88,103	2 1/2
1898-1899	2,14,09,805	4 1/8	1,60,63,496	2 1/3
1899-1900	2,09,34,201	4	1,37,44,745	2 1/4
(First Eleven months)				

On Wylie's suggestion, Bir Shamsher invited Sir Frederick Roberts, the Commander-in-Chief of India, and his wife to visit Nepal in 1892. In March 1892 Sir Frederick and Lady Roberts were presented with a guard of honour and received at the border post by a Nepali General who escorted them on their long journey on horseback to Kathmandu across the difficult mountain terrain.

In Kathmandu an impressive ceremonial parade of 18,000 soldiers was held in honour of the Indian Commander-in-Chief. Dev Shamsher, the then Commander-in-Chief of Nepal, under special instructions from the Maharaj spared no efforts to make it a success in every way. Money was lavishly spent in importing the outfit, equipage and accouterments of the troops. Ceremonial dresses, plumed helmets, high boots and Sam Browne belts must have cost a fortune in themselves, and on top of that, colourful uniforms for officers and men were custom-made by the most expensive English tailors in Calcutta, Ranken and Company.

All this was purposely done to impress upon the ranking visitors that the Shamsher brothers were very friendly and not uncouth, as their detractors claimed. The march past amply served its purpose, firstly because the visitors were very much impressed by the turnout and performance of the Nepali troops, and also because it helped Bir Shamsher make friends with Roberts and through him make the British Government better appreciate Nepal's position and friendly attitude towards the British. What Sir Frederick (later Lord Roberts of Kandahar and a Field marshal) wrote in his autobiography bears testimony to this:

> Notwithstanding the occasional differences which have occurred between our two governments and the Nepal Durbar, I believe that, ever since 1817, when the Nepal war was brought to a successful end by Sir David Ochterlony, the Gorkhas have had a great respect and liking for us; but they are in perpetual dread of our taking their country, and they think the only way to prevent this is not to allow anyone to enter it except by invitation, and to insist upon the few thus favoured traveling by the difficult route that we traversed. Nepal can never be required by us for defensive purposes, and as we get our best class of native soldiers thence, everything should, I think, be done to show our confidence in the Nepalese alliance, and convince them that we have no ulterior designs on the independence of their kingdom.[14]

Roberts went back to India highly impressed by Bir's "greatest civility" and his brothers' "quiet and easy manners" and their complete lack of awkwardness. Roberts found Bir "very intelligent" and his administration both efficient and benevolent in character. According to him, the Maharaj was not only interested in military matters but also in hospitals, schools and sanitary improvement in Kathmandu. Bir and Roberts hit it off with each other so well that the Maharaj did not even hesitate to introduce his wife to the Commander-in-Chief of India, perhaps the first European to be shown that gesture which was characterized by the Viceroy, Lord Lansdowne, himself as a "significant event." Roberts also noted Bir Shamsher's special interest in music when he wrote that "The Maharaj is extremely musical and has several well-trained bands taught by an English bandmaster."[15] Thus the money, time and efforts spent by Maharaj Bir and his brothers in organizing the friendly reception and the parade in honour of Roberts were not spent in vain.[16]

Both Roberts and Wylie were in favour of the removal of restrictions on the purchase of arms by Nepal from India because they thought that this would kill any incentive for Nepal itself to manufacture arms whereas Durand had unsuccessfully opposed the supply of even rifles to Nepal. Wylie now advocated the same kind of arms policy for the British Government towards Nepal as it had pursued towards Afghanistan.

According to Wylie's estimate, the Nepali army consisted of 44,000 of all ranks, and Roberts felt that they were as good as their own men. The Nepali soldiers were armed with martini and Snider rifles. Cables and devices for detonating mines and the machinery for making rifled cannon had also been imported from India. Dev Shamsher, the Commander-in-Chief of Nepal, had given Roberts an exaggerated account of the scale on which rifles and ammunition were being manufactured in Nepal. Both Roberts and Wylie felt that if the Nepal Government's fear and suspicion of the British intention were removed by some means, the military resources of Nepal could be an additional asset to the British in India.

As a measure of conciliating Bir Shamsher, they influenced Lansdowne to secure for the Maharaj the title of Knight Commander of the Star of India (K.C.S.I.) in May 1892, after Bir had already been given the title of Tiung-ling ping ma Kuo Kan Wang (Commander-in-Chief of the forces and truly valiant prince) by China in 1889. The British made another conciliatory gesture towards Bir about the same time by instructing their agents and officials along the border that "sufficient surveillance should be exercised over the (Nepali) refugees to prevent their making British territory a base for hostile activities against the Nepal Darbar.

In February 1893, Bir Shamsher paid a visit to Calcutta as a state guest. At his meeting with the Maharaj, Lord Lansdowne (1888-1893) stated his preference for Magars and Gurungs in the British Indian Gorkha regiments and asked Bir not to enroll all of them in his own army. Bir assured Lansdowne that he would treat the Resident also in a better way. Lansdowne in his turn promised his assistance in enabling Nepal to purchase arms and ammunition from England and India without paying duties on them on the condition that Nepal should not try to procure arms by clandestine means, and that it should inform the

Resident of its "reasonable" needs. The Governor-General also asked for an undertaking from Nepal that it would not pass on those arms to Tibet-- an undertaking which was actually unnecessary in view of Nepal's hostile relations with Tibet.

Within a year of his visit to Calcutta, Bir Shamsher put in his request to the Resident for the purchase of 8,000 Martini-Henry rifles and 300 rounds of ammunition per rifle along with a complete set of plant and machinery for the manufacture of field guns, ammunition, and rifles. Lord Elgin (1894-1899) had by that time taken over from Lord Lansdowne as the Viceroy, and he was hard put to it to explain his Government's attitude on this question of the supply of arms to Nepal. Lord Elgin told Nepal that Lord Lansdowne's commitment did not imply an unlimited supply of arms to Nepal but meant only Nepal's "reasonable" needs. While respecting Nepal's autonomy and cherishing every goodwill towards it, Lord Elgin refused to supply machine-guns to Nepal for fear that Nepal might start making them themselves after discovering their mechanism. However, Bir was supplied 8,000 Martini-Henry rifles and six seven-pounder field guns. An agreement was also reached between Nepal and British India in 1894 on the conditions of the purchase and supply of ordnance in the future.

When Bir wanted to go to England in 1896, Lord Elgin pleaded with his Government that if the Maharaj were offended, the relations between the two Governments might be strained and for that reason he should be invited there. But the India Office refused to fulfill Bir's condition that he should be treated the same way as Jang Bahadur, as an Ambassador of his King, for fear that Nepal might seek relations with Russia as well in due course, if she were treated as a fully independent state, with France, Germany, Japan, and China.

Bir Shamsher refused to accept a lesser status for himself and his country. Lord Elgin and Ex-Viceroy Lord Lansdowne finally succeeded in persuading George Hamilton, the Secretary of State for India, to meet Bir's wishes but by that time Bir had changed his mind because of Nepal's preoccupation with Tibetan affairs. However, to mollify Bir, Elgin saw to it that Bir was awarded G.C.S.I. (Grand Commander of the Star of India) in 1897.

With its general decline in power and prestige towards the end of the 19th century, China was fast losing its shadow of authority in Tibet. Tibet very much resented China's helplessness against the British Government's penetration into Sikkim forcing the Tibetans to withdraw from there in 1888. The Anglo-Chinese convention of 1890 recognizing Sikkim as a British protectorate and the 1893 agreement granting commercial rights to the British in Tibet did not have the prior consent nor the signature of any Tibetan representatives, and therefore Tibet did not regard them as binding on it.

The 13th Dalai Lama had just come of age and in seeking to assert his authority was having difficulties with the Chinese Amban. The god-king believed that among the Russian Czar's Buddhist subjects in Siberia and Mongolia a sizable number were devoted to him, and he knew that both Britain and China feared Russia's designs against them. It was, therefore, only natural for him to exploit the possibility of enlisting Russia's support for himself.Many Mongolian Buriats who were studying in Lhasa's monasteries could be used as instruments of communication with Czar Nicholas II who might well have been as interested in Tibet as in Afghanistan for the scope it provided to put pressure on the British in India.

Nepal's misunderstanding with Tibet reached an all-time high in 1895-96. Lord Elgin had thought of assuring Bir Shamsher, at least orally, that the British Government would bring Chinese pressure to bear on Tibet to settle its disputes with Nepal amicably. But the India Office stopped Lord Elgin from doing so because it felt that it would not be politic for the British Government to involve China under any pretext in the settlement of affairs between Nepal and Tibet when China had not itself done so nor had either party to the dispute sought British assistance. If Britain asked China to do something about the dispute, China might interpret the British suggestion as British recognition of China's suzerainy over Nepal.

The India Office, while approving of the sale of arms to Nepal, wanted Lord Elgin to let the dispute between Nepal and Tibet take its own course. The British Government reasoned that China's war with Japan in 1894-95 would prevent China from intervening in favour of Tibet, and that, left to itself, Tibet was not in a position to defeat Nepal. The India Office thought that only Nepal's defeat by Tibet would create a real embarrassment for Britain by compelling it to take steps for its own security in India, and, luckily for all parties concerned, the dispute between Nepal and Tibet did not lead to war between the two countries.

Lord Curzon (1899-1904), who succeeded Lord Elgin as Viceroy of India in 1899, was convinced that the Tibetan problem could not be solved through China. His imperial outlook and temperament made him press for what was described as a 'forward' or more aggressive policy everywhere vis-a-vis Russia. He strongly suspected Russia's interest in Tibet because between 1899 and 1901 many reports were in circulation about the growing contact between the Dalai Lama and the Czar through a Mongolian Buriat monk named Dorjieff.

Lord Curzon's outlook on relations with Nepal proved to be different from that of his predecessors. He did not want Nepal to have anything to do with China, and he sought to make Nepal accept a role of complete subordination to India. Several points of irritation soon developed.

In June 1899 Bir paid a visit to Calcutta to meet Lord Curzon as the new Viceroy of India. The description by the British Indian authorities of this visit as "a complimentary mission" to Lord Curzon created friction with the Nepali Government which felt that as in the past the head of the mission on such an occasion should have been recognized as an Ambassador of the King of Nepal. In 1900, Bir unsuccessfully opposed Calcutta's decision to send a Gorkha regiment to deal with the Boxer Rebellion in China.

Maharaj Bir did not accept Lord Curzon's proposal for a visit to Kathmandu, and it was with considerable reluctance that he agreed to invite Lord Curzon for a shoot in the tarai in April 1901 after telling the Viceroy that he would not be there in person to receive him for reasons of health. Perhaps as a retaliatory gesture for treating his visit to Calcutta as a complimentary mission, Bir put Harka Jang Thapa and Jit Bahadur Khatri in sole charge of Curzon's hunting trip despite the fact that their official position and rank were not befitting the hosts of a Viceroy, Lord Curzon.

Bir's plea of ill health was genuine: he died from an aneurism on 5 March 1901 at the age of 49. Commander-in-Chief Chandra Shamsher persuaded the new Maharaj Dev Shamsher, Chandra's brother, to change the arrangements and let himself look after Lord Curzon during the hunt.

It is difficult to believe that when these two clever and ambitious men met at Morang in eastern tarai in April 1901, they just hunted tigers and did not discuss internal Nepali politics and the situation in Tibet. This meeting between Chandra and Curzon may indeed be treated as a prelude to the coup d'etat against Maharaj Dev and to the Younghusband mission to Tibet, which will be discussed in the subsequent chapter.

Let us conclude this account of Maharaj Bir's administration with the following estimate of his character said to have been given by one who knew him well:

> He was endowed with a sound common sense which he brought to bear upon every question before him and thus helped him to solution which, though it might not have been brilliant, was in most instances on the right side.[17]

NOTES

1. Perceval Landon, *Nepal* (Kathmandu: Ratna Pustak Bhandur, 2nd reprint 1976), Vol. II, p. 74.
2. Kashinath Acharya Dikshit, *Bhayeko Kura* (Actual Facts) (Kathmandu: Narendramani Acharya Dikshit, 1974) (V.S. 2031), p. 28.
3. Foreign Service-E, February 1887, No. 405 (National Archives of India), cited in Asad Husain, *op.cit.*, p. 145.
4. Asad Husain, *op.cit.*, p. 143.
5. Asad Husain, *op.cit.*, p. 144.
6. Kanchanmoy Mojumdar, *Political Relations between India and Nepal* (Delhi: Munshiram Monoharlal Publishers, Prt. 40, 1973), pp. 54-56.
7. General order issued by the Nepal Government dated 1943 V.S. (August 1886), Ministry of Foreign Affairs, Bundle (Poka) No. 30, cited in Tri Ratna Manandhar, *Some Aspects of Rana Rule in Nepal* (Kathmandu, 1983), p. 101.
8. Kashinath Acharya Dikshit, *Bhayeko Kura* (Actual Facts), edited and published by his son, Narendramani Acharya Dikshit (Kathmandu, 1974, V.S. 2031), pp. 32-33.
9. Kashinath Dikshit, *op.cit.*, pp. 37-39.
10. Perceval Landon, *Nepal* (Kathmandu: Ratna Pustak Bhandar, reprinted in 1976), p. 74.
11. Telegram from British Resident E.L. Durand to Foreign Secretary H.M. Durand, 4 August 1888, Foreign Secret-E, September 1888, No. 190, N.A.I. (New Delhi).
12. Kashinath Acharya Dikshit, *op.cit.*, pp. 80-82.
13. Kashinath Dikshit, *op.cit.*, p. 26.
14. Lord Roberts of Kandahar, Field Marshal, *Forty-one Years in India*, Volume II, p.452 (London: Richard Bentley and Son, 1897), p. 452.
15. Roberts *op.cit.*, p. 536.
16. Lansdowne Papers, Vol. VII, Roberts to Lansdowne, 30 March 1892, Lansdowne to Roberts, 9 April 1892, cited in Kanchanmoy Mojumdar, *op.cit.*, p. 58; Roberts, *op.cit.*, Vol. II, pp. 449-52.
17. Cited in Dr. Ishwari Prasad, *The Life and Times of Maharaja Juddha Shamsher Jung Bahadur, Rana of Nepal* (New Delhi: Ashish Publishing House, 1975), p. 36.

12

Bir's Three Successors: Maharaj Dev, Chandra and Bhim Shamsher

A. Dev Shamsher, the Maharaj for One Hundred and Fourteen Days

Bir was succeeded, one after another, by three of his half-brothers all of whom were born of the same mother. Although they were brothers, relations amongst them were no more cordial than their relations with Bir had been as we shall presently see. The three of them had combined against Bir at one particular instance in the past, but this demonstration of unity was forged out of sheer desire to promote their own immediate self-interest much in the same way as they had previously sided with Bir against their own brother, Khadga.

Though the Rana family rule may be characterized as a patriarchal system in general terms, it did not always conform to it in form and spirit and was full of aberrations. But what is remarkable about the Rana system of government is that it worked despite its frequent aberrations, and it kept the brothers and the half-brothers, their sons and nephews united up to a point in protection of their familial interests against the general public, who remained helpless against them for a period of one hundred and four years.

As soon as Bir died on 5 March 1901, Dev Shamsher, Commander-in-Chief and the next in line of succession to him, went to Bir's residence and had the dead body of Maharaj brought down from his room to the open courtyard of his Lal Darbar residence. After that Dev went back to his own residence at Thapathali with the Maharaj's security guards.

He also took along with him in a guarded carriage three articles-- the Maharaj's *pagari* or *tin chand*, the picturesque headdress heavily inlaid with pearls, diamonds, emeralds and other precious stones and peaked with the plumes of a bird of paradise; *Lal-Peti* or the red box containing the *Lal Panja* or the original document with the King's palm-print in red, delegating sovereign authority to members of the Rana family on the roll of succession; and the Maharaj's ceremonial sword of state. Once back in his residence, Dev Shamsher profusely garlanded himself, put the Maharaj's headgear on his head and auspicious red and vermilion mark or *tika* on his forehead and retired to his private chapel for worship to invoke divine blessings on himself.

He then drove in a carriage straight to the royal palace and presented *nazar* or coins to the King in order to secure formal confirmation of his succession to the high office of the Maharaj of Kaski and Lamjung and that of the Prime Minister and Supreme Commander-in-Chief of Nepal. From the royal palace, he rode in his carriage as the newly proclaimed Maharaj at the head of triumphal procession to the Parade Ground in the heart of Kathmandu where he received the salute of the officers and men of the army, the civilian officials and all others who were assembled there.

After all this was over, he returned to his Thapathali residence and then issued orders for the state funeral of his deceased half-brother, Maharaj Bir Shamsher. General Bhim Shamsher, who was the Commanding General in charge of the east, was entrusted with the supervision of the funeral procession and other arrangements for the performance of the rites of cremation and mourning. If Kashinath Acharya Dikshit's account as an eyewitness is to be believed, he found Bir's Lal Darbar almost deserted when, under instructions of General Bhim, he went there to help Bir's wives perform their rites of mourning. He himself had to carry pitchers of water for the ladies to bathe as all of the servants had abandoned their posts to wait on the newly proclaimed Maharaj for fear of being victimized by him. The desertion of the deceased Maharaj's residence at the time of succession became common practice henceforth because the successor tended to persecute those who had been close to his predecessor.

Dev Shamsher was thirty-nine years old when he became Maharaj and Prime Minister. As he had been adopted by Commander-in-Chief Krishna Bahadur Kanwar Ranaji as a godson, he did not share the initial hardships of life with the rest of his sixteen brothers and half-brothers. Bir had always trusted him and Bhim Shamsher much more than Chandra Shamsher. Dev Shamsher had served under Bir for thirteen years successively as Commanding General, Senior Commanding

General and Commander-in-Chief and had given his predecessor full satisfaction.

But Chandra Shamsher had found Dev too liberal and progressive for his taste and had set to work against him even before Dev became Prime Minister. Dev was frank and amiable and readily trusted people. In the secretive and conspiratorial atmosphere that prevailed in the court politics of Nepal, Dev Shamsher was foredoomed to failure even in normal circumstances. But the fact that Dev was pitted against Chandra, a cunning rival who was a past master in the art of intrigues and pulling strings from behind, hastened his downfall. Chandra was a shrewd observer of men and knew the strengths and weaknesses of every one of his brothers and half-brothers. He had thus always succeeded in getting others to pull his chestnuts out of the fire. His role in the ousting of his own brother Khadga in Bir's time is an example in point.

Dev Shamsher aired liberal ideas light-heartedly but did not have the capacity for sustained effort nor the sense of restraint and discipline needed to translate them into enduring measures of public policy. He has very often been projected by the present generation of Nepali historians as a liberal, well-intentioned ruler who fell an easy prey to his successor's intrigues and unscrupulous methods. Dev's present-day evaluation has been partly a result of the backlash of popular resentment against his younger and more successful brother and successor, Chandra Shamsher, who ruled Nepal for twenty-nine years with an iron hand after removing Dev from power within less than four months of his assumption of office, and partly that of lurking sympathy for a hapless victim of a truly ruthless adversary who was more than a match for him in the risky game of political intrigue.

During his rule of one hundred and fourteen days, Dev started the first Nepali language newspaper, called *Gorkha Patra* which is still published as an official daily. He manumitted female slaves in his kingdom of Kaski and Lamjung and also in the Kathmandu Valley. He is credited with devising a scheme for the abolition of all slavery, which his successor put into effect. He also proclaimed a scheme for universal primary education. A network of Nepali language primary schools, called *Bhasa Pathshalas*, was started during his time.

As an example of his interest in public welfare and personal benevolence, it may be mentioned that even before he became the Maharaj, as a tribute to the memory of his first wife and out of deference to her own pious desire, he had imaginatively accomplished the work for supplying water to wayfarers at a site midway on an eight-mile stretch of road that passed through dense forests and connected Bichakhori with Simra on the main route from Kathmandu to the railhead at the Indian border. The conduit out of which the water flowed was artistically covered from above with exquisitely wrought designs of the outstretched and turned down forearm, hands, and fingers unmistakably of a noble lady. He also put up boxes at public places in the capital and invited people to deposit their suggestions and gave them the assurance that their identity would not be revealed to anyone.

There is yet another example of his desire to promote a certain measure of popular consultation and participation. In the groundfloor hall of his residence Dev convened an assembly of the officers of the army and the civil service, certain members of the religious, trading and landowning communities and also persons from other walks of life including some members of the untouchable castes. He reportedly inaugurated the assembly from a marble chair placed on a raised platform and told the gathering that they were free to discuss any matters not relating to the crown, the appointment and succession of the Prime Minister and the beliefs and practices of the Hindu religion. The meeting had no fixed agenda or terms of reference, but in his formal address the Maharaj invited suggestions for the improvement of the administration and judicial process with an eye to the quick redress of popular grievances and also for the development of trade and industries. The first and the only assembly of this kind held during the Rana period came up with many suggestions including that of encouraging cottage industries.

We have enumerated above some of the redeeming features of Maharaj Dev's short-lived administration, but it had serious lapses as well, for he was excessively fond of pomp and show and had a real weakness for women, luxuries and other pleasures of life, and these proved to be his undoing. He spent lavishly on his own inaugural ceremony. As a departure from the established tradition and for no good reason, he actually had three inaugural ceremonies on three different days, one at each of the three towns of the Kathmandu Valley. On these occasions, Dev in his splendid white ceremonial robes as the Maharaj of Kaski and Lamjung sported an eye-catching necklace of deep coloured emeralds on his neck and chest, and sparkling rings of precious stones of different kinds and colour shone on his fingers while the picturesque official headgear of the Maharaj peaked by the plumes of a bird of paradise majestically adorned his head.. Thus dressed and bedecked with jewels, Dev rode to each ceremony in the ornamentally upholstered open *howdah* on the back of a richly caparisoned tusker that moved leisurely at the head of a triumphal procession through the main thoroughfares of each of the three towns of the Valley. The procession consisted of a long train of Government servants from the highest to the lowest, a vast concourse of commoners, military bands playing martial tunes and assorted groups of local singers, dancers, and players of musical instruments who demonstrated their own indigenous forms of performance. These events were invariably followed by the announcement of public holidays for gambling which was the most popular form of recreation during the entire period of the Rana rule. According to a noted Nepali historian, Baburam Acharya, there was a record number of public holidays for gambling during the short-lived administration of Maharaj Dev.

Much time, effort and money was spent by Maharaj Dev on these extravaganzas and on pageants such as the ladies' court. This court was attended by all the ladies of the Rana and the Shah royal families dressed to appear like European Victorian ladies in their full-blown skirts and whalebone stays. The Nepali ladies actually wore baggy trousers of fifteen to twenty yards of heavily starched cotton fabric, and their maidservants worked for a considerable time stretching the different parts of the trousers in such a way as to make the winding sheet of cloth retain its stiffness and give the appearance of being a full-blown victorian skirt.

Dev's indulgence in these light-hearted pursuits enabled his detractors, and his own brother and successor Chandra Shamsher among them, to project the image of the Maharaj as essentially a lover of idle pastimes and pleasures without the strength of determination and character needed to conduct the affairs of state.

Partly to cover himself by forewarning the British, and partly to facilitate British recognition of his regime after his plan for the coup d'etat against Maharaj Dev Shamsher had materialized, Chandra chose to write a letter to Colonel Wylie, a former British Resident who had retired from his post in Nepal in 1899. In this letter, Chandra went so far as to state that he "did not mean to sit down quietly if opportunity should occur to better his position" and assured Colonel Wylie that the intended coup would involve "no loss of life and everything (would) be done in such a way that nobody could be shocked or annoyed."[1] Aware of the difficulty Maharaj Bir had experienced in obtaining formal

British recognition of his regime in the wake of the assassination of Maharaj Ranoddip, Chandra was consciously making a case for a coup d'etat against Maharaja Dev without bloodshed and violence. Chandra was no doubt mindful of Viceroy Dufferin's warning to Bir that violence and bloodshed should be avoided at all costs in future. In view of all this, when Chandra met Lord Curzon at Morang in April 1901, it is highly probable that he discreetly sounded out the Viceroy on his plan for action against Maharaj Dev. The fact that Chandra, after his coup against Dev, did not experience the same difficulty as Bir in securing British recognition seems to corroborate this conjecture.

Within Nepal for the success of his venture against Dev, Chandra needed the whole-hearted cooperation of Dev's aide-de-camp, General Fatte Shamsher, who was in charge of the Maharaj's security forces, and also of Bir's eldest and most gifted son, General Gehendra Shamsher, who was a close personal friend of the twenty-eight year old King, Prithvi Bir Bikram Shah Dev. To begin with, Maharaj Dev's relations with the two Generals were much better and closer than Chandra's relations with them. But Dev was an open-hearted person, too unsuspecting and temperamentally unfit to keep secrets. Dev once told Chandra himself in a light-hearted and careless manner that General Fatte had warned him against Chandra. It was his failure to keep to himself what General Fatte had told him in all confidence about Chandra's designs that eventually turned his aide-de-camp against Dev.

Maharaj Dev, General Fatte, and General Gehendra used to drink together whereas Chandra did not drink and kept himself aloof from their drinking parties. Dev and Gehendra not only drank together but also shared a taste for the pleasures of flesh, and they would frequently go to the royal palace together to witness performances by the dancing and singing girls and make passes at them. But just before Dev was overthrown, he developed a serious misunderstanding with General Gehendra over a particular girl who had all along been the General's favourite. Gehendra was more interested in his mechanical workshop than in anything else, but he was of a highly sensitive nature and was piqued by Dev's attitude.

Chandra, a master conspirator, was watching all these developments with keen interest. After making sure that the Maharaj and the General had fallen out with each other for good, Chandra showed his cards to General Gehendra. He was next in line of succession to Maharaj Dev, and he reportedly told Gehendra that he did not mind even yielding his own place to the General but the time had come to remove the Maharaj at all costs in the interests of both the Shamsher family and the country.

It was through General Gehendra that Chandra approached General Fatte for the second time, and he also sought Gehendra's help in enlisting the support of the King for him. The Maharaj's personal bodyguard, Lieutenant-Colonel Indra Bahadur Shahi, who was married to Chandra's politically minded sister Khadga Kumari alias Kahili Maiyan's adopted daughter, Liku Maiyan was prevailed upon by his wife and mother-in-law to join the conspiracy against Dev. Thus, did Chandra Shamsher prepare the ground for taking decisive action against Maharaj Dev.

They set a date for the final move to remove Dev from office: 27 June 1901. It was initially planned to arrest Maharaj Dev in Chandra's own residence where he was supposed to go that day to see their ailing sister, Kahili Maiyan, who had just been brought to Chandra's house for medical treatment. But then the conspirators made a last minute change in their plans, and Maharaj Dev went to Darbar School to give away prizes on the occasion of its annual prize distribution ceremony. After the ceremony was over, Maharaj Dev was reminded by his aide-de-camp, Hazuria General Fatte, of his appointment at the late Maharaja Bir Shamsher's residence to adjudicate a domestic dispute concerning the partition of the building among Bir's sons. The Maharaj unsuspectingly accepted the proposal and went there. Once Dev was inside the house, his brothers and nephews presented him with an ultimatum and forced him to sign his resignation in the presence of King Prithvi.

Every detail of what happened after Maharaj Dev reached Tundikhel or the Parade Ground on his way to Darbar School on that fateful day has been recorded in a contemporary private diary on the basis of an eyewitness's account. The unfolding of the dramatic sequence of events affords an insight into the mind, character, and temperament of the main actors on the stage, all of whom were destined to play an important role in Nepal's history in the immediate future. For these reasons, the following excerpts are lifted as they were from the book[2] which published them for the first time:

> The official landau of the Prime Minister, while passing through the Tundikhel parade ground halted for a while and Bhim Shamsher, the Jangi Lath (Senior Commanding General in charge of the

west), commanded the army forces to present arms to the Prime Minister. Dev took salute and then moved towards the school in a very cheerful mood. The Jangi Lath gave temporary command of the parade ground to General Juddha Shamsher and followed the Prime Minister in his Victoria.

After distributing the prizes at the school, the Prime Minister boarded the carriage and was about to proceed to Thapathali. There the Hazuria General reminded him of the case at Seto Darbar and requested him to visit there. Dev agreed and everybody including a company of the Prime Minister's *Bijuli garat* (Special and Personal Bodyguards) followed the Prime Minister's official landau.

It was exactly 4.30 p.m. when the Prime Minister and party arrived at Seto Darbar. There they were formally received by Gehendra Shamsher and at his request the party walked inside the courtyard. The Hazuria General ordered the guards to stay at the courtyard on the excuse that their family dispute should not be exposed to everybody. Only Lieutenant Colonel Indra Bahadur Shahi, the commanding officer of the guards, was allowed to go inside while the guards stayed outside. Gehendra guided the Prime Minister and party to the disputed room. Bhim was there in his service uniform with his service sword in his Sam Brown Belt.

When everyone entered the room, Chandra shouted, "What are you looking for?" It was a signal to the conspirators and General Gehendra and Colonel Durga Shamsher (both of whom were body builders) grabbed and overpowered the Prime Minister. Within seconds Bhim Shamsher drew his service sword and pointed it at the neck of Lieutenant Colonel Indra Bahadur Shahi. On the point of the sword, Shahi's rifle was snatched by the conspirators.[2]

Dev Shamsher was stunned at this dramatic arrest and shouted what the hell they were doing. Chandra moved forward and told him that he was already deposed by the order of King Prithvi Bir Bikram Shah Dev. In the meanwhile, the conspirators pulled off his white cummerbund and tied the hands of the deposed Prime Minister behind his back. Dev was kept in the room under the care of Colonel Durga and four strong guards, and the others left the room. While coming out of the room, some of the conspirators shouted. "Behold! If anything happens to the King, everybody shall be killed." Chandra himself pointed the rifle at the courtyard and shouted out that His Majesty the King had dismissed Dev Shamsher and everybody should obey his orders.

The Company of the *Bijuli garat* (Special and Personal Bodyguards) was commanded by an ensign. The commander was bewildered and did not respond to the call of Chandra. Once again the unfaithful Hazuria General ordered the ensign to obey the orders of the new Prime Minister. King Prithvi was also present there. The King reluctantly confirmed the appointment of Chandra. Then, the ensign cried that the guards would obey the order of anyone to whom the King would grant authority and ordered the guards to present arms. The King and the new Prime Minister then left for Tundikhel in a carriage, heavily guarded by security forces.

Hazuria General Fatte Shamsher and General Tej Shamsher took a waiting phaeton and rushed to the ex-Prime Minister's house and brought the *Tin Chand* (headress of the Prime Minister) on the pretext that Dev needed it for a special triumphal procession. Chandra Shamsher put on the headdress and appeared before the assembled forces at Tundikhel.

At Seto Darbar, the room was opened after one hour and the hands of Dev were freed and he was allowed to sit in a chair. Bhim was instructed to make necessary arrangements to send away the deposed Prime Minister to Dhankuta in eastern Nepal. By 8 p.m. the arrangements were ready and Dev was put in a closed palanquin and taken out by the side exit of Hiti Darbar. The palanquin was closely guarded by men of the armed forces. At midnight the party reached Bhaktapur and halted for a while. There Dev was joined by his spouse who was brought from her residence. The party moved forward, crossed the Sanga Pass and halted for the night at a place called Bhatay Dhikro.

It will be best to conclude our account of the prime ministership of this simple, unsuspecting, open-hearted, well-meaning, fun-loving and frolicsome Maharaj by mentioning two episodes at the end of his career, both of which reflect on the kind of the man he was.

The day on which he was arrested and deprived of his office and power, Dev was wearing a valuable necklace of emeralds he had borrowed from Maharaj Bir's widow, Shree Tin Kanchha Bada Maharani. He wanted to hand it over to Chandra to be returned to her, but Chandra proved generous to his elder brother at somebody else's cost and asked him to keep the necklace for himself on the plea that their sister-in-law had many such necklaces.

The other episode is rather touching and sad. While nobody among Dev's relatives and retinue was bold enough to display any concern for the Maharaj's sad plight, one of the dancing girls in the royal palace named Gul Bafa, who seemed to be head over heels in love with the deposed Maharaj, wept bitterly and hurled abuse at Chandra himself when he went there. She was overpowered by grief at the deposition of her Maharaj and was completely dazed and went into hysterics. She went without food and water for seventeen days before she died.

Dev introduced the practice of having cannons fired in Kathmandu to signal midday. The custom had endured to this day as a reminder of Dev's prime ministership.

B. Chandra Shamsher's Era of Twenty-Nine Years

The 29-year-long era of Chandra Shamsher's unassailed sway over the affairs of Nepal began with the deposition of his elder brother, Maharaj Dev, on 27 June 1901. Chandra Shamsher was not only the most educated but also the most cautious, the most careful and the cleverest of the Shamsher brothers. He was always feared and respected rather than loved by his sixteen brothers and half-brothers. None of his own brothers–Khadga, Dev, and Bhim – not to speak of Bir and his other half-brothers, trusted him but they could not help playing into his hands and serving as mere instruments of his selfish designs more than once. The people in general, including civil and military service personnel, were also afraid rather than fond of him, but they respected his authority and proved more than willing to carry out his will at all times.

Chandra did not indulge in drinking or womanizing vices which all of his brothers shared in common. A born conspirator and a past master in the art of intrigue, he also knew how to exercise authority to his own advantage and purpose. His success in acquiring power and in exercising unchallenged authority for a long and unbroken period of twenty-nine years amply proves his political acumen. But unlike his great predecessor, Jang Bahadur, Chandra was not innovative nor was he as adventurous. He was not inclined to take risks. If Chandra erred at all, it was always on the side of excessive caution and restraint.

Chandra, unlike Bir, did not have to wait for British recognition of his assumption of power in Nepal as he had, as we have seen earlier, carefully prepared for it by sounding out Colonel Wylie and perhaps the Viceroy, Lord Curzon, himself beforehand on his move. British recognition was automatic. Although Chandra was reported to have said to Resident Durand once during the prime ministership of his elder half-brother, Maharaj Bir, that Nepal was subordinate to China but in no respect so to the Government of India,[3] he did not allow himself to be guided by the spirit of this statement after he himself became Maharaj. He avoided incurring the displeasure of the British in every matter and sought to gain his ends by pleasing them in every possible way.

The following excerpt from a letter written by Maharaj Chandra to the Viceroy, Lord Curzon, sometime in early 1903 truly reflects the essence of Chandra's policy towards the British Government in India:

> I shall take this opportunity of assuring Your Excellency's Government that I shall always deem it a sacred duty and valued privilege, not only to cultivate and continue unimpaired the friendly relations subsisting between the governments of India and Nepal, but to strengthen and improve them, so that we may realize all those expectations which the association with such a power like that of England naturally raises in our mind. I am fully conscious that our interests can best be served by the continuance of friendly relations between India and Nepal.[4]

The British Government has always had a preference for Chandra Shamsher over his brother, Dev Shamsher. Wylie, the former Resident in Nepal wrote to W. Lee Warner, the political secretary, immediately after Chandra's bloodless coup against his brother that the change was "a good one" as Chandra Shamsher was "cleverer, sharp, and quite ready to be loyal" whereas Dev Shamsher was "much addicted to drink, conceited, and overbearing".[5]

Born on 8 July 1863, Chandra was 38 years old when he became the Maharaj and Prime Minister. He was the first and the only Rana Prime Minister to have passed the entrance examination of the Calcutta University in 1883.

In 1903 Chandra's elder brother, General Khadga Shamsher, who had been expelled by Maharaj Bir Shamsher to Palpa and was later appointed Governor there dispatched the Sabuj regiment of soldiers from Palpa as had been desired by Maharaj Chandra, but then he suddenly left Palpa for India. His unexpected departure from Palpa aroused strong suspicions in the mind of the Maharaj about his elder brother's hostile intentions and these were subsequently corroborated by the revelation of a secret plot by some officers and men of the Sabuj regiment itself.

Maharaj Chandra Shamsher attended the Imperial Darbar in Delhi as a representative of the King in the same way as his father, Dhir Shamsher, had attended one earlier, sitting along with the ambassadors of other countries in the special enclosure for the representatives of foreign Governments rather than in the main hall where the rulers of native states in India were seated.

Records in the Nepali Foreign Office and the National Archives of India give a reliable clue that Maharaj Chandra Shamsher might have had something more to do with the Younghusband mission than having merely assisted it after it was already undertaken. It was Chandra's casual reference in conversation with Acting Resident Colonel Pears to a news item in the *The Pioneer*, an Indian English language daily newspaper, about the Czar receiving a Tibetan mission that eventually led to the use of the Nepali permanent mission in Lhasa for supplying information regularly about events in Tibet to the Viceroy through the Nepali Maharaj.[6] Again, Chandra while on his way to Delhi to attend the Imperial Durbar insisted on having a private meeting with the Viceroy in Calcutta in the midst of his pressing engagements. The meeting took place at noon on 31 December 1902. The interview actually began with the expression of gratitude by the Viceroy to the Maharaj for supplying him regularly the news received from his Representative in Lhasa.[7]

At this point, it may be useful for us to take advantage of hind-sight and look at the actual state of international relations at the time. As long ago as 1870, Colonel Prejavalsky had made an unsuccessful attempt to get to Lhasa, and Russo-British rivalry during the period between 1881 and 1895 in Tibet would certainly have affected the pattern of relationship between British India and the kingdoms on the southern side of the Himalaya. The prevailing British Indian attitude on the matter is summed up in the saying that "Tibet is the first buffer for Czechuan, and Nepal is the immediate buffer for Tibet."

The rumour picked up by British newspapers about a secret understanding between Russia and China on the basis of the surrender of Tibet by China to Russia in exchange for concessions by Russia elsewhere may have aroused the suspicion of Britain. The suspicion was further strengthened by the Dalai Lama's dealings with Russia through Dorjieff, a Buriat Mongol Lama, who, while a subject of the Russian Czar, had lived and studied for a long time in Lhasa and enjoyed the confidence of the Dalai Lama. Dorjieff was said to have succeeded in making Czar Nicholas II in St. Petersburg believe that the Czar was regarded by the Lamaic church as Maitreya, the future reincarnation of Buddha. In Lhasa, the Dalai Lama was said to have been assured by Dorjieff that the Czar had become a convert to the Buddhist faith.

Maharaj Chandra was said to have met with a ranking Tibetan Lama who was in Kathmandu apparently on a religious pilgrimage. The Lama told Chandra that a Tibetan mission had gone to India through Nepal sometime previously, but the Lama was not sure whether the same delegation had also visited Russia. He spoke to Chandra about the growth of anti-British feeling in China, Tibet and Ladakh which had led these three countries to form an alliance against the British with the support of Russia, and he reportedly went so far as to predict an attack by these countries on British India in 1904.[8] Though Chandra was not initially inclined to believe what the Lama had reported to him, yet his suspicion about the involvement of the Dalai Lama in dealings with the Czar was further confirmed by Ekai Kawaguchi, a Japanese monk, who happened to pass through Kathmandu at the time. Kawaguchi informed Maharaj Chandra of Russia's influence and close relations with the Dalai Lama and his associates.[9]

Chandra Shamsher, as suggested, proved to be "one of the more assiduous abettors of British Russian rivalry"[10] without being able to gain anything for himself or for his country. The situation in Lhasa in all probability did not warrant the dispatch of a British military expedition. Lord Curzon's undue concern for the defence of the frontiers of the Indian empire is reflected in what is described as his aggressive or 'forward' policy and his imperious and impetuous temperament were responsible for the Younghusband mission which literally had to shoot its way into Lhasa.

Curzon wrote to his home government on 8 January 1903, not long after his historic meeting with Maharaj Chandra Shamsher on 31 December 1902, as follows:

> We should contemplate acting in complete unison with the Nepalese Durbar throughout our proceedings, and we should even invite them, if thought advisable, to take part in our mission. We believe that the policy of frank discussion and cooperation with the Nepalese Durbar would find them prepared most cordially to assist our plans. Not the slightest anxiety has been evinced at our recent forward operations on the Sikkim frontiers; and we think that, with

judicious management, useful assistance may confidently be expected from the side of Nepal. Our anticipations on this point may have been confirmed by a recent interview between His Excellency the Viceroy and the Prime Minister of Nepal, Maharaj Chandra Shamsher Jang, at Delhi. The Nepalese Government regards the rumours of intrigue in Tibet with the most lively apprehension, and considers the future of the Nepal State to be directly involved; and further the Maharaj is prepared to cooperate with the Government of India in whatever may be thought most desirable, either within or beyond the frontier, for the frustration of designs which he holds to be utterly inconsistent with the interests of his own country.[11]

In mid-1903 Lhasa was not willing to negotiate with British India and even expressed its determination to resist the British mission with force should that be necessary. The British Government in London reluctantly gave a green signal to Lord Curzon to go ahead with his plan for sending the so-called Younghusband mission to Tibet. It must have been influenced by happenings in China, as well as the probability of a war between Russia and Japan (with whom the British had concluded the Anglo-Japan alliance in 1902) in finally yielding to Lord Curzon's pressure for immediate action against Tibet under the instigation of Maharaj Chandra Shamsher, the Prime Minister of Nepal.

The Younghusband mission had first gone to the Sikkim-Tibet border to negotiate with the Tibetans. It was now empowered to proceed beyond the border and occupy the Chumbi Valley, and to march to Gyantse in the Tsang province of Tibet if this was found necessary. In December 1903 Colonel Younghusband, at the head of a strong military force including the 8th Gorkha Rifles, crossed the Jelep La into Tibetan territory. Attempts of the poorly-trained and equipped Tibetan forces to resist him came to nothing, and after defeating them in a number of engagements, Younghusband marched first to Gyantse and later on to Lhasa. By 3 August 1904 Lhasa lay prostrate at the feet of the Younghusband mission, and the Lhasa convention was signed on 9 September 1904.

The Nepali representative in Lhasa, Captain Jit Bahadur Khatri, who was Colonel Fauda Singh Khatri's son, and who had kept his Government informed of the developments in Lhasa, played an important part in the negotiation of the Lhasa convention. Lord Curzon had referred to Colonel Jit Bahadur in his conversation with Maharaj Chandra on 23 January 1904 as "a clever and sensible sort of man"; and the Maharaj also expressed satisfaction with his role as Nepal's representative in Lhasa.

Maharaj Chandra's advice to the Tibetans, like that of his predecessors Maharaj Jang and Maharaj Bir, had been to make peace with the British by accepting their terms. Chandra put his own construction on the terms of the 1856 Treaty between Nepal and Tibet by suggesting that it did not oblige Nepal to extend armed assistance to Tibet. According to him, Nepal's duty was merely to extend advice and counsel to Tibet.

But the fact was that the Younghusband mission did not benefit Nepal in any way. It might have brought Chandra the British title of Grand Commander of the Star of India in January 1905 but it actually harmed Nepal's trade interests by further strengthening the British move since 1900 to have a direct trade route between British India and Lhasa through the Chumbi Valley in Tibet. This direct route became famous as the Kalimpong route to Lhasa, and its opening greatly diminished the volume of trade that passed through Kathmandu by the Kuti and Kerung passes.

Chandra Shamsher had sought to impress his countrymen as the person who had played the grandiose role of a peacemaker between British India and Tibet, but Lord Curzon would never have let him perform that function. Chandra was merely used by the Viceroy as an agent for carrying out his wishes in disregard of his own country's interests and also despite Nepal's solemn treaty obligations towards Tibet. Chandra's role was more or less actually confined to supplying the Younghusband military expedition with porters and with 4,000 yaks, of which only 150 survived partly because of the spread of the rinderpest epidemic and partly because of the mishandling of the animals by the British transport officer.

However, Perceval Landon, an English journalist commissioned by Maharaj Chandra Shamsher to write a comprehensive book on Nepal, not only tends to highlight the Maharaj's role as a peacemaker even at the cost of Nepal's own interest but also to justify the utility and timeliness of the Younghusband mission, to which he had been attached as a correspondent of the London *Times*. Although the present author's views are altogether different from Landon's on both points, the following excerpts are reproduced verbatim from Landon's book in all fairness to Landon himself and also for the benefit of the readers who may profit by comparing the two diametrically opposite views on the subject matter:

> It is more to the Maharaj's credit that he undertook the office of the peacemaker, because there is no doubt that one of the results of this settlement, the opening of the direct Chumbi Valley route has to a great extent diminished the volume of trade that had hitherto ebbed and flowed along the Kirong or Kuti roads through Nepal. Nor was the Marshal blind to the probability that as a result of the expedition and the consequent weakening of Tibet's power of resistance the Government of China might be aroused, and might even re-establish its waning authority in the country in a manner that would not fail to affect the interests of Nepal. But confident not merely in the military strength of his country but in the excellent relations which had been established between Nepal, India, Tibet, Chandra did not hesitate to adopt the policy of intermediation which has been described.[12]

The proposed visit to Nepal of King George V as the Prince of Wales had to be abandoned because of the outbreak of a cholera epidemic among thousands of beaters collected for the hunt.

Chandra, like his predecessor Bir, expressed his inability to invite Lord Curzon to Kathmandu because he represented the British Crown in person as the Viceroy and might have difficulty in paying homage to Nepal's King. The reason given was, however, that "the bigoted and conservative class of officers (in Nepal) was even opposed to his expression of devotion to the British throne."[13] Like Bir, Maharaj Chandra also invited the Indian Commander-in-Chief to Nepal, and in the autumn of 1906 Lord Kitchener was honoured with a full parade of the Nepali army. He was full of praise for the Nepali army and the Gorkhas of the Indian army: "Should it fall to my lot to be appointed the leader of troops in case of serious war, I should feel proud to have under my command the army of Nepal and to associate it with the Gorkhas of our army, who have long been recognized as some of our bravest and most efficient soldiers."[14] Lord Kitchener also took the opportunity of his visit to confer on Chandra the rank of General in the British army and appointed him Honorary Colonel of the 4th Gorkha Rifles.

In 1907 Maharaj Chandra once again visited Calcutta to meet the Earl of Minto (1905-1910) who must have sounded highly liberal to his guest from Nepal during their conversation. On this occasion the 4th Gorkha Rifles presented Maharaj Chandra Shamsher with an address and a sword of honour.

Chandra's Visit to England

The next year Chandra undertook a journey to Britain. The British Government made sure that he would have no false illusions about his status by warning Resident Manners-Smith beforehand that he was suffering from megalomania about Nepal and might cause trouble. The Resident had suggested that Maharaj Chandra should not be treated as an Indian Maharaja but should at least be set on the same footing as Sardar Nasrullah Khan, the Prime Minister of Afghanistan. But after he was rebuffed by the India office, Manners-Smith must have secured an undertaking from Maharaj Chandra that he would not "discuss affairs of state in England, and that his dealings in all such matters rest with the government of India." Prime Minister Jang Bahadur, who did not even have the title of the Maharaj when he visited Europe in 1850-51, was the only Rana Prime Minister who was actually treated by the British Government, press, and public as an ambassador of an independent country, though the British Government discouraged him also from discussing political affairs directly with the members of the Government in England.

Chandra was given a salute of 19 guns, two more salutes than the Nizam of Hyderabad, but in the interviews which the Maharaj had with King Edward VII, his Prime Minister, and the Secretary of State for India, nothing of substance was discussed.[15] Chandra Shamsher thus merely served as an object of curiosity to the British press and public, whereas his predecessor Jang Bahadur, even without any knowledge of English, had made a great impact on both the British and French press and public as his country's true ambassador. The newspaper reports and editorials in the English press at the time of Chandra's visit were not even half as complimentary and colourful as those in the English and French Press during Jang's visit. Compared with the impressive and extensive coverage of Jang's visit, the write-ups about Chandra's visit read like notices of events.

The London *Times*, for example, published an account of Chandra in the court circular and carried a one column-story entitled 'The Prime Minister of Nepal, Reception by King' and the Leeds *Mercury* gave a one-column headline – 'The King and Deewan, Nepali Ruler's visit to Buckingham Palace'. *The New York Herald* also gave a one-column headline, 'Indian Ruler at Court in London, Dewan of Nepal and Suite Lend Greater Brilliancy to the Royal Reception.'[16]

Chandra had left Kathmandu for Britain on 6 April 1908. Accompanied by a group of eleven Englishmen including Major Manners-Smith V.C., who was detailed to act as the Maharaj's political attache during his visit to Europe, Maharaj Chandra and his party of twenty two Nepalis left for England by the steamship 'City of Vienna'. They landed at Marseilles on 6 May and reached London on the afternoon of 8 May.

Chandra was awarded the Grand Cross of the Order of the Bath, and as an exceptional honour for Chandra, King Edward had the star set in diamonds before he pinned it on the Maharaj's breast. Maharaj Chandra received the honorary degree of Doctor of Civil Law of Oxford University from the hands of its Chancellor, Lord Curzon.

On his way home, Chandra halted in Paris, and then travelled across Europe with brief stops in Milan and Rome to Naples, from where 'The City of Vienna' brought the Maharaj and his party back to India, to Tuticorin, at the southern tip of the peninsula. From there a trip to the island temple of Rameshwaram by rail and boat for ritualistic purification was relatively easy. Maharaj Chandra reached Kathmandu via Calcutta on 27 August 1908.

Upon his return home, Chandra had to face the strains in the relations between Nepal and Tibet that had been in evidence in the early months of the year 1908 itself. These were not due to the longstanding difference over the boundary line in the Kuti and Kerung areas but to the activities of the Chinese High Commissioner in Lhasa during the absence of the Dalai Lama and his entourage in Urga, Kansun and Peking between the years 1904 and 1908. Chang Yin-tang who had been the junior Amban in Lhasa since 1906, indirectly raised the question of suzerainty of China over Nepal while claiming the right to enlist in Tibetan security forces the Bhebons (people of mixed Nepali and Tibetan blood), who were Nepali citizens under the terms of the understanding reached at the time of the conclusion of the Nepal-Tibet Treaty of 1856.

Maharaj Chandra, with the backing of the British Indian Government, rejected this demand. In addition, he stopped the quinquennial mission from Nepal to Peking following the 1911 revolution in China. The last mission from Nepal reached Peking in April 1908 and returned to Nepal via Batang and Lhasa in 1909.

It may be pointed out here that London by then had had second thoughts on the utility of the Younghusband mission itself when the flight of the Dalai Lama from Lhasa in search of protection from Russia and China had imposed great strains on British relations with the two nations. At the home Government's insistence, the British Indian Government had withdrawn the expeditionary force from Tibet on terms less punitive than those sought to be imposed on the Tibetan

Government by the Lhasa convention. In another move to reassure Russia and China, Britain secured the consent of China which had refused to sign the Lhasa convention, to a new agreement in London on 27 April 1906. Under this agreement, London agreed "not to annex Tibetan territory or to interfere in the administration of Tibet" and Peking approved of the Lhasa convention as amended by it and undertook "not to permit any other foreign state to interfere with the territory or internal administration of Tibet." As a matter of fact, the Younghusband military expedition to Lhasa had thus proved to be an exercise in futility for Great Britain, India, and Nepal in both the short and the longruns.

In 1910 the Dalai Lama once again fled Lhasa. He went to India this time for fear of being persecuted by the Chinese authorities, just as he had earlier escaped to Mongolia and China in 1904 in order to avoid British retaliation in the wake of the Younghusband military expedition. During the period of the Dalai Lama's refuge in India, Chang Yin-tang urged upon Maharaj Chandra Shamsher the blending of the five colours–China, Tibet, Nepal, Sikkim, and Bhutan. The Chinese Amban compared Nepal, Sikkim, and Bhutan to the molar teeth lying side by side in a man's mouth.

On 31 March 1911, China which had practically put an end to its imperialist expansion, again claimed its right to recruit bodyguards for its Amban from among the Nepali-Tibetan halfbreeds. In May 1911 the British Government declined to recognize China's claim and expressed its determination to resist any attempt on the part of China to enforce it. China was further told by the British Government that it would protect the integrity and rights of Nepal, Bhutan and Sikkim. In view of the Chinese attempt at encroachment, the British Indian Government dispatched a special supply of munitions to Kathmandu in December 1911.

In 1912 the overthrow of the Chinese imperial regime encouraged the Tibetans to throw the Chinese officers out of Lhasa, and it was through the intervention of the Nepali Government that the Chinese officials could go back to China through India without suffering reprisals at the hands of the Tibetans. The Peace Agreement of August 1912 brought compensation to Nepal for the material losses its nationals suffered during the period of Chinese intrusion. But Lhasa persisted in its claim to recruit Bhebons for its military and paramilitary forces. Chandra could have forestalled the Tibetans by announcing the occupation of the Tibetan ends of the Kuti and Kerung passes, but he was discouraged by the British from doing so.

Meanwhile, King Edward VII had passed away on 6 May 1910 and a 101 gun salute was fired in Kathmandu as a parting tribute to him. On 11 December of the following year, King Prithvi Bir Bikram Shah Dev also died and was succeeded by his five-year-old infant son, King Tribhuvan Bir Bikram Shah Dev (1911-1955).

Nepal was still mourning its King's death when King George V, with apparent reluctance, accepted Maharaja Chandra's invitation to hunt at Sukibhar at Thori in the Nepal tarai for about ten days. To guard against the contingency of the hunt being cancelled in view of King Prithvi's failing health, Chandra had earlier gone to attend the Imperial Durbar in Delhi equipped with a personal letter to the Emperor of India from the dying King himself. The letter contained a passionate plea that King Prithvi's own death should on no account be allowed to interfere with the royal hunt which had involved great preparations redounding to the credit of Nepal.

The hunt took place as planned from 18 to 27 December 1911 notwithstanding King Prithvi's death and the British royal party returned to India on 28 December. The hunting camp at Sukibhar was at a distance of thirty-two miles west-north-west from the Indian railhead of Bikhna Thori on the border. Twenty-one tigers, ten rhinoceroses, and two bears fell to King George V's rifle, and the total bag consisted of thirty-seven tigers, eighteen rhinoceroses, and four bears. It excelled the record of his own father King Edward VII who, during his hunting trip to Nepal in 1876, had shot only fifteen tigers out of a total bag of twenty-three tigers.

On Christmas Eve, the insignia of a Grand Commandership of the Royal Victorian Order and a Knight Commandership of the Victorian Order were conferred on Maharaj Chandra Shamsher and Commander-in-Chief Bhim Shamsher respectively. The Maharaj also received a gold coronation medal and a salute of nineteen guns on Indian soil. Nepal received a gift of two thousand Lee Metford rifles and five million rounds of ammunition on the occasion.

King Tribhuvan's formal coronation took place on 20 February 1913. Fifteen thousand poor were fed and a sizable number of prisoners convicted of minor offences were released in celebration of the event. There were also military displays and public decorations on the occasion. The boy King also received the formal congratulations of the Government of India through the British Resident, Colonel Showers, four days after his coronation had taken place.

The Great War of 1914-18

After the assassination of the heir to the Austrian throne Maharaja Chandra had begun to feel strongly that the event might lead to a continental war in Europe. He brought up the matter several times in his discussion with the British Resident and others in the course of the month of July 1914. As a matter of fact, Chandra anticipated the involvement of Britain in the war earlier and more correctly than some of the British cabinet ministers themselves, as indicated by Landon and even before all the member states of the Triple Entente had quite made up their minds about which side to join.

On 3 August 1914 Chandra personally went to the British Residency to convey to Resident Manners-Smith the following message for transmission to the Viceroy:

> The war cloud looks very threatening. In the event of a continental war, Great Britain will in all probability be involved. I have come to request you to inform His Excellency the Viceroy and through him His Majesty the King Empreror that the whole military resources of Nepal are at His Majesty's disposal. We shall be proud if we can be of any service however little that may be. Though far from the scene of actual conflict, we yield to none in our devotion and friendship to His Majesty's person and Empire. We have spoken of our friendship on many occasions. Should time allow, we hope to speak in deeds. I may say I am speaking in the double capacity, firstly as the Marshal of the Gorkhas and secondly as Major-General in His Majesty's army.[17]

The Government of India at once thanked the Maharaj for his offer of help and told him that it would not hesitate to accept it should the necessity arise. It also reciprocated Chandra's gesture in a highly appropriate manner when Prime Minister Asquith described Nepal's assistance to England at a Guildhall meeting on 19 May 1915 in these words: "It was not founded upon obligation but upon goodwill and sympathy." As a matter of fact, Nepal actually joined the British side without even declaring war against Germany and other European powers. It loaned six thousand of its own troops for general service within the borders of India. General Padma Shamsher and General Tej Shamsher commanded three regiments each in the Northwest Frontier and the United Provinces respectively, whereas Chandra's second son,

General Babar Shamsher who was junior in rank to the other two Generals in the Nepal army, was appointed Inspector-General of the Nepali contingent and was attached to British Army Headquarters in India. Reinforcements and additions were sent until a total of 16,554 Nepali army men had been put at the service of the British Indian regiments.

The Gorkhas directly recruited for the British Indian regiments covered themselves with glory in France, Mesopotamia, Palestine and Salonika, according to Viceroy Chelmsford (1916-21). Two hundred thousand Gorkha soldiers must have left the country for all military purposes if we take into account twenty-six thousand Gorkhas forming part of the regular Indian army in 1914 and reinforcements including non-combatant contingents. A new intensive system of recruiting was put into effect. Nepal lost more soldiers than any one of the warring countries in proportion to its total population which was about five million at the time.

Nepal also sought to render material and financial help to the British Government. A substantial loan of Indian silver coins was made to meet the shortage of coins in India, and Chandra gifted cash to the British Viceroy from time to time for any use he thought proper. In 1914, 1916, and 1917, a cash donation of 300,000 was made each year and in 1918 Rs. 200,000 was given in connection with the silver wedding anniversary of the King. Thirty-one machine guns purchased from Vickers Armstrong were presented to King George V in London on the occasion of his birthday in 1915. The same year 71 mechanics were sent by Nepal from its arms factories and workshops to work in India. Forty thousand pounds of cardamom, 84,699 pounds of tea, 200 jackets and 12 great coats were supplied to the British soldiers, and 200,000 broad gauge sleepers and 220 sisum logs were supplied to the railways free of cost.[18]

By mid-1917, the King of Nepal was requested in a letter from the German Imperial Chancellor to assist in the efforts of the entire population of the Indian subcontinent "to set up a big force state by destroying the abominable British rule." The letter further added that "In this war of independence, the Rajas and people of India look upon you as their leader and it is only through your help that their wishes will be fulfilled."[19] This move of Germany appears to have been made under the influence of Indian revolutionaries such as Raja Mahendra Pratap and Teja Singh, whom it was using to hinder the Indian contribution to the British war effort in every possible way. Mahendra

Pratap himself wrote a letter to the King of Nepal and to the Prime Minister tempting them to assume the leadership of the popular movement against the British.

Teja Singh who, according to the Government of India's information, was involved in the Lahore conspiracy case, visited Kathmandu in 1917. He informed Chandra of what Afghanistan, Persia, and Indian revolutionaries such as Mahendra Pratap had planned to do against the British and tried to impress upon the Maharaj that Britain was bound to lose the war. Nepal, therefore, should join the forces against the British so that it might be able to share the benefits of the plan the Germans had for the independence and welfare of Asia as a whole, he argued. Prince Nasrullah Khan of Kabul was also used as an intermediary by the Germans in communicating with the King and the Prime Minister of Nepal.

Maharaj Chandra, far from listening to them and being a party to their campaign against the British, dutifully passed every bit of information he had from these sources on to the British Resident. At the same time, Chandra also complained to the British that Nepal's status as an independent country was being undermined, and it was becoming difficult for him to resist the pressure of the anti-British hardliners in the court politics who tended to judge him by what Jang Bahadur had achieved in the way of independence and status for Nepal. Chandra's complaints were not entirely groundless. The Imperial Gazetteer of India of 1908 had referred to Nepal as "a native state on the northern frontier of India" and described its political status as being "intermediate between Afghanistan and native states of India" whereas the 1881 Imperial Gazetteer listed Nepal as an "independent state." The British had started giving the Prime Minister of Nepal a 15-gun salute instead of his earlier 19-gun salute. In a book entitled *England's Work in India* (by N.N. Ghosh), which was a prescribed textbook for the only school in Nepal as it was affiliated with the Calcutta University, the country was again called "a native state on the frontier of India," thereby arousing misgivings in the minds of the English educated Nepalis and giving them an opportunity to talk slightingly of Chandra. When Chandra visited Britain, he had not been treated in the same way as Jang Bahadur as the ambassador of an independent country but as a 19-gun feudatory prince favoured by the King with an interview. Bir Shamsher had refused to accept less than the status given to Jang Bahadur and for that reason cancelled his visit to England initially, thereby forcing the British Government to change its attitude on the question. Though Bir himself did not actually go there, Jang Bahadur had remained a friend and ally of Britain without being a feudatory, but partly because of the impact of time and partly because of his own obsequious attitude towards the British, Chandra Shamsher was finding it hard to project the same image of himself as Jang Bahadur's.

The British were not prepared to define the status of Nepal clearly because once they accepted Nepal as a fully independent nation, they would not be able to put restrictions on the import and purchase of arms by Nepal from other sources, nor would they be able to check Nepal's flirtation with other powers like Russia, Germany, or Japan. Whenever the question of its independent status was raised by Nepal, the British would merely reply that the independence which Nepal had "hitherto enjoyed" would not be interfered with.

At the end of the Great War, the Japanese had begun to show their interest in Lhasa, and the Dalai Lama was said to have obtained Japanese rifles through Mongolia. This must have made the British and Nepal also uneasy. The defeat of Russia by Japan in 1904-1905 had its impact on the whole world and projected the image of Japan as an emerging world power. Chandra Shamsher himself was impressed by Japanese success and had sent six students to Japan rather than to England in 1902 for technical training.

Japan also seemed to be interested in developing contact with Nepal. Japanese scholars were desirous of coming to Nepal for study and travel. Ekai Kawaguchi, who is considered to have been a Japanese expert on Tibet and Nepal, visited Nepal in 1899 and once again went to Nepal in 1902 with a Japanese scholar. Kawaguchi was in touch with the Indian revolutionaries such as Tarak Nath Das and Rash Behari Bose in Japan and was sympathetic towards the anti-British nationalist movement. He had sought to find out whether the Nepali authorities would be interested in assisting India to be free from the British rule but found to his disappointment that they were not at all interested in doing so. Chandra Shamsher's interest in securing Britain's formal recognition of Nepal's independence has to be viewed against the above background.

In May 1919 after the signing of the armistice in Europe, another war broke out between British India and Afghanistan. Amir Amanullah who succeeded his father, King Habibullah, following his assassination, started creating trouble for the British by flirting with Soviet Russia in a bid to modernize his country. Nepali troops were again sent to

Waziristan to the aid of the British.

Britain's reward to Nepal for its assistance in World War I was an annual payment of one million rupees in perpetuity, but Nepal's request for the retrocession of all its territory ceded by it to British India as a result of the 1815 Treaty of Sugauli was not granted.

The Maharajadhiraj began to be addressed as 'His Majesty' by the Viceroy, Lord Chelmsford (1916-1921), being the first Viceroy to do so in his letter of 27 December 1919 in which he conveyed the offer by the Indian Government of an annual present of one million rupees. Maharaj Chandra, who had been promoted to the rank of Lieutenant-General in the British army in 1915, was appointed full General after the war and awarded the Grand Cross of the Order of St. Michael and St. George. In January 1920 the British Government agreed to call in future the 'Residency' a 'Legation', the Resident their 'Minister', and the Residency Surgeon 'Legation Surgeon'; and in official correspondence the Nepal Durbar began to be referred to as the 'Government of Nepal.'

In view of the fact that the 1815 Treaty of Sugauli itself referred to the British and Nepali representatives at each other's court as accredited ministers, the changes in the names were no real gain for Nepal. They were merely intended as a sop to the Maharaj's pride. But these changes helped Chandra's coteries to advertise that Chandra had actually enhanced the country's prestige while countering the criticism of Chandra by a handful of English-educated Nepalis who had come under the influence of the nationalist movement in India.

Maharaj Chandra Shamsher, keen though he was on securing independence for his country at least in form, was in practice greatly flattered by the titles and gun salutes bestowed upon him by the British Government in India. In this he was just like the rulers of Indian native states from which he ironically always wanted Nepal to be distinguished as an independent country.

In October 1920, the Viceroy of India addressed the Maharaj by the courtesy title of His Highness. Although Chandra's acceptance of the title may be interpreted as his being degraded to the role of the Maharaj of the native states in India and in a way was not quite complimentary to Nepal and Chandra himself, one cannot help noting the comment on it in Perceval Landon's book (in which according to the author himself, "For the first time, the story of the court of Kathmandu has, in these pages, been willingly told in its fullness by the government itself":[20] "This change in style symbolized the recognition of the unique position of the Prime Minister and Marshal of Nepal, and raised him to plenipotentiary rank implying direct and permanent representation of his sovereign that no other public office in the world bestows on a temporary dignity."[21]

The above comment merely represents an attempt by Landon to rationalize his patron's action with the advantage of hindsight. But the fact remains that heads of government of all independent states are addressed by each other as 'excellencies' and the title "His Highness" in the British usage merely showed the feudatory status of the recipient vis-˜-vis the British crown or its representative in India, the Viceroy. Chandra's sycophants inside Nepal welcomed this gesture of the Viceroy as implying that Chandra had acquired a higher status than his predecessors including Jang Bahadur all of whom were addressed by the British Government as "excellencies" and not "highnessess."

Chandra continued his policy of being almost obsequious to visiting members of the British Royal family while at the same time putting off any meeting between them and the Nepali royal family. He explained that he could not think of allowing his King to be subordinate even to the British King and such a probability would arise if the meeting between them took place. This was the same plea the Rana Prime Ministers had previously advanced for preventing the Viceroy, as the representative of the British crown in India, from visiting Kathmandu where Nepali King resided.

King Edward VIII as the Prince of Wales visited Nepal on Maharaj Chandra's invitation in 1921 and hunted in Chitwan between 14 and 21 December. The party consisted of 49 Europeans and 243 Indians. The more prominent among the European members of the party were the Earl of Cromer, Vice-Admiral Sir Lionel Halsey, G. de Montmorency, Colonel R.B. Worgan, Sir Godfrey Thomas, Lieutenant-Colonel F.O. Kinealy, Captain Dudley North, R.N., Captain the Honourable Piers Legh, Lieutenant the Honourable B.A.A. Ogilvy, Lieutenant-Colonel C.O. Harvey, Surgeon-Commander A.C.W. Newport, H.A.F. Metcalfe, D. Petrie, Captain E.D. Metcalfe, Captain S.F. Poynder, Lieutenant Lord Louis Mountbatten, Sir Percival Phillips, Professor Rushbrook Williams, Perceval Landon and E. Villiers together with official photographers and cameramen. These hunts were always treated as events of national importance by Maharaj Chandra and the entire machinery of the Government was geared to make them a success. Four hundred and twenty-eight elephants were collected for the hunt including the Government's herd of elephants and other elephants requisitioned from private owners and rented from India for the purpose. Thousands of beaters and soldiers had to be maintained in the campsite for a considerable period of time. All this involved a lot of expenditure and effort on the part of the host Government. The total bag of the hunt consisted of 18 tigers, 8 rhinoceroses, 2 bears, and 2 leopards. According to the official historian, Perceval Landon, "the days of the Prince of Wales's visit were spent in the pleasantest surroundings and in a luxury that was known to no Mogul on the march." The Maharaj's own sons, General Babar and General Kaiser, who were in charge of all the arrangements for the hunt, were regularly in attendance at the Prince of Wales's camp and joined in the entertainment, pastimes, and pleasures of the night.

At the end of the hunt, the Prince of Wales was presented with a well-assorted collection of animals and birds, just as his father and grand-father, King George V and King Edward VII had been offered, and, as in the past, this was subsequently housed in the London Zoological Gardens. In return the Maharaj also received the customary letter of thanks from the Prince of Wales for the hospitality he had received in Nepal. The letter referred gratefully to the services rendered by Nepal in the recent war and contained the usual assurance of the King Emperor's "grateful confidence in the Maharaja's devotion and fidelity."

However, by 1919 the British Government seems to have begun to realize that it might be advantageous for it to keep Nepal distinct and different from the native states of India in order to use it as a countervailing force or a breakwater to the mainstream of the Indian nationalist movement for independence, as a counterweight to Afghanistan and the Muslim movements to its west and north and together with Tibet as a buffer on the northeast. The following excerpt from the memorandum prepared by the Foreign and Political Department of the British Government in India attests to this:

> The services rendered by Nepal in the Mutiny, at the time of Tibet expedition, and above all in the present war are a matter of common knowledge. It is only necessary to mention that without Nepalese goodwill we should lose beyond the possibility of replacing the flower of the Indian army. But Nepal's importance is not limited to that. Nepal is in a position to exercise a powerful influence in Indian internal politics and if it were disaffected, the anarchist movement in India would achieve a much more serious

> aspect. Externally this state is important to us from two points of view, (1) it forms a very valuable counterpoise to Afghanistan and Moslem movements to the West and North of Afghanistan, (2) the political situation on our North-Eastern frontier is very unstable. We have released Tibet from China, but Tibet cannot stand alone and we cannot support her very effectively against Chinese aggression.[22]

It is the kind of perception reflected by the above quotation that seems to have made the British Government evolve a change in its attitude about concluding a new treaty with Nepal over a period of five years after the end of the First World War. A new pact, signed in 1923, did not bring about any significant change in Nepal's status. Nepal would have been independent after the withdrawal of the British from India in the same way as Bhutan even if it had not concluded the 1923 Treaty with the British.

The treaty was concluded because it served the interests of both the Rana Prime Ministers and the British rulers of India at the time. It served the British interests because they could tell the Rana Prime Minister that they had recognized their services by enhancing the status of their country without having to do anything more. It served the interests of Maharaj Chandra Shamsher and the later Rana Prime Ministers to insulate the Nepali people from the impact of the Indian nationalist movement and to maintain their own personal power intact. It was another matter that the common people of Nepal were short-changed in the deal.

The 1815 Treaty of Sugauli provided, among other things, that accredited ministers of each signatory should reside at the court of the other. We have already seen that the representation clause makes the East India Company's treaty with Nepal resemble more the treaties with the frontier states of Afghanistan (1879) and Iran (1841) than those with Hyderabad (1798) and Mysore (1799), which belonged to the Company's system of protectorates and subsidiary alliances, and for whom the Company had assumed responsibility for internal peace and stability. However, by the treaty of Sugauli, Nepal relinquished its right -- generally enjoyed by independent states – to choose its officials and advisers from any country it liked. Nepal was not to employ any European or American or even any British subject without the consent of the Company's Government. The Company also acquired the right to mediate in any dispute that might arise between Nepal and Sikkim.

As a psychological concession to the Rana Government, the British Government later officially recognized Nepal Government's practice of employing British subjects without previous reference, and in June 1923 that part of the engagement of 1839 by which Nepal undertook to have no dealings with the dependent allies of the East India Company beyond the Ganges was cancelled. All this was done by the British to meet the Rana Government's concern about the maintenance of Nepal's formal independence.

A fresh treaty was concluded between Nepal and Great Britain on 21 December 1923 to emphasize, at least in principle, that the relationship between them was one between two independent countries. The ostensible purpose of the treaty was to strengthen the friendship which had existed since 1816. Its most important provision was a confirmation of all treaties subsequent to and including the 1815 Treaty of Sugauli except in so far as they might have been altered by the new treaty.

Article 3 of the 1923 Treaty also provided for close consultation and cooperation between Nepal and Great Britain through exchange of information should any serious friction or misunderstanding arise between the signatory states and their neighbours. Article 4 of the Treaty obliged each of the High Contracting Parties to "use all such measures as it may deem practicable to prevent its territories, being used for purposes inimical to the security of the other." This article came in very handy for both the Rana Government and the British Indian Government in denying the right of asylum to political opponents of the other Government and this arrangement hindered the growth of political consciousness and human rights awareness among the Nepalis in both India and Nepal. Article 5 expressed the British willingness to let Nepal import "arms, ammunition, machinery, warlike material or stores" from or through British India, with due respect by both sides for any international convention for the regulation of the arms traffic as and when such convention might come into force.

Article 6 provided that the Government of Nepal could import any goods from overseas, for its own direct use, through India without payment of duty. The Treaty in respect of all trade goods provided for a rebate of full duty paid on such goods upon their entry into India, on the production of a certificate issued by the proper Nepali authority that the goods had arrived in Kathmandu "with the customs seals unbroken and otherwise untampered with." While the Treaty of 1923, out of respect for the Barcelona Convention on freedom of transit, apparently provided for immediate transmission of trade goods to Kathmandu without "breaking bulk", Nepal's imports in actual practice were subject to the treaty stipulation that "such goods may break bulk for repacking at the port of entry," under the supervision of the Indian customs. This article enabled the Rana Prime Ministers to import goods from overseas without payment of duty in the name of the Government and sell them in the market at a profit. Chandra Shamsher had actually got his favourite private trader to set up a shop called 'Bhadrakali House' to sell imported goods and merchandise.

The Treaty was accompanied by a letter from the Prime Minister of Nepal to the British envoy at the Court of Nepal, dated 21 December 1923, committing the Government of Nepal to furnish the British envoy with detailed lists of the arms and ammunitions to be imported in order to facilitate customs clearance at the British Indian ports. The exchange of ratifications took place in Kathmandu on 8 April 1925.

However, despite the fact that the very first article of the Treaty provided that the two Governments agreed to acknowledge and respect each other's independence, both external and internal, Nepal's foreign relations in fact continued to be conducted through New Delhi, and the nature of the relationship between Nepal and Great Britain did not show any change. The same arrangement continued even after a Nepali legation was set up in London in 1934 ostensibly to facilitate relations between Nepal and Great Britain but in fact to prepare for the day when India would achieve independence. All that can be said to the credit of Chandra Shamsher and his other Rana successors is that they managed to retain the formal independence of Nepal even by being obsequious to the British Government and letting it have everything it wanted without much exertion.

The signing of the Treaty was treated as an event of national importance to create a misleading impression inside and outside Nepal that Chandra Shamsher had brought independence to the country as if it had not been independent before his time. Two days' public holiday was announced in Kathmandu and a general remission of three months was granted to prisoners other than those held for life. Food and clothes were distributed among the poor and there was illumination in Kathmandu for several days in celebration of the occasion.

In addition to this treaty with Britain, it has been customary for sympathetic authors to mention the abolition of the practices of Sati, or widow self-immolation and of slavery as the other highlights of Maharaja Chandra's administration. The custom of a wife having to burn herself with the dead body of her husband was banned in Nepal in 1920, almost a century after it was abolished in India by Lord William Bentinck (1829-1834) in December 1829. Slavery was abolished in 1924. There were other changes in Chandra's time. The 14-mile cableway for carrying goods from Dhursing to Matatirtha in Kathmandu was started by 1924 and the Pharping hydro-electric work was completed in 1911. A metre gauge railway line from Raxaul to Amlekhganj was constructed in 1927. Tri-Chandra College, until 1951 the only college in Nepal, was established in 1918 and while laying the foundation stone of its building, Chandra reportedly said that what he was doing might ruin the political future of his family, but he could not help moving with the time. The Gorkha Bhasa Prakashini Samiti was set up in 1913 for publishing and censoring books in Nepali. In 1901, the number of students admitted to the only English school in Kathmandu was 17 but by 1919 their number had increased to 147. About a dozen middle schools were opened in different parts of the country.

Although several students were sent to Japan in 1902, Chandra put out a story that the suggestion to send students to study overseas was rejected by his counsellors or Bhardars. From then until after the abolition of the Rana family's rule, Nepali students were not permitted to go overseas for higher education. A handful of them who defied the ban had to suffer exile and loss of caste. On the other hand, soldiers in the British Gorkha regiments who were taken overseas got back their caste upon the payment of a nominal fee to obtain religious dispensation from the Royal Preceptor for their purification.

Let us now turn to Chandra's internal policy and administrative and court reforms. The roll of succession to the prime ministership of Nepal drawn by Maharaj Chandra Shamsher Jang Bahadur Rana and published in Appendix III of the first volume of Landon's book on Nepal is as follows:

1. Maharaj-Prime Minister and Marshal Chandra Shamsher Jang Bahadur Rana (son of General Dhir Shamsher J.B.R.), G.C.B. (1908), G.C.S.I.(1905), G.C.M.G. (1919), G.C.V.O. (1911), D.C.L. (1908).
2. Commander-in-Chief General Bhim Shamsher J.B.R. (son of General Dhir Shamsher), K.C.S.I. (1917),K.C.V.O (1911).
3. Senior Commanding General Juddha Shamsher J.B.R. (son of General Dhir Shamsher J.B.R.), K.C.I.E. (1917).

4. Commanding General Dharma Shamsher J.B.R. (Eastern Command) (son of Maharaj Bir Shamsher J.B.R.).
*5. Commanding General Rudra Shamsher J.B.R.(Southern Command) (son of Maharaj Bir Shamsher J.B.R.).
6. Commanding General Padma Shamsher J.B.R. (Northern Command) (son of General Bhim Shamsher J.B.R.).
*7. General Tej Shamsher J.B.R. (son of Maharaj Bir Shamsher J.B.R.), K.C.I.E.(1919), K.B.E. (1921).
8. General Mohan Shamsher J.B.R. (son of Maharaj Chandra Shamsher J.B.R.), K.C.I.E. (1924).
*9. General Pratap Shamsher J.B.R.(son of Maharaj Bir Shamsher J.B.R.).
10. General Babar Shamsher J.B.R.(son of Maharaj Chandra Shamsher J.B.R.), G.B.E (1920), K.C.S.I. (1919). K.C.I.E. (1916).
11. Lieutenant-General Kaiser Shamsher J.B.R. (son of Maharaj Chandra Shamsher J.B.R.), K.B.E. (1924).
12. Lieutenant-General Bahadur Shamsher J.B.R. (son of General Juddha Shamsher J.B.R.).
13. Lieutenant-General Agni Shamsher J.B.R. (son of General Juddha Shamsher J.B.R.).
14. Lieutenant-General Singha Shamsher J.B.R. (son of Maharaj Chandra Shamsher J.B.R.).
15. Major-General Hari Shamsher J.B.R. (son of General Juddha Shamsher J.B.R.).
16. Major-General Prachanda Shamsher J.B.R. (son of General Fateh Shamsher J.B.R.).
17. Colonel Bhupal Shamsher J.B.R. (son of General Fateh Shamsher J.B.R.).
18. Major-General Krishna Shamsher J.B.R. (son of Maharaj Chandra Shamsher J.B.R.).
19. Lieutenant-Colonel Surya Shamsher J.B.R. (son of General Juddha Shamsher J.B.R.).
20. Major-General Bishnu Shamsher J.B.R. (son of Maharaj Chandra Shamsher J.B.R.).
21. Major-General Shankar Shamsher J.B.R. (son of Maharaj Chandra Shamsher J.B.R.).
22. Lieutenant-Colonel Narayn Shamsher J.B.R. (son of General Juddha Shamsher J.B.R.).
23. Major-General Madan Shamsher J.B.R. (son of Maharaj Chandra Shamsher J.B.R.).

Then according to seniority the sons of those who are in the roll of succession from their legally wedded wives with whom rice can be partaken.[23]

Landon adds a footnote as follows after giving the names of those in the roll of succession at the time of Ranoddip's death in 1885. "Note: The names marked with an asterisk are illegitimate. Rice cannot be partaken with them or with their families by the other members in the Roll."[24]

This was a timebomb planted by Maharaj Chandra Shamsher to have Maharaj Bir's three sons, Generals Rudra, Tej, and Pratap, removed from the roll of succession in due course of time so as to pave the way for the promotion of his own older sons in the roll. It seems that Chandra himself had by 1928, i.e., one year before his death, decided not to tamper with the existing roll of succession immediately in the hope that Juddha, the third half-brother in line of succession, would do so himself in order to move up his own sons in the roll of succession. Chandra's sons also would automatically benefit from Juddha's action since most of them were higher up in the roll of succession than Juddha's own sons.

It is sometimes alleged that Maharaj Chandra had himself asked Juddha to do it because Chandra knew that after he died his brother, Commander-in-Chief Bhim Shamsher, was going to include some of his own sons born out of wedlock in the roll, and Bhim Shamsher himself was already 64 years old, less than two years younger than Chandra. Whatever may have been the case, Chandra had given a clear warning to his successors in the roll through Landon who writes as follows on the subject:

> Elsewhere will be found a chart pedigree to which a note is attached indicating three recognized classes of wives. The first are those of equal caste with their husbands. Those have not been distinguished in the chart by any accompanying symbol. Below them are wives taken from a caste which had every right of association with caste of the husband other than that of eating rice together. *The third class consists of wives with whom no eating in common is possible.* In the interests of all concerned, and certainly that of the country, the present Maharaj has only permitted those to be added to the roll of succession who are children by wives of the first class. But he has been unable to make the decree retrospective; he has not amended the list of succession which he received from his

predecessor. It will, therefore, be seen that in the line of near succession on the Prime Ministership are three candidates for the highest office in the state who do not fulfil the qualification laid down by Chandra for future observance. These are the sons of Maharaj Bir Shamsher by wives who were not of the same caste as his own. *In view of the new and stricter conception of the descent of the title and powers of the Maharaja, it is obvious that difficulties are not unlikely to arise when these candidates have a claim to assume one of the senior offices in the state."*

Not being content with sounding a clear and ominous note, in this respect, Landon proceeds to refer to the same matter in the genealogical table of the Rana family up to the year 1923, given at the end of his book, in such a way as to exclude the sons and grandsons of the above mentioned sons of Maharaj Bir Shamsher from the roll of succession itself by marking them 'C' or illegitimate while leaving the names of those born of lawful marriage without any marks and those born of lawful but unequal marriage as 'B'. Landon's overemphasis or focus on this matter clearly shows that he was allowing himself to be used by Maharaj Chandra as the instrument of his will.

Apart from this, Chandra must be given credit for getting Landon to assemble in his book's appendices some scientific papers by B.H. Hodgson on mammals and birds, on fauna of Nepal by H.S. Prater, C.M.Z.S., on flora of Nepal under the authority of the Director of the Royal Botanical Gardens, Kew, on forestry of Nepal by J.V. Collier, and on coinage by H.G. Bannerji, thereby adding to scientific knowledge of Nepal. Secondly, the map in Landon's book is the first scientific map of Nepal ever published and is based on the Survey of India map recorded between 1925 and 1927. Thirdly, it was Chandra who subsidized the publication of Ralph Turner's etymological dictionary of Nepali which, apart from being the first and most authentic Nepali-English dictionary, led to the publication of the 12 volume Indo Aryan dictionary by the same author. Chandra's patronage of Landon led to the wider dissemination of scientific knowledge about various aspects of Nepal including culture, architecture and relations with China in the past.

Chandra also made reforms in the court system. The legal code, introduced by Jang Bahadur and modified by Bir Shamsher, was twice revised during the administration of Chandra Shamsher. The object of revision was to bring about uniformity of law in all parts of the country and to mitigate the severity of punishment. According to the revised laws, prisoners for civil offence were not to be put in the irons. Printed copies of the legal code were made available for the first time. The obsolete systems of the courts in Nepal consisted of four lower courts–*Itachapali, Koteling, Taksar*, and *Dhansar* with the *Adalat Goswara*, the supreme court of appeal, over them. They were allotted jurisdictions of different kinds, but an overlap of civil and criminal jurisdictions existed in all of them. The legal rights of Nepalis depended so much upon local custom that assessors were frequently called in to assist the judges. The courts ordered trial by ordeal in difficult cases.

Maharaj Chandra abolished Taksar and Dhansar courts and also sought to draw a distinction between civil and criminal jurisdiction by making *Adalat Diwani Koteling* responsible for civil cases and the *Fauzdari Adalat Itachapali* responsible for criminal cases. Judicial duty was separated from the task of carrying into effect the decisions of the court.

In 1906 a *Bhardari* court consisting of 5 to 10 Bhardars was created and in 1908 the appellate jurisdiction was reformed. The new tribunal became the court of appeal for the decisions of two Sadar courts– the *Adalat Diwani Koteling* and the *Fauzdari Adalat Itachapali*. The *Fauzdari Itachapali* and *Adalat Diwani Koteling*, besides being courts of first instance, had previously acted as courts of appeal for the decisions of the provincial magistrate of the *Gauda* courts in the hills and the *Goswara* courts in the tarai. This appellate jurisdiction was given to the Bhardari court in Chandra's time.

The *Adalat Diwani* was divided into four courts including the court of registration. There were two sections of the criminal court because of an increase in the work-load. The first and the second *Fauzdari* courts decided criminal cases of all kinds except those which the *Sadar Jangi Kotwali* or court martial and the *Thana* were empowered to deal with. Besides, there were *Amini Goswara* courts that dealt with reports from the Amini Courts generally handling cases to which one or both parties were foreigners. The appeal against the decisions of the Bhardari courts lay in the Niksari courts of which the judges were "drawn from very high families, General, or Commanding Colonels, the chiefs of subordinate principalities of Nepal, the family of Raj Guru, and a group of men of long experience in law and practices. The Niksari dealt with the petitions to the Prime Minister and Maharaj who was, of course, the final court of appeal and justice in Nepal.

Influence of Indian Reformist and Political Movements

The Arya Samaji reformist influence penetrated into Nepal from India in the last decade of the 19th century. Swami Dayananda, the founder of the Arya Samaji movement, advocated reforms in orthodox Hindu rites and practices on the basis of his reinterpretation of the ancient Vedas. The movement blamed the corrupt role of the Hindu priesthood in the post-Vedic period for the prevalence of such social evils as child marriage and forced widowhood. Though essentially religious in nature, it also stood for social reforms.

The first Arya Samaji reformist to appear on the Nepali scene was Madhav Raj Joshi of Kathmandu. He had come back from his visit to Varanasi, deeply impressed by the thoughts and methods of Swami Dayananda, and in 1893 he started propagating reformist ideas in Pokhara and Kathmandu. As Maharaj Bir Shamsher remained indifferent to his activities, Madhav Raj Joshi succeeded in setting up a centre in Kathmandu in 1895 notwithstanding the propaganda of orthodox Brahmins against it.[25]

But soon the priestly establishment composed of the Pande family of the Raj Guru (royal preceptor) and the Raj Purohit (royal priest) viewed the spread of reformist ideas as a direct threat to their vested interests. One of the important sources of the income of the Raj Guru consisted of payments made to him by tens of thousands of Gorkha soldiers for his formal permission to dispense with the strict observance of caste rules while in service. The rates of fees to be paid for dispensation varied with the degree of seriousness of caste pollution. Very nearly all the members of the Pande family, who served as preceptors and priests to Ranas as well as to the royal family, had long given up the hardships and austerities of scholarly and intellectual discipline and opted for an indolent life of luxury. It was only natural for them to oppose the egalitarian and anticlerical spirit of the Arya Samaji movement.

Even Maharaj Chandra Shamsher did not discourage the spread of reformist ideas initially, and the impression gained ground that he was not totally opposed to religious reforms. On what appeared to be Madhav Raj Joshi's own initiative and suggestion, a scholarly debate was held in 1905 on the interpretation of Hindu scriptures in the presence of the Maharaj himself. Though none of the members of the higher priestly establishment themselves took part in this debate, they had other Brahmans on their behalf debate the religious issues and, at the end, had Madhav Raj Joshi badly beaten up on the allegation that he had balsphemed against the deities of Nepal in the course of the discussion.

Joshi was paraded through the streets of Kathmandu in disgrace and sentenced to two years' imprisonment. His followers and benefactors were penalized in different ways, his two sons were expelled from school, and Gunadatta, an Arya Samaji missionary from the Panjab, who was Madhav Raj's associate, was turned out of the country. Though Madhav Raj Joshi succeeded in securing his release before his prison sentence had expired, he found it difficult to live in his own country. He went to Darjeeling and carried on his reformist activities there.[26] In Nepal the persecution of the Arya Samaj continued and in 1910 Dr. Kartik Prasad, an assistant surgeon in Bir Hospital, was dismissed on the charge of having correspondence with Bhai Parmanand, a prominent Arya Samaji leader in India.[27]

However, two of Madhav Raj's sons, Bakpati Raj Joshi and Amar Raj Joshi subsequently returned to Kathmandu and set up a centre at Bange Muda for propagating religious and social reforms. They enlisted the cooperation of Fatte Bahadur, Chandra Man Maskay, Tulsi Mehar, Chakra Bahadur Amatya and others in carrying on its activities. When their reformist efforts were once again stopped by the Government in 1920, they had already created a sufficient measure of popular consciousness and some of the youths founded a new organization called "Malami Guthi" (Funeral Trust) to escape official persecution and continued to propagate reformist ideas. But its chief manager, Satyacharan, was fined 480 rupees and the two Joshi brothers were eventually expelled from Nepal.

Although signs of popular discontent with the Rana regime were not much in evidence inside the country in the first decade of the twentieth century, as early as 1907 Nepalis living in India were attacking Chandra Shamsher's policy through such newspapers as *Gorkha Sathi*. The British Government was worried about the army in north India being subjected to seditious influence as the terrorist movement had gained momentum in Bengal in the wake of its first partition in 1905. In May 1907 a dismissed Gorkha soldier by the name of Prithiman Thapa, who was said to have links with Bengali terrorists, addressed public meetings and raised subscriptions for running a newspaper with a view to inculcating love of their mother country in the minds of the Gorkhas living in India. Prithiman at first sought support for the *Swadeshi* movement through Nepal's official representative in Calcutta, Colonel Bahadur Jang Rana, and also wrote to Maharaj Chandra Shamsher himself for financial help for his paper. After his efforts to enlist the cooperation of the Government of Nepal for his cause failed, his paper *Gorkha Sathi* started attacking the pro-British policy of the Rana rulers directly. The British Indian Government banned its circulation among the Gorkha ranks but at the same time turned down Chandra Shamsher's request for Prithiman's extradition in keeping with its traditional policy of non-extradition of political offenders to Nepal.[28]

In 1908, the *Bande Mataram*, a revolutionary newspaper of Calcutta, printed an article criticizing Chandra Shamsher for his failure to promote the development of Nepal.[29] The Maharaj reacted against it by admonishing the people in general and the Bengali employees of the Nepal Government in particular not to have anything to do with Indian political agitators. Indian newspapers critical of the policies of the Nepali and British Governments were banned in Nepal and their subscribers were put under strict surveillance.

Bringing a foreigner, even an Indian, into Nepal without the prior approval of the Rana Government was a criminal offence; even Indian pilgrims for the Shivaratri festival were compelled to leave the country immediately after the festival was over. Thus, it is noteworthy that on at least one occasion Chandra Shamsher, in clear violation of Nepal's traditional closed door policy, allowed four British Indian detectives to conduct a search inside Nepal for some Bengali revolutionaries reported to have been manufacturing bombs and training the local people in their use.[30]

Factors in the growth of political consciousness

World War I and the 1920 Indian civil disobedience movement were the two external events that contributed the most to the growth of political consciousness among Nepalis during Chandra's administration. Nepali soldiers, who fought bravely in different international theatres of war, were exposed to modern influences and enthused with the hope of excelling in peacetime activities as they had done in war. But Chandra Shamsher sought to suppress their desire for change at home. He asked the British authorities not to promote Nepali soldiers beyond the rank of a non-commissioned officer and also insisted on the strict observance by Nepali soldiers of *pani patiya*, the rites of religious purification on their return home. The result was the large-scale migration of Nepalis to India in the post-war years because of their growing dissatisfaction with the conditions of life inside their own country.

The hill areas experienced an acute shortage of labour even for normal agricultural operations. The conditions of "acute scarcity bordering on famine" in the hill areas portended ill for the future. At least one-third of the Gorkhas whom the Indian Army disbanded after the war did not return to Nepal but settled down in India because of better prospects there for work and living. The Nepali army began to feel a shortage of recruits as the hill people preferred serving in the Indian army with its higher pay scales and better prospects in every other respect. Chandra Shamsher was forced by these circumstances to raise grudgingly the salary of men and officers of the Nepali army.

Nepal was thus confronted with the deep-rooted problem of economic discontent which had serious long-term consequences not only for the Rana Government but also for the British in India. The British Indian Government came forward to cooperate with Chandra Shamsher in checking Nepali migration to India. Chandra did not want his people to be politically spoilt by contamination with the Indians, but he suggested to the Indian Government that non-military employment of the Gorkhas might affect their fighting quality. This seemed to convince the British military authorities. Under this pressure from Chandra Shamsher, the Indian Government banned the employment of Gorkhas not only in tea gardens and other non-military services but also in the military police.

Chandra Shamsher also imposed strict limits on the recruitment of Gorkhas for the Indian army from the Kathmandu Valley and the neighbouring districts. The total strength of the Gorkha corps in the Indian army at the end of the war consisted of thirty-three regiments with 42,500 men. Out of this only twenty regiments with 18,542 men were retained and the rest were disbanded. Under the changed circumstances not more than 1,800 recruits from Nepal were needed annually to reinforce the numbers of the Gorkha regiments in India. The Assam Rifles and police battalions also were not to be reinforced henceforth with recruits from Nepal and were to be in due course formed entirely of Indian-domiciled Gorkhas.

If the British were worried about Indian political unrest in the 1920s, they were also concerned about its influence being transmitted to Nepal through the educated Nepalis living and working in India. As both Governments had a common stake in checking the growth of political consciousness among the Nepalis in their respective countries, their policies showed a convergence of aims and interests. However, even well-conceived Government policies cannot always check the flow of ideas and stem the tide of events.

One concrete result of the exposure of Gorkhas to outside influences during World War I was the establishment of the All India Gorkha League at Dehra Dun in 1921. Though it remained apolitical for the first six years, the Gorkha League was turned into a dynamic organization by Thakur Chandan Singh after his election as its president in 1926. Thakur Chandan Singh had creditably served in the Indian army during World War I and acted as an assistant to the Maharaja of Bikaner after the war. He was married to one of the daughters of General Khadga Shamsher, Maharaj Chandra Shamsher's elder brother who had been dismissed as Commander-in-Chief of Nepal in 1886. Singh had once belonged to the Indian National Congress and taken part in the Congress movement but left it in 1922.

The second annual session of the All-India Gorkha League which elected Thakur Chandan Singh president, was attended by many retired Gorkha Subedars and received complimentary messages from the Gorkha regiments and also from the rulers of several Indian states such as Jhalwar, Garhwal and Sikkim. Resolutions were passed calling upon the Rana Government to lift the ban on overseas travels by Nepalis. The League also favoured reforms in Nepal along the lines followed by Amir Amanullah in Afghanistan.

Thakur Chandan Singh edited a paper called the *Himalayan Times* and later another paper, the *Tarun Gorkha*, a Nepali weekly published from Dehra Dun. The *Tarun Gorkha*, renamed as the *Gorkha Samsar*, became the mouthpiece of the League. The League's connections with the All India Hindu Mahasabha had made it very anti-Muslim. Thakur Chandan Singh attended the Delhi session of the Hindu Mahasabha in 1921 and gave up his war decorations and medals. In 1927-28 the Maharaja of Kashmir was offered the League's services for the restoration of peace in his state which was rife with communal violence at the time. However, the League adopted a highly conciliatory attitude towards the Rana Government and the British Government towards the end of the decade and went so far as to condemn the Indian civil disobedience movement after some of the leaders of the League were bought over by Maharaj Chandra.

Nonetheless there was no dearth of supporters of the Indian civil disobedience movement among the Gorkhas in India. A prominent one was Khadga Bahadur Bista, a student of the Law College in Calcutta, who was convicted of murdering a Marwari businessman in cold blood for purchasing a Nepali girl for immoral purposes. Although he was initially sentenced to eight years' rigorous imprisonment, his sentence was remitted on appeal, and he was released by March 1929. Meanwhile his case had aroused great interest among the Nepalis in India and in the course of his short imprisonment he had gained immense popularity among the Nepalis and had become a hero of Nepali women in particular. He subsequently turned out to be the most effective propagandist against the British among the Gorkhas.

Khadga Bahadur wrote an article in the *Bombay Chronicle* exhorting his countrymen to make amends for the folly of their kinsmen who had fought against their own Indian brethren. He and another dismissed Gorkha soldier by the name of Dhanpati Singh had joined the Indian National Congress and campaigned for it in several villages of the Dehra Dun district. Khadga Bahadur was in close touch with Congress leaders such as Motilal Nehru and Sardar Vallabhbhai Patel and was arrested in November 1930 while raiding the Darshana salt depot along with other Congress volunteers. After serving his term of imprisonment in India, Khadga Bahadur was suspected by the British Indian Government of having joined Nepal's army under a different name. Whatever may have been the case, Khadga Bahadur faded into oblivion after winning the admiration of the Nepalis both inside and outside Nepal for a brief period of 4 years or so.

By the first quarter of the twentieth century resourceful commoners from Nepal, who managed to get themselves educated in western style schools in India, had acquired new ideas about political and social change in their homeland. Thanks to their education in Indian schools and their exposure to the Indian nationalist movement, quite a few educated Nepalis had begun to feel that the fate of the Rana regime was inextricably bound up with that of the British rule in India. No wonder that some of them even joined the Indian National Congress and the mass movements launched by it in the 1920s, the 1930s and the 1940s.

Subba Devi Prasad Sapkota, a former officer in the Nepali foreign office, was dismissed by Maharaj Chandra Shamsher for opposing Nepal's support of the 1904 Younghusband military expedition to Lhasa as being inconsistent with Nepal's treaty obligations to Tibet. He then exiled himself to Varanasi with his family and was educating his children there. In 1921, he started a weekly periodical in Nepali called the *Gorkhali*. Varanasi had traditionally been a sanctuary for

Nepali political dissidents and rebels. The weekly demanded democratic rights for the people of Nepal and at the same time called upon them to take part in the non-cooperation and satyagraha movements launched by the Indian National Congress. Among other politically conscious and educated Nepalis who were connected with the paper were Nain Singh Gurung, Lakshmi Prasad Sapkota, Dharani Dhar Koirala, Dinanath Sharma and Krishna Prasad Koirala.

The British Indian Government and the Rana Government had a common interest in suppressing political consciousness among the Nepalis. This was that the British envoy of the time wrote to his Government about the *Gorkhali* weekly:

> It seems certain that artificially introduced dissatisfaction with their condition, such as the *Gorkhali* sets itself to bring about, can neither lead to any beneficial change in the form of government nor to improvement in material prosperity.[31]

However, his real purpose in discouraging or banning the publication was succinctly expressed by him in the same context:

> In view of the great importance to India of the preservation of the political status quo in this country and the supply of Gurkha recruits unstained with Indian advanced sentiment, our interest in this matter coincides with those of the Nepal Government.[32]

The Government of India first demanded a security bond from the *Gorkhali* weekly as provided by the law, and the periodical itself was banned by 1922. The Government also kept a strict watch on all those who had been connected with the publication. In connection with activities outside Nepal aimed at awakening nationalist feelings among Nepalis through the printed word, mention must also be made of Dharani Dhar Koirala's poems and Surya Bikram Jnawali's historical books in Nepali published from Darjeeling

Inside Nepal itself, educated Nepalis were under constant watch of the Rana Government and therefore were not as free to carry on political activities as Nepali expatriates were in India. In Kathmandu, their efforts were limited to airing their grievances through their writings. The prosecution of Subba Krishna Lal, an officer in the legal office of the Rana Government, is a telling instance of repression during the administration of Maharaj Chandra Shamsher. In the preface to his book on the cultivation of maize, Krishna Lal had merely stated that "Ease loving and lazy dogs of foreign breeds were being prized in Nepal, but for protection against thieves native dogs were the only useful animals." This simple statement was taken by the Rana Government as implied criticism of its pro-British attitude, and the author was sentenced to 9 years' imprisonment. Krishna Lal died in prison before his term had expired.[33]

Chandra Shamsher's 29-year old administration was not altogether free from opposition from the King's side. In 1903, King Prithvi Bir Bikram Shah, like his father Crown Prince Trailokya Bikram Shah, had sought to restore his traditional royal authority by forming a group of his sympathizers and supporters. The group consisted of Dambar Bahadur Shah, Colonel Kumar Jang Rana, Captain Jag Narsingh, Captain Ganga Bahadur Basnyat, Jangbir and Durga Nath Adhikari. But Durga Nath Adhikari revealed the secret to Maharaj Chandra, who lost no time in expelling the rest of the King's supporters to different parts of the country.[34] The King's move, though not much of a threat to the Maharaj's position, was thus rendered altogether ineffective. King Prithvi's death in 1911 at the early age of 36 and the accession of King Tribhuvan as a minor to the throne gave Chandra a free hand in running the administration. He remained very much in control until his death.

On 25 November 1929 Maharaj Chandra Shamsher breathed his last a few days after he had caught a chill at a farewell garden party given by him in honour of the outgoing British envoy, Wilkinson.

C. Thirty-three Months of Maharaj Bhim's Administration

Prospects of War with Tibet

Maharaj Bhim Shamsher was confronted with the very real prospect of a war with Tibet when he succeeded his elder brother Chandra Shamsher as Maharaj and Prime Minister at the age of 64. The extraterritorial status gained by Nepal in Tibet as a result of the 1856 treaty had been a source of friction and had led to frequent disputes. The deterioration in the relations between Nepal and Tibet had for long been the subject of comment by several British officers including Sir Charles Bell, who blamed the Nepalis for their arrogant attitude.

Earlier in 1929 a most flagrant breach of international etiquette had been committed by Tibet in the case of an accused person named

Gyalpo, about whose nationality a difference had arisen. Gyalpo, most probably a Nepali subject of mixed origin, had been a personal servant of Captain Lal Bahadur Basnyat, who was Nepal's Vakil or representative in Lhasa, at the time. Gyalpo had been arrested by Tibetan authorities on some charge but escaped from their custody and sought refuge in the Nepali agency claiming to be a Nepali subject. Notwithstanding the protest of the Nepali representative, he was forcibly removed by the Tibetans and subjected to torture, which caused his death. The British Indian Government offered arbitration in the case and advised Nepal and Tibet to adopt a conciliatory attitude. The Nepal Government at first demanded a written public apology and the punishment of the individuals concerned.

This had happened during the last year of Chandra's administration. Dissatisfied with the British role and bitterly disappointed at Britain's failure to take his side, Chandra Shamsher was making hectic preparations for going to war with Tibet and at his death left tens of millions of rupees in the teasury for the purpose. Maharaj Bhim was not as enthusiastic as his brother about waging a war against Tibet. Apart from his age, Bhim was far from robust. Basically he was a kind-hearted man of religious temperament "with a conservative and domestic turn of mind", to borrow Daukes's expression. All that Bhim wanted was to follow quietly in the footsteps of his famous brother and avoid trouble during the few years that he might live as the Maharaj. From the beginning of his rule he was inclined to smooth over the friction with Tibet which might land him in a difficult situation, for it was clear that the British Government would view with grave concern a threat of war between two countries with both of whom it claimed special relationship.

On the other hand, the Maharaj's position was delicate and insecure because he was under constant pressure from Maharaj Chandra's sons, who wanted him to continue their father's policy towards Tibet. Maharaj Bhim could not always override the views of the powerful Chandra family led by Generals Mohan, Babar and Kaiser.

Nepal sought assistance from the British Indian Government in making Tibet accept its terms for reconciliation and even threatened to stop the recruitment of Gorkhas for the Indian army if its call for help remained unanswered. It was only under considerable pressure that the Nepal Government reduced its original demand for a public apology and punishment for the offenders to one for a simple apology.

An outbreak of hostilities between Nepal and Tibet at a time when the 1930 Naval Disarmament Conference was about to be held in London would have also caused embarrassment to the British. Under these delicate circumstances the British Indian Government decided to send an emissary to Lhasa with a personal letter from the Foreign Secretary to be delivered to the Dalai Lama, and the Nepal Government was persuaded not to dispatch troops to the frontier pending the outcome of this direct effort to secure an amicable settlement. The emissary chosen by the British Government for the purpose was Major Laden La, a Darjeeling Lepcha with Tibetan connections. After some abortive and trying negotiations, the Dalai Lama at long last agreed to send an unconditional apology to the Nepali Prime Minister in March 1930. This satisfied the Nepal Government and the relations between Nepal and Tibet were normalized.

Maharaj Bhim was really fortunate to have the problem with Tibet resolved without recourse to war and without loss of face for Nepal. But he was very much subject to the pressures of domestic politics inherent in the system of the family oligarchy under a titular king. The following extracts from British Envoy Sir Clendon Daukes's note on Nepal to his home government vividly picture the state of politics in Nepal at the commencement of Maharaj Bhim Shamsher's administration:

> The tension which arises and which always must arise on the death of a Maharaja of Nepal is due to the fact that he is essentially an autocratic ruler, who is himself the head of the Army and of every branch of the administration. To a considerable extent this is dependent on the man himself but in the case of a strong personality his word is absolute law.
>
> His position carries with it not only great power but great wealth (the late Sir Chandra is believed to have been worth about 20 to 50 million sterling when he died). The prize therefore is immense.
>
> His Majesty the Maharajadhiraj remains in the background at these junctures and becomes himself one of the suspected potential claimant. It is never forgotten that he is the direct descendant of Prithvinarayan Shah the original conqueror of the country who was deprived of power by Jang Bahadur, nor that he or some party active in his name might attempt to regain it.

Status of His Majesty the Maharajadhiraj

> He does not legislate or take any part in the administration of government but is the head of the aristocracy and the fountain head of honour and his confirmation is essential to all titles and precedence. In his case sovereignty is the equivalent of the power of the nation and is a term descriptive of the will of the community as expressed through its administrative and executive head–namely through His Highness the Maharaj.
>
> The word "reigning" in the definition is inaccurate and "titular" seems a better description. His Majesty is accepted as the head of the aristocracy and that, in practice, is all. Among the people, he is but a name, while the Maharaj is a very actual force.
>
> It was in these circumstances that Bhim Shamsher "succeeded" to the Maharaj of Nepal but his position was not secure and it was evident he felt the strains and was himself aware of the fact.
>
> The illegitimate party (consisting of some of Bir's and Bhim's sons on the roll of succession) were not, at that time, to the fore and danger lay chiefly in some combination among Sir Chandra's powerful sons. After such a long period of office as that which had been enjoyed by Sir Chandra, this sudden turn of fortune's wheel, which pushed them into the political background, inevitably created heart burnings. There is good reason to believe that Sir Chandra, who was an extremely acute and farseeing statesman, sensed the danger and it is generally believed that he summoned General Sir Mohan Shamsher to his bedside and enjoined him to support his uncle Sir Bhim whose name stood next on the Roll of Succession.[35] (Information in brackets added.)

When Commander-in-Chief Bhim Shamsher with tears in his eyes went to pay his respects to his ailing brother Maharaj Chandra Shamsher the day before he died, the Maharaj had told his brother that it was not time for him to cry and he should go back to his own residence and take the necessary precautions to ensure his own succession to the high office. It is said that Chandra's sons kept waiting for a very long time Bhim Shamsher's son, Hiranya Shamsher, who had gone to Singh Darbar to fetch the Prime Minister's headdress and the red box containing the Lal Panja, the paper with the King's palm-print in red, granting the office of the Maharaj to the Rana family in perpetuity. Then Senior Commanding General Juddha Shamsher, accompanied by several of his sons who were equipped with handguns in holsters, approached Chandra's sons and firmly told them to hand over the headdress and the red box to Bhim's son without delay. When Chandra's second son, General Babar Shamsher, complained against Juddha's high-handedness, Juddha was said to have replied to him that sentiments had no place in politics. Juddha was due for promotion to the number-two rank of Commander-in-Chief with his elder half-brother Bhim Shamsher as the Maharaj and Prime Minister. Juddha was said to have been rewarded by Bhim in cash for his intervention at this juncture.

Soon after he became the Maharaj and Prime Minister, it was clear that Maharaj Bhim Shamsher was feeling insecure and showing signs of strains. The shadow of rigid control and authority his brother Chandra Shamsher had exercised over him for 29 years haunted him till the end of his life. The first step he took upon becoming the Maharaj was to take revenge against the officials who had affronted him in his brother's time. Chandra's favourites like Kashi Nath Acharya Dikshit's sons and Colonel Shiva Pratap Shamsher Thapa were publicly insulted and expelled from Kathmandu. Only the scene created by Kashi Nath crying loudly and rolling on the ground prevented the confiscation of the property of one of his sons.

Balakrishna Sama, a well-known Nepali poet, dramatist and painter, has, in his autobiography, mentioned a few incidents which indicate an obsessive sense of fear and insecurity which Maharaj Bhim suffered from.[36] One day a legal case which had been carefully decided by General Mohan Shamsher was brought before the Maharaj in open court for his final approval of the decision. But the Maharaj reversed Mohan's decision without any ground, and everybody present in the andience was surprised. After some time the Maharaj said, "As I have received several anonymous letters saying that the administration is still in the hands of Chandra's sons and even now Mohan's writ runs in the country, I have reversed Mohan's decision just to disprove this." On another occasion while promoting one Major Ghale to the rank of Lieutenant-Colonel, the Maharaj was heard to say loudly, "If you bring others' tales to the Prime Minister, you are promoted."

The Maharaj's utterances and behaviour in public were thus causing concern to the members of the Rana family and other officials. The Maharaj, having dealt with court cases and litigations of all kinds during his 29-year-old apprenticeship to his elder brother, had acquired considerable expertise in handling these affairs. But after he had himself become all in all, he started acting arbitrarily and in a high-handed manner by relying too much on intelligence reports which were specially tailored by interested parties to arouse his anger and suspicion. Some of his sympathizers blamed everything on his age and senility.

Maharaj Bhim Shamsher had several 'C' class sons (according to Landon's definition as furnished by Chandra) and so ignored Chandra Shamsher's roll of succession altogether. He drew up yet another roll allegedly under the advice of Eastern Commanding General Tej Shamsher, who was the wealthiest and the most politically active of Bir's sons on the roll of succession, and one of the three whom Chandra through Landon had made the target. It is understandable that Commanding General Tej might have put pressure on Bhim to put some of his own sons born out of wedlock on the roll of succession in order to counter Chandra's move. Bhim's revised roll of succession resulted in the demotion of some of his 'A' and 'C' class nephews already on the roll.

As Maharaj Bhim Shamsher was always afraid of the designs of his brother Chandra's sons against him and his family, he initially tended to placate them by appointing General Mohan additional Commanding General and by making all of Chandra's and his own grandsons Major-Generals. This unfortunately gave offence to the members of the Bir and Juddha families.

Bhim wanted to continue more or less the same policy as his elder brother Chandra in relation to British India. The visits of the Commander-in-Chief of India to Kathmandu were taken very seriously by every one of the Maharaj Prime Ministers. Like the visits of Lord Roberts in 1892 and of Lord Kitchener in 1906, the visit of Sir William Birdwood, the Commander-in-Chief of India in 1930, was regarded by Maharaj Bhim Shamsher as recognition by the British Government of the new regime and the strengthening of his own personal position. The visit proved to be an unqualified success and the Commander-in-Chief was given a most enthusiastic reception. Twenty-two thousand troops took part in the review held in his honour, and Sir William Birdwood was invested with the full insignia of Nepali General at a special ceremony or Darbar held for the purpose. His successor, Sir Philip Chetwode, was also invited and similarly honoured in October 1931.

In the winter of 1931-32, Maharaj Bhim Shamsher paid an official visit to India as guest of its Government. During his visit, he took the salute at a special review of troops in Calcutta and was present at the Proclamation Parade on 1 January 1932. He attended a special aeroplane exhibition, inspected a warship, and was also present at various other functions including the Calcutta races. The visit was quite a success from the Maharaj's point of view as the Viceroy announced the grant of G.C.M.G. to him at its end.

In February 1932 Chang Ming, the Chinese Consul-General in Calcutta, visited Kathmandu and conferred on the Maharaj the first class P-ao Ting decoration (a newly instituted national order of the "Precious Tripod") together with the rank of "Lu Chun Shang Chiang" or full general in the Chinese army. Two military attaches were sent by the Chinese Government to report on the Nepali army but they returned to China on the outbreak of hostilities with Japan without visiting Nepal. This was the first resumption of relations with China since Maharaj Chandra had discontinued the quinquennial missions to China and as such may perhaps be regarded as recognition by China of the independent status of Nepal.

In 1930 a social worker by the name of Tulsi Mehar, sent by Chandra Shamsher himself on scholarship for training in cottage industries to the Gandhi Ashram, was arrested for popularizing the spinning wheel in the Kathmandu Valley. Maharaj Bhim Shamsher felt that the movement for the spinning wheel might arouse political consciousness among the people in Nepal by exposing them to the influence of the nationalist movement for democracy and independence in India.

Like his elder brother Chandra, Bhim Shamsher was basically conservative and rigid in his outlook. In the same year 45 to 46 young men, who had petitioned the Maharaj for permission to set up a public library in Kathmandu, were arrested. Their case was given a political colour by representing it to the Maharaj as a plot against him that had allegedly been joined by one of his grandsons and his son. The Maharaj's grandson, Basanta Shamsher, who was implicated in the plot, happened to be Commanding General Padma Shamsher's son and the motive of those who involved him in the plot was to further spoil the already cool relations between the Maharaj and his eldest son. Yajna Shamsher, one of the Maharaj's own sons, who was not included in the roll of succession along with others, was also said to be an accomplice. This was the doing of General Rama Shamsher, who wanted to impress upon his aging father's mind that he was the only son on whom the Maharaj could really count. Rama Shamsher had also created differences between his own elder brother, General Hiranya Shamsher, and his father, the Maharaj. Among those who were arrested in connection with petitioning for a public library were Yog Bir

Singh, Hari Krishna Shrestha, Baikuntha Prasad Ṣhrestha, Lakshmi Prasad Devkota, Krishna Prasad Khatwida, Dharma Raj Thapalia, and Chittadhar Upasak, but the trumped-up charge of political conspiracy was ultimately dropped against them all and they were fined one hundred rupees each and released.

In April 1931 Bhim Shamsher's administration had to face domestic and political complications created by the flight from Nepal to England of Major-General Bishnu Shamsher, sixth son of Maharaj Chandra and his eldest son by his second wife, Bal Kumari, the Junior Bada Maharani, who had survived the Maharaj. The austere and ascetic atmosphere of Nepal where there was no entertainment other than gambling even for the rich and the powerful, did not appeal to Major-General Bishnu, who was young, wealthy and English-educated and who sought the kind of social life that was available to a man of means in western countries. He had converted his property into securities outside Nepal (since no one leaving the country could draw his income from it), ignored all caste restrictions and sailed with his newly married wife and a nurse for England from Bombay on 11 April 1931. He is said to have obtained a passport secretly and fraudulently with the help of one of his distant cousins, Major Nripa Jang Rana, who also sailed from Bombay a week after Bishnu had left. Bishnu's letter of resignation from the roll of succession was posted to the Maharaj from Calcutta on 18 April 1931.

Bishnu's flight from Nepal created a great stir and led to considerable misunderstanding between Maharaj Bhim and his brother's widow, the mother of Bishnu Shamsher. The role of the widow's stepsons, Generals Mohan, Babar and Kaiser, was not helpful either as they did everything they could to create distrust between the Maharaj and the step-mother they did not like.

The Maharaj took a very serious view of his nephew's escapade. He informed the British envoy that he had washed his hands of Bishnu and requested the envoy to inform all whom it might concern that Bishnu henceforth would have no claim upon him and should be regarded as an ordinary private individual unrelated to the ruling family of Nepal and should not, therefore, be received in society as a Rana. Bhim also expressed the hope that Bishnu would not be allowed to re-visit England if he should return to India.

As a result of the Bishnu episode there was a lot of ill feeling between Chandra's Junior Bada Maharani, Bal Kumari, and Maharaj Bhim. Bishnu later on wanted the Maharaj to condone what he had done and his mother also strongly supported her son's plea. But the Maharaj remained unmoved.

Meanwhile Chandra's second wife went to Calcutta to meet with her son in 1932 and returned to Nepal only under pressure from the Government of India. Bishnu came back to India briefly in the summer of 1932 only to return to Europe again on the plea of his wife's medical treatment. Maharaj Bhim relaxed the prohibition on his return in view of the alleged serious illness of Bishnu's wife and the impossibility of maintaining such an attitude vis-a-vis an individual from whom he had dissociated himself. To the last, however, Maharaj Bhim remained adamant in his uncompromising attitude and by this time he was strongly enough established to make his will prevail in such a matter–even over the Chandra group (Generals Mohan, Babar and Kaiser).

Even after her return to Nepal, Chandra's widow continued to intrigue against Bhim, and the strained relations between them finally resulted in an open breach. For a while it appeared that she might even seek refuge in the British Legation; Maharaj Bhim warned the British envoy of this possibility and the envoy requested him to do everything in his power to prevent such a situation. But nothing of the kind happened, much to the relief of everyone concerned.

This was how the British envoy had initially depicted the crisis:

> The danger of the position lies in the fact that she constitutes a focus of disaffection in the very heart of the ruling family and is thus a source of encouragement to any disaffected elements which do or may exist."

But at the end the envoy, Sir Clendon Daukes, summed up the situation as follows:

> He (Maharaja Bhim) has been made a G.C.I. and G.C.M.G. and had visited India as the guest of the Government of India and with the lapse of time had otherwise consolidated his position as Maharaja of Nepal. But the Chandra family, Bishnu's brothers, with a more enlightened and advanced outlook, refused to accept the uncle's view of the case and feeling consequently ran high, while the fact that Bishnu had taken his wife with him introduced the woman element which plays such a large part behind the scenes. That there was much to be said from the Maharaja's point

of view had been demonstrated by after events. Bishnu's career had tended to discredit his country.

A real conspiracy to overthrow Maharaj Bhim was unearthed in July 1931, and a distant member of the royal family was a party to it. The conspirators called themselves "Prachanda Gorkha" (lit. Terrible Gorkha). An eyewitness account of the trial of the conspirators staged in one of the courtyards of Maharaj Bhim Shamsher's Tangal residence is given below along with the same perceptive observer, Balakrishna Sama's analysis of the political situation at the time:

> The trial was held in the open stone-paved courtyard to the western side of the Tangal Palace. It was enclosed by walls on the west and the south, and there stood a dense forest of tall trees on the north. There were in the courtyard several long benches facing the main building. Maharaj Bhim Shamsher brought King Tribhuvan to the courtyard from inside by offering his hand for the King to lean on for support. The Maharaj seated the King on one of the benches and himself sat next to him. All other members of the Rana family and officers stood behind the bench and I was also one of the spectators.
>
> By command of the Maharaj all the convicts were made to stand in a line before those assembled in the courtyard: Sahebjyu Umesh Bikram Shah, one of the royal collaterals, Captain Khanda Man Singh, Khadga Man Singh, Maina Bahadur, Ranga Nath Sharma, etc. Pointing at Umesh Bikram Shah, Maharaj Bhim said to King Tribhuvan, "I am going to expel to Palpa this mean fellow who had harboured an evil design on Your Majesty's life and throne. What would Your Majesty command?" After obtaining the royal consent, Bhim directed his attention to Captain Khanda Man Singh and said to him "You mean fellow wanted to kill me and become prime minister!" Forgetting about his gout, the Maharaj abruptly stood up and walked up to Khanda Man Singh pouring abuse and scorn on him and started beating him with his stick. But after others had joined him in beating Khanda Man Singh, Bhim returned to his seat. After Khanda Man Singh fell down to the ground under the impact of blows and started crying, Bhim's bodyguards, who were wearing heavy duty boots, started kicking him to a pulp. Khadga Man Singh, who was very young, and Maina Bahadur were also beaten up very badly. I learnt later on that

Umesh Bikram Shah had also been subjected to severe beating inside the Palace itself. All of them were sentenced to life imprisonment. At the end Bhim reported, "They should have been given capital punishment but they escaped it because I have tentatively done away with it on an experimental basis".

* * *

As a result of this conspiracy, there arose a situation leading to friction between the Maharaj and his half-brother, Commander-in-Chief Juddha, who was next to him on the roll of succession. Umesh Bikram's uncle Bhupatendra Bikram's son Chandra Bikram Shah alias "Lakshman Raja" was also a party to the conspiracy. But as Chandra Bikram Shah happened to be Juddha Shamsher's son-in-law, Juddha saved him by telling the Maharaj that his son-in-law had turned out to be an informer and reported the conspiracy to him. Maharaj Bhim had retorted to Juddha that if it had been the case, how was it that he had not informed the Maharaj earlier? To this Juddha had replied that he was waiting to find out more about the conspiracy through his son-in-law. But Bhim did not find Juddha's plea convincing. It had caused a deep-seated misunderstanding between the two brothers leading to a situation in which Juddha might have had to resign. But Generals Mohan, Babar, Kaiser saved the situation for Juddha by their efforts at bringing about reconciliation between him and the Maharaj. Now there had been two clear factions among those on the roll of succession, one consisting of those born of wedlock and the others consisting of those born out of wedlock. The First Group was composed of Juddha, Dharma, Padma, Mohan, Babar, Kaiser, Bahadur Shamsher, etc., and the Second Group consisted of Rudra, Tej, Hiranya, Pratap, Rama, etc. The Second Group enjoyed the blessings of Maharaj Bhim himself. Bhim had planned to win over King Tribhuvan also to his side by having one of his own daughters and grand-daughters betrothed to Crown Prince Mahendra. The Second Group was led by Tej Shamsher. He had plans to expel the members of the First Group from Nepal and retain only the members of the Second Group on the roll. The two groups were very much afraid of one another. The Land Reform Commission called "Ukhada Janch Commission" was sent to different districts under General Tej Shamsher with a view to boosting his personality among the people. Reforms in the court-system and administration were also introduced through Tej. Mahila Gurujyu Hem Raj Pande lost his charge of Bir Pustakalaya on the allegation that he had misappropriated manuscripts and books, and Bada Gurujyu Tarka Raj, a supporter of the Second Group, was appointed in his place. This replacement seemed awkward to the intelligent public. The atmosphere was tense and everyone was anxiously waiting for something startling and terrible to happen. Every morning I used to attend on Rama Shamsher on horseback when he went out on horseback riding in the streets of Kathmandu. He was accompanied by a large number of people on horseback and even General Krishna Shamsher used to be one of them. It was a sense of fear and not that of love or respect that dominated the scene. Rama Shamsher's brother-in-law Rana Jang Shah had mainly spread terror.

* * *

By 1932 Senior Commanding General Dharma Shamsher fell seriously ill. Gangrene set in and his leg had to be amputated. After he went to Calcutta for treatment, Rudra took over his functions. As portents of the event were beginning to appear, General Tej Shamsher had a stroke of paralysis, and was permanently confined to bed. The conspiracy broke down without coming to the surface. The Second Group felt as if it had lost its mainstay. The First Group could hardly conceal its glee. The people in general heard that the two leading Ranas had fallen prey to disease and inside the ruling clique many dreams were shattered to pieces. Tej also went to Calcutta for treatment. Referring to him, Bhim said in the open court, "I have lost my right hand."[37]

During Bhim Shamsher's administration capital punishment was abolished except in cases falling under military law and high treason. The abrogation of capital punishment had the incidental effect of removing the anomaly of discrimination in favour of particular sections of the community. Under the law Brahmins and women were exempt, being subject to imprisonment for life when found guilty of murder. On conviction a Brahmin was adjudged *ipso facto* to have lost his caste.

The Times (London) of 25 July 1931 commented favourably on the achievements of Bhim's administration during the first ten months:

> During the short administration the Prime Minister had done much to deserve the gratitude of his subjects. He has abolished the duties on salt and cotton, on pasturage, and feeding cattle, lightened the burden of taxes upon the poor, increased the pay of all soldiers in the army, and bettered their equipment. He has appointed a reforms committee to enquire into the details of administration, and to devise means to carry out improvements wherever needed. He has promulgated new laws to prevent the delay and miscarriage of justice. He had pursued a policy of gradual decentralization of powers and responsibility to the heads of different departments of state.

But as he advanced in years, he seemed to lose his grip on the administration and began to show signs of excessive insecurity and senility. The quarrel between two of his sons, Generals Hiranya and Rama, on whom he had relied for the conduct of the administration, made things worse for the Maharaj. General Padma had all along been living separately with his mother who was estranged from the Maharaj long ago, and in the closing years of Bhim Shamsher's administration, General Hiranya had also drifted away from his father and was spending his time in Calcutta on the pretext of his wife's medical treatment. The Maharaj was entirely playing into the hands of his youngest wife, Sita Maharani, whom he had promoted to the rank of Bada Maharani, and his fourth son, General Ram, who had apparently been able to win her favour.

After General Tej's restraining hand was removed from the Maharaj (after the General had had a paralytic stroke), General Rama and his brother-in-law Major Rana Jang Shah had a free hand in running the administration, but they failed to take a single constructive or popular step. The Land Reform Commission established under General Tej had introduced measures to protect the rights of the tenant cultivators in the central tarai districts of Butwal, Bhairawa and Taulihawa, but they were not fully implemented. The reforms would have gone a long way in affording relief to the poor peasantry as is apparent from the hue and cry raised by the vested interests against them through the Hindi language newspapers across the border. In the course of a note under the heading "Propagation of Communism in Nepal", the *Pratap* wrote:

> This year the government of Nepal had decided to propagate communism in the district of Butwal. The government has even promulgated communist laws there which will give equal rights to all. The Zamindars and capitalists of the district have been ruined. The Nepal government has decided to establish the communistic regime.[38]

It was during Bhim Shamsher's administration that the practice of observing Saturday as a public holiday every week was introduced, there was no provision for a weekly holiday before that. The working hours in Government offices were fixed as being from 10 a.m. to 4 p.m. Provisions were made for the supply of piped water for the first time in the district of Morang where the quality of drinking water was supposed to be excessively bad, and in the Kathmandu Valley also measures were taken to expand the facilities for the supply of piped water. Maharaj Bhim's religious concern for the cow and compassion for the poor and the needy made him eliminate pasture taxes for bovine animals and import levies on salt and cotton.

As an example of the role of ritual in the politics of oriental countries may be mentioned the performance of a *Koti Hom* in the Maharaj's residence. A *Koti Hom* literally means 10 million libations and offerings to the sacred fire, a religious performance which keeps nearly 200 priests employed day and night for two months and is followed by a big *dana*, or gift of gold, raiment and food to the holy.

Maharaj Bhim had been lucky financially since he had at his disposal the crores of rupees Maharaj Chandra had left in the public treasury to meet the contingency of a war with Tibet. He used this fund to import silver and gold from overseas and to have coins minted for himself and his favourites as the prices of silver and gold had fallen very low at the time as a result of the worldwide economic depression. But Bhim did not live to enjoy this luck for very long. He died on 1 September 1932 at the age of sixty-eight.

Among the direct beneficiaries of Bhim's newly acquired wealth were his sons and grandsons who were included by him in the roll for succession after he became Prime Minister. Some of them such as Commanding General Hiranya Shamsher and his son Major-General Subarna Shamsher along with Bhim's other grandson, Major-Gerneral Mahabir Shamsher, played an important role in organizing the overthrow of the Rana rule in 1950-51. General Padma Shamsher, Bhim's eldest and only son born of his legally wedded wife, had had no share in this inheritance because he and his mother were living separately. But Padma subsequently became Maharaj and Prime Minister in his own right.

NOTES

1. Kanchanmoy Mojumdar, *Political Relations between India and Nepal, 1877-1923* (Delhi: Munshiram Manoharlal Publishers Private Ltd., 1973) p. 101.
2. Description of the event by Khamba Shamsher Rana who was himself an eyewitness to the entire sequence of events as recorded by Colonel Nara Raj Shamsher in his personal diary and cited in Pramode Shamsher J.B. Rana, *Rana Nepal: An Insider's View* (Kathmandu, 1978), pp. 111-113.
3. Report by Resident Durand, Foreign Secret-E, October 1890, Nos. 88-89 (National Archives of India), cited in Asad Husain, *op. cit.*, p. 134.
4. Landon, *op. cit.*, Vol. II, p. 108.
5. Political and Secret Letters from India, Vol. 134, Reg. No. 772; Wylie to Lee Warner, 2 July 1901, cited in Kanchanmoy Mojumdar, *op. cit.*, p. 101.
6. Political and Secret Home Correspondence, Vol. 198, No. 2429, Chandra Shamsher to Pears, 13 July 1901; Political and Secret Letters, Vol. 142, Regd. No. 448, Chandra to Pears; Mojumdar, *op. cit.*, p. 106.
7. "Conversation Between H.E. The Maharaja and H.E. the Viceroy in 1902", Basta No. 47 (NEOK); reproduced verbatim in Appendix VIII, Husain, *op. cit.*, pp. 354-56.
8. Ekai Kawaguchi, *Three Years in Tibet*, pp. 526-29.
9. *Ibid.*, pp. 685-713.
10. Leo E. Rose, *Nepal--Strategy for Survival* (Berkeley: University of California Press, 1971), p. 154.
11. *Ibid.*, pp. 155-56.
12. Landon, *op. cit.*, Vol. II, pp. 12-13.
13. Husain, *op. cit.*, Appendix IX, p. 360.
14. Landon, *op. cit.*, p. 119
15. Husain, *op. cit.*, Appendix 10, pp. 362-69. Verbatim records of seven interviews between Maharaj Chandra and British leaders including the King and also the translation of the petition from the Maharajadhiraj to the King Emperor and a Kharita from Lord Minto, Viceroy of India, to the Maharajadhiraj, Basta No. 49, of the collection in Nepal's Foreign Office are given in this Appendix.
16. Husain, *op. cit.*, p. 161.
17. Letter from Maharaja Chandra to the Resident, Basta, No. 63, Ministry of Foreign Affairs, Nepal, cited in Husain, *op. cit.*, pp. 183-84.
18. Husain, *op. cit.*, p. 190.
19. *Ibid.*, p. 193
20. Landon, *op. cit.*, Preface, p. 10
21. Landon, *op. cit.*, p. 149.
22. Memorandum. Foreign and Political Department, Secretary, Internal Proceedings, July 1919, Nos. 35-36 (National Archives of India).
23. Landon, *op. cit.*, Vol. I, p. 249.

24. *Ibid.*, p. 250.
25. Balchandra Sharma, *Nepalko Aitihasik Ruprekha* (lit. Outline of the History of Nepal) (Varanasi: Madhav Prasad Sharma, 3rd edition, 1969), p. 399.
26. Balachandra Sharma, *op. cit.*, p. 400.
27. Kanchanmoy Mojumdar, *Nepal and the Indian Nationalist Movement* (Calcutta : Firma K.L. Mukhopadhyay, 1975), p. 4.
28. Kanchanmoy Mojumdar, *op. cit.*, p. 3.
29. *Ibid.*, p. 4.
30. *Ibid.*, p. 4.
31. Cited in Mojumdar, *op. cit.*, p. 26.
32. *Ibid.*, p. 27.
33. Sharma, *op. cit.*, p. 365.
34. Sharma, *op. cit.*, p. 359.
35. Sir Clendon Daukes's note on Nepal 19/29-34 attached as an enclosure to his letter to the Rt. Hon'ble Sir John Simon of 15 January 1935.
36. *Mero Kavita Ko Aradhana (My Devotion to Poetry)*, Part II (Kathmandu : Sajha Prakashan, 1972), p. 120.
37. *Mero Kavita ko Aradhana* (lit. *My Devotion to Poetry*), Vol. II, Balakrishna Sama (Kathmandu: Sajha Prakashan, 1972), pp. 128-33.
38. C.T. Daukes's letter to the Secretary to the Government of India in Foreign and Political Department in Simla of 13 August 1931.

13

Maharaj Juddha, the Last of Dhir Shamsher's Sons

Bhim Shamsher was succeeded by his younger half-brother Juddha Shamsher as the Maharaj and Prime Minister of Nepal on 1 September 1932. Juddha was Commander-in-Chief Dhir Shamsher's last son to become the Maharaj. After him the position passed to the third generation of the Dhir Shamsher branch of the Rana family consisting of his grandsons, and only two of Dhir's grandsons subsequently held the coveted position before the system of hereditary Rana prime ministers was abolished in 1951.

Born on 19 April 1875 Juddha Shamsher was 57 years old when he became the Maharaj. Unlike his predecessors, Juddha refused to permit celebrations marking his elevation to this office until after the 13-day period of ritual mourning for his deceased half-brother had ended. His formal inaugural ceremony was held on 14 October 1932.

It is said that on the very morrow of Bhim Shamsher's death Juddha was approached by Chandra Shamsher's sons and Bhim's son, Padma Shamsher, with the suggestion that Bir Shamsher's and Bhim Shamsher's illegitimate sons be immediately removed from the roll of succession with a view to consolidating the position of the legitimate Ranas. Bir's son, General Rudra Shamsher, who was going to be next in line of succession to the prime ministership, was amongst those to be dropped. Instead of being automatically promoted to the rank of Commander-in-Chief, he was asked to attend to the affairs on the parade ground for an hour or two while the other senior Ranas on the roll of succession were closeted with Juddha at his residence to deliberate on the future ruling setup. But Juddha apparently asked for more time to execute their common design to remove Bir's and Bhim's sons from the roll, and Rudra was appointed Commander-in-Chief that day. No action was taken against him or against some of his brothers and cousins on the roll of succession until 18 months later.

This was how the British envoy, Sir Clendon, had depicted the situation in Nepal at the time:

> Perceiving that the first essential at such a moment was to seize the power he (Juddha) came to terms with Rudra, and outwardly adopted the view that though the principle of the inclusion of illegitimate children was a bad one and would be discontinued, the existing roll of succession must be followed.
>
> For several days, however, troops were kept under arms and were in constant movement around Kathmandu.
>
> Sentries were posted by day and night over the approaches to the Legation, both on account of the prevailing feeling of unrest and also in view of the possibility of an invasion by refugees seeking sanctuary. Had Sir Juddha refused to accept Rudra as the Heir Apparent, it was almost certain that bloodshed would have resulted since Rudra was in temporary command of the army because of the death of Senior Commanding General Dharma Shamsher only a week prior to the passing away of Maharaja Bhim.
>
> Sir Juddha's action, however, in coming to a seeming understanding with Rudra and first obtaining confirmation of his own elevation and that of Rudra as their heir apparent from His Majesty the King disarmed the suspicions of the illegitimate party. Any doubts which they may have still entertained were still further allayed by the new Maharaja's declaration of policy in this respect which he communicated to the British envoy and which was to the effect that the existing roll would be adhered to.[1]

Fire at a Historic Building

In the spring of 1933 the famous Main Hall (Thulo Baithak) of Maharaj Bir's Seto Darbar (The White Palace) was reduced to ashes by an accidental fire that raged for several hours whilst almost the entire ruling Rana hierarchy and their troops and officers helplessly stood by without being able to do anything to save what was, in Maharaj Juddha's words, "the pride of Nepal", a hall that displayed valuable paintings and tapestries, antiques and *objets d'art* – both indigenous and imported – and a marble floor covered with Persian and Turkish rugs of the finest quality. Just the crystal pillars and chandeliers along with bigger-than-life-size wall mirrors imported from Osler and Company in London and brought to Kathmandu over the shoulders of men across the mountain ridges must have been worth a fortune. Their price including the cost of transhipment and porterage was put at 5 million rupees at the time.

The fire may have taught a useful lesson to Nepal insofar as it led Maharaj Juddha to set up the first fire brigade in Kathmandu with modern fire-fighting equipment. But it forebode ill to the members of the Bir Shamsher branch of the Rana family because within less than a year of the event all the seniormost members of this branch were removed from the roll of succession to the prime ministership and the Bir family's influence in Nepali politics was as good as dead.

The Great Earthquake of 1934

If the fire that had burnt down the White Palace was an unfortunate man-made accident of limited consequence, the severe earthquake that struck large parts of Nepal on 15 January 1934 proved a disastrous natural calamity with widespread effect. It caused a heavy loss of life and property in the Kathmandu valley and eastern Nepal as a whole. The following on-the-spot report on the earthquake by the British Legation surgeon, Lieutenant-Colonel C.H. Smith, presents a memorable account of the shock and its aftermath at Kathmandu.

> "The shock occurred about 2.15 p.m. As the vibration became more violent, I lost no time in getting downstairs and outside.
>
> From the (Legation's) garden there is an extensive view of the valley and many of the palaces of the leading family are in sight.
>
> When I got out of the house, it was difficult to walk, the motion of the ground was like that of the deck of a P and O liner in a gale of wind with a cross sea, but one was not actually thrown down.
>
> It was an awe inspiring sight as palace after palace crashed to the ground and the ruins were enveloped in a cloud of dust.
>
> With the Nepalese officers and three Mukhias laden with dressings, splints, etc., I went to the city. We were in the city by 3.30 p.m.
>
> Many of the public buildings were down and all, with one exception, seemed to be so badly cracked as to be unsafe. The exception was the electric offices. The hospitals were partly demolished and those remaining were so badly cracked as to be useless.

The city itself was a dreadful sight. At least one house in five had completely collapsed and very few seem to have escaped uninjured.

Every hundred yards or so the narrow streets were blocked with piles of debris twenty feet high over which we had to climb.

The inhabitants were behaving splendidly. There seemed to be no panic; the people were hurrying out of the narrow streets towards the various open squares with goods and chattels they had been able to save and were settling down in family groups in those open spaces preparing to pass the night as best as they could.

* * *

The first news we received on the morning of the 16th was that the pipe water supply was not working. Fortunately there is a spring just outside the legation which supplied for our needs.

Casualties were pouring into the Legation Hospital. The sub-assistant surgeon and staff were quite capable of coping with the work. The Nepalese Officer and myself started for the city.

Just inside the city we met one of the Nepalese doctors who told us that the medical staff were still busy straightening up their hospital and had not been able to arrange anything in the way of first aid.

The people were now collected in the various squares and open spaces. They were quiet and orderly, sitting in family groups cooking what food they had.

They had no shelter, and might have spent a very unpleasant night, as there was a heavy ground frost.

On the 17th (January) I heard that the Nepalese had their medical arrangements in full swing, so I did no further first aid work in the city.[2]

So much for my personal experience."[2]

An earthquake of great intensity with its epicentres probably at Kathmandu, Monghyr and Bhagalpur had, in the form of an ellipse, swept the country southwards from the Everest region and had devastated large parts of eastern Nepal and the Indian province of Bihar. Some 7,000 people had lost their lives in Nepal, and over one-half of these deaths had occurred in the Kathmandu Valley alone. A few members of the elite families including two daughters of King Tribhuvan died in the earthquake. King George V sent condolences to the King not directly but through Maharaj Juddha after a good deal of bureaucratic discussion on the correct protocol and traditional practice; in the end it was decided that death resulting from an earthquake should not be treated as a private matter since an earthquake was in itself a public event.

All communications between the Kathmandu Valley and Raxaul, the nearest Indian railhead to the south, were totally disrupted. Kathmandu was full of the usual wild rumours that Calcutta, Banaras and Delhi had been virtually wiped out. The price of whatever little foodstuffs were available in the Kathmandu market had risen sky high, and there were several incidents of looting at night. But the administration lost no time in issuing orders that looters were to be shot at sight, and stern steps were forthwith taken to stop profiteering and black-marketing.

By 17 January telephonic communication with Raxaul was restored. The situation in the Valley also showed an all-round improvement. The people once again appeared to be on their best behaviour. Strict measures adopted by the Government had produced the desired effect. Looting and profiteering had stopped altogether by 18 January. The pipe-water supply had been partially restored, and water was made available for part of the day. The hydroelectric station had escaped damage, as though by a miracle. The cableway had started operating again and supplies had begun to arrive in the Valley. On 19 January all the main streets were lit by electricity and this had a tremendous effect on the morale of the people.

All tents in the possession of the Government were issued to the people who sorely needed protection against the winter cold. As the Government's stock of tents was not found adequate to meet the public needs, improvised tents made of ordinary thick cloth, gunny bags and coarse matting as well as corrugated iron sheets and tents requisitioned from traders and other private parties were made available for the purpose. The speedy supply by cableway and porters of foodgrains and other necessaries of life to the Kathmandu Valley prevented their price from rising and made it possible for rice to be sold at 8 kilos per rupee. A fair price market set up on the parade ground for the sale of foodgrains and other essential goods also had a good effect on the people's morale.

As communications were restored, reports of death and devastation from the outlying region started flowing into the capital. The western hills along with the tarai experienced only mild tremors. But eastern

Nepal as a whole was seriously affected by the earthquake and suffered not only casualties and damage to houses but also ecological and environmental disturbances. The districts of Bhojpur and Udaipur in eastern Nepal experienced landslips on a wide scale, and rivers were blocked causing a shortage of water. Landslips continued for months in the wake of the earthquake. The eastern tarai districts of Rajbiraj and Mahottari suffered the worst calamity as they were situated quite close to the epicentres of the earthquake in Bihar. All the buildings in the districts collapsed and the ground cracked at several places letting water gush out and flood the roads and agricultural land for days on end.

In the absence of the Maharaj in the tarai, Commander-in-Chief Rudra Shamsher entrusted to his cousin, Senior Commanding General Padma Shamsher, the entire charge of organizing relief operations in the Valley. Luckily the quake had struck the Kathmandu Valley at a time when the soldiers were assembled on the parade ground for their routine afternoon drill. Padma, who was in direct charge of the army as *Jangi Lath* in the Rana hierarchy, rushed to the parade ground within minutes of the earthquake and called upon the soldiers to do their duty by the country at the hour of its trial and suffering. Though the soldiers were themselves deeply concerned about the safety of their own family members in their distant home districts, they responded to duty's call and took upon themselves the task of rescuing people from under the debris and exhuming dead bodies and also that of protecting private and public properties and maintaining law and order.

On the morrow of the earthquake, General Padma convened a conference of high-ranking Government officials, prominent merchants and traders and other notables and addressed them in a touching manner: "Brothers, many people are lying beneath the debris. Some of them must have already died. They must be dug out. You will acquire considerable religious merit if you perform the deed well. Those who have relatives around, should be entrusted to their care. You must see to it that no man lays his hand on somebody else's property".[3]

In response to General Padma's appeal for help and cooperation, students and staff members of the medical department pooled their resources to provide first aid care, medicine and other relief measures to the earthquake-stricken people. Bhotahiti and Asan, the hub of commercial activity in the Kathmandu town, were densely populated and congested with houses on narrow lanes and therefore suffered the worst consequences. General Pratap Shamsher, whose residence was adjacent to this section of the town, put up temporary sheds of corrugated iron sheets and canvas cloth in the open area inside his own private compound and made them available to those who were rendered homeless. Major-General Brahma Shamsher formed a relief committee mainly of students and public-spirited Government servants and merchants to carry on voluntary relief work. It was perhaps for the first time that many Nepalis including the Ranas themselves got an opportunity to render voluntary social service in their private and individual capacity.

Maharaj Juddha Shamsher himself was at his hunting camp on the bank of the Mahakali river in the far western tarai when the earthquake occurred. The Maharaj and his entourage, who were out on elephant-back hunting in the forest that day, did not even realize that there had been an earthquake. Even those members of the Maharaj's party who were resting at the camp had felt but a mild tremor. It was not until Friday, 18 January, that Juddha had received the tragic news from the capital. The earthquake had also disrupted the railway and the telegraphic lines in the adjoining Indian provinces with the result that a telegraphic message which would have in normal times reached the Maharaj's hunting camp in a matter of hours had to be brought from Kathmandu by special couriers with considerable delay.

After breaking the news of the natural calamity to the members of his entourage at the camp, Juddha lost no time in sending a message back to Kathmandu expressing his sorrow at what had happened and calling upon his relatives and officers of the state to leave no stone unturned to provide relief to the victims of the disaster. Meanwhile earnest efforts were made in cooperation with the British Indian authorities across the border to restore the telegraphic lines and repair the railway tracks expeditiously so that the Maharaj and his party might be able to return to Kathmandu without much delay.

However, it was not until 4 February 1934 that Maharaj Juddha himself could return to the capital. Although he was not well-educated, Juddha, who had a good voice for public speaking, was fond of making speeches and quite adept at projecting a favourable image of himself to his audience as a simple, guileless and benevolent ruler. He was given to histrionic gestures, and his speeches, though always ghost-written, were delivered by him with great effect. On the very day of his arrival in Kathmandu, the Maharaj, with tears in his eyes and in a voice choked with grief, addressed a large gathering of the people on the parade ground from the historic platform under the chalk tree (Khari

Ko Bot) and conveyed to them his deep sense of sorrow and sympathy at the fate that had overtaken the country. At the same time he reminded his audience of the example of Japan where the people, though frequently subjected to the ravages of earthquakes, had invariably emerged stronger and better off from their ordeals time and again. His speech had also a touch of appeal based on religious superstition: he announced that he was going to dedicate the merit he might have acquired, by giving away 1,000 cows in charity on the bank of the Mahakali river, to those who had died in the earthquake. Death as a result of natural disasters was considered to be inauspicious and the victims were said to need special treatment for their salvation. Juddha loudly lamented that the earthquake had wrecked his earnest plans to promote the welfare of the people. Thus did he speak in an impassioned manner with overtones of pathos but with a firm political purpose:

> I had hoped to construct barracks for the benefit and comfort of the soldiers and to make the people happy and prosperous by developing trade and industries and by creating facilities for increasing the use of machinery in factories and workshops. Such were my hopes but behold what has happened. It seems God has ordained that my desire should not be fulfilled, for henceforth I shall have to concentrate all my heart, soul and energy on redeeming the city from the havoc created by the earthquake. I am already engaged in this work. If each of you does what he can, I have no doubt, our ruined condition will improve.[4]

It must be said to the credit of Juddha that he undertook to provide relief to the earthquake-stricken population on his own without even availing himself of the generous offer of help by the Governments and voluntary organizations of other countries. Maharaj Juddha set up the Earthquake Relief Funds (Bhukampa Kosalaya) with a capital of 5 million rupees for the disbursement of interest-free loans to the inhabitants of the Kathmandu Valley and the township of Banepa outside it. The Funds were placed under the supervision of Mahila Gurujyu Hem Raj Pande, who saw to it that only those who were really in need were the beneficiaries of the loans. No individual was entitled to receive more than 1,500 rupees. These loans went a long way in helping a large number of people meet the cost of rebuilding their houses.

Later in the same year, Juddha started another loan-giving agency called Funds for Relief Loans to the Earthquake-Stricken (Bhukampa-Pidit-Sahayak Rin) again with a capital of 5 million rupees. Those desirous of obtaining loans could borrow reasonable amounts without interest for four years on the security of their land and houses. The loans were made repayable in instalments or in a lump sum within a specified period depending on the convenience of the borrowers.

However, subsequently on Friday, 2 September 1938, the Maharaj assembled members of his family, officials and merchants and other people on the parade ground at 3.30 p.m. and proclaimed that he had written off all outstanding loans from both of these agencies, a total of Rs. 24,21,360/62. Even those who had already made partial repayments on their loans were refunded whatever they had paid.

The cancellation of these loans, even though setup with public funds, shows a measure of personal generosity on Juddha's part if we take into account the fact that under the Rana system of government no practical distinction was made between the public treasury and the private coffer of the Maharaj. It also reflects credit on Juddha that he proved himself capable of meeting the crisis created by the earthquake without help from outside. The foreign press also gave him well-deserved praise for his success in providing immediate relief to the people and also for helping them rebuild their houses and towns within a short period of two years or so. New Road, also called Juddha Road, which passes through the most modern section of the town, was constructed after the earthquake and is still the main shopping centre and hub of business and commerce in Kathmandu. New Road stands to this day as a tribute to Juddha's success in meeting the situation created by the earthquake.

The Political Purge of 18 March 1934

Only two months after the earthquake, Juddha decided to resolve the problem of the growing tension between the 'legitimate' and the 'illegitimate' Ranas on the roll of succession. It has already been noted that ever since he had become Prime Minister, Juddha had been under steady pressure from Chandra's sons to remove some of Bir's and Bhim's sons from the roll of succession on the ground of 'illegitimacy' as propounded by Maharaj Chandra Shamsher through Perceval Landon's book on Nepal, which had been published in London one year before Chandra's death. The present author was also told by

Juddha's eldest surviving son, General Bahadur Shamsher, that Chandra had actually made Juddha promise that he would remove some of Bir's and Bhim's sons from the roll during his prime ministership. It is also said that Chandra's sons compelled Maharaj Juddha to act in a precipitate manner because they had sensed that the Maharaj had unwittingly revealed their design to Commander-in-Chief Rudra Shamsher who was his close boyhood friend.

Apart from Juddha's previous commitment to his half-brother Maharaj Chandra Shamsher to retain only the 'legitimate' Ranas on the roll of succession, Juddha might have also profited by the mistake of his hero and idol, Maharaj Jang Bahadur Rana, who had actually sown the seed of dissension in the Rana family by adding some of his younger sons by his favourite mistresses on the roll of succession and also by assigning them a higher rank of precedence over those already on the roll. Juddha also would have had to accommodate too many of his own sons on the roll and would have in the process aroused the animosity of not only his sons kept off the roll but also of his half-brother's sons who were already on it.

Juddha sought to solve this problem for himself by giving his favourite mistresses titles of Maharani and Ranisaheb, which brought them status and handsome allowances even without their sons being included on the roll of succession. But Juddha's innovative solution also could not keep his immediate family united because his elder sons by his non-title-holding mistresses tended to side with the Chandra faction of the family, while the power of his eldest son on the roll, General Bahadur Shamsher, was undermined by the friction between him and Juddha's youngest Maharani, who began to stand up for her sons.

Whatever Juddha's reasons, General Babar Shamsher, Chandra's second son, suggested to the Maharaj soon after the earthquake that as the sons and grandsons of Bir and Bhim they were thinking of expelling from Kathmandu had their houses heavily damaged or demolished by the earthquake, it would be in the long-term interests of the victims themselves if they were expelled from the capital before they had actually started spending money on building or repairing their houses. This sugges-tion somehow appealed to Juddha and he at once made up his mind about putting into effect his plan to purge the roll of succession of the Ranas designated as "C" class in Landon's book.

The following account of what happened on 18 March 1934 and the three days preceding it is literally translated into English from the autobiography of a celebrated Nepali literary figure, Balakrishna Sama who, though a Rana himself, was not directly involved in the conflict and was actually present when this live drama of the political purge was enacted. Balakrishna Sama's analysis of the day-today happenings immediately preceding the purge and his vivid description of what actually happened on that fateful day is based partly on his own personal observation and partly on what he was told by the principal parties involved in the crisis. Sama's narration runs as follows:

> "After General Tej Shamsher, known to be the richest and the shrewdest of Bir's sons, had had a paralytic stroke in early 1932 and after the death of Bir's eldest surviving son, Senior Commanding General Dharma Shamsher, and of Maharaj Bhim Shamsher within an interval of a week in the same year in the autumn, the faction, consisting of Bir's and Bhim's sons on the roll of succession, had already lost its potentiality for effective action against their adversaries. There was no chance of their being able to put up successful resistance with 50 odd rifles at their disposal to the incumbent Maharaj Juddha who had the backing of his own and Chandra's sons solidly entrenched behind him.
>
> Lt. Col. Yajna Raj Shamsher, the second son of General Tej Shamsher, who had been away in Calcutta for medical treatment, died on 14 March 1934. The annual military sports on the occasion of the horse festival (Ghoda Jatra) were held on Thursday, 15 March, that year. Sporting events including the horse races had just taken place on the parade ground. Maharaj Juddha, Commander-in-Chief Rudra and Generals Padma, Mohan and Pratap were sitting on the historic platform under the chalk tree at the centre of the parade ground. Juddha commanded Rudra to notify everyone concerned that a meeting was going to be held in Singha Darbar, the prime minister's official residence on Sunday, 18 March, and almost immediately after that Rudra was further instructed by Juddha to assemble three battalions on the parade ground on Sunday itself at 12 noon. After that Juddha proceeded to his carriage, but I noticed a sudden change of expression on Rudra's face although he had said yes to the Maharaja's command. Meanwhile I could not help overhearing a piece of conversation between Commander-in-Chief Rudra's son, Colonel Ishwar Shamsher, and General Prachanda Shamsher. General Prachanda was asking Ishwar to inform his father of what he had told him despite Ishwar's assertion

that what Prachanda has told him was not plausible. Prachanda contended that what was being done was of course improper and that was why it had also appeared to be implausible.

By Friday, 16 March, Rudra had had the additional instruction that the soldiers of the three battalions to be assembled on Sunday were to be issued with 10 rounds of ammunition each and some of the retired old-time officials of the Chandra Shamsher period such as Subbas Ram Mani, Bharat Mani and Govinda Prasad were also to be asked to be present on Sunday. This must have made Rudra feel that his days as Commander-in-Chief on the roll were numbered. Rudra had also learnt by then that his own military aide-de-camp Lt. Col. Hem Bahadur Malla had all along been in the pay of General Mohan Shamsher, to whom he was supplying information about the goings-on in Rudra's household.

On Saturday, 17 March, Commander-in-Chief Rudra discussed what they were up against with four of his sons by his third wife, Ishwar, Gopal, Shyam and Dhairya. As his sons by his first and second wives had already separated themselves from Rudra, they did not enjoy his confidence. When his sons suggested that Generals Hiranya and Pratap be also taken into confidence and the matter thrashed out with them, Rudra told them that the two generals would find themselves as helpless as he was and any move to get together with them might expose all of them to their adversaries in the most unfavourable light.

By Sunday, 18 March, the 'A' Ranas were through with their ritual 5-day mourning over General Tej's son's death whereas the 'C' Ranas had to observe mourning for eight more days. The fateful meeting was deliberately scheduled for Sunday by taking this into consideration.

All the Ranas on the roll of succession with the exception of General Hiranya Shamsher reached the prime minister's official residence on that fateful day at the appointed hour. As they arrived they were asked to sit for sometime in a large Swiss cottage tent which was pitched in front of the billiards pavilion to the northeast of the main Singha Darbar building. By a quarter after 12 noon all those summoned were assembled there. Although some of those present were seen whispering with one another, there prevailed tense silence around where Commander-in-Chief Rudra was seated. It was already past 12.30 p.m. when one of the Maharaj's personal guards officers announced that the Maharaj wanted the

Commander-in-Chief and all those on the roll of succession to go to the main hall upstairs and the rest of them to proceed to the hall on the ground floor and remain there.

Before they could even enter the main hall on the first floor of Singha Darbar, General Surya Shamsher, one of Juddha's sons, with a revolver in his hand, searched the pockets of General Pratap and Major General Mahabir asking them if they had brought some weapons along. This made everyone all the more tense. All of those on the roll of succession entered the hall and sat according to their warrant of precedence on the sofas and couches placed on both sides of the water fountain inside the hall. The fountain was not at work and there prevailed pin-drop silence in the hall. The glass windows and doors on the side of the hall next to the terrace, where Commander-in-Chief Rudra was sitting, were closed except the one next to the stairs leading to the ground floor. After about an hour General Agni Shamsher entered the hall by the open door and walked down a few steps to unbolt the second glass door. From the terrace outside entered King Tribhuvan Bir Bikram Shah Deva wearing a white cap and a white overcoat and with canvas shoes on and took his seat on the couch in the middle. Everybody got up from his seat, saluted him and sat down. Silence grew all the more. The glass door was once again closed.

King Tribhuvan had had a meeting with Maharaj Juddha before the King came into the hall. The King lighted a cigarette and appeared to be absorbed in deep thought as he was puffing on his cigarette and exhaling the smoke. After he had smoked two cigarettes, King Tribhuvan left the hall and was followed by his Equerry-in-Chief, General Agni Shamsher, Juddha's third son.

At 2.50 p.m. the very same second glass door was opened by another son of Juddha, General Hari Shamsher, and the Maharaj himself entered the hall by it with loaded revolvers in each of his hands and stood in the middle of the hall while his eldest son, General Bahadur, with a loaded revolver in hand, stood behind him. Ladies holding pistols in their hands meanwhile appeared at the small crystal glass windows above the hall.

Juddha looked straight at the Commander-in-Chief and said to him, "I gave the two parties 18 months to settle their differences and become one but there were no signs of unity between them. On the other hand, I was myself faced with the danger of sharing Ranoddip Singh's fate. That is why I have finally decided to remove one faction from the roll. You yourself go to Palpa. Hiranya is of a sickly disposition and let him go to Dhankuta. Sanu Raja (General Pratap's pet name) go to Ilam. Rama Shamsher is out on a tour of inspection and we shall find a place for him on his return".

Rudra replied, "I do not think I have done any wrong, your Highness." And Juddha rejoined, "I never said that I had anything against you but one or two of your sons were showing off and making all kinds of pretences." Rudra said at the end with emotion, "If you feel threatened like Ranoddip, send me away by all means and I shall gladly go." And Juddha responded with a touch of warmth and affection, "I shall see to it that every one of you continues to draw the same salary. Your father Bir had given brother Khadga a salary of 40 thousand rupees a year. But as you have a large family, I shall grant you a salary of 60 thousand rupees right away and I shall increase it in future depending on your work.

Rudra wanted to bow down at Juddha's feet but Juddha put out to him the back of his right hand with a revolver in the fist. Pratap and others also touched their head at the same hand and left the hall. As Rudra was being driven away in a car, his cousins, Padma, Mohan, Babar and Kaiser saluted him. Rudra's parting words to them were, "Cousins, I had always been true to the salt while working under the Maharaj and I hope you will also remain as loyal and devoted to him as I was." Rudra had earlier entered the main gate of Singha Darbar with a number of cavalry guards riding in front of his car but now the car carrying him was followed by a truck-load of soldiers and headed for the south gate and went out of it." [5]

It is said that Maharaj Juddha had at first invited King Tribhuvan to the meeting on that fateful day at Singha Darbar with a definite purpose in mind. The Maharaj had at one stage thought of openly accusing the 'illegitimate' Ranas in the King's presence of their design to debase the royal family by obtaining the King's consent for the betrothal of Crown Prince Mahendra to an illegitimate daughter and granddaughter of Maharaj Bhim Shamsher. Juddha had second thoughts after a meeting with the King in private and had him merely appear before the assembled Ranas prior to the Maharaj's formal announcement of the purge without any reference to the above-mentioned accusation. Juddha probably thought that even the King's casual appearance on the occasion would help to create the impression that the

Maharaj had also obtained the royal consent for the purge and also that the King had disapproved of the matrimonial proposals for his son previously endorsed by him. The 'legitimate' Ranas sought to make political capital out of the Crown Prince's betrothal for propaganda purposes. This is borne out by the following excerpt from the British envoy's note on the subject:

> The betrothal of the Crown Prince to an illegitimate daughter and granddaughter of the late Maharaja (Bhim Shamsher) was given prominence by the Nepal Government as the decisive factor in the upheaval, but the real cause, as already explained, was undoubtedly the realisation of the ruling family of their danger.[6]

The 1934 purge of a section of the Ranas did not produce any immediate impact on the internal politics of Nepal, and Juddha was in full control of the situation. The British Indian Government of the day also had reasons to believe that the removal of some of the seniormost Ranas from the roll of succession was not going to make a basic difference to the internal situation in Nepal and therefore passed over this action of the Maharaj as if it were a routine matter. Most of the sons and grandsons of Maharaj Bir and Bhim, who were victims of the purge, went to the different districts and accepted this new assignment quietly. The only one who refused to accept the assignment was General Pratap Shamsher, who was seen by many actually in tears, after Juddha first made his announcement about the purge. Once in India, the General showed signs of being Juddha's most formidable adversary but this was for only a very short time. He met Mahatma Gandhi as a prelude to his preparations for organizing popular opposition to native despotism among the Nepalis in Nepal and India. This caused some concern to the ruling Rana oligarchy before he suddenly died at Darjeeling in August 1934.

This was what the British envoy of the time, Sir Clendon, had to say about the purge:

> "Juddha with the support of the legitimate members of the roll carried out a coup de main directed against the illegitimate party in the Government. The leaders of the political party and in particular H.E. the Commander-in-Chief, Rudra Shamsher, who was heir apparent to the Maharajaship were arrested by a carefully planned plot, in which troops and machine guns were employed, and they

were banned from Kathmandu. They were offered and accepted employment in the outlying provinces of Nepal.

The removal of so highly placed a person as the Commander-in-Chief created a considerable stir but this had died down and for the moment the danger appears to be scotched through the dissemination of disaffected elements to distant parts of the country but is likely to give difficulties to the administration of the future."[7]

True to Daukes's prediction, the long-term results were disastrous for the Rana regime. Some of the rich and influential Ranas who had themselves been victims of the purge joined hands with anti-Rana elements in bringing about the abolition of the age-old system of hereditary prime ministership 17 years after they were purged.

Assessment of the Reformed Roll of Succession

The following extract from the communication of another British Minister, Sir Geoffrey Betham, to his Government presents a true picture of the reformed roll of succession:

"Sir Padma Shamsher is the first on the roll. Next come three sons of Chandra Shamsher, viz. Generals Sir Mohan, Sir Babar and Sir Kaiser, followed by two legitimate sons of the present Prime Minister, i.e., Sir Bahadur Shamsher and General Agni. Agni is a man with no personality, culture, education or any other quality. Then come Singha, Krishna, Shankar and Madan all sons of Chandra, except that between Singha and Krishna come Hari, son of Juddha and Prachanda, son of Fatte Shamsher to whom the remarks applicable to Agni apply equally."[8]

The struggle for power between Juddha's sons and Chandra's sons characterized the remaining 17 years of the Rana regime. Rivalry and tension between them came to the fore after they had successfully combined against Bir's and Bhim's sons.

The relative position and merits of Juddha and his sons on the one hand and Chandra's sons on the other and their mutual jealously and rivalry are clearly brought out in the following comments by Sir Geoffrey himself in another context:

"Generals Mohan, Babar, Kaiser and Krishna (all sons of Chandra) are really far ahead of His Highness in education and culture. I feel sure that the fact that General Bahadur takes such a leading part in the administration irritates the three eldest brothers of the family. This is readily understandable in view of the act of His Highness not reinstating General Sir Kaiser Shamsher (3rd son of Maharaja Chandra) as Foreign Secretary on his return from the mission at the time of the Coronation (The 1937 Coronation of King George VI) and the appointment of General Bahadur to the post for General Kaiser is an exceptionally well-read and cultured man. This has given considerable powers to the latter and the impression one gets is that General Bahadur is running his father and is, in fact, if not in name, the actual ruler of Nepal. This has caused considerable resentment to the Chandra group, who, I feel sure, would not be sorry to see the back of Sir Juddha break."[9]

Later on when the Rana regime was called upon to meet the challenge of the anti-Rana Movement, which enjoyed the backing of the King, the relations between the Juddha and Chandra Shamsher factions of the Rana family had almost reached the breaking point. This was reported by Sir Geoffrey in his communication to the home government:

"I have reported from time to time that the Chandra family would like to see the back of H.H. Juddha and of his son Bahadur Shamsher broken and are only biding their time. I also reported on one occasion (see my endorsement dispatch No. 12, date the 2nd April 1940) that H.H. complained that the subversive would not have reached the present stage had the Generals used their influence to pacify the people. On that occasion Sir Bahadur advised his father to get rid of the Chandra family.

Taking everything into consideration I have reluctantly come to the conclusion that the Chandra family headed by Sir Mohan Shamsher have deliberately done nothing to suppress the agitation against him (Juddha). It may be noted that General Mohan Shamsher is very popular with the army. He frequently distributes largesse amongst the troops.

The object, of course, is obvious. With the departure of Sir Juddha Shamsher from the scene, Sir Padma will assume the reins of office, but will not, I consider, remain long on the gaddi. The power in the country will then pass into the hands of the Chandra family who will retain it from generation to generation. With the aid of the army they will be able to suppress any attempts of the people to depose them. They will, I feel sure, pacify the latter by giving them some, though perhaps not much say in the Government."[10]

The first two paragraphs quoted above clearly reflect the situation at the time. With respect to the predictions in the last paragraph, the first one regarding the future of Padma Shamsher, the then Commander-in-Chief, came literally true but the second about the prospects of the Chandra family proved to be completely off the mark as we shall see in due course.

Juddha's Foreign Policy Initiatives

When Juddha's predecessor Maharaj Chandra Shamsher had, after the conclusion of the 1923 treaty with Great Britain, made the suggestion about having a diplomatic establishment in London, the British Government was not overly enthusiastic about it for several reasons. First, it was convenient and more practical for the British to continue conducting relations with Nepal through the external affairs department of the Government of India in Delhi. Second, the opening of a diplomatic mission by Nepal in London would prompt other powers also to seek diplomatic relations with Nepal and break Britain's monopoly in diplomacy with it. Chandra Shamsher was politely told by the British Government that it would be an unnecessary expenditure for him to open a mission in London because Britain would as usual continue to deal with Nepal through its external affairs department in India.

Maharaj Juddha Shamsher also, like Maharaj Chandra, sought to secure the formal trappings of Nepal's independence as far as circumstances permitted. Arrangements were made with the Indian Government for the use of Nepali stamps, hithertofore valid within Nepal alone, throughout India as well.

Juddha, like his predecessors, had always been highly sensitive to the question of his country's independent status and had wanted Nepal to appear different from the native states of India in every respect. Even before the establishment of Nepal's diplomatic mission in London, Juddha had told some of the British envoys to their face that despite their exalted titles, they still continue to be political officers with the status of Residents in second class states in India. Before the Government of Nepal agreed to the appointment of Colonel Bailey as Minister to Nepal in 1935 it had had considerable correspondence with the British Government. The Government of Nepal wanted to make sure that the colonel would not revert to the Indian Political Department which provided Residents in Indian states because it was Nepal's view that the standing of the ministers reflected the status of the country to which he was accredited and the appointment of India political officers would mean that Nepal was being regarded as being of the same status as an Indian state. In the course of correspondence the Government of Nepal were informed that the Minister represents His Majesty and His Majesty's Government and not the Government of India, and ceases on appointment to be an official serving under the Government of India; that H.M.G. are constitutionally responsible for India's foreign relations so that all international questions between India and foreign countries including Nepal must be referred to H.M.G. for final decision; and all problems of more than local importance will be dealt with in direct communication between the Secretary of State for Foreign Affairs and the Minister. While the Government of Nepal was assured that Colonel Bailey would not revert to the Political Department, the British Government did not assure the Government of Nepal that the Kathmandu post would not be confined to the Political Department.

Juddha's grievance against having the second-class Indian states' residents as envoys and ministers to Nepal was not removed until after the end of the Rana regime. Yet Juddha himself persisted in airing his grievance on this account as long as he remained the Maharaj Prime Minister. This was what he once said to Sir George A. Falconer:

> "Forgive me when I say that circumstances compel me to remark that for all your Excellency's uniform and in spite of your 17-gun salute you are shown and seem to be no better than a Resident of the second class."

Despite the fact that the 1815 Treaty of Sugauli between Nepal and the United Kingdom provided for the stationing of accredited ministers at each other's courts, it was only 120 years later that the treaty provision was actually implemented. In March 1934, the British monarch approved raising the British post at Kathmandu to that of an envoy extraordinary and minister plenipotentiary and consented to accept the Glorious Order of Rajanya from the King of Nepal. Juddha's eldest son, General Bahadur Shamsher, left Nepal for London in April 1934 as the head of a mission to confer, on behalf of the Nepali King, the highest order of Nepal on King George V, and Bahadur stayed on as Nepal's first Minister Plenipotentiary and Envoy Extraordinary at the court of St. James's from June of the same year. At the same time the status of the political agent or representative of the Government of Nepal in Delhi was raised to that of a Consul General, a permanent Nepal House was constructed there for his office and residence. The motive prompting the Government of Nepal to have its minister stationed in London and the status of the British envoy in Kathmandu accordingly raised was its concern about its prestige and its desire to obtain recognition of equal status with other countries.

This was what Sir Clendon, the British envoy in Kathmandu at the time, wrote about General Bahadur's historic mission to the United Kingdom:

> "The Nepali mission is the third visit to England since a British representative was first appointed in Nepal in 1802, but unlike the former mission, marks the opening of a new policy in that, for the first time in her history Nepal will retain a representative at a European Court. This is in accordance with the old treaty of Sugauli 1815, to which however, effect had never been given."[11]

Owing to changing times, Maharaj Juddha found it easier than his predecessors to diversify Nepal's official contacts with other major powers in the world as well. In the mid-1930s Italian, French, Chinese and other missions were vying with one another in conferring suitable honours on the Maharaj on behalf of their Governments. Though the British Government was naturally inclined to view these overtures as an eventual threat to its monopoly in diplomacy with Nepal, it did not discourage them because Britain was by then more or less reconciled to the emerging situation in India.

The Nepali side, in its turn, in view of the British offer of provincial self-government to India by 1935, was very much concerned about defining its relations with British India in such a way as to maintain and doubly ensure its independent and sovereign status in future. Besides, the Rana government was also, for their own selfish reasons, interested in insulating the people of Nepal from the influence of the democratic movement in India as far as possible.

The following comments of the British envoy, Sir Clendon, reflects the British perception of Nepal's increasing concern about its international status:

> "And the arrival of an Italian Envoy and Minister Plenipoteniary with credentials from the King of Italy further served to emphasise the anomalous character of the status of Nepal. The British representative in Nepal was known as the British Envoy but was not credentialled by the King Emperor.
>
> The point had not escaped the notice of the Nepal government who had long felt that they had not been treated squarely in this deal and nursed a grievance concerning it, which had caused them to regard proposals emanating from us with some suspicion. It had, however, been decided by Sir Chandra that it was not worthwhile taking up the matter unless they were themselves prepared to send a Minister to the Court of St. James's in London, which involved raising the ban on overseas residence which, except on certain rare and exceptional occasions, had been accepted as a principle of Nepalese faith for many years.
>
> But in the light of recent events, and under the influence of the younger Nepal party, the question was not reopened and without in any way attempting to justify Bishnu's caste-breaking example (Chandra Shamsher's sixth son, who had chosen to live in Europe and America in self-imposed exile so that he might take full advantage of his inherited wealth and enjoy the pleasures of modern life), it was pointed out that in the service of the state and with proper regard to caste restrictions, it was possible to take a hand in outside affairs. The Reform deliberations in regard to India had also an undoubted effect on the younger Nepalese generation in this matter who felt that the moment was ripe to define Nepal's position before the advent of a new Indian Constitution (The Government of India Act, 1935), vis-a-vis of whom (sic) unknown complications might arise. With such considerations before them the Nepal government resolved to press immediately for a full recognition of their status and for the appointment of a Nepalese Minister in London."[12] (Information in brackets added.)

Lord Clydesdale's Flight over Mount Everest

Apart from Nepal's exchange of official missions and diplomatic contacts with overseas countries to which we shall presently turn, it may not be out of place here to refer to an instance in which the Nepali Government for the first time seemed to have got over its traditional fears and superstitions about Europeans and permitted an aerial survey of the Everest area: this also marked a slight change in its closed door policy. In April 1933 Lord Clydesdale and his friends had organized a flight over Mount Everest under the auspices of the Houston Expedition. Its project involved crossing eastern Nepal by air from southeast to northwest. As the request for the project enjoyed the backing of the British Indian Government, the late Maharaj Bhim Shamsher had sanctioned it subject to certain restrictions with respect to the route and height of flying. Maharaj Juddha rendered it every possible help and also granted its request for a second flight. This expedition was regarded as the greatest flying feat of the year. Lord Clydesdale and his friends, despite a dangerous downward air current, flew over Mount Everest at a height of some 30,000 feet in the face of a gale blowing at a speed of 100 miles per hour.

Foreign Missions to Kathmandu

The Italian mission was the first of the kind to arrive in Nepal during Maharaj Juddha's administration. Professor Giuseppe Tucci, a famous orientalist with specialization in Sanskrit and Tibetan religious, cultural and literary lore, was the first to cable the Nepal Government on 21 March 1933 that Italy had decided to confer an honour on the Maharaj. Within less than a month an official communication to the same effect was received by the Government of Nepal from the Italian Consulate in Calcutta. Subsequently the Italian mission consisting of Consul General Dr. Gino Scarpa and his assistant Dr. Domenicone, along with a Bengali photo-grapher and two servants, arrived in Kathmandu on 4 May to invest the Maharaj with the Order of S.S. Maurizio and Lazzaro (Ordine deil Santi Maurizo e Lazzaro).

The Maharaj was honoured for the statesmanlike qualities said to have been shown by him in leading Nepal to greatness and a higher position in the world and also for his assistance to Professor Tucci in his researches and through him to the Royal Italian Academy. The insignia was presented to the Maharaja at his Jawalakhel residence with the following comments:

> "The present and the modern thought have their starting point in the Renaissance of Italy. Mazzini called back Europe from the path of individualism and materialism into which it had fallen after the French and Industrial Revolutions. Mussolini is continuing the mission of Mazzini.
>
> Nepal is the depository of the most glorious and vital traditions of India – the tradition of the great Hindu Kingdoms, and the tradition of the three *darshanas* which form the very soul of Indian culture are among the highest spiritual productions of humanity I mean, the Vedic, the Tantric and the Buddhist.
>
> Tradition when not creative may become a burden and a handicap, but it is, at the same time, the very foundation where a nation can renew itself, it is the vital seed which, when the old tree decays and dies, produces the new tree.
>
> Vedic and Tantric knowledge is, therefore, today not only of scientific and historic importance, but is also the source wherefrom India will derive her inspiration and guidance. Not only *Shastras* and *Sadhanas* are of value, which by giving an aim to education and culture, will make people able to face boldly the reality of life and the hard problems of modern existence.
>
> When Italy after centuries of division became united, she remained for a period of three-fourths of a century, uncertain without self-confidence, till a man of destiny showed to her the path which was hers and led her with a firm hand to accomplish the mission she has in the world.
>
> In no other period of our history, perhaps, so vivid has been the vision of the past and at the same time so prominent the consideration of modern needs, so dominant the prestige of tradition and so radical and dynamic the policy of the government at the elimination of all forms and institutions which had become dead or had remained unassimilated and were killing the spirit.
>
> It is very fortunate for your country to have, as a ruler, a man who is in the same way, conscious of modern necessities, who feels the glorious ambition to prepare his country for a historic mission, who in spite of the short period of the rule, has already carried out important reforms preliminary to broader and more audacious ones in future."[13]

After paying a glowing tribute to the contributions of the Roman and the Hindu cultural traditions to the world and emphasizing their importance as a source of inspiration enabling man to face the problems of modern times, the Consul-General also complimented Maharaj Juddha Shamsher as Nepal's man of destiny leading Nepal along the same line as those on which Mussolini was guiding Italy.

The Italian Consul General's remarks have been reproduced at length to provide a concrete example of the approach of the Fascist countries to the eastern world and that of their style of diplomacy and manner of speaking before and during World War II. The emphasis on national and cultural tradition as a source of inspiration in meeting the challenge of modern times was intended to gain the willing support and sympathy of the autocratic regimes in the East, who prided themselves on their traditional glory as opposed to democratic trends. The Italian Consul General's speech was much to the liking of the Rana rulers. It echoed their own cherished view of the role of the man of destiny in enhancing the glory of the nation by drawing inspiration from its past tradition and culture, as distinct from the modern concept of democratic mobilization on the basis of every citizen's individual freedom and dignity. The reference to Mazzini's alleged role in turning Europe back from the path of individualism and materialism shown by the French and Industrial Revolutions must have also struck a sympathetic cord in the hearts of the Ranas and their henchmen. Concrete proof of the success of the Italian mission was that several photographs of the Duce appeared on the walls of the drawing rooms of the Ranas and their courtiers even before the Consul General and his party left Nepal.

The Italian Consul General's remarks also contained a thinly veiled suggestion to the Maharaj that he should set an example to the rest of India in revitalizing the common religious and cultural tradition in such a way as to meet the challenge of modern times effectively as Italy under Mussolini had done. But it may be pointed out here that the potentiality of Nepal as the only independent country in inspiring and fostering an anti-Britain movement in the subcontinent along the revivalist lines was exaggerated and misconstrued not only by the Fascist powers but also by other interested parties in utter disregard of past experience and the reality of the situation. These overtures from different sources flattered the vanity of the rulers of Nepal, who even encouraged them as long as it did not cost them to do so. The Italian mission, the first of the kind from a European country other than Britain, gave much satisfaction to Nepalis who had long been highly sensitive to the question of foreign recognition of their independence and sovereignty and the richness of their religious and cultural heritage. But when it came to the crunch, the powers-that-be in Nepal had always sided with the paramount power in India for geopolitical, economic and other considerations.

The day after the Maharaj was presented with the insignia of the Italian order, the Consul General was also granted a public audience by the King himself in a formal Darbar at the Hanuman Dhoka Palace. After the routine exchange of *pan* (betel leaves with nuts and paste of catechu and lime) and *attar* (perfume), the Maharaj presented the visiting Consul General to His Majesty, the King who expressed his pleasure at the fact that the Italian Government had conferred a high honour on the Maharaj.

Another Darbar was held at the official residence of the Maharaj, Singha Darbar, the same day at 4.30 p.m. On this occasion, the Maharaj invested the Italian Consul General with the honorary order of Pradipta Manyabar Tara (The Refulgent Star of Nepal). At a dinner given by the Maharaj in honour of the Italian Consul General at which none of the Nepalis present drank or ate, the Maharaj's eldest son, General Bahadur Shamsher, proposed a toast to the health and happiness of His Majesty King Victor Emmanuel of Italy. The Maharaj's gift for the Duce consisted of a *Khukri* in a leather scabbard mounted with gold filigree work and a sword in a gold-mounted velvet scabbard. The Consul General and his assistant were also given presents as mementos of the Maharaj's goodwill. General Bahadur Shamsher subsequently led a mission to Italy later in the year to confer the highest Nepali honour on the King of Italy on behalf of the King of Nepal.

The French Mission

Like Professor Giuseppe Tucci of Italy, Professor Sylvain Levi, an internationally known French orientalist reputed for his studies in Buddhism, had first visited Nepal at the turn of the century and several times since, spending a considerable length of time in remote parts of the country. He was assisted by the Nepali Government in his researches in Buddhism and also in ancient and medieval Nepali history and culture. These two European scholars had in their own way played a part in getting their Government interested in cultivating relations with Nepal because they were fully aware of Nepal's status as an independent country and were anxious to promote its wider recognition. Their initiative was most welcome to the Maharaj, who was as much interested in getting foreign decorations as in having first-hand contact and acquaintance with the representatives of countries other than Great Britain.

Though the French Consul General in Calcutta, M. Danjou, had himself visited Nepal the previous year and met the Maharaj, yet a diplomatic mission led by him to invest the Maharaj with the insignia of the Grand Croix de la Legion d' Honneur (The Grand Cross of the Legion of Honour) followed the Italian mission within less than three weeks. The second mission with another member, M. Vissiere, arrived at Kathmandu on 23 May 1934.

The investiture ceremony was held this time on the *Tundikhel*, the parade ground, where a spacious shamiana or marquee was pitched for the purpose. Flags and buntings were displayed all over the parade ground, lending a festive air to the occasion and adding to its colour and pageantry. The French Consul General drove to the parade ground in a carriage-and-four escorted by a Nepali General and a protocol officer, and as the party left the guest house, a salute of 21 guns was fired. When the Consul General reached the parade ground, he was received by the Maharaj, who himself escorted him to the dais beneath the marquee.

While presenting the insignia of the Grand Cross of the Legion of Honour to the Maharaj, M. Danjou made a speech in which he touched briefly on Nepal's military assistance to the Allied Powers during World War I and the gallantry of the Gorkhas. He spoke of France's friendly feeling for Nepal, and of the highest esteem in which the Maharaj was held by the President of the French Republic. The French Consul General also expressed France's appreciation of General Kaiser Shamsher's contribution to the cause of learning and research and invested him also with a Grand Officer de la Legion d' Honneur. After the ceremony was over, a guard of honour was presented to the Maharaj and a salute of 19 guns was fired. The French national anthem was played and a salute of 21 guns was fired in honour of the French President.

The Maharaj, while appreciating the French token of friendship, referred to the friendly feeling between Nepal and France since World War I during which soldiers of the two countries fought shoulder to shoulder in many a battle. The Maharaj spoke of Nepal's assistance to Professor Sylvain Levi in his research on the ancient and medieval history and culture of Nepal and also expressed his satisfaction at the French recognition of his nephew General Kaiser's contribution to the cause of learning. The Maharaj was followed by Commander-in-Chief General Padma Shamsher who also spoke on the occasion. He lauded the Maharaj's administrative ability and achievement on the domestic front and in foreign policy. At the end, he thanked the French President for honouring Nepal by conferring an order on the executive head of its Government and also for showing appreciation of General Kaiser's assistance in furthering learned researches.

M. Danjou and M. Vissiere were invested with the insignia of the Order of Refulgent Star of Nepal and the Order of the Puissant Right Hand of Gorkha respectively at a ceremony also held beneath a marquee on the parade ground the following day. After the members of the French mission were presented to the King on 25 May, a dinner was held in their honour at which General Singha proposed a toast to the French President on behalf of the Maharaj. In his speech General Singha suggested that all of them were peacefully assembled in the hall as the concord of peace had replaced the din and bustle of the war that had brought together the sons of Nepal, and Britain and France on the battlefields of France and Flanders.

The Chinese Mission

The republic of China also sent its mission to Kathmandu in June 1934 to confer the military rank of Luh Chuan Shang Chian of the Chinese army on the Maharaj. The mission consisted of Consul General C.P. Liang and his deputy Daniel Lee among others. Beneath a commodious shamiana or marquee put up on the parade ground, the investiture for the Maharaj was held in the midst of great festivity and rejoicing with the Brahmin priests chanting Vedic benedictions. The investiture ceremony was attended by civil and military officers, college and school teachers, doctors, leading traders and merchants. The Consul General, in the course of his statement on the occasion, referred to the age-old friendship between the two countries and religious and cultural exchange between them across the common land frontier over the centuries. He noted that Nepal and China were neighbours and not strangers. At the end he conveyed to the Maharaj the best wishes of the President of the National Government of the Republic of China, Marshal Chiang Kai-Shek, and the Chinese people for his personal happiness and for the welfare and prosperity of the people of Nepal, and the

Consul General also added his own wishes and prayers for the longevity and happiness of the Maharaj. The Chinese Consul General, like his Italian and French counterparts, was invested with the Second-Class Order of the Star of Nepal (Pradipta Manyabar Tara).

Other Delegations

Missions from Belgium and the Netherlands were also received by the Maharaj with usual hospitality in 1935. Belgian Consul General H. Marcel Ulser invested the Maharaj with the Grand Cordon de l'Order de Leopold, the highest Belgian order. In the course of his formal address on the occasion of the Maharaj's investiture, the Belgian Consul General spoke of the memorable assistance extended by Nepal to the Allied Powers during World War I and told the Maharaj how their heroic fight under the leadership of King Albert I and the sacrifice of their lives by many Gorkhas in the battlefield of Flanders for the common cause had become part of history. The Consul General and his colleague, M. Robert Beruck, were also given the Second Class Order of the Star of Nepal and that of the Order of the Right Hand of Gorkha respectively.

The Dutch delegation consisting of Consul General Allard Menes and Vice-Consul Lankeer Petrus Lohames visited Nepal in 1940 to confer on Juddha on behalf of Queen Wilhelmina the Order of the Knighthood of the Netherlands on the Maharaj, an honour he was said to share "with the mightiest sovereigns and heads of states" in other parts of the world. The Dutch Consul General in course of his public statement emphasized the heroic character and the fighting qualities of the freedom-loving Nepalis and also referred to his nation's 80 year-old struggle for its independence and its love of liberty. He said that the love of independence was something which his country and Nepal shared in common. The Maharaj also invested the Consul General and his colleague with the Second Class Order of the Star of Nepal and that of the Right Hand of Gorkha respectively.

The arrival of German mission in Kathmandu in 1937 created a lot of public stir and enthusiasm because Germany by then had emerged as a major power in the world once again. The mission consisted of Count Von Pode-Wils-Durnitz, the Consul General, and Dr. Richter, the Vice-Consul, from the German consulate in Calcutta and its purpose was to confer the Order of the Star of the German Iron Cross on the Maharaj. The investiture for the Maharaj was held this time in the

Gallery Baithak, a spacious reception hall specially built by Maharaj Juddha inside the Singha Darbar compound for holding public receptions. The German delegation also presented the Order of the German Iron Cross to Commander-in-Chief General Padma Shamsher in recognition of his meritorious work at the time of the 1934 earthquake. In his formal statement the Consul General, while assuring the Maharaj of the endeavour of the German Government to promote good relations and friendship between Germany and Nepal, disavowed his country's political interest in this part of the world and stressed the prospects for peaceful cooperation between the two countries in the spheres of trade and spiritual understanding. The Maharaj in his reply paid tribute to the German achievements under the country's leader, Herr Hitler, in the following words:

> "We yield to none in our admiration of the wonderful qualities of head and heart displayed by your great leader, Adolph Hitler, and his inspiring rebuilding of the German nation. Great as he is, he has, after achieving rehabilitation with honour, pledged himself to peace, a consummation devoutly to be wished for, by our traditional friends, the British, and to the safeguarding of the civilisation to which the world owes so much."[14]

Juddha had been very much impressed by what Hitler had accomplished for his defeated nation and initially tended to share the British view about Hitler's peaceful intentions. The Maharaj invested the Consul General and his colleague with the Second Class Order of the Star of Nepal and that of the Right Hand of Gorkha respectively.

In November 1937 an investiture ceremony was held in the Gallery Hall once again to confer the order of Finland on the Maharaj's seniormost wife, the Bada Maharani. The Maharaj himself decorated his wife with the medal, and she received congratulations from all those present for the honour that had been bestowed on her by a foreign power.

All these diplomatic missions to Kathmandu helped to publicize Nepal's independent and sovereign status in the world. Besides, they also had the effect of widening the political horizon of the rulers and the people of Nepal to an extent. Maharaj Juddha was keen to expand Nepal's international relations. At the same time, however, he was fully aware of the political and economic leverage the British in India had on Nepal. He never lost sight of the reality that in vital matters relating to war and peace Nepal could not act independently of Britain.

It was this consideration that led him to help Britain in World War II in the same way as his predecessors Maharaj Jang Bahadur and Maharaj Chandra Shamsher had gone to the aid of Britain in previous times of crisis.

Although Juddha himself was not a little impressed by the meteoric rise of Hitler and Mussolini as world leaders and also admired Japan's spectacular rise as a major world power, his faith in the intrinsic superiority of the western powers in respect of industrial and military potentiality was never shaken even when the allied powers initially suffered a series of reverses in the war. He believed in the ultimate defeat of the Axis Powers despite the doubts shared by the entire Rana family and the court of Nepal. Maharaj Juddha undoubtedly chose to back the right side in the war, but he, like many others, did not foresee the impact of the great awakening brought about by the war throughout the world and particularly in India. Juddha, as we shall see presently, not only failed to cope with the emerging change in the regional and global environment but also created problems for himself and his successors by trying to move against the current of the times.

It was not that the Rana rulers were altogether blind to the political change that was taking place in India. They seemed to go all out to secure British guarantees for the protection of the interests of their country and themselves in view of the implementation of the 1935 Government of India Act which had provided provincial autonomy to India while reserving defence, foreign relations and other vital matters exclusively to the Central Government. But the Ranas were, apart from securing the formal independence of Nepal, mainly interested in obtaining assurance about the future position of the Gorkha regiments and the continuance of payment of annual subsidy to Nepal as a reward for its military assistance to Britain in World War I. But the British guarantees could not possibly have protected them against popular unheavals inside Nepal itself but that was something about which the Rana rulers of Nepal seemed to remain unconcerned till the end.

General Bahadur Shamsher, Nepal's Minister in London, was told by Samuel Hoare under instructions from Sir John Simon in a letter of 20 June 1935 that:

> "When the Government of India Bill (1935) comes into operation, there will still remain complete control by His Majesty's Government in the U.K. in matters concerning Nepal since the Bill provides for the reservation of the spheres of Defence and Foreign

> Affairs to the Governor-General, who in exercising his functions with respect to those subjects, will be under the general control of and comply with such particular directions as he may receive from the Secretary of State for India.
>
> The payment of the annual payment which India makes to the Government of Nepal would of course be a matter fully within the sphere of Foreign Affairs. His Majesty's Government will give most careful consideration, in consultation with the Government of India, to the note on the subject after which they will be in a position to address your government further regarding the points raised."

Assurances were also sought by the Government of Nepal from the British Indian Government at a later stage about the effects of the constitutional developments in India on two main issues: first, the safety of Nepal's boundaries with India in the tarai and, second, the maintenance of the Gorkha regiments in the Indian army. The first point was met by the assurance that no dominion within the British Commonwealth could contemplate aggression against the frontiers of a neighbouring country. The second point was explained as an issue of political importance both to India and Nepal. However, all that the British Government was prepared to say at the moment was that "the military association of Nepal with the British empire in the present war can only reinforce the century-old tradition whereby Nepal has contributed to her own name and the security of the British Commonwealth and India, and we see every reason why at the conclusion of the war further association of the Gorkhas with the Indian army should be established on an enduring basis of that tradition."[15]

Juddha's Historic Visit to India

Juddha was not invited to visit India until two years after he had become Prime Minister. The British Government in India seemed to be watching carefully his foreign policy moves and initiatives. The Consuls General who had visited Nepal to confer honours on him on behalf of their Governments were based in India and must have had prior consultations with the British Indian Government about their missions in Nepal. The British Indian Government in its turn must not have failed to realize the significance of the new Maharaj's attempt to expand his country's relation with other world powers particularly in view of his move to establish Nepal's diplomatic mission in London itself. But

Crown Prince Trailokya Bikram Shah (born 30 November 1847, died 30 March 1878)

Dip Kumari, also known as Bagh Ko Kanchi Maiyan, who was the sister of King Prithvi's mother and married to the King's first cousin, Dhirendra Bikram Shah. She played an important part along with her sister in the 1885 *coup d'etat* on behalf of Dhir Shamsher's sons.

Crown Princess Lalita Rajyalakshmi (Married to Crown Prince Trailokya Bikram Shah in April 1860 and mother of King Prithvi Bir Bikram Shah Dev)

King Prithvi Bir Bikram Shah Dev, father of King Tribhuvan (19 May 1881 - 11 December 1911)

Commander-in-Chief Dhir Shamsher (1882-1884) with his 17 sons and some of his grandsons. Five sons and two grandsons became **Maharaj** Prime Ministers and thus the Dhir Shamsher branch of the Rana family, dominated Nepal for a period of 65 years (1885 through 1950)

Maharaj Bir Shamsher Jang Rana Bahadur
(22 November 1885 - 5 March 1901)

King Prithvi Bir Bikram Shah Dev, sitting on the floor (centre) and leaning against his third queen; with his fourth queen sitting to his left, and his first and second queens sit behind them on two sides of his mother, Dowager Maharani Lalita Rajyalakshmi Devi Shah in the 1890s.

King Prithvi Bir Bikram Shah Dev (centre) and his third and fourth queens with the queens' parents Maharaj Prime Minister Bir Shamsher and his Kancha Bada Maharani, Toph Rajyalakshmi, standing behind them in the 1890s.

Commander-in-Chief Khadga Shamsher Jang Rana Bahadur (22 November 1885 - March 1887)

Maharaj Prime Minister Bir with the Duke of Orleans in the Nepal Tarai in 1888.

1. H.I.H.Archduke Franz Ferdinand of Austria, whose assassination in 1914 at Sarajevo triggered off World War I, on a hunt in the Nepal Tarai (in 1893) with; 2. Lt. Khadga Singh; 3. Col. Keshar Singh Thapa; 4. Captain Prem Shamsher Thapa (son of Keshar Singh); 5. Captain Dilli Bahadur and 6. Major - General H.Wylie, British Resident

Maharaj Prime Minister Dev Shamsher Jang Bahadur Rana (5 March - 27 June 1901)

Lord Curzon, Governor - General and Viceroy of India, with two middle level Nepali officers, Harka Jang Thapa and Jit Bahadur Khatri in Nepali dress to his right and left during a hunt in Morang (Eastern Tarai in April 1901)

Maharaj Prime Minister Chandra Shamsher Jang Bahadur Rana (27 June 1901 - 25 November 1929)

King Prithvi Bir Bikram Shah Dev (left) and General Juddha in 1900s

Maharaj Prime Minister Chandra and his entourage with British guests in England (1908)

Maharaj Prime Minister Chandra Shamsher with King George V in the Nepal Tarai in 1911

King George V with Maharaj Prime Minister Chandra, his sons and other Nepali members of the hunting party (December 1911)

King Tribhuvan's Coronation: Maharaj Chandra on the King's right and C-in-C Bhim on the left (20 February 1913)

Maharaj Prime Minister Chandra Shamsher with the Prince of Wales (Later King Edward VIII) in the Nepal Tarai (December 1921)

The Prince of Wales (Later King Edward VIII with other British and Nepali members of his hunting party in the Nepal Tarai (December 1921)

Queen Lakshmi Divyeshvari (left) with her son King Tribhuvan Bir Bikram Shah Dev and Maharaj Chandra's second wife, Kancha Bada Maharani Bal Kumari Devi

Maharaj Prime Minister Bhim Shamsher Jang Bahadur Rana (25 November 1929 - 1 September 1932)

Maharaj Prime Minister Juddha Shamshe Jang Bahadur Rana (1 September 1932 - 29 November 1945)

King Tribhuvan Bir Bikram Shah Dev (11 December 1911 - 13 March 1955)

Maharaja Juddha playing host to Governor-General Lord Wavell, 1944

Maharaja Prime Minister Padma Shamsher Jang Bahadur Rana (29 November 1945 - 30 April 1948)

Maharaj Padma Shamsher with his aide-de-camp, General Krishna Shamsher (left) and C.-in-C. Mohan Shamsher's son, Major-General Bijya Shamsher, in 1947

Maharaj Prime Minister Mohan Shamsher Jang Bahadur Rana (30 April 1948 - 12 November 1951)

Tanka Prasad Acharya, founder of Nepal Praja Parishad and acting president of Nepali National Congress.

Bishweshwar Prasad Koirala, founder of the Nepali National Congress, one of the leaders of the 1950-51 revolution and Home Minister in the interim Rana-Congress coalition Government.

Major-General Subarna Shamsher Jang Bahadur Rana, one of the top leaders of the Nepali Congress, Commander-in-Chief of its liberation army, Mukti Sena and Finance Minister in the interim Rana-Congress coalition government as one of the Congress members

Dr. Kunwar Indrajit Singh, one of the leaders of the 1950-51 revolution who opposed the Delhi Compromise and fled to China.

King Tribhuvan on the day of his triumphant return from New Delhi (15 February 1951)

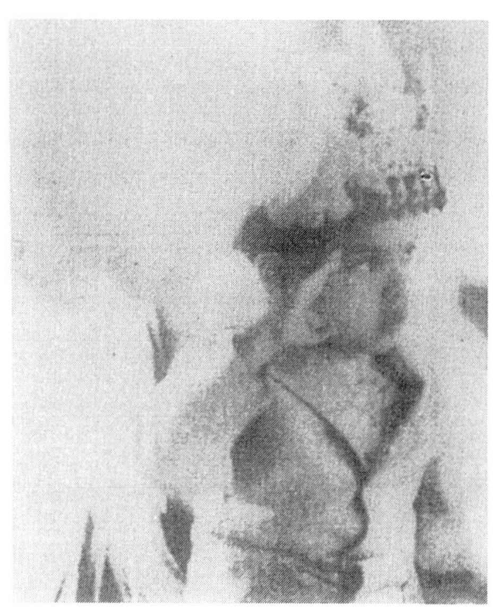

Prince Gyanendra Bikram Shah being crowned king on 7 November 1950

Matrika Prasad Koirala, first commoner Prime Minister of Nepal after the 104-year-old-Rana rule.

King Tribhuvan with some of the members of his first council of ministers headed by a commoner prime minister (from left to right) Assistant Minister Dharma Ratna Yemi, Bhadrakali, Mishra, Narad Muni Thulung, Surya Prasad Upadhyaya Prime Minister Matrika Prasad Koirala, Mahendra Bikram Shah, King Tribhuvan B.B. Shah Dev, Major-General Subarna Shamsher Jang Bahadur Rana, General Kaiser Shamsher Jang Bahadur Rana, Major General Mahabir Shamsher Jang Bahadur Rana.

Crown Prince Mahendra Bir Bikram Shah Dev and Crown Princess Ratna Rajyalakshmi Devi who were married on 10 December 1952.

General Kaiser Shamsher Jang Bahadur Rana, who headed the government of Royal Councillors (14 August 1952 to 15 June 1953) following the collapse of M.P. Koirala's first cabinet.

Major-General Bijaya Shamsher Jang Bahadur Rana, who died as Nepal's ambassador to India in 1953 and had played a key role in the Delhi negotiations culminating in the formation of the interim Rana-Congress coalition cabinet.

King Mahendra Bikram Shah Dev, who ascended the throne on 13 March 1955

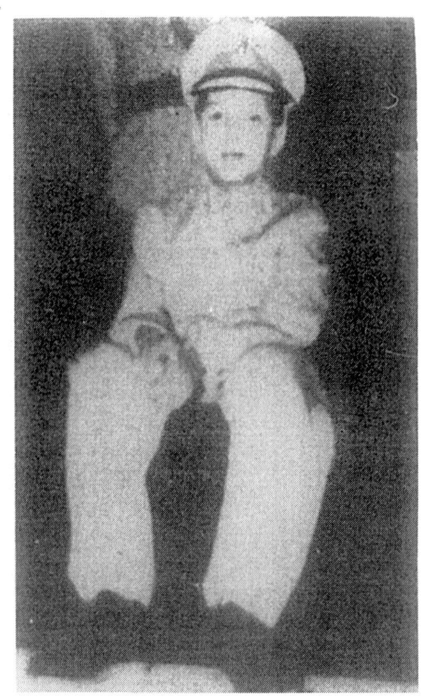

Crown Prince Birendra at the age of nine

with the steady growth of the nationalist movement in India, the British were, ever since the 1920s, more inclined to recognize Nepal as an independent country with a view to using Nepal as a breakwater to the mainstream of the Indian nationalist movement. As long as the Rana rulers of Nepal were indifferent to India's independence struggle, the British Indian Government did not mind their reinforcing Nepal's formal status as an independent country.

Maharaj Juddha Shamsher's visit to Delhi in January 1935 must be viewed in the changed context of his Government's having already appointed a resident minister of its own at the Court of St. James's. Nepal's maintenance of a legation in London did not mean that it was dealing with the British Government entirely through the British foreign office or through the India office in London. Yet the Nepali diplomatic presence in London helped Nepal to pressure the external and political department of the Government of India through the British foreign office and the office of the Secretary of State for India under special circumstances. It must, however, be borne in mind that Britain conducted its relations with Nepal through the external and political department of the Government of India until India became independent in 1947.

Maharaj Juddha very much wanted to go on a pilgrimage to the Dwaraka Dham in Gujarat, and he felt that it would not be advisable for him to pass through Delhi without paying a call on the Viceroy. Even though there was no special reason for the Viceroy to meet Maharaj Juddha, Lord Willingdon invited him to Delhi after he was informed of the Maharaj's pilgrimage plans.

The Maharaj left Kathmandu on 16 January 1935. His party consisted of 143 persons including 110 attendants. Among the important persons in the Maharaj's suite were Senior Commanding General Mohan Shamsher, Commanding General Kaiser Shamsher, General Surya Shamsher, General Narayan Shamsher, Bada Kazi Marichi Man Singh, Kazi Ratna Man Singh and Rajguru Pandit Hem Raj Pande. They left Raxaul by a special train on 21 January and after halts at Jaunpur and Agra reached Ballabhgarh, a wayside station 22 miles away from Delhi, on 23 January. The Maharaj was received at the station by the Commander-in-Chief of India and the Nepali Consul General and driven to a camp specially set up for him and guarded by units of Gorkha regiments.

On 24 January at 10 a.m. the Maharaj was escorted by Sir Philip Chetwode, the Commander-in-Chief, and his A.D.C. to see the manoeuvres of the Eastern Command. The manoeuvres were held in the midst of persistent rains and the Maharaj was impressed by them. On the morning of 25 January the Maharaj was taken to Delhi by a special train decorated with Nepali flags and was received there with a salute of 19 guns and the playing of Nepal's national anthem. The Maharaj was taken from the station to the Nizam's Hyderabad House in a viceregal carriage drawn by four horses. At the entrance to Hyderabad House thousands of people had gathered to extend a hearty welcome to the Maharaj as the de facto ruler of the only independent Hindu kingdom of the world. A 30-member deputation of the Hindu Mahasabha led by no less a person than Pandit Madan Mohan Malaviya and including Pandit Din Dayal, Bhai Parmanand, and a few Hindu Mahasabha members of the Central Assembly, waited upon the Maharaj in the reception hall of Hyderabad House. Pandit Madan Mohan Malaviya, while presenting the address of welcome to the Maharaj on behalf of the Hindu Mahasabha, praised the administration of Nepal which according to him was conducted in accordance with the principles of Hindu religion and politics. He singled out for special mention the establishment of the Nepali legation in London and also referred to the peace and stability that prevailed in the kingdom while at the same time praising the Maharaj's interest in promoting Nepal's trade and industries. The Hindu Mahasabha's interest in Nepal is summed up in the following excerpt from Pandit Malaviya's speech:

> "It is your independent and progressive state which makes the Hindus raise their head with pride even today. You are a protector of Hindu religion and Aryan culture. If there is any place in the world where our ancient culture still survives intact, it is your religiously minded country. It is natural, therefore, that the Hindus should entertain feelings of affection and kinship towards Your Highness's Government and the brave Gorkha nation."[16]

The Maharaj thanked the members of the delegation for their love of his country and asked them to remain firm in their religion.

It may be pointed out here that the Indian National Congress and the Hindu Mahasabha had been at cross purposes with each other in India because the Mahasabha did not at all approve of the Congress's emphasis on secularism. The British Indian Government was also in its own way playing off the Hindu leadership of these organizations against one another. The Mahasabha had always been more pro-British than the Congress and had at one time seriously thought of enlisting Nepal's support for their cause. But the Rana Maharajs though always afraid and suspicious of the Congress leaders' intentions against them, did not go beyond merely flirting with the Hindu Mahasabha just to create an impression that they enjoyed the sympathy of the Hindus in India. The Indian National Congress had nothing to do with Nepali politics or the Rana rulers until the attainment of Indian independence became certain. It was only then that the Congress made known its concern for the cause of democracy in Nepal.

On the very day of his arrival in Delhi the Maharaj was taken to see the military manoeuvres in the afternoon when he happened to meet Lord and Lady Willingdon by chance and exchanged pleasantries with them. Lady Willingdon seemed to have made quite an impression on the Maharaj by saying that as they would not allow her to be present when the Maharaj went to her residence for a formal call on the Viceroy, she would watch the occasion through a hole in the screen.

The Maharaj had quite a busy week in Delhi. On 26 January the Maharaj drove in state to pay a formal call on the Viceroy at his residence in the morning. It was quite a procession in front of which rode two policemen on their horses followed by two troopers of the 19th K.G.O. Lancers. Behind them were four more lancers who held out their lances as if to clear the way. Those who rode in the carriage along with the Maharaj were the British Minister in Nepal, the Military Secretary to the Viceroy, the Under-Secretary of the Political Department and one of the Viceroy's A.D.Cs. In the following carriage were the high-ranking members of the Maharaj's entourage wearing their resplendent uniforms complete with their picturesque headdresses peaked with the plumes of a bird of paradise. The procession must have proved a real spectacle to the spectators who lined both sides of the route.

When the party reached the Viceroy's residence, the Maharaj was received by the Foreign Secretary on behalf of the Viceroy and a procession was formed consisting of the Foreign Secretary, other British Officials and the ranking members of the Maharaj's entourage with the Maharaj himself at the head. When they reached the reception room, the Viceroy rose from his seat and advanced a few steps to receive the Maharaj and offered him a seat on his right. All the members of the Maharaj's entourage were introduced to the Viceroy, and a conversation followed in the course of which the Maharaj chose to pay his compliments to the Vicereine's "wit, hard work and amiable disposition." The Viceroy was apparently pleased and agreed that he had in her a wonderful wife who helped him in all things. After the interview the Maharaj accepted the pan and *attar* (perfume) offered to him by the Viceroy and took his leave. Before the Maharaj left the Viceroy's residence he inspected a guard of honour, and a salute of 19 guns was fired from the Delhi fort in his honour.

The same day at noon the Viceroy drove in a six-horse-drawn carriage to Hyderabad House in order to return the Maharaj's call. The Viceroy was accompanied by the Foreign Secretary, his Private Military Secretary and the Under-Secretary in the Foreign and Political Department, as well as his personal staff. As the Viceroy alighted from his carriage he was received by the Maharaj along with the British Minister in Nepal. The Maharaj conducted the Viceroy to the reception hall and offered him a seat to his right. The Viceroy was presented a guard of honour both on his arrival and departure and a salute of 31 guns was also fired in his honour.

One additional feature of the ceremony in the Maharaj's residence that was in keeping with Nepali practice consisted of the use of *chobdars* or mace-bearers who, like the *naquibs* of Muslim courts in the middle ages, showered in their own tongue praise and benedictions on the dignitaries in a loud voice: "The image of auspiciousness, the Viceroy and the Governor-General of India, may you live long. May auspiciousness always attend the meeting of two great personages who are like the sun and the moon. May they be cheerful! May peace and happiness dwell in their hearts! May friendship and affection (between them) subsist for ever ! Hail Victory! Victory to the Viceroy! Victory to the Maharaj, the very embodiment of piety."

Processions in horse-drawn-carriages through the roads of Calcutta or Delhi were a regular feature of the official visits of the Maharaj Prime Ministers of Nepal. These ceremonial processions were always full of colour and pageant and were talked about long after the visits were over. Though it was a waste of time and effort for both parties involved, the practice was continued till the very end of the British Raj as if it would impart a sense of participation to the common people in the grandiose affairs of state.

In the evening Maharaj Juddha was also invited to the dinner given by the Maharaja of Bikaner in Bikaner House in honour of the Viceroy and Vicereine. After Juddha had been introduced to all the guests present, Lady Willingdon, who was seated next to the Maharaj, entered into a conversation with him. She said that if they had the Maharaj's permission, she and her husband would sometime fly to Nepal, meet him and return to Delhi after having their tea in the British Legation. The Maharaj could not flatly refuse the lady's well-meaning request. He extricated himself from a delicate situation by professing great solicitude for their physical safety and expressing his own unwillingness to have any responsibility should an accident occur by chance. Lady Willingdon did not press her suggestion further. After the European guests had departed, the Maharaj spent some more time with the ruling princes of India reminiscing about the valour and glorious deeds of the Sisodias of Mewar and the Rathors of Bikaner before he returned to Hyderabad House.

The Maharaj was busy during the visit receiving at his residence unofficial visitors and deputations of all kinds in addition to the Government of India officials and members of the consular corps in Delhi.

The All-India Sanatan Dharma Mandali, the Punjab Sanatan Dharma Pratinidhi Sabha, and the New Delhi Sanatan Dharma Sabha held a joint function in honour of the Maharaj, In his address Pandit Madan Mohan Malaviya thanked the Maharaj for protecting Brahmins and cows in accordance with Hindu principles and referred to the services he had rendered to his people during the earthquake.

On 28 January the Indian army held a special march past of 15,000 troops at which the Maharaj took the salute along with Sir Philip Chetwode, the Commander-in-Chief of India. At the end of the march past, the Maharaj in a short speech thanked the Commander-in-Chief for his hospitality and praised the discipline and efficiency of the British Indian army while expressing his pride in Nepal's being united with the British Government in "bonds of indissoluble friendship."

In the evening Field Marshal Sir Philip Chetwode held a reception at his residence and presented Juddha with a general's sword as the Maharaj had recently been given the rank of Honorary Lieutenant-General in the British army. The Maharaj buckled on the sword and expressed his appreciation of the honour bestowed on him.

At the Commander-in-Chief's reception, there occurred an incident of human interest involving the ladies. The Maharaj's ceremonial headdress studded with emeralds and diamonds and surmounted by the plumes of a whole bird of paradise attracted the attention of the ladies present in the ball room and turned out to be the favourite subject of conversation. Some of them approached the Maharaj and expressed their desire to take a closer look at his picturesque headgear. The

Maharaj readily handed his headgear to them and one of the Maharaj's A.D.C.'s, explained the history of some of the precious diamonds and emeralds. Needless to say the ladies were very much impressed by the dazzling splendour of the Maharaj's unique headdress, and one of them, who proved to be more forward than others, said to the Maharaj in jest, "Will Your Highness be pleased to gift your headdress to me as I am so much attracted by it?" The Maharaj's instant reply was, "All right, if you desire to have it, it is yours. I shall get another one." All the ladies were taken aback by the Maharaj's gesture. The lady who had asked for it apologized to the Maharaj afterwards and told him that her request was never meant seriously. When the headdress was being curiously examined by the ladies in another room, the Commander-in-Chief, who saw the Maharaj wearing another ordinary cap, felt disturbed and remonstrated with the ladies by saying that the Maharaj whom he had invited to do honour was dishonoured by them by depriving him of his headdress. The party broke off just before midnight.

On 29 January the Maharaj visited the legislature and spent about an hour in the Viceroy's box watching its proceedings. But the discussions there did not seem to enthuse him. From there he went to see the Red Fort. The Assistant Director-General of Archaeology was on hand to receive him and show him round the place. After the tour, the Maharaj presented the official with a pin of gold as a memento. The day ended with the Maharaj's attendance at a reception for 300 people at the Viceroy's residence where he met the ex-King of Greece and a number of Indian ruling princes along with high officials. The Maharaj was also given a tour of the Viceroy's House by his host and the hostess.

On 30 January the Maharaj received a deputation of the ten Gorkha regiments in the Indian army including their commanding officers. Major-General W.L. Turiss made a speech on behalf of the deputation complimenting His Highness for the qualities of leadership he had shown in providing prompt relief to his earthquake-stricken people and also as the Honorary Colonel of the Gurkha Regiments with a 120-year history and magnificent fighting record in many parts of the world. The Maharaj reciprocated the sentiments of kinship with the Gorkha regiment in a fitting speech and concluded with the assurance that Nepal would always be ready as in the past "to come forward for the defence of India if approached by the British Government."

Before the Maharaj left Delhi, he also attended one of the biggest reviews held in the Delhi cantonment in which 15,000 troops had taken part. The last function in connection with the Eastern Command manoeuvres the Maharaj attended along with the Viceroy, Lady Willingdon and the Commander-in-Chief was a musical band display in aid of charity held on 1 February 1935 at the Irwin Amphitheatre.

In the evening the Maharaj attended an important unofficial function organized by Pandit Madan Mohan Malaviya and his friends in the Talkatora Gardens, New Delhi, as a farewell gesture. This function was also attended by leading Congressmen such as Babu Rajendra Prasad, an ex-president of the Congress, Dr. Ansari and Bhulabhai Desai. In attending this function Maharaj Juddha made a departure from the traditional policy of the Maharaj Prime Ministers of Nepal of having nothing to do with Indian politicians in opposition to the British Government. Juddha's attitude towards the Congress leaders might also have slightly changed in view of the fact that they were likely to come into power in most of the provinces after the constitutional reforms envisaged by the Government of India Act 1935 were implemented.

As the programme of the Maharaj's visit in Delhi was coming to a close, he personally saw to it that the Viceroy, Lady Willingdon, the high Indian Government officials and other distinguished persons were given suitable presents. The Maharaj's presents to the Viceroy consisted of a photograph of the Maharaj in a silver frame, a dagger and a Khukri with a jewelled hilt. Those for Lady Willingdon were a rich variety of articles: besides a photograph of the Maharaj in a silver frame, the gifts included an ivory temple of Buddha, a Chinese tablecloth, a jewellery box which served also as a musical instrument, a flower vase made of the leg of a rhinoceros, a pair of brass lions, a necklace of musk bedecked with diamonds and a carved ivory tusk.

When the Maharaj paid a private call at the Viceroy's residence on 2 February 1935, he took along with him two of his younger sons in compliance with Lady Willingdon's wishes. After saying good-bye to Lord and Lady Willingdon, the Maharaj and his entourage left Delhi in the afternoon for Dwaraka by train.

Exchanges of Visit with Governor-General Linlithgow

As we have covered Juddha's first historic visit to India in some detail, it will not be necessary for us to deal with the routine formalities and ceremonies connected with such visits in future. But before we come to Maharaj Juddha's official visit to Calcutta in 1939 on the invitation of

Lord Linlithgow, let us take a look at the Viceroy's visit to the Nepal tarai for a hunt in 1938 on the invitation of the Maharaj.

Juddha, although known to be an Anglophile, could not possibly think of inviting the Viceroy to the capital because, it was explained, that would place the Viceroy in the embarrassing position of having to pay homage to the Nepali King in the capacity of a high-ranking dignitary governing as a deputy for his sovereign. All the Maharaj could do under the circumstances was to invite Lord and Lady Linlithgow and their daughters to a hunt in the tarai. The hunting camp was pitched at the same site at Thori where King Edward VIII as the Prince of Wales had hunted in 1921. The Viceroy and the party arrived at the border on 3 December 1938 and left Nepal on 11 December 1938. The shoot was a complete success, the total bag being 14 tigers, 3 rhinoceroses and one sloth bear.

In October, the Maharaj was invited by Lord Linlithgow to visit Calcutta as a guest of the British Indian Government in December 1939. The Maharaj reached Howrah on 22 December by a special train and was warmly received by the ranking officers of the Government of India on behalf of the Viceroy. Among the non-official prominent Indian citizens on hand to receive the Maharaj was Dr. Shyama Prasad Mookerjee on behalf of the Hindu Mahasabha. The Maharaj was taken to his residence in the state coach in a procession and a salute of 19 guns was fired in his honour from Fort William.

At a special function held by the Viceroy in Government House, the Maharaj was invested with the Grand Cross of the Most Honourable Order of the Bath (G.C.B) on behalf of the British monarch. The Maharaj thanked the Viceroy in a brief speech befitting the occasion.

The Maharaj inspected a Royal Air Force unit and was also shown different kinds of aerial manoeuvres and exercises. He took a keen interest in watching how a bomb was loaded on a war plane and personally got into it to see the cockpit and the gun turret. The Maharaj also visited the Government ordnance factory.

The Hindu Mahasabha's formal address of welcome to the Maharaj followed more or less the same lines on which he was previously welcomed by it in Delhi in 1935. The Mahasabha's interest in Nepal was thus expressed in a succinct manner:

> While strictly adhering to the highest ideals of Pan Indian Nationalism this Mahasabha is seeking to bring about Hindu

solidarity and Hindu well-being; and in our endeavours to preserve Hindu culture, we hope to receive your Highness's approbation and sympathy.

Juddha replied to the welcome address in Hindi expressing his wish to see Bharatavarsha strong and united and free from friction and conflict based on caste and creed.

The Calcutta Municipal Corporation also held a civic reception in honour of the Maharaj. Its address of welcome mentioned the Maharaj's Indian ancestry and emphasized the fact of Nepal's independence while expressing appreciation of the warmth of hospitality Indian visitors had always received in Nepal.

Among the prominent non-official Indians who called on the Maharaj in Calcutta was the internationally known Bengali poet and Nobel laureate Rabindra Nath Tagore whom the Maharaj warmly thanked for treating his sons with affection and kindness when they were studying at the poet's university in Santiniketan. The Maharaj also took this opportunity to make a cash donation to Vishwa Bharati, the university founded by Tagore.

Maharaj Juddha went to Delhi again in September 1943 to say good-bye to Lord Linlithgow. His purpose in making this informal visit to the Indian capital was to sound the retiring Viceroy and through him the British Government in London on Nepal's hope that it would be rewarded suitably and substantially for its help to the Allied Powers after their victory in the war. The Maharaj also told the Viceroy that he had no specific request to make and would leave everything to the good sense and discretion of the British statesmen. He, however, chose to make it clear to Lord Linlithgow that he was not interested in titles and honours for himself but wanted to have tangible gift which would prove to be an enduring gain for the country.

Like his predecessor Lord Linlithgow, Lord Wavell also enjoyed the hospitality of the Maharaj's shooting camp in the tarai in January 1945. Lord Wavell and his party had an excellent shoot at Jhuwani in Chitaun. Sir Claude Auchinleck, the Commander-in-Chief of India, visited Kathmandu in October 1945 and was treated much in the same way as his predecessors who had visited Kathmandu earlier. Auchinleck, accompanied by Major-General J.G. Bruce, Brigadier Desmond Young, Lieutenant-Colonel Ridgway and two A.D.Cs., arrived in Kathmandu on 24 October and stayed at the British Legation as the guests of the British Minister. King Tribhuvan conferred on Auchinleck the First Class Order of the Star of Nepal and also the rank of General in the Nepal army. Major-General Bruce received the Second Class of the same Order. On 27 October Auchinleck reviewed the 9 regiments comprising the Nepal contingent sent to India and took the salute at the march past on the central parade ground. Auchinleck and his party left Kathmandu on 28 October.

The Anti-Rana Movement

As was hinted earlier, the Rana rulers had chosen to completely ignore the possibility of popular upheaval inside Nepal. Signs of popular discontent were, however, already in evidence. In 1939 handwritten pamphlets were found in circulation sometimes threatening Juddha with death or at other times stating that his days were numbered as he was suffering from leprosy. Articles attacking the Rana regime in the most scathing terms appeared in Indian Hindi periodicals such as *Janata, Naya Hindusthan* and *Agragami* during the 1938-40 period. Following the example of Mahatma Gandhi, who had established in India Rastriya Vidyapiths (Nationalist institutes of education as distinct from the British Indian Government – recognized regular colleges and universities), a number of enterprising youths decided to set up Mahavir School in Kathmandu in 1935-36 with a view to imparting a sense of civic and democratic consciousness to the students. The school was established at the Khimhla Tole mainly, by the efforts of Fatte Bahadur, Chiniyaman, Rameshwar and Anandaman. By May-June 1937 they had drawn up their own syllabus of studies for the school, and Purna Bahadur, Tanka Bilas, Vakpatiraj Joshi, Indra Prasad Pradhan, Siddhi Charan, Surya Bahadur Bharadwaj and others started teaching classes in the school. But 28 teachers of the school were arrested in October 1940 along with those connected with the circulation of revolutionary leaflets in the name of a political organization called Praja Parishad (People's Conference). Chiniyaman, and his elder brother Fatte Bahadur were sentenced to life imprisonment and the former died in prison. Among other teachers Purna Bahadur and Chandra Man Maskay were sentenced to 18 years and Siddhicharan to 12 years in prison. The rest of those connected with the school were fined ten rupees four paisas each.

In 1937-38 another group of twenty-one social workers, consisting of Shukra Raj Joshi, Kedar Man Vyathit, Muralidhar Sharma, Ananda Ram and Shankar Prasad Sharma among others, set up an organization called Nepali Civil Rights Committee. Its members were engaged in creating an awareness of the need for social reforms among the people mainly through writings and discourses on religious literature such as the Gita and the Puranas. Shukra Raj Shastri was arrested in November 1938 for giving a lecture on the Gita and was offered release in 1939 on certain conditions. But he told the Government that even before he could consider its terms for his release, it should apologize for arresting him and sentencing him to 6 years' imprisonment for giving a religious discourse on the Gita at Indrachok. His associates had planned to continue courting arrest by continuing discourses on the Gita, but Ganga Lal, a fiery student at the time, showed up on the spot unannounced and gave a hard-hitting speech for which he was temporarily detained. But the plan Shukra Raj Shastri's colleagues had for courting arrest by giving religious lectures by turns on the same spot came to an end. Most of Shastri's associates along with Ganga Lal were rounded up after the Praja Parishad secret was revealed to the Government notwithstanding the fact that most of them had nothing to do with it.

As early as 1936, a handful of disaffected youths had founded an underground political organization called Nepal Praja Parishad with a view to bringing about the overthrow of the Rana rule. Tanka Prasad Acharya, Dasarath Chand, Dharma Bhakta, Jiv Raj Sharma and Ram Hari Sharma were among its founder members.

By May-June 1940 leaflets condemning the Rana rule in harsh words and blaming it for all the ills of the country were circulated in Kathmandu itself. One of the three pamphlets was addressed exclusively to the youths exhorting them to rise against the Ranas. Maharaj Juddha's sex scandals and misappropriation of public funds and land to meet the increasing needs of his huge family were also the talk of the town, and the rival faction of the Chandra Shamsher family was secretly encouraging a smear campaign against Juddha's personal life.

This was what Sir Geoffrey Betham, British Minister in Nepal, had to say about the seamy side of Juddha's life:

> "There is no doubt that Sir Juddha Shamsher is a naughty old man and his way of life has left much to be desired and for all the number of his illegitimate children are said to have been a legion (sic). A conservative estimate is one hundred sons and daughters spread all over the length and breadth of Nepal. Officially he claims 19 il-

legitimate sons(daughters not mentioned). It has been and still is as far as I am aware his practice to pick up any damsel that takes his wayward fancy and then to return her, with a few rupees clutched in her hand, to her parents or her husband. Naturally this kind of behaviour does not earn him the respect or affection of the masses in Nepal. Like his predecessors, he has since his accession pocketed the whole of the surplus revenue of Nepal and he is now reputed to be an extremely wealthy man though his large family must cost him a pretty penny to support. I understand he supports any illegitimate sons that may be born to him but not many of the daughters. Although Sir Juddha is not peculiar in this respect, times have changed since the practice of pouching as much of the public money as possible by the reigning prime minister was started, and not only the people but also the royal family are complaining. His general universal behaviour has naturally antagonized the priesthood or at least given them a broom with which to beat him. This was not improved by his unfortunate shooting of a cow in the tarai last winter and his refusal to earn absolution by paying the enormous sum demanded by the priest."[17]

The Praja Parishad Affair

Maharaj Juddha Shamsher was called upon to deal with the situation created by the Praja Parishad's activities in Nepal itself at a time when he was busy making hectic preparations for helping the British war effort. Even before World War II actually broke out on 3 September 1939, Juddha had personally taken the initiative in sounding out the British Minister in Kathmandu on Nepal's plan to assist the British in the event of war. He had informed the British Government that Nepal would need at least two months' notice in advance to prepare for sending its troops for garrison duties in India as in World War I. We shall in due course discuss Juddha's contribution to the war effort at some length. But for the present let us concentrate on the internal crisis that confronted Juddha.

Twenty persons were arrested on 18 October 1940 and further arrests continued to be made daily for some time to come. Among the detainees was Tanka Prasad Acharya, who appeared to be the leader of the Nepal Praja Parishad (the Nepal People's Conference); he was picked up at Janakpur in the tarai on 29 October 1940. Seven months previously leaflets in the name of the above organization had been circulated, but it was not until Vakpati Raj Shastri alias Ramji, one of the members of the organization, had chosen to become an informer that the Government of Nepal could find out anything about it or its activities.

After arrests were made on a large scale, the organization was accused of plotting mass-assassination of all the leading members of the ruling Rana family. Every year the ruling Ranas went to the Royal Palace during the Diwali festival to present Nazar (coins) to the King as a mark of their homage.[18] The plot alleged to have been hatched by the Nepal Praja Parishad was to have the King's private cinema hall, where the Ranas were to be invited, blown up while the show was in progress after the King himself had temporarily retired from the hall.

The involvement of King Tribhuvan in the plot presented a serious problem to the Rana Government. The Ranas of course knew that the King was dissatisfied with the treatment he had received at their hands. But none of them including Maharaj Juddha had expected the King to be a party to their assassination. Maharaj Juddha's granddaughter, Indra Rajyalakshmi, had been married to Crown Prince Mahendra only that spring and the wives of three of Chandra Shamsher's sons, Commanding General Kaiser and Generals Singha and Krishna, who were among the prominent Ranas on the roll of succession, were King Tribhuvan's own sisters.

Even the British Minister in Kathmandu, Sir Geoffrey Betham, had at first refused to believe that the King was a party to the plot until he had a chance to see a copy of the intercepted letter written by Maharaj Juddha to his nephew, General Singha, who was Nepal's Minister at the Court of St. James's:

> ". . . and the position relating to the King has been confirmed to me by the Nepali officer attached to the Legation on December 2nd (1940) when he drove with me to Thankote. At the time I wrote the above letter (No. 2/363-C dated 28 November 1940) I could not given credence to the story that His Majesty was a party to the plot to blow up the Ranas, but, as stated above, there apparently was truth in the story, though I am still of opinion that it was much more foredoomed to failure than the "Gun Powder" plot on 5th November 1605.
>
> During the course of my conversations with the Nepalese officer attached to the legation I confirmed that the story reported by me in the above quoted letter was in fact correct and that His

> Majesty and his sons were indeed, if not active, at least passive participants but the Nepalese Government were in a quandary as to what to do with His Majesty the King–banish him to a distant province, imprison him in Nepal or ask the Government of India to take him over.
>
> The most recent information is that the King has been cleared of any participation in the movement. The only reason I can think that this is now said is because the Nepali Government do not know what to do with him for he is definitely antagonistically inclined against the Maharaj, the Ranas and the present regime. He wants to rule as a King, to have a paid and elected, or selected Maharaj with a council and a Treasury which goes on for all time instead of being emptied every time a Maharaj dies."[19]

According to the second report received from the British Indian Intelligence Bureau, Maharaj Juddha had at one stage even thought of replacing King Tribhuvan by his son, Crown Prince Mahendra, who was married to the Maharaj's son's daughter:

> "The present King certainly dislikes the Maharaj. However when late in November (1940) and early in December (1940) there was talk of putting the Crown Prince as King in his father's place, he is said to have refused point blank saying that if his father went he would go too. Rumour had it that Prince Himalaya (Mahendra's brother) was rather pleased that this would mean that his turn might come."[20]

The anti-Rana movement initiated by the Nepal Praja Parishad was definitely a revolutionary movement. Out of the 43 persons who were arrested in 1940, three were hanged, 14 given life sentences, 20 received sentences between 3 and 8 years, and four were banished from the capital. Dharma Bhakta Mathema who gave the King lessons in wrestling was hanged from a tree on the night of 24-25 January 1941 on the road leading to the temple of Pashupatinath. Three nights later Dasarath Chand and Ganga Lal were shot to death on the bank of the Bishnumati river on the western outskirt of Kathmandu near the temple of Sobhabhagavati, and their bodies with bullet marks were left tied to posts till 12.30 p.m. the next day. Subba Purna Narayan Pradhan, who had also been sentenced to death, was spared capital punishment by the Maharaj's peremptory command at the last minute.

Shukra Raj Shastri who had been imprisoned on 26 November 1938 for voicing the demands for civil rights and social reforms through religious lectures on the Gita was at that time in prison serving a 6-year sentence after refusing to accept the Government's terms for release; he too was hanged on the night of 24-25 January 1941. His body was left hanging till 5 p.m. the following afternoon with a placard tied round his neck stating that "such would be the plight of men endeavouring to mislead the people."

Shastri had had nothing to do with the Praja Parishad. He had advocated non-violent methods to gain popular support for civil rights and social reforms. Apart from other considerations, to hang a person who was already in prison on one charge for another offence for which he cannot possibly be held responsible, was, to say the least, the most inhuman and barbaric act of gross injustice. The execution of Shukra Raj Shastri on a vague and general charge which could not stand even for a moment is the blackest spot on Juddha's administrative career and has tarnished his image in history for good.

As early as 4 November 1940, Juddha had given the British Minister, Sir Geoffrey Betham, an inkling of what he was going to do and Betham had warned him against inflicting the death penalty unless murder had been committed. According to the British Minister, several years previously it had been announced to the world that Nepal had abolished capital punishment, and it would now appear as though the Government had backed down from the position it took in the past if it imposed death penalty. The British Minister's other pleas were as follows:

> "I also warned him against degradation of people particularly degradation of a bestial nature and also particularly with people of high caste. I told him that the world of the 20th Century simply would not stand for it. Moreover, I stated the punishments of the description contemplated would be learned of in India where they would be greatly resented by the Hindu community from which His Highness is not excluded but on the contrary he is very much inclined. I repeated my warning in a few words to General Krishna but they have not and will not bear fruit. It is partly because I am slightly of the opinion that these punishments will have greater repercussions inside Nepal and outside it than the revolution itself. The death penalties would have been tolerated, I fancy, had they been carried out with decency either inside the jail or in public and

> had the relatives of the executed men been allowed to take away the corpses to burn them. The bestiality with which the executions were being carried out and the bestiality of the treatment of two Brahmins will, I felt sure, have their repercussions.[21]

The two Brahmins referred to above were Tanka Prasad Acharya, President of the Nepal Praja Parishad, and Ram Hari Sharma, one of its founder members. Both of them, with their heads shaven cross-wise and with piglets dangling on their chest from a rope round their necks, were marched through the streets to the prison, under heavy guards. They were being led by a person of the scavenging caste who drew the attention of the householders and the onlookers by clanging the cymbals as a clerk of the court proclaimed aloud that the two had been deprived of their caste and their religious threads and were thus degraded for their heinous crime.

After the executions had been carried out and the most humiliating treatment had been meted out to the two Brahmins, whose lives had been spared only because of their high caste, the British Minister expressed his opinion about the likely consequences of the these brutal acts in strong terms:

> "It is my considered opinion that the public executions carried out as they have been are a very grave political mistake and His Highness was ill advised to order them. From observations made of reactions of people to the public display of those executed it was apparent that the people of the valley – mainly Newars–although afraid openly to express their feelings were very bitter against the Maharaj for the degradation of fellow Newars and the sullen expression on their faces boded ill towards those responsible for the executions. Large crowds went to view the dead bodies and many were observed surreptitiously to pay respect to them. The refusal of Ganga Lal to appeal for mercy had been secretly applauded and I fear that rather than having the effect of stamping out the movement these gruesome spectacles will have entirely the opposite effects for feelings against His Highness in particular have been heightened and extended. Active agitation may die down for a time, but it is my opinion that it will break out again and will not be easily suppressed. I would not be surprised if desperate attempts are made at some time on the life of His Highness."[22]

It has already been pointed out that the Chandra Shamsher faction of the Rana family, according to the British Minister, was in its own way trying to make things difficult for the Maharaj instead of cooperating with him in handling the situation. Betham wrote to his government about it in this vein:

> "On that occasion he (Juddha) showed heat against me and irritation which savoured to me at the time of the exasperation of a man advised by others, whose advice he could not easily disregard, to act contrary to my advice."[23]

The advice referred to in the above context was certainly that of Chandra's sons.

Popular Resentment against Executions

Though the people were too poor or too ignorant to protest against Juddha's excesses and were even afraid of talking about them except in whispers, two examples of concrete manifestations of popular resentment, which were of course silent, sullen and covert, may be cited.

A placard in Nepali found on 27 January on the tree on which the corpse of the first man to be hanged had been left dangling read as follows:

> "Please carry out the death sentences as soon as possible as the authors of this placard wish to carry out the sentences which they have imposed on those responsible for awarding death and other sentences to their friends."

This was the first visible popular reaction against the executions carried out by the Rana government.

The second instance consisted of an attempt to affront Juddha personally by making an insulting gesture to his statue on the night of 28 January 1941. The British Minister's report on the incident runs as follows:

> "There is a statue of H.H. Juddha in Juddha Road, the main road into Kathmandu City. It is situated close to the Fire Station and also not far from the Nepal Bank. (The statue still stands on the same spot; the roads branching off in four different directions from its pedestal

are now named after the four persons whom Juddha had martyred.) Four men drove to the statue in a closed car. They got out and draped Sari round the statue. They then smeared the Sari in certain places with blood. Further explanation in official and decent correspondence is unnecessary. They then drove away. Some men of the Fire Brigade saw them but have been definitely unable to name them."

The report further adds:

"These two inicdents infuriated the Maharaj but also appears to have to a certain extent broken his heart as it were for he has said that if his people do not realise that he is doing his best then he might as well leave the valley."

It may not be out of place here to refer to the official Rana version of the long-term objective and plan of the Praja Parishad as conveyed to the British Minister by Maharaj Juddha himself. Juddha's account is deliberately tailored to make the Praja Parishad appear merely a Newari venture which was not only anti-Rana but also anti-King and anti-British in its aim and outlook. The Rana version seeks to make political capital out of the passing reference in the Praja Parishad pamphlets to the fact that the outcome of the war might not be favourable to the Ranas and their British allies, and it is wilfully conceived to rally the ignorant and illiterate hill people behind the Rana Government by projecting the Praja Parishad as also anti-King. The following account of Juddha's view about the character and objective of the Praja Parishad which was conveyed to the British Government appears to be a well-concocted attempt at disinformation:

"The plan was essentially and basically the Newar Plan. It had as its objective the breaking of the Rana power and regime either by removal or assassination of the Ranas. They have Jang Bahadur's coup of 1846, the French and the Russian Revolutions as the precedents for action.

The royal family was also to be disposed of in due course and a republic set up.

The story told me by the Nepalese officer attached to the legation on 2 December 1941 of the plan to assassinate as many Ranas as possible by blowing them up in a cinema hall was not news to me as I had already reported this story, vide my letter No. 2/363-G, dated 25 November 1940, although it did not fit in exactly with what the Maharaj had told me on 4 November 1940. He told me that the plan was to be worked out in stages and the coup de grace was not to be given till after the present war is ended. The plan was as follows:

(a) Disaffect the Nepalese contingent in India as being the easiest to disaffect.
(b) Spread insidious propaganda through the provinces so as to disaffect the fighting elements.
(c) Poison the minds of the Nepalese army of 45,000 men.
(d) All the time try and disaffect the Gurkhas in the Indian army.

Then at the end of the war when the newly recruited Gurkha battalions are disbanded and the personnel of them, together with the Nepalese contingent, return to Nepal, breathe disaffection into their hearts by telling them that we have treated them scurvily while the Maharaj and the Ranas have only sent them off as cannon fodder to obtain decorations and honours themselves from the British Government.

It was thought that the plan would succeed and the Ranas would be overthrown by the fighting classes, the Gurkhas and the Newars would get the powers into their hands by filling the lucrative and official posts.

Then a Republic would be formed with all the power in the hands of the Newars."[24]

It was far from true that the Praja Parishad was in any way dominated by the Newars or was seeking to spearhead a narrowly selfish Newari plan of action aimed at establishing a republic against the interests of the King and the hill people with a view to having the key positions occupied by the Newars. As the Praja Parishad had its origin in the Kathmandu Valley which had a large Newari population, and as the Newari community was also widely educated and politically conscious, it was but natural that it had a fair sprinkling of Newari members. However, among its five founders there were only one Newar, three Brahmins and one Thakuri. Among the members there were several Chetris who belonged to military families, though none of them was actually serving in the army.

Again, the pamphlets circulated in the name of the Praja Parishad were sympathetic towards the King in tone and indeed found fault with the Ranas for not treating him properly and for denying him the role that was due to him as the King of the country. The Praja Parishad did not seem to have a long-range plan of action as ascribed to it by the Ranas in the above account. Its founding members were idealistic, educated youths from the bureaucratic and land-based feudal middle and lower middle classes, who were just carried away by the romantic thought of bringing about a revolution. Some of them might have read about the French and Russian revolutions and also about the Kot Massacre, but they were far from being indocrinated and trained revolutionary workers.

Nor were the Praja Parishad leaders in any position of vantage to spread disaffection among the Nepali soldiers of the Indian and Nepali army. The movement was far from being broad-based or organized in a real sense. It depended for its internal and external propaganda mainly on the articles published in some of the Indian periodicals in Hindi such as *Janata*, *Agragami* and *Naya Hindustan*.

In putting together their piece of disinformation partly for the British and partly for popular consumption inside and outside the country, the Ranas had merely projected their own fears and suspicions about the potential threat against their authority. Though the Ranas had no doubt about the involvement of King Tribhuvan and some other members of the Royal family in the Praja Parishad, yet they thought it expedient to win the royalty over to their side gradually by making them feel that the ultimate aim of a popular organization like the Praja Parishad was or had to be anti-King. The Ranas knew better than anybody else that effective opposition to their authority could eventually come from the King who could serve as a rallying centre for unified popular action against the Rana regime.

Once Juddha found himself helpless to do anything against the King and the royal family, even after he had had convincing proof of their involvement in the Praja Parishad activity, he made a determined bid to win them over in every possible way. He started taking the King and his sons to the tarai, on hunts, in winter. He even sent two younger sons of the King to Calcutta in the winter of 1941 accompanied by Juddha's grandson, General Nara Shamsher. After the hunt in the winter of 1944; he sent King Tribhuvan himself to northern India–Puri, Calcutta, Lucknow, Agra and Delhi– on an icognito visit accompanied by Crown Prince Mahendra and General Bahadur Shamsher, Juddha's eldest son. They left the Nepal tarai for India on 20 November 1944 and returned to Kathmandu on 10 December 1944. This was the first time that a Nepali King was allowed to go beyond the frontiers of his own country after Jang Bahadur Rana had come into power.

Juddha further strengthened matrimonial ties with a view to cultivating the royal family. As we have seen one of Juddha's granddaughters was already married to Crown Prince Mahendra on 9 May 1940. Mahendra's two brothers, Princes Himalaya and Basundhara, were married to great granddaughters of Juddha named Princep and Helen in March and June 1945 respectively. These matrimonial ties served the Juddha Shamsher faction of the Rana family not only during the Rana administration but also after the Rana system of hereditary prime ministers was abolished. Both the present King and Queen of Nepal, Birendra and Aishwarya, are themselves Juddha's great grandchildren and both of the present King's brothers have also married the present Queen's sisters. By early 1940 King Tribhuvan had attracted the attention of the British Minister as a strong personality in his own right. This is what Betham wrote about him: "The King does not strike me as being a non-entity and a man lacking in character. He has become a King at the age of 6 and he has been a virtual prisoner in his palace. Since then everything he has said or done has been reported to the Maharaj. The only thing is that at the Crown Prince's wedding on 9 May 1940 when something went wrong with the arrangement and the King happened to be kept waiting, I then saw and heard him rant at the Maharaj, which showed anyhow, he not only realised what his position was as King but was not afraid of saying so to the Maharaj." [25]

About Maharaj Juddha himself, the same British Minister recorded the following judgement: "I cannot altogether agree that the present Maharaj is not a clever man. He is certainly not well-educated and I think he had several advisers who gave him bad advice (on purpose) but in many ways he is astute, quite fearless and can have the expression "Big" attributed to him for there is certainly nothing small about him."[26]

This is how Sir Geoffrey Betham had assessed the future of the anti-Rana movement represented by the Praja Parishad:

> "No one can say whether the anti-Rana movement has been scotched or not but I give it as my personal opinion that it has only been sup-

> pressed for a while and the time is not far distant when the agitation will again break out, but with renewed vigour."[27]

Betham, however, seemed to have a very poor opinion of General Bahadur Shamsher, who played a key role during his father's administration. This was what the British Minister had to say about Bahadur after he returned to Nepal from India in November 1940 after the unearthing of the Praja Parishad plot:

> "It will be all right if Padma or Mohan succeeds but if Bahadur succeeds all will not be well because I do not think I can say the same about Sir Bahadur Shamsher as I consider that he is inclined to be hot headed and unbalanced and have no great opinion of his brain power or personal ability. As far as Nepal is concerned he is cordially disliked and practically friendless. There he would, in my opinion, automatically be useless with the portfolios of friendship in his hand."

Again in his 1940 annual report to his Government, Betham assessed General Bahadur thus:

> "Bahadur is not a courageous man but a complete egoist and takes very much to heart anything directed against himself. Also from a talk H.M.'s minister had with him it is apparent that he is not a courageous man and any threats of personal violence do not leave him, as they do his father, unmoved.
>
> His fears were such that he so far lost control of himself to embark on a tirade against the King and his sons and various members of the Chandra family, whom he referred to as in the 'C' group."

However, it was initially expected of Bahadur, as the eldest son of his father on the roll of succession, to play a more useful and constructive part in shaping the long-term goals and policies of Juddha's administration by acting as a link between his father and Chandra's sons, who were high up on the roll of succession. Even as late as 1935, Sir Clendon Daukes in his communication to the home government had this to say about Bahadur:

> "The present Maharaj is a man of apparent robust health and energy and it may be hoped that another change is not imminent. He is the

last of the old generation but his eldest son, Commanding General Bahadur Shamsher, was brought up and educated with the Chandra family and he therefore constituted a very valuable link between the new generation and his father."

But it did not take Bahadur long to completely belie the above expectations. Bahadur over the years developed an uneasy relationship not only with Chandra's sons but also with his own father, who during the first half of his administration had completely relied on him.

Chandra's son General Kaiser Shamsher and General Bahadur were about the same age and had grown up together. But Kaiser was much more educated and cultured and far abler than Bahadur or any of the other contemporary Ranas for that matter. Juddha, in recognition of Kaiser's qualifications for the job, had initially put him in charge of Nepal's foreign relations. But when General Kaiser went to London to represent Nepal at the coronation of King George VI in 1937, General Bahadur took charge of the foreign office and did not hand it back to Kaiser upon his return to Nepal.

Juddha, however, proved politically shrewder than his son in every respect and sought to give Chandra's sons their due share of responsibility in the administration. Commanding Generals Mohan and Babar, two of Chandra's eldest sons, were assigned major responsibilities in supervising the military and civil services on the domestic front. Chandra's other two younger sons, General Singha and Krishna, were regularly given foreign assignments or else retained as the Maharaj's Hazuria General or the chief of his personal staff during General Bahadur's absence from the country. General Singha served as the head of the Maharaj's personal staff and General Krishna remained in charge of the foreign office when Bahadur was away as Nepal's first Minister at the court of St. James's in London. After Bahadur's return from London, General Krishna Shamsher was appointed Minister in London and held this position until his elder brother General Singha replaced him in 1939. Although General Bahadur Shamsher was appointed first General Officer in command of the entire Nepali contingent of troops sent to India for garrison duties in 1940, Juddha replaced him with General Krishna Shamsher in 1943.

Juddha seemed to enjoy Kaiser's wit and intelligence and was also aware of his intrinsic merit, but the Maharaj probably found him a little too independent and clever. Kaiser had gone on his own to Austria in 1939 for a medical check-up as he was suspected of having throat cancer. He had expected in his heart of hearts that the Maharaj might appoint him as Minister in London to facilitate his treatment. But the Maharaj passed him over and appointed his younger brother General Singha to that position during his absence in Europe. Juddha was reported to be very angry with General Kaiser for applying for an American visa without the Maharaj's prior approval. General Kaiser returned to Nepal disappointed after undertaking a round-the-world trip at his own cost.

Nepal and World War II

Juddha had made a tentative offer of military assistance to the British Government long before World War II had actually broken out and even before the Munich Pact was signed in September 1938. When the Maharaj learnt in the last week of August 1939 from his Minister in London about the likely outbreak of war, he once again conveyed to the British Minister his offer of 8,000 troops for garrison duties in India through General Bahadur Shamsher, Director-General of Foreign Affairs and Bada Kazi Marichi Man Singh, the permanent head of the Nepali foreign office as Principal Private Secretary to the Maharaj. Even before he had been aware of the formal declaration of war, Juddha went to the parade ground on 4 September 1939 for personal inspection of the troops to be sent to India and told the British Minister the same day that the Nepali troops were ready to leave for India whenever required. It was only on the evening of 4 September that the Maharaj was informed of the formal declaration of war between Britain and Germany.

By March 1940 the Nepali army contingent arrived in India. The first Jangi Auxiliary Pioneer Battalion and the Jagannath Auxiliary Pioneer Battalion were the first to leave Kathmandu. Eight battalions of regular Nepali troops, four under the command of Major-General Ekraj Shamsher and four under that of Major-General Brahma Shamsher were sent for garrison duties to Kakul in the North-Western Province and Dehra Dun in U.P. respectively. General Bahadur Shamsher, the Maharaj's eldest son, was put in charge of the entire Nepali contingent as G.O.C.-in-C. and was attached to the Indian army's high command in Delhi.

But as the war progressed, it was agreed to mobilize the Nepali contingent for active duties, and its command was also reorganized. Two brigades commanded by Juddha's sons, Brigadier Nir Shamsher and Brigadier Kiran Shamsher, were stationed in Rawalpindi and Calcutta respectively and General Bahadur continued as G.O.C.-in-C. as before. It was further agreed at the time that while on active duty the Nepali battalions would be attached to the British army like other Indian army battalions. As a result three Nepali battalions, Kali Bahadur, Sher and Mahendra Dal, saw action in the Assam-Burma theatre of war as part of the 14th Army under General Slim.

With the Maharaj's ready consent, the peacetime strength of the Brigade of 20 battalions was doubled. The number of men recruited from Nepal during the course of the war totalled about 160,000. The quality of the recruits from Nepal fell only very slightly, even at the end. This was quite an achievement for a country with a total population of only about 6 million. Nepal suffered a higher percentage of dead and wounded per total population than any other country involved in the war.

The Maharaj further obliged the British Government by permitting the Gorkha units of the British Indian army to go overseas. They were sent to Iraq and Malaya with their divisions. In April 1941 they landed in Basra, some of them proceeding north to Mosul and subsequently to Tehran under General Slim to forestall the advancing Russian army and others moving from Basra to protect the oil wells at Abadan and Ahwaz which were being threatened by the Persians under the instigation of the Axis Powers. In April 1942 the Gorkha units were taken to Cyprus by land and sea routes. By June 1942 Gorkha battalions were being involved one after another in ill-planned military operations in the Western Desert from Gazala to Alamein where they, like all others, underwent immense suffering to no purpose whatsoever.

The Gorkhas also took part in the famous battle of Alamein and were called upon to encounter Germans in the Matmata hills as the 8th Army crossed into Tunisia. From there to Wadi Akarit where Subedar Lal Bahadur Thapa of the 2nd King Edward VII's own Gorkha Rifles showed exemplary valour and capacity for leadership during the Allied attack on Rass Az Zondi feature and won a Victoria Cross. There ensued a period of hand-to-hand fighting between the Gorkhas and the Germans who met on the bare rocks of Garci.

The Gorkhas were fighting shoulder to shoulder with their British and Indian comrades-in-arm at Medjera on a dark night when they smashed the Axis Centre and sent the 7th Armoured Division to capture the Tunis town. From Tunis the Gorkhas proceeded to Italy and Greece in due course.

On the eastern front the Gorkhas had disembarked at Port Swettenham in Malaya in September 1941 and for no fault of theirs they along with others suffered the worst reverses because of the failure of the high command in Malaya to guide them properly. By mid February 1942 the survivors had become prisoners of war.

In January 1942 the Japanese proceeded north to attack Tavoy in Burma and they were engaged by the 16th and 46th Indian Brigades each of which had a Gorkha battalion. The Gorkha battalions gave a very good account of themselves by launching skilful and dashing counterattacks even while retreating. The Gorkhas were involved both in the 'first Arakan' and Wingate's first Chindit Expedition both of which proved futile and also in the general advance of 1944 both in the Assam-Burma and the European theatres of war. The numerous awards of bravery in the field, including no less than ten Victoria crosses, to men of Gorkha regiments of the Indian army are an eloquent testimony to their achievement in World War II. Subedar Lal Bahadur Thapa, Havildar Gaje Ghale, Rifleman Ganju Lama, Nayak Agam Singh Rai, Subedar Netra Bahadur Thapa, Rifleman Lakshman Gurung, Rifleman Tul Bahadur Pun, Rifleman Sher Bahadur, Rifleman Kaman Gurung and Rifleman Bhanubhakta were those who won the Victoria Cross.

But as the war came close to India with the Japanese invasion of Assam in March 1944, three of the regiments of the Nepali contingent in India were also involved in actual fighting. Two of these regiments, Kali Bahadur and Sher, were engaged in checking the onward march of the Japanese towards Delhi. The Mahendra Dal regiment, though initially commissioned to protect the Silchar-Bishanpur track, had had a few encounters with the Japanese army during the siege of Imphal, but after the Burma campaign began to gain its momentum, the Nepali regiment actually marched into that country and pushed ahead against heavy odds. Captain Bal Bahadur and Commander Sailendra Bahadur Mahat of the Mahendra Dal regiment won military crosses in this campaign.

In Nepal itself, Juddha never lost his confidence in the ultimate victory of the Allied Powers notwithstanding the serious reverses they had suffered in the first year of the war. Betham, the British Minister in Kathmandu, stated in the report to his Government on Nepal for the quarter of the year ending 30 September 1940:

> "His Highness's enthusiastic support of Britain's cause remains unabated. He continues to demonstrate his determination to do all in

his power to render whatever help Nepal can give and we owe His Highness a heavy and increasing debt for all he had done, particularly in bolstering up the nervous element in the country and for his assistance in obtaining the additional recruits for the Indian Army."

After successful British resistance to Germany's "blitzkrieg" on England, other senior members of the ruling Rana hierarchy also began to think that the chances of British victory were better than before.

In 1941 an act of indiscipline by a section of the Nepali contingent at Kohat (N.W. Frontier Province) was taken seriously by both the Nepali and the British authorities. Twenty-two ring leaders were sent back to Nepal for disciplinary action against them. Subedar Megh Bahadur was sentenced to death and hanged and one soldier was sentenced to life imprisonment. The remaining 20 received prison sentences varying from 6 to 8 years.

Juddha was in the habit of sending congratulatory messages to Prime Minister Winston Churchill himself whenever and wherever the Allied Powers won worthwhile victories in the course of the war. Churchill's reply to Juddha's congratulatory telegram on the success of the Allied offensive in Egypt in the fall of 1942 paid tribute to the role of the Gorkha units in its success:

> "I have received with much pleasure Your Highness's heartening congratulations on the success of the Allied offensive in Egypt and in other spheres, and your kind references to myself. You will be glad to know that Gurkha troops, those valiant fighters, played their part in the great victory of the Eighth Army in Egypt. Let us pray that these events are but the prelude to yet bigger successes."

In 1942 Nepal itself had to face two problems created by war – that of the refugees from Burma and the effects of the anti-British Quit India movement in India.

Refugees from Burma

The fall of Burma to Japanese forces in March 1942 posed an unprecedented problem to Nepal. By June quite a large number of refugees and evacuees from Burma flooded the Gorkha recruiting depots in India and some of them even entered Nepal. Nepal undertook to shoulder the burden of rehabilitating refugees and evacuees from Burma, who had not completely lost the Nepali orthodox mode of living and religion. But the Nepal Government asked for three months' time to make the necessary arrangements for resettling refugees in Nepal and requested the British Indian authorities to keep them in India until then.

On 3 August a Gorkha evacuee camp was opened at Motihari, which is equidistant from Muzaffarpur and Raxaul. The First Secretary of the British Legation in Kathmandu acted as a temporary commandant assisted by a small civil and medical staff brought from there. The Bazar camp set up at a new market place belonging to the Bettiah Estate and the polo ground camp accommodated 400 and 600 evacuees respectively. The Nepal Government eventually resettled them in the Nepal tarai by providing them with land and building materials such as timber, bamboos and thatch free of charges.

Effect of the Political Unrest in India

The Indian National Congress gave a call for a mass political movement on 8 August 1942 with a view to forcing the British to quit India. By 9 August all the important Congress leaders were rounded up and the party itself was declared illegal. As there was no definite leadership or organization to conduct the movement, sporadic incidents of violence and sabotage occurred on a large scale in different parts of India. According to official sources, more than 60,000 people were taken into custody, 18,000 jailed without trial, 940 lost their lives and 16,030 sustained injuries as a result of police and military firing during the last five months of 1942. Although strong repressive measures adopted by the Government proved effective in the end, there prevailed a state of utter chaos and disorder for the first two weeks after 8 August.

The state of political unrest in India resulted in the complete breakdown of all kinds of communication, railways, posts, telegraphs and road as far as Nepal was concerned. Disturbances proved to be worse in north Bihar and the three eastern districts of the U.P. on which Nepal borders. They virtually led to the blockade of Nepal as the only route for imports to Nepal's capital lay through north Bihar. No wireless transmitting set existed in Nepal nor was there any airfield in Nepal. Under the circumstances it was not possible to get in touch with the outside world or with the Government of India from Nepal.

Maharaj Juddha did not accede to British Minister Betham's request for loaning him one or two battalions of Nepali troops so that the

Minister might with their help clear up Raxaul and put an end to the sabotage of railway lines leading to Raxaul. But the Maharaj permitted Col. Betham to build under his direct supervision a landing strip for Tiger Moth planes near the Simra railway station in the tarai. An east-west runway, 630 yards long and 50 yards wide, was built. Two landing strips were actually prepared and levelled by 25 August 1942 to enable Tiger Moth planes to land, bringing letters from the Governor of Bihar, the General office commanding and Lines of Communication Division, Patna. As the Bihar Government had only two Tiger Moth planes to maintain communication in Bihar, the Governor approached the viceroy for sending an extra plane to keep up communication with Nepal. It was only on 27 August that Lieutenant Falcon arrived at Raxaul with 30 British troops and the first train came to Raxaul on 28 August. The following day Colonel Betham returned to Kathmandu with his purpose accomplished.

But the effects of the political unrest in India were long felt in Nepal. The infiltration of political refugees and fugitives into Nepal across its free and open border with India proved to be a continuing problem despite the most effective cooperation between the border officials of the two governments. On the night of 22 May 1943 an armed party of about 50 Congressites entered Nepal from north Bihar and, after burning some huts and firing indiscriminately, fell upon the Nepali police post at Hanuman Nagar. They killed and wounded the police guards and carried off seven detainees among whom were some of the leading Indian socialists, Jayaprakash Narayan, Dr. Rammanohar Lohia and Achyut Patwardhan, who had gone underground in India to conduct the anti-British movement in the absence of the Congress stalwarts who were in prison. Only one of the seven rescued persons was immediately arrested in India, although the Nepal Government had given the Indian authorities the names of all of them.

The annoyance caused by the armed raid on the Hanuman Nagar police post to free 7 Congress leaders served to drive the Maharaj into action against the continued existence of the Congress workers hiding in Nepali territory. This forced leaders such as Jayaprakash Narayan, whom the British record describes as "whales" to go back to India whereas quite a few "minnows" were still left behind.

Colonel Som Shamsher, the Bada Hakim of Biratnagar, who since May had been placed on special duty for rounding up fugitive political offenders in the districts of Biratnagar and Saptari, came up to Kathmandu about the middle of September with 25 prisoners consisting of

Nepali landlords and others harbouring Jayaprakash Narayan and his party. The Maharaj was reported to have personally questioned the prisoners brought by Colonel Som Shamsher. Among them Krishna Bir Kami and Abdul Miya died in prison and Rameshwar Singh, Chaturanand Singh, Yamuna Prasad Singh, Jaya Mangal Singh, Min Bahadur, Tarini Prasad Singh, Ramji Singh, Bishnu Bhakta, Kisan Dusadh and Nebu Mandal were released after about two and a half years in prison.

By the end of July 1943 only 123 mostly minor Congress fugitives out of the original total of 487 were believed to be still in Nepal. The search for most of them presented immense difficulties as the Bihar police quite naturally could not say where they were in Nepal. However, one or two arrests were made every week. Even some of the wanted persons, who did not come under the purview of treaty offences, were, at the suggestion of the British Minister, surrendered by the Nepali Government as undesirable aliens.

According to Betham's report to his Government "the use of His Highness's discretionary prerogative in extraditing some of these objectionable people has had a salutary effect." When he wrote this in connection with the Congress fugitives, he must have also been thinking of how the Maharaj had earlier in December 1940 agreed to expel from Nepal Dr. Filchner, whose services the Nepal Government had itself requested from the German Government, and his two associates, Dr. Schubert and Herr Hermann, for internment in India even when Nepal itself had never declared war against Germany. It may also be pointed out here that the British before the war had refused to extradite or even arrest Bhed Narayan Shrestha, whose extradition the Rana Government had demanded on the allegation that he had abducted one of the daughters of General Pratap Shamsher and had also written anti-Rana articles published in the Hindi magazine called *Janata*. But after the war, as a quid pro quo for the Rana gesture in extraditing 'objectionable people' from the British point of view, the British Indian Government had extradited Agni Prasad Kharel and his brothers to Nepal and had jailed in India under the defence of India rules some of the prominent Nepalis such as Dilli Raman Regmi, Surya Prasad Upadhyaya, and Rajeshvari Prasad Upadhyaya in Varanasi, Subba Adi Bhakta in Calcutta and Hari Prasad Pradhan, Dharani Dhar Sharma and Surya Bikram Jnawali at Darjeeling. Raja Jaya Prithvi Bahadur Singh of Bajhang was also interned in Bangalore.

Having dealt with some of these side-effects of the war on Nepal and its relationship with British India, let us turn our attention once again to the main trend of the war itself. The victories in 1943 and specially in 1944 brought great satisfaction to Maharaj Juddha, who had unfalteringly supported the Allied cause all through. The Allied successes in Africa and the defeat of the Italians were celebrated in Kathmandu with illumination of public buildings and holidays for licensed gambling as a gesture of popular rejoicing. The British Minister of the time had this to say about the Maharaj's attitude towards the Allied successes in 1944:

> "H.H. The Maharaj, who from the outset has never wavered in his belief of an ultimate British triumph, was greatly cheered by the series of great allied victories during 1944. To those who were pessimistic about allied chances at the beginning of the war and the wisdom of Nepal throwing in its lot with them, the Maharaja was about to say with much personal satisfaction I told you so."

With the tide flowing strongly in favour of the Allies, the year 1945 opened in a very confident atmosphere in Nepal. Because the ultimate defeat of Germany had been apparent for some months previously, the end of the Hitler regime did not seem to cause the same amount of spontaneous jubilation as in the case of the previous Allied victories. Nevertheless there was a feeling of relief that the major enemy had at last been defeated and the event was celebrated with a military parade in the presence of King Tribhuvan himself. As usual there was an exchange of complimentary speeches between the Maharaj and the British Minister at the end of the parade. Feeding the poor, illuminations and the usual licensed gambling completed the show.

The sooner-than-expected collapse of Japan, though it marked the end of the war, seemed to produce even less excitement than the surrender of Germany. This was so perhaps because the Maharaj planned to have a grand victory celebration after the return of his troops to Kathmandu. In spite of this the defeat of Japan was also marked by a parade and illumination of some public buildings.

In Churchill's reply of 13 October 1945 to Juddha's letters of 31 July and 20 August, both of which had apparently reached him after he had lost his office as a result of his party's defeat in the General Elections, the outgoing Prime Minister, while expressing his gratefulness for the Maharaj's appreciation of his work and kindly sentiments towards him, thus paid handsome tribute to the role of the Maharaj and the Gorkhas in the war:

> "No one in Britain will ever forget what your Highness and the heroic Gurkhas have done throughout the war to bring about the downfall of the German and Japanese tyrants and aggressors."

Following the defeat of Germany the Maharaj moved for the return of the Nepali contingent to Nepal. He was anxious to retire from the prime ministership to a life of prayer and meditation and desired the return of the Nepali troops before doing so. Consequently it was agreed that the Nepali contingent should be released and the last of the nine units arrived in Kathmandu in October 1945. All regiments were personally welcomed back by Maharaj Juddha himself and were given a warm reception by the people in general.

The Nepali contingent was allowed to bring back to Nepal its modern standard equipment valued at 330,000 rupees. As a war memorial to the men of the Nepali contingent four life-size plaster statues of Gorkha soldiers in full battle dress were placed on pedestals round the permanent platform at the centre of the parade ground in Kathmandu.

The British Government deemed it appropriate that any recognition of Nepal's war services (as was made after World War I when also Nepal had sent a contingent) should be announced before the retirement of Maharaj Juddha so that he might deservedly claim the credit for the benefits to be conferred on Nepal by virtue of the British award. Thus, on 12 November 1945, prior to the British Minister's announcement about the British Government's recognition of Nepal's war services at a meeting in Singh Darbar, Juddha gave a long address to the assembly in which he recounted the achievements of his Government during his tenure as Prime Minister and thanked those present for loyal services to him. He afterwards distributed farewell gifts of framed photographs and silver boxes to them.

The British Minister at the request of the Maharaj read out to a large assembly at the Singha Darbar a communication addressed to the Maharaj expressing the thanks and appreciation of His Britannic Majesty's Government and the Government of India for Nepal's services. The communication further stated that in recognition of those services the Government of India with the concurrence of the British Government proposed to increase the annual present to Nepal of one million Indian rupees to two million, and further, in deference to Nepal's long-expressed wish, they were prepared to agree to the capitalization of up to fifty per cent of the enhanced annual present to assist the Nepal Government in financing post-war development in the country.

This offer of capitalization of a part of the annual present gave much satisfaction to the Nepal Government. The actual amount was subsequently fixed at 2.5 million rupees. The British Government also took note of Nepal's desire for facilities for industrial development and promised detailed proposals at a later date.

Maharaj Juddha was obviously very satisfied with the recognition of Nepal's war services and asked that his expressions of gratitude be conveyed to the British and the Indian governments. He had reasons to be pleased at the promptness with which recognition of Nepal's war services was made.

To mark the end of the period of his prime ministership during which the Pandits had prophesied ill-luck for him, Maharaj had already on 31 October 1944 performed the supreme Hindu charity of *Tula Dan* by having himself weighed against gold within the precincts of the temple of Pashupati. He tipped the scale 11 stone 10 lb. at a cost of 200 to 300 thousand rupees. Half of the amount was set aside for progressive religious work, one-fourth of it was distributed among Pandits and priests and the remaining one-fourth was divided into one tola (equivalent to 10.2 grams) and half tola pieces of gold and distributed among the poor and the infirm.

Achievements during Juddha's Administration

A little more than a month before his demission from the office of Prime Minister, Juddha, while unveiling the statue of King Tribhuvan on 16 September 1945, listed the achievements during the King's reign and also mentioned three critical problems that Nepal had so far faced--World War I, the Great Earthquake of 1934, and World War II. Some of the achievements he had listed namely, the abolition of slavery and the introduction of technical innovations such as the ropeway, rail and the establishment of the hydroelectric power stations and the arms and ammunition factories in Kathmandu, in part belonged to the period of his half-brother Chandra Shamsher's administration (1901-1929). But the rest of the achievements listed were made during his own tenure of office. These were: the extension of telephonic lines to the eastern districts of Jhapa, Biratnagar, Dhankuta and Saptari; the opening of the Nepal Bank; the establishment of a General Provident Fund scheme for the benefit of civil and military servants; the promulgation of a pension scheme for all Government servants; and the concessions of a rebate of Indian customs duty on goods imported into Nepal from foreign countries. For the first time in the history of Nepal, Nepali currency notes were put into circulation on 16 September 1945. A new railway line from Janakpur to Jaynagar on the Indian side was opened on 19 April 1940. The ropeway was also extended from Matatirtha to the customs office in Kathmandu in Juddha's time.

Juddha also introduced reforms in the civil and military administration and the judicial system. In the field of social reforms, he succeeded in imposing some restrictions on early marriage and discouraged extravagant expenditures on marriage ceremonies. He also reduced the period of ritual mourning from one year to that of 13 days and also sought to do away with the restrictions on dress to be worn during the period of mourning.

Juddha paid attention to both agricultural and industrial development. He set up a board of agriculture to promote agriculture in the country. Foreign agricultural experts were hired by it to provide facilities for watershed management and irrigation in the hills and the plains and to modernize agriculture by introducing improved seeds and implements. Irrigation canals were dug out of the River Bilhul in Saptari, River Manusmara in Rautahat, River Banganga in Khajahani, River Sisiya in Birganj and at Sifale Bas in Syangja. During Juddha's administration irrigation channels in Bhaktapur and at Ichadol and Bansbari were repaired and new irrigation channels were constructed at Lele, Pharping and twelve other villages in the Kathmandu Valley. Two per cent of land taxes collected in the tarai was set aside for expenditure on irrigation, and improved seeds--both locally processed and imported from abroad--were distributed among the farmers. Agricultural technicians were sent to the different areas to teach improved methods of agriculture to the peasants. To meet the shortage caused by war of imported machine-made fabrics, Juddha decided to encourage the production of cloth through cottage industries and also the cultivation of cotton in Nepal itself. The office for the spread of cottage industries set up by the government achieved considerable success in meeting its goal. Beekeeping was encouraged as a home industry. A cow exhibition was held at Jawalakhel in 1934 and the owners of cows of the best breed were handsomely rewarded. An office called Kathmahal Report Adda (Office for report on forests and timber) was set up and with the help of a foreign forestry expert, E.A. Smythies, a plan for the conservation of forests and the prevention of indiscriminate felling of trees was prepared.

Juddha also turned his attention to industrial and commercial development. Electricity, first introduced in Kathmandu in 1912, was extended with the opening of a second hydroelectric plant at Sundarijal in 1933. In 1936 the Nepal industrial board was set up with the Maharaj's eldest son General Bahadur as its chairman and Sardar Gunja Man Singh as its secretary. A new Nepal Company Act was promulgated with a view to encouraging private management and investment in the industrial sphere. As a result, a jute mill, two match factories in Birganj and Biratnagar, a cotton mill at Birganj, the Nepal Plywood and Bobbin Company and the Morang Hydroelectric Supply Company were set up in addition to a few rice mills. Nepal Bank Ltd., the first bank to be established in the country, was opened on 23 October 1937. Two biennial industrial exhibitions were held in 1937 and 1939 to boost the production and sale of indigenously produced cloth, handicrafts, and other goods and commodities along with preserved fruits, fruit juice, jelly, marmalade and pickles.

As long ago as 1934 the Bombay-based National Mining Syndicate and Trading Company had been given licence to work the cobalt mines in Palpa and in the districts of Kavre Palanchok and Sindhu Palchok to the east of the Kathmandu Valley. The Government of Nepal had also obtained before the war the services of German experts through the German Government to conduct a geomagnetic survey of the country. Dr. Filchner and his associates, Dr. Schubert and Herr Hermann, were working in Nepal on this project, until they were compelled to leave the country in December 1940. A.V. Corry, a mining engineer connected with the Metal Reserve Company Ltd. of the U.S.A., visited Kathmandu on 17 November 1944 to examine beryl deposits on behalf of the Himal Mining Syndicate, a company in which some of the members of the Rana family were believed to have interests. The company had applied to the Government of India for Indian import permits and dollar exchange to enable them to import mining machinery from America. H. Wilt and Lieutenant Alfred D. Brown of the U.S. Foreign Economic Administration arrived in Kathmandu in September 1945 to advise the company in mining copper and zinc and to further inspect quartz and beryl deposits.

The Nepali Government also formed a committee to advise the Government on post-war development projects. But according to th British Minister's report to his Government for the year 1944, "outwardly the committee has shown but little activity though it was learned unofficially that the Director General of Industry and Development (Major-General Bijaya Shamsher), who is a member of the committee, submitted a 10-year development plan to H.H. the Maharaj, involving an expenditure of twenty million rupees (one and a half million pound sterling). This would-be progressive Director was afterwards warmly taken to task by his own father (Senior Commanding General Mohan Shamsher) for recommending to the Maharaj so ambitious a plan which he declared Nepal could not possibly afford. As the father is next but one on the roll of succession as Maharaj, his personal interest in the allocation of Nepal's surplus revenue during the next ten years or so is not altogether surprising."

This merely attests to the validity of the following perceptive observation made by charge' d'affaires J. Rodgers of the British legation as long ago as 1938:

> "So long as the present practice continues of Prime Ministers being allowed to recompense themselves with the surplus state revenue after deduction of expenditure there will always remain the temptation for them to economise on expenditure for the public welfare with the result that the progress of the country economically, industrially and socially will continue to be slow. Due to their poverty the people are as easily receptive to insidious Congress propaganda from India which has recently been creeping in."

The Nepal Government was reportedly planning to undertake two post-war projects: (1) telephonic connection between Kathmandu and district headquarters and important towns throughout the country, and (2) a hydroelectric power station on the Trishuli river in the Nagarkot district. But the end result was that their plans came to nothing.

An annual contribution of Rs. 200,000 from the British Indian Government to the post-war military reconstruction funds was used to open two centres in the east and the west where ex-servicemen and their family members could be given training in improved methods of agriculture, animal husbandry and cottage industries. Juddha also contributed to it Rs. 200,000 on his own for village development.

Ever since the beginning of his rule Juddha had been very keen on having an Anglo-Nepali trade convention drawn up. Bada Kazi Marichi Man Singh, the permanent head of the foreign office, as long ago as May 1939 had expressed resentment over the British delay in responding to Nepal's proposal about this convention. Betham wrote to his Government in his report ending 15 May 1939 that "the interview was the most strained that I have experienced since I came to Nepal." Even during his informal visit to Delhi in 1943, Juddha brought up his proposal to enter into a trade convention with the Government of India. Although by treaty and usage Nepal had been able to import seaborne goods free of duty and similarly to export anything which she may have for export, Nepal was not a party to the Barcelona convention of 1921 and therefore wanted to secure freedom of transit and tariff for itself by entering into a trade convention with the Government of the coastal country. The British Indian Government, in its turn, offered Nepal through Sir Allan Lloyd a proposal for a customs union, but Juddha rejected it.

The proposal for having a trade convention with the British Indian Government was steadfastly pursued by Bada Kazi Marichi Man Singh until he died in Kathmandu on 22 October 1945. For the quarter of a century before his death his opinion carried considerable weight in all matters relating to Nepal's foreign relations. He served as a foreign policy adviser to three Rana Maharaj Prime Ministers. His family was called the Munshi Khalak (the foreign office family) as it had been in charge of the foreign office and served as advisors in foreign policy since the 1830s.

Juddha Shamsher sought to introduce a basic reform in the judiciary by separating the judiciary from the executive at the district level. He deprived the Bada Hakims or the chief district officers of their judicial powers and functions which they had traditionally enjoyed. Again, he wanted justice to be dispensed cheaply, expeditiously and in a fair and impartial manner as he had always felt that the common people found the burden of litigation too heavy, cumbersome, expensive and time-consuming.

The translation of a public notice posted by Juddha on his planned judicial reforms and asking for the election of the four members of the court is as follows:

> "The existing courts of justice in Nepal at the time in order of priority are Tallo Adda (court of the first instance), Diwani (Civil),

Fauzdari (Criminal), Sadar Amini and Thana at the capital; in the tarai, the Amini and in the hills, the Adalat. There are appellate courts – Goshwaras in the tarai, Gaundas in the hills and Appeal in the Valley.

Justice is being dealt to the people by these courts, but cases have occurred when one party or the other, consistently losing from the lowest court to the court of appeal, are still not satisfied, would bring his case to the Maharaj as the final court of appeal and justice. On personal enquiry and investigation the Maharaj found that not even one per cent of such cases was justified. He felt that most of his and the Commander-in-Chief's time and efforts had been wasted in hearing these cases whose number had of late greatly increased under these conditions. They could not find time to attend to the other more important state affairs with the result that the people were feeling dissatisfied and discontent.

In the circumstances it is decided to open for the benefit and satisfaction of the public four centres of appeal in the tarai, four centres in the hills and two in the Kathmandu Valley. Over these courts there will be a final court of justice consisting of the following five members: one General to be elected from amongst the generals from the Senior Commanding to the last general on the roll, two members to be elected from among the colonels, kazis and sardars and two members to be elected from among the subbas and mir subbas. The general was to be the head of the court and other four members were to be his subordinates. The decision of the court was to be final, neither the Maharaj nor the Commander-in-Chief having any power over the decision."

A notice containing the above particulars was posted on a small temple near the parade ground. A box was kept below the notice in which the public were requested to put in the voting slips indicating their choice for the members of the above court. If no votes were cast the Maharaj was to appoint members he considered competent to carry out the duties of the court. The box was to be opened on 15 July 1939.

Nothing much, however, came out of the balloting except that it was rumoured for a while that General Bahadur, the Maharaj's eldest son, had received the largest number of the votes that were cast. But this innovative and elective scheme devised by Maharaj Juddha for the highest court of the country proved to be a non-starter because of the indifference and lack of cooperation of other senior members on the roll of succession (mostly Chandra Shamsher's sons) who viewed the scheme as a design to put them in the wrong box. The Maharaj had to go back to the old method of appointing members of the court himself and endorsing the final judgements of the court as before.

Juddha was not a well-educated man himself and was, like his predecessor Chandra Shamsher, said to regard the introduction of English education as the beginning of the end of the Rana regime in Nepal. Yet Juddha made efforts to encourage the publication of books in Nepali through the Nepali Bhasa Prakashini Samiti (lit. Committee for the publication of the Nepali language books) which was also entrusted with the charge of censoring them. Quite a few original books on different subjects and translation of classical literary works from foreign languages in Nepali were published by the Government Publishing Agency and the authors were paid for their writings. The Bhasanuvad Parishad (Council for Translation in Nepali) was established as part of the Government Publishing Agency to get suitable works translated in Nepali through writers employed on a permanent basis. The *Gorkhapatra*, the oldest weekly in the country, was made biweekly on 6 October 1943. Two Nepali literary magazines, *Sharada* and *Udyog*, were published in Nepal for the first time during Juddha's administration.

A new private higher secondary school named after him as Juddhodaya Public High School was allowd to be opened in Kathmandu along with two other private higher secondary schools in the country. A Board was established in Nepal for conducting the School Leaving Certificate examinations and its certificates were recognized by universities all over India.

Balakrishna Sama's Nepali dramas staged by students and other private dramatic performances in Nepali received personal encouragement from Maharaj Juddha who made the New Road City Hall available for the purpose. On 24 May 1943 Juddha established the Juddha National Art Museum to exhibit Nepali works of art and sculpture along with other objects of historical and cultural value. Juddha also financed the construction of the Dhir Dham Temple at Darjeeling to enable the Darjeeling Nepalis to practise their traditional modes of prayer and worship.

In November 1934 a tuberculosis clinic was set up at Tokha in the Kathmandu Valley. In Juddha's time a hospital and a sales dispensary were started at Lalitpur and 40 beds were added to the Bir Hospital. A hospital was set up at Makwanpur as well, and Juddha introduced veterinary treatment for the first time in the country and appointed 21 veterinary doctors at different places.

Juddha's Demission from Office

Juddha was the only Maharaj Prime Minister to relinquish office voluntarily and retire to a life of prayer and meditation. He had toyed with the idea of retirement even since 1938. Then the war came and Juddha had to send Nepali troops to India. After that Juddha began to plead that he would resign his office as soon as the troops sent to India were back in the country.

But what was the real reason behind his retirement? In his farewell speech on the day of his resignation, he made it clear that it was not because of his age or illness or because of the pressure of his nephews on the roll and the friction in his own immediate family, as is sometimes alleged, that he was going to lay down the burden of office. The ostensible reason he gave for his retirement was that as a devout Hindu he wished to make good his next life as well by doing penance when he still had enough physical strength to observe the discipline and austerities of an ascetic's life in the forest (Vanaprastha Dharma).

But his decision to retire was, after all, a political decision. If we examine it in depth against the background of his past life we shall see how faith in religious soothsayers can influence vital decisions of even otherwise strong and stubborn actors on the political stage. Juddha claimed himself to be the only one among Dhir Shamsher's sons to be born of a Rajput mother. This claim of his subtly implied that all his half-brothers who had preceded him as Maharaj Prime Ministers were born of inferior local Khatri-Chhetri mothers--Basnyat and Thapa. He proudly put forward this claim when he, as the Maharaj Prime Minister, unveiled the statue of his mother, Juhar Kumari Devi, at Jawalakhel in Patan.

Though always in robust health after he became the Maharaj, Juddha had been a sickly child of feeble constitution and suffered from chronic dysentery for 7 years until the age of 19. His oldest half-brother Bir Shamsher eventually cured him of it by giving him an Ayurvedic medicine called Rasparpati. Juddha always had gout and was once confined to bed for 9 months at a stretch. Besides this, he met with several accidents in life and effected hairbreadth escapes many a time.

Toward the end of 1927 Juddha as Senior Commanding General was seriously ill. Dr. Waterfield, who was brought from England to treat Maharaj Chandra Shamsher, examined Juddha and gave no hope of recovery. In the last resort local doctors were invited to show their skill with the promise of a suitable reward, but they also proved helpless. At this critical moment a young man, who later on became quite well known as Resunga Prabhu (lit. the lord spiritual of Resunga), entered into Juddha's life and gave him a few marigold petals besprinkled with water to take as medicine. As a result of this, Juddha was miraculously saved, and he gradually regained his health and vitality under the constant care and treatment of a Nepali Ayurvedic physician named Kabiraj Shiva Nath Rimal. Further, this young mendicant friar, whom Juddha apparently owed his life to, had also prophesied that he would become the Maharaj Prime Minister at a particular date. This prophecy also literally came true. No wonder that this religious man enjoyed Juddha's patronage and became his confidant. It is said that he further won Juddha's confidence by making correct predictions in other matters to help him.

In the kind of medieval atmosphere that prevailed in Nepal at the time, the Resunga Prabhu (who was an ordinary Nepali Risal Brahmin to begin with) received a lot of popular attention and attracted the notice of the governing elites in particular. When Juddha announced his plan for relinquishment of his office, it was widely rumoured in the valley that Senior Commanding General Mohan Shamsher on behalf of the Chandra Shamsher branch of the Rana family had bribed the Resunga Prabhu to advise Juddha to resign. But the present writer, because of his interest in decision-making as a student of political science, always had an interest in finding out whether Maharaj Juddha was actually persuaded by the Resunga Prabhu to resign the prime ministership. Just a month or so before the Resunga Prabhu passed away, this writer had a chance to meet him in Kathmandu in 1967. He was told by the Resunga Prabhu personally that he himself had wanted to teach Juddha a lesson by telling him that he was going to die within a year from 1945 because the Maharaj and his favourite wife, Kanchha Maharani, had been reluctant to grant his request in full for funds to meet the growing expenditure of his *ashram*. The Resunga Prabhu was in stitches while answering the writer's question, and the obvious implication was that he had deliberately caused Juddha to suffer the pain and frustration of life for six more years as punishment for not obliging him.

Juddha, like his predecessor Maharaj Chandra Shamsher, attached a lot of importance to testimonials and awards of merit from the British monarch and ministers of the crown. The British Government saw to it that the complimentary messages to Maharaj Juddha reached him before the day set for his demission. The message from Lord Pethick Lawrence, the Secretary of State for India, was delivered to the Maharaj on the morning of 28 November 1945. The same day the message from King George VI to the retiring Maharaj Prime Minister was read out by British Minister Lieutenant-Colonel G.A. Falconer at a ceremonial Darbar in Kathmandu.

The message of King George VI referred to the "undaunted valour" and "the unstinted devotion to be expected of as faithful an ally." It recorded fond recollections of the visit of King George V and King Edward VIII as Prince of Wales for big game shooting in the tarai forests and also contained the King's promise to accept the Maharaj's invitation when he had an opportunity to visit India. It ended with a "most cordial wish for a long life for the enjoyment of the tranquillity which your steadfast labour for Nepal has so well earned."

Ever since Maharaj Juddha Shamsher had made known his desire to retire voluntarily, everybody was anxiously awaiting the day on which he might do so. Finally the long-awaited day arrived. On the morning of 29 November 1945 the Maharaj convened at his official residence, Singha Darbar, an assembly of his ranking nephews and other members of the Rana family, priests and preceptors, high-ranking civilian and military officials, traders and merchants, and other notables to stage the final act of renunciation in a dramatic manner. In a wide-ranging speech the Maharaj summed up the achievements and failures of his 13-year-old administration and also indicated the lines along which reforms might be introduced. It was a lengthy speech which was read by the retiring Maharaj only in parts and the rest was read by Naib Bada-gurujyu Pandit Hem Raj Pande. The speech made a reference to Rajdharma as laid down by ancient sages and emphasized the need to do penance for the attainment of spiritual ends while one was physically and mentally fit. He told the audience that it had been his long-cherished desire to renounce office of his own volition and thanked God for giving him the strength to translate his wish into a reality. All that he wished in the twilight of his life was to retire to the inner recesses of the hills in Nepal itself and spend his days in penance and prayers until such time as his body, reduced to ashes would become part of Nepal's natural elements from which it had sprung. He said all this without betraying the slightest trace of emotion.

He also made it a point to praise every one of his ranking successors including his eldest son Bahadur Shamsher. He reminded the audience of the noble services that his successor-designate Padma Shamsher had rendered during the 1934 earthquake and expressed his satisfaction at being able to entrust the administration of the country to one who enjoyed his complete trust and confidence. But he did warn Padma against being carried away by his predilection for the parliamentary form of government which might not suit the objective conditions of Nepal. At this point the Maharaj quoted Shakespeare and said "uneasy lies the head that wears the crown." Turning to Senior Commanding General Mohan Shamsher, who was next in line of succession after Padma, Juddha asked him in particular to be loyal and faithful to his brother like Bharat. General Bahadur received thanks for his services in the past and also other sons along with him for their filial devotion indicated by their offer to follow their father in his retirement, but they were told to remain in the service of their country as they were not yet old. He expressed the hope that as his successor's favourite deity was Rama, he would be able to usher in an era of Rama Rajya in Nepal. Finally, in a touching gesture of farewell to all present, he asked to be forgiven and forgotten and sought benedictions from the preceptors and the priests and best wishes and prayers from others for the realization of his supreme goal.

Though most of the audience including the Maharaj-to-be broke into tears and sobs as they heard the concluding line of his speech, the retiring Maharaj himself remained calm and dignified. He asked his nephew not to cry but to move forward to wear the headdress of the Maharaj Prime Minister, which he put on Padma Shamsher's head at 1.55 p.m. that day.

Immediately following his resignation, Juddha left Singha Darbar in an open carriage wearing a pale green and gold *safa* (long-flowing turban) through the crowded streets where he was loudly acclaimed. He passed the night at Kalimati, one-and-a-half-mile away from Kathmandu, and left the Valley the following morning on the first stage of his journey to Raxaul. A special train in due course took him from Raxaul to Nautanwa in northern U.P. from where he proceeded by road to his new residence on the bank of the Kali Gandaki at Ridi in the district of Gulmi in western Nepal. After spending a little more than a year at Ridi, he moved his residence to Dehra Dun in Uttar Pradesh in India.

Juddha died in Dehradun on 20 November 1952 at the age of 77, a bitter and frustrated man angry with his successors for the manner in which they had hastened the collapse of the 104-year-old Rana regime. In a letter to one of the former British Ministers, who had served in Nepal during his administration, Juddha bewailed his own lot by saying that it would have been much better for him if he had not lived to see the abolition of the system of hereditary Rana prime ministers, a proud legacy he had himself inherited from his worthy ancestors.

This was what Sir Georges Falconer had heard from Juddha in reply to his letter that he was retiring at the end of April 1951 and had done his best to bring Nepal in line with other countries, particularly India:

> "I understand how kindly you have advised my successors to move with the times and try to get more in step with other countries. I had also written to them to do so, but as they thought themselves learned and over-wise, their pride never allowed them to see things in the real light. It is indeed a great pity that the Rana Regime came to an inglorious end so suddenly. I do not think the Ranas will be able to do anything in the administration of the country. I am sorry to have survived to see these events. I wish the day of my departure had come sooner."

Falconer had the following remark to make on what Juddha had written to him:

> "This comment on his successors by elder-statesman Juddha is illuminating for he himself was a diehard in his day but was wise enough to retire from office at the height of his fame. It seems he has little confidence in the Ranas being able to weather the storm and I am beginning to think he may be right. For the remnants of the family were not pulling together even now. Several seniors have gone 'on leave' to India, probably never to return, like rats leaving a sinking ship."

NOTES

1. Sir Clendon Daukes's secret letter No. 2/147C to the Rt. Hon'ble Sir John Simon dated 15 January 1935.
2. India Office Record L/P&S/12/3036 No. 21/25.
3. Ishwari Prasad, *The Life and Time of Maharaja Juddha Shamsher* (New Delhi: Ashish Publishing House, 1975), p. 80.
4. *Ibid.*, p. 83.

5. Balakrishna Sama, *Mero Kavita Ko Aradhana* (My Devotion to Poetry) (Kathmandu: Sajha Prakashan, 1972), pp. 228-34.
6. *Op. cit.*, Daukes's Secret Letter of 15 January 1935.
7. Sir C. Daukes's note on Nepal 19/29-34 attached as an enclosure to his letter to the Rt. Hon'ble Sir John Simon of 15 January 1935, IOR/L/PS/12/305 21/40.
8. Sir Geoffrey Betham's letter to Sir Olaf Caroe, Secretary to the Government of India, Political Department, of 22 August 1939.
9. Betham's letter to Sir Aubrey Metcalfe, Secretary to the Government of India, External Affairs Department, of 12 July 1939.
10. Betham's letter to Caroe of 28 January 1941 giving the substance of Maharaj Juddha's conversation with him on 26 January 1941.
11. Sir C. Daukes's note on Nepal, *op. cit.*
12. Sir Clendon Daukes's note on Nepal, *op. cit.*
13. Ishwari Prasad, *op. cit.*, pp. 111-12.
14. Ishwari Prasad, *op. cit.*, p. 126.
15. The Government of India to the Secretary of State for India in London on 7 August 1940.
16. Ishwari Prasad, *op. cit.*, p. 136.
17. Sir Geoffrey Betham's letter of 17 August 1939 to Sir Olaf Caroe, Secretary in the External Affairs Division of the Political Department of the Government of India.
18. The Raktapat Mandal (Bloodshed Group) under the direct control and guidance of the King himself was said to have been entrusted with the charge of actually carrying out the plot against the Ranas by blowing up the King's private cinema hall with dynamite or by setting it on fire by means of the use of electrical or explosive devices or by both. The person in immediate charge of the group was Ram Das Khawas, one of the King's confidants or the Navagrahas, the nine planets or satellites as they were called. Others who belonged to it were Ganesh Raj Gorkhali, one Sharma and the driver and the electric mechanics in the Royal household, Marich Man and Katak Bahadur, who were probably included as the performance of the plot required mechanical skill. Chandra Man Saijun, a medical aide in the royal palace, who was also a member of the Praja Parishad, served as the only link between it and the Raktapat Mandal.
19. Sir Geoffrey L. Betham to Sir Olaf Caroe, Secretary to the Government of India in the External Affairs Division of the Political Department in New Delhi. Letter No.2/363-C dated February 1941 on the Anti-Rana Movement in Nepal (IOR/L/PS/12/30/27).
20. *Ibid.*
21. *Op. cit.*, Betham's letter to Caroe of 28 January 1941.
22. *Op. cit.*, Betham to the Secretary to the Government of India in the External Affairs Department, Delhi, dated 7 February 1941 (IOR/L/PS/12/ 30/27).
23. *Ibid.*
24. *Ibid.*
25. *Ibid.*
26. *Ibid.*
27. *Ibid.*

14

Padma Shamsher: The First of Dhir Shamsher's Grandsons to be the Maharaj Prime Minister

With the installation of Padma Shamsher as the Maharaj Prime Minister on 29 November 1945 the position passed from the second generation to the third generation of the Dhir Shamsher branch of the Rana family. Born on 1 January 1883, Padma became the Maharaj Prime Minister at the age of 62. The outgoing Maharaj Juddha no doubt made a generous gesture when he himself put the Maharaj Prime Minister's headgear on his nephew's head. But it is also a fact that the new Maharaj inherited a legacy of problems from his well-meaning uncle.

Juddha Shamsher had been blissfully unaware of the wind of change that was blowing across Asia and the whole world as a result of World War II. Though the critical situation now confronting Nepal was not entirely of Juddha's own making, yet his forcible suppression of even a peaceful movement for civil rights inside the country and his opposition to the Indian independence movement compounded the problems facing his successor.

Furthermore, as Juddha had a huge family of 20 sons and almost as many daughters, he took such an immense sum from the public treasury and requisitioned such a large area of public and private land for his children that his successor Maharaj Prime Minister Padma Shamsher is said to have inherited an empty treasury. In his monthly report to his Government for January 1946, British Minister Sir George A. Falconer had this to say:

> "It is reliably learnt that after Maharaja Juddha's departure the Government Treasury was heavily depleted. This came as some-

thing of a shock to the new Maharaja though he has not openly referred to it."

Again Maharaj Padma inherited a delicate problem of adjudging the claims of Juddha's numerous sons, who had previously been controlled by their father with an iron hand. Before his departure, Juddha promoted to the rank of major-general only some of his sons by his mistresses holding the titles of Maharani and Rani Saheb, though some of his older sons by his non-title-holding concubines had also on the basis of seniority in age and experience justifiably pressed their claims for the same rank. Maharaj Padma was said to have incurred the displeasure of his retired uncle himself by promoting one of the older sons, Dhruba Shamsher, to the rank of major-general in recognition of his claim. Thus, in addition to having to manage the inherent friction between Chandra's sons and Juddha's sons on the roll of succession, Maharaj Padma also found himself in an unenviable position of having to settle claims and counterclaims among Juddha's innumerable sons based on sibling rivalries.

When he became Maharaj Prime Minister, Padma's one serious disadvantage was that he was not at all rich by the Rana standard and also had no brothers of his own to support him. He was the eldest son of Bhim Shamsher, but had been a loner all his life as his father, long before he became Maharaj Prime Minister, had cut him off. He, therefore, had had no share in the wealth his father had acquired as Maharaj, and his wealthy half-brothers, whom Juddha had removed from the roll of succession, were living most of the time outside Nepal.

Thus Maharaj Padma had no choice other than to lean on the Chandra and the Juddha branches of the Shamsher family for carrying on the administration. Fully aware of the inherent weakness of Maharaj Padma's position in the ruling family hierarchy, Chandra's and Juddha's sons wanted to exploit it to the best of their advantage. Maharaj Padma started with General Bahadur Shamsher as his chief personal aide-de-camp or Hazuria General as a gesture of goodwill towards Juddha and also as an expedient device to reinforce his own position vis-a-vis Chandra's sons. But it did not take Chandra's sons long to split General Bahadur from Maharaj Padma whose temperament and political outlook were altogether different from General Bahadur's.

Once the Chandra and the Juddha branches of the family closed their ranks against him, Maharaj Padma was rendered helpless for all practical purposes, though he attempted to enlist the 'support and cooperation of the well-meaning liberal members of the Chandra family such as Commanding General Kaiser Shamsher and General Krishna Shamsher. Kaiser sought to keep himself out of the political arena by having Padma appoint him Ambassador at the Court of St. James's and the first Nepali Minister to the U.S. After Bahadur's resignation, Krishna became Maharaj Padma's chief aide-de-camp, until he was forced by personal circumstances to resign the position in his turn and eventually to leave the country after voluntarily resigning his position on the roll. Like a drowning man proverbially catching at a straw, Padma was briefly tempted to take the help of his own half-brothers and their sons and also that of Bir Shamsher's grandsons such as Lieutenant-General Ekraj Shamsher and his brother Lieutenant-General Sura Shamsher to counter the combined pressure of Chandra's and Juddha's sons, who held top administrative positions at the time. But the Maharaj's efforts in this direction were of no avail in the end.

Though the British ministers and envoys in Kathmandu had nothing against Padma, they consistently felt that he would not last long as the Maharaj Prime Minister. As early as January 1935 Sir Clendon Daukes assessed Padma's position thus:

> "The next Maharaja Apparent is Sir Padma Shamsher, son of the late Bhim Shamsher. He is a good soldier, and has a good record as commander of a Brigade of the Nepali Contingent loaned to the British in World War I, but he plays a lone hand and his position will not be an easy one in Nepal vis-a-vis the powerful Chandra group with whom his family is not in sympathy."[2]

Again, in 1938, Sir Geoffrey Betham, while lightly dimissing the probability of Juddha's resignation at the time, had the following comment to make on the succession in case of that unlikely event:

> "Senior Commanding General Mohan (Head of the Chandra family and second in line of succession) is strongly fancied as his (Juddha's) successor as he is undoubtedly more able, more influential and much richer than H.E. Padma Shamsher, the C.-in-C., who though first in line of succession is comparatively very poor and appears to lack personality."[3]

The Rana regime's failure to adjust itself to post-war changes in the world resulted in its collapse. During the closing year of the 1940s it was confronted with the gravest crisis in its history following the withdrawal of the British from India and the establishment of the communist government in China. At such a critical time the Rana Government proved to be a house divided against itself.

By the time Padma became Maharaj Prime Minister, there had been ominous developments both inside and outside the country. The return of thousands of demobilized Nepali soldiers exposed to modernizing influences abroad but without any future prospects at home posed a threat to internal stability. The Rana Government's immediate fear was that even men and officers of their own ill-paid and poorly maintained army might be disaffected by the returning soldiers' accounts of what they had seen in different parts of the world.

At the same time a cabinet mission sent by the newly elected Labour Government in Britain arrived in India in March 1946 to prepare the way for the transfer of power to Indian hands. It appeared as though India were on the threshold of independence, and the small but vocal group of anti-Rana Nepalis in India felt encouraged for the first time to organize themselves politically. An Ad Hoc Committee of the All-India Nepali National Congress was formed in Varanasi on 31 October 1946 with Subba Devi Prasad Sapkota as its Chairman, Balchandra Sharma as its Vice-President and Krishna Prasad Bhattarai and Gopal Prasad Bhattarai as its General Secretary and Publicity Secretary respectively. In November 1946 D.N. Pradan and D.B. Pariyar formed the All-India Gorkha Congress.

Maharaj Padma was thus called upon to formulate innovative policies to meet these emerging threats to the Rana rule. If only Padma had been able to combine his own political insight with the firm resolve and courage of his predecessor, the Rana regime might have been spared a sudden and abrupt collapse, and a systematic process of liberalization could have been initiated in the larger interests of the country.

With these preliminary observations let us now examine the record of Padma's brief administration chronologically. Immediately after his predecessor Juddha had left Singha Darbar on 29 November 1945, Padma, visibly saddened at his uncle's departure, appeared on an open terrace as the new Maharaj Prime Minister to receive the salute of those assembled on the ground below. In a voice choked with sobs

Padma declared, "I regard myself as the servant of the nation" and then withdrew from public view with tears rolling down his cheeks. Though he retained all his life the epithet of 'the weeping Maharaj' that he had earned that day, yet his dramatic statement, so untypical of a Rana, touched the heart of many Nepalis, who felt that he had come closer to themselves as a relatively poor, neglected and weak Rana, disowned by his own father and deserted by his eldest son.

This was how the British Minister's report to his Government depicted the situation at the commencement of Padma's administration:

> "A man of simple tastes and mode of living, Maharaja Padma has acquired the reputation of wholehearted application to the task in hand and early indications are that he is taking his new responsibility very seriously. Sandwiched between the two more powerful factions of the Rana hierarchy, the wealthy Chandra and Juddha branches, with no brothers and only one of his sons (only Narendra Shamsher was living with him as Padma's eldest son Basanta Shamsher, who was on the roll of succession, had separated himself from his father long ago), Maharaja Padma made very cautious moves in establishing himself in his new office. (Information in brackets supplied.)
>
> Compared with other senior members of the Rana family he is not well off and it was something of a shock to him when he found that about two-thirds of the amount he expected to find in the government treasury went with the Maharaja's demission. However, the country has one big advantage in this Maharaja; he has not a large family to be maintained and enriched from the revenues.
>
> He was with the Nepalese contingent in India during the war of 1914-18 and created a very favourable 'impression' there. He frequently recalls with pride his association with British officers during those years and although he admits he had doubts at the commencement of the last war about the ultimate success of the Allies, there is no doubt that his sentiments are strongly pro-British.
>
> Maharaj Padma on several occasions proclaimed his earnest desire to maintain, and if possible to strengthen, the traditional friendship between the British Commonwealth and Nepal.

Succession Changes

Consequent upon the succession of General Padma as Prime Minister, the following promotions according to the roll of succession were made: Commander-in-Chief General Mohan Shamsher, G.C.I.E., G.B.E., Senior Commanding General Babar Shamsher, G.B.E., K.C.S.I., K.C.I.E., Eastern Commanding General Kaiser Shamsher, G.B.E., Southern Commanding General Sir Bahadur Shamsher, G.B.E., K.C.B., Northern Commanding General Agni Shamsher.

The next three to the Prime Minister on the roll of succession are sons of the late Maharaja Chandra and they are followed by two sons of Juddha. All are between 50 and 60.

As Hazuria General to his father during the greater part of the latter's 29 years of office as Prime Minister, the new Commander-Chief possesses considerable administrative knowledge. He is a very shrewd, reserved and orthodox person wielding much influence."

Padma's Policy Statement

On 10 December 1945 Maharaj Padma addressed a large assembly of officials and the general public on the Central Parade Ground in Kathmandu outlining the policy and aims of his administration. He stressed greater educational facilities as the first need for Nepal's advancement and expressed his intention to open primary schools throughout the country. Hydroelectric development was emphasized as the primary requisite for industrialization, and the audience was told that plans were under preparation for the further development of the ropeway, railway and the road systems in Nepal. Finally, the Maharaj announced increases in the pay of the lower grades of civil and military employees and also provision of rice to the army personnel at subsidized rates.

In his report to his Government Sir George Falconer, the British Minister, commented on the speech thus: "Although the value of his declaration of policy and aims depends upon the speed and extent of effect given to it, it has the merit of avoiding extravagant promises which would have little prospect of fulfilment. It also reflects the sober and well-balanced outlook of the new Maharaj."

Padma's Foreign Policy

Maharaj Padma impressed upon the British Minister his earnest desire to maintain the firm friendship between Nepal and the British Commonwealth. He explained that he was a blunt soldier by training and not a diplomat and stated that there would always be a frank exchange of views between the British Minister and himself.

The following excerpts from the British Minister's report to his Government reflect Maharaj Padma's views on Nepal's relations with India:

> "With regard to Nepal's future relations with India, he had caused his views to be conveyed to certain political leaders in India (he did not say who they were or whether they had sought his views). These views are that while he, the Maharaja, had much sympathy with India's desire for political advancement, he thought that as long as it was of the Dominion Status variety within the British Commonwealth all might be well; but that if India broke off from the connection, she would surely come to grief.
>
> The Maharaja said he desired that His Majesty's Minister should know of this so that if his message to Indian leaders was quoted by them, especially if it was partially quoted or distorted, he would not be misunderstood by the British Government or the Government of India. He was not, he further explained, a partisan of Indian politics but was naturally interested in political developments in the country in so far as they may react on Nepal."

Padma's Faith in the Younger Generation

In January 1946 Major-General Mrigendra was sent to India to study the educational system there. He visited Lucknow, Agra, Delhi and Lahore and came back very much impressed by the prospect for the introduction of Gandhi's 'basic education' as the prototype educational system for Nepal. Though the experiment in 'basic education' was actually launched in Nepal in 1947, it became suspect in the eyes of the Nepali educated elites who viewed it as Mrigendra's device to exploit Gandhi's name and programme to discourage and finally displace the western-style education system which the Ranas did not find conducive to their political interests. Mrigendra's grandfather Chandra Shamsher had sought to use the 'Charkha' (spinning wheel) programme of

Gandhi's movement to counteract popular enthusiasm about sending children to schools where English was taught. Chandra had sent Tulsi Mehar, a young social worker, on a Government stipend to Gandhi's Ashram for training, and encouraged him upon his return to Nepal to organize training centres and workshops in the Kathmandu Valley to teach boys and girls how to spin.

Likewise, in February 1946 Major-General Bijaya Shamsher, Director-General of the Industrial Development Board, was sent to India to visit industrial centres in the U.P. and the Punjab. Major-General Subarna Shamsher, son of Padma's half-brother General Hiranya Shamsher, whom Juddha had removed from the roll of succession, and a young commoner, Purna Bahadur, M.A., who had a degree in statistics and was politically persecuted by the previous administration, were also deputed by the Maharaj to study the industrial centres in South India.

Padma showed in dispatching these young men on study tours that he was very keen on associating the younger generation with policy-making during his administration. As British Minister Falconer points out in this context in his report to his Government for February 1946, "he (Padma) had greater confidence in the younger generation than Maharaja Juddha or at least he is prepared to give them better chance to prove their worth to Nepal."

A conference of the Zamindars of the tarai was convened by Maharaj Padma in March 1946 so that they might give suggestions for improving conditions in the tarai. As that region was more open and vulnerable to political influences from India, the Rana Government wanted to ensure stability in southern Nepal by securing the support and cooperation of the Zamindars, whose vested interest lay in backing the *status quo* in Nepal.

Though Padma believed in cultivating friendly relations with Indian Congress leaders, more than any other senior members of the Rana family did, yet he was equally interested in expanding Nepal's relations with other powers in the world so as to protect Nepal against India's high-handedness. The Rana Government was inclined to believe that the growing instability and the general breakdown of law and order might prevent the transfer of authority to the Indian Congress. Even though this belief of theirs was in a way substantiated by the riots in August 1946 following the Muslim League's call for direct action, Viceroy Wavell's invitation to Nehru the same month to form an interim government must have made the Ranas view the situation in a different light.

On 23 April 1946 General Bahadur was sent by Maharaj Padma to Delhi in order to present Viscount Wavell with the insignia of the Star of Nepal (First Class). At the invitation of the British Government the Government of Nepal sent to the United Kingdom a contingent of their army consisting of 3 general officers, 3 staff officers, 24 other ranks (also 1 civil officer and 17 public and private servants).[4] Prominent in the contingent were Senior Commanding General Babar Shamsher (leader of the contingent), Lieutenant-General Ekraj Shamsher and Major-General Kiran Shamsher. They left Kathmandu on 26 April 1946 en route to Bombay and sailed from Bombay in early May.

Senior Commanding General Babar and his party went to the U.S.A. in October as a guest of its Government. Babar was received by President Truman on whom he conferred the Order of Om Rama on behalf of the King of Nepal. This visit to the U.S. was followed by the arrival in Kathmandu of George R. Merrel, U.S. charge d'affaires in India, in November 1946 to prepare for the visit of a U.S. mission in April 1947.

In May 1946, Admiral Lord Louis Mountbattern, Supreme Allied Commander South-West Asian Command, accompanied by his wife, Major-General R.F.S. Denning, Squadron Leader C. Harris and Captain Lord Brabourne arrived in Kathmandu on 9 May 1946 and left on 13 May. King Tribhuvan invested Admiral Lord Louis Mountbatten with the Star of Nepal (First Class) at a ceremonial Darbar held for the purpose and on 11 May Mountbatten took the salute at the march past held in his honour.

A Chinese mission headed by Tsunglien Shu arrived in Kathmandu on 26 November 1946 to present the insignia of Teh Tsung Dah Sew Pao Ting Hsun Chang (Grand Order of the Sacred Tripod) to the Maharaj and the Grand Order of the Cloud and the Banner to the Commander-in-Chief on behalf of the chinese government. A mission led by Lieutenant-General Krishna Shamsher consisting of himself, Colonel Dhruba Shamsher and Captain Padma Jang Thapa left Kathmandu on 3 April 1947 en route to China and embarked at Bombay on 18 April to present the insignia of Ojaswi Rajanya and Subikhyat Trishakti Patta to President and Madame Chiang Kai-Shek respectively. But the exchange of these missions did not result in anything of diplomatic or political consequence: the Nationalist Government in China was near its end.

The first year of Maharaj Padma's administration had also had its share of unofficial delegations from India and Ceylon. In September 1946 Dr. B.S. Moonje of the Hindu Mahasabha visited Nepal along with a son and personal secretary. Though he described his visit as a pilgrimage to Pashupatinath, he had several meetings with the Maharaj. The All-India Hindu Mahasabha had for years been pro-Rana and extolled the Rana rulers as the guardians of the only Hindu state in the world. The Mahasabha denounced the secular political programmes of the Indian National Congress and were pledged to the setting up of a truly Hindu state in India also. The Rana rulers had always sought to use the Hindu Mahasabha to project a favourable image of themselves to the Indian public. Moonje was presented by Major-General Mrigendra Shamsher, Director-General of Public Instruction, to a gathering of students and teachers at Tri-Chandra college before he addressed them. Moonje bestowed high praise on the Ranas for their pursuit of the principles and goals of Hindu policy in Nepal, and he bitterly criticized the Indian National Congress leaders and also Mahatma Gandhi himself for their secularist programmes and policies. Also in September a goodwill mission from Ceylon consisting of Narad Maha Thera and Piadasi Thera visited Nepal and pleaded with the Government for greater freedom for Buddhist missionary activities.

A delegation led by Dambar Singh Gurung, President of the All-India Gorkha League, arrived in Kathmandu on 26 November 1946. Though it brought good wishes to the Maharaj from the Nepalis domiciled in India and also obtained a modest donation from him to its funds, Dambar Singh Gurung and his colleagues did not spare the Rana regime in their public speeches and plainly told their audiences that the Ranas had done nothing so far to deserve the goodwill and trust of the Nepalis in India.

Maharaj Padma's inaugural had been held on 9 June 1946. It was a simple ceremony as compared with the inaugurals of his predecessors and successor and was completely bereft of pomp and show. He announced remission of long outstanding dues of land tax, the exemption of cotton from import duty and the raising of the Bhadgaun Middle School to the level of a high school as his goodwill gestures to the people on the occasion.

Even after his formal inaugural, he refused to move to the official residence of the Maharaj Prime Minister, Singha Darbar, even though he came under heavy pressure from his cousins and other high-ranking officials to do so. However, General Bahadur Shamsher, Equerry-in-

Chief to the Maharaj, occupied Singh Darbar from August 1946 with Maharaj Padma himself attending to business there three times a week. The Maharaj told the British Minister that he was attached to his own residence at Bishalnagar, in which he had lived for the last 44 years and though it was small, he felt that it was his home and did not anticipate taking up his residence in Singh Darbar. As a matter of fact, Padma Shamsher never did live in the official residence.

Maharaj Padma relaxed restrictions on the King and his sons and allowed them to travel to India for health reasons. King Tribhuvan accompanied by his two younger sons, Princes Himalaya and Basundhara, and attended by Commanding-General Bahadur Shamsher and Major-General Subarna Shamsher left Kathmandu on 17 December 1946 on a three-week private visit to Calcutta for treatment.

In his annual report to his Government for the year 1946, British Minister George Falconer has objectively assessed Padma's first year as the Maharaj Prime Minister thus:

> "Administratively it cannot be said that Maharaja's first year of office was of the material progress for Nepal. When it comes to making decision on any major problems, Maharaja Padma appears to lack the courage of conviction. So far he has been a little disappointing as a ruler but he may be a 'dark horse' and has got to show his hand. Meanwhile the administration drifts along."

The prospect of the British withdrawal from India proved ominous for the Rana regime in many ways. The All-India Nepali National Congress was established on 31 October 1946 in Varanasi and the All-India Gorkha Congress was also formed the same year at Darjeeling. The two political organizations set up by Nepali political exiles and Indian domiciled Nepalis merged into one to form a mass political party under the name of the Nepali National Congress following their conference on 24-25 January 1947. The conference was attended by educated Nepali youths from Varanasi, Calcutta, Patna, Darjeeling and different parts of Nepal itself. Among those who attended it was Ganesh Man Singh who had already become a popular hero because of the thrilling manner in which he had made good his hairbreadth ascape from the Kathmandu prison. In the small hours of 20 June 1944 he had managed to scale the high walls of the heavily guarded prison where he was serving a life sentence for his involvement in the Praja Parishad activities. Under Ganesh Man Singh's persuasive influence, this new party elected as its President in absentia Tanka Prasad Acharya, who had been in prison since 1940, and B.P. Koirala its Acting President. The declared objective of the party was to establish through non-violent methods a democratic system of government in Nepal under a constitutional monarch. Its conference received written messages of goodwill from Acharya J.B. Kripalani, then President of the Indian National Congress, Vijayalakshmi Pandit, Acharya Narendra Deva, Jayaprakash Narayan, Rammanohar Lohia and others.

Juddha's brutal suppression of the activity of a small group of social and religious reformers and of an underground political organization, the Nepal Praja Parishad, in the thirties and the early forties had not succeeded in containing unrest within Nepal. Discontent was fast spreading in Kathmandu and also in the districts adjacent to India where the Rana authority could be more easily challenged. Meanwhile the British Government formally announced on 20 February 1947 that it would withdraw from India not later than June 1948. The British withdrawal from India was going to deprive the Ranas of powerful external support, and the new Indian Government would not be sympathetic towards the Rana regime.

Nepal under Maharaj Padma participated in the historic Asian Relations Conference convened by the Indian Council of World Affairs in Delhi in March-April 1947. Though leading members and representatives of Governments and political movements along with other eminent men in literary and cultural fields from 28 countries took part in the conference, it was described as unofficial and cultural only; this was in order to avoid international misunderstanding about the ulterior motives of the newly established Government of India which was yet to be independent. None the less the Asian Relations Conference in Delhi paved the way for the 1955 inter-governmental Afro-Asian Conference in Bandung.

The Nepali delegation to the Delhi conference was led by Major-General Bijya Shamsher and consisted of four other delegates and three observers. The delegates were Sardar Narendra Mani Acharya Dikshit, Professor Ratna Bahadur Bisht, Surya Prasad Upadhyaya and Principal Rudra Raj Pande, and the observers were Major-General Subarna Shamsher, Lieutenant-Colonel Khadga Narsingh Rana and Sardar Gunja Man Singh.

In his opening statement as the leader of the delegation, Bijaya Shamsher described the conference as "a unique occasion, when for the first time in history the representatives of many races and peoples in Asia, the home of more than half of the entire population of the world, should have gathered together on a common platform to discuss common problems and to exchange information and views." He also bestowed fulsome praise on Jawaharlal Nehru, the guiding spirit behind the conference, as one who "possesses those qualities of sagacity, sincerity and strength, which will be invaluable in the counsels of Asia and the World."

It was more than just a coincidence that labour strikes and political demonstrations inside Nepal occurred about the same time as the Nepali delegation was taking part in the Asian Relations Conference in Delhi. The newly formed Nepali National Congress, which was agitating for democratic rights in Nepal from its base in India, took advantage of the situation of unrest in the Biratnagar Jute Mill in the spring of 1947. The Nepali Government was no longer in a position to send troops quickly to the disturbed areas by Indian railways and it took a long time for the troops to be sent to Biratnagar by the long and circuitous hill route. In the meantime Congress leaders, including Acting President B.P. Koirala, had involved themselves in the mill workers' strike, which started on 4 March and continued till 27 March 1947. The cooperation of the Congress had been sought by leaders of the mill workers such as Tarini Prasad Koirala, Girija Prasad Koirala, Man Mohan Adhikari, Gehendra Hari Sharma and Yuvaraj Adhikari, all of whom worked in the mill. B.P. Koirala and other Congressmen reached Biratnagar on 9 March and led the strike peacefully till 24 March. On 23 March 250 troops sent from Kathmandu arrived at Biratnagar and on 25 March Bishweshar Prasad Koirala, Balchandra Sharma, Gopal Prasad Bhattarai, Girija Prasad Koirala, Man Mohan Adhikari, Gehendra Hari Sharma, Tarini Prasad Koirala, Yuvaraj Adhikari and a number of workers of the Indian Socialist Party from the Purnea district were arrested.

Immediately following these arrests the millowners and the district authorities accepted most of the demands of the mill workers, but the workers did not go back to work in protest against the arrest of their leaders. The strike continued for two more days under the leadership of Matrika Prasad Koirala, and the troops opened fire to disperse the procession of the mill workers. On 27 March B.P. Koirala's mother, two of his sisters, his cousin's widow Kamini Devi and some more Indian socialist workers were arrested.

Meanwhile a meeting of the working committee of the Nepali National Congress was convened in Calcutta. It called upon the Rana Government to release the arrested persons and change its policy of repression by 13 April 1947. As there was no response from Kathmandu, the Congress held a delegates' conference on 9 and 10 April at Jogbani across the border in Bihar, to endorse the decision of the working committee and to launch a countrywide satyagraha or civil disobedience movement on the Indian model.

Accordingly this anti-Rana movement, the first of its kind in Nepal, started on 13 April as planned and quite a number of Nepalis courted voluntary arrest at Biratnagar, Birganj, Janakpur and Kathmandu. There were demonstrations and processions in the Kathmandu Valley itself on 30 April and 4 May 1947, and several volunteers were detained in the Bishalnagar and the Lakshmi Nivas compounds of the residences of the Maharaj and the Commander-in-Chief. Prem Bahadur Kansakar, who had first returned to Kathmandu after completing his studies at Patna, was the main person behind these political activities in the Kathmandu Valley.

As nothing like this had ever happened before, the Rana rulers did not know how to tackle the situation. Finally, after several weeks of feverish consultations with his cousins and others, Maharaj Padma Shamsher made a historic speech on 16 May 1947 expressing his desire to associate the people with the administration in a meaningful way. He also publicly announced his decisions (1) to set up a reforms committee and to invite an eminent constitutional lawyer to advise on constitutional reforms suitable for Nepal, (2) to set up elected municipalities and district boards in the capital and elsewhere to whom local authority would be transferred, (3) to establish an independent judiciary, (4) to extend education and introduce female education by opening seven new schools in the Kathmandu Valley, (5) to publish the national budget annually, and (6) appoint consuls at places in India and Burma where necessary to protect the interests of Nepali subjects. The reforms committee set up by the Maharaj started work from 28 May 1947.

The Maharaj's announcement seemed to satisfy the Congress and the movement was formally called off on 2 June 1947. But even before that, all those detained in connection with the Satyagraha, with the exception of B.P. Koirala and a few others, were released after the Maharaj's historic pronouncement. By August 1947 B.P. Koirala was also set free on health grounds as a result of Mahatma Gandhi's intercession after requests from several other Indian leaders had proved to be of no avail.

But after the release of B.P. Koirala, there was a split in the party because its general conference had elected D.R. Regmi Acting President on the assumption that B.P. Koirala was not going to be liberated soon. After his release B.P. Koirala stated that he had taken over leadership of the party, and this started a conflict between him and Regmi, who insisted on serving as President for the full term. The conflict continued until April 1950 with both factions functioning under identical names and flags.

Some members of the Chandra and the Juddha branches of the Rana family suspected that Maharaj Padma was in personal contact with the leaders of both the Indian National Congress and the Nepali National Congress and was acting hand in gloves with them. But the Maharaj's links with them were at best tenuous. Surya Prasad Upadhyaya had met Mahatma Gandhi as the Maharaj's unofficial ambassador in 1946 and presented the Indian leader with a Cashmere shawl on Padma's behalf. In 1947 the Maharaj helped Hora Prasad Joshi and Kedar Man Vyathit escape to India and join the Nepali National Congress after he found it difficult to withstand his cousins' pressure to arrest them for political agitation.

Let us now turn to the initial reaction of the India office in London to the announcement of the reforms by Maharaj Padma Shamsher on 16 May 1947. This was what British Minister Falconer had to say about these reforms in his dispatch to Lieutenant-Colonel Crichton, Secretary to the Government of India, dated 26 May 1947:

> "I have no doubt as to the sincerity of the Maharaja in these matters, but it remains to be seen to what extent circumstances obtaining here permit the implementation of the changes foreshadowed in the announcement."

It seems that British Minister George Falconer, who was inclined to overrate the Chandra branch of the family like his predecessors and was close to some of its senior members, must have been fully aware of their determination to oppose the reforms when he wrote the above letter to his superior in the External Affairs Department in New Delhi.

But the India office minutes in London view Maharaj Padma's reforms from various angles and on the whole reflect a favourable opinion of them. The notings of the officers through whose hands the file on the subject passed were highly perceptive. This was what I. Ross had stated as his opinion:

"This is a bold step for the autocratic Rana regime to take but is a clearly wise one in anticipation of events. The stability of the Shamsher Jang Bahadur Rana family is a matter for speculation. Sir Girija Bajpai who generally accompanied General Lyne to Kathmandu for discussion on the future recruitment of the Gurkhas expressed the opinion that the Rana family were firmly in the saddle, backed by the army. I would say that Sir Girija knows nothing about the horse; the anti-Rana movement is certainly not dead. If HMG's negotiations to recruit Gurkhas fail, and India accepts only 8 battalions as against 20 pre-war, much discontent will be felt in Nepal which will scarcely be balanced by these proposed reforms. The reforms in any case will hardly be felt in the countryside. Nevertheless they are a welcome sign of progress and it is hoped that it will be the preliminary to the opening up of the country to the outside world."

Another officer in the India office, P.J. Patrick, attributed the Maharaj's reforms to American pressure and recorded his opinion as follows:

"I should be disposed to connect the announcement with the recent USA mission to Nepal which I understand was intended to be a prelude to Nepal's recognition by America. For exchange of representation there may be a price to pay, e.g., the constitutional lawyer."

American pressure on the British Government itself to grant independence to India and America's professed concern for the spread of democracy in the world as a whole might have led Patrick to think along the above lines.

Yet another member of the India office bureaucratic hierarchy, E.P. Donaldson, seemed to relate the Maharaj's announcement of reforms to his immediate plan to apply for Nepal's membership in the United Nations. This was what he had to say on the subject.

"I gather that Bajpai was speaking to a brief given by Weightman, who does hold that the Rana regime is a good jockey to follow — largely because there is no other party in the state capable of taking its place in the saddle. But Maharaj Padma seems to have seen the red light and before we know where we are we may see Nepal applying for membership of U.N.O."

The British feared that in the event of the refusal of the new Government of India to retain more battalions than there had been before the war and if the Nepal Government should be unwilling to permit Britain to retain some of the Gurkha battalions for services overseas, there might be instability in Nepal because of the lack of prospects for employment for the demobilized soldiers. However, negotiations began on the possibility of concluding a tripartite agreement amongst Nepal, India and Great Britain on the future employment of the Gorkhas in July 1947. General Lyne and Sir Girija Shankar Bajpai went to Kathmandu to conduct negotiations on behalf of the Indian Government. An agreement was finally concluded by the three countries in November 1947 under which India retained 12 battalions of Gorkha soldier while eight battalions were transferred to Britain on the condition that Britain would in the future recruit Gorkha soldiers only after India's requirements had been satisfied. India, however, retained an option to raise the number of Gorkha battalions to 20 during an emergency.

As to American pressure on the Maharaj to introduce political reforms in Nepal, all that can be said is that the U.S. mission led by J.C. Satterthwaite had arrived in Kathmandu on 13 April 1947 to a salute of 17 guns about a month before the announcement of the reforms by the Maharaj. It is likely that the 6-man American mission might have impressed upon the Nepali authorities the need for political reforms, but the Rana Government, apart from securing international recognition of the independent status of the country, was chiefly interested in obtaining American aid after the exchange of diplomatic relations between the two countries.

A friendship and commerce agreement was signed between Nepal and the U.S.A. on 25 April 1947 which among other things provided for the exchange of diplomatic and consular relations between them. This finally led to the accreditation of representatives to the two capitals at the ministerial level in February 1948. *The Times* (London) of 12 May 1947 wrote that by exchanging diplomatic representation with Nepal, the Americans were seeking to fill up the power vacuum created by the British withdrawal from India. However, the *New York Times* of 22 March 1947 had commented thus on the planned American mission to Nepal:

> "Although Nepal lies in a region where Soviet influence might extend, should it spread throughout the Middle East as a result of the current crisis surrounding Greece and Turkey, the Department (the State Department) said there was no connections between this fact and the forthcoming Mission."

Although 'Point Four', President Harry Truman's call for aid to the underdeveloped nations, figured for the first time only in his 1949 inaugural address, the policy of containing communism on a global basis was already taking shape in the U.S. as is reflected in the above comment of the *New York Times*.

Though one cannot be certain whether Maharaj Padma's announcement of political reforms was intended to facilitate Nepal's entry into the United Nations, yet it was only in February 1949 that Nepal applied for membership in the United Nations. Had Nepal applied for membership immediately after World War II or even in 1946, it would have perhaps got into the U.N. without any difficulty. But Padma was discouraged by his cousins from applying for U.N. membership out of their sheer personal jealousy: they did not want him to receive the credit for getting Nepal into the U.N. Nor was Britain very enthusiastic about Nepal's U.N. membership.

Nepal's application for U.N. membership came up for consideration in May 1949. The brief honeymoon spell in international relations among the victorious war allies immediately after World War II was followed by intense cold war tension and polarization of the great powers, and in 1949 even the question of Nepal's admission to the U.N. became a part of the greater cold war issue which completely dominated the thinking of the great powers at the time. But when the membership committee considered Nepal's application in May 1949, seven members supported it but, as anticipated, the U.S.S.R. and Ukraine, citing provisions in the 1815 and the 1923 treaties, alleged that Nepal was, in effect, a British colony and requested proof of Nepal's independence. It was only in December 1955, eight years after it had applied for membership, that Nepal was at last admitted to the U.N. with twelve other countries as a result of the so-called 'package deal.' (The Soviet Union, which doomed Nepal's previous application by veto in the Security Council in 1949, later on made it clear that it had no objection individually to the admission of Nepal. The Soviet objection had been that other similarly qualified countries were not being allowed membership.)

Within Nepal people began to take advantage of Maharaj Padma's liberal attitude and started setting up libraries and social organizations. A literary organization called the *Nepali Sahitya Parishad* (lit. Council of Nepali Literature) was founded by the efforts of a number of private individuals in May 1947, and a conference was held under its auspices on 28 May in Kathmandu. It was the first such conference to be held in the history of Nepal. Major-General Mrigendra Shamsher, the Director-General of Public Instruction, permitted the conference to be held, and Nepali writers and poets gave renderings of their works to an appreciative gathering of several hundred people. The Parishad also published its own organ called *Sahitya Srot.*

In pursuance of the reforms announced by the Maharaj earlier, a municipal election was held in Kathmandu on 11 June 1947. The town was divided into 21 wards and each of the wards was entitled to elect one representative to the municipal council. In seven of these wards candidates were returned unopposed while in the remaining fourteen wards 9,332 persons out of 12,069 voters or, in other words, 77 per cent of the electorate recorded their votes. Among the twenty-one newly elected municipality councillors seven members were from the business community, seven from the scholastic professions, and seven from other occupations. The Council also had ten nominated members. At its first meeting held on 21 July 1947 for the swearing in of the members, Shankar Dev Pant and Purna Bahadur, M.A., were respectively elected its Chairman and Vice-Chairman.

In July 1947 students of the Sanskrit Collegiate School at the capital staged a strike demanding a higher scale of pay for their teachers, better facilities for them in the hostel and the modernization of their curriculum for studies by including such subjects as history, economics and other social sciences. The agitation of the Sanskrit students called Jayatu Sanskritam (lit. Victory to the cause of Sanskrit) was directed as much against the Rana regime as against the Brahmin priests, who were in charge of the school. The movement was called off on the Maharaj's assurances that the students' demands would be fulfilled shortly. But Mohan Shamsher, who was the Commander-in-Chief and the next in line of succession to the office of the Maharaj Prime Minister, and Mahila Gurujyu Hem Raj Pande reportedly had the leaders arrested after the movement was suspended and expelled them not only from the hostel but also from Kathmandu itself. Some of the leaders of the movement including Rajeshwar Devkota, Shri Bhadra Khanal,

Kashi Nath Gautam and Gokarna Raj Shastri went to India and joined the Nepali National Congress.

In response to the Maharaj's request to the Government of India, an Indian team of constitutional advisors consisting of Sri Prakash Gupta, a personal friend of Jawaharlal Nehru, and a member of the Indian Constituent Assembly, and Professor Ram Ugra Singh, Dean of the faculty of law in the Lucknow University and a member of the U.P. Council of State, accompanied by several assistants had arrived in Kathmandu on 13 June 1947. Sri Prakash Gupta, after several rounds of conference with the Reforms Committee and talks with the Maharaj, handed over to the Maharaj a draft constitution before he and the other members of the Indian team returned to India on 26 June 1947. Thereafter the Reforms Committee engaged itself in the task of preparing a report on the draft constitution for submission to the Maharaj.

There was no visible sign of progress in preparing the final draft constitution for quite some time after the departure of Sri Prakash Gupta and his party from Kathmandu. Several sub-committees charged with the responsibility of finalizing the draft of the constitution met regularly, but they failed to reconcile the views of the pre-eminent Ranas themselves on its basic features. In July, General Bahadur Shamsher resigned his appointment as President of the main Reforms Committee reportedly due to a difference of opinion with other members of the Committee on the extent of reform in Nepal. General Bahadur also resigned his post of Hazuria General or Chief aide-de-camp to the Maharaj, a post that had made him head of the foreign department. He was succeeded by General Singha as the President of the main Reforms Committee and as Hazuria General by General Krishna Shamsher.

On 11 July 1947 the Government of Nepal had announced agreement with the British Government to raise the status of their present legations in Kathmandu and London to embassies. The Maharaj informed the British Minister that his Government proposed to appoint a change d'affaires in New Delhi pending the appointment of an ambassador and transter the consulate-general to Calcutta. Commanding General Singha was expected to be the first Nepali Ambassador to India and his role as the President of the main Reforms Committee in Nepal was viewed merely as a stop-gap arrangement.

Following his father's resignation as Maharaj Padma's Hazuria General, Bahadur's son, Major-General Nara Shamsher, also resigned his appointment as the Director-General of Police and General Shankar

Shamsher, Commander-in-Chief Mohan's most loyal half-brother, was appointed head of the police. Maharaj Padma's position was becoming weaker every day and he was feeling beleaguered by his foes; pressure was being brought to bear from all sides to deter him from introducing political reforms. But the Maharaj remained determined to announce his Constitution of Nepal at all costs, albeit in the whittled-down form, before leaving for India in early 1948.

Padma's simple and austere life-style had never appealed to the British representatives in Kathmandu, and the Maharaj's move to introduce political reforms in the country did not receive the support and encouragement which he had expected from the British representative of the time, G.A. Falconer. When Falconer was informed by Padma on 29 October 1947 of his intention to resign, the envoy did not even make the gesture of trying to persuade the Maharaj to change his mind. On the other hand, the British Minister, while conveying the Maharaj's intention to London, tended to give the impression that Padma's exit from Nepal would be a good riddance. This was what Falconer wrote to Ernest Bevin, the British Foreign Secretary, on 1 November 1947:

> "This (ill-health) combined with the difficult problems of post-war development and the introduction of reforms in Nepal in which he has met with some opposition from other members of the Rana family, has proved too much for him and in my opinion his impending retirement will be in the best interests of Nepal.
>
> His anticipated successor according to the roll of succession will be the present Commander-in-Chief General Mohan Shamsher, aged 62, eldest son of the late Maharaj Chandra Shamsher. By (sic) his (Mohan's) succession to the prime ministership will bring back to power the Chandra branch of the family and he will have the support of the next two on the roll of succession, Generals Babar and Kaiser (the present Nepali Ambassador in London) who are his younger brothers. By comparison General Mohan is a much stronger character than the present Prime Minister and can command a greater support and respect from other members of the Rana family, and I think, from the majority of the people also than Maharaja Padma could ever hope to achieve. During his father's 26 years (sic) as Prime Minister General Mohan acquired considerable experience in administration which he should be able to put to good account. He strikes me more as an administrator than a soldier and I

think Nepal needs a Prime Minister with the former qualities more than the latter at this critical period of her history.

Whatever Sir George Falconer might have had to say about the relative qualifications of Padma and Mohan for the high office, both of them miserably failed. The last two hereditary Rana Prime Ministers were very much unlike their strong predecessors. They possessed neither the courage nor the shrewdness of their forerunners in meeting the challenge of the changed circumstances. But it may be pleaded in favour of Maharaj Padma Shamsher that he at least had the correct insight, though he did not possess the strength of personality to bring about change against the opposition of Chandra's and Juddha's sons, who held most of the top positions. However, his successor Mohan Shamsher, who was so highly rated by the British representatives in Kathmandu, had to preside over the liquidation of the 104-year-old Rana regime within less than three years of his becoming the Maharaj Prime Minister.

The 1948 Constitution, as it was announced, was not entirely to the satisfaction of the Indian constitutional advisers and the Government of India because it took for granted the hereditary right of succession of the Ranas to the office of the Maharaj Prime Minister "for all time inalienable and unalterable" and did not contemplate any changes in the prerogatives of this office. The Indian advisers under instructions from the Government of India pressed for the inclusion of the expression "with the ultimate aim of responsible and representative government. Maharaj Padma Shamsher himself was quite amenable to their suggestion but most of the leading members of the Chandra and the Juddha branches of the family opposed it tooth and nail.

General Krishna Shamsher who had succeeded General Bahadur as Maharaj Padma's Chief aide-de-camp or Hazuria General and was at the time generally regarded as a fair-minded and well-meaning member of the Rana family, told the author long after the abolition of the Rana rule in Nepal that despite his best efforts he could not get support for the above reference to the ultimate aim of responsible and representative government even from educated persons like Major-General Mrigendra Shamsher and Sardar Gunja Man Singh not to speak of other diehard members of the ruling hierarchy and the officialdom. This despite the fact that Sri Prakash Gupta had told General Krishna Shamsher that even just the mention of this goal in vague and general terms would ensure the support of the Prime Minister of India for the Rana Government in future.

It may be pointed out here that General Krishna's brief association with Maharaj Padma was misunderstood by his own brother Mohan Shamsher, who succeeded Padma as the Maharaj Prime Minister, and General Krishna Shamsher therefore first resigned his appointment as Maharaj Padma's aide-de-camp to remove his own brother's misgivings about his personal loyalty and subsequently resigned his position on the roll of succession itself on health grounds soon after Mohan's inaugural. Krishna's voluntary resignations may be taken as friendly warnings to his elder brothers to change their traditional modes of thought and action and also as an earnest of his support for liberal reforms. Krishna made over his palatial residence to the state as a public-spirited gesture so uncharacteristic of a Rana.

As his scheduled departure for India was fast approaching, Maharaj Padma decided to make his constitutional offer to the people anyway, though he was not sure whether the reforms would be implemented in the same spirit in which he had introduced them. It was on 26 January 1948 that the first written constitution of Nepal was proclaimed jointly in the name of the King and the Prime Minister as the Government of Nepal Act, V.S. 2004 (A.D.1948). It was to come into force on 14 April 1948.

Despite its shortcomings, it was a positive and constructive step taken by the Rana regime to meet the challenge of the times. It failed to do so not because of the lack of cooperation from the people in working it but because of the reluctance of Padma's successor. Maharaj Mohan, and his advisers to implement it in the proper spirit. However Maharaj Padma cannot escape his share of the blame for leaving the country for good even before the reforms he had introduced were supposed to come into force.

As has been indicated, the 1948 Constitution retained the prerogatives of the Rana Prime Minister intact and did not even contemplate changing them in future. It envisaged the establishment of a Council of Ministers, a bicameral legislature and a High Court (Pradhan Nyayalaya). The Rana Prime Minister was vested with absolute authority as Head of the Government and Chairman of the Council of Ministers. The Prime Minister was to appoint five ministers to the council and they were to have a tenure of four years. The Constitution provided that two of the ministers be appointed from among the elected members of the legislature. The Prime Minister had the right to dismiss any or all ministers if they lost his confidence, and he also enjoyed a wide measure of discretionary powers such as those of suspending and modifying the Constitution by enacting special ordinances having the force of law for six months. The Council of Ministers was to conduct the executive business of the Government and "to define policies of the government, scrutinize the budget of the various departments, give final consideration to the government bills to be placed before the legislature, and bring about coordination and cooperation between various departments of the government."

The constitution provided for the setting up of the panchayat councils at the village, town and district levels as units of local self-government. The primary units of local government were the village panchayats (village councils) consisting of 5 to 15 elected members and representing one or more villages and the nagar panchayats (town councils), composed of 10 to 15 elected members and representing a town or city. Above the village and town panchayats were the zilla panchayats (district councils) which were composed of 15 to 20 members elected by the chairmen of the town and village panchayats. The panchayats at all levels were authorized to spend whatever revenue they could raise by local taxation and whatever grants they received from the Government at the centre to provide such services to the people as education, health, transport, public buildings and water-supply systems.

The legislature was to consist of two houses, the Rastra Sabha (National or Lower Council) of forty-two elected and twenty-eight nominated members, and the Bhardari Sabha (the Council of Nobles) consisting of twenty to thirty nominated members. The elected forty-two members of the Rastra Sabha were to be the chairmen of the thirty-two district panchayats, the chairmen of the four town panchayats of Kathmandu, Patan, Bhaktapur and Birganj, and the remaining six members were to be elected to represent different professional and economic interests and the intelligentsia with one each to represent merchants and traders, landlords and Birta holders, Government servants, labour, and two to represent the intelligentsia. The minimum qualification for being able to elect the representatives of the intelligentsia was the matriculation or Madhyama examination and that for being a candidate for election was a college degree. Merchants paying Rs. 100 or more as customs duty could elect one from among themselves as their representative in the legislature, and landlords owning 20 ropanis or 10 bighas of land or their equivalent in the hill district were entitled to elect one representative in the legislature. Rules for the election of one representative each from among the Government servants and labour were left to be framed by the Government.

The two houses of the legislature were to meet at least twice a year. The President of the Rastra Sabha was to be nominated by the Maharaj and its Vice-President elected from among its members. The Maharaj had the right to veto any motion or question, and his authentication was required for any bill to be a law. The annual budget was to originate with the Maharaj, who would cause it to be laid before the legislature.

The following items were not to be submitted to the decision of the legislature: (1) civil lists of the King and the Prime Minister, (2) expenditure on the armed forces, (3) pay and pensions of the public servants appointed by the Maharaj, (4) expenditure on foreign affairs.

The Judicial Committee, consisting of 10 members of the legislature and two from outside it and to be appointed by the Prime Minister, was to act as the Supreme Court of Appeal in special cases. The committee was also empowered to frame rules and regulations for the administration of justice. The High Court, called a court of records, was to exercise supervision over all other lower courts and to consist of one chief justice and twelve judges; the Prime Minister had the discretionary power to appoint or dismiss any judge of this court.

The more important provisions of the Constitution from the people's point of view were, apart from the recognition of the concept of representative and responsible government at the local level, the external or formal safeguards against arbitrary government such as the Auditor General's office and the Public Service Commission. Above all, the 1948 Constitution for the first time in Nepal's history permitted the exercise of civil rights and liberties such as the freedom of speech and assembly on a limited scale.

The following excerpts from the letter of Sir G.A. Falconer to Sir Ernest Bevin, the British Foreign Secretary, dated 19 March 1948 reflect the British views of the 1948 Constitution:

> "It will be seen that while the Act associates the people of Nepal with administration of the country in greater measure than ever before, discussions on all important matters including finance rest in the end with the Prime Minister, or the Maharaj as he is popularly called in Nepal; indeed in the Act the designation 'Prime Minister' is not employed at all. Thus the position of the Rana

family as the purveyors of Prime Ministers for Nepal remain unimpaired and the Act goes so far as to declare their right of succession to the post as inalienable and unalterable for all time. It is I think significant that the latter declaration is applied in one and the same (article) (3) to the roll of succession relating to His Majesty the Maharajadhiraj and the Maharaj Prime Minister.

Criticism of the Nepal Act and its shortcomings must be tempered by conditions at present prevailing in the country. With the exception of the thickly populated valley of Kathmandu and a few other centres, the six to seven million inhabitants are scattered over 54,000 square miles of a territory seldom better than a rough mountain track. It is hardly surprising that the majority of the people have had little or no education whatever and no training to fit themselves for the responsibility of even local self-government. To introduce democracy into Nepal it is therefore necessary to begin at the bottom. To begin at the top or even halfway as the few anti-Rana agitators in India would have it will merely produce chaos and the condition of the people will be worse than before.

The sincerity of the declared policy of the Ranas to associate the people more and more with the administration of the country by progressive stages, will be judged by the steps taken during the next few years to fit the people for political advancement. With conditions in Nepal as they are, the task will not be easy! But I believe it can be achieved, given time and the will to achieve it.

Needless to say that the Nepal Constitutional Act does not satisfy the Nepali National Congress, a body established in India, largely composed of persons of Nepali descent domiciled in that country and organised and led by a few malcontents and political adventurers. It exercises little influence inside Nepal."

The bias of Sir George Falconer, the British Minister on the spot, with his experience and background in life as a Resident in a second class Indian native state, against the Congress political leaders comes out in the raw in the last paragraph, though his comments on other aspects of the 1948 Constitution are by and large sound and valid. What his ingrained prejudice prevents him from perceiving is that even the most genuinely Nepali political leaders in the absence of minimal rights of freedom inside the country had no option other than to work for democracy from outside the country. The British Minister also makes a factual error in his letter inasmuch as the leaders of the Nepali

Congress ceased its agitation as a concrete gesture of satisfaction with the Maharaj's constitutional offer.

The comments of Peter Murray, a concerned high ranking British government official in the London Foreign office, are free from any such bias, and are factual and perceptive:

> "Evidently the Nepalese government has seen the writing on the wall and decided to spring clean and redecorate its house in the latest democratic fashion. This must have been prompted by Indian influence — possibly by Indian pressure — and by the spectacle of the Indian states tumbling over themselves to show how progressive they have become. It remains to be seen how serious the government's intention is, and how effective the changes will be."

The pith and marrow of Peter Murray's observation on the 1948 Constitution is contained in the following sentence:

> "The Constitution is obviously eyewash to disarm criticism from progressives while retaining powers firmly in the hands of the Rana family."[5]

Many Nepali historians and publicists, while praising Maharaj Padma's political foresight and liberal intentions, have blamed him for his failure to implement the political reforms envisaged by his Constitution. Balchandra Sharma, a noted Nepali historian, has concluded that he "proved to be an excessively religious, god-fearing and timid prime minister" while conceding that "he would have earned a special place for himself in the history of Nepal, if he had only implemented the constitution promulgated by himself notwithstanding its deficiencies".[6]

Maharaj Padma left Kathmandu on 21 February 1948 and crossed the frontier into India a week later. Before he left Kathmandu he had already wound up his domestic affairs in Nepal and made up his mind about resigning the prime ministership and settling down in India. According to Falconer's report to his government, the Government of India had allotted to Padma 40 acres of land in Ranchi (Bihar) at a nominal price for 99 years and there the ex-Maharaj proposed to build several houses for himself and his family. He took along his cousin and his successor-designate Mohan Shamsher's second son Major-General

Bijaya Shamsher, through whom he was supposed to send in his formal resignation from India in writing.

Maharaj Padma was originally expected to hand in his resignation by 29 March 1948. But when Bijaya Shamsher came back empty-handed from India merely with the message that Maharaj Padma would send in his resignation from Ranchi in due course, Maharaj Mohan and his other brothers and cousins were quite concerned, especially because Mohan had already moved to the official residence of the Prime Minister. Commanding Colonel Dambar Shamsher Thapa, one of Padma's boyhood friends, and Mohan's trusted military aide-de-camp Captain Khadga Bahadur Singh, were sent to Ranchi on a special mission to bring back Padma's resignation by all means. According to one Nepali source, Padma gave his resignation to Mohan's military aide-de-camp on the condition that Commanding Colonel Thapa was going to be held up in Ranchi until such time as the retiring Maharaj had had acknowledgment of his resignation from his successor-designate Mohan in Kathmandu.[7] According to another Nepali source, it was Sardar Narendra Mani Acharya Dikshit who had brought Padma's resignation from Ranchi.[8]

Whoever might have carried Padma's resignation to Mohan, he was feeling disturbed until he had had his cousin's resignation in his hands. As early as 9 March 1948, Falconer wrote to Ernest Bevin that Acting Prime Minister Mohan told him that "even if Maharaj Padma changed his mind 'they' would not accept his doing so." General Mohan added that "he and other senior members of the government had had a very difficult and exasperating time with the Maharaja during the past 6 or 8 months and the state of affairs could not continue any longer."

Even after Padma reached Ranchi on 3 April 1948 and had already been there for quite some time, he was apparently hesitating to resign. It was only on 17 April 1948 that once again communication was received from Padma that he would definitely issue a letter of resignation on Friday, 30 April 1948. But even this did not apparently allay the fears and anxieties of the interested parties. This was what Falconer wrote to Ernest Bevin on 22 April 1948:

> "There is some reason to believe that he (Maharaja Padma), is being urged by certain illegitimate collaterals extended in India not to resign in the hope of personal advantage to themselves. There are others too who would prefer the inert administration of Maharaja

Padma to continue rather than it be replaced by that which will emerge from the stronger character of General Mohan.

Short of a volte face on the part of Maharaja Padma, which I fear could only lead to dissension and ultimate disturbance in Nepal, I think he has gone too far with the arrangements for his retirement not to go through with it. In my opinion, and knowing the man's character, a likely explanation of his procrastination is that he believes he will get more consideration from the Indian authorities in the settlement of his property and other personal matters in India as Maharaja than as General Padma, ex-Maharaja. I think, too, there is some question concerning Indian Income Tax on his investment income which is not yet settled and anything touching his pocket will influence Maharaja Padma greatly. Whatever the reason, one thing is certain; he will never be allowed by General Mohan and other senior members of the Rana family to return to Kathmandu as Prime Minister. On this point they are adamant, for Maharaja Padma has tried their patience too long.

There is not doubt that the 'Weeping Maharaja' as Maharaja Padma has been nick-named even by the Nepali National Congress, has proved himself a complete failure as the Prime Minister of Nepal and the country will be much better off without him."

The present writer finds the British Minister's judgement on Padma's role as the Prime Minister of Nepal a little too harsh and overly biased. Everybody is of course free to form his own opinion about the worth and character of important public figures. But as someone who had had the privilege of knowing Maharaj Padma from close quarters, the writer cannot help feeling that he was inspired by the best of intentions in doing whatever he did. If he had on the one hand genuinely felt the need for the introduction of liberal reforms in the long-term interests of the family, he was, on the other, obsessed with the thought of avoiding the situation in which he could even remotely appear to be a direct instrument of the destruction of the future interests of the family. He had always had his instincts in the right place, but his failure as a practical politician or statesman resulted from his inability to reconcile the interests of his family with those of the people at large about which also he had a deep concern. It is true that their interests proved irreconcilable in the end, but Maharaj Padma certainly deserves credit for making efforts in the right direction though they were not successful. Padma's formal letter of resignation was at long last received by his successor-designate Mohan Shamsher just on time to enable him to announce his succession as the Maharaj Prime Minister on 30 April 1948. But the succession served to aggravate rather than mitigate the circumstances confronting the Rana rule in Nepal with the result that Mohan Shamsher was not able to rule as the hereditary Prime Minister for more than three years.

NOTES

1. India Office Library Record L/PS/12/3105.
2. Sir Clendon Daukes's note on Nepal (1929-1934) attached as an enclosure to his letter to the Rt. Hon'ble Sir John Simons of 15 January 1935 (India Office Library L/PS/12/305/21/40).
3. Betham's report to his Government ending 15 October 1938.
4. It was because of their old-fashioned and orthodox ways of eating and living that the military delegation needed so many servants.
5. Foreign 5058, Peter Murray 9/4/1948.
6. Balchandra Sharma, *op. cit.*, p. 389.
7. Pramode Shamsher Rana, *Rana Nepal—An Insider's View* (Kathmandu, 1978, p. 160.
8. Sardar Bhim Bahadur Pande, *Tyas Bakhat Ko Nepal* (Nepal of that time) (Kathmandu, 1981), p. 255.

15

Mohan Shamsher, the Last Hereditary Maharaj Prime Minister

Even before he formally became the Maharaj Prime Minister, Mohan Shamsher had banned the Nepali National Congress in mid-April 1948 after he had assumed full powers as Acting Maharaj upon Padma's departure to India in February. His action against the party at the time when the 1948 Constitution was scheduled to come into effect was a clear indication of the policy he would follow.

However, in his speech as the Maharaj Prime Minister on 30 April 1948, Mohan Shamsher did not completely back down from his predecessor's political commitments to the people. While addressing a gathering in the grounds of his official residence, he made a reference to the recently promulgated constitutional reforms and expressed his Government's intention to implement them smoothly with the goodwill of the people. But his lukewarm attitude towards the 1948 Constitution and his reluctance to implement it enthusiastically cost the Rana regime dearly in terms of popular support when it was most needed.

Both Mohan Shamsher, who became Prime Minister at the age of 63, and his younger brother Babar Shamsher, 61, whom he promoted to the rank of Minister and Commander-in Chief on 3 July 1948, were completely lacking in the political vision needed to cope with the challenges of the time. They were unable to realize the significance of the new forces of nationalism, anti-imperalism and communism that were already at work in the post-war world. Nor in respect of foreign affairs were they even conscious of the need to gear their policy to the changes that had taken place in both the regional and global environments. They hardly seemed to realize till very late in the day that Great Britain, the greatest imperialist power in the world at one time, had now become one of the second-rate powers. The withdrawal of the

British from India had deprived the Rana regime of its main source of external support. The attainment of independence by India with the Indian National Congress party at the helm at nearly the same time as the establishment of the communist government in China and its assertion of authority over Tibet inevitably accelerated the pace of events in Nepal. But even this seemed to be beyond the grasp of the two brothers, who were compelled by circumstances beyond their control to forge a new strategy for their political survival in a fast-moving world. Maharaj Mohan and his brothers, his sons and nephews, with all their long accumulated administrative experience and with the built-in-advantages of their wealth, foreign travels and education utterly failed in the task of coping with the changed situation both at home and abroad. Thus they belied the high expectations of them by the British envoys over the last two decades.

At a time when the Rana regime was faced with the most serious crisis in its history, the Maharaj seemed to be more concerned with the increase in the number of gun salutes for himself and his brother and with the standardization of the English spelling of his and his family's surname than with meeting the political challenges. The Maharaj was obviously more interested in attending to the details of his Sindur Yatra (vermilion procession) in celebration of his elevation to the high office and of his formal inaugural which he did not hesitate to call his coronation, than in coming to grips with the political crisis that confronted him.

Even as late as 1948 Sir George Falconer, the British Ambassador who had been his country's representative in Nepal since 1945, wrote this to his Government in his letter of 8 June

> "In my opinion the reasonable expectations of the people will be realised under Maharaja Mohan's regime. He is a capable and level-headed administrator and, jealous of his present and future prestige in the country, would not make promises which he did not think he could fulfil or had no intention of doing so."

Not only the British representatives in Nepal for the last 25 years, but also a large section of the Nepali governing elite had felt ever since the death of Maharaj Chandra in 1929, or even before, that Nepal under Chandra's sons would witness unprecedented stability, development and prosperity. It was said that there was unity among Chandra's sons, who were more wealthy, educated and cultured compared with other Ranas, not to speak of the common people of Nepal. But despite all these advantages, how was it that Chandra's sons under Mohan, who was the eldest of them all and had himself served a 29-year old apprenticeship to their father as his chief of personal staff, failed the test when their turn came?

The primary reason, as we have already indicated, was that they especially Maharaja Mohan and Minister and C.-in-C. Bahar, completely failed to understand the trends of the time and adjust their thinking and policies accordingly. Even some of their more enlightened brothers such as Generals Kaiser and Krishna and their university-educated sons and nephews could do very little to rid the two elders of the family of their traditional notions. Furthermore the so-called unity among Chandra's sons also proved to be a myth. They might have combined successfully against other branches of the family in the past when they had a common stake, but there was considerable feuding between the brothers themselves. General Kaiser, who was on all accounts the best educated, most enlightened and ablest of them all, had a very poor opinion of both of his elder brothers and felt unsafe specially with his second brother Babar. He had probably anticipated serious friction between Maharaj Padma and his two first cousins next to him in the line of succession to the prime ministership and therefore left Nepal as an ambassador to avoid taking sides in their quarrel despite the fact that his rank as the fourth man in the hierarchy was too high for an ambassadorship. Again, General Krishna, Maharaj Mohan's youngest brother, voluntarily withdrew from the arena probably because of the persistence of his two elder brothers in their traditional methods of running the Government.

To turn to the record of Maharaj Mohan's administration, he completely underestimated the need for domestic political reforms and focused his attention on establishing relations with more countries with a view to obtaining aid from them for Nepal's economic development. The Maharaj seemed to take a highly simplistic view of modernization. What he had failed to realize was that the expansion of diplomatic relations and the acceptance of foreign aid were merely superficial features of modernization, and there was going to be no modernization in the real sense unless the Nepali people themselves were involved in the process and enabled to change their basic outlook on life and society. And it was precisely for this reason that political reforms had been the crying need of the hour.

This was what Maharaj Mohan said in his policy statement of May 1948:

> "In modern times it is neither possible nor desirable for any state to keep itself in isolation from world affairs. It shall be our policy therefore to enter into diplomatic relations with all such countries that seek our friendship. It is evident that we shall require much help and cooperation from abroad in our nation-building projects. We hope we shall obtain such needful assistance and cooperation from our neighbouring and friendly countries."[1]

As if he had suddenly become aware of Nepal's diplomatic isolation from the world after the British withdrawal from India, Mohan wanted to make amends for it by establishing diplomatic relations with foreign countries including the United States, France, the Netherlands, Brazil and Belgium. The India-based Ambassadors of the United States and France, Loy Henderson and Daniel Levi respectively, were concurrently accredited to Nepal and presented their credentials to King Tribhuvan in 1948 and 1949 respectively; Nepal's application for membership in the United Nations signed by Major-General Bijaya Shamsher as the Director-General of Foreign Affairs, was filed with the U.N. Secretary-General in February 1949, as has been earlier pointed out; and a Nepali decoration was conferred on the Brazilian Minister to India in August 1949. Mohan appeared to be relying more on diplomatic assistance from outside than on internal political reforms for strengthening the foundation of the Rana rule in Nepal.

Mohan was also interested in cultivating the Congress Government in India mainly with a view to avoiding its pressure on him to introduce political reforms in Nepal. India's turbulence following partition afforded the Maharaj a chance to buy the goodwill of the Nehru government by lending Nepali troops to India for garrison duties as in the past. In keeping with Nepal's traditional practice, he offered help to India during the Hyderabad and Kashmir crisis in mid-1948 against the advice of the British Ambassador to Nepal. Ten battalions of Nepali soldiers were sent to India with the Maharaj's eldest son, Major-General Sarada Shamsher, as the G.O.C.-in-Chief. They released Indian troops to take part in active duties when the resources of the Indian army were strained to the utmost.

During his state visit to India in February 1950, Mohan Shamsher went to the extent of stating publicly that Nepal would always answer

India's call for help. All this was intended to placate the Indian Government so that it might not support the anti-Rana elements in Nepali politics. But Maharaj Mohan did not attach much importance to Jawaharlal Nehru's well-maning advice that if Nepal did not keep pace with the march of time, it would be in for serious trouble. The Maharaj came back from Delhi with the impression that he would be able to mollify the Government of India by signing the drafts of the treaty he was given there.

Further, in view of the Chinese communist threat to liberate Tibet, which was broadcast over Radio Peking in November 1949, Mohan sought to allay India's axieties on that account by merely emphasizing his Government's strong anti-communist predilections. But the Nehru Government rightly felt that the Maharaj's negative attitude towards communism would not in itself protect Nepal against this ideology unless the Maharaj could mobilize popular support inside his country for himself and his Government.

This was how Jawaharlal Nehru, the Prime Minister of India, explained the basic principle of his policy to Parliament on 17 March 1950:

> "We have advised in earnestness the Government of Nepal, to the extent a friendly power can advise an independent nation, that in the inner context of Nepal, it is desirable to pay attention to the forces which are moving in the world, the democratic forces and forces of freedom, and put themselves in line with them."[2]

While setting aside the suggestion of a military alliance between the two countries Nehru added:

> "Apart from any kind of alliance, the fact remains that we cannot tolerate any foreign invasion from any foreign country in any part of the Indian subcontinent. Any possible invasion of Nepal would inevitably involve the safety of India."

Mohan's second son, Bijaya Shamsher, visited Delhi in April 1950 to tell the Government of India as Nepal's Director-General of Foreign Affairs that Nepal would sign the treaties more or less as proposed provided India did not insist that the signing should also be marked by the introduction of political reforms. As the Chinese were already in the process of establishing their authority in Tibet, India wanted to conclude the treaties without any delay, and treaties of peace and friendship and of trade and commerce were signed in Kathmandu on 31 July 1950 by Maharaj Mohan and the Indian Ambassador, Chandreshwar Prasad Narayan Singh, and were ratified by their respective Governments in due course.

Treaty of Peace and Friendship

Articles 1, 2, 5, 6 and 7 contain the most important elements of the 1950 treaty of peace and friendship. But there was something more: the letters accompanying it, which had the same binding force but which were not published till 1960.

The key paragraph of the letters was disclosed to the public for the first time by Prime Minister Jawaharlal Nehru while responding to Prime Minister B.P. Koirala's reaction to his earlier statement following the Kor Là (Pass), Mustang incident on 28 June 1960. Immediately after the incident Nehru made a public declaration that any attack on Nepal would be regarded as an attack on India. In an obvious response to the Indian Prime Minister, B.P. Koirala, then Prime Minister of Nepal, issued a diplomatically worded statement which deserves to be quoted in full:

> "Nepal is a fully sovereign independent nation. It decides its external and home policy according to its own judgement and its own liking without ever referring to any outside authorities. Our Treaty of Peace and Friendship with India affirms this. I take Mr. Nehru's statement as an expression of friendship that in case of aggression against Nepal, India would send help if such help was ever sought. It would never be taken as suggesting that India could take unilateral action. Is there apprehension of danger from any quarter? The answer is definitely no. We are at peace with everybody and we do not apprehend any danger from any quarter."[3]

Nehru's reaction to B.P. Koirala's statement also needs to be reproduced in full:

> "I think what the Prime Minister of Nepal, Mr. B.P. Koirala, has said is completely true. The statement I made struck many people as perhaps a novel statement but it was merely stating what the position has been for the last ten years, you may say even more than

ten. I am saying ten years because there was a treaty ten or nine years ago with Nepal.

That treaty is the Treaty of Peace and Friendship between the Government of India and the Government of Nepal, 31 July 1950. Article I of the Treaty stated that "the two governments agree to acknowledge mutually and respect the complete sovereignty, territorial integrity and independence of each other." Article II: "The two governments hereby undertake to inform each other of any serious friction of misunderstanding with any neighbouring state, likely to cause any breach in the friendly relations existing between the two governments".

There is much else in the Treaty, but attached to the Treaty were letters that were exchanged on that very day, as is often done. In these letters, apart from other matters, there is a paragraph: "Neither government shall tolerate any threat to the security of the other by a foreign aggressor. To deal with any such threat, the two governments shall consult with each other and devise effective countermeasures." (This occurs in both the letters, the letter from Nepal to India and that from India to Nepal.)

It is not a military alliance by any means but a mutual assurance between friendly countries. I had that in mind. I was not aware, even, that I was making some novel statement and Mr. B.P. Koirala has correctly interpreted it. There is no question of India or any country taking unilateral action. That is absurd. It is a question of functioning as friendly countries and being helpful to each other in case of danger."[4]

One is inclined to believe that it was only Prime Minister Nehru's allergy to the mention of military alliances that made him describe the understanding between Nepal and India on mutual security as a mutual assurance rather than a pact. What is devising countermeasures to meet the threat of a foreign aggressor but taking military steps to meet it?

Article 5 recognizes Nepal's right to import "arms, ammunition or warlike materials and equipment necessary for the security of Nepal." The Nepal Government was keen on including this provision in view of the difficulties it had had in the past with the British Indian Government's policy to control and regulate the import of arms into Nepal. Though this article of the treaty contained the proviso that the procedures "for giving effect to this arrangement" would be worked out through joint consultations, no formal or procedural restriction was ever imposed on Nepal's right to acquire arms.

Article 6 lays down that "each government undertakes, in token of the neighbourly friendship between India and Nepal, to give to the nationals of the other, in its territory, national treatment with regard to participation in industrial and economic development of such territory and to the grant of concessions and contracts to such development." However, in the text of the letters exchanged at the time of the signing of the treaty, it is stipulated in paragraph 3 that "in regard to Article 6 of the Treaty of Peace and Friendship which provides for national treatment, the Government of India recognizes that it may be necessary for sometime to come to afford the Nepalese nationals in Nepal protection from unrestricted competition. The nature and extent to the protection will be determined as and when required by mutual agreement between the two governments."

Though it was recognized that Nepal and its nationals will not be able to compete with India and its nationals in industrial and economic enterprises on a footing of equality, nothing was done subsequently to determine the nature and extent of protection to be given to the Nepalis as nationals of a relatively underdeveloped country.

Article 7 of the same treaty guarantees the nationals of one country in the territory of the other reciprocity in the matter of "residence, ownership of property, participation in trade and commerce, movement and privileges of a similar nature." Despite this provision the Government of Nepal was not in a position to allow unrestrained immigration of Indian nationals into the country. The Government of Nepal had always had a law forbidding the sale of land to foreigners, including Indians, even in the tarai. Again in view of the fact that neither Nepali nor Indian law allows double citizenship to its nationals, the reciprocity given by the treaty stipulation has created a state of uncertainty about the citizenship of quite a large number of inhabitants in both countries. If this stipulation in the treaty is not revised realistically, Nepal and India may also be involved in the kind of citizenship disputes that have characterized the politics of Sri Lanka, Burma and East Africa.

Further, paragraphs in the letters accompanying the treaty may be cited as an example of how old-fashioned and ridiculous some of the stipulations were in the context of the mid-twentieth century world. It binds both Governments not to employ "any foreigners whose activities may be prejudicial to the security of the other" and further states that "either government may make representations to the other in this behalf, as and when occasion requires." The acceptance of restrictions in the matter of employing foreigners prejudicial to the security of the other only serves to remind the Nepalis of the unequal 1815 Treaty of Sugauli restricting employment by Nepal of British subjects or subjects of other European and American states without the consent of the British colonial government. This stipulation in the letter was once invoked by the Indian Ambassador, C.P.N. Singh, in the early 1950s to make the M.P. Koirala cabinet send back an American professor of political science, who was visiting Nepal as a tourist after having met Sheikh Abdullah in Kashmir before the Sheikh's dismissal as the Chief Minister.

The letters couched in identical language and exchanged at the time the treaty of peace and friendship between Nepal and India was signed, furnish the basis of subsequent and present arrangements for mutual security between Nepal and India, though a separate tripartite agreement signed by Nepal, India and Britain in November 1947 provided for the retention of the specified number of the existing Gorkha battalions by India and Britain and for the continued recruitment of Nepali nationals for the Indian and the British armies. A close scrutiny of the contents of the letter will reveal that most of the items mentioned therein, with modifications, were borrowed from the 1815 peace treaty of Sugauli and the 1923 treaty between Nepal and Great Britain.

The 1950 Treaty of Trade and Commerce

Until 1950 there was no trade treaty between Nepal and India. But the treaty of trade and commerce signed by Nepal and independent India on the same day as the treaty of peace and friendship aroused a good deal of controversy in Nepal from the very beginning. "Subject to such agreements as may be agreed upon between the two governments", the treaty recognized, in favour of the Government of Nepal, full and unrestricted right of commercial transit of all goods and manufactures through the territory of India as provided in Articles 2, 3 and 4. Each of these articles began with a reference to the arrangements to be agreed upon. But such arrangements were never agreed upon during the 10-year period covered by the treaty.

Nepal's imports from overseas were, until 1960-61, subject to the rigid control and regulation of Indian customs and tariffs because the 1950 Treaty of Trade and Commerce with India obliged Nepal to impose the same amount of levy as India on both imports from a third country and on exports to it. Such an undertaking very much hampered considerable expansion of Nepal's trade with other countries and virtually subjected Nepal to India's jurisdiction in matters of trade and tariff. Any demand for a change in the said treaty stipulation was met with the argument that if the same rates of export and import levy were not charged by India and Nepal on goods coming from outside, there would be wide scope for illegal trade in imported goods between the two countries.

The Nepalis strongly resented the treaty stipulation which required Nepal to put the same amount of levy on its exports overseas so that they might not be able to undersell Indian exports in the world market. The Nepali opinion holds that this treaty was the main obstacle to the expansion of international trade before 1960. Mohan Shamsher's Government was openly accused of accepting an "unequal treaty" to appease the Indian Government for its selfish ends. But Maharaj Mohan and his advisers regarded the conclusion of the treaties of peace and friendship and of trade and commerce with the Nehru Government as a triumph of their policy. The Maharaj naively believed that his loan of Nepali troops to India and his acceptance of most of India's terms in the newly concluded treaties would ensure him the enduring support of the Government of India and also secure him its cooperation in neutralizing the efforts of Nepali politicians who were clamouring for political reforms in Nepal.

Treaty of Peace and Friendship with Great Britain

After the withdrawal of the British from India, an informal suggestion for a new treaty between Nepal and Britain seemed to come for the first time from the Nepali Ambassador to the United Kingdom, General Kaiser Shamsher, at a luncheon meeting with Earnest Bevin, the British Secretary of State for Foreign Affairs, on 16 July 1948. General Kaiser, who was returning to Nepal after about a month to take up his new position as Senior Commanding General, or the third man just below his two brothers in the Rana hierarchy, might have deemed it fit to sound, even though unofficially, the British Government on a new treaty before he left his post in London. However, such a treaty was not concluded with Britain until after Nepal formalized its treaty relations with independent India, and it was only on 30 October 1950 that Nepal signed a new agreement with Great Britain.

One of the preambular paragraphs mentions that a new treaty had been necessary because of the inapplicability of certain provisions of the earlier treaties under the changed circumstances resulting from the establishment of the two independent states of India and Pakistan. Article I states that 'there shall be perpetual peace and friendship between the governments of Nepal and the United Kingdom." Article II acknowledges each other's independence, both external and internal, and Article III provides for the continued diplomatic representation in the two countries. The other articles deal with commercial relations and Article V(a) and (b) extends the most-favoured nation treatment to Nepal while making it clear that this arrangement does not imply the kind of special treatment accorded by the commonwealth countries to one another. Article V(c) states that the Nepal Government in turn shall not be bound to extend to the United Kingdom the advantages accorded to adjacent countries in order to facilitate frontier traffic.

The National Economic Planning Committee

On the domestic front, Maharaj Mohan felt that popular discontent was more economic than political and he would be able to satisfy the people by making promises of economic development, which he hoped to promote with the help of technical and financial aid from the rich industrial countries of the West. The Maharaj inaugurated the National Economic Planning Committee on 26 September 1948 by giving a wide-ranging speech in which he emphasized the primary importance of supplying the basic needs of the people for food, clothing and shelter by increasing production and ensuring proper distribution of what is produced. He called upon the committee to draw up a 15-year plan with these ends in view, giving priority "to transport, agriculture, mines, industry, forests, vegetation, model settlements, education, the common living standard, industrial raw materials and goods, electricity, etc." He told the committee to give careful attention to the question of resources for the plan and added that it should cut its cost according to the cloth it had.

The Maharaj agreed to become the patron of the committee and to chair its crucial meetings himself or have his brother, Minister and Commander-in-Chief Babar, chair them should the necessity arise. He entrusted the committee to the charge of his younger son Bijaya Shamsher as its President. Several sub-committees were set up to consider the tentative proposals invited from various government departments for incorporation in the plan. But nothing came out of the committee in the end because other Ranas, who were senior to Bijaya on the roll of succession and were also departmental heads, viewed the planning committee merely as his political stratagem to exercise control over their departments. In due course, the Maharaj himself lost interest in it as he had pressing political problems to face.

Mohan's Attitude Towards Political Reforms

Maharaj Mohan's lukewarm attitude towards political reforms initiated by his predecessor had already made him suspect in the eyes of the people. He could not have backed out of those reforms without personal loss of face because he had also endorsed them in his inaugural address. He, however, implemented them in a haphazard manner. Elections were held to a few village panchayats over the years and when he came under real political pressure in 1950, he tried to save his face by pleading that 150 village panchayats had been elected on the basis of adult franchise. He also claimed that the Bhaktapur, Lalitpur and Birganj municipalities had begun functioning, though he conceded that 11 out of the 21 elected members of the Kathmandu municipality had resigned. And, in a move to placate India, Mohan Shamsher made the pretence of convening his so-called Parliament on 22 September 1950 and even co-opting two elected commoner members of Parliament as members of his non-existent council of ministers in compliance with the provisions of the 1948 Constitution.

But what Maharaj Mohan had actually done during the first two years of his administration was to put into effect repressive laws drastically curtailing freedom of expression and association. It was clearly laid down that anything said or written that might adversely reflect on the interests of the regime would be treated as a punishable offence in law and harsh punishment from rigorous imprisonment to death sentence was prescribed for those who were found guilty of violating the rules framed to regulate the working of the Constitution. The Kathmandu municipality lost even the limited freedom of action it had enjoyed under Maharaj Padma, and civil liberties were suspended in the Kathmandu Valley. The opening of private schools, reading rooms and libraries was discouraged. The establishment of a university and a Sanskrit college never materialized notwithstanding the creation of a commission for the purpose. In short, Maharaj Mohan wanted to put the clock back by reversing the process of liberalization initiated by his predecessor.

Anti-Rana Political Activities

Political activities continued inside Nepal even after the Nepali National Congress had been banned by Maharaj Mohan in mid-April 1948. Thanks to the efforts of Tripurwar Singh and Gopal Prasad Rimal a new political party called the Nepal Praja Panchayat came into being in Kathmandu in September 1948. Its declared aim was to cooperate with the Rana Government in putting into effect the 1948 Constitution in a constructive spirit and it voiced its demands for the implementation of the Constitution by holding open-air meetings and popular demonstrations in the Kathmandu Valley towns.

By October 1948 the party started satyagraha against the policy of repression after it had come to the conclusion that Mohan Shamsher had changed his mind about implementing the reforms. B.P. Koirala accompanied by K.P. Bhattarai and Kedar Man Vyathit arrived in Kathmandu incognito in October 1948 as the satyagraha movement launched by the Nepal Praja Panchayat was gaining momentum. They tried to establish contact with the local leaders of the movement, but the local men, suspicious of the Congress moves, did not respond favourably to the overtures from its leaders. As the Nepali National Congress had split into two factions in India after the return of B.P. Koirala from Nepal following his release from detention in 1947, the local Praja Panchayat leaders sought to avoid taking sides in that factional dispute by remaining cool to B.P. Koirala's gestures.

B.P. Koirala was arrested a few weeks after his arrival in Kathmandu, and his faction of the Nepali National Congress decided to launch a non-violent movement in Nepal for political rights. B.P. Koirala and three of his party colleagues who were also in detention began a 21-day fast on 1 May 1949 to protest against the lack of political freedom in the country and the denial of proper treatment to them as political prisoners. Meanwhile the Socialist Party of India under Dr. Rammanohar Lohia's leadership observed 'Nepal Day' all over India in the last week of May 1949, and on 25 May Dr. Lohia was arrested along with 50 of his colleagues in New Delhi while staging a demonstration in front of the Nepali embassy. Jayaprakash Narayan sent a telegram to the Maharaj complaining against the "barbarous ill-treatment" of B.P. Koirala and his colleagues and stating that "the Indian people cannot brook tyranny in Nepal." Several Indian leaders including the Indian Prime Minister himself intervened in B.P. Koirala's case. After Koirala had given up his fast on 28 May 1949 the Maharaj released him as a goodwill gesture. The Koirala faction of the Nepali National Congress withdrew its call for the commencement of the satyagraha in response to his appeal to cancel it. But now the movement for democracy in Nepal had lost its earlier momentum because of the split in the Nepali National Congress despite the fact that the B.P. Koirala faction retained the bulk of the party workers and enjoyed the active support of the Socialist Party of India.

Meanwhile the Nepal Democratic Congress with Mahendra Bikram Shah, son of Colonel Raja Birendra Bahadur Shah of Jumla, as its Secretary-General, came into existence in Calcutta in August 1948. The present author, who was teaching in Tri-Chandra College in Kathmandu, was one of its founder members. The party enjoyed the blessings of Major-General Subarna Shamsher and Major-General Mahabir Shamsher, who were living in self-imposed exile in Calcutta at the time. The party did not have any President to begin with and looked to Somendra Nath Tagore, the leader of the Revolutionary Communist Party of India, for inspiration and guidance. The organization initially started as a rival to the Indian Socialist Party-sponsored Nepali National Congress and opposed it for splitting the democratic movement in Nepal, but the Nepal Democratic Congress also aimed at the establishment of a responsible democratic government in Nepal, with the King as a constitutional monarch, through a popular legislature elected on adult suffrage.

The main office of the Nepal Democratic Congress was first located at 'Leslie House' in Chowringhee Road, Calcutta, but was shifted in April 1949 to Patna after the party had changed its top organizational structure by making Mahendra Bikram Shah its President and Surya Prasad Upadhyaya its Secretary-General. The head office at Patna was not, however, much used and for all practical purposes the party continued to function from Calcutta where Mahendra Bikram Shah resided. After the present author persuaded Jiv Raj Sharma, one of the founder members of the Nepal Praja Parishad, to join the party and sent him to India. Jiv Raj and another long-time political worker, Shankar Prasad Sharma, started looking after the official organ of the party, *Nepal Pukar*, which was published from Patna with Babu Lal Moktan as its editor. The journal was predictably soon banned by the Nepal Government.

The Nepal Democratic Congress had no connection with any other political group to begin with but was in touch with some of the Nepali communists in India like Ratna Lal Bahun and others. After Surya Prasad Upadhyaya became the Secretary-General of the party, it began to turn to the Indian National Congress leaders such as Rafi Ahmed Kidwai and Keshav Dev Malaviya for advice and guidance. Some of the wealthy Calcutta Ranas like General Hiranya Shamsher and Major-Generals Subarna and Mahabir Shamsher openly came out in support of the party after Maharaj Mohan Shamsher had seized their property in Nepal. An effort was made by Mahendra Bikram Shah to organize branches on the Nepal-Bihar border and at Guwahati and Kathmandu.

A few meetings and a conference were held during the latter part of the 1948 and the first quarter of 1949. But in spite of these activities the Nepal Democratic Congress was not able to make much headway. In April 1949 negotiations were started with a view to amalgamating both the factions of the Nepali National Congress with the Nepal Democratic Congress, but the talks broke down. Since then there was no appreciable activity on the part of the parties in India working for democracy in Nepal. The way in which Maharaj Mohan Shamsher was cordially received by the Nehru Government in Delhi in January 1950 seemed to dampen the hope and enthusiasm of these parties about their immediate success. But Mahendra Bikram Shah, always thinking in terms of armed revolution, led the Nepal Democratic Congress in setting up a cell of some of the Nepali officers who had served as part of Subhas Chandra Bose's Indian National Army. These men included Dilman Singh, Puran Singh and J.B. Yakthumba with Thir Bam Malla in charge of it for recruiting armed volunteers as and when necessary.

In early 1950 a fresh proposal was mooted for the merger of the Nepali National Congress (Koirala) and the Nepal Democratic Congress with a view to consolidating the struggle for democracy in Nepal. On 27 March 1950 M.P. Koirala, President of the Nepali National Congress, and M.B. Shah, President of the Nepal Democratic Congress, issued a press statement emphasizing the necessity for the merger of the two parties. As a result, a joint conference of the delegates of the two parties was held at the Tiger Cinema in Calcutta on 9 April 1950, and thus was born a new party called the Nepali Congress out of the Nepali National Congress, with an avowed policy of non-violence, and the Nepal Democratic Congress, pledged to overthrow the Rana regime by any means. The new Nepali Congress adopted the flag and the mouthpiece, *Nepal Pukar*, of the Nepal Democratic Congress and elected M.P. Koirala of the Nepali National Congress as its President.

The revolutionary plan of the Nepali Congress was to abduct King Tribhuvan and take him to western Nepal, probably to Palpa, and set up a parallel government under him. This move was to be followed by a revolt by disaffected sections of the army against the Rana regime. King Tribhuvan was to be seized during the week-long Indra Jatra festival in September with the help of some Rana and Shah officers who were supposed to mobilize a section of the army for the purpose.

On 5 September 1950, Crown Prince Mahendra's first wife Princess Indra Rajya Lakshmi Devi Shah, died following a miscarriage. The royal family had reason to be angry with Maharaj Mohan and his brothers for they neither sent her to India for the delivery nor did they bring a reputed gynaecologist and nurses trained in midwifery from India to take care of her.

On 24 September 1950 volunteers of the Nepali Congress including Dil Man Singh and others were arrested with arms in their possession. Other Nepali Congress organizers and volunteers including Sundar Raj Chalise and his wife were also detained along with them as their accomplices. Those arrested also included army officers in active service such as Colonel Toran Shamsher Rana, Captain Pratap Bikram Shah, who was Subarna Shamsher's sister's husband, and Captain Mohan Bikram Shah, who was Subarna's wife's brother, together with several retired army officers such as Colonel Nod Bikram Shah, who too was Subarna's sister's husband. An official press statement stated that arms, ammunition and wireless equipment had been seized in Captain Pratap Bikram Shah's house. It was alleged that the recorded statements of those arrested implicated Tribhuvan himself in their plot and for that reason the King had stopped paying routine visits to the Prime Minister in order to avoid interrogation on this question.

Meanwhile the Nepali Congress convened its delegates' conference at Bairgania in northern Bihar on 26-27 September 1950 and decided to launch as soon as possible a movement for the establishment of democracy in Nepal. Dictatorial powers were given to its President, Matrika Prasad Koirala, for the duration of the movement, in view of the fact that it might take the shape of an armed struggle.

At this time a crucial change was taking place in Nepal's region of the world, and this accelerated the pace of events in Nepal itself. On 7 October 1949 the Tibetan garrison at Chamdo was overrun by the advancing Chinese troops and on 25 October the Peking Radio announced that the People's Liberation Army had been ordered to 'liberate' the whole of Tibet. China's reply to India's complaint against its use of force in Tibet was that as Tibet was an integral part of China, it would brook "no foreign interference." British India's traditional China policy of treating Tibet more or less as an autonomous buffer zone between India and China had been abandoned by independent India, and Tibetan appeals for help from India and Nepal remained largely unheeded. India told Tibet to seek on its own the best available terms with China.

However, the Indian Government wanted to show its resolve not to let the Chinese influence extend beyond the Tibetan frontiers. To achieve this India determined to strengthen its hold on Nepal through support for the King and the nascent democratic movement.

The arrest of armed Nepali Congress volunteers along with some of the officers in the Nepali army had already created a serious problem for the King. During his unofficial visits to India in 1946 the King had had a chance to establish links with the anti-Rana elements through Major-General Subarna and Major-General Mahabir, who were at the time in the good books of Maharaj Padma. Therefore, there was every room for the suspicion that King Tribhuvan himself was involved in the Nepali Congress's attempt to stage a coup in September. Furthermore, the King was afraid that he might be forced to give the royal sanction for the execution of some of those who were under arrest. Embarrassed by these circumstances, the King at last decided to extricate himself. He drove to the Prime Minister's residence alone on 5 November by pre-arrangement and obtained his permission to go on a hunting trip on the morning of 6 November.

It was against the background of these events inside and outside Nepal that King Tribhuvan, accompanied by his two queens and his three sons, Crown Prince Mahendra, who was a widower, Prince Himalaya and Prince Basundhara with their wives, and Mahendra's 5-year old son and heir apparent Prince Birendra, left the Royal Palace by car on the pretext of going hunting in a forest to the north of Kathmandu on the morning on 6 November 1950. As they drove north, they approached the Indian Ambassador's residence, Sheetal Nivas at Maharajganj, and suddenly the King and his sons, who were driving their own cars, swung through the embassy gates to the shock and bewilderment of the Rana government's guards posted outside the embassy.

The Rana Government did not know till the early afternoon that the King and other members of the royal family had sought asylum in the Indian embassy. The British Ambassador to Nepal, Sir George Falconer, had invited to lunch that day a visiting Indian, Deputy Inspector General Waryam Singh, who was staying with the Indian Ambassador. Sir George's luncheon guest, though fully aware of the King's flight to the Indian embassy, did not disclose anything about it to his host until 2 p.m. when he saw the Nepali officer attached to the embassy hurriedly approaching the Ambassador with the news.

According to the intelligence report of the Rana Government, two embassy cooks had arrived by air the day before the King's party sought shelter, and senior members of the embassy staff were there at the ambassador's residence within 15 minutes of the arrival of the King's party. According to the British Ambassador, "from one or two incidents which are alleged to have since come to light, the Prime Minister is very suspicious that the Indian ambassador was not really without knowledge of the King's intention before he arrived at the embassy."

It was thus for the first time in history that a reigning monarch had sought asylum in a foreign embassy. The Rana Prime Minister was belatedly informed of the dramatic event only after 1 p.m. by his brother, Minister and Commander-in-Chief Babar Shamsher. Babar was first given this piece of information on the telephone by a Rana relative, who had by chance overheard on his radio a wireless message being transmitted to New Delhi from the Indian embassy concerning the King's presence there.

Reportedly the first reaction of the top Ranas was to use force, if necessary, to have the Indian embassy surrender the royal family. But they feared the consequences of military action against a foreign embassy and decided instead to send two emissaries to the Indian Ambassador's residence to request the King to return to the royal palace. Accordingly, Major-General Arjun Shamsher and Major-General Bijaya Shamsher were sent there to call on King Tribhuvan, but the King refused to meet them.

An emergency session of Nepal's Parliament and a Bhardari, an assembly consisting of the nobility, Rajgurus and state officials was convened to consider the situation created by the royal flight to the Indian embassy. They met at 7 a.m. on 7 November and declared unanimously and emphatically in writing that according to the laws, usage and constitution of Nepal, Maharajadhiraj Tribhuvan Bir Bikram Shah Deva and the members of the royal family had by their action forfeited their right to the throne. Prince Birendra, the minor eldest son of the Crown Prince, should be given a chance to return; failing which, the next rightful heir should forthwith be proclaimed King to ensure peace and tranquillity in the realm.

Major-General Arjun Shamsher and Major-General Bijaya Shamsher were sent once again to meet the King and apprise him of this decision of the Bhardari. King Tribhuvan met Bijaya alone and said that he did not recognize the decision of the Bhardari nor did he intend to abdicate. The King also declined to allow the eldest son of the Crown Prince to return to the palace.

Meanwhile the Ranas had found still in the Royal Palace the King's second grandson, four-year-old Prince Gyanendra, along with his ten month–old younger brother and their three sisters. When the Rana Government was informed of what Major-General Bijaya was told by the King, Prince Gyanendra was proclaimed and enthroned King at 2:45 p.m. on 7 November 1950.

B.P. Koirala, one of the Nepali Congress leaders, issued a statement the same day from Patna to the effect that by his abdication the King had denounced the present Government of Nepal as that of usurpers, and the end of the regime of the Rana family was now only a matter of days. India's stand on the developments in Nepal was described next day to Britain's envoy in New Delhi by Sir Girija Shankar Bajpai, Secretary General of India's Ministry of External Affairs, who said it was his government's intention to resolve the dispute between the Maharajadhiraj and the Maharaj through its good offices. According to him, it was the duty of the Government of India to find out the implications of recognizing the new King before doing so. As King Tribhuvan could be the centre of agitation on Indian soil, the Government of India had only taken note of his desire for medical treatment.

Bajpai further added that there was no question of the Government of India treating the Government of Nepal on a basis of paramountcy as if it were an Indian state. But the fact remained that Nepal was entirely dependent upon India, more especially in the existing world situation with the new threat to Nepal from communist China. It would therefore be very short-sighted on the part of the Maharaj to proceed in the matter as he had done without consultation with the Government of India and without paying due regard to their views. India would insist on the King coming to India unconditionally and they would take their time over deciding their attitude towards recognizing the new King. According to Bajpai the Government of India was angry and indignant over the Maharaj's action and they seemed to be prepared to crack the whip if he failed to toe their line. He pointed out that the Maharaj could not have chosen a more awkward moment for his rash action from the viewpoint of the state of international relations. It was particularly awkward for the Government of India as it had given an excuse to the many Indian critics of the Government of Nepal for finding fault with it. Bajpai complained that over the past two years the Maharaj had paid no attention to constant Indian advice and practical suggestions for making his regime more democratic.

Bajpai referred to the future problems created for India by the Chinese victory in Tibet. He was concerned that the more democratic elements inside and outside Nepal might turn to communist China for support. Bajpai's plea was that the British and the American Governments should adopt a policy similar to that of India with regard to the recognition of the new King and to the other aspects of the policy towards Nepal lest any divergence should be exploited by the Chinese.

Bajpai was assured by the British High Commissioner that the British Government would be in close touch and form a policy in consultation with the Government of India. The American Ambassador to India, Loy Henderson, who was concurrently accredited to Nepal, asked his Government to act in consultation with the British Government in London.

The Government of India would stand by King Tribhuvan who, according to Bajpai, had not abdicated and would not give the assurance that he would refrain from political activity in India.[5]

Yet another crisis in the Nepal-India relations occurred on 8 November 1950 when Maharaj Mohan Shamsher objected to India's refusal to describe King Tribhuvan as ex-King and when he declined to grant landing permission that day for a special Indian aircraft to be sent for King Tribhuvan. Without giving the required month's notice Mohan also withdrew the permission for Indian commercial planes to land in Nepal. The Indian Ambassador now feared that the Rana Government might even use force to take the royal family back to the palace, for the embassy had been put under strict surveillance.

The Government of India at this juncture made it clear to the British High Commissioner through Bajpai and also to the Rana Government that it had no hidden motives, but it would act if the Rana Government laid an indefinite siege on the Indian embassy while

Tribhuvan stayed there or if it sought the removal of the King and his family by force. It could not let moderate Nepali political elements go over to the Chinese side, and it also had to take into account the sympathy amongst Indian political leaders for the Nepali Congress.

The Indian Deputy Prime Minister and Home Minister, Sardar Vallabhbhai Patel, reputed to be India's iron man, stated on 9 November that India could not possibly have refused asylum to the King and that Nepal's internal feud had laid India's frontiers in the north open to danger. He had prefaced it with the following cryptic remarks: "Those who are wielding real power today do not accept the Raja as the head of the state. They have installed the Raja's three-year-old grandson on the Gadi. They want us to accept the position. How can we do so?"

By 9 November London had asked its ambassador to Nepal to urge upon the Nepal Government the importance of ending the present crisis by letting King Tribhuvan go to India immediately. London's view was that the recognition of the new King was not an immediate problem and it should present little difficulty if Nepal could be persuaded to allow the ex-King to go to India. The British Government, however, would regard the change of monarchy as an internal matter of the Nepal in which it was not concerned.[6]

On 10 November the Indian Ambassador to Nepal, Sir C.P.N. Singh, conveyed to Maharaj Mohan the oral message of the Indian Prime Minister, Pandit Jawaharlal Nehru, that Tribhuvan would not be allowed to take part in any political activities in India. This apparently enabled the Maharaj to rescind without loss of face his earlier decision not to let the Indian aircraft land in Nepal and next day Tribhuvan and other members of the royal family were flown out of Kathmandu by two Indian Air Force planes. On his arrival at Palam airport together with his family the King was presented a guard of honour and was received by the Indian Prime Minister himself.

General Shankar Shamsher, Nepal's Ambassador to the United Kingdom, had met the British Foreign Secretary Bevin at 10.45 a.m. on 10 November 1950. Following their meeting a cabinet paper covering the whole question was ordered. The British Secretary of State for Foreign Affairs himself was inclined to recognize the new King as quickly as possible in order to forestall difficulties with India.[7]

A telegram sent by Sir G.A. Falconer to the Foreign Office on 10 November accused his Indian counterpart and the Government of India of "erring in international law on two counts: (i) In voluntarily affording asylum to the King and his family, whose persons were in no physical or political danger from the legal government; there being no record of the government having conceded to envoys the right of granting asylum by fact or usage, unless by act of abdication asylum was sought to ensure safe conduct out of the country, and (ii) By arranging with his government (the Indian government) for immediate removal to India of the King and all his family without first consulting the government of Nepal or at least informing them of his intention." The reason said to have been given by the King for asylum was "to arrange to go to India for medical treatment."

Now the Nepali Congress swung into action. On 10, 11 and 12 November there were unauthorized flights of aircraft dropping Nepali Congress leaflets in the Kathmandu Valley, Birganj and several places between them. The Nepali Congress "insurgency" seemed to coincide with the arrival of the King and other members of the royal family in New Delhi. In the small hours of 11 November, two or three hundred armed men made a surprise attack on Birganj, a frontier township in south central Nepal, which had always served as the main gateway to Kathmandu from India for purposes of both travel and commerce. The armed Nepali Congress volunteers were said to have used forty trucks bearing the marking and numbers of Bihar state in India and received reinforcements from the Indian side of the border. The Nepal army garrison at Birganj were heavily outnumbered but offered resistance till the last round of ammunition was spent. The Congress volunteers captured the Bada Hakim or the Governor, Colonel Som Shamsher Rana, and other officials with their familities and took them away to the Indian side of the border. (On 12 November the Governor was released from captivity by the Government of India.) The Congressmen had accomplished their task but lost their commander, Thir Bam Malla, who was shot at from close range by a Government soldier and died as he was being taken by his men to the Duncan Hospital at Raxaul. Several others were wounded.

The volunteers lost no time in proclaiming a revolutionary government under the Mukti Sena, the Liberation Army of the Nepali Congress, and from 12 November they started spreading towards Kalaiya while one truck headed for Simra. The success of the Nepali Congress volunteers in capturing Birganj and retaining its control for a week boosted their morale and also helped them gain sustained favourable reports in the Indian press.

Though the Indian press widely publicized a report that large bodies of armed men were assembling in India with a view to crossing into Nepal at nine points, the nine-pronged attack never materialized and even attacks on one or two other district headquarters bordering on India were not successful. Biratnagar, an industrial town in the Morang district in the eastern tarai, was attacked on 11 November from Jogbani in India, but the attack was repulsed by the Government forces stationed there. At 5 a.m. on 15 November armed volunteers of the Nepali Congress attacked Bhairahawa, the headquarters of the Butwal district in the mid-western tarai. Their strength was of one hundred to one hundred and fifty well-trained men and about two hundred followers. They used a smokescreen and automatic weapons, and heavy and constant exchange of fire occurred between the two sides. By 8 a.m. the Government side had killed about twelve and wounded about the same number of Nepali Congress armed volunteers, and an hour later the Congress force had dispersed except for a few groups of eight or ten taking defensive positions in the mill areas. Reports of the volunteers gathering on the Indian side of the border in the Darjeeling district for an attack on Ilam were published.

On 13 November 1950 a plane carrying Nepali Congress leaders with a quantity of arms and 3.5 million rupees, which they had taken from the Birganj Revenue Office, was intercepted by the Indian authorities in Delhi and the money was held by the Government of India pending arrangements for its return. By 16 November the Government of India issued strict orders to the Governments of West Bengal, Bihar and the United Provinces not to allow armed men to go either way across the border. Four days earlier the British Deputy High Commissioner in India, Sir Frank Roberts, had been informed by the Government of India that it had no knowledge of insurrectionary activities on the border.

However, George Falconer, the British Ambassador in Nepal, was pressing his Government to extend recognition to the new King without delay. This was what he had said in his telegram of 13 November 1950 to the Foreign Office in London:

> Events in Nepal are moving fast and I think time has come for plain-speaking. I am now convinced in my mind that the ex-King is an intriguer and a proved liar; the actions of the Indian ambassador are gravely suspicious and the attitude of the Government of India towards Nepal in this affair and the events leading up to it are 'unfriendly' to say the least.

> No greater justice will be done to Nepal and its people than speedy recognition of its Parliament's action in declaring the throne vacant and proclaiming the new King. They are becoming disheartened at our delay in recognising their first major decision as a common assembly. I therefore hope that speedy recognition will be given.

On 13 November itself, Sir Frank Roberts in Delhi telegraphed to the Commonwealth Relations Office in London that:

> In this connection I should mention in strict confidence that I have reliable information that Pandit Nehru himself rather regretted the Maharaja's climb down (on allowing Tribhuvan to be flown out of the country) as he was prepared in the case of obduracy to push through what he considers essential reform.

Krishna Menon, the Indian High Commissioner to the United Kingdom, met the Labour Prime Minister, Clement Attlee, on 13 November and told him that some of the reformist parties in Nepal had wanted to get into contact with the communists of China. Attlee's reply was that his colleague "the Foreign Secretary would not like to let the issue of recognition remain unresolved."

On 14 November General Shankar Shamsher, Nepal's Ambassador in London, met Sir William Strang, Private Secretary to the British Foreign Secretary. The British Government did not know how to say no to the Nepali Ambassador, if he pressed for the immediate recognition of the new King. They thought that "if it was argued that formally speaking, the King had not abdicated, then he (the Nepali) ambassador would remind us that James II had not abdicated from the throne but by abandoning the reins of the Government, had left the throne vacant and had thus enabled the Prince of Orange to ascend the throne by constitutional means." When General Shankar pleaded that delay in recognition would be dangerous, Sir William said that he would bring everything to the attention of his Secretary. Subsequently the Nepali Ambassador was told that the recognition question would be raised in the cabinet on 20 November and the decision would be in favour of the recognition of the new King.

On 14 November the Commonwealth Relations Office sent the following telegram to the United Kingdom High Commissioner, Sir Archibald Nye, in Delhi:

> A decision on recognition cannot be delayed and the matter will probably be raised in the cabinet on Monday the 20th November. This will probably be in favour of recognition on the grounds that this is an internal matter for the Nepalese government and depends primarily on the question of fact whether the new regime is firmly installed and in effective control of the country.
>
> We recognize Indian interest in Nepal. We are in sympathy with her wish for the introduction of democratic reforms in Nepal but we cannot be a party to interfering in the internal affairs of an independent country, and it is our experience that reforms of this nature cannot be hurried and attempts to use pressure defeat their own ends. The return of the old King of Nepal at this stage might cause the downfall of the present regime and might lead to further disorder and bloodshed in Nepal. Stability is at present the prime necessity, both in view of the international situation and because of the likely unfortunate effect on recruitment of Gurkhas of any change in the government at present.
>
> Please approach the Government of India on the above lines informing them that (a) we are anxious to take an early decision, and (b) that we would if possible like to keep in line with Indian policy.
>
> You should telegraph the reply as soon as possible, in any case to reach me not later than the 18th of November.

Loy Henderson, American Ambassador to India and Nepal, had suggested to his British counterpart in New Delhi on 13 November that "it might not be in the interests of stability in the present international situation to do anything to weaken the Rana regime in Nepal."

Sir Geoffery Betham, British Minister in Nepal from 1938 to 1944, called on Peter Scott, Head of the South East Asian Department, on the morning of 16 November 1950 at the request of the Nepali Ambassador, and pressed for the early recognition of the new King by Great Britain. The British Ambassador to Nepal had also informed the Foreign Office that the Government of Nepal had no intention of sending a representative to discuss the question with the Government of India. It was also reported by the British High Commission at the time that India contemplated withdrawing its Ambassador from Nepal.

As far as the British Government was concerned, the relevant facts were that the established and recognized Government of Nepal had formally stated that the accession of the new King was in accordance with the Nepali law, usage and custom; and the regime with the new King was firmly established. But in his note on the file dealing with the recognition of the new King in Nepal dated 18 November 1950, J.S. Oliver, a ranking officer in the British Foreign Office, made the following observation:

> India is unlikely to be deterred from her present course by agreements or appeals or even by a personal message from Bevin. It is just possible that by our announcing clearly that we ourselves intended to recognise the new King, whatever the Indian attitude, Nehru might be given cause to think.

However, P.H. Scott was not in favour of giving an ultimatum to India, and he told the Nepali Ambassador that consideration of the question by the cabinet had been deferred till 23 November 1950.

As the interview between the Indian Prime Minister and the British High Commissioner on 19 November 1950 covered a wide range of issues relating to the recognition of the new King of Nepal, excerpts from Sir Archibald Nye's account of this interview with Nehru as transmitted to the British Commonwealth Relations Office Secretary are reproduced below:

> I opened by pointing out that it was our sincere desire to march with India on this as on any other question of importance and we would only decide to take a view contrary to that of the government of India, if we honestly felt that we were unable to subscribe to India's views and we would do so with extreme reluctance.
>
> The object of my interview was to get Nehru's views on a number of specific points so that before HMG made its decision they would be fully apprised of what was in his mind and would take the decision with their eyes open and well aware of all the consequences.
>
> This was the great value of pre-consulation within the Commonwealth. If after the closest exchange of views we found ourselves unable to agree, it would mean an agreed disagreement carried out with mutual understanding and with mutual respect and would not, we hope, have any adverse effect on our general relationship. We still hope that we would be able to come to some understanding.
>
> Nehru gave me a very long reply speaking for over one hour reviewing the situation from many years back in great detail and his

remarks though quite interesting were largely irrelevant and added little to our knowledge of the situation or the government of India's views about it. The major points which emerged are as follows:

(a) The present Maharaj was an obstinate and stupid reactionary and there is no hope of any progress in Nepal so long as he remains in his present position.
(b) The Rana regime cannot possibly last. It may continue for a few months or a few years but it is bound to collapse.
(c) Public opinion in India is very strong against the existing regime in Nepal and there is great anger at the behaviour of the Nepalese government. No prime minister could fail to take note of these sentiments and he himself is in entire agreement with public opinion in this matter. Were the Government of India to recognise the infant King they would be condemned throughout the country as having done a dastardly act.
(d) The Soviets were successful in giving the impression that they were a liberating force even although we know that is not the case. It is essential that we must not appear as a reactionary force giving our backing to outworn feudal regimes.
(e) It would be very unwise for the Government of India to throw its weight on a side which, it is quite convinced, must fall. So far as world opinion is concerned, he is not worried. He thought that the great majority of countries would regard the recognition of the infant King as Gilbertian.
(f) He complained about the reactionary attitude of the British ambassador in Kathmandu who had, he understood, strongly advised the Nepali government against any form of change.
(g) He failed to understand on what ground we could conceivably say that the selection of the new King was based on law. On the contrary in his view it had no legality, indeed it was stamped with illegality.

I made the obvious replies to these points but only two of which call for special attention:

(a) I strongly denied the allegation against Sir George Falconer who I said had consistently advised the Nepal government to liberalise the constitution. Nehru was glad to hear this.

(b) As to the question of the legality of the accession of the new King I said it was wholly irrelevant whether we considered the question of Nepal to be a good one, a liberal one, a feudal one or an archaic one. The fact remained that it existed and even if it was as Nehru described it solely the will of the Maharaja, no one could call into question its legality. Most of us heartily disliked certain regimes, e.g., those in the communist countries which were regarded not merely as illiberal but in many respects quite revolting but it did not occur to us to call into question their right to their own governments, to make their own laws and to have their own constitution.

I then asked him if he could give me some idea of the practical effects which would follow from any recognition which the Government of India might give to the old King. Would it merely be a paper transaction or would he continue to live in Delhi or elsewhere in India or might he go to Monte Carlo and disappear from the scene. If so the practical effects might be relatively small or would he on the other hand be allowed to remain in India to go through the process of starting up a provisional government, of collecting discontented Nepalese around him, of indulging in political and possibly military activities using India as a base because if such consequences were to follow they would be serious in the extreme. Nehru was in an obvious difficulty in answering this question and it was quite evident that he had not given any precise consideration to it. He said he thought it would not be a transaction and that the ex-King would be allowed to remain in India but the Government of India would have to consider very carefully if he proposed to indulge in any political activities which might prove embarrassing to them.

I then pointed out that there were 24 battalions of Gurkhas in India, 12 under the Tripartite Agreement of 1947 and 12 'wartime' battalions still on loan from the government of Nepal. I asked him what would be the attitude of the Government of India if Nepal asked for the return of the extra 12 battalions. He said he did not know and he would have to think this over. I asked him if there were any efforts to persuade these Gurkha troops to give their allegiance to the ex-King, whether the Government of India would permit him to take command of them and to attempt any invasion of Nepal. He said they would not allow the ex-King to do any such thing.

I said to him the crux of the whole matter seemed to be this. Even if we allowed that the regime in Nepal is reactionary, even if we allowed that there is some discontent, that there may be confusion or chaos in the country in course of time, that it may come under communist hands and that it may therefore constitute a threat to the security of India (making it clear that I did not subscribe to all these propositions), one nevertheless had to face the fact that Nepal was an independent country. If India claimed as she apparently did claim a particular interest because Nepal's borders were adjacent to hers, would she similarly claim that if she was dissatisfied with conditions in say Burma and Pakistan that she had a right to interfere with their system of government and to ask them to send their representatives to Delhi to discuss the matter. And conversely if Pakistan and Burma or Nepal find themselves dissatisfied with the method of the Government of India as a possible threat to their security by India's failure to deal with her communist agitators and requested India to send their representatives to Rangoon, Karachi or Kathmandu, what would be the reaction of India in such circumstances. It appeared to me that India was enunciating a theory of international relations which would not bear any examination. Surely we are all entitled as independent and friendly countries to offer each other advice, suggestions, exhortations and criticisms but there was a very definite limit as to how far we could go and it behoved us all not to step beyond a certain line which would amount to nothing more or less than interference. He denied with some warmth that India had so far done anything which could be regarded as interference with another country or that the action which they proposed could possibly be construed in that way. I told him that I hoped that he would be able to convince other countries that this was so but I had considerable doubts whether he would be successful.

I said I assumed that he would withhold any further action in this matter until the reply from HMG was received.

He said the matter was an urgent one and he would do his best to take no action until he had heard from London. I said his best was not good enough and I would assume that he would wait to hear the considered reply from HMG before he took further action.

> The interview was very friendly and he warmly reciprocated the sentiments which I had expressed about the good relations which existed between our two governments and the desirability of maintaining them. I spoke with extreme frankness but he did not seem to resent any representations I made. Nevertheless my impression is (and indeed Bajpai has privately informed me) that he has already made up his mind and no arguments we may produce are likely to have any effect on him. The most I think we can hope is that whilst he will undoubtedly disagree with the attitude which we propose to adopt, he is not likely to attribute to us any unfriendly motives.[8]

On 21 November the United Kingdom High Commissioner met the Secretary-General of the Indian Ministry of Commonwealth and External Relations and told him that it would be unfortunate if their countries took diametrically opposite views on the important question of recognizing the new King of Nepal, but they must necessarily do what they thought was right even if the result was a deterioration in their general relations.

Back in Nepal, the insurrection was faltering. An attack by 200 Congress armed volunteers on Jhapa, the eastern-most district in the tarai, on 19 November was repulsed by Government forces. Ten days after Birganj had fallen into the hands of the Nepali Congress, the Nepal Government forces, apparently under the overall command of Lieutenant-General Ekraj Shamsher and Major-General Brahma Shamsher but actually led by Colonel Giri Raj Ghale in the field under instructions from the Maharaj himself in Kathmandu, recaptured it at 2 p.m. on 20 November. Two persons were killed, eighty were taken prisoners and the rest of the armed volunteers fled Birganj. The delay in its recapture was mainly due to the absence of a unified command of Government forces and their inability to make a correct assessment of the strength of the armed volunteers. Following the Government forces' success at Birganj, there was a complete lull in insurrectionary activities for more than a month until the last week of December.

On 20 November a message from Nehru to Attlee on the recognition of the old King in Nepal was handed over by the Indian High Commissioner to the United Kingdom, Krishna Menon. Another Nehru letter was delivered to Attlee by Krishna Menon on 22 November in which the Indian Prime Minister acknowledged the message from the British Prime Minister convened through Sir Archibald Nye. Nehru assured Attlee of his "desire to maintain unity of understanding and action with the United Kingdom in all matters of common interest" but expressed his inability to change the earlier decision of the Indian Government to withhold recognition of the new King even after the fullest consideration of the points that the British High Commissioner had urged. When Menon once again raised the question of the British recognition of the new King, Attlee gave him an evasive reply.

According to what General Shankar Shamsher, then Nepal's Ambassador to the United Kingdom, told the present author, Foreign Secretary Bevin had definitely promised him a favourable decision with regard to the British recognition of the new King in Nepal by 23 November. But after the British Foreign Secretary was informed by Krishna Menon that a high-power Nepali delegation consisting of Eastern Commanding General Kaiser Shamsher and Major-General Bijaya Shamsher was due for arrival in New Delhi on 24 November for discussions with the Indian Government, Bevin told the Nepali Ambassador that under the circumstances he could not immediately announce the British decision to recognize the new King as such an action might unduly prejudice Indian feeling against the British Government.

Krishna Menon, then Indian High Commissioner, also told the present author long after the collapse of the Rana regime that after he had received information through his sources about the British plan for the immediate recognition of the new King in Nepal, he sought to placate Attlee by promising to withhold the announcement of the Indian decision not to recognize the new king until after further consultations between the Governments in view of the outcome of the discussions and negotiations in Delhi between the Nepali delegation and the Indian Government. On the whole, Menon's well-planned tactic of delaying the British recognition of the new King helped his Government fulfil its end eventually without much embarrassment.

On the evening of 24 November Senior Commanding General Kaiser Shamsher, the number-three men in the ruling Rana hierarchy, and Bijaya Shamsher, the Director-General of Foreign Affairs and the favourite second son of the incumbent Maharaj himself, arrived in Delhi and began talks with the Government of India immediately. But the arrival of the Nepali delegation seems to have further strengthened Nehru's resolve to announce India's non-recognition of the new King. Nehru became impatient to do so whereas President Rajendra Prasad and former Governor-General Rajagopalachari were in favour of playing for time, partly because the Commonwealth Prime Ministers' conference in London was only six weeks away.

On 25 November Sir Archibald Nye telegraphed his Government his increasing anxiety about the very serious consequences for the relations between the British and the Indian Governments that might flow from the recognition of two different kings by them. When Sir Archibald Nye handed Nehru the personal message from Attlee on the evening of 24 November, Nehru launched a tirade with great heat and passion and lost control of himself. He said he would bear the attitude of the Rana Government no longer. But Nehru was told by Sir Archibald that he had no ground for withdrawing the Indian Ambassador because the Rana Government was in effective control of the country and the accession of the new King was in proper constitutional form.

Nehru was actually threatening to refuse to go to the Commonwealth Conference. The American Ambassador to India and Nepal, Loy Henderson, had earlier sought permission from his Government to warn India that it should not expect American sympathy in the United Nations or elsewhere if it failed to live up to its international obligation in respect of Nepal. But now the U.S.A. was becoming concerned at the open divergence of policy between the U.K. and India on the matter of the recognition of the new King. Apart from the international consequences which might ensue in Nepal, the U.S. Government were apprehensive about the relationships between India and the United Kingdom which would make their own position invidious. The U.S.A. also appeared to be in favour of the deferment of the question of recognition.

Nehru was reported by Reuter to have said on 26 November in a speech at Jamshedpur that "we cannot recognize a 3-year-old boy as King." His plea was that Nepal was an independent country but was in many respects interlinked with India. "We cannot, therefore, watch developments in Nepal as silent spectators. It is desirable that there should be a democratic Government there. But in spite of the desire it is not possible for me now to say what course of action the government of India will take in regard to the problem in Nepal."

These remarks by Nehru were apt to arouse misunderstanding in the U.K. about his earlier promise not to announce the non-recognition of the new king except in consultation with the British Government. Krishna Menon hastened to mollify the British by writing to the Commonwealth Relations Secretary, Gordon Walker, the same day that

> the Prime Minister spoke in Hindi and the reporter came from Calcutta and he must have found it difficult to understand the Prime Minister properly.
>
> The Prime minister did not say, as the reporter alleges, that we cannot recognise the boy King. What he said was the Government was carefully considering the whole question of Nepal and the King but in any event we have felt the need for reforms in Nepal.

Meanwhile, since their arrival in Delhi on 24 November General Kaiser and Major-General Bijaya had had meetings with Nehru, Patel and Bajpai. On the question of the ex-King, General Kaiser said that he was no longer acceptable to the people of Nepal; as regards reforms Kaiser cited what had been done during the past two years: constitutional acts, panchayats, the convening of the Assembly last September. Kaiser desired to know what India really wanted and it was arranged for the Nepalis to have a further meeting with Bajpai.

At a meeting on 30 November, Bajpai, presumably under instructions from Nehru, put forward India's suggestions as follows:

(a) return of the ex-King as a constitutional monarch,
(b) speedy formation of a representative assembly,
(c) meanwhile the immediate creation of an executive council to include representatives of the Nepali Congress from India.

Kaiser reiterated that the ex-King had been deposed by the Nepal parliament as established under the Act in force and was therefore unacceptable, and he also pointed out the inevitable obstacles to the speedy creation of a national assembly on a truly representative basis. The Nepali delegation were agreeable to having an executive council with wide powers, but strongly objected to the inclusion of those persons who had taken up arms against the Government and were residing in India. The meeting failed to reach any agreement and both sides decided to refer back to their Governments.[9] While showing him the communication from the Nepali delegation in Delhi, the Maharaj told the British Ambassador to Nepal in strict confidence that so far Pakistan had indicated its intention to recognise the new King, but the Nepali Government were awaiting the reply from some other Governments before making any public announcement. Falconer, however, advised the Maharaj to have the most friendly relations with India and expressed the hope that the present differences would be resolved to mutual satisfaction and regard. Falconer did not think that the government of India would take any armed action against Nepal. He also told the Maharaj that he could not speculate on the attitude of the United Nations should the government of Nepal in the last resort make a representation to it. At the end the British Ambassador requested the Maharaj not to make any hasty decision.

General Kaiser gave the British Deputy High Commissioner, Sir Frank Roberts, more or less the same account of their discussions with the Indian leaders, though not in the same detail as given above. Sir Frank had made it clear to the Nepali delegation at the very beginning that his purpose in meeting them was not one of mediation. Kaiser began by saying that "the Indians were insisting upon the return of the old King but later stated that this was not correct and all that they said was they were still examining the question of recognising the new King." Kaiser was not unduly worried about the question of reforms and seemed to think that the Nepali Government could accept the Indian suggestion for reforms if it did not mean the inclusion of the Nepali Congress leaders in the Government, which was out of question.

In Kaiser's view the crux of the matter was the question of the King. He was turning over in his mind the possibility of a compromise based upon some council of regency, and he and Bajpai both agreed that there was no need for haste in regard to recognition by either India or the United Kingdom. Indeed they both volunteered that it had been very fortunate that the British Government had refrained from recognizing the new King hurriedly and thus avoided precipitating a crisis with India.

As the talks had reached a stage when references to Kathmandu were necessary, Kaiser asked Roberts 'to take a full report from them to the Maharaja.' Kaiser further indicated that he expected to receive his final instructions after Sir Esler Dening, a high-ranking officer from the British Foreign Office, had seen the Maharaj and on the return of Dening and Roberts to Delhi. Roberts agreed to act the part of courier and take a sealed packet to Kathmandu. General Singha, the Nepali Ambassador to Delhi and Kaiser's brother, told Roberts that while the situation was very serious he thought that wise counsels were beginning to prevail in India and that if precipitate action from any side could be avoided, and if the U.K. could continue to exert its helpful influence behind the scenes in Kathmandu and Delhi, a solution might now be found.

Though Lloyd V. Steere, Counsellor in the U.S. Embassy in Delhi, arrived in Kathmandu for an on-the-spot study of the situation immediately after the British mission, his visit did not create any commotion and passed off quietly. However, the much publicized British fact-finding mission composed of Sir Esler Dening and Sir Frank Roberts, upon its arrival in Kathmandu on 3 December was greeted by a rather hostile demonstration of about 30,000 people who were shouting slogans such as "Long Live King Tribhuvan", "Down with Rana autocracy", and "Go Back British Mission". This was obviously intended to convince the British Government about the popularity of the King in exile and the lack of popular support for the Rana rule. Already the Rana Government's firing on popular demonstrations at Kathmandu on 26 and 28 November resulting in the death of at least two demonstrators had vitiated the atmosphere for the British mission.

The British mission was in Kathmandu for about 5 days and had several meetings with the Maharaj and other leading members of the Rana family. The Maharaj called a meeting of his cabinet at 5 p.m. on 5 December to send General Kaiser that evening their reaction to the proposals received from India because Nehru had insisted on Nepal's reply before the debate on foreign affairs in the Indian Parliament on 6 December. The Maharaj apparently played for more time by giving New Delhi a non-committal reply that his own proposal would be sent there as soon as possible.

On the same day, 5 December, after he had been informed by the Maharaj that the Indians were insisting on Nepal's reaction to their proposal and, asked by the Maharaj for his thoughts, Sir Esler Dening put forward the following purely personal suggestion for Mohan's consideration. It was that the Maharaj should make a public statement within the next week and with the maximum publicity. *India should be informed in advance and thus be given an opportunity to comment, without being specifically invited or encouraged to do so.*

Sir Dening then suggested that the Maharaj should review the progress already made in constitutional reform, e.g., establishment of panchayats, summoning of National Assembly stating the target date (as shortly as possible) for completion of reforms already envisaged in the Constitution Act of 1948. There are genuine difficulties about this: the establishment of executive council with defined functions including non-Rana and elected members of the Assembly, budgetary controls by Executive Council (these last two reforms can and will be executed immediately), creation of an effective bicameral legislature and separation of the judiciary from the executive. The Maharaj's statement should indicate that all these reforms, far-reaching, though they are in the present stage of Nepali constitutional developments and given limited political consciousness of the Nepali people, were only a first step leading to the eventual goal of full representative government and election by adult suffrage of a constituent assembly (clearly no such election could take place now and the essential inevitable protracted preliminary, as India herself is finding, would be a census and preparation of electoral rolls). Finally it was suggested that the Maharaj should make it clear that all Nepalis now abroad, against whom no criminal or treasonable charge lay, would be welcomed back to contribute to Nepal's progress on the above lines. Sir Dening and Roberts emphasized that the statement should be couched in such terms as to make the greatest possible appeal to India and world opinion.

The Maharaj seemed to approve of the above proposals which were very much in line with his own thinking. But he had doubts whether such a programme of reforms would satisfy the Indian Government and wanted to know what should be done if his doubts on this account proved to be true. The British mission's reply to the Maharaj was as follows:

> We said while we could not speak for India, our personal view was that such a programme effectively presented and executed sincerely and as rapidly as possible, should satisfy any reasonable criteria of what is practicable and desirable for Nepal at the present stage of development.

On the second issue of the acceptance of the old King the Maharaj preferred to Regency solution and intended to establish a Council of Regency for the infant King. As he wanted to know whether foreign envoys should be accredited to the Council or to the infant King, and whether they should present their letters to the Council as a body or to one of its members, the British mission undertook to inform him of the practice in the U.K. and elsewhere, or he could seek guidance directly from the British Foreign Office on the point.

But the British mission also put in the following recommendation to its own Foreign Office:

> While we did not say this to Maharaja, we hope you will be prepared to urge India if necessary nearer the acceptance of the

above solution. We are satisfied that it is reasonable and goes as far as it is consistent with Nepalese stability and the practical realities of the situation.

Kaiser and Bijaya were still in Delhi when Nehru fulminated in the Indian Parliament on 8 December 1950:

From time immemorial, the Himalayas have provided us with magnificent frontiers. . . . We cannot allow the barrier to be penetrated because it is also the principal barrier to India. Therefore, much as we appreciate the independence of Nepal, we cannot allow anything to go wrong in Nepal or permit the barrier to be crossed or weakened, because that would be a risk to our own security.[10]

Nehru made it clear that "India would continue to recognize" King Tribhuvan and asked the great powers to do everything possible to solve the present crisis in Nepal by "negotiation or other peaceful means." As a piece of warning to the U.K. and the U.S.A. Nehru stated that "we are a patient government. Perhaps we are too patient sometimes. I feel, however, that if this matter drags on, it will not be good for Nepal and it might even make it more difficult to find the middle way we have been advocating."

On 7 December Sir Esler Dening and Sir Frank Roberts were back in Delhi, and the very next day Senior Commanding General Kaiser and Major-General Bijaya left for Kathmandu after calling on King Tribhuvan and issuing a brief communique to the effect that the points raised in the discussions between the two Governments would receive full and sympathetic consideration from the Government of Nepal. Before the Nepali delegation returned home the Government of India, however, presented it with a memorandum containing the following set of proposals elaborated on the basis of suggestions made to the Nepali delegation by Bajpai on 30 November. The memorandum stated:

The Government of India's primary objective is that Nepal should be independent, progressive and strong. For this purpose they regard immediate constitutional changes which will satisfy popular opinion and be acceptable to important non-official organizations of Nepalese nationals as urgent. They suggest the following measures: (1) that a Constituent Assembly composed entirely of properly elected members should be brought into being as soon as possible to draw up a constitution for Nepal; (2) pending the meeting of the Constituent Assembly mentioned above an interim government, which will include persons representative of popular opinion and enjoying public confidence should be established. This body should also include members of the Rana family, one of whom should be Prime Minister. This body should act as a cabinet on the principle of joint responsibility and should frame its own rules of business; and (3) King Tribhuvan should continue as King in the interests of the realm.

It must be pointed out here that the Nepali delegation had not called on King Tribhuvan until the day of its departure from Delhi and also that Senior Commanding General Kaiser, the leader of the delegation, upon his arrival in Delhi had made it clear in reply to a correspondent's question that their meeting with the King depended entirely on his (the ex-King's) pleasure thereby forestalling the situation in which any kind of a meeting with Tribhuvan could be in any way interpreted as their recognition of the King in exile.

On the other hand, in all those discussions between the Nepali representatives and the Indian officials prior to the handing over of the above memorandum, it had appeared as though the Indians were representing not only their own Government but also both King Tribhuvan and the Nepali Congress. Although India had apparently taken both the King and the Nepali Congress under its wing, yet no direct contact was allowed between them until very late in the day. In other words, India had planned from the beginning to impose on Nepal what Nehru regarded as the middle-way solution using all its unofficial talks with the Rana Government, King Tribhuvan and the Nepali Congress at various levels with that particular end in view. The dependence of both the King and the Nepali Congress on India for all practical purposes gave them no option but to toe the Indian line, and the Rana Government, in its turn, proved incapable of a bold political action based on courage and vision.

However, it cannot be gainsaid that the leader of the Nepali delegation played his role in Delhi with great skill and ability at the time. He made an effective use of his innate gift for wit and sarcasm by directing his barbs against the Indian attitude in the apparently innocuous off-the-cuff rejoinders to the pressmen's queries on the Nepali Congress's insurrection: "It is a P.T.I. war. The reports are louder than the guns. The booming of the guns is not heard in Kathmandu." Besides that, he made a pious and polite statement already referred to without any specific reference to the memorandum as such. As a matter of fact, it was not until 19 December that the Rana Government even acknowledged the memorandum.

The Rana Government had more than 12 days to act along the lines contemplated at the crucial meeting between the Maharaj and the British delegation on 5 December 1951, i.e., to present the Indian Government with a *fait accompli* by announcing its own set of reforms and setting up a Regency Council. At a time when prompt and decisive action would have made all the difference, Maharaj Mohan listened to his many advisers and confidants for too long a time and failed to make up his own mind. The result was that he missed another chance of securing Anglo-American recognition of the new King as he had missed his first chance by deciding one day too soon to send a delegation to India.

As we have seen, Senior Commanding General Kaiser was the first to come up with the suggestion of the Regency Council which had found favour with the British delegation and, on its evidence, even had the approval of the Maharaj. Kaiser had come back from India without even formally acknowledging the Government of India's memorandum, thereby giving the Maharaj and his Government plenty of time to act in a decisive manner. Instead, the Maharaj took a long time to decide what to do next, and delay proved dangerous to him. The Government of India, had on the other hand, more time to bring pressure on the Maharaj in different ways to make him accept the set of reforms proposed by them.

It is difficult to explain what made the Maharaj take such a long time even to acknowledge the memorandum if he had not contemplated some sort of action on his own, and also what made him desist from the act of setting up a Regency Council after he had announced to a special session of his Parliament his proposal of reforms more or less along the lines discussed and approved at his meeting with the British delegation on 5 December 1950. But the fact remains that the Maharaj formally acknowledged only on 19 December the Indian memorandum handed to Senior Commanding General Kaiser on 8 December before his departure from Delhi.

Following Nepal's acknowledgment of the memorandum India also made King Tribhuvan throw his weight on its side by issuing a press statement from New Delhi on 23 November to the effect that he hoped for a new political order in Nepal based on popular participation and representation.

The delay in Nepal's acknowledgment of the Indian memorandum had caused concern to India because India was worried about Nepal's next move and was intensifying its diplomatic pressure. But Kaiser had, at least for the time being, proved more than a match for a noted Indian diplomat, Sir Girija Shankar Bajpai, at his own game. Bajpai told Sir Archibald Nye as early as 14 November that the brief communique published on the eve of the departure of Kaiser and Bijaya from Delhi was clearly not enough to satisfy parliamentary curiosity and the plan was to lay before Parliament, probably not before 20 or 21 December, the communication handed to him. If a reply had come from Kathmandu meanwhile, it would have been possible for the Government of India to say whether it appeared satisfactory or not. If the reply were of a provisional nature the Government of India would point out that matters were still under discussion and refrain from expressing any final decision. While acquainting Sir Archibald Nye with the main features of the memorandum, Bajpai was at pains to point out that the document had been couched in the form of advice. "When Sir Archibald Nye referred to the probable difficulty about the references to the desirability of maintaining the old King on the throne, to the Regent acting for him and to King appointing the new cabinet, Bajpai drew my attention pointedly to the fact that the document nowhere stated that India refused to recognize the new King."[11] Indian diplomacy had for quite a while centred upon quibbling on non-refusal to recognize the new King and the continuance of the old King or the ex-King as if they were not exclusive of each other while doing meanwhile everything possible to secure the restoration of King Tribhuvan to the throne.

But against this background Maharaj Mohan Shamsher proposed his own reforms to a special session of Parliament on 24 December but they fell short of setting up the Regency Council which was the crux of the proposal. Even the proposal for reforms was thus oddly and belatedly launched, depriving it of all its force and impact, and by Mohan's seeking to obtain advance Indian agreement to his reforms, the Indian side was enabled to lengthen its bid for the approval of its own proposals. It is not known as to who was actually responsible for making the Maharaj give up his previous plan of informing the Indian Government of the reforms in advance just as a formality without even giving India enough time to react to them and presenting yet another more vital fait accompli by appointing a Regency Council promptly. The matter had gone so far that the British Foreign Office had had even provided at one stage whatever advice or guidance it could about the appointment of regency apropos of the Maharaj's talk with Sir Esler Dening along these lines:

> We have no Regency precedent in this country, but there are or have been precedents in other countries, notably Iraq and Thailand (noting on the margin). Surely we did in the reign of George III when the future George IV "Prinny" was more than once Regent during his father's period of insanity. But it may not help this issue. In the former (Iraq) there is Regent and in the latter (Thailand) there was until recently a Council of Regency. In both cases foreign diplomatic representatives are or were accredited to the King, as the lawful head of the state, the letters themselves being presented to the Regent or the Council of Regency in accordance with the prescriptions of the local protocol.
>
> It is worth recording that on recent occasions when in this country the crown has been placed in commission (e.g., during the illness of King George V and during the present sovereign's state visit to South Africa in 1947) the custom has been for newly-arrived foreign ambassadors or ministers to present their letters to such of the councillors of state as have been readily available for the purpose. This on the earlier of the two occasions mentioned we have record of the presentation of several sets of credentials to the Prince of Wales and one set to the Duke of York: on the more recent occasion two sets of credentials were presented to the Duke of Gloucester and the Princess Royal jointly.

Whatever might have made the Maharaj change his previous plan for action, which he had approvingly discussed with the British Mission, Major-General Bijaya Shamsher and Sardar Narendra Mani arrived in New Delhi on 25 December 1950 for the second round of talks on this occasion particularly to clear with the Government of India the reforms proposed by the Maharaj and already approved by the Nepal Parliament. Sir George Falconer had suggested to the Maharaj through his eldest son, Major-General Sarada, that it would be much better to send Kaiser as before. Falconer's plea was that because of his ability, experience and stature, Kaiser could hold his own in discussions with the Indian officials. However, Senior Commanding General Kaiser told the present author sometime after the collapse of the Rana regime that he kept himself out of the delegation because he had already sensed the mood of the real decision makers.

Anyway, the Maharaj's favourite son and sole confidant, Major-General Bijaya Shamsher, was given the entire responsibility for concluding the final deal with the Government of India. Nobody knows what his terms of reference were. Bijaya after his discussions with Bajpai on 27 December, felt that India was showing "a spirit of dictation rather than negotiation" when Bajpai refused even to entertain Bijaya's suggestion to have the return of the ex-King decided by the Constituent Assembly and insisted that "a major King" was absolutely necessary to decide any deadlock, to establish peace and security. There was then a suggestion that a Regent be appointed by the ex-King for two to three months pending his own return to the country. Subsequently the appointment of Crown Prince Mahendra himself as Regent or the establishment of a Regency Council was suggested.[11] But the Government of India remained firm in its demand for the return of the old King.[12]

By 2 January 1951 Major-General Bijaya accepted the return of the old King subject to the approval of the Nepal Parliament, and another leading member of his mission, Sardar Narendra Mani Dikshit, assured the Indian press that he did not expect any difficulty about the parliamentary approval of the restoration of King Tribhuvan.

As Major-General Bijaya's interview with Sir Archibald Nye on 2 January 1951 affords a real insight into the mind of the Chief Nepali negotiator, the U.K. High Commissioner's account of this meeting to the Commonwealth Relations Office is reproduced in full here:

> I saw Bijaya yesterday and he told me that there seems to be comparatively little difference between the Government of Nepal and the Government of India on the question of reforms. He clearly did not regard this issue as one which would cause any great difficulty.
>
> He said, however, that India was very insistent on the question of the recognition of the old King and it was, therefore, agreed that the question should be referred back to the Nepalese Parliament. He said this was a matter on which the Government of India appeared to feel very strongly and he got the impression that Nehru regarded it as a personal issue.
>
> In response to his questioning I said that in my view the Government of India really regarded reforms as a major issue and

in particular that whatever reforms were agreed upon should in fact be carried out, that whilst they no doubt would very much like the Government of Nepal to recognise the old King again that this was really in their minds a secondary issue.

He asked me for advice as to what attitude the Government of Nepal should take about recognition of old King. This was a matter on which nobody could give advice but one on which his Government must make up their own minds. If they were prepared to have back the old King and thus win the goodwill of the Government of India it was their own affair. Similarly it was for them to decide if they felt no independent Government could be expected to give way to this extent. (Emphasis added.)

In subsequent discussion I got the impression that Bijaya himself would as a last resort be prepared to recommend the infant King to be dethroned and the old King recognised. But he would prefer if it were possible that there should be a tacit understanding that the old King should be given an indefinite leave from Nepal and be represented by a Regency Council. (Emphasis added.)

I now learn that Dikshit, the leading official in Bijaya's staff, disclosed to press correspondents yesterday that the Nepalese government had yielded to Indian assistance on this question also, to the extent of agreeing to the restoration of the old King, subject to the approval of Nepalese Parliament. Dikshit added that Parliament was unlikely to reject the proposal and this is prominently featured in today's Statesman, under headline "Nepal agrees to King's return" and impression given that this is decided in principle subject to a few formalities.[13] (Emphasis added.)

Major-General Bijaya returned to Nepal on 3 January after tentatively accepting the Indian proposals. On 8 January 1951 Maharaj Mohan made his proclamation on reforms and announced the reversal of Parliament's decision of 7 November 1950 regarding the succession of the boy King. He gave two reasons for this: first, the failure of his Government to obtain foreign recognition of the new King and India's advice to continue King Tribhuvan as King of Nepal and, second, the growth of lawlessness in the country as a result of the King's absence. He pleaded that King Tribhuvan should return to the country or else should be authorized to appoint a Regent in his absence. The other changes the Maharaj proclaimed were: (1) elections to a constituent assembly to be held on the basis of adult suffrage not later that 1952, (2) an interim cabinet to be formed with an equal quota of Ranas and of the representatives of the people, and (3) a general amnesty for political prisoners.

By his proclamation Maharaj Mohan accepted the so-called 'advice' given by India with the exception of three suggestions: (1) that the proclamation be issued by the King, (2) that no reference be made to the earlier constitutions including the 1948 Government of Nepal Act framed largely on Indian advice, and (3) that popular elements be given a majority in the interim cabinet.

King Tribhuvan welcomed the Maharaj's proclamation of reforms by issuing the following public statement on 10 January 1951:

> I welcome the announcement of constitutional reforms made by my government at Kathmandu on January 8th. This is the first and important step in the reconstruction of the government of our dear and sacred land on democratic lines. I now appeal to my people to do everything that is necessary to restore order and peace at once and to give the fullest cooperation in all the steps to be taken in giving effect to the constitutional change now announced. No political changes will be beneficial unless all leaders of popular opinion worked in close harmony, having the good of people at heart and avoiding all rivalries and personal aspirations. I appeal to all to maintain the good tradition and culture we have inherited. Let the task of peaceful reconstruction be taken as a sacred obligation. I shall do my part in this with a full sense of duty and having the good of my people as my only concern.

It appeared as though the political movement for democracy in Nepal had been split by the Maharaj's proclamation. On the one hand, M.P. Koirala, leader of the Nepali Congress which had conducted the fighting, described the royal proclamation in a public statement of 10 January 1951 as a 'disillusionment' and said that any arrangement short of the complete transfer of power to the Nepali Congress would hinder it in achieving its declared goals, the liquidation of the feudal regime, and the establishment of full democracy in Nepal. Another spokesman of the Congress stated that the party had not been consulted about participation in the cabinet and would probably carry on its programme until victory was achieved.

On the other hand, the Nepali National Congress which had previously given general support to Koirala without taking an active part in the fighting, took a more conciliatory line. Its leader, Dilli Raman Regmi, speaking in Calcutta on 9 January 1951, dissociated his party from the activities of the Nepali Congress, criticized the activities of the "freedom fighters" who had harassed the common people, and welcomed the proposal for the setting up of a constituent assembly, the restoration of King Tribhuvan and the release of political prisoners.

By 16 January M.P. Koirala, President of the Nepali Congress, obviously changed his previous stand on Maharaj Mohan's proclamation of 8 January and came out with the following statement:

> After consultation with the Government of India about the situation arising out of the declaration of the Prime Minister of Nepal and the statement issued thereupon by His Majesty the King of Nepal, and in response to the appeal made by the Prime Minister of India, we have decided that in order to create suitable conditions for negotiations there should be a cessation of all operations at once. We, therefore, direct all workers to stop hostilities of every kind and we appeal to everyone in Nepal to assist in the restoration of peace. We are grateful to the Government of India for all that they have done in the cause of reforms and progress in Nepal. We accept the advice given by the Prime Minister of India at this juncture and we fully trust that the problem of Nepal will soon be solved satisfactorily.

King Tribhuvan and his sons were at the airport on 22 January 1951 when Nehru returned after attending the Commonwealth Prime Ministers' meeting in London.

Let us now consider in some detail the background and role of the Nepali Congress, the third important party, other than the King and the Rana Government, to the Delhi agreement on political reforms in Nepal achieved through the good offices of the Nehru Government. To begin with, the Indian Congress leaders were not all willing to encourage an armed revolution in Nepal for fear that it might lead to the total disintegration of the country and also for their own ideological considerations. They had wanted the Nepali Congress to adopt non-violent methods to bring about conditions in Nepal for the establishment of a like-minded Government sharing their own faith in democratic values and institutions. However, the Indian Congress leaders had, in view of the adamant attitude of Maharaj Mohan and his brothers and cousins on the question of political reforms, slightly changed their position on the use of violent methods by the Nepali Congress and had agreed to let them do so without compromising the position of the Government of India. This was an indication to the Nepali Congress that it could arrange on its own to secure a supply of arms for its political purposes.

The Nepali Congress obtained its first consignment of arms from the socialist Government of Burma with the Indian socialist leaders acting as intermediaries. Just on the eve of the armed insurrection by the Nepali Congress a plane-load of arms was brought from Burma in one of the commercial aircrafts of the Himalayan Aviation of which Major-General Mahabir Shamsher, one of the financiers of the Nepali Congress, was the managing director. The plane landed at an abandoned World War II airstrip in north Bihar and the arms and ammunition were promptly distributed among the volunteers of the Mukti Sena (liberation army) units of the Nepali Congress deployed along the Nepal-India border. The Indian Congress leaders had wanted this supply of arms from sources other than Indian Government as a cover for the involvement of their own Government not only in meeting its arms requirement but also in providing training to the volunteers in the use of arms.

After imposing strict limitations on the supply of arms and the movement of armed volunteers for about a month from 20 November till 20 December 1950, the Government of India tended to relax these restrictions in view of the British and American procrastination on the issue of the recognition of the King and the inflexible stand of the Rana Government itself. Biratnagar, the only industrial township near the Indian railhead at Jogbani in the Purnea district of Bihar, was captured by the armed volunteers of the Nepali Congress on 23 December 1950. Just before that, the Nepali Congress was allowed to obtain another supply of rifles and ammunition from Sheikh Abdullah in Kashmir, once again to provide a cover for the Government of India to provide arms and ammunition to the Nepali Congress volunteers through its own sources. The result was a remarkable upsurge in the insurrectionary activities.

On 4 January 1951 the regular but locally recruited garrison of Palpa defected to General Rudra who had held the nominal title of Commander-in-Chief of Western Nepal till the previous November, when he had been relieved of his position and confined in his official residence at Tansen for his sympathy with the Nepali Congress. In the wake of these defections in Palpa, the armed volunteers moved further north and east and occupied Syangja. By the time Maharaj Mohan had accepted the Indian proposal for reforms on 8 January there had already been instances of lawlessness in different parts of the country, and with the further weakening of the central authority and with King Tribhuvan still in New Delhi, the law and order situation in Nepal became still worse. This also caused serious embarrassment to the Government of India as it had to send its own constabulary forces to different areas in the western tarai even after the return of the King to Kathmandu and the establishment of an interim government in Nepal.

The Government of India, which was playing the role of a midwife in delivering democracy to Nepal, was very much afraid of the aggravation of the law and order situation in the country. It used its powers of both persuasion and coercion to secure a consensus on the shape of the future political set-up on the basis of India's proposal as endorsed by Maharaj Mohan in his proclamation of 8 January.

Not all sections of the Nepali Congress were happy at the Delhi compromise, but under no circumstances could the Congress have prevailed against the combined weight of the King, the Rana Government and Prime Minister Nehru of India, whose steady pursuit of a 'middle way' policy seemed to bear fruit in the end. The Nepali Congress felt left out because it was not directly associated with the Delhi discussions at the initial stage.

The dash to New Delhi of the two most influential leaders of the Nepali Congress, B.P. Koirala and Subarna Shamsher, on 14 January 1951 to convey the general feeling of the Nepali Congress in favour of continuing their armed struggle had no effect on the Indian authorities. In view of the rapid deterioration in the law and order situation throughout Nepal, the Indian Government was more keen than ever on the immediate establishment of a revamped central authority capable of restoring and maintaining the peace and stability needed for the implementation of the proposed political reforms.

The solution with regard to the future governmental set-up did not, however, satisfy all sections of the Nepali Congress. Several breakaway sections of the Congress refused to respect the cease-fire order of its President, M.P. Koirala, and they continued their insurrectionary activities further by taking advantage of the indifferent attitude of the local authorities of the Rana regime in the wake of the announcement of the cease-fire and the start of the Delhi talks.

One particular section of the Nepali Congress in the west led by Dr. K.I. Singh came out openly against any compromise with the Ranas and the Delhi talks and continued its armed struggle unhampered. This necessitated joint military action by the Nepali troops and the Indian Maratha regiment against Dr. K.I. Singh and his followers in the summer after the interim government was set up in Kathmandu.

Another breakaway section of the Nepali Congress led by Bhairav Prasad Acharya at Jhapa in the eastern tarai had also initially professed opposition to the Delhi talks and favoured the continuation of the armed struggle. They, however, eventually yielded to the persuasion of the Nepali Congress leadership.

The Communist Party of Nepal (CPN) was founded by Puspa Lal Shrestha, Nara Bahadur Karmacharya, Narayan Bilas Joshi, Niranjan Gobinda Baidya and Moti Devi on 22 April 1949 in the house of a Bengali gentleman at Shyam Bazar in Calcutta. The CPN's first manifesto was made public on 15 September 1949. A Central Organizing Committee consisting of Man Mohan Adhikari, Tulsi Lal Amatya, D.P. Adhikari, Shailendra Kumar Upadhyaya, Hikmat Singh Bhandari and a representative of the Communist Party of India, Ayodhya Singh was set up under the leadership of Puspa Lal Shrestha at the first conference of the CPN held from 27 September through 2 October 1949.

The CPN was also opposed to the Delhi compromise of 15 January 1951 and in the course of the popular movement launched against it some of the front organizations such as All Nepal Trade Union, All Nepal Peasants' Organization, All Nepal Students' Union and All Nepal Women's Organization appeared upon the scene as the standard bearers of the CPN. Later on in 1951 Puspa Lal Shrestha was replaced by Man Mohan Adhikari as the Secretary General of the CPN.

It was only in early February 1951 that direct talks between the Rana representatives and the Nepali Congress leaders took place in Delhi under the guidance of King Tribhuvan with the Indian Government advising and manipulating all the three of them from the sidelines. An agreement which came to be known as the "Delhi Compromise" was hammered out by 7 February 1951 and under it a 10-man cabinet with equal representation for both the Rana and the Nepali Congress sides was to be set up with Maharaj Mohan Shamsher himself as the interim Prime Minister.

Even as the negotiations among the parties concerned on the future political setup were under way in New Delhi, the political atmosphere in the Kathmandu Valley had undergone a dramatic change. On 17 January as many as 217 political prisoners were released by the Rana Government, whose attitude towards political activity had considerably altered even without any formal declaration or enactment.

Some of the important members of the Nepali National Congress led by Dilli Raman Regmi, who had been an advocate of nonviolent methods all along, arrived in Nepal on 23 January with the professed intention of testing new reforms. But, even though they were allowed by the Rana Government to hold open-air meetings criticizing it and welcoming the proposal for the restoration of the King and the interim government, the Regmi faction had to face considerable opposition at the popular level because the people had reasons to be suspicious that the Nepali National Congress might have had a secret understanding of some kind with the Rana Government.

However, spontaneous demonstrations had become the order of the day in the Kathmandu Valley. There was a widespread feeling of joy and enthusiasm among the people at the prospect of being freed from the stranglehold of the Ranas, and the peak was reached when King Tribhuvan and his family along with the topmost Nepali Congress leaders returned to Kathmandu on 15 February 1951. Their triumphant returned served as a prelude to the abolition of the 104-year old Rana rule in Nepal.

NOTES

1. The *Gorkhapatra*, 14 Jyestha 2005 (27 May 1948).
2. Parliamentary Debates, Part II, 17 March 1950, Cols. 1697-98.
3. A.S. Bhasin, *Documents on Nepal's Relations with India and China, 1949-66* (Bombay: Academic Books, 1970), p. 27.
4. *Ibid.*, p. 28.
5. British High Commission in India to the Commonwealth Relations office in London on 8 November 1950.
6. Telegram 183 to Sir G.A. Falconer in Nepal by P.H. Scott, Head of South East Asian Department in the British Foreign Office, of 9 November 1950.
7. Murray's transcript of the meeting on 10 November 1950.
8. Sir Archibald Nye's Telegram 3277 of 19 November 1950 to the Secretary for Commonwealth Relations Office.
9. FO 371/84295/ Falconar's letter to the Foreign office of 1 December, 1950 giving an account of his meeting with the Maharaj the previous day.
10. Jawaharlal Nehru, *India's Foreign Policy: Selected Speeches, September 1946-April 1961* (New Delhi, Ministry of Information and Broadcasting), 1961, *op. cit.*, p. 252.
11. Sir Archibald Nye's telegram of 14 December 1950 to Falconer in Kathmandu, which reached him at 12:50 p.m. on 15 December.
12. (PRO) FO 371/92901/Falconer's telegrams Nos. 200 and 201 to the Foreign Office of 29 November 1950.
13. FO 371/920901 Priority No. 9 Confidential, the U.K. High Commissioner to the Commonwealth Relations Office (3 January 1951).

16

Rana Rule in Retrospect

Nepali history during the Rana period contained few developments of any broad significance to the people in general and centred upon the acquisition and transfer of the prime ministership, accompanied by several violent deviations from the established roll of succession from time to time. The basic objective of the Rana regime was to keep the power with the family by maintaining the *status quo* in every field. In the sphere of internal affairs, every effort was made to insulate Nepal from the impact of western influence and ideas, which was being felt in Asia during the latter part of the 19th and the beginning of the 20th century. In accomplishing this policy of isolation the Ranas were aided by the geographical location and topography of Nepal. The Nepali people were not merely deprived of the influence of western ideas but were also discouraged from coming into contact with the neighbouring people of India. This is evident from the fact that during the first half of the 20th century the popular mass movements in India produced only a ripple in the stagnant waters of Nepal.

Until 1951, Nepal was largely an anachronism, and remained one of the few strongholds of feudal autocracy and medieval obscurantism. It was a closed book to the outside world and was hermetically sealed off against the beneficent influences of modern life, thought and civilization. Though its free and open border with India on the south prevented it from being a 'Forbidden Land' in the same sense as Tibet, yet Kathmandu, the capital of Nepal, was virtually a forbidden city to which not only outsiders, but also Nepalis from the outlying part of the country itself, were denied access without a special permit from the Rana Government. Foreigners, especially the Americans and the Europeans, were not, as a rule, allowed to visit the country unless they were passed as desirables by the so-called Political Department of

British India, with which the Rana administration always acted in close consultation.

In those days, as even now to an extent, Kathmandu presented a striking picture of contrast between extreme poverty and vast wealth. On the one side there stood clustered together red and yellow mud hovels in the congested section of the city, which with its dirty, narrow and winding lanes was largely reminiscent of the ghettos in some of the European cities in the medieval times. In contrast to this were the vast and glittering palaces of the Ranas in the Greco-Roman style, with balustrades and pillared columns, standing amidst spacious grounds enclosed by high compound walls. Public buildings such as courts, hospitals and colleges suffered in comparison with the private residences of the Ranas and their favourites. This pattern of contrast was fairly widespread and, generally speaking, was true of the country as a whole, though its effects in Kathmandu might have been heightened.

The family oligarchy of the Ranas, despite their concern about the formal independence of the country, stunted the growth and development of nationalism by limiting the decision-making power to a few members of the Rana family. The people in general were denied opportunities or encouragement to cultivate any interest in national history, art, architecture, tradition and culture. History was so distorted as to make the people feel that the Rana era was the most glorious in the country's history. Ranaism or Ranarchy engendered such a narrow and parochial outlook on life and art as to make them lose all their interest and meaning for the people. Instead of drawing on Nepal's own rich tradition of art, architecture and sculpture for their models, the Ranas like their predecessors, Bhimsen Thapa and Mathbar Singh Thapa encouraged cheap imitations of the Anglo-Indian style in decor and building with the result that there was a sharp decline in the artistic value of the Rana-time works and designs. The Belvedere Palace or the Government House in Calcutta seemed to have served as a model to the palatial buildings of the Ranas who were more attracted by the crystal chandeliers and vases manufactured in Europe than by the bronze and stone pieces of exquisite craftsmanship produced in Nepal.

Change of any kind was suspected of weakening the foundations of the Rana rule. Educational development was very slow, and the number of high schools and colleges could be counted on one's fingers. Public works programmes during the Rana period were almost non-existent and particularly deficient in respect of transportation and communication. Worst of all, the nation's limited resources were exploited by the Ranas for their own personal enrichment rather than for public benefit.

It is ironical but true that there was a good deal more pre-industrial manufacturing activity in the first decade of the last century than during the greater part of the Rana period. Until about 1850 cotton was grown extensively in the hill areas. The neighbouring hill areas supplied the Kathmandu Valley with considerable quantities of cotton, both raw and ginned. This enabled the Kathmandu Valley to be self-sufficient in the production of cloth for at least the lower and middle class people. The processing of sugarcane was also known to the people and brown sugar made in Nepal, according to William Kirkpatrick, who visited Kathmandu in 1793, was "much more refined . . . than that which is met with in Bengal."

The earliest Chinese visitors to India, Fa-Hien and Hiuen Tsang mentioned Nepal in their travelogues as a country that exported iron and copper. Land in the hill areas was rich in mineral wealth. Copper, iron and lead deposits were exploited to some extent, together with gold, cinnabar and other minerals. According to Kirkpatrick, "the iron of Nepal is not, perhaps, surpassed by that of any country" and Nepali copper was sold for a higher price than European copper in the Calcutta market. Baglung and other western hill areas supplied large quantities of copper to India. Individuals acquired the right to work mines on the condition of payment of rent to the Government in the form of metal. According to Francis (Buchanan) Hamilton, who visited Nepal in 1803, both copper and iron ore were dug from near the surface and mines were not worked deep underground.

The extension of the Indian railway system to the Nepal tarai at the turn of the century would have been a windfall. It did accelerate the pace of settlement in the tarai. The Rana Government encouraged people to settle there in large numbers with the object of exploiting the Indian market for the sale of the forest resources and agricultural produce of the region. But although the Ranas did this, they prevented Nepal from getting the maximum benefit from a transport system that touched her southern border in many places. At that time, Nepal could have paved the way for long-term economic growth by starting consumer goods industries. Such a step would have exploited the new monetization of the regional economy and the increased purchasing power of the people. But the Rana Government was afraid of introducing technical innovations for fear that it might bring about changes in the values and aspirations of the people.

Again in 1923, the Ranas, ignoring local potential, concluded a treaty with British India, which encouraged an unrestricted flow of British goods into Nepal. This not only killed the Nepali incentive to start new industries but also accelerated the decline and decay of traditional handicrafts and cottage industries in Nepal already suffering from British competition. Once the potential level of technology was exploited, the economy of the tarai remained stagnant until World War II, which gave a sudden boost to the prices of agricultural produce in India.

Just as there had been a lack of economic development during the Rana regime, so also social reforms were hindered by its beliefs in rigid forms of Hindu orthodoxy. Sati (widow-burning) and slavery were in due course abolished. But discrimination on the grounds of caste and religion were continued till its very end. Even the Mulki Ain, the Legal Code introduced by Jang Bahadur after his return from his visit to Europe, while mitigating the severity of punishment for criminal offences, laid down clearly that punishment be determined both by the degree of the seriousness of the offence and the caste of the offender. The roots of the Rana conservatism may, however, be traced back to national attitudes evolved long before the rise of Jang Bahadur as Nepal had even since the days of Prithvinarayan Shah endeavoured to guard its independence and its Hindu identity from the lengthening shadow of the British power by avoiding contact with it as far as possible. Prithvinarayan's professed aim in his *Divine Message* was "to make Nepal into a genuine piece of Hindusthan or a model of the genuine tradition of the Hindus."

Jang Bahadur's travels in Europe, however, convinced him that Britain's military and industrial power was overwhelming. He decided that the safest course for Nepal was friendship with Britain as long as it allowed Nepal to follow its traditional policy of isolation, exclusion of foreigners, and reducing even official contact with the British to the barest minimum. These basic guidelines for Nepal's foreign policy were followed till the very end of the Rana regime and it was this policy which more than anything else enabled Nepal to retain its formal independence and separate entity during the time when the more powerful states of the Sikhs and the Marathas were merged into British India.

Jang Bahadur, the founder of the Rana system of government, by acquiring power with considerable daring and skill and concentrating it solely in his own hands and those of the family, had succeeded in putting an end to feuding among the elite families including the royal family, which had characterized the court politics of Nepal before Jang's rise. Jang Bahadur must no doubt be given credit for restoring order and stability in the land at the most critical time when the British, who had already consolidated their position in India, would not have tolerated a volatile and unstable situation in its northeastern frontier much longer.

However, the royal family and the remnants of the elite families such as the Thapa, Pande and Basnyat were not easily reconciled to the ruthless treatment they had received at the hand of this upstart leader who belonged to one of the less important families. Jang Bahadur's attempt to win them over through matrimonial exchanges, free-hold land grants and job opportunities at the middle level civil and military administration mollified them only partially. Most of the old nobility, who were biding their time to seek vengeance on Jang Bahadur and other members of the Rana family resorted from time to time, without success, to the traditional forms of oppositional tactics known to the Nepali courts—plots, counterplots and assassinations.

On the domestic scene, Jang Bahadur established a system of hereditary prime ministers with a novel method of succession regulated by a predetermined roll. He set the pattern of government that lasted with certain aberrations for 104 years. It is known as the Rana regime since he took the name of Rana for his family.

Jang Bahadur had temporarily resigned the prime ministership in August 1856 in favour of his brother Bam Bahadur in a manoeuvre to gain greater power for himself. He was made a Maharaj, and he obtained a written undertaking from the King that both the monarch and his Prime Minister, Bam Bahadur, would abide by the Maharaja's advice in all matters of state policy. They would even allow themselves to be restrained and disciplined by the Maharaj, if necessary, with the help of the army commanders and troops who had clear instructions to carry out Jang Bahadur's orders even when in conflict with the command of the King himself. The Maharaj was also given the power to inflict capital punishment on all those who might plot against his kingdom and his life.

These rights were made inheritable by the Maharaj's children, and the same document provided a predetermined roll of succession for the office of the Prime Minister. The office of the Prime Minister was to go to the eldest agnate of the Rana family. After the generation of brothers, in the second and subsequent generations, seniority would still prevail among the eligible candidates for office.

This amazing document wrested power from the helpless reigning monarch, King Surendra Bikram Shah (1847-1881). It served as the legal basis for the Rana regime for ninety-five years, for it led to the institutionalization of the Rana family within the political structure.

According to Jang's dispensation, his eldest son, General Jagat Jang, should have inherited the office of the Maharaj with absolute powers and the prime ministership should have gone to Ranoddip Singh as the eldest agnate of the family. But after Jang died in 1877, his brothers manipulated King Surendra and had Ranoddip appointed both Maharaj and Prime Minister. Thus a precedent was created and maintained throughout the Rana period that one man should hold both positions.

Jang's nephew, Bir Shamsher, and his brothers killed Maharaj Ranoddip Singh (1877-1885) in November 1885 and had Bir appointed Maharaj and Prime Minister by King Prithiv Bir Bikram Shah (1881-1911) who was hardly 10 years old. They retained the members of their own family on the roll of succession by removing all the descendants of Jang and his five brothers. The Shamsher faction of the Rana family remained in firm control of Nepal till 1951.

Subsequent division of the Rana family on the caste and sub-caste lines seriously affected the working of the system in practice. The Rana system was not free from internal dissension and sabotage. The Rana practice of marrying several wives and having concubines to boot resulted in oversized families with a large number of progeny and descendants. This combined with a roll of succession based on seniority by birth set an ideal framework for the growth of intra- and inter-family misunderstanding and discontent. Again, the division of the Rana family by Maharaj Chandra Shamsher in 1928 into 'a', 'b' and 'c' classes, without tampering with the existing roll of succession, sowed the seed of dissension within the family, with the Ranas low on the roll or excluded from it because of the caste of their mother, or the whims of the Rana Maharaj, more than willing to conspire against those high up in the ruling hierarchy. His successor and brother Maharaj Bhim Shamsher (1929-1932) ignored this division and included in the roll some of his sons born out of wedlock. But Juddha Shamsher (1932-1945) decided to recast the roll in accordance with the caste principle propounded by Chandra Shamsher, and this finally destroyed the solidarity of the Rana family, with the result that a number of wealthy and influential 'c' class Ranas joined hands with other non-Rana disaffected elements in bringing about the overthrow of the Rana family in 1951.

All told, the abrupt and sudden collapse of the Rana regime in 1951 resulted from its failure to adjust itself to the regional and global changes in international politics following World War II. Though the Ranas had for a period of 104 years successfully dealt with oppositional threats of a traditional type such as intrigues, conspiracies and assassinations, they were helpless against the circumstances created by an alliance between the King and the popular forces. The Nepali political activists, with the moral support of the Indian National Congress, rallied the people in the name of democracy behind the King , who, in spite of being neglected and kept without power for over a century, had not lost his utility and effectiveness as a centre of loyalty. It may be pointed out here in passing that the popular movement for democracy in Nepal, which was all along being organized from India because of the denial of even the minimal civil and political rights and the rule of law inside Nepal, had received a sudden boost after the attainment of independence by India under the Indian National Congress whose struggle for democracy had also inspired the democratic-oriented Nepalis both inside and outside Nepal.

In Nepal the march of democracy was not initially characterized by the struggle between the King and his subjects as in Great Britain and elsewhere, because the Rana system acted as sort of a safety valve for the King or monarchy by taking all the blame and responsibility for the errors and omissions of the Government.

The King's position during the Rana period was truly that of a reigning monarch. In Nepal both the King and the people found themselves pitted against the Ranas. With the abolition of the Rana system of the hereditary Maharaj Prime Ministers as the *de facto* rulers, there has, however, been a steady growth of the tension between the royalist and the popular forces in the politics of Nepal and its final result is yet to be seen.

17

The Post-Revolutionary Tribhuvan Era (1951-1955)

India's firm political and diplomatic pressure combined with the insurrectionary tactics of the Nepali Congress resulted in King Tribhuvan being restored to the throne and in his historical declaration of 18 February 1951 expressing his resolve that "the government of our people be carried on henceforth according to a democratic constitution prepared by a constituent assembly elected on the basis of direct universal suffrage."

By this royal proclamation, in which King Tribhuvan pledged to establish democracy in Nepal, the 104-year-old Rana system of hereditary prime ministership officially came to an end. Having spent the previous 45 years as a figurehead monarch under a succession of five Ranas who were the actual rulers, Tribhuvan now for the first time exercised his sovereign royal powers and constituted an interim cabinet, provided for in the Delhi compromise, to run the Government until a new, truly democratic constitution could be framed by a constituent assembly, which was to be convened by 1952. Although the incumbent Rana Prime Minister, Mohan Shamsher, was reappointed as Premier and indeed half of the new cabinet were Rana men, the other half were not, and the hereditary nature of the premiership was clearly ended.

The following chart lists the members of the interim Rana-Congress coalition cabinet with their portfolios and political persuasions:

The cabinet was thus composed of equal numbers of Nepali Congress nominees, representing the popular elements, and nominees of the Rana regime representing the *status quo*. There was a last-minute difference as to whether B.P. Koirala or Babar Shamsher should be

The Rana-Congress Joint Cabinet of 1951

Name	Position	Portfolios	Political persuasion
	(I) The Rana Side		
Mohan Shamsher	Prime Minister	Foreign Affairs	The last hereditary Rana Maharaj and the seniormost member of the erstwhile ruling Rana family.
Babar Shamsher	Minister (ranking number 2)	Defence	The next in line of succession to the hereditary Rana prime ministership and Commander-in-Chief under the old system of the Rana Government.
Chudaraj Shamsher	Minister (ranking number 5)	Forests	Himself an 'A' Rana on the roll of succession and a direct nominee of the Prime Minister.
Nripa Jang Rana	Minister (ranking Number 7)	Education	Representative of the Ranas outside the roll of succession; a civil engineer holding at one time the rank of major in the old regime.
Yajna Bahadur Basnyat	Minister (ranking number 9)	Health and Local Self-Government	Representative of the non-Rana officials in the Rana regime; a lieutenant-colonel and an engineer by training.
	(II) The Congress Side		
Bishweshwar Prasad Koirala	Minister (ranking number 3)	Home	One-time Acting President of the Nepali National Congress; a member of the

			Working Committee of the Nepali Congress.
Subarna Shamsher	Minister (ranking Number 4)	Finance	Leader of the Nepal Democratic Congress; treasurer of the Nepali Congress.
Ganesh Man	Minister (ranking number 6)	Industry and Commerce	One-time member of the Praja Parishad in 1940; leader of the Nepali National Congress and the Nepali Congress.
Bhadrakali Mishra	Minister (ranking number 8)	Transport	Nepali Congress nominee on the suggestion of the Indian Ambassador, C.P.N. Singh; said to be a social worker in the Nepal tarai.
Bharat Mani Sharma	Minister (ranking number 10)	Food and Agriculture	Nepali Congress leader of the Dang Deukhuri region in the inner tarai

number 2 in the cabinet, and the swearing-in ceremony was actually delayed by half an hour or so. But the matter was amicably settled when B.P. Koirala made a generous gesture out of consideration for the age of his colleague and relinquished what was his by right on the basis of political considerations.

To Prime Minister Nehru, who had always been in favour of a "middle way" political solution in Nepal and was nurtured in the British liberal tradition, this interim cabinet was an ideal arrangement: it represented a working compromise between the conservative and liberal traditions, one complementing the other and together presumably making for ordered and stable progress in a manner envisaged by Lord Morley in his famous essay, *On Compromise* (1874). But in practice, the interim cabinet, as we shall presently see, could not function effectively because of the pulls in opposite directions exerted by the antagonistic elements.

The change in the political system necessitated constitutional and administrative innovations. The setting up of a British Indian style bureaucratic machinery geared to the needs of a parliamentary monarchy based on the Westminster model was the primary need of the hour. Therefore a central secretariat was established at the Rana Maharaj Prime Minister's 1,000-room official residence known as Singh Darbar. Ministries and departments with secretaries and directors running them as permanent civil servants under the political direction of cabinet ministers were improvised along modern lines. The country's first budget was prepared and a civil service with new and higher grades was created and pay-scales were also revised.

It now became possible for the first time for any qualified Nepali, irrespective of his caste or family, to become not only the Prime Minister of Nepal but also the Commander-in-Chief of the army and the Chief Secretary of the Government. In other words all these high offices were at least in theory thrown open to all Nepalis on the basis of their merit and qualification. This was an epoch-making change if one takes into consideration the fact that in the previous regime no non-Rana could aspire to the rank higher than that of a Commanding Colonel in the army and that of a Bada Kazi in the civil administration.

The 1951 Antarim Bidhan or the Interim Constitution

This interim constitution was granted by the King to the people "on the advice of the Council of Ministers" and came into effect on 11 April 1951. It was a short document consisting of 47 articles in all. Nineteen articles, numbered 2 to 20, dealt with directive principles of state policy. Though they were not justiciable and could not be enforced by courts, yet they served as sort of a blue-print to the newly established Government for directions of policy. Most of the articles in the 1951 Interim Constitution of Nepal are bodily lifted from the Indian Constitution.

Article 3 was the most comprehensive in its scope and promised more to the people than any other article. It said "the state shall strive to promote the welfare of people by securing and promoting as effectively as it may a social order in which justice–social, economic and political–shall inform all the institutions of national life." Thus did the interim constitution lay the basis for a future social welfare state in direct contrast to the police state which the previous Rana regime had typified.

Article 5 stressed the setting up of units of local self-government called panchayats. Article 6 promised the right to work, education and public assistance in cases of unemployment, sickness, old age etc. Article 9 emphasized the need for a uniform social code and Article 13 that for "equality before the law or the equal protection of law." Article 19 advocated abolition of forced labour and traffic in human beings and Article 20 pleaded for the abolition of exploitation of children below the age of 14.

Article 12 required the state to endeavour "to promote international peace and security", "just and honourable relations between nations", "foster respect for international law", and "encourage settlement of international disputes by arbitration."

Article 16 guaranteed citizens the well-known rights of freedom of speech and expression, of assembling peacefully without arms, of forming association or union of moving freely, of residing and settling in any part of Nepal, of acquiring and selling property and of practicing any profession, occupation, trade or business.

These 19 articles aimed at projecting Nepal as a modern state oriented towards freedom and welfare, equality and social justice. They were obviously intended for opening up new vistas of progress for a primitive obscurantist feudal society struggling to be ushered into the modern age like many other third-world societies.

The Executive or the King-in-Council

Articles 21 to 28 transferred the powers previously enjoyed by the Rana Maharaj Prime Minister to the King-in-Council. Article 21 clearly stated that: "The executive power of the state shall be vested in the King and his Council of Ministers and shall be exercised by him in accordance with the advice of his ministers." The implication was that the King could not act except on the advice of his ministers and had to function as a constitutional monarch. It was on this condition that "the supreme command of the Defence Forces of Nepal" was vested in the King by Article 21(2), and Article 22(1) gave him powers "to grant pardon, reprieves, respites or remissions of punishment." Article 25(1) required all the business of the Government of Nepal to be executed in the name of the King.

The Council of Ministers was held "collectively responsible to the King" according to Article 24. Because of the special and delicate circumstances in which the interim cabinet was formed and expected to function in Nepal, Article 26 empowered the King to ask for information from the Prime Minister and transmit for consideration by the Council any matter decided upon by a minister but not the Council.

The King was also authorized by Article 29(1) to promulgate ordinances on the advice of the Council of Ministers, but such ordinances as provided for in Article 29(2)(a) were to expire automatically three months after the validly constituted legislative body had met or assembled. Some of these articles were obviously intended to put a check on the exercise of arbitrary power by the King.

The Judiciary

Article 30(1) provided for Pradhan Nyayalaya, the "highest court of justice" to act as a court of record with the full authority vested in it by Article 31 "to punish for contempt of itself". Article 30(1) also empowered the King to appoint the Chief Justice and other judges of the High Court. The judgement of the Pradhan Nyayalaya could not be reversed by the King or the Prime Minister unlike under the 1948 Constitution. The 1951 interim constitution thus effectively ensured the separation of the executive from the judiciary at the highest level.

External or Formal Safeguards of Democracy

The Antarim Bidhan or the 1951 Interim Government Act provided for various formal or external safeguards of democracy through the Public Service Commission (Article 37), the Election Commission (Articles 41, 44) and the independent audits and accounts under a Comptroller and Auditor-General of Nepal (Articles 33, 35).

This interim constitution marked a radical departure from the past administrative tradition and practice under the Shahs and the Ranas. It was not envisaged as a gift from the ruler to the people like the Government of Nepal Act, 1948, or, for that matter, the latter constitutions (of 1959 and 1962). As it was an Act promulgated by the King on the advice of his Council of Ministers and not by virtue of his inherent power derived from hereditary tradition, it presupposed the concept of the King-in-Council, which was of the very essence of constitutional monarchy and implied that the King could act only on the advice of his Council of Ministers. Although the interim constitution was merely termed as a fundamental law for regulating the conduct of the Government pending the framing of a new constitution by the duly elected constituent assembly, it proved to be the most progressive of all constitutional documents in Nepali history to date from the viewpoint of the rights granted to the people.

Immediately after the King's return to Kathmandu a Civil Liberties Union was formed under the chairmanship of Chudananda Vaidya, and two Nepali periodicals, the daily *Awaz* and the weekly *Jagaran*, was published with Krishna Murari and Hridayachandra Singh Pradhan respectively as their editors. Another organization called *Paropakar*, a voluntary social organization, though originally set up with the blessing of a section of the Rana Government, switched its allegiance overnight to the King and the Congress after February 1951 and became quite active because it had had an organizational network throughout the Kathmandu Valley, which none of the political parties including the Nepali Congress initially had.

The relations from the very beginning between the Nepali Congress and the Rana elements in the interim cabinet were uneasy, to say the least. Apart from their inherent suspicion of each other, the role of the King also could not possibly have been impartial between the two sides against the background of the immediate historical circumstances which we have already examined. The King had reasons to be favourably disposed towards the Congress and prejudiced against the Ranas, and it was precisely this attitude of his that prevented him from playing a wholly constructive role during the period.

The Gorkha Dal Incident

B.P. Koirala, who was the leader of the Congress side in the Government, told the present author long after the event that it was under undue pressure from the King himself and some of Koirala s Congress party colleagues, particularly Major-Generals Subarna and Mahabir Shamsher, that he had to take a rather precipitate action against the Vir Gorkha Dal (literally Brave Gorkha Organization), a political party started by one of the grandsons of the Defence Minister, Babar Shamsher, with tacit if not active support of the Rana side in the Government. B.P. Koirala deliberately sought to provoke the Rana prime minister into action so that it might be used as a cause for his removal. It was alleged even before the formal opening of the party that it was intended as a cover for an organization seeking to overthrow the new Government by subverting the army. Without informing the Prime Minister or the cabinet, Home Minister B.P. Koirala precipitated a crisis by ordering the arrest of several members of the Gorkha Dal on 11 April 1951 under the Public Security Act even a few hours before the Act had obtained the royal assent.

In the small hours on 12 April Bharat Shamsher, a grandson of Defence Minister Babar Shamsher, along with other members of the Gorkha Dal including Ranadhir Subba, an erstwhile leader of the Darjeeling-based All-India Gorkha league, were arrested. But that very day Bharat Shamsher, Ranadhir Subba and a few other Gorkha Dal leaders were brought out of the Kathmandu prison by a crowd of supporters and sympathizers who thereafter thought it fit to demonstrate in front of Home Minister Koirala's residence hardly five hundred yards away from the prison. Koirala was reported to have himself shot to death one of the demonstrators, Sukul Dhoj, who was allegedly attacking the Home Minister with a khukri, but in fact, it was one of his party colleagues who had actually killed the demonstrator.

The demonstration, luckily for all concerned, was joined by recruits in mufti and not by the regular soldiers who were engaged in their routine drill on the parade ground. The attack on the Home Minister's residence did not appear to be pre-planned nor did the open and vociferous appeal of the demonstrators to the troops to join them seemed to have had the official backing of the Ranas in authority. Senior commanding General Kaiser Shamsher, who was in command of the troops assembled on the parade ground, saw to it that they did not join the demonstration.

Kaiser also showed a rare sense of calm and courage in sending back a truckload of armed men and officers of the Congress Mukti Sena (the Liberation Army) who had appeared upon the scene after a section of their comrades-in-arm had arrested Bharat Shamsher, who was riding in his car at the northern end of the parade ground, and taken him to their camp at Lain Chaur. An unruly mob in a state of frenzy meanwhile burnt Bharat's car, and all the Congress ministers sought shelter in King Tribhuvan's palace.

There was a state of panic in the town because the people felt that the Prime Minister himself must have been behind the Gorkha Dal demonstrations aiming at counter-revolution. But all this proved to be a storm in a tea cup because Maharaj Mohan, who was still occupying Singha Darbar, his official residence as the Prime Minister, refused to use the two crack regiments of the Nepali army at his disposal, First Rifle and Kali Bahadur, for any counter-revolutionary purpose.

An emergency cabinet meeting was convened on 13 April 1951 under the chairmanship of the King himself. It was held in the royal palace, where a large body of the King's bodyguards were quartered, because Tribhuvan suspected a coup might be attempted. Mohan Shamsher had to be brought to the meeting by Major-General Nara Shamsher by special command of King Tribhuvan. Mohan was blamed by his cabinet colleagues for the attack on the Home Minister's residence. Only Chudaraj Shamsher, Minister for Forests, stood by the Prime Minister while the Defence Minister, Babar Shamsher, was away in Bombay for medical treatment. Two of the Ministers of the Rana side, Nripa Jang Rana and Yajna Bahadur Basnyat, deserted the Prime Minister on this issue. Under the circumstances the Prime Minister had no option other than to offer to resign and he was more than willing to do so.

The Indian Ambassador, Sir C.P.N. Singh, happened to be out of the country on that fateful day and India requested King Tribhuvan and everyone concerned to withhold the cabinet's final decision until after his return to Kathmandu the very same afternoon. It was not until the evening that the Ambassador could return to Kathmandu by a special plane because of weather conditions. With the support of the King solidly behind him, the Indian Ambassador succeeded in playing the proverbial role of a monkey between two cats quarrelling over a piece of bread. Koirala later told the present author that the Ambassador appealed to his generous impulses by saying that Mohan was after all going to resign in a few days' time as he had already agreed and therefore, the Home Minister should not put the Prime Minister to disgrace by insisting on his tendering resignation then and there. The cabinet decision of 13 April recording the offer of the Prime Minister to resign was signed by Mohan Shamsher under duress on 14 April to avoid an immediate crisis.

By 13 April 37 Gorkha Dal members ana sympathizers had been arrested and by 29 April, 20 of those arrested had been released. But the Gorkha Dal incident, because of its counter-revolutionary overtones, adversely affected the position of the Rana Prime Minister in the cabinet, although his instant resignation in disgrace had been forestalled by the Indian Ambassador's intervention.

The immediate result of the Gorkha Dal episode was the assumption of the command of the army by the King as the Supreme Commander-in-Chief and the transfer to the royal palace of the crack regiments guarding Singh Darbar, where Maharaj Mohan Shamsher was still residing (Mohan Shamsher moved to his private residence at Maharajganj on 20 April.) There were other changes in the command of the army. Though Senior Commanding General Kaiser was promoted to the office of the Commander-in-Chief of the army, General Kiran Shamsher was appointed Deputy Commander-in-Chief with wide powers of independent action. General Nara Shamsher was appointed Inspector-General of Police. The Gorkha Dal incident gave the Nepali Congress a pretext for retaining the party's Mukti Sena, the liberation army, as a paramilitary force, renamed the Raksha Dal (Security Force).

Prime Minister Mohan Shamsher's complaints against Home Minister B.P. Koirala were meanwhile forwarded to Nehru through the Indian Ambassador on 16 April. Though the Home Minister had actually misused the Public Security Act, the Prime Minister felt compelled to sign the cabinet decision of 13 April against his will only to avoid an immediate crisis, he explained, and a cabinet reshuffle was essential for the maintenance of the parity. Otherwise no useful purpose would be served by his continuing in office. He would like to discuss the situation with Nehru in Delhi.

Major-General Bijaya told the British Ambassador, Sir George Falconer, that if the Delhi talks were not satisfactory, the Prime Minister would not return to Kathmandu. As he was leaving, Bijaya added "strictly *entre nous*" that: "I think it will be better if my father does go, he has suffered enough at the hands of the Congress and will never be strong enough to stand up to the class of persons in the cabinet." Falconer urged that he should not take hasty action in a vital matter of this kind and suggested that when the facts were known in Delhi, some move to restore the situation might be initiated from there without the necessity of the Prime Minister's going to Delhi.

This was what Falconer had reported to his Government on these development:

> B.P. Koirala was opposed to the Prime Minister going to Delhi because the people would think that he was acting under Nehru's instructions which would be a loss of prestige both for Nepal and the Maharaj. The aim of both Subarna Shamsher and Koirala was the maintenance of the country's independence and progress along democratic line.
>
> In the event of Mohan's resignation either Kaiser or Singha might fill the bill according to Koirala. Koirala obviously respected

Kaiser for his erudition. Subarna thought that the next Prime Minister would not be a Rana. The Congress could not agree to having a Rana Prime Minister. After discussing the pros and cons, Subarna, however, agreed that Kaiser would be the most suitable Rana Prime Minister. Neither would agree to Babar who, according to them, was more dyed in the wool than Mohan. Falconer advised Koirala to release all those who were arrested to earn the goodwill of other parties. He would do that and asked Falconer to talk to Subarna along those lines.[1]

Both Mohan Shamsher and B.P. Koirala were summoned to Delhi for talks with Nehru so that the crisis might be resolved. Mohan was originally supposed to go to Delhi on 30 April, but his visit was later postponed till 6 May. Maharaj Mohan was strongly advised by Nehru not to resign, and this came as a shock to B.P. Koirala. Further, Koirala himself was kept waiting indefinitely in Delhi for an interview with Nehru even after the die was cast. B.P. Koirala told the author that Jayaprakash Narayan, who happened to be in Delhi at the time, advised him to leave for Kathmandu if he had any sense of self-respect as a minister of the Government of an independent country. The Home Minister acted on his advice and left Delhi abruptly. Probably the Secretary-General of the Indian Ministry of External Affairs had this incident in mind when he told the British High Commissioner, Sir Archibald Nye, after the minister's return that "Koirala was getting too big for his boots." However, within a few days Koirala's colleagues in the Congress and members of the Rana faction apparently resolved the cabinet crisis under the advice and guidance of Prime Minister Nehru and the Indian Ministry of External Affairs and returned to Kathmandu to work in a spirit of harmony and cooperation.

A complete agreement between the two sides was made known to the press and public through a joint statement on 16 May to the effect that "the Nepali cabinet would work in a cooperative and progressive spirit for the political development and economic prosperity of Nepal."[2] There was further agreement that there should be only minor changes in the cabinet and that a nominated Advisory Assembly should be set up to serve as a "little parliament" imparting thereby a more representative character to the interim governmental set-up.

Nehru's Visit to Kathmandu

Prime Minister Nehru was scheduled to visit Kathmandu in mid-June, and this seems to have provided the urge for all parties concerned to improvise a settlement of their differences. In keeping with the terms of the agreement reached in Delhi in May, the entire cabinet offered its resignation to King Tribhuvan through Prime Minister Mohan Shamsher on 9 June. The following day King Tribhuvan announced a reconstituted cabinet replacing Babar Shamsher by Singha Shamsher in the Rana group of ministers and Bharat Mani Sharma by Surya Prasad Upadhyaya in the Congress group.

But certain unforeseen circumstances seemed to threaten the prospect of the Indian Prime Minister's visit on the appointed day. There had been incidents of attack on some Indian merchants' shops and houses at Birganj, a border township in the tarai. The Indian embassy laid down a condition that the Indian Prime Minister's visit would be cancelled if within 72 hours a board of enquiry with an Indian representative on it was not set up to investigate the Birganj events. The Indian condition was accepted and the Indian Prime Minister's visit was confirmed.

Nehru's first visit to Kathmandu from 15 through 17 June did not prove to be as great a success as it was expected to be. Though he was enthusiastically received by the King himself at the airport, he was greeted by hostile black flags on his way to the town. There was no doubt that he attracted a mammoth gathering on the parade ground, where he made a speech from the historic platform under the chalk tree in the company of the King, the Prime Minister, the cabinet and Nepali Congress and other political party leaders. The same evening there was a gala banquet in the royal place given in his honour by the King. Sudden brief torrential rains temporarily interfered with the elaborate open-air arrangements made for the banquet in the spacious lawn in front of the palace. But once the rains stopped and the moon and the stars came out, the party was moved to the front lawns as planned in the midst of great enthusiasm and jubilation and continued till the early hours of the morning.

After being shown round the important temples and other places of interest in the Kathmandu Valley, Nehru addressed another open air meeting at which the microphone and loudspeakers were not properly fitted. Nehru probably forgot that he was in a different country and said publicly half in jest and half in annoyance that the hill people were known for their lack of intelligence–a remark which certainly did not go down well with the huge crowd that was assembled to hear him at Lain Chaur.

Arrest of Opposition Leaders

During September several political events of note took place in Nepal. Dilli Raman Regmi, President of Nepali National Congress, along with the publisher and the printer of the Nepali National Congress bulletin, Tejkanta Silwal and Keshav Dev Pande, were held guilty of the contempt of court by Hari Prasad Pradhan, the Chief Justice of the Pradhan Nyayalaya, (the High Court) and sentenced to 18 months' imprisonment and a fine of two thousand rupees on 9 September. They were convicted for contempt for printing in their bulletin a news item concerning the delay in the disposal of the case of Rishikesh Shaha, the present author, who had been arrested for taking out a procession after an incident on the football ground and detained by the order of the Home Minister, B.P. Koirala, but had since been released by the High Court.

Rishikesh Shaha denied in the hearing of the contempt case that he had assured the Chief Justice that he would get the news item contradicted. The news item had merely stated that political leaders like Shaha were hindered in their work because the judges and the courts had tended to put oil into their ears (a Nepali idiom which means sleeping) over the periodicals' pleas for the expeditious disposal of their cases. The Chief Justice took exception to the use of the expression "putting oil into the ears" as derogatory to the court. But Rishikesh Shaha and his colleague, Shankar Prasad Sharma, were not sentenced to imprisonment the same day as others but were asked to present themselves at the court the following day, respectively accused of stating a falsehood and committing a misdemeanour. Sharma had refused to accept summons by the Chief Justice of the highest court on the ground that his signature was in the Roman script and was illegible.

Strangely enough Shaha and Sharma were not sentenced to prison because there were no laws for punishing offences of the kind they had committed. (The Home Ministry was instructed to draft legislation to correct this.) It was probably the public furor over the sentencing of Regmi and others the previous day that had deterred the Chief Justice from sentencing them. It may be pointed out here that King Tribhuvan himself heard arguments between Shaha and Sharma on the one hand and Chief Justice Hari Prasad Pradhan on the other in his own drawing room. But even this meeting, at which the party leaders seemed to score points against the Chief Justice, failed to ensure Regmi's release.

By July 1951, the National People's United Front was formed on the initiative of the Communist Party of Nepal consisting of itself, the Nepal Praja Parishad, the Nepal Youth Organisation, the All-Nepal Workers' Organisation, the All-Nepal Women's Organisation, the Social Reforms Organisation, the All-Nepal Students' Federation and the Progressive study circle with Tanka Prasad Acharya and Shailendra Kumar Upadhyaya as President and Secretary.

In due course the Nepali National Congress under the leadership of Rishikesh Shaha and Shankar Prasad Sharma formed a joint action committee with the leftist United Front led by the Praja Parishad to launch a struggle for the repeal of the Public Security Act and the release of all political prisoners including Dilli Raman Regmi. After the joint action committee had organized a successful strike in the valley through a campaign of posters and bulletins against the high-handedness of the I.G.P. and the Police Force, 11 political leaders including Tanka Prasad Acharya, Juju Bhai and Bal Mukunda of the Praja Parishad, Rishikesh Shaha, Shankar Prasad Sharma and Murali Dhar Sharma of the Nepali National Congress, Tilak Raj Shahi of the Communist Party, Agni Prasad Kharel of the All-Nepal Rastriya Mahasabha, and Mangal Man, Shankar Prasad Joshi and Iswari Raj Sharma, were arrested under the Public Security Act on 24 September and sent to prison.

This was how the British Ambassador, C.H. Summerhayes, reported the situation marked by the above events in September 1951:

> During recent months there has been a growing opposition to the uneasy Rana-Congress coalition and this was mainly led by a certain Regmi, who was, till he objected to the violence of the last year's coup, himself a Congress leader and who had incidentally been imprisoned as such at Rana request during our control in India. Shortly after the recent return of Koirala from his tour in eastern Nepal this man was arrested on the charge of having brought local justice into contempt by criticising the impartiality and competence of the new chief justice. He was sentenced to rigorous imprisonment and a fine, though apparently it was not correct to have given a double sentence. This brought about further strikes of students and others and there was general protest even to the King.
>
> Then a week ago a row flared up after a football match at which the Crown Prince and most ministers were present and anti-government shouts were heard. The unpopular Congress special

police behaved roughly and a number of people were damaged, so opposition leaders of various parties protested by bulletins and by arranging a brief strike, besides requesting the removal of the Inspector-General of Police, Major-General Nara, who had previously shown his stupidity here and also in London over a police case that you may remember but who is a palace favourite having married off his two daughters to the younger princes.

Two days ago at least eight of these leading critics were also arrested by order of the Home Minister, for the new democracy here does not seem to recognise that outspoken criticism is a part of their declared system and that having preached this doctrine they cannot easily apply the old fashioned Rana control.[3]

Towards the Collapse of the Rana-Congress Joint Cabinet

Though King Tribhuvan was advised by Nehru not to help the Nepali Congress keep Prime Minister Mohan Shamsher out of political councils there was no love lost between the Prime Minister and the King whose sympathy lay completely with the Nepali Congress. This became quite clear when King Tribhuvan announced a 35-member Advisory Assembly on 2 October 1951 without consulting the Prime Minister. An overwhelming majority of the nominees belonged to the Nepali Congress and the rest were independents; other parties and the official Rana side were left without any representation at all.

Both the Indian and the British Ambassadors also seemed to agree that opposition leaders should have also been released and some of them nominated members of the assembly. More importantly, on 8 October Prime Minister Mohan Shamsher publicly aired his grievance that the King had announced the Advisory Assembly without consulting the cabinet.[4] The Nepali Congress leaders interpreted the Prime Minister's statement as a challenge to the King's constitutional right and asked for Mohan Shamsher's resignation.

As this internal crisis in the Government was building up, on 6 November a procession of students was fired on by the police resulting in the death of a youth named Chiniya Kazi. Prime Minister Mohan Shamsher came out with a public statement on 9 November regretting the tragic incident and conveying condolences to the bereaved family. B.P. Koirala took the statement as the Prime Minister's violation of the principle of collective responsibility and also publicly accused the Indian Ambassador of interfering in the internal affairs of the country after he had made enquiries from the Home Minister about the firing incident.

Following a stormy cabinet meeting at which B.P. Koirala was blamed even by his own colleague in the Congress group, Bhadrakali Mishra, known to be the Indian Ambassador's agent, the Home Minister spoke over Radio Nepal on 10 November, the first anniversary of the start of the 1950 revolution. In an emotional speech he made a plea for a complete revolution as the revolutionary objectives had only been partially achieved, and he tendered his own resignation and that of all the other Congress ministers, demanding a homogeneous cabinet to replace what he described as an "unnatural coalition." He also ordered the release of all political prisoners to enable "progressive forces to re-examine the situation."

The very same day the Congress group of ministers reinforced Koirala's statement by handing their resignations directly to the King and not to the Prime Minister, who did not learn of their mass resignation until the following night. It was only on 12 November that the Rana bloc of ministers resigned, leaving the King free to set up a new Government.

The outgoing Home Minister's order for the release of all political prisoners was only partially carried out after a delay of at least 36 hours. Tanka Prasad Acharya, the present author and others were set free on 12 November, whereas Dilli Raman Regmi, Bharat Shamsher and others were freed only after the new cabinet was formed. But Dr. K.I. Singh and his followers were allowed to languish in detention indefinitely.

After the release of their leaders the opposition political parties held open-air meetings to share their views with the people on the political crisis. The Praja Parishad and the Nepali National Congress expressed their opposition to the formation of a Nepali Congress Government in view of its nine months' record of arbitrary administration, and they demanded an all-party Government as a fair and just solution to the political problem facing the country. The so-called independents of Kathmandu were also disillusioned with the Nepali Congress as a result of the recent firing incident, and they too came out against the Congress being given sole charge of the Government.

By November India's attitude towards Prime Minister Mohan Shamsher seemed to have changed. Bajpai told Ganer, the Acting British High Commissioner in Delhi, that Mohan had failed to provide stability and an effective Government. According to Bajpai, Mohan behaved well but dissensions and intrigues in the Rana family prevented him from playing the role the Ranas were expected to play.

Bajpai found fault with B.P. Koirala, whom he regarded as "an irresponsible intriguer." B.P. Koirala's resignation had taken the Indians by surprise. It was clear that the Indian Government favoured the reconstitution of the Government under the leadership of a Nepali Congress representative, most probably M.P. Koirala.[5]

It appears that King Tribhuvan sought the advice of the British Ambassador, Summerhayes, about the reconstitution of the new Government. This was what the Ambassador wrote to the Foreign Office on 13 November:

> "Consistent with my view I submitted to His Majesty the King my proposals for reconstituting the cabinet and making it more broad-based and representative. Soon thereafter the Congress group of ministers in the cabinet submitted their demand to HM the King for the formation of a homogeneous cabinet or, in case this was not possible, for the acceptance of their resignations. In view of both these letters, it has become necessary for HM the King to reconstitute the cabinet as early as possible. I have full hope that the reconstituted cabinet will be representative in character and will be able to look to the needs." [6]

It is interesting to note that by this time the British envoy had established a personal rapport with the King, who was himself full of admiration for the British tradition of constitutional monarchy. The Ambassador's reference to the King's connection with the Gorkhas as their future natural leader seems to be highly perceptive:

> "The King, whose unmartial figure went round the local golf course with me yesterday on a first appearance there for over 20 years, will sooner or later have to have closer connection with 'our' Gurkhas, if his country avoids absorption despite all the jealous splits."[7]

There were serious dissensions in the ranks of the Nepali Congress itself following the resignation of B.P. Koirala and other Congress ministers. The majority of the party's Working Committee wanted B.P. Koirala to lead the Congress Government whereas a small but influential minority favoured the party's acceptance at least for the time being of the King's choice–M.P. Koirala, B.P.'s elder half-brother–as the Prime Minister. It was with some reluctance that the Working Committee approved of M.P. Koirala as the Prime Minister and submitted to the King a list of eight Nepali Congress members and six independents to the King for inclusion in the new Council of Ministers.

M.P. Koirala thus became the first commoner Prime Minister after 104 long years of Rana rule. The ex-Maharaj Prime Minister, Mohan Shamsher, at the age of 65, left for India on 14 December 1951. His departure from Nepal must have indeed been a sad event for the Maharaj because, apart from all other considerations, fate had made him a direct party to the abolition of the Rana regime. He lived a retired life in Bangalore, India, until his death in 1965 at the age of 80.

The First M.P. Koirala Government (16 November 1951 to 14 August 1952)

On 16 November 1951 King Tribhuvan proclaimed the establishment of a new Council of Ministers under the prime ministership of Matrika Prasad Koirala. The King admitted that the Rana-Congress coalition cabinet had failed to satisfy the people, and he stressed the need for a broad-based and representative Government reiterating his long-term commitment to "a fully democratic system functioning in accordance with a constitution prepared by a Constituent Assembly." But he stated that for the time being the best he could do was to ask the leader of the largest party to form a Government broadly representative of ethnic and territorial divisions in the country. The new Prime Minister was exhorted to pursue an enlightened policy based on statesmanship and carry on the administration in such a manner as to ensure the "continued goodwill, impartiality and respect of the people toward the government."

The Prime Minister was asked to ensure the enjoyment of civil rights by the people without prejudice to public security and the existing laws. The Council of Ministers was collectively required to set up an independent judiciary, to make sure that the Public Service Commission functioned freely and impartially, and to take the necessary steps to hold elections to the Constituent Assembly by April 1953 if possible. The King concluded his proclamation with an appeal to the people to cooperate fully with the Government and with a call for the civil servants to carry on their duties regardless of political changes.

The members of the new Council of Ministers under the prime ministership of M.P. Koirala are given below:

The Nepali Congress Government of 1951

Name	*Rank*	*Portfolios*	*Political persuasion*
(1)	(2)	(3)	(4)
Matrika Prasad Koirala	Prime Minister	Foreign Affairs and General Administration	Nepali Congress
Surya Prasad Upadhyaya	Minister	Police, Jail, Broad-casting and Food	Nepali Congress
General Kaiser Shamsher	Minister	Defence	Independent
Subarna Shamsher	Minister	Finance	Nepali Congress
Naradmuni Thulung	Minister	Local Self-Govt. and Health	Nepali Congress
Mahendra Bikram Shah	Minister	Industry, Commerce and Civil Supplies	Nepali Congress
Manajor-General Sarada Shamsher	Minister	Education	Independent
Bhadrakali Mishra	Minister	Transport	Nepali Congress
Mahabir Shamsher	Minister	Planning and Develop-ment, Mines, Forests and Electricity	Nepali Congress
Ganesh Man Singh	Minister	Agriculture, Animal Husbandry and Land Reform	Nepali Congress
Khadga Man Singh	Minister	Parliamentary Affairs	Independent
Bhagavati Prasad Singh	Minister	Law and Justice	Independent
Nara Bahadur Gurung	Deputy Minister	Health	Independent
Dharma Ratna "Yami"	Deputy Minister	Forests	Independent

The new Council of Ministers contained representatives from the eastern and the western hills and the tarai and also from the ethnic groups such as the Kirati and the Gurung. However, there were still four Ranas in the cabinet—two from the Congress and two from the old regime.

Though the independents were technically nominated by M.P. Koirala with the King's approval, yet they looked to the King for guidance and acted for all practical purposes as the King's men in the cabinet. Conflict inside the Nepali Congress tended to increase the importance of the role of these independents.

The number of portfolios had had to be increased primarily to accommodate a larger Council of Ministers than before, and new ministries such as General Administration, Planning and Development, Land Reform, Parliamentary Affairs and Law and Justice had to be created. The Home Ministry's original jurisdiction was drastically curtailed because M.P. Koirala took charge of General Administration which not only allowed him general supervision of all departments and ministries but also gave him specific charge of cabinet affairs, Government appointments, the Public Service Commission, the coordination of the different ministries and the supervision of district administration. The new Home Minister was left in charge of only Police, Jail and Broadcasting.

The Rift between the Koirala Brothers

The full-fledged Nepali Congress Government started with a serious handicap because it did not enjoy the whole-hearted support of B.P. Koirala, the charismatic leader of the party to whom not only the rank and file but also some of the senior party leaders within the Government owed personal allegiance. B.P. Koirala was not at all happy at M.P. Koirala's choice of the independents, most of whom did not share the party's thinking on the vital issues that had to be confronted in the interim period if a smooth transition to a new fully democratic order were to be ensured following elections to the Constituent Assembly. M.P. Koirala felt that it would not be opportune for the party during the interim period to emphasize the strict enforcement of the principle of constitutional monarchy or to insist on the immediate implementation of the party's programme of economic and social welfare. According to M.P. Koirala, the task of the interim government was just to carry on the day-to-day administration of the country smoothly until such time as elections to the Constituent Assembly were held and the constitution was framed.

Both these points of view were valid up to a point, and if they could have been reconciled in practice not only would the future of the party have been assured but the history of the country might have taken a different course. But in actual practice the differences between the two half-brothers, as we shall presently sec, degenerated to the level of a personal feud with political overtones, and this caused a serious split in the country's major political party with far-reaching consequences not only for its own future but also for the future of the nation and for democracy.

M.P. Koirala, who had himself recently been a civil servant in the Rana regime, did not perhaps find anything wrong in making use of the services of the old-time civil servants and Rana supporters. The first administrative reorganization under M.P. Koirala as the Prime Minister was announced on 28 November 1951 and the key positions in civil service went to Sardar Gunja Man Singh and Colonel Chandra Bahadur Thapa, who were respectively appointed Cabinet Secretary and Home Secretary. B.P. Koirala himself had not hesitated to entrust the charge of the Home Ministry to Kul Nath Lohani and Tilak Shamsher Thapa, who were also among the erstwhile supporters of the Rana regime. The reason for this was partly the paucity of qualified persons outside the Rana-time bureaucracy and partly the reluctance of the political leaders themselves, despite their professed revolutionary zeal, to entrust the younger people with responsibility. Even worse than this, the command and composition of the old Rana-time army were left intact notwithstanding much talk about the democratization of the political and social order.

In February 1952 Prime Minister M.P. Koirala as the head of the civil offices coordinating committee, composed entirely of officials from the Rana period, increased the King's privy purse in the budget 100 per cent over that previously made available by the Rana-Congress coalition Government. This brought him criticism from the party as a seeker of the King's favour for selfish purposes.

Taking advantage of the overall decline in his brother's reputation in and outside the party, B.P. Koirala made known on 20 February his intention to run for the presidentship of the party. B.P. Koirala's position was that one and the same person should not be both Prime Minister and party President. He accused Indian Ambassador C.P.N. Singh of playing politics in Nepal by setting one leader against another and asked for Singh's replacement in the long-term interests of Indo-Nepal relations. While condemning the Nepali Government's policy of banning the Communist Party as "unwise", he pleaded for an effective economic policy which might "prevent the Chinese Communists from taking advantage of the situation in Nepal with the help of Dr. K.I. Singh.[8]

M.P. Koirala's immediate response to his younger brother's challenge was to put off the annual session of the Congress on the pretext that more time was needed for the election of delegates from the different districts in view of the increase in membership. On 1 March B.P. Koirala openly challenged the contention of his brother bringing the differences between the two men into the open. This split both the Party and the Government into two factions.

Jayaprakash Narayan invited the brothers to Calcutta and sought to bring about a reconciliation between them. On 8 March the Koirala brothers were back in Nepal together having reached an understanding on several points: mutual recriminations should cease forthwith; a contest for the party presidency must be avoided; the same person should not hold the offices of both Prime Minister and party President; the party should not interfere with the day-to-day administration of the Government and the Government should follow as far as possible the policies and programmes adopted by the party's annual.conference.[9]

It seemed for a while that the two brothers were truly reconciled. M.P. Koirala withdrew his candidature for party presidentship in favour of B.P. Koirala. But B.P. Koirala's election as President did not help improve his relations with M.P. Koirala, who seemed to turn more to the King than to his party colleagues for political support. The Prime Minister was said to have announced on 2 July 1952 the King's birthday honours list without first consulting his colleagues. It was also held against M.P. Koirala that he did not associate his colleagues with preparing the speech from the throne delivered at the first inaugural session of the Advisory Assembly on 7 July. B.P. Koirala was highly critical of the address on the floor of the Assembly, saying that it was out of step with the times, its land reforms programme was vague and meaningless and the Government's commitment to the Constituent Assembly was "casual."

The quarrel between the two Koirala brothers had thus assumed crisis proportions in the first half of July 1952. Out of the 14 members of the Nepali Congress Working Committee selected by Prime Minister M.P. Koirala, ten sided with the party President B.P. Koirala. They agreed with B.P. that the presence of too many independents in the cabinet was responsible for delay in the implementation of the party's economic and social welfare programmes and for a revival of the influence of reactionary and conservative elements in Nepali society. M.P. Koirala was not prepared to incur the displeasure of the King by dropping the independents, most of whom enjoyed royal favour.

The Working Committee, in the absence of the Prime Minister, decided on 19 July 1952 that the numerical strength of the cabinet be reduced from eleven to seven members, and they forwarded a list of nominees: five Nepali Congress members and two independents. The Prime Minister was said to have objected to the inclusion of the hard-core trinity of the Nepali Congress, Subarna Shamsher, Surya Prasad Upadhyaya and Ganesh Man Singh, whom he held mainly responsible for dissension in the cabinet.

Prime Minister M.P. Koirala's reply to the Working Committee the following day found fault with its directives on the reconstitution of the Government. According to him, the Working Committee was interfering with the Prime Minister's acknowledged right of selecting his own team to run the Government and it was also disregarding the gentlemen's agreement between the two brothers that the party President was not to interfere in the routine administration of the Government. The Prime Minister also expressed his dissatisfaction with the reasons given by the Working Committee for reconstituting the cabinet.

The Working Committee's next move was to demand the resignation of M.P. Koirala and his colleagues from the Government. Prime Minister M.P. Koirala contended that the nominated Working Committee had no right to ask for the Government's resignation and demanded an immediate meeting of the All-Nepal Nepali Congress Central Committee. The Working Committee in its turn asked M.P. Koirala and his colleagues to submit their resignations to the King within 48 hours or face suspension from active membership in the party for a period of three years.

Three Nepali Congress ministers, Subarna Shamsher, Surya Prasad Upadhyaya and Ganesh Man Singh, resigned from the cabinet as required by the Working Committee. But three others, Naradmuni Thulung, Mahendra Bikram Shah and Mahabir Shamsher sided with the Prime Minister and did not tender their resignation on the grounds that the Working Committee's decision was not constitutional. The Prime Minister and the three refractory ministers were expelled from the party in the last week of July and the M.P. Koirala cabinet ceased to be a party cabinet thereafter.

Following the King's acceptance of the resignation of the three Nepali Congress ministers from the cabinet on 29 July, B.P. Koirala, the party President, arranged to hold an open-air meeting the next day. The gathering was broken up by paid agents of the Government hired from other parties, and the Nepali Congress leaders were roundly manhandled. Summerhayes, the British Ambassador, made the following comment on the incident in his dispatch to his Government: "They asked for trouble by attempting such a public appeal before the present cabinet dispute is discussed at the end of August by the main Congress Committee (Central Committee). The objectors at the meeting were mainly from other opposition parties and not Communist or Congress supporters of the Prime Minister. Such potentially dangerous clashes are likely to recur while the cabinet crisis lasts.[10]

On 6 August 1952 Prime Minister M.P. Koirala told a meeting of his supporters in the party that he was himself willing to resign, but he accused the three ministers who had already quit of conspiring against him since 21 February, the day on which he had put off the annual session of the party as its President. On 10 August M.P. Koirala tendered the resignation of his Government and soon thereafter expressed his intention to face the Central Committee of the Nepali Congress as a "common soldier of the Congress and not as the prime minister.[11]

The following account contained in the Acting U.K. High Commissioner's report to his Government before M.P. Koirala's resignation, while affording an insight into M.P.'s own thinking, also shows how Nehru felt that the Nepali Prime Minister should resign.

1. Nepalese ambassador (Bijaya Shamsher) told me today that M.P. Koirala had informed that he was ready to continue as Prime Minister but wished to know what Mr. Nehru's views on the present situation were. Bijaya has accordingly had a long discussion with Nehru in the course of which the latter said:

   (I) He approved the stand which M.P. Koirala had taken hitherto; he endorsed his action and entirely agreed that he was right not to submit to the dictation of the Congress Working Committee.

   (II) From the Indian point of view he would be very happy to see M.P. Koirala continue as Prime Minister.

(III) On the other hand he was very concerned at recent developments and disturbed at the lack of moral authority for continuance of the present regime. It was clear that the Congress Party itself was hopelessly split in two and not even certain that M.P. Koirala could secure a majority at a meeting of the full Congress.

(IV) Nehru was particularly concerned at what he feared might be a breakdown in the machinery of the government; three key ministers had resigned and it was essential that the work must go on.

2. Nehru's own view was that the right course would be for M.P. Koirala to resign. This should strengthen his position in the country and would remove any criticism that he was merely insisting on clinging to office. A new government could not be formed until after the full Congress had met and therefore for the interim period he was in favour of the King assuming direct responsibility for the administration assisted by a small advisory council. The council should be composed of independent members and should not include any persons with marked political affiliations.
3. Bijaya himself is rather surprised and distressed at this advice since he feels:

(I) That the King has neither the character nor the ability to run the administration himself, and there is a danger that once he has tasted power, he may be difficult to dislodge.

(II) It is almost impossible in present circumstances in Kathmandu to find really independent and impartial advisers.

(III) The advisory council will not be in a strong position and there will be endless scope for all the intrigues to continue to cause every possible trouble (including going direct to the King behind the council's back).

4. Bijaya endeavoured to put some of the points to Nehru though he did not like to press them, and he found that Nehru still had considerable confidence in the King personally. Bijaya asked Nehru whether what he had said represented his considered opinion; Nehru replied that he was giving the best advice he could but no one at a distance could judge precisely how the situation should be handled and his views were not to be accepted rigidly.

5. Bijaya had communicated with the King and the Prime Minister accordingly; he has little doubt that the King will be attracted by Nehru's advice and the Prime Minister will feel bound to give it very serious weight.
6. Nehru also confirmed that it was his intention to move Indian Ambassador as soon as convenient but said that he would not make change until the present crisis was over.
7. Incidentally Bijaya added that there were constant rumours that he would be summoned to Kathmandu either to join the cabinet or the advisory council if it were set up. If he were to receive such an invitation he would be faced with a very difficult situation.[12]

Summerhayes in Kathmandu was categorically told by his Foreign Office not to give advice to the Nepali Prime Minister because "it would be most undesirable to be drawn into the position of giving advice diametrically opposite to advice repeatedly given by Nehru to Nepalese Ambassador."[13]

Nehru's advice prevailed in the end and M.P. Koirala resigned as we have already seen. Thus did the first Nepali Congress Government come to an end after only nine months, a period dominated by the rift between the two Koirala brothers but also including other developments which interfered with the smooth functioning of the Government. The Government had been called upon to meet two serious challenges to its authority: an armed revolt in the Government's armed police in January 1952 and a lightning strike by the low-grade employees in the Government secretariat in June.

The Raksha Dal Mutiny

On the night of 22/23 January 1952 a section of the Government's special armed police force, the Raksha Dal, largely composed of volunteers and men of the Nepali Congress's Liberation Army, the Mukti Sena, mutinied against the Government and captured key Government offices and installations, such as the Central Secretariat at Singh Darbar, the airport, radio station, jail, wireless and telephone offices, and ordnance depots and factories. Though they numbered hardly one thousand in all, the rebels succeeded in assuming control of the capital for about twelve hours from midnight till noon on 23 January. During that period of time, they threw open the central jail in Kathmandu and released a number of political leaders including Agni Prasad Kharel of

All-Nepal Rashtriya Mahasabha and Ram Prasad Rai of the secessionist Kirati organisation. They also freed Dr. K.I. Singh, who had been under detention in Singh Darbar since September 1951.

Although most of the mutineers belonged to eastern Nepal and had nothing to do with Dr. K.I. Singh during his insurrection, yet they thought of projecting him as the leader of their mutiny because of the popular sympathy he had received when the joint Nepal-Indian military action was launched against him and his men in the summer of 1951. Dr. K.I. Singh was feeling uncomfortable as the leader of this 1952 revolt from the very beginning and only waited for his men in the Nakkhu prison at Lalitpur to be freed by the mutineers so that he and his associates might escape from the Kathmandu Valley. He saw to it that the mutineers held Singh Darbar Secretariat until he and his own followers had had sufficient time to make good their escape from the Valley.

Meanwhile that morning Dr. K.I. Singh received at Singh Darbar political leaders of different parties such as Tanka Prasad Acharya of the Nepal Praja Parishad, Food Minister Ganesh Man Singh of the Nepali Congress itself and Shankar Prasad Sharma of the Nepali National Congress. Dr. K.I. Singh conveyed to the King through them two political demands on behalf of the mutineers: the formation of an all-party interim government and the maintenance of equal friendship with both India and China, but added on his own that he wanted to avoid bloodshed at all costs. But before these leaders returned from the royal palace to acquaint the rebels with the King's and the Government's response to their demands Dr. K.I. Singh and his close followers had already left Singh Darbar on their way north to the Rasuwa pass by which they subsequently crossed into safety into Tibet.

It was late in the afternoon of 23 January that the state troops had recaptured Singh Darbar, though they had regained control of other installations by noon. Both Agni Prasad Kharel and Captain Tek Bahadur Malla, who were credited with organizing the group, were arrested on 23 January itself. One driver of the armed police force and a civilian lost their lives in the course of intermittent firing by the mutineers from Singh Darbar, and two or three other persons were wounded.

The Indian Ambassador made frantic requests to his Government on behalf of the Nepal Government for reinforcements of 2,000 Indian troops by air on 23 January. But these demands were not met for political reasons and also for the practical consideration that the mutineers were in control of the only airport in Kathmandu. It must be said to the credit of the old Rana-led army, whom the King had good reasons to thank afterwards, that the situation was restored to normal without outside aid by the end of the day.

In the wake of the Raksha Dal mutiny, the Communist Party of Nepal was banned on the allegation that it had willfully attempted to exploit the situation politically by seeking collaboration with the mutineers. However, in 1952 itself Gauribhakta Pradhan, brother of the wives of the two top communist leaders of that time, Puspa Lal Shrestha and Man Mohan Adhikari, secretly made his way to China for political training.

The Government was not seriously weakened by this small revolt, which had quickly collapsed, but the King and his ministers were taken by surprise despite repeated warnings by the Nepali National Congress in particular among the opposition parties and by other well-meaning observers of the Nepali scene against the threat from the politicized security forces. M.P. Koirala merely reprimanded his colleague, Food Minister Ganesh Man Singh, for having contacted the rebels before obeying a summons to the royal palace but took no further action against him. King Tribhuvan however had lost no time in declaring a state of emergency and authorizing Prime Minister M.P. Koirala to act, if necessary, without consulting the cabinet. As its leader Agni Prasad Kharel was actively involved in the revolt, the Rashtriya Mahasabha was banned, as was the Communist Party of Nepal because of their quick efforts to exploit the mutiny by claiming that they had organized it. The situation returned to normal quickly, and the King deemed it safe to fly to Calcutta on 30 January 1952 after announcing a pay increase for the regular army.

The Indian embassy's requests for permission to land troops in Nepal on 31 January apparently at the behest of the Nepali Government had aroused Nepali sensitivity on the issue of Indian soldiers on Nepali soil. British Ambassador Summerhayes made the following observation to his Foreign Office:

> But I'd just like to say that in my opinion many Nepalese would have turned to Communism as the nearest hope of help if the Indians had flown in troops during the last bother here. Though not a single shot had been fired, this was seriously considered on the 23rd January and again with less reason on the 31st (after Communications and Forest Minister Bhadrakali Mishra, known to be

the Indian Ambassador's agent in the government, had made strong pleas in his memorandum to the cabinet for the bringing in of the Indian troops with tanks) I am not sure whether it was the King or certain Nepalese Ministers or the Indian Ambassador who passed panic requests before trying local action.[14]

Despite the success of the Nepali army in meeting the situation created by the Raksha Dal revolt, the brief crisis seemed to provide the Delhi Government with an added incentive for the prompt dispatch of an Indian Military Training Mission to Nepal on 27 February 1952 even without any advance formal agreement. Since the beginning of the year when the Nepali Prime Minister and ministers were in New Delhi, the Indian Government had urged that it would be more economical and efficient to dispatch a military mission to Kathmandu than to have Nepali troops brought to India for training. The Nepali ministers, however, expressed difficulties about accepting the Indian suggestion without first consulting the Commander-in-Chief of Nepal's army. They undertook to consider the matter further on their return to Kathmandu and let the Government of India know their mind. The Government of India also offered to train a small number of Nepali officers in Indian training schools and this offer was readily accepted by the Nepali ministers.

The Indian Military Mission, which suddenly appeared as an aftermath of the Raksha Dal mutiny, was supposed to remain in Nepal for only one year, but it stayed on for about six years. Its presence proved to be a contentious issue in Nepal's politics as we shall see.

The Low-Grade Government Employees' Strike

The Union of the Low-Grade Government Employees, the *Nyuna Vaitanik Karmachari Sangha*, was organized on 2 March 1951 immediately after the 1951 political change. It functioned as it saw fit notwithstanding a circular issued by B.P. Koirala, then Home Minister, asking Government employees not to take part in any kind of party or trade union politics. It even presented him with a list of its demands on 25 May 1951.

This same union a year later submitted its demands to the M.P. Koirala Government on 16 May 1952. This time it notified the Government that its members would take strike action from 31 May unless suitable measures were taken to remove their grievances. The Government did not take the strike threat seriously, so the low-grade Government employees, mostly the clerical staff, went on strike from the announced date. The strikers received a good deal of support and encouragement from students and the opposition political parties,who organized a general strike in sympathy by providing pickets and propagandists. A Government press communique issued on 2 June dismissed all striking employees. But the strike continued until King Tribhuvan's Royal Proclamation of 6 June granted the low-grade Government employees revised pay scales and a minimum salary of thirty rupees per month.

This successful strike was the first of its kind in Nepal's history, and it indicated the possibility of the Government services being politicized and infiltrated by the leftist political parties. However the M.P. Koirala Government, wholly preoccupied with its own internal party politics involving the growing rift between the two Koirala brothers, failed to recognize this.

The Janakpur Session of the Nepali Congress (25 May through 28 May 1952)

The long-postponed annual session of the Nepali Congress was held at Janakpur in the last week of May. Though the Koirala brothers had patched up their differences with the intervention of Jayaprakash Narayan and had agreed to B.P. Koirala as the sole candidate for the party presidentship, the annual meeting did not go as smoothly as expected. B.P. Koirala easily trounced his only rival, Kedar Man Vyathit, by an overwhelming majority of votes. However, trouble came not too unexpectedly from the Communications and Forests Minister, Bhadrakali Mishra, a particular associate of the Indian Ambassador, who apparently walked out of the Congress meeting and with the defeated Vyathit staged a rival session of the Congress. The Mishra-Vyathit conclave claimed to cancel the choice of B.P. Koirala as President and set up a presidium after banning from the party the Prime Minister, his half-brother, and other Congress leaders.

It is obvious that Mishra had overplayed his cards, and even the Indian Ambassador with all his influence in Kathmandu could not save him this time. The day after the King returned from India on 3 June, he held a meeting of the Council of Ministers at which it was decided to drop Bhadrakali Mishra. However, it was only on 6 June that after some hesitation the King actually ordered the dismissal of the Communications Minister.

B.P. Koirala had, however, told British Ambassador Summerhayes that he anticipated trouble at the party's annual conference from the tarai separatists, from supporters of the old regime and, finally, from the Indian interests whose domination of Nepal he had resisted.[15] The following account of the Janakpur session of the Nepali Congress and the analysis of the character and implications of Bhadrakali Mishra's role in it by Summerhayes in his dispatch to his Foreign Minister deserve notice because of their objectivity and perceptive quality:

> This was the first conference of the kind inside Nepal and ever since the Nepali Congress obtained power in 1951 there have been disputes and jealousies, and in this loose-knit and inefficient country a good deal of confusion was only to be expected. A large percentage of the delegates had no proper credentials and a lot of discontent was caused by preliminary efforts to sort them out.
>
> Bhadrakali Mishra, who was Minister of Communications and Forests, worked quietly up till the last moment on the committees that organised the conference and that agreed on the delegates, but he asked to be allowed to speak just before the poll on May 25th, when the only two candidates were B.P. Koirala and a much less likely choice Kedar Man Singh Byathit.
>
> What he (Mishra) said was a violent attack on B.P. Koirala in whose favour he had previously stood down, and on the prime minister and in fact on all the government and leading Congressmen. The last-minute effort to upset the conference was much resented and Bhadrakali Mishra was shouted down often with cries that he was an Indian and an Indian tool—and he fled from the meeting with about 20 per cent of the men there.
>
> The meeting went on to elect B.P. Koirala by a large majority of 258 votes against 2 for Kedar Man Singh while another 68 votes went to the Prime Minister who was not standing for election.
>
> In my telegram No. 100 which first reported this trouble I said that personal jealousy and tarai disaffection were its main causes, for I was naturally reluctant to suggest Indian interference again, but the fact that Bhadrakali Mishra, who is indeed more Indian than Nepali, has consistently acted these last 18 months in very close collaboration with the Indians, has on several occasions been reported. The Prime Minister and others said that Bhadrakali

Mishra's act must have been with Indian agreement. I think that his hope was and still is to become a Prime Minister of Nepal under still more Indian protection than is at present the case. Rumours of his dishonesty particularly over forest contracts have been too frequent and I have for long been told that he is a leading critic of our Gurkha recruitment.

Following this election Bhadrakali Mishra staged a counter show after collecting disgruntled and unaccepted delegates and a crowd of outsiders, and at this meeting declarations were made about starting a new congress, dissolving the present government, expelling the Koiralas and others, and creating a presidium. There was a lot of shouting but few heads were broken.

All these opposition efforts were given full and rapid publicity in the Kathmandu press, for it seems that Bhadrakali Mishra, whose ministry controlled the telephones, prevented the passing of other news.

The old Congress now under the presidency of B.P. Koirala, later voted that Bhadrakali Mishra should be expelled from the party and the Government should get rid of him from the cabinet.

One another minister, Narad Muni Rai (Thulung), who was sore about representation from eastern Nepal, started to join the opposition group but soon feared that they would ruin the country and ceased protests.

The conference continued till the 28th (May) hearing reports, and its most interesting session was about foreign affairs when, as reported in my telegram No. 103 the Prime Minister effectively defended the present foreign policy of the government in reply to those who urged closer terms with China. Only a Congress official, a secretary, Krishna Prasad Upadhyaya, recommended the withdrawal of Gurkha troops from Malaya. This did not lead to any discussion and was, I hope, no more than a gesture that the old declaration on the subject by Congress had not been forgotten.

The Indian Ambassador remarked to me on June 1st that the Prime Minister seemed to have no constitutional right to request Bhadrakali Mishra's resignation. The Prime Minister later—at the party here on the Queen's birthday when Bhadrakali Mishra was also present—asked me urgently for any indication of the British practice regarding the authority of the head of the government. While emphasizing that Nepal was different because of the absence of Parliament, I quoted the relevant comments in Trevelyan's History of England and this apparently helped him on the following day to persuade the hesitant King who had returned from India on June 3rd to endorse the decision of the Prime Minister and Cabinet that the rebel minister should be dismissed rather than that the whole cabinet should be reformed, as some were urging.[16]

The Indian Ambassador, Sir C.P.N. Singh, who was in his own right a highly ambitious, intriguing and vindictive person, never forgave the Nepali political establishment of the time for dismissing his protege Bhadrakali Mishra unceremoniously. His sense of irritation and disappointment with the Nepali Congress leaders in general, who had had to put up with his imperious temperament and high-handed gestures, made him act towards the end of his tenure in Kathmandu in excess of his authority without regard to his Government's instructions. If B.P. Koirala were the first to join issue with Ambassador Singh in public on many an occasion, none of the other leaders and politicians were happy with him partly also because they felt he had double-crossed them at one time or the other. Subarna Shamsher and Surya Prasad Upadhyaya told the present author that they had resigned from M.P. Koirala's cabinet at the end of July only after they were told by the Indian Ambassador that Nehru wanted them to quit the Government. But Nehru denied having advised them so when they met him later. By that time Nehru had, however, made up his mind about removing Sir C.P.N. Singh from Nepal, as we have already seen, as soon as the cabinet crisis was over. In October he was replaced by Bala Krishna Gokhale, who was a career diplomat.

The First "Little Parliament" convened by the King

The 35-member Advisory Assembly, announced by King Tribhuvan in October 1951 without consulting the interim cabinet headed by the Rana Prime Minister, was never actually convened. It was subsequently expanded from 35 to 62 nominated members under the first Nepali Congress Government led by M.P. Koirala and was intended as the "Little Parliament" for the interim period.

The first meeting of the expanded Assembly was convened on 29 June 1952 and Krishna Prasad Bhattarai, a prominent leader of the Nepali Congress, was elected Speaker. The session was addressed by the King on 4 July. In his speech from the throne, Tribhuvan hoped that his country would adopt the parliamentary institutions of Britain with whom Nepal had a long friendship. He said that his first duty was to hold elections to the Constituent Assembly as soon as the electoral rolls were ready.

Six members of the "Little Parliament" had formed a parliamentary opposition group and obtained the Speaker's official recognition as such. The six were Kedar Man Vyathit, Lakshmi Prasad Devkota, Mrs. Punyaprabha Devi Dhungana, Shiva Prasad Rauniyar and Gulab Narayan Jha, and their leader, Rishikesh Shaha, who was recognized by the Speaker as the leader of the opposition. This group had earlier opposed Bhattarai's election to the speakership on the ground that he was not a full-fledged Nepali citizen, and they put in a petition to the King challenging his citizenship. As a protest against having received no reply to their petition and as a mark of their disapproval of the choice of the Speaker, the six who formed the entire opposition remained standing throughout the King's lengthy speech.

However, after this rather unpleasant start the Speaker and the Opposition worked in perfect harmony and the six-member group was afforded ample opportunity to make their mark in the proceedings of what proved to be a brief session of a short-lived interim legislature. The British Ambassador's report to the Government on the performance of the Speaker was also favourable. "Some who would not be biased in this young speaker's favour have told me that so far he has shown sense and fairness in the assembly."[17]

B.P. Koirala, the leader of the Nepali Congress, as has already been mentioned, himself criticized on the floor of the Assembly itself the speech from the throne, and as the differences between the party and the Government were likely to be exploited by the opposition and played up in public, the session was hastily adjourned till 16 August and the "Little Parliament" itself was dissolved within three weeks. It was prorogued by the King upon the establishment of the Royal Councillors' regime, which replaced M.P. Koirala's Government on 14 August 1952 following the rift between the two Koirala brothers and the split in the Nepali Congress, which we have already discussed at length.

The King's Dependence on Delhi

The annual political report of the British Ambassador to his Government for the year 1952 highlighted King Tribhuvan's dependence on India in its very opening sentence: "The King of Nepal was in India when the year opened and again at its close and also on four different occasions in between and this was an indication of his dependence on them." The same report in due course rightly states that "Much of the popularity he (King Tribhuvan) had gained as the champion of the people's rights has been affected by his subservience to India."[18]

The King and his Prime Minister M.P. Koirala were in Delhi in January 1952 discussing defence in particular, but Defence Minister Kaiser Shamsher was not associated with the talks. It was agreed that an Indian military mission, about 25 officers and a hundred other ranks, and also engineering units, should be sent to Nepal.

The Prime Minister and two other ministers went again to Delhi in April to discuss a loan and a large Indian civil mission to Nepal. The financing was for the construction of the Kathmandu-Raxaul road and the improvement of the Kathmandu airport. The ways and means of meeting the expenses of the Indian advisers in Nepal were discussed.

In the first half of the year India informed foreign countries that it had assumed protection of Nepali interests wherever there was no Nepali mission. Nepal had apparently asked India to do this only when requested in special cases and India was reported to have admitted later that it had moved incorrectly. The Nepali position on this matter was made clear only after the British Government had requested elucidation about the position in Malaya where there was a Nepali liaison officer with the Brigade of the Gorkhas.

When the Nepali Government enquired whether the Government of India would have any objection to Nepal receiving aid under America's Point Four aid programme, the Indian representatives replied that they saw no objection whatsoever, provided (as was the case with their own agreement with the U.S.) no political strings were attached.

About the establishment of a U.S. aid mission in Kathmandu, India while leaving the final decision to Nepal, expressed its apprehension that such a move would lead the Chinese to demand the establishment of their mission as well, thereby causing embarrassment to the Government of Nepal. The Indian Government had made it clear to the Nepali authorities that according to Indian information, the Chinese missions in Burma and Indonesia were acting as centres for communist activities. If a Chinese mission with full diplomatic privileges were established in Kathmandu, it would be impossible for the Nepalis to exercise control over the movement of communist agents into Nepal.

The Nepali Government was satisfied that there was no serious infiltration of communist agents from Tibet at that time and were not seriously bothered by the threat of communism in the immediate future provided that they themselves could produce progress on the political and economic front in Nepal and could keep the local communists under control. It had been agreed, however, that there should be an exchange of intelligence between the Indian and the Nepali Government, and the Director of the Bureau of Intelligence of the Government of India was willing to help Nepal in building the nucleus of an intelligence service. It had also been agreed that district officers on both sides of the border should keep in touch with a view to controlling the movement of undesirables.

Tibet

In early January 1952 Nepal reminded India that a periodic mission from Tibet was expected in the near future and would probably raise three matters: (1) extraterritoriality, (2) annual tribute, and (3) Nepal's representative in Lhasa. The Indians advised the Government of Nepal not to insist on the first two points as they had become obsolete but at the same time not to volunteer to give them up except as part of a general settlement. As regards the third point, there were considerable advantages in Nepal having a mission in Lhasa, and the Indians advised the Nepalis not to raise the question themselves but to try to retain the status quo. If the Chinese raised the question of a Chinese mission in Kathmandu in this context, the Indians advised the Nepalis to stall. The Indians expected that on his early return to Peking Sardar K.M. Panikkar, Indian Ambassador to China, would have some discussion with the Chinese authorities on such questions as India's interests in Tibet, and the Indian Government thought it would be better that the Nepalis should stall off discussion until these talks had taken place. (The Chinese had previously suggested that there should be tripartite talks among China, India and Nepal but the Indians had objected to this.)

Though Delhi had begun to feel by July 1952 that M.P. Koirala should at least temporarily resign from the prime ministership in view of the political crisis created by his own party, yet he had initially created quite a favourable impression in the Indian circles. This was what Bajpai had told the British High Commissioner in Delhi about M.P. Koirala:

> Bajpai commented that Koirala had created a good impression in

> Delhi. He appeared to be straightforward, honest and sincerely anxious to develop his country. At the same time he was modest and fully conscious of his own limitations.[19]

The Royal Councillors' Regime (14 August 1952 to 15 June 1953)

The Interim Government Act, 1951 (The *Antarim Bidhan*) had had no provision for direct rule by the King through a nominated Council of advisers. Such an arrangement was provided for in the Special Circumstances Act, 1952, which retroactively suspended all clauses with respect to the cabinet and vested the King with all executive powers.[20] This Act at least for the time being voided the original concept of the King-in-Council and provided the legal basis for the King's absolute authority in political affairs. As Bhuwan Lal Joshi and Leo E. Rose have rightly observed, "The Councillors' regime also marked the beginning of the Crown's direct participation in the political process during the period of democratic experimentation. The King had now veered away from his original intention to assume a constitutional role and allow popular representatives to run the government, and took an increasingly active part in decision and policy making."[21]

The continuation of the Advisory Assembly was also rendered anomalous by the promulgation of the Special Circumstances Act, 1952. After setting up the Councillors' regime, the first thing King Tribhuvan did was to prorogue the Assembly, which was eventually dissolved in September when the Nepal Interim Government (Second Amendment) Act was suspended on the advice of the Royal Councillors.

The following chart gives the composition of the Royal Councillors' Government proclaimed by King Tribhuvan on 14 August 1952:

(The Royal Proclamation listed only five councillors, but a notification of the Royal Palace Secretariat dated 26 August added the name of Sarada Shamsher as an adviser with the education portfolio.)

General Kaiser Shamsher Rana, always regarded as the ablest and the most cultured of the Ranas, was called upon by the King to shoulder the responsibility for administration notwithstanding the fact that their personal relations were far from happy for the General had long been estranged from his first wife, the King's favourite eldest sister. Major General Sarada Shamsher, who had also been Minister for Education in M.P. Koirala's Nepali Congress cabinet as an independent, was Maharaj Mohan Shamsher's eldest son. The two non-Rana councillors, Lieutenant-General Surendra Bahadur Basnyat and Kazi Manik Lal Rajbhandari, were from the prominent Kshatriya and Newari families long associated with the Rana military and civil service respectively. Only two of the councillors had some kind of political background: Mahabir Shamsher who was a member of the Nepali Congress until he resigned from the party a few hours before becoming a councillor; and Khadga Man Singh, who had been in prison for almost 20 years during the Rana rule for his complicity in the 'Prachanda Gorkha' conspiracy and joined the Nepal Praja Parishad briefly after his release, but had been an independent since July 1951.

The Royal Councillors' Government

Name	*Rank*	*Portfolios*
Kaiser Shamsher Rana	Chief Councillor	General Administration, Finance, Defence.
Mahabir Shamsher Rana	Councillor	Home, Planning and Development.
Surendra Bahadur Basnyat	Councillor	Industry, Commerce, Food and Civil Supplies
Manik Lal Rajbhandari	Councillor	Public Works and Comunications, Law and Parliamentary Affairs, Health and Local Self-Government.
Khadga Man Singh	Councillor	Foreign Affairs, Revenue, and Forest.
Sarada Shamsher Rana	Adviser	Education

This was what the British Ambassador, C.H. Summerhayes, had to say about the Royal Councillors' regime:

> . . . The five consisted of one experienced Rana (General Kaiser), one of the previously banished and quite irresponsible 'C' Ranas (General Mahabir) and three loyal men of mediocre ability

(Surendra Bahadur Basnyat, Manik Lal Rajbhandari and Khadga Man Singh). The King assumed the burden of presiding at all councils, a task which was too heavy for his liking, his experience or his health, but he certainly stuck it for four months and did not delegate authority—a step which would have provided a useful buffer.

The organisation of the Council was the final effort here of Sir C.P.N. Singh, who had as ambassador so strongly helped the Congress effort of less than two years previously. He saw to it that the Indian adviser (Gobinda Narayan) attended all councils, replacing the Nepalese Secretary and was in a position to ensure that Indian wishes were followed. Next in influence with the King was General Mahabir and in addition to the portfolio for planning and development that he had badly neglected in the last government he was now put in charge also of Home Affairs.

The Advisory Council was announced as a temporary arrangement but it was hoped that the country's administration could be carried on more quietly by it till elections were possible. However, before the end of the year, when the King went to India, the leaders of the various political parties, who, of course wanted power, had stirred up discontent about the ineffectiveness of the Council and it seemed that some sort of political cabinet would be tried again soon. Though the Congress had lost its unity and its various factions commanded little confidence, B.P. Koirala's claim was that M.P. Koirala had put the country's interest only after his obedience to the Indian-influenced King, but personal ambition and jealousy also did much to make the rift between these half-brothers sadly deep.

The Royal Councillors' regime had a shaky start because its members did not know how long it was going to last. Further, the councillors had reasons to feel all the more uneasy because the King had soon made up his mind to have a political party government as soon as possible in view of his indifferent health. They had a creeping suspicion that the King wanted to bring in M.P. Koirala by the backdoor. The King's most trusted councillor Mahabir Shamsher, under instructions from the King, continually hobnobbed with the leaders of different political parties to see if a broadbased Government could be established under the elder Koirala's prime ministership.

The Fragmentation of Political Parties

The establishment of one-party Government under M.P. Koirala after the fall of the Rana-Congress coalition Government had already given an impetus to a blind and selfish race for power among the leaders of various other political parties none of which had sound ideological and organizational foundations. However, partisans were never short of arguments to justify their splits on ideological or constitutional pleas.

The Nepali Congress, which had played the most active role in bringing democracy to the country and was reputed to be by far the largest party, was the first to splinter with the formal separation of the M.P. Koirala faction following the annual party congress and the cabinet crisis leading to the resignation of the M.P. Koirala Government in August 1952. The same session of the Nepali Congress also witnessed the secession of two other groups which briefly maintained their separate entities as the Leftist Nepali Congress, under the leadership of Balchandra Sharma and Kedar Man Vyathit, and the Nepali Jana (People's) Congress led by Bhadrakali Mishra.

Even the efforts of King Tribhuvan and some Indian political leaders failed to unite the two major factions of the Nepali Congress led by the Koirala brothers. M.P. Koirala and two of his former Cabinet colleagues—Mahendra Bikram Shah and Narad Muni Thulung—were suspended from the active membership of the party for three years in August 1952 when the Central Committee of the Nepali Congress endorsed the earlier decision of its Working Committee against them by 118 to 7 votes. M.P. Koirala's camp followers refused to accept the decision and at once formed an 'Ad Hoc Central Committee' to carry on their struggle against the current leadership of the Nepali Congress.[22]

Once again the Indian socialist leader, Jayaprakash Narayan, sought to help the Koirala brothers settle their differences in the autumn of 1952, when they took separate trips to meet him in Poona in September and October. But the Indian leader's efforts had the effect of widening rather than narrowing the differences between them as mutual recriminations in the succeeding months vitiated the atmosphere for unity and cooperation between the two sides.

In March 1953 M.P. Koirala claimed that about 60 out of the 150 members of the Central Committee of the Nepali Congress had switched their allegiance to his side.[23] Further, M.P. Koirala accused B.P. Koirala of rejecting his proposal to bring back into the parental organization the three Nepali Congress factions led by himself, Balchandra Sharma and Bhadrakali Mishra by giving adequate representation to each of them in the Working Committee of the party. According to M.P. Koirala, his brother asked for the dissolution of the Ad Hoc Committee as a precondition for unity talks. B.P. Koirala, in his turn, however, contended that the strength of the three seceding factions put together did not represent more than 20 per cent of the total strength of the Nepali Congress. Thereafter M.P. Koirala formed his new party called Rashtriya Praja Party (National People's Party) and put forward his bid to form a new Government, which was in due course recognized by King Tribhuvan.

Following the ban on the Communist Party in January 1952 the United Front had become almost defunct with the Praja Parishad shouldering single-hand most of its political responsibilities. Under the circumstances it did not take the Praja Parishad too long to lose interest in its collaboration with the communists, and the Parishad officially withdrew from the United Front in September 1952.

The Nepali National Congress also split in May 1952 with the party President, Dilli Raman Regmi, expelling four leading members of his Working Committee—Rishikesh Shaha, Jib Raj Sharma, Shankar Prasad Sharma and Sobha Mohan Bhattarai. On 3 June they set up a parallel Nepali National Congress and expelled Regmi, accusing him of violating the party constitution and misusing party funds. On 25 October 1952 the Nepali National Congress (Shankar-Rishikesh faction) came together with Nepali Jana Congress (Bhadrakali Mishra) and set up a coordinating committee of eleven members with Jiva Raj Sharma of the Nepali National Congress faction as Chairman and Bhadrakali Mishra as General Secretary. This alliance, did not last for more than seven months. On 23 June 1953 B.P. Koirala, President of the Nepali Congress, and Jiva Raj Sharma, President of the Nepali National Congress (Shankar-Rishikesh faction) announced that their respective parties had formed the Nepali Congress (National Congress Associated) with an eye to the eventual merger of the two parties following their respective conventions. After this B.P. Koirala dissolved and reconstituted the Working Committee, Parliamentary Board and all sub-committees of the Nepali Congress to accommodate the new entrants and appointed Rishikesh Shaha General Secretary. At the same time the Nepali Jana Congress and a dissident Nepali Congress held a joint conference of their delegates on 28 June to form the All-Nepal Jana Congress with Bhadrakali Mishra as its President.

As the so-called national parties were preoccupied with their internal bickerings, tactical manoeuvres and shifting alliances, two professedly parochial and regional parties, the Gorkha Parishad and the Tarai Congress, took full advantage of the confused political situation and stepped up their activities. The Tarai Congress was established in 1951 with three declared goals to secure: the establishment of an autonomous tarai state, the recognition of Hindi as a state language, and adequate representation for the tarai people in the Nepali civil service. The Tarai Congress leader, Vedananda Jha, claimed in May 1953 that his party had a membership of 60,000 and demanded adequate representation for the tarai in the proposed Assembly.

The Vir Gorkha Dal, which was banned after the attack on Home Minister B.P. Koirala's residence in April 1951, was reorganized as Gorkha Parishad in February 1952. It sought to rally behind it the support of the people in the hills by exploiting their fear and distrust of the non-Gorkha elements in the tarai and the Kathmandu Valley. As most of the Gorkha Parishad leaders had been closely associated with the Rana regime, they could not avoid headlong conflicts with local Nepali Congress leaders as shown by the events in Pokhara in January 1953.

These disturbances resulted in police firing and the detention under the Public Security Act of the leaders of several political parties including Bharat Shamsher, the General Secretary of Gorkha Parishad, Sobha Mohan Bhattarai of the Nepali National Congress, and Nirmal Lama of the Communist Party of Nepal. However, a judicial commission set up by the Royal Councillors' regime to enquire into the incident found fault with the local administration and the police, and it ordered the release of the political detainees.

It was under the Nepali Congress Government in 1952 that Nepal for the first time decided to avail itself of scholarships offered by the British Council and the Colombo Plan to send students overseas for higher education and training. Accordingly, under the councillors' regime two students were sent to the United Kingdom and four to Australia for training in Geology, Animal Husbandry and Aeronautics. Four students were also sent to the United States for in-service training in public administration. According to an official Nepali news bulletin issued in mid-1952, there were 40 high schools, 150 middle schools, 380 primary schools, 75 basic schools, 274 Sanskrit schools and 2 intermediate colleges in all of Nepal.

Two British lady doctors with four other ladies as staff were allowed by the councillors' regime to open a dispensary in Pokhara in

October 1952 in the hope that a permanent hospital would soon be set up in the centre of western Nepal.

It was only in December 1952 that Crown Prince Mahendra was reluctantly permitted by King Tribhuvan to marry his deceased wife's sister, Ratna Rajyalakshmi Devi. King Tribhuvan had initially opposed his eldest son's marriage to the lady for the simple reason that she belonged to Maharaj Juddha Shamsher's family, who were considered highly reactionary in their political attitude. The relations between the father and the son had once become so strained over the question of this marriage that in the previous year Crown Prince Mahendra had actually handed his formal resignation to Home Minister B.P. Koirala, who returned it to him after a talk with the King. B.P. Koirala told the present author that when the king charged his eldest son with seeking to marry a daughter of the Gorkha Dal, the Home Minister humbly pleaded on behalf of the Crown Prince that the Gorkha Dal could not possibly have a daughter and it did not behove the King to give a political colour to a truly human relationship. Even after that, King Tribhuvan on all evidence needed to be convinced a good deal by his personal confidants and political advisers before he grudgingly consented to his son's second marriage to the lady of his choice.

King Tribhuvan did not personally attend the Crown Prince's wedding on 10 December 1952 but left Kathmandu the day before the ceremony was held at the Nagarjun forest resort just outside Kathmandu. The king's plea was said to be that if his son felt himself free to marry anyone he liked, he also considered himself free to do what he liked and was not, therefore, going to attend his son's wedding. He also asked his two queens to do what they liked but both of them, who were in Kathmandu at the time, did not go to the wedding nor did they even receive the bride ritually as she was brought to the palace.

Apart from reasons of the heart, Crown Prince Mahendra seemed to have also a practical consideration in marrying his deceased wife's sister, that she would raise her sister's children as her own. And by seeing to it that he had no children by his second marriage, the Crown Prince completely ruled out the chances of family feuds which had marred the rule of the Shah dynasty in the 19th century.

The British Ambassador in his report to his Government commented: "It was hoped that the King's permission, however grudging, for the marriage of the Crown Prince to his deceased wife's sister in December indicated an improvement in their relations, for this eldest son, who is only 14 years younger than his father, seems to be more respected, though he is retiring and does not seek popularity.[24]

Mount Everest was climbed by Edmund Hillary and Tenzing Norgay on 29 May 1953. Though the news of the ascent of Everest had reached the British embassy on the evening of 1 June and had been immediately passed on to London just in time for Queen Elizabeth's coronation, it was only on 2 June that the King of Nepal and the Chief Royal Councillor, General Kaiser Shamsher, were informed of it by the British embassy. The Indian press played up this apparent neglect of the Nepal Government by the British embassy, but the Nepalis themselves did not seem to have been overly worked up. The reception in celebration of the coronation on 2 June at the embassy was attended by King Tribhuvan and other important Nepali leaders and officials. Ambassador Summerhayes's explanation that as a special gesture he wanted to keep this piece of news a secret for the British Queen to hear first of all on the occasion of her coronation, seemed to have satisfied the Nepali authorities.

By May 1953 the political parties were once again showing signs of impatience to get into the Government. The M.P. Koirala faction of the Nepali Congress had held its conference at Birganj in April and declared itself as a new party called Rastriya Praja Party with M.P. Koirala as its President and Mahendra Bikram Shah its General Secretary. M.P. Koirala held a general meeting of his party in May and issued a statement claiming that he should be asked to form a cabinet again. The purpose in naming his party Rashtriya Praja Party was perhaps to bring into its fold eventually the Nepali National (Rashtriya) Congress and the Praja Parishad by making the name of the new party contain parts of the names of each of them.

Though M.P. Koirala did not succeed in uniting these parties under a single name and banner, his bid for forming a cabinet immediately and expanding it into a broad-based national Government found sympathy with the King, who was in a haste to replace the councillors' regime by a party cabinet before he went to Europe for a medical check-up. B.P. Koirala, who had in 1952 brought about the expulsion of his brother from the Nepali Congress, inadvertently seemed to help M.P. by conducting a no-rent campaign against the Royal Councillors' regime in the tarai. The Royal Councillors' Government was ended on 15 June without much fan-fare and were on the same morning replaced by a cabinet with M.P. Koirala as the Prime Minister.

The Second M.P. Koirala Government (15 June 1953 to 18 February 1954)

The following chart presents the composition of the cabinet of the Rashtriya Praja Party (National People's Party):

Name	*Rank*	*Portfolios*
M.P. Koirala	Prime Minister	Foreign Affairs, General Administration, Finance.
Narad Muni Thulung	Minister	Defence, Revenue, Forests.
Tripurwar Singh	Minister	Health and Local Self-Government, Education, Public Works, Communications.
Suryanath Das Yadav	Minister	Law and Parliamentary Affairs.
Mahabir Shamsher Rana	Minister	Home, Planning and Development, Industry and Commerce, Civil Supplies and Food.

The assumption of office by the Rashtriya Praja Party helped it expand its membership, and its important organs were at once filled with opportunists and careerists of all kinds. The newly-formed party apparently attracted such a large following as to make its leader M.P. Koirala claim the most important position for it in Nepali politics. In his estimate the Nepali Congress came next in strength and popularity followed by the Gorkha Parishad and the Communist Party, in the descending order.

But the Royal Proclamation ushering in the Rashtriya Praja Party Cabinet frankly stated that the King had no way of finding out the relative strength of the parties until the elections were held, and he expressed a sense of bewilderment at the fragmentation of public life and the lack of national outlook among the political leaders:

It is difficult to determine which party is big and which small before general elections are held. And, as every party claims itself to be the largest, our difficulty is made worse and not simple. If the politicians had only given up their selfish and partisan outlook and taken a national view, this problem would have been solved and our burden, too, which we have been compelled to carry on, contrary to our taste and health, would have been lightened. The Prime Minister shall, with our consent, be entitled . . . to make any alteration in the portfolios of the ministers as and when necessary. . . ."[25]

The King's Proclamation apparently gave M.P. Koirala a blank cheque to make changes in the cabinet as long as he obtained the King's consent before actually introducing them. The King's pronouncement also made the people feel that the new cabinet was a make-shift arrangement which was apt to be replaced by a more representative and broad-based set-up in due course. If this arrangement, on the one hand, tended to silence the opposition by giving every political party or leader some hope of being accommodated in the Government at a future date, on the other hand it adversely affected the effectiveness of the Government by creating the impression that it was a temporary arrangement.

The formation of the Rastriya Praja Party cabinet by King Tribhuvan with its leader having the authority as Prime Minister to negotiate with other parties the expansion of the cabinet and the changes therein, subjected the King to the charge of unduly favouring M.P. Koirala, who enjoyed the backing of the King's favourite and confidant, Mahabir Shamsher Rana, on whom the King tended to lean heavily in his failing health. The hasty and casual manner in which the cabinet was sworn in seems to have prevented the inclusion of even Tanka Prasad Acharya and Dilli Raman Regmi in it at the beginning. Both Acharya and Regmi in a joint statement on 20 July stated that they had returned from the Royal Palace on 15 June without taking part in the swearing-in ceremony because they did not wish to be hustled into the cabinet. It may also be pointed out that the President and the General Secretary of the Rastriya Praja Party under Mahabir Shamsher's direction had earlier met Shankar Prasad Sharma, Jiv Raj Sharma, Sobha Mohan Bhattarai and the present author at his residence and made overtures to their faction of the Nepali National Congress which, however, decided to associate itself with the Nepali Congress rather than to join the Government. The Rastriya Praja Party leadership thus saw to it that the cabinet did not initially include anyone who could have posed a threat to M.P. Koirals's domination of the Government.

However, unlike the previous Royal Councillors' regime, the Rashtriya Praja Party cabinet contained representatives from the hills and the tarai, such as Narad Muni Thulung and Suryanath Das Yadav respectively. Tripurwar Singh, who was one of the leaders of the Praja Panchayat in 1948 and had subsequently joined the Nepali Congress and, after the split in it, the Rastriya Praja Party, represented the Kathmandu Valley.

The problems that initially confronted the second Government of M.P. Koirala's were the fast decline in the exchange rate of the Nepali rupee in relation to the Indian rupee and the spread of lawlessness in some of the districts in the western tarai. The Government lost no time in calling a joint conference of political leaders, Government officials, and economists on 4 July 1953 to devise measures to solve the currency problem, but nothing came out of it.

On the law-and-order front, a well-known local political worker by the name of Bhim Datta Pant had raided the police station at Brahmadev Mandi in the western tarai and seized the Government treasury with the help of his followers. This was described by the Government as nothing more than a daring act of robbery, but certain political elements thought of Bhim Datta Pant in the image of K.I. Singh as a Robinhood-style adventurer given to looting the oppressors and the rich and also the Government as their custodians, and distributing the bounty among the sufferers and the needy. Pant's armed activities in defiance of the Government spread to other districts of the far-western tarai such as Kanchanpur and Belauri, and the Government in Kathmandu was initially helpless against them because of the logistic difficulties involved in sending troops to the area.

On 19 July Prime Minister M.P. Koirala went to New Delhi to ask the Nehru Government for help in restoring law and order in the far western tarai districts bordering India. A joint military mopping-up operation against Bhim Datta and his followers was launched by Nepali troops and the Uttar Pradesh Armed Constabulary. Initially two rebels were killed, 50 injured and 276 taken prisoners. Pant himself was shot dead on 23 August.

M.P. Koirala was also said to have taken on this trip to Delhi and a draft outline of Nepal's first Five-Year Plan with a view to asking for India's advice and assistance in implementing it. But nothing was said about it afterwards. M.P. Koirala's programme for the Government had nothing to offer the public as it was vague and general. His land reforms envisaged the conversion of Birta (tax-free) lands to Raikar (Government) lands and the security of tenure to the tillers, but no concrete measures were taken to implement them. He talked about introducing income-tax and death duty to reduce economic inequality but did nothing about them either. Similarly his plans for the reorganization of the army and the police and the development of communications, industrialization and education were not even seriously drawn up. Prime Minister M.P. Koirala's time and efforts were entirely taken up with political talks and manipulation.

The day before M.P. Koirala's second Government was announced, 14 Nepali Congress volunteers were arrested in connection with the no-rent campaign which the Nepali Congress had earlier launched against the Royal Councillors' regime. Although the establishment of a political party Government had slowed down the tempo of the no-rent campaign, yet additional troops were flown out of Kathmandu to Biratnagar to reinforce the garrison there. The M.P. Koirala cabinet released all the detainees by 1 August and claimed that the no-rent campaign had proved to be a flop as the Government had been able to realize the revenue in full.

King Tribhuvan's indifferent health influenced Nepali politics more than anything else from 1953 till his death in March 1955. He was not strong enough to talk personally with all the leaders of the different political parties and mediate between them. The result was that other parties were disadvantaged in discussing ministry-making with M.P. Koirala who, as a leader of one of them, had partisan interests of his own and could not therefore be fair and impartial in adjudging claims for representation in the Government.

King Tribhuvan went to Calcutta on 12 August 1953 for a medical check-up and stayed there more than a month for the treatment of his heart condition. He was briefly back in Kathmandu for three days in September before he left for Europe, where he had to stay four months for more medical care. During the first half of 1953 the agenda and timetable for political action by various parties were largely determined by the dates of the King's arrival in and departure from Kathmandu.

Elections to the Kathmandu municipality were held in September 1953. Almost all of the 73 candidates took part in the elections as independents, for the very considerable decline in the prestige of the political parties led candidates to pose as independents even when they enjoyed the full support of their parties. Fifty-three per cent of the total number of 56,000 electors cast their votes. The Municipality Act did not at that time provide for the direct elections of the Chairman and the Vice-Chairman of the municipality; both were to be chosen indirectly by the representatives elected from the different wards into which the town was divided.

The attention of the entire country was focused on this election because Kathmandu was the capital and had been the hub of political activity, and because most people were inclined to take them as a political barometer for all of Nepal, specially in view of the fact that there had so far been no elections elsewhere in the country. All the parties campaigned vigorously for their candidates.

Out of 16 councillors elected from 16 wards, six were supported by the Communist Party, four each by the Nepali Congress and the Nepal Praja Parishad and one by the Gorkha Parishad, and the remaining four were independents. The outstanding success of the banned Communist Party of Nepal in the Kathmandu municipality elections and the first party congress being held about the same time at Patan proved the growing strength of the communist movement in the Valley.

The results of these municipal elections exposed the hollowness of the claim of M.P. Koirala's party about its popularity because it did not win a single seat in the municipality. The election results came as a shock to the Nepali Congress as well. All the democratic parties used this apparent increase in the popularity of the communists in Kathmandu as a pretext for applying further pressure on the King and M.P. Koirala to reconstitute the Government before the King's departure for Europe, but to no avail.

King Tribhuvan, who had returned to Kathmandu from Calcutta on 17 September, left for Europe on 21 September after setting up a Regency Council with limited powers. It consisted of his two queens, Kanti Rajyalakshmi Devi Shah and Ishwari Rajyalakshmi Devi Shah, and Crown Prince Mahendra.

During the King's absence in Europe, Prime Minister M.P. Koirala was authorized by Royal Proclamation of 20 September to continue his efforts to expand or broad-base the cabinet with the inclusion of the representatives of other parties and independents. Three parties, the Nepali Congress, the Praja Parishad, and the Nepali National Congress (Regmi), were highly critical of the delegation of the royal authority to M.P. Koirala. They formed a council of action consisting of B.P.

Koirala, Tanka Prasad Acharya, Dilli Raman Regmi, Chuda Prasad Sharma, Subarna Shamsher and K.P. Rimal and pledged publicly to cooperate with one another on the basis of a common programme. B.P. Koirala was interned in the Kathmandu Valley by the order of the magistrate on 21 September on the charge of attempting to suborn civil servants, but on appeal this order was annulled by the supreme court, the Pradhan Nyayalaya.

On 23 September 1953, just two days after King Tribhuvan left Kathmandu, the three parties announced the formation of what they called a "League of Democrats" on the basis of equality. They published their agreed 9-point minimum programme with an anti-Indian thrust: foreigners not to be associated with internal administration; foreign economic and technical aid should be accepted only if it does not impinge on the independence of the country; treaties with foreign Government should be revised in such a way as to remove articles which are not found to be in keeping with the prestige and interests of Nepal; foreigners should not be allowed to own land; Nepali currency to be made the sole legal tender throughout the country; membership in the United Nations should be secured; all kinds of imperialist forces should be opposed; early elections should be pressed for and a coalition cabinet of democratic parties should be formed.

These nine points were calculated to exploit popular sentiment against the armed personnel of the Indian military mission and the Indian advisers attached to various ministries including the law and the finance ministries. They were really more slogans than commitments to any serious long-term programme. Unity among the three constituent members of the League of Democrats was not real but was based on expediency to extract favourable terms for themselves in talks with M.P. Koirala on ministry-making. The constituents had, however, no definite understanding even about their respective shares in the Government.

M.P. Koirala did not fail to exploit this serious flaw in the organization of the league by publicly offering four Government seats to the Nepali Congress on 16 October and giving it the option of filling them with other members of the league if it so desired. This move at once brought about the disintegration of the league, with Tanka Prasad Acharya and Dilli Raman Regmi finding fault with M.P. Koirala's refusal to deal directly with the league as a group.

The Nepali Congress no doubt ignored the League of Democrats because its other two constituents had also indirectly blamed it along with M.P. Koirala. But the Nepali Congress sounded M.P. Koirala, Mahabir Shamsher and the Indian Ambassador, B.K. Gokhale through Subarna Shamsher, and the present author who was at the time the General Secretary of the Nepali Congress (Nepali National Congress Associated) on the probability of the royal acceptance of the names to be included in the cabinet. Mahabir had told Subarna Shamsher and the author categorically that if B.P. Koirala's name were suggested for the ministry there would be no expansion of the cabinet. But upon the assurance by M.P. Koirala and the Indian Ambassador that there would be no objection to B.P. Koirala's inclusion in the cabinet, the author, under his signature as the General Secretary, forwarded to Prime Minister M.P. Koirala on behalf of the Working Committee of the Congress the names of B.P. Koirala, Subarna Shamsher, Surya Prasad Upadhyaya and Rameshwar Prasad Singh as the Congress nominees to the Government.

The four names were even broadcast in the news over Nepal Radio as the Congress cabinet nominees, but these Nepali Congress representatives were never accommodated in the Government. The end result proved Mahabir Shamsher right and left no doubt in the minds of all concerned that he was more influential with King Tribhuvan than anybody else. As far as the League of Democrats was concerned, it had a stormy meeting on 2 November and was dissolved after two hours of inconclusive and recriminatory exchanges of views. After the league became defunct, M.P. Koirala and Mahabir Shamsher in their turn started fresh talks once again with Tanka Prasad Acharya, Dilli Raman Regmi, and Bhadrakali Mishra and eventually succeeded in making them join the so-called national cabinet.

One important event at the end of 1953 was the accidental death of the Nepali Ambassador to India, Mohan Shamsher's son Major-General Bijaya Shamsher. He was electrocuted when the electric heater fell into his bathtub at his residence in New Delhi. A career full of promise was tragically cut short; many felt later that Bijaya would have played a major political role in Nepal during King Tribhuvan's reign if he had lived longer.

As the annual report by British Ambassador Summerhayes for the year 1953 presents an objective and perceptive review of the important political developments during the year, it is reproduced here in full:

> . . . Nepal at the close of 1953 was quiet and the general atmosphere has kept cooler than was the case during the previous two

years. Yet there is little sound progress to report and the administration has been drifting along. The national discipline and the simplicity of the bulk of the population have kept things going and the people deserve better leadership to give a reasonable chance for the future.

King Tribhuvan after more than two months' treatment for heart and other ailments in France is preparing now to fly back to India, and he may come on without delay to Nepal. He was in India when 1953 opened and spent some four months there at various times during the year, over and above his time in Europe. Though it was realized that he was unwell, people got somewhat dubious about his keenness and ability to serve his country usefully. The return of an ailing and inadequate monarch is unlikely to help much, but a King is a specially necessary symbol of independent sovereignty of Nepal, and the people want to be loyal. *India must want this particular King back in his country at present, for they forced his return here three years ago to further their policy.* (Emphasis added.)

During the latest absence of the King there has been a council of state of two Indian-born queens and the Crown Prince. A Council was appointed somewhat on British lines, rather than a Regency, partly because the Crown Prince, despite his apparent correctness, is still viewed with some jealousy by the King. The Council's power is very limited and collectively the members are not thought to have taken any significant action.

Nepal was badly in need of some quiet time so that steady work might be done in organizing the administration, but this chance has not been used well and great uncertainty continues.

Whereas the Advisory Council (the Royal Councillors' regime), whose fairly decent but unforceful members represented the government for 10 months till summarily dismissed in June were constantly declared to be temporary stop-gap while the King continued to consult their colleagues about replacing them, the succeeding government under M.P. Koirala as Prime Minister have again failed quite as badly, and with less excuse to inspire confidence among officials and others.

M.P. Koirala, though often accused of weakness and incapacity is thought to be the best local leader available and he has proved reliable, if slow, in his dealings with Her Majesty's Embassy. It is probable that the present Indian representative here will back him sincerely. The other four in the cabinet, of whom only the irresponsible General Mahabir has much influence, are most inadequate and there are now clear signs that M.P. Koirala, the step-brother and other Nepalese politicians realize the straits to which their jealousies and disputes have brought their country. Just at the close of the year the situation has been worsened by the tragic early death of the Nepalese Ambassador at Delhi, who was the best link not only with India but also between all past and present Nepalese leaders. Sound men are extremely scarce here.

Ever since M.P. Koirala resumed the office which he had lost a year previously owing to having temporarily forfeited Indian support he has been trying to get others to strengthen his weak team. He had himself charge of five ministries and even in the small country they are too many. It has repeatedly been announced by himself and by others that changes were imminent, so in the absence of a reliable civil service this has resulted in a sad drift in the general administration, as also in public confidence and welfare. The government seem little more democratic and certainly no more efficient than was the case three years ago, and prospects of the promised elections that were to ensure a better representation still seem distant.

With Communist China settling along the northern frontier and with a form of discontented Communism having easy access from India where some who oppose that creed are either acquisitive or else rashly nervous about Nepal this drift here just now imperils her continued existence as a friendly and nominally independent state.

Talks starting at present in Peking about Tibet between India and China must have some bearing on Nepal which has no direct contact with China and there is only an uncommunicative and temporary Nepalese representative at Lhasa. India has, at Nepal's request, promised full information about these talks. China has been acting carefully and Tibet must take a lot of absorbing, but the chances of objection from there has a bearing on Nepal's relations with the distant western world. Those who come down from Tibet speak of difficulties and much increased cost of living there, so the change does not yet sound attractive to Nepalese.

This review has got off to a gloomy start. There fortunately are better aspects to the situation.

Much of the long pent up political agitation in the valley and parts of the tarai against past conditions has now been released without severe internal strife and men are less prone to be excited by any demagogue. Some cohesion remains.

India's great influence, which increases in unstable days here, is being used with more wisdom and patience. The Indian Military Mission has certainly improved a very sleepy army without exciting much resentment and the Indian army has pushed through a first road link to this valley. The immediate need may have been greater for Indian political and strategic reasons than for Nepal's economy, but in every sense a road was inevitable and this work is being done speedily and peaceably, though compensation is not being paid to those who have lost land along it.

The Colombo Plan has helped to pioneer this road and it is to aid other development of communications and power. While India wants to appear as the main benefactor, she has proved more ready to allow aid to Nepal from other free countries. So far British aid has taken the form of training formalities in the United Kingdom but technical equipment has recently been requested also.

The American Team under Point 4 have also been able to work more effectively on agricultural lines and their plans are less suspect than was the case in the previous year, though at the moment the talk of an American pact with Pakistan is having a bad press presumably at Indian instigation.

Nepal remains keen on membership of the United Nations. Through the efforts of a Swiss 'forward' team she joined Food and Agriculture Organization a couple of years ago but owing to local difficulties most of the small team of experts left here in 1953. Now Nepal planned to have been accepted by United Nations Educational Scientific and Cultural Organization and World Health Organization.

Even in the Valley medical arrangements continue to be most primitive and there have recently been considerable outbreaks of cholera, typhoid and smallpox. Tuberculosis is very prevalent and British aid has just been requested again. A British medical mission has been the first to be given permission to build inside the country at Pokhara.

Nepali currency fell in terms of Indian currency by 17 per cent in 1953 after other falls in the previous years. Indian visitors tend to swamp the valley and their economic competition is feared.

At the beginning of 1953 the future of the recruitment of the Gurkhas for HM's forces seemed to be uncertain. It was a relief

> when in July after one of the first meetings of the new cabinet of former Congress supporters, the Prime Minister came immediately to tell me that the formula proposed by HMG had been agreed and that recruitment inside Nepal for the first time could be carried out for a minimum period of 5 years.[26]

We have already seen what happened to the list of the Nepali Congress nominees to the Government after it was submitted to M.P. Koirala on an agreed basis. However, M.P. Koirala and Mahabir Shamsher must have been talking to leaders of other minor parties privately and informally all along. By 10 January 1954 M.P. Koirala informed pressmen in Calcutta that talks on the cabinet expansion had reached a final stage and new ministers, though picked up from various parties, would be included in the cabinet on an individual basis.[27] After a few days M.P. Koirala made it known that the new cabinet would have 10 to 15 ministers and he would set a closing deadline for talks with other political leaders.

The new, so-called national cabinet actually was much smaller than this. Furthermore it was formed without the participation of the most important political party in Nepal.[28] It contained two representatives from M.P. Koirala's own party, one representative each from the Praja Parishad, the National Congress (Regmi faction) and the All-Nepal Jana Congress plus two independents.

The So-called National Coalition Cabinet
(18 February 1954 to 2 March 1955)

When King Tribhuvan returned to Nepal in January 1954 from his long stay in Europe for medical treatment, the stage had been set for the replacement of the one-party Rastriya Praja Party Government with four-party coalition Government, euphemistically called a 'national cabinet.' The new Government was from the very beginning plagued by internal dissensions, which came into the open almost immediately and which later assumed all the more series proportions during the sessions of the Advisory Assembly. The following chart presents the composition of the so-called national coalition cabinet of 1954, which was announced by King Tribhuvan on 18 February, Nepal's 'National Day':

Name	*Rank*	*Portfolios*	*Political persuasion*
(a)	(b)	(c)	(d)
M.P. Koirala	Prime Minister	General Adminstration, Finance	Rashtriya Praja Party
Mahabir Shamsher	Minister	Planning and Development, Agriculture and food, Indutry and Commerce	Independent
Narad Muni Thulung	Minister	Revenue, Forest	Rashtriya Praja Party
Kaiser Shamsher Rana	Minister	Defence	Independent
Dilli Raman Regmi	Minister	Foreign Affairs, Education, Health, Local Self-Govemment.	Nepali National Congress
Tanka Prasad Acharya	Minister	Home	Praja Parishad
Bhadrakali Mishra	Minister	Public Works, Communications, Law and Parliamentry Affairs	All-Nepal Jana Congress

The cabinet was national only in name, not in reality, because the Nepali Congress was not represented. The Gorkha Parishad and the banned but still active Communist Party had not even been associated with talks on ministry-making. Both the King and members of the coalition cabinet should have had a guilty conscience at calling it a national cabinet even without the participation of the Nepali Congress.

On 20 February, two days after the formation of the 'National Cabinet', M.P. Koirala announced that two Nepali Congress members and an independent would be added to the Government. However, on 2 March, the Working Committee of the Nepali Congress passed a resolution expressing its opposition to the new Government which, according to it, had been formed as "a private affair" like a managing committee of a private estate. Incensed at the alleged deviousness and duplicity of M.P. Koirala, the Working Committee decided to start a popular agitation against the curtailment of the powers of the Supreme Court and to observe an 'Anti-Black Act Day' on 28 March against the Royal Proclamation of 10 January.

On 10 January 1954 King Tribhuvan had issued a proclamation for removing misunderstanding about the power of the judiciary and its first paragraph read as follows:

> It is the prevailing tradition and custom of our land since the days of our great ancestors that the highest powers of the executive, the legislature and the judiciary vest in the King by virtue of inherent royal sovereignty and prerogatives of the Crown. This power, as delegated to them by our distinguished predecessors, was for some time exercised by their prime ministers. As our proclamation of 18 February 1951 has voided the delegation of such authority the supreme power in every sphere now vests solely in us.

The historic Royal Proclamation of 18 February 1951, without mentioning the transfer of arbitrary authority to the King from the Rana Prime Ministers, had stated the King's resolve to have the country governed by a Constitution drafted and approved by the Constituent Assembly to be elected by the people on the basis of direct adult suffrage, and for the interim period it provided for the Council of Ministers to carry on the Government and hold elections to the Constituent Assembly in due course. The Nepali Congress (National Congress Associated) felt that the 1954 Royal Proclamation was the reversal of the spirit of constitutional monarchy, which required the King to be bound by the advice of the Council of Ministers in the administration of the country.

The call of the Nepali Congress for the restoration of an independent judiciary elicited limited support from parties such as the Communist Party and the Gorkha Parishad. The Communist Party was interested in having its ban lifted and was conducting activities for the realization of this objective through its front organization called the Janadhikar Surakshya Samiti (Committee for Protection of the People's Rights). Both the Communist Party and the Gorkha Parishad were happy that they had a weak Government to deal with.

But the proposed movement of the Nepali Congress in protest against the Royal Proclamation of 10 January had not deterred King Tribhuvan from reaffirming his royal prerogatives again on 13

February when the power of the judiciary was greatly reduced through the Third Amendment of the Interim Government Act, 1951. The King asserted in no uncertain terms the absolute power of the hereditary King based on the nation's tradition:

> The inherent sovereignty of the monarch and his special prerogatives over the executive, legislative and the judicial wings as the supreme head have been handed over to us by the tradition and customs of the country. For some time the prerogatives of the King were exercised by the Prime Ministers by virtue of the rights vested in them by our illustrious forefathers. Since these rights were ended by the proclamation of 18 February 1951 the supreme authority in all affairs of the state now rests in us.[29]

The day on which the Nepali Congress observed the 'Anti-Black Act Day,' 28 March 1954, the culmination of its 3-week long schedule for processions and street-corner protest meetings, B.P. Koirala and 18 other leaders were arrested at a public meeting but were released the same day after being held in police custody for six hours. The open-air meeting attracted an unusually large gathering and concluded peacefully.

Gulzari Lal Nanda, then Indian Minister for Planning, arrived in Kathmandu on 23 April 1954 and three days later an 18-point agreement on the Kosi River Project between the Governments was signed by him and his Nepali counterpart, Mahabir Shamsher, who had returned from his visit to India with the King just for this purpose. The agreement was widely criticized as Nepal's surrender of territorial rights to India at the project site without any *quid pro quo*.

Prime Minister M.P. Koirala, however, defended it by saying that 2,000 square miles of fertile land in Nepal would be protected against erosion annually and that irrigational and power benefits would also be available to the country. His plea that in the past also land had been bought by Nepal at Raxaul and Jayanagar and sold to a foreign country, in those cases to the British Residency in Kathmandu, failed to convince his critics.

British Ambassador Summerhayes's report to his Government at the time throws a flood of light on the actual state of Nepali politics at the time—both domestic and foreign:

> Both M.P. Koirala and B.P. Koirala who in spite of various attacks

on India still court her favour--went to the Indian Congress meeting at Kalyani (near Calcutta).

* * *

The King and three of his ministers were also away in Delhi. He wanted more ear, throat and nose treatment and rather than fetch a doctor up here where there are no proper facilities for X-ray or laboratory work he decided to go to India despite the present heat. He is expected back next week. There are to be ceremonies later this month, for the new Advisory Assembly was to meet on or about the 24th of May while we have been offered 26th for the long-delayed sword presentation. I am awaiting confirmation from Perowne.

Mahabir went as usual with the King; he had come back for the signing of the Kosi Dam agreement and it is understood that a reason for his rapid return to India is in connection with the settlement of his own income and taxation matters. Regmi, who incidentally when in opposition criticized the fact that the ministers were travelling to Delhi by special planes, followed the King down in a special plane with Bhadrakali who when previously a minister had been specially in India's pocket. The Prime Minister indicated that he had not wanted them to go and that Regmi had no instructions from the cabinet to raise matters of Tibet. He has previously talked too freely about that and also about other matters that are less his concern to the ever inquisitive and flattering press correspondents.

My Indian colleague, with whom it is still a pleasant relief to talk after his difficult predecessor speaks in the same way of Regmi. I wish he had kept him away from Foreign Affairs. I am sending a dispatch about Tibetan Affairs.[30]

Indian interference in Nepal was another issue on which most of the parties in Nepal were united. Rumours were afloat that a secret aide-memoire was discussed in New Delhi in May when some of the ministers, namely, Mahabir Shamsher, Dilli Raman Regmi and Bhadrakali Mishra were there.

The text of this aide-memoire, which was published in one of the Nepali periodicals long after the event was as follows:

It has been accepted that the governments of India and Nepal should in mutual interest coordinate their policies in foreign and international affairs. In order to further the coordination in the policies of the two governments, discussions were held in the month of May between the Prime Minister of India and Foreign Minister and other Ministers of the Government of Nepal, and the following agreements were reached:

1. The two countries will hold special discussions on matters of mutual interest in the area of foreign policy and relations.

2. The Government of India will consult with the Government of Nepal on any matter under consideration that is related to Nepal.

3. The Government of Nepal will consult with the Government of India on such matters and will seek advice and opinion from the latter on matters of establishing relations with any foreign country with a view to promoting better coordination in the policy of the two countries.

4. Especially on matters of Nepal's relationship with Tibet and China, special advice will be sought from the Government of India.

5. The Government of India is willing to represent Nepal and to take care of Nepali interest through its missions in countries desired by the Government of Nepal.

6. All Indian missions abroad will be instructed to accord all possible assistance to Nepali citizens abroad.

7. The two governments will hold consultations and exchange information on matters concerning foreign affairs and relations.[31]

The note must have been drafted by the Indian Government and was never formally endorsed by the Nepali Government. But at his press conference on 8 May, D.R. Regmi, then Nepal's Foreign Minister, declared that there should be frequent consultations between the Foreign Ministers of the two countries.[32] Though nobody was aware of the exact wording of the aide-memoire at the time, its substance was being widely discussed in the political circles in Kathmandu and the public impact of this was both immediate and far-reaching. The matter assumed a greater importance following Prime Minister Nehru's specific statement to the Indian Parliament on 18 May that he had 'reiterated' to King Tribhuvan and D.R. Regmi that "Nepal should coordinate its foreign policy with India."[33] This was used as further proof of India's desire to control Nepal's foreign policy.

It was against the above background that a parliamentary goodwill mission from India, consisting of Radha Raman, N.R. Malkani, Keshav Ayengar, Gobinda Reddy, Gopal Rao Vaishnav, Balwanta Singh Mehta, Bhagwat Jha 'Azad' and Maya Devi Kshetri, arrived in Kathmandu on 28 May 1954 to attend the inaugural session of the second Advisory Assembly. The visiting Indian parliamentarians were greeted at the airport by hostile demonstrators shouting anti-Indian slogans such as "Go Back Parliamentary Mission", "Down With Indian Interference." and "Repudiate the Kosi Project Agreement and Revise the 1950 Treaties." The embassy car carrying them and the Indian Ambassador, B.K. Gokhale, was stoned and its wind-screen was cracked. The demonstration was jointly organized by the Nepali Congress (National Congress Associated) and the Gorkha Parishad.

Leaders of both parties were arrested by the Government. Among those detained or arrested were Mrigendra Shamsher, Bharat Shamsher, Ranadhir Subba, Subha Shamsher Thapa, Jagdish Shamsher—all of the Gorkha Parishad, and Shankar Prasad Sharma, editor of the party organ of the Nepali Congress (National Congress Associated), *Nepal Pukar*. Ganesh Man Singh, a prominent leader of Nepali Congress, was also arrested and detained for months under the Security Act after he and the present author had addressed an open air meeting on the small parade ground about the same time.

Opposition party leaders interpreted the demonstration as a spontaneous outburst of popular feeling against the policy of their own Government and that of the Indian Government. Disowning his party's responsibility for the mob violence at the airport, B.P. Koirala depicted the situation as follows: "The Kosi agreement, the presence of an Indian Military Mission, a large contingent of Indian advisers and technicians, and the India-Nepal trade agreement have been irritating the national sentiments of the Nepalese people. . . . The incident at the airport was not an organized event but an outburst of pent-up feeling."[34]

King Tribhuvan himself thought it fit to reply to these allegations against India by stating in his inaugural address to the Advisory Assembly on 28 May 1954 that "India's assistance constituted no interference in Nepal."[35] M.P. Koirala, while seeking to turn the tables on B.P. Koirala and other Nepali Congress leaders, who, as members of the Rana-Congress coalition, had initially brought in the Indian advisers, vehemently denied the allegations of Indian interference:

> The Indian Military Mission came to train and reorganize the Nepalese army at our request during the Rana-Congress coalition

government in 1951. There was not a single adviser for the government. Certain Indian officers were here for public relations. I definitely know that those who shout at the top of their voice about Indian interference had sought the help of Indian advisers themselves to the extent of taking them into cabinet confidence themselves and associating them in every administrative execution. During recent times these practices have stopped completely."[36]

The second Advisory Assembly nominated by King Tribhuvan on 13 April 1954 was convened on 25 May, and only 61 out of 113 members appeared for the inaugural of its budget session. Originally, the Prime Minister's Rastriya Praja Party had 12 members: the Nepali Congress eleven, the Nepali National Congress (Regmi) eight, and the All-Nepal Jana Congress and Gorkha Parishad had one each. On 11 May eight more names were added to increase the membership for All Nepal Jana Congress and the Praja Parishad. Dilli Raman Regmi's Nepali National Congress did not join the Advisory Assembly though Regmi himself was a member of the government, whereas the Nepali Congress (National Congress Associated) did not accept nomination in the Advisory Assembly and took out a peaceful procession to register the protest against it on 28 May 1954, the day on which it was inaugurated. All the eleven members of the Nepali Congress (National Congress Associated), including B.P. Koirala and Rishikesh Shah, the President and the General Secretary of the party, who were nominated by the King to the Advisory Assembly, abstained from taking part in it throughout the period of its existence.

Prime Minister M.P. Koirala by virtue of his official position became the leader of the House, and Balachandra Sharma was elected Chairman of the Advisory Assembly on 1 June 1954. The Assembly was in session for about 11 weeks till 17 August with its proceedings characterized by spirited debates, sharp exchanges and at times by bitter criticisms of the Government. Most of the time the party whips were not headed by their members who chose to function as royal nominees in their individual capacities rather than under the guidance of the party.

Members of the Advisory Assembly freely vented their anti-Indian feeling. One of the members even ascribed the fluctuations in the exchange rate between the Nepali and the Indian currency to a wilful design of the Indian Government to destabilize Nepal. The question of the withdrawal of the Indian Military Mission and the Indian army checkposts on Nepal's northern frontier along with the question of the recruitment of the Gorkhas for the British and Indian armies were persistently raised to harass the Government.

The intention of the interpellators was not only to corner M.P. Koirala as the Prime Minister but also to put two of his ministerial colleagues, Tanka Prasad Acharya and Dilli Raman Regmi, in the wrong box because they had been vociferous in their demand for the ban on the recruitment of Nepali nationals for foreign armies before joining the Government. As confirmed by the British Ambassador's report to his Government at the time, the members had rightly sensed that these two colleagues of the Prime Minister had not even formally raised the matter in the cabinet.

On 23 July, M.P. Koirala presented the statement of expenditure for the financial year 1953-54 (ending on 16 July) and the statement of estimated expenditure for the 4 months of the current financial year for a vote on accounts. When one member, Krishna Gopal Tandon, asked for 24 hours to study the bill, his request was rejected by the Government. But another member's resolution to put off consideration of the bill by 24 hours was immediately approved by the House. At this the Prime Minister left the Assembly hall in a huff. This was just the beginning, but the best was still to be seen. On 5 August Home Minister Tanka Prasad Acharya's bill delegating extensive powers to magistrates and public officers was rejected by a majority in the Assembly. Common knowledge of serious division between the leading members of the Government encouraged members of the Advisory Assembly to attack some ministers and side with others depending on the exigencies of the situation.

As the Assembly session was in progress there had been widespread floods as a result of heavy rain both in the hills and in the tarai, with 300 casualties and heavy damage to crops, roads and bridges. A fifteen-member Flood Relief Committee was formed by the Assembly under its Speaker, Balachandra Sharma, but the Speaker soon resigned as chairman of this committee on the ground of lack of cooperation from the cabinet. The first session of the second Advisory Assembly was adjourned by Crown Prince Mahendra on behalf of his father on 17 August 1954 so that the members might go back to their constituencies and take part in flood relief work.

The following paragraph in the report of C.H. Summerhayes, the British Ambassador, to his Government succinctly and objectively depicts the general political situation:

> The main political parties have broken into fragments and not one could stand by itself—yet each is loud in the abuse of others. Those of the people who concern themselves with politics—and they are not in a large proportion anywhere outside Kathmandu--are taking an unwholesome interest at present in Communism as an alternative to the futility of the present political squabbles.
>
> A close second to the government as recipients of abuse are the Indians and particularly the Indian Military Mission. The Nepalese are waking up to the fact that Indians are steadily consolidating their position here, but instead of putting their own house in order—the only way in which they could resist this infiltration—they content themselves with futile abuse and recriminations about who first let them in. Meanwhile the civil servants, true to form and tradition, do nothing.[37]

Internal dissensions in the Government became worse after the adjournment of the Assembly session. Both Tanka Prasad and D.R. Regmi in their heart of hearts felt that they would make better Prime Ministers than M.P. Koirala. However, Tanka Prasad had expressed his inability to take over as Prime Minister when King Tribhuvan, partly in joke and partly in irritation, once told him in the presence of the incumbent Prime Minister that he would be glad to appoint the Home Minister as Prime Minister if the Home Minister were only sure he could make a better Prime Minister. Mahabir Shamsher, because of certain differences with Prime Minister M.P. Koirala at the time, was in a subtle and cunning manner seeking to fuel Regmi's ambition to become the Prime Minister. By pitting Regmi and Bhadrakali Mishra against M.P. Koirala in the struggle for power, General Mahabir wanted to warn the Prime Minister that he was in for serious trouble unless he made up with the General.

Immediately after the adjournment of the Advisory Assembly, Prime Minister M.P. Koirala went to Calcutta for an appendicitis operation. The Prime Minister was called back to Kathmandu by the King on 11 September before his five-week convalescence there had got him quite fit.

After the ban on the Communist Party of Nepal in January 1952 had compelled it to go underground, its activities were carried on with considerable success under the name of the Jana Adhikar Suraksha Samiti (Committee for the Protection of People's Rights) and other front organizations such as the Kisan Sangh (Peasants' Organization) throughout 1952 and 1953. By August and September 1954 the underground Communist Party proved itself capable of staging impressive anti-Indian and anti-American demonstrations at Nepal's capital Kathmandu itself. The steady growth of anti-Indian sentiments ever since the establishment of the so-called national cabinet under M.P. Koirala in February, reached its peak on 21 September when a public demonstration was organized by the Jana Adhikar Surakshya Samiti, the front organization of the Communist Party, as 'Anti-Indian Interference Day.' But even before that the Jana Adhikar Surakshya Samiti, with the backing of the banned Communist Party and the pro-communist Kisan Sangh, the Peasants' Organization, had staged an anti-American rally on 8 August complaining against American 'imperialist' activities in Nepal. The apparently angry crowd burnt the effigies of Eisenhower and Dulles as a protest against American designs. It was rather strange that even Prime Minister M.P. Koirala's party regretted its inability to send volunteers for active participation in the demonstration and sent a message of sympathy and support for it.

The M.P. Koirala Government either played into the hands of the Communists or else were motivated by their desire to placate India when it had arrested Major-General Mrigendra Shamsher, a leader of the Gorkha Parishad, on 5 June following the demonstrations against the Indian parliamentary delegation. Though the Supreme Court granted their habeas corpus petitions on three different occasions during the period of the continued detention of Mrigendra and other members of the party, the court's order was not respected even once.

Mrigendra was even charged with illegally importing four American-made wireless transmitters with the inscription, "Signal Corps, U.S. Army." His explanation was that these walkie-talkies were purchased from army surplus stores. The communists exploited this incident to accuse the United States of seeking to establish a pro-western Government in Nepal. This matter was blown up in certain sections of the Nepali and Indian press. George Allen, the American Ambassador to Nepal and India, had thought it fit to pay a hurried visit to Nepal on 12 June 1954 to clear the misunderstanding about American interference in Nepal's internal affairs. He felt very frustrated after he failed to persuade the Government to show him the wireless equipment allegedly supplied by the U.S.A., and he came out with the following statement at a press conference in Kathmandu:

I have begged, implored, and beseeched the Nepalese officials to

> give the details of the equipment to help us find out how and from where it came. No details have been given to me yet, and I have been told that they would be supplied if the necessity arose.[38]

In the autumn it was necessary for the King to leave for further medical care. On 25 September he announced a 3-member Regency Council with more or less the same powers as its predecessor in 1953 had. This time it consisted of his three sons, Crown Prince Mahendra, Prince Himalaya and Prince Basundhara, with the Crown Prince as its chairman. But his actual departure for Europe was delayed by intra-cabinet dissensions at the last minute. As the British Ambassador put it, "the cabinet was being battered by the repeated stupid and unauthorized pronouncements of the Foreign and Home Ministers." We have already seen that both the British and the Indian Ambassadors had a rather poor opinion of Regmi as Foreign Minister, and in the British Ambassador's view Home Minister Tanka Prasad: "had had only modest education and owed his influence to courage rather than to the wisdom of his talk."

M.P. Koirala told press correspondents on 28 September 1954 that he had informed the King of his intention to resign if proper understanding was not restored among his ministerial colleagues. The King held a special meeting of all the ministers in the palace and told them to put their disputes before him freely and frankly. After the King had helped them patch up their differences, the ministers, along with the Prime Minister, issued the following joint statement:

> Minor differences of opinion are unavoidable, but press reports in this connection have been unduly exaggerated. To remove any misunderstanding in the public mind, we feel it our duty to announce that we have renewed our pledges before His Majesty the King, prior to his departure, to work in absolute harmony and cooperation for the proper functioning of the government and for the peace and prosperity of the country.[39]

King Tribhuvan said good-bye to his subjects in a radio message on 2 October and also informed them that the ministers had solemnly undertaken to work together harmoniously. The very next day he left for Switzerland on a visit from which he never returned alive.

October and November 1954 were not easy months for this so-called national cabinet, for it was in fact a house divided against itself notwithstanding the fact that it had been formed in February on the basis of a 40-point 'minimum' programme incorporating the essential features of the manifestos of all the constituent parties. It had now become clear that neither the parties nor the Government were intent on implementing the programme.

There was considerable unrest in different parts of the country at this time. Even a local branch of the Prime Minister's own party carried on a satyagraha movement for 24 days in the Palhi district in the midwestern tarai. Additional troops had to be dispatched post-haste from Kathmandu to Dang in order to reinforce the strength of the armed forces already engaged in restoring law and order in the district. Bardia, further west from Palhi and Dang, was also said to be tense and on the point of exploding into an outburst of anti-Government activities. And a detachment of the armed police force was also sent to the northeastern hills to suppress the activities of Agni Prasad Kharel, who had escaped from detention after his arrest following the collapse of the Raksha Dal mutiny in early 1952.

Home Minister Tanka Prasad Acharya, having lost faith in the Government's own strength and capacity to tackle the situation of widespread unrest in the country, came out with the suggestion for an all-party conference to devise ways and means of dealing with the subversive elements. The Working Committee of the Prime Minister's party also adopted a resolution which expressed great concern "particularly because of the present political atmosphere in which a general feeling of hostility and indifference towards the government predominates." Contrary to the spirit of the pledge made to the King on 2 October the resolution blamed "the political elements who had recently joined the cabinet" for the prevailing state of affairs.

It was against the background of such unfavourable circumstances that Crown Prince Mahendra inaugurated the second session of the Advisory Assembly on 17 November 1954. Although the session was thinly attended, discussion on the formal speech from the throne continued for six days and as many as 134 amendments were suggested to the Government's policy statement.

A series of articles written by a special representative of the Indian English language daily, *The Statesman*, vividly pictured the contemporary scene and the Nepali political actors involved in it. This has what the article entitled "Nepal in Ferment" with the subheading "struggle for power" had to say about the state of M.P. Koirala's 'national' cabinet in November 1954:

If they (the quarrelsome ministers) have not succeeded in wrecking the cabinet, it is due to the King's reluctance to permit drastic changes.

In such a setting of inner discord, it is natural for the administrative machinery to go to pieces. But what amazes a visitor is the utter callousness with which important members of the government carry on the work regardless not only of public weal but of their own political fortune.

The fact is that the present government is exceedingly unpopular among all sections of the people, including those reputed to be behind the Prime Minister.[40]

The second article in the series discussed the key figure in the Government, Mahabir Shamsher: "A man on the Nepalese scene today on whom much may depend is Mr. Mahabir Shamsher. He was with M.P. Koirala but now functions in the cabinet as an independent. He has great influence on the King and is regarded as a maker of ministries. As he has seemingly abjured party moorings his undoubted influence evokes pungent comment from party leaders."[41]

The Nepali Congress leadership was reviewed under the subhead "Many Parties But No Stability":

Within Mr. B.P. Koirala's Nepali Congress, there are many wings. There is the unsuitable "B.P." himself an attractive, politically virile, though temperamentally somewhat inscrutable, personality. Among his party secretaries are Mr. Rishikesh Shah, an intellectual and writer of some repute who once functioned with Professor D.R. Regmi and also for a period counted himself among Dr. K.I. Singh's friends. Mr. Shaha is a Rana (sic) and he has close family and other ties with the Gurkha Parishad leadership and with the continuing juntas in the army.

Mr. K.P. Upadhyaya is another General Secretary. He has been a staunch follower of "B.P." but appears these days to be suffering from a sense of frustration which threatens to push him into extremes of philosophy. He seems to be particularly embittered against India, ostensibly because of "Indian intervention" or interference in Nepalese affairs but perhaps largely because India has not "intervened" to force M.P. Koirala out of the government. The Nepali Congress has a sage adviser in S.P. Upadhyaya who for some time was the Home Minister, and Subama Shamsher who took a most effective part in the revolution against the Rana regime. There are indications that Mr. Subarna Shamsher is these days spiritually worried and therefore, his next step if any may have political significance.[42]

On 11 December 1954 the Prime Minister suggested the merger of all major parties into one on the plea that there was a lack of adequate cooperation and homogeneity in the Cabinet. M.P. Koirala frankly stated that as supporters of some of the cabinet ministers were going against the Government instead of backing it, he would soon have to do something about this.

The Government suffered a serious loss of face on 23 December when a non-official resolution, denying the Government the power to make laws by ordinances when the assembly was not in session, was passed by the Advisory Assembly. This was the first defeat suffered by the Government in this session and it had suffered as many as five defeats in the earlier session. Although the assembly had no mandatory power and the Government was not obliged to resign even after it was defeated in it, yet the failure of even a nominated assembly with an overwhelming majority of Government party members to support the Government showed that there was something rotten in the hard core of the cabinet, and its internal dissensions were so deep-rooted that they could not be eliminated.

After Tanka Prasad had succeeded in improvising a joint meeting of Praja Parishad, Jana Congress, Nepali National Congress and Nepal Congress leaders, the Rastriya Praja Party felt isolated and its General Council on 30 December retaliated against Tanka Prasad's move by complaining publicly that "it was impossible to work in the government in the present form.[43]

The Nepali Congress Satyagraha

Ever since it boycotted the Advisory Assembly, the Nepali Congress was preparing for a trial of strength by starting a satyagraha movement for "safeguarding the interests of democracy." The party announced a six-point programme for the agitation: restoration of peace and security; protection of civic rights and establishment of an independent judiciary; abolition of the "farcical" Advisory Assembly and the holding of early general elections; reduction in the general price level and particularly in the price of rice; currency control and reduction in the exchange rate; and protection of national independence and preservation of the "prestige" of the nation.

Prime Minister M.P. Koirala reacted by saying that the Nepali Congress could implement those demands by joining the Government. The Gorkha Parishad leadership criticized the Congress demands as "all vague except the one for an independent judiciary." The pro-communist Janadhikar Surakshya Samiti alleged that the motive of the Nepali Congress was to strengthen its bargaining position with M.P. Koirala.

But the Nepali Congress President, B.P. Koirala, launched the satyagraha campaign by appealing to the people to stop paying taxes, to boycott Government offices and to join general strikes from 10 January 1955. A Nepali Congress procession led by Subarna Shamsher and joined by the Janadhikar Suraksha Samiti went round Kathmandu asking for the fulfilment of the above six demands. It proceeded to the royal palace, and the Chairman of the Regency Council, Crown Prince Mahendra met a delegation on behalf of the processionists consisting of Subarna Shamsher and Rishikesh Shaha. In the presence of Prime Minister M.P. Koirala, Crown Prince Mahendra as the Chairman of Regency Council assured them that their demands would be fulfilled.

After two days B.P. Koirala, President of the Nepali Congress, received a letter from Crown Prince Mahendra as chairman of the Regency Council assuring him of the fulfilment of the Congress's demands for an independent judiciary, general elections and the restoration of peaceful conditions in the country as soon as possible. The Congress satyagraha was immediately called off, for the Congress party leaders held this as their success. But the communist-led mobs tried to raid the Nepali Congress office in Kathmandu because they claimed that the Congress had betrayed the people's movement. The pro-communist group wanted to continue the movement on their own, but it soon took a violent turn and on 17 January 26 persons were arrested including the sons of Prime Minister M.P. Koirala and Foreign Minister D.R. Regmi.[44]

The Nepali Congress's satyagraha move had demoralized the Government and the Prime Minister had relieved Tanka Prasad and Bhadrakali Mishra of their portfolios and himself taken over the Home Ministry. On 17 January Tanka Prasad staged a walk-out with five members of his party after the Speaker had disallowed an adjournment motion, which was introduced by Ratna Prasad Kharel of the Praja Parishad and which stated that the Regency Council's assurances to the

Nepali Congress amounted to a censure of the Government.

On 23 January, M.P. Koirala presented his Government's budget for the financial year 1954-55 to the Assembly. Thirty-six members of different parties spoke against the budget. Even a member of the Prime Minister's own party condemned the budget as "an insult to the party manifesto and resolutions."[45] The imposition of a ten per cent surcharge on land taxes and the exemption of Birta land from taxation came up for a good deal of criticism. As a result the surcharge on land taxes was dropped and the provisions for income-tax and for taxation of the Birta land were included in the budget.

On 30 January, Foreign Minister, D.R. Regmi moved demands for grants for the Foreign Ministry. Out of the seven cut motions initially tabled, five were withdrawn; but two introduced by Ratna Prasad Kharel were adopted by a vote of 43 to 39 with members of the Praja Parishad, the Jana Congress and even some of the Rastriya Praja Party voting for them. The same evening Matrika Prasad Koirala submitted the resignation of the so-called national coalition cabinet to the Regency Council. It was forwarded to the ailing King in Europe. The Regency Council did agree to a month's adjournment of the Advisory Assembly.

The Government was in a state of disarray. The payment of Government bills had to be put off since the sanction of the Regency Council for the budget had not been obtained, and indeed could not be, since the Assembly was adjourned rather than prorogued. On 9 February 1955 Crown Prince Mahendra left for Europe after ordering the dismissal of Tanka Prasad and Bhadrakali Mishra and proroguing the Assembly on the advice of the Prime Minister.

Crown Prince Mahendra returned from Europe on 16 February and two days later, on the National Day, King Tribhuvan's message delegating full royal powers to the Crown Prince was broadcast over Radio Nepal and the Regency Council was dissolved. In his message to the nation, Crown Prince Mahendra first listed the measures he had adopted as Chairman of the Regency Council and proclaimed that he would assume personal charges of the Anti-Corruption Department, Public Service Commission, Central Intelligence Bureau, and Civil Servants' Registration Office. He promised that he would within 15 days clarify the position of the Supreme Court. On 2 March, he accepted the resignation of M.P. Koirala and his cabinet, which had remained pending for two months.

Thus did the dismal experiment in the so-called national coalition come to an ignominious end. Within less than two weeks of the formal exit of M.P. Koirala's truncated cabinet, on 13 March 1955 King Tribhuvan passed away in Zurich, Switzerland, and the post-revolutionary Tribhuvan era in the history of Nepal ended with his death.

Though the ultimate sovereignty of the King had been legally established during King Tribhuvan's reign itself, absolute monarchy existed in Nepal only in theory and not in practice during his rule as the Council of Ministers enjoyed considerable political power. The Government of India, which had played a great part in ushering in the post-revolutionary Tribhuvan era, could have assumed a more constructive role in promoting democracy in Nepal. But it took an ambivalent attitude, at times supporting the political parties and at other times the King. It was not clear what India really wanted in Nepal: stability or democracy. The same political parties sided with the King or with India, or against the one or the other or both at different times. Instead of building up their strength among the masses, they relied on the King or the Government of India to provide them with positions of power. Disenchantment with the democratic process and increasing apathy towards politics and political parties were the inevitable reactions of the Nepali people.

The net result of all this was a steady decline in the strength of democratic institutions established after 1950, and a corresponding rise in the trend towards the traditional absolutism of the King. By the time King Mahendra had succeeded King Tribhuvan to the throne, there were few impediments to making absolute monarchy a fact in Nepal.

Foreign Policy

After the 1951 political change in Nepal, every political party with the exception of the communists advocated a foreign policy compatible with that of India's. King Tribhuvan declared in 1954 that "It is an undeniable fact that no nation can in the context of the modern world have an isolated existence. The age demands that all nations, big and small, must draw close together and contribute to the welfare of humanity as a whole. It follows therefore that we must develop good and friendly relations with nations of the world without attaching ourselves to any particular power group. In such a policy alone lies our welfare."[46]

Like India Nepal characterized its foreign policy as independent rather than "neutral" because the concept of neutrality in international law presupposed a state of belligerency and bore no application in times of peace. Unlike Switzerland, Nepal did not decide on a policy of permanent neutrality in the event of war between other countries and was prepared to undertake military obligations under the United Nations Charter. Hence Nepal insisted on following an independent foreign policy of judging every issue on its merit without consideration of anybody's fear or favour and without committing itself beforehand to the support of one bloc or another. Thus non-alignment with any military power bloc was the logical corollary of its independent foreign policy.

However, it goes without saying that in actual practice the conduct of independent foreign policy is influenced by "such considerations as would prevail in international life in any case." Apart from Nepal's close ties of religion and culture with India, no country has as great a political and economic leverage on Nepal as India.

Nepal's foreign policy since the political revolution of 1951 was described by the Nepalis as "special friendship with India" and interpreted by other powers as "paramountcy of India's interest and influence in Nepal." India's influence remained dominant in Nepal up to 1955 because the King and the political elements that came into power were obligated to India for its support in their coming to power. But during the period India was not enthusiastic about Nepal's move to expand its diplomatic contacts with other countries, as has been indicated earlier, and wanted Nepal to coordinate its foreign policy with India's.

What perturbed politically conscious Nepalis was the impression created by the Indian press and Indian politicians in the post-1950 years that Nepal was some kind of an area of Indian influence and that India must oversee Nepali independence and sovereignty. The Government of India at times did not even seem to regard Nepal as an equal and independent country. In September 1951, the Chinese Premier, Chou En-lai, suggested a tripartite conference of China, India and Nepal to discuss the question of Tibet. However, India ignored the suggestion without even the courtesy of informing Nepal about it.[47]

In this connection, it may be appropriate to refer to China's attitude toward Nepal's rights in Tibet under the 1856 treaty. Kathmandu was naturally concerned about them after China had acquired control of Tibet. Nepal felt somewhat relieved when an emissary of the Dalali Lama arrived in Kathmandu on 7 March 1952 with the annual subsidy of Rs 10,000. A letter from the Dalali Lama handed over to the Nepali

Vakil in Lhasa on 14 March gave some satisfaction to the Nepali Government that the Nepali-Tibetan relations were not going to be substantially changed. The Dalali Lama wrote in the letter: "I have every hope that there will be no hindrance to continuing the age-old relations between my government and yours. I pray to God that our relations may become stronger than ever."[48]

At this time there appeared to be a slight difference between the Nepali and the Indian stand on China's status in Tibet. The Government of India ended direct relations with the Dalai Lama's Government and recognized China's sovereignty in Tibet by signing an agreement with China on 15 September 1952 and by turning the Indian mission at Lhasa into a consulate-general. Prime Minister M.P. Koirala even as late as 5 April 1954 was still referring to Nepal's relations with Tibet as "independent of Chinese control", thus by implication if not directly questioning Chinese sovereignty in Tibet.[49] It was rather strange in view of the fact that China had already asked the Dalai Lama to stop the annual payment to Nepal in 1953, and the Nepali Vakil at Lhasa was told that his right to hear cases to which the Nepali subjects were a party would no longer be recognized.

It was only on last day of 1953 that talks between India and China were started in Beijing on the Tibetan question. After four months of negotiation an agreement was reached between the two countries on the regulation of trade and pilgrim traffic between India and Tibet and on the number and location of trade agencies the two Governments were to be permitted to set up on each other's territory. The set of five principles which subsequently became famous as the Panchashila formed the preamble of this 1954 Indo-Chinese Agreement concluded on 28 April 1954. In early May, Dilli Raman Regmi flew to Delhi to meet King Tribhuvan who had already gone there for medical treatment and to hold talks with the Government of India. Regmi must have been advised to place Nepal's relations with Tibet also on a new footing. The Nepali Foreign Minister told the press on 8 May that should China approach Nepal formally, "We will do the right thing at the right moment."[50]

However, as late as September 1954, D.R. Regmi was still contradicting press reports that the M.P. Koirala Government were considering "normalizing" relations with China.[51] But three weeks later Regmi welcomed Premier Chou En-lai's suggestion to exchange diplomatic relations with Nepal by saying that "we are willing to give serious thought to the proposal when it reaches us."[52]

In October 1954, Nepal-China relations formed one of the subjects of discussion between Nehru and Chou En-lai during the Indian Prime Minister's official visit to China. The Nepali Prime Minister, M.P. Koirala met Nehru in Calcutta both before he went to China and after he returned from there. The Nepalis at the time acquired a feeling that the Chinese Government had agreed to consult the Indian Government in every matter relating to Nepal, and that China and India had struck a secret deal between themselves as to their respective areas of influence at the time of the relinquishment by India of certain privileges and interests in Tibet inherited by it from the British-Indian Government. The Chinese Ambassadors in this period, even after signing the protocol for the exchange of diplomatic relations which made them concurrently accredited to Nepal and India, would not mention Nepal independently of India in their private and public utterances even inside Nepal.

Assessment of the Post-Revolutionary Tribhuvan Era

The Antarim Bidhan, the new organic law called the Interim Government Act, 1951, in English, abolished for good the Rana Maharaj Prime Ministers' rule by peremptory command as laid down in the 1856 Lal Panja, the Red Seal document with the King's palm-print, and also in the 1948 Constitution of Nepal. The traditional rule by peremptory command (personal edict or fiat) was at least temporarily replaced by the modern constitutional concept of the King-in-Council implying a sharing of power between the King and his ministers as popular representatives. The Interim Government Act initially imposed statutory restrictions on the powers of both the King and the Prime Minister in the new set-up. The position of the hereditary Maharaj Prime Minister himself as the head of the interim Government was relegated to that of the appointed head of the Council of Ministers which was collectively responsible to the King. Like a constitutional Prime Minister he was to inform the King in a routine manner of all decisions of the cabinet with regard to the administration of the country, to provide such information as may be requested by the King on any administrative matter and to submit to the cabinet, as and when desired by the King, any matter on which the decision had been taken by an individual minister without discussion in the cabinet as a whole. The King-in-Council also had the authority to promulgate ordinances with the force and the effect of the laws subject to the condition that they would cease to be effctive three months after the convening of a validly constituted legislative body.

The Interim Government Act for the first time in the history of Nepal gave effect to the principle of the separation of the executive from the judiciary at the highest level. The Act clearly laid down that the Pradhan Nyayalaya or the High Court was the highest court of justice in the land beyond which there did not lie any appeal to the King or the Prime Minister as in the past when one or the other of the two had always served as the final court of appeal. The High Court was designated a court of record and was also empowered to punish for contempt of itself.

The Interim Government Act also provided for the other formal or external safeguards of democracy like the Public Service Commission, independent audit and accounts, and the Election Commission. The Public Service Commission was set up to ensure fair and impartial recruitment of civil servants on the basis of merit and their promotion on the basis of efficiency and seniority. An independent audit and accounts under a Comptroller and Auditor-General was provided for to prescribe the form in which the Government accounts were to be kept and to submit to the King every year reports as to whether they had been maintained properly.

The Act also laid down the duty of the interim government as that of creating "conditions as early as possible for holding elections to a constituent assembly, which will frame a constitution for Nepal." With this end in view an Election Commission was to be set up with full responsibility for "the superintendence, direction and control of the preparation of the electoral rolls for, and the conduct of these elections" on the basis of universal adult suffrage.

The interim constitution contained a lengthy section called "Directive Principles of State Policy" modelled on the Indian and Irish constitutions. The goal of the state was defined as the promotion of "the welfare of the people by securing and protecting as effectively as it may a social order in which justice—social, economic and political, shall inform all the institutions of the national life." Apart from introducing the concept of the welfare state, the interim constitution also sought to ensure for the citizens the rights to freedom of speech and expression; freedom of assembly, association, travel and residence throughout the country; and the right to private property and pursuit of any profession or business. Though the realization of the concept of the welfare state and that of the civic and political rights might not have been realistic and feasible in the Nepali context, yet the interim constitution visualized a political and economic order for Nepal as conceived by the advocates of political democracy.

Advisory Assemblies were set up to act as "Little Parliaments" during the interim period with a view to affording popular representatives a greater participation in the administration of the country. These Assemblies, however, did not possess mandatory powers but would offer such assistance and advice to the King and the cabinet as they were capable of. The members of the Assembly were nominated by the King with the cabinet ministers as its ex-officio members.

A new administrative machinery had to be created to suit the needs and purposes of a modern democratic Government. The traditional civil administration was nothing but a shadow of the Rana-dominated military hierarchy. There was, to begin with, an utter lack of trained administrative personnel. Though most of the Rana-time civil servants were not suited, by temperament or training, for the new system of administration, yet most of them had to be retained for practical considerations, and no radical change was brought about in the composition and character of the civil service. Only three new secretaries were recruited from among the western-educated elite and they were put in charge of such minor ministries as Health, Local Self-Government and Parliamentary Affairs. Even rules of procedure for the new administrative set-up were drawn up on the model of the Indian Secretariat manual with the help of three senior members of the Indian Civil Service who were in Nepal for about a year and had also had a hand in shaping the Interim Government Act, 1951. The Nepali Government drew on the small community of college and school teachers to man some of the newly available positions in the administrative set-up.

Singh Darbar, the official residence of the Rana Prime Minister, with 1,000 rooms, was converted into a Government Secretariat and 10 ministries were established in accordance with the portfolios announced by King Tribhuvan on 18 February 1951. Every ministry was assigned a permanent secretary under a politically appointed minister and was assisted by deputy secretaries, assistant secretaries, non-gazetted officers, senior and junior clerks who together constituted the civil service. Government offices previously scattered all around the town were consolidated and subjected to the jurisdiction of the appropriate ministry.

The first team of Indian experts with the exception of the Principal Secretary-cum-Adviser to the King left Nepal in February 1952, and a new team called the Buch Committee after its leader, N.B. Buch, arrived in July to undertake a thorough survey and scrutiny of the administrative machinery with a view to suggesting reforms in it. The Buch Committee submitted its report about the time when the Royal Councillors' regime came into power and the councillors were instructed by the King "to establish immediately a system of administration consisting of honest, loyal, unprejudiced, impartial and public welfare-minded officials, and to draft laws and rules for every part and branch of administration."[53] The secretariat was reorganized into eleven departments as suggested by the Buch report and the administrative personnel at the district level were also changed. But the district administration remained as politicized as before because what had happened in most cases was the replacement of the officials appointed by B.P. Koirala as the Home Minister by the favourites and relations of the royal family or the councillors. By September 1952 new pay-scales for Government servants were announced. A Civil Service Screening Committee was set up after a few months to examine the competence of civil servants, and a curriculum for examinations in different grades of civil service was published. All Government employees were for the first time divided into two categories: the Nepal Civil Service and the Nepal Technical Service. These were the preliminary steps taken to set up that most intricate of modern organizations—the machinery of Government.

The reorganization of the administrative machinery continued under M.P. Koirala's 'national' cabinet and the Police Department was reorganized under Tanka Prasad as Home Minister. According to the reorganization plan, the existing five different forces discharging police duties—the 2,000-men strong civil police, the 500-men strong Ram Dal, the Rakshya Dal having 4,500 men, the militia consisting of 15,000 men and the military detachment of 1,000 men, also part of the police force— were to be integrated into a single unit of 6,500 officers and men, a drastic reduction from 23,000. The local militia in the hill districts were to be remodelled as a 'road army'.

It was for the first time in November 1954 that the Bada Hakims, as district executive officers were called at the time, were incorporated into the regular civil service; previously they had been appointed on an ad hoc political basis.

By the end of the post-revolutionary Tribhuvan era, the form and structure of the administration of Nepal had undergone a substantial change with the establishment of ministries in charge of public welfare activities in addition to those for collecting revenue and performing security functions which had remained the main concern of the administration since the Rana days. But these changes in the external form did not affect the spirit and mode of the administration which was dominated by the Rana time psychological outlook.

In the traditional pattern of Nepali Administration under the Ranas no distinction had been made between the public treasury and the private coffer of a ruler who was not held responsible to the people for spending tax money. The account of Government income and expenditure was made public for the first time during the post-revolutionary era, thereby making the people realize the significance of the financial accountability of the government. On 2 February 1952 Finance Minister Subarna Shamsher for the first time in the history of Nepal presented an annual budget (for the year 1951-52) and compared it with an estimated budget for the previous year which of course had not been published. The financial assets left by the last Rana Government in the form of gold, silver, old coins, Indian coins, Nepali and foreign currency notes, and shares in the Nepal Bank roughly amounted to 80 million Nepali rupees. Out of what was left, the Finance Minister established a Currency Reserve Fund, an Exchange Stabilization Fund, and a Budget Equalization Fund of fifty, twenty and ten million rupees respectively.

The post-revolutionary era released the creative energy of the people stifled by the repressive and oppressive Rana regime for a period of 104 years. The pent-up feelings of the people found their outlet in the literary, artistic and cultural spheres. Kathmandu, the traditional centre of political and cultural elites, was overwhelmed by these spontaneous activities of the Kathmandu intelligentsia composed of the English educated, the writers, the pamphleteers, the newspapers editors, the popular speakers and the politicians.

The creatve impulses of the people also manifested themselves in the phenomenal expansion of educational opportunities on private initiative and efforts. There was an enormous rise in the number of new schools and colleges, adult education and vocational training centres and reading rooms and libraries throughout the country. Women's education received a tremendous boost as girls in open defiance of the existing social taboos sought admission into schools and colleges.

Another effect of this remarkable flow of popular energy was the rapid growth of political and social organizations covering a wide range, from those that voiced the aspirations of various organized interests in society to those that were capable of formulating public policies by reconciling conflicting interests as far as possible and casting them in a coherent form with a view to providing guidelines to the organization of the state itself. As examples of corporate activities along these lines may be mentioned trade unions of taxi drivers and tailors to protect their interests, organizations of untouchables and 'depressed' classes to fight for social equality, associations of women and youth to ensure their rights and better prospects in future and, above, all, political parties with their manifestos and programmes of public policy.

However, the Nepali Congress was the only political party that could have played a major role in the immediate post-revolutionary era by steering the country through the difficult transitional years. But it lacked the experience and wisdom of the Indian National Congress and failed to act as a rallying point for diverse elements in the country. In the first flush of its success, the Nepali Congress forgot to its cost that the constitutional scheme forged in Delhi had after all to strike roots in Nepal. The interim constitution no doubt brought the beginnings of democracy to the people, but these political gains and opportunities were lost one after another in the course of the next two or three years as the first Congress Government under M.P. Koirala and subsequent cabinets under him disintegrated in a conflict of personal interests and ambitions slightly tinged by ideological differences.

As the political process deteriorated as a result of the fragmentation of public life and political parties stemming from a clash of personal interests of the leaders, the embryonic plan for democracy as envisaged by the interim constitution was subjected to serious strains and aberrations. As we have already seen, the Interim Government Act, 1951, and the High Court Act, 1951, were revised and amended several times during the following years with the result that by February 1954 both the concept of the independence of the judiciary and that of a King-in-Council requiring the King to act on the advice of his ministers, had become completely modified. The King was once again restored to the position of a traditional monarch as the source and respository of the executive, legislative and judicial powers with the High Court and the Government functioning within the limits or framework of authority and powers granted by the King. The 'Directive Principles of State Policy' envisaging the evolution of a society based on legal equality and social equity and guaranteeing fundamental rights of freedom to the people, was declared to be non-justiciable in a court of law. The

Constituent Assembly, which King Tribhuvan had expected to convene first by 1952 and then by not later than April 1953, appeared to be as remote as ever at the time of his death in 1955. During the four years between King Tribhuvan's historical proclamation of 18 February 1951 and his delegation of all powers to Crown Prince Mahendra on 18 February 1955, the democratic experiment in Nepal suffered several aberrations. Thus did the post-revolutionary Tribhuvan era come to an end on a dismal note of mounting political frustration and economic degeneration.

But it must be said in fairness to King Tribhuvan that despite the constitutional amendments that restored him to the theoretical position of a traditional or despotic monarch, he allowed his ministers to exercise their powers fully and also allowed the people to enjoy their rights of freedom to the utmost. And as long as he was alive he never backed out of his firm pledge to the nation to have the country governed in accordance with a constitution drawn up by the representatives of the people elected on the basis of universal adult suffrage. The Interim Government Act, 1951, marked the fulfilment of King Tribhuvan's lifelong mission to end the Rana system of government and held the promise of a constituent assembly to the people. King Tribhuvan did not live long enough to redeem his solemn pledge to the people. His failing health prevented him from playing his role fully in consolidating the new democratic order as he was compelled to depend on the judgement of the few people who enjoyed his personal confidence.

Unlike traditional oriental rulers, King Tribhuvan did not seem to relish the taste of power and was temperamentally suited to be a purely constitutional monarch. The present author once seriously suggested to him that he should take a stronger hand in running the Government, at least during the interim period. But he replied to him categorically that he was not at all inclined that way because he had, as a matter of principle and conviction, visualized the same role for himself in the Nepali context as that of a Swedish monarch, although the King was prepared to concede that Nepal was not politically and economically as developed as Sweden.

However, most of his people, who were imbued with the traditional Nepali culture, had expected him to adopt a paternalistic attitude. They felt that he proved himself incapable of giving a strong Government to the country in a transitional period, that the cabinets formed during the post-revolutionary Tribhuvan era suffered from a lack of firm royal guidance. But it may be pleaded on behalf of King Tribhuvan that as a democratically-oriented King, he believed that the popular representatives, left to themselves, would learn their lessons by trial and error, and he did not therefore wish to impose himself on them at any stage.

Though King Tribhuvan proved to be a unique King who had actually staked his life and throne for the liberty of his subjects, yet even his own son and successor, King Mahendra, was not impressed by the achievements of the post-revolutionary Tribhuvan period. The speech he made as Crown Prince with full royal authority on the fifth anniversary of the introduction of democracy, on 18 February 1955, was highly critical of its record.

Less than a month before his father's death, Crown Prince Mahendra declared:

> Today marks the completion of four years of democracy in the country, but it is a matter of great shame that we cannot point to even four important achievements that we have made during this period. If we say that democracy is still in its infancy, we have seen such qualities as selfishness, greed and jealousy which are not found in an infant. If we say that it has matured, unfortunately we do not see it flourishing anywhere, and I presume, this is not hidden from anyone in the country.[54]

The inflamed and unrestrained letters of the two dismissed ministers of the so-called national cabinet, Tanka Prasad Acharya and Bhadrakali Mishra, to their restwhile leader in the Government, Prime Minister M.P. Koirala, in mid-February 1955 also served as a sad commentary on the entire Tribhuvan period:

> The independence of the judiciary is lost. All over the country, anarchy, famine, corruption, bribery, unemployment and inflation are rampant. The currency situation has reached a dangerous state. Irrigation, education and public health are almost nonexistent. The lawful rights of students, labour, women and merchants have been ruthlessly suppressed. Reactionary elements are receiving full encouragement from you. Big landlords and capitalists are having a field day in exploiting the people and the resources of production.[55]

Nevertheless, whatever other prejudiced persons and detractors might have also had to say, King Tribhuvan's democratic intentions and honesty of purpose were seldom questioned by his countrymen.

After critically examining the trends and events, Bhuwan Lal Joshi and Leo E. Rose have concluded that "It was only right and proper, therefore, that King Tribhuvan should be acclaimed as 'the father of the nation' and 'the chief architect of Nepali democracy'."[56]

NOTES

1. Deputy High Commissioner in Calcutta in his dispatch to the Foreign Office and Commonwealth Relations Office on 10 May 1951
2. *The Hindu* (Madras), 17 May 1951.
3. FO 371/92906, Summerhaye's letter of 26 September 1951 to Murray (Public Record Office).
4. Grishma Bahadur Devkota, *Nepalko Rajnaitik Darpan*, second edition (Kathmandu, 1979), pp 113-14.
5 FO 371/92907, U.K. High Commissioner's telegram No. 1659 to Commonwealth Relations Office of 7 November 1951 (PRO).
6. FO 371/92907, Summerhayes's letter to the Foreign Office on 13 November 1951 (PRO).
7. Summerhayes to J.S. Oliver in the British Foreign Office on 3 November 1951.
8. *The Times of India* (Bombay), 22 February 1952.
9. *The Hindustan Times* (New Delhi), 8 July 1952.
10. FO 371/101145, telegram No. 159 of Summerhayes to the British Foreign Office on 31 July 1952.
11. *The Hindustan Times* (New Delhi), 8 July 1952.
12. FO 371/101150/101151 (PRO), Acting U.K. High Commissioner to Commonwealth Relations Office.
13. F/O's telegram No. 954 of 2 August 1952.
14. Summerhayes's letter to J.D. Murray in the British Foreign Office of 8 February 1952.
15. Summerhayes's letter to the Principal Secretary of State for Foreign Affair s on 5 May 19.
16. Summerhayes's dispatch to the British Foreign Secretary of 9 June 1952.
17. Summerhayes's despatch No. 32 of 16 July 1952.
18. FO 371/106865 (PRO), Annual Political Report for 1952.
19. F.O 371/101145 (PRO), Sir Archibald Nye to the Commonwealth Relations Office on 11 January 1952.
20 *Nepal Gazette*, Vol.II, No.5 (September 1952).
21. Bhuwan Lal Joshi and Leo E. Rose, *Democratic Innovation in Nepal*, (Bermeley: University of California Press, 1966), p.169.
22. *The Amrita Bazar Patrika* (Calcutta), 8 March 1953.
23. *The Free Press Journal* (Bombay), 25 March 1953.
24. *Op. cit.*, Summerhayes's Annual Report for 1952 to the British Foreign Office.
25. The *Gorkhapatra*, 17 June 1953.
26. The British Ambassador's Report to the British Foreign Secretary on 2 January 1954.
27. *The Statesman*, 10 January 1954.

28. The Nepali Congress in 1959 won a two-thirds majority in the first-ever general elections to partliament while all other parties included in M.P. Koirala's 1954 cabinet secured just two seats.
29. The *Nepal Gazette*, Vol. IV, 15 September 1954.
30. Summerhayes to Tahourdin in South-East Asian Department of the British Foreign Office on 8 May 1954.
31. *Jhyali*, 7 July 1958.
32. *The Statesman*, 9 May 1954.
33. *The Hindu*, 20 May 1954.
34. *The Statesman*, 2 June, 1954.
35. Grishma Bahadur Devkota, *Rajnaitik Darpan* (First edition), pp. 250-52.
36. *The Statesman*, 6 June 1954.
37. Summerhayes's report to his government for the month of August.
38. *The Statesman*, 13 July 1954.
39. *The Statesman*, 5 October 1954.
40. *The Statesman*, 27 November 1954.
41. *The Statesman*, 28 November 1954.
42. *The Statesman*, 28 Novemebr 1954.
43. *The Statesman*, 31 December 1954.
44. *The Times of India*, 18 January 1954.
45. *The Statesman*, 25 January 1955.
46. *The Statesman*, 18 June 1954.
47. Narendra Goyal, *Political History of Himalayan States — Indian's Relations with Himalayan States since 1947*, (New Delhi: Cambridge Book and Stationary Store, 1964), second edition, p. 24.
48. *The Statesman*, 15 March 1952.
49. *The Hindustan Times*, 2 May 1952.
50. *The Hindustan Times*, 8 May 1954.
51. *The Statesman*, 8 September 1954.
52. *The Hindustan Times*, 28 September 1954.
53. *Nepal Gazette*, Vol. II, No.30, 10 Bhadra 2009 V.S. (26 August 1959).
54. Grishma Bahadur Devkota, *Rajnaitik Darpan*, first edition, pp. 155-57.
55. *Ibid.*, pp. 273-74.
56. Bhuwan L. Joshi and Leo E. Rose, *Democratic Innovations in Nepal*, Berkeley: University of California Press, 1966), p. 147.

Chronology

1885 (22 November)	- Assassination of Maharaj Prime Minister Ranoddip Singh; Bir Shamsher proclaimed Maharaj Prime Minister.
1885-1901	- Rule of Maharaj Bir Shamsher.
1885 (23 November)	- By the morning of 23 November two other important personages had lost their lives the eldest son and grandson of Maharaj Jang Bahadur, General Jagat Jang and General Yuddha Pratap Jang.
1885	- Some of the surviving sons of Jang Bahadur and Badri Narsingh along with the King's uncle, Narendra Bikram Shah and the two ladies of high rank, the King's stepmother, the eldest dowager Maharani Tara Kumari and the murdered Prime Minister's first wife, Haripriya Devi, fled to the British Residency for their safety. All of them except the King's uncle, Narendra Bikram Shah, made their way to India.
1886 (20 January)	- Ex-C.-in-C. Jit Jang Bahadur Rana's meeting with Viceroy Dufferin.
1886 (1 February)	- Dowager Maharani Tara Kumari, the King's stepmother's meeting with the Vicereine.
1886 (March)	- The British Government extended recognition to the new regime in Nepal.
1887 (March)	- Dismissal of C.-in-C. Khadga and expulsion of his associates by Maharaj Bir.

1888 (August)	- Unsuccessful plot by his brothers against Maharaj Bir.
	- General Ranabir Jang organized unsuccessful military expedition into the central tarai from India.
1888	- Maharaj Bir's official visit to Viceroy Dufferin in Calcutta.
1888	- Marriage of two of Bir's daughters by his second wife to King Prithvi Bir Bikram Shah Dev, who had already married two other Rajput brides from India in 1887.
1892 (March)	- Visit of Sir Frederick Robert, the C.-in-C. of India and his wife to Kathmandu.
1893	- Maharaj Bir's visit to Viceroy Lord Lansdowne in Calcutta as a state guest. Another abortive attempt by General Ranabir Jang's followers to create disturbances in eastern tarai.
1896	- Proposed visit to England postponed by Bir.
1899	- Description of Bir's visit to meet with Lord Curzon in Calcutta as "a complimentary mission" created friction between the two governments.
1901	- Bir did not accept Curzon's proposal for a visit to Kathmandu but with considerable reluctance, agreed to invite Lord Curzon for a shoot in the tarai in April 1901.
1901 (5 March)	- Death of Maharaj Bir Shamsher and accession of Dev Shamsher to the office of the Maharaj Prime Minister.
1901 (5 March-27 June)	- Rule of Maharaj Dev Shamsher.
1901 (27 June)	- Deposition of Maharaj Dev as a result of a bloodless coup and accession of Chandra Shamsher to the office of the Maharaj Prime Minister.
1901-1929	- Maharaj Chandra Shamsher's rule.
1902	- Several students sent to Japan for training.
1902 (31 December)	- Meeting between Curzon and Chandra in Calcutta.

1903	- Former C.-in-C. Khadga, Maharaj Chandra's elder brother, left Palpa for India after the revelation of his secret plot against the Maharaj.
1903 (December)	- Younghusband military expedition entered Tibet from India.
1904	- Lhasa subjugated by 3 August and the Lhasa convention signed on 23 January 1904.
1906 (autumn)	- Lord Kitchener's visit to Kathmandu.
1908 (April-August)	- Maharaj Chandra's trip to Europe.
1908-1909	- Last Nepali mission to Beijing following Nepal's rejection of Amban Chang Yin-tang's claim to Chinese suzerainty.
1910	- Dalai Lama's flight to India.
1913	- Nepal intercedes on behalf of Chinese officials expelled from Lhasa.
1910 (6 May)	- 101 gun-salute was fired in Kathmandu on the death of King Edward VII.
1911 (11 December)	- Death of King Prithvi Bir Bikram Shah Dev and accession of King Tribhuvan Bir Bikram Shah Dev.
1911-1955	- Reign of King Tribhuvan.
1911 (18-27 December)	- King George V's hunt in the tấrai.
1914-1918	- During World War I 16,554 men of the Nepal Army were put at the service of the British in India, and two hundred thousand Gorkha soldiers must have left the country for all military purposes.
1918	- Tri-Chandra College founded.
1919 (May)	- Nepali troops sent to the aid of the British in a war with Afghanistan.
1919 (27 December)	- Maharajadhiraj was addressed as "His Majesty" by the Viceroy, Lord Chelmsford, the first viceroy to do so. He offered an annual present of one million rupees in perpetuity.
1920 (January)	- British "Residency" called "Legation" and the Resident "Minister."

1920 (October)	- Maharaj addressed by the Viceroy of India by the courtesy title of "His Highness."
1921 (14-21 December)	- Visit of Prince of Wales (later King Edward VIII) for a hunt in Chitwan.
1923 (21 December)	- A fresh treaty concluded with Britain to confirm all treaties subsequent to and including the 1815 Treaty of Sugauli.
1924	- Abolition of slavery.
1929 (25 November)	- Death of Maharaj Chandra Shamsher and accession of Maharaj Bhim Shamsher.
1929-1932	- Rule of Maharaj Bhim Shamsher.
1930 (March)	- War with Tibet averted following its unconditional apology to the Nepali Prime Minister.
1930	- Abolition of capital punishment on an experimental basis.
1930	- Visit of India's C.-in-C. Sir William Birdwood to Kathmandu.
1931 (April)	- Flight of Maharaj Chandra's son, Major-General Bishnu Shamsher to England.
1931 (July)	- Plot to overthrow Maharaj Bhim unearthed.
1931 (October)	- Visit of Sir Philip Chetwode, C.-in-C. of India to Kathmandu.
1931-1932 (Winter)	- Maharaj Bhim's visit to India.
1932 (1 September)	- Death of Maharaj Bhim Shamsher and accession of Maharaj Juddha Shamsher.
1932-1945	- Rule of Maharaj Juddha Shamsher.
1933 (May)	- Visit of the Italian Consul General to Kathmandu to invest the Maharaj with an Italian order.
1934 (15 January)	- The Great Earthquake.
1934 (18 March)	- The Political Purge removed the 'C' class sons of Maharajs Bir Shamsher and Bhim Shamsher from the roll of succession.
1934 (April)	- General Bahadur left for London as Nepal's first Minister Plenipotentiary and Envoy Extraordinary.
1934 (23 May)	- Visit of the French Consel General to Kathmandu to invest the Maharaj with a French order.

1934 (June)	- Visit of the Chinese Consel General to Kathmandu to invest the Maharaj with a Chinese order.
1935 (January)	- Maharaj Juddha's visit to Delhi to meet Viceroy Willingdon.
1935	- Visits of Dutch and Belgian Consuls Generals to Kathmandu to invest the Maharaj with orders.
1938	- Viceroy Lord Linlithgow's visit to the tarai on a hunt.
1939	- Visit of the German Consul General to Kathmandu to invest the Maharaj with an order.
1939	- Maharaj Juddha's visit to Calcutta on the invitation of Lord Linlithgow.
1939 (3 September)	- Declaration of World War II and Juddha's moves to aid British war efforts.
1940 (9 May)	- Marriage of Maharaj Juddha's grand-daughter Indra Rajyalakshmi to Crown Prince Mahendra Bir Bikram Shah.
1940 (October)	- Arrest of Praja Parishad leaders and workers and revelation of their plot to overthrow the Ranas.
1940	- Involvement of King Tribhuvan in the plot presented obvious difficulties to the Rana government. Crown Prince Mahendra said to have turned down the offer of the Crown to him by Maharaj Juddha.
1940	- Trial prolonged.
1941 (October)	- Of 43 persons who were arrested in 1940, three were hanged, 14 given life sentences, 20 received sentences between 3 and 8 years and four were banished from the capital. King Tribhuvan and other members of the royal family were absolved from complicity in the plot.
1941 (Winter)	- Maharaj Juddha made determined efforts to cultivate the royal family after the Praja Parishad episode by taking the King and his sons to the tarai on hunts. Princes Himalaya and Basundhara were sent to Calcutta accom-

	panied by Juddha's grandson Major-General Nara Shamsher.
1942	- Influx of refugees from Burma into Nepal and the Quit India Movement of 8 August 1942.
1944 (20 November to 10 December)	- Maharaj Juddha sent King Tribhuvan himself to northern India (Puri, Calcutta, Lucknow, Agra, and Delhi) on an incognito visit accompanied by Crown Prince Mahendra and General Bahadur Shamsher, Juddha's eldest surviving son.
1945 (March)	- Marriage of Maharaj Juddha's great-granddaughter Princep (Major General Nara's daughter) to Prince Himalaya Bir Bikram Shah, King Tribhuvan's second son).
1945 (June)	- Marriage of another great-grand-daughter Helen (Major General Nara's second daughter) to Prince Basundhara Bir Bikram Shah, King Tribhuvan's youngest son from his Junior Queen.
1945 (October)	- Return of the last nine units of the Nepali troops from India to Kathmandu.
1945 (12 November)	- Annual present of two million rupees announced by the British Minister as a recognition of Nepal's services in war and the capitalization of up to fifty per cent of the enhanced annual present to assist Nepal in financing post-war development.
1945 (29 November)	- Relinquishment of his high office by Maharaj Juddha in a colourful ceremony and accession of Maharaj Prime Minister Padma Shamsher.
1945-1948	- Maharaj Padma's rule.
1946 (March)	- Conference of the tarai Zamindars.
1946 (9 June)	- Maharaj Padma's inaugural.
1946 (September)	- Visit of Dr. B.S. Moonje of the Hindu Mahasabha to Kathmandu.
1946 (November)	- Arrival in Kathmandu of the Gorkha league delegation led by its President, D.S. Gurung.
1946 (17 December)	- As a result of relaxation of restrictions by Maharaj Padma on the King and his sons, King Tribhuvan, Princes Himalaya and

	Basundhara, attended by Commanding General Bahadur Shamsher and Major-General Subarna Shamsher, left Kathmandu on three-week visit to Calcutta.
1947 (24-25 January)	- All-India Nepali National Congress and All-India Gorkha Congress set up by Nepali political exiles and Indian domiciled Nepalis in Varanasi and Darjeeling respectively merged into one to form a political party under the name of the Nepali National Congress.
1947 (March-April)	- Nepal participated in the historic Asian Relations Conference in New Delhi.
1947 (4-27 March)	- Mill workers' strike at Biratnagar and arrest of several workers and Nepali National Congress leaders including B.P. Koirala.
1947 (17 April)	- The Nepali National Congress launched its first countrywide Satyagraha or civil disobedience movement.
1947 (25 April)	- A friendship and commerce agreement signed with the USA.
1947 (30 April – 4 May)	- Demonstrations and processions in the Kathmandu Valley.
1947 (16 May)	- Maharaj Padma's historic speech stating his desire to associate the people with the administration in a meaningful way by introducing constitutional reforms and publishing the national budget annually.
1947 (2 June)	- The Congress called off its Satyagraha and all detained in connection with it except B.P. Koirala and a few others were released.
1947 (June)	- Municipal elections held in Kathmandu.
1947 (13-26 June)	- An Indian team of constitutional advisers under the leadership of Shri Prakash Gupta handed over to the Maharaj a draft constitution.
1947 (11 July)	- The status of British and Nepali legations in London and Kathmandu raised to embassies.
1948 (26 January)	- The first written constitution of Nepal proclaimed to come into force on 14 April 1948.

1948 (21 February)	- Maharaj Padma left Kathmandu for India.
1948 (30 April)	- Maharaj Padma issued his letter of resignation from Ranchi in India and formal accession of Maharaj Mohan Shamsher.
1948-1950	- Maharaj Mohan's rule.
1948 (May)	- In his policy statement Maharaj Mohan showed a lukewarm attitude towards Padma's reform.
(Mid-1948)	- Ten battalions of Nepali soldiers sent to India during the Hyderabad and Kashmir crises against the advice of the British Ambassador to Nepal.
1948 (26 September)	- Maharaj Mohan inaugurated the National Economic Planning Committee.
1948-1949	- The India-based ambassadors of the United States and France were concurrently accredited to Nepal in 1948 and 1949 respectively.
1949 (May)	- B.P. Koirala arrested earlier in Kathmandu, went on a 21–day hunger fast on 1 May and was released on 28 May.
1949 (25 October)	- Beijing Radio announced the People's Liberation Army had been ordered to 'liberate' the whole of Tibet.
1950 (9 April)	- A new party called Nepali Congress born out of a merger between the Nepali National Congress (B.P. Koirala) and the Nepal Democratic Congress (M.B. Shah).
1950 (31 July)	- Treaties of peace and friendship and of trade and commerce signed with India.
1950 (5 September)	- Crown Prince Mahendra's first wife, Princess Indira Rajyalakshmi, died following a miscarriage.
1950 (24 September)	- Arrest of Nepali Congress armed volunteers in Kathmandu and of several relatives of General Subarna Shamsher and others in the army.
1950 (26-27 September)	- Nepali Congress' decision at Bargania in northern Bihar to launch a movement for the establishment of democracy in Nepal.

1950 (6 November)	- King Tribhuvan, accompanied by his two queens, three sons two daughters-in-law and a grandson, sought asylum in the Indian Embassy in Kathmandu.
1950 (7 November)	- Prince Gyanendra crowned King at Kathmandu.
1950 (11 November)	- King Tribhuvan and other members of the royal family were flown out of Kathmandu in two Indian Air Force planes.
1950 (11 November)	- Birganj captured by Nepali Congress armed volunteers.
1950 (24 November)	- Senior Commanding General Kaiser and Major-General Bijaya arrived in Delhi for talks with the Indian government.
1950 (3-7 December)	- Sir Esler Dening and Sir Frank Roberts visit Kathmandu.
1950 (8 December)	- General Kaiser and Major-General Bijaya left for Kathmandu after calling on King Tribhuvan.
1950 (24 December)	- Maharaj Mohan proposed his own reforms to a special session of his parliament.
1950 (25 December)	- Major-General Bijaya Shamsher and Sardar Narendra Mani Dixit arrived in Delhi for second round of talks.
1951 (2 January)	- Major-General Bijaya's most revealing interview with Sir Archibald Nye, the U.K. High Commissioner in Delhi.
1951 (3 January)	- Major-General Bijaya's return to Kathmandu after tentatively accepting the Indian proposal for the return of King Tribhuvan to throne.
1951 (8 January)	- Maharaj Mohan made his second proclamation of reforms and announced reversal of parliament's decision regarding the succession of Prince Gyanendra.
1951 (10 January)	- King Tribhuvan welcomes Maharaj Mohan's proclamation of reforms.
1951 (7 February)	- Agreement known as "Delhi compromise" was hammered out under which a cabinet with equal representation for the Rana and Nepali Congress sides was to be set up under

	Maharaj Mohan Shamsher as interim Prime Minister.
1951 (18 February)	- King Tribhuvan's historical declaration expressing his resolve that "the government of our people be carried on henceforth according to a democratic constitution prepared by a constituent assembly elected on the basis of direct universal adult suffrage." His Majesty also announced a Rana-Congress joint cabinet under Maharaj Mohan Shamsher.
1951 (11 April)	- The interim constitution (also called the Interim Government Act) granted by the King to the people "on the advice of the Council of Ministers" came into effect.
1951 (12 April)	- Bharat Shamsher, a grandson of Defence Minister Babar Shamsher and leader of Gorkha Parishad, and others arrested but immediately released by a crowd of supporters who thereafter demonstrated in front of Home Minister B.P. Koirala's residence nearby. Sukul Dhoj shot to death.
1951 (14 April)	- Cabinet decision of 13 April recording the offer of the Prime Minister to resign was signed by Maharaj Mohan under duress.
1951 (6 May)	- Maharaj Mohan visited Delhi and was strongly advised by Nehru not to resign prime ministership.
1951 (10 June)	- Reconstituted cabinet replacing General Babar Shamsher by General Singh Shamsher and Bharat Mani Sharma by Surya Prasad Upadhyaya.
1951 (15-17 June)	- Prime Minister Nehru's first visit to Nepal.
1951 (September)	- D.R. Regmi held for contempt of court and T.P. Acharya, Rishikesh Shaha and other 9 opposition leaders arrested under the Public Security Act.
1951 (6 November)	- Police firing resulted in death of a student, Chiniya Kazi.
1951 (10 November)	- Home Minister B.P. Koirala speaking over Radio Nepal tendered his own resignation and

	that of all the Congress ministers demanding a homogeneous cabinet.
1951 (12 November)	- The Rana ministers resigned leaving the King free to set up a new government.
1951 (November)	- All political prisoners duly released after T.P. Acharya, Rishikesh Shaha and others were set free on 12 November.
1951 (16 November)	- First M.P. Koirala Government of the Nepali Congress was proclaimed.
1952 (22-23 January)	- Raksha Dal armed police force mutiny and escape of K.I. Singh and his men to China.
1952 (25-28 May)	- Janakpur session of the Nepali Congress.
1952 (3 June)	- Bhadrakali Mishra dismissed from cabinet.
1952 (29 June)	- First meeting of expanded advisory assembly convened and addressed by King Tribhuvan 5 days later.
1952 (14 August)	- Royal Councillor's regime established and assembly prorogued.
1952 (14 August) to 1953 (15 June)	- The Royal Councillor's regime.
1952 (10 December)	- Marriage of Crown Prince Mahendra to his deceased wife's sister, Ratna Rajyalakshmi.
1953 (29 May)	- Mount Everest climbed by Edmund Hillary and Tenzing Norgay.
1953 (15 June) to	- Second M.P. Koirala government of the Rashtriya Praja.
1954 (18 February)	Party (National People's Party).
1953 (21 September)	- King Tribhuvan left for Europe for medical treatment after setting up a Regency Council consisting of his two queens and Crown Prince Mahendra.
1954 (18 February)	- Four-party coalition cabinet called a "national cabinet"
to 1955 (2 March)	under the Prime Ministership of Matrika Prasad Koirala.
1954 (28 May)	- Demonstration in Kathmandu against Indian Parliamentary Mission.
1954 (1 June – 17 August)	- Session of Advisory Assembly.
1954 (September)	- Demonstrations by Jana Adhikar Suraksha

	Samiti as "Anti-Indian Interference Day."
1954	- Arrest of General Mrigendra of Gorkha Parishad and his associates notwithstanding the repeated release order of the Supreme Court.
1954 (12 June)	- American Ambassador George Allen's visit to Nepal.
1954 (25 September)	- 3-member-Regency Council consisting of Crown Prince Mahendra and his two brothers announced but King Tribhuvan's departure was delayed owing to intra-cabinet dissensions.
1954 (3 October)	- King Tribhuvan's departure for Switzerland for more medical treatment.
1955 (10 January)	- Nepali Congress procession led by General Subarna Shamsher and joined by Jana Adhikar Suraksha Samiti assured by Crown Prince Mahendra that their demands would be fulfilled.
1955 (30 January)	- Budget session of the Advisory Assembly adopted two amendments rejecting two demands for grants for the Foreign Ministry; M.P. Koirala submitted resignation of the national cabinet and the Regency Council agreed to a month's adjournment of the Advisory Assembly.
1955 (9 February)	- Crown Prince Mahendra left for Europe after ordering the dismissal of Tanka Prasad Acharya and Bhadrakali Mishra from cabinet.
1955 (18 February)	- King Tribhuvan's message delegating full royal powers to Crown Prince broadcast over Radio Nepal. Regency Council was dissolved.
1955 (2 March)	- Crown Prince Mahendra accepted the resignation of M.P. Koirala and his cabinet.
1955 (13 March)	- Death of King Tribhuvan in Zurich, Switzerland and accession of King Mahendra Bikram Shah Dev.
1955-1972	- Reign of King Mahendra Bikram Shah Dev.
1972 (31 January)	- Death of King Mahendra Bikram Shah Dev and accession of King Birendra Bikram Shah Dev.

Appendices

Genealogies

These genealogies are not complete and are meant merely to show the relations between individuals figuring in the narrative. The charts are primarily based on the tables in Perceval Landon, *Nepal*, 2 Volumes, London: Constable and Co., 1928; Baburam Acharya, *Prithvinarayan Shahko Samkshipta Jivani,* 4 Volumes, Kathmandu: Royal Palace Secretariat, 1967/1968; Ludwig Stiller, *The Silent Cry etc.*, Kathmandu: Sahayogi, 1976; Bhim Bahadur Pande, *Rastrabhaktiko Jhalak*, Kathmandu: Ratna Pustak Bhandar, 1977/1978; John Whelpton, *Kings, Soldiers and Priests etc*. New Delhi: Manohar, 1991.

Appendix 1
SHAH (RULING HOUSE OF NEPAL) THE REGNAL YEARS FOLLOW NAMES OF KINGS

GENEALOGY OF THE SHAH DYNASTY

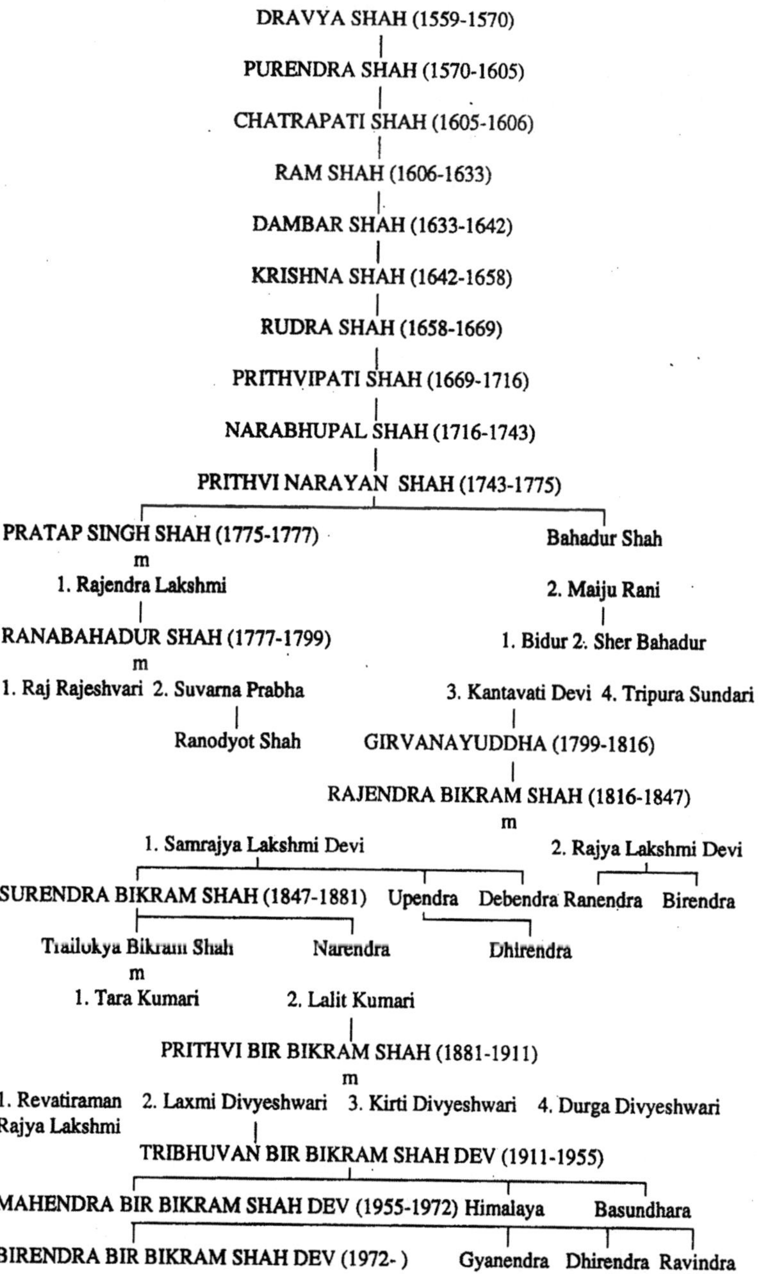

N.B.

A. Two of Maharaj Jang Bahadur Rana's daughters, Tarakumari and Lalitkumari were married to Heir Apparent Trailokya Bikram Shah.

B. Two of Maharaj Bir Shamsher Rana's daughters, Kirtidivyeshvari and Durgadivyeshvari were married to King Prithvi Bir Bikram Shah Dev.

C. Two of the daughters of General Hari Shamsher Rana, son of Maharaj Juddha Shamsher Rana, were married to King Mahendra Bikram Shah Dev and two of the daughters of General Nara Shamsher Rana, son of General Bahadur Shamsher Rana and grandson of Maharaj Juddha Shamsher Rana, Princep and Helen were married to Prince Himalaya and Prince Basundhara

D. Three daughters of General Kendra Shamsher Rana, son of General Agni Shamsher Rana and grandson of Maharaj Juddha Shamsher Rana, Aishvaryarajyalakshmi, Komalrajyalakshmi and Preksharajyalakshmi were married to King Birendra Bikram Shah Dev and Prince Gyanendra and Prince Dhirendra.

Appendix 2
GENEALOGY OF THE RANA FAMILY

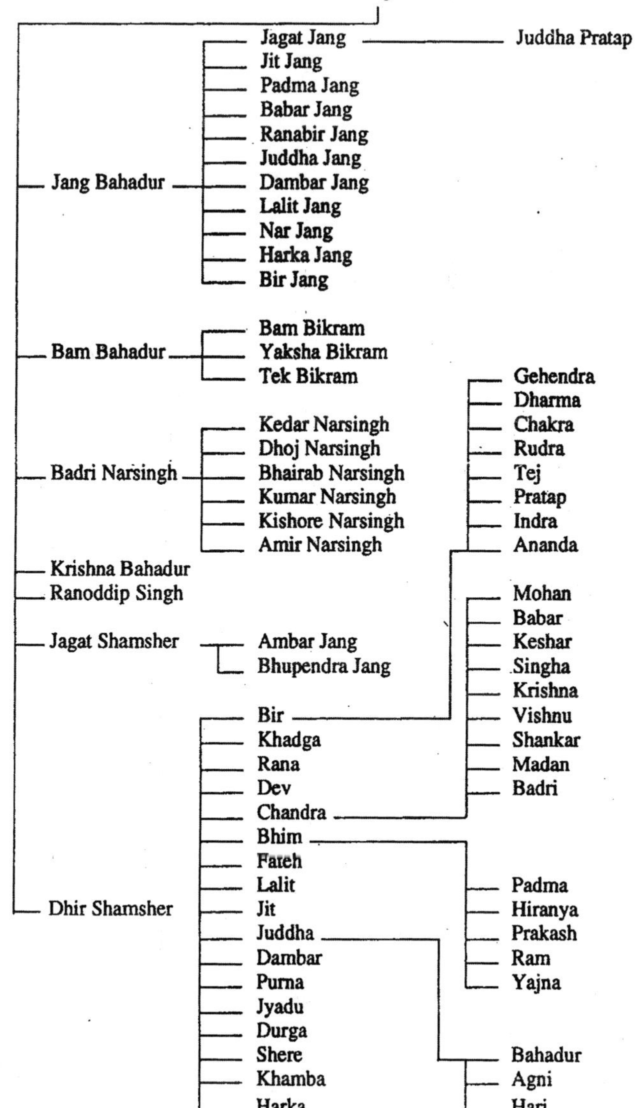

Appendix 3

KANWAR (JANG BAHADUR)

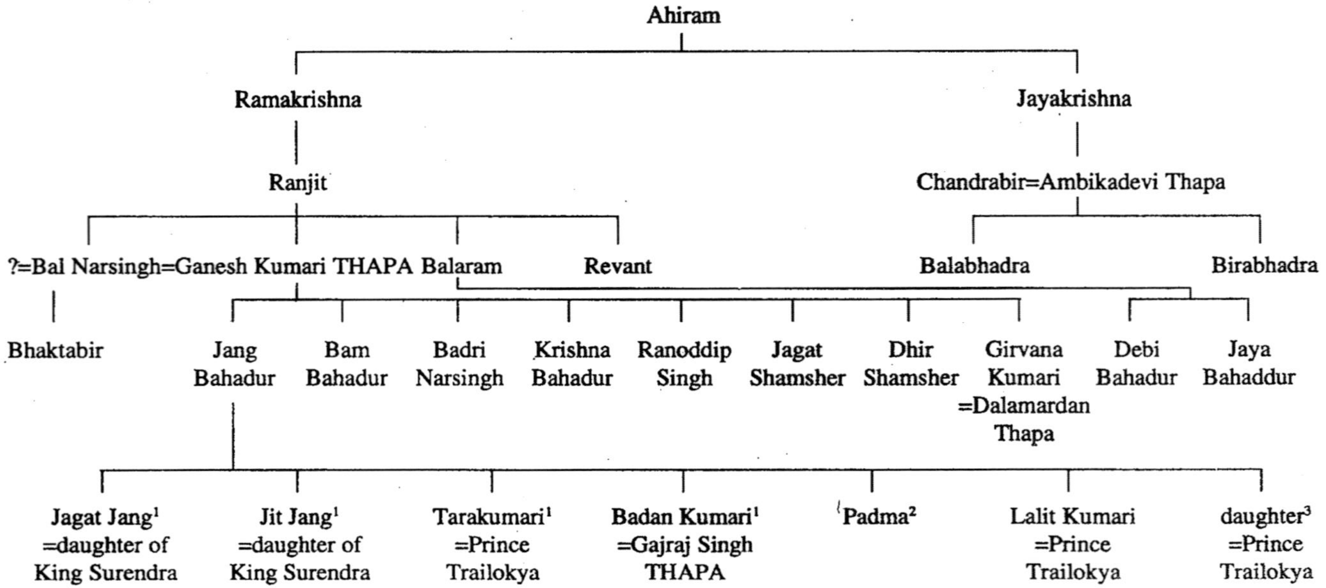

Ahiram

- Ramakrishna
  - Ranjit
    - ?=Bal Narsingh=Ganesh Kumari THAPA
      - (by ?) Bhaktabir
      - (by Ganesh Kumari THAPA) Jang Bahadur, Bam Bahadur, Badri Narsingh, Krishna Bahadur, Ranoddip Singh, Jagat Shamsher, Dhir Shamsher, Girvana Kumari =Dalamardan Thapa
    - Balaram
      - Debi Bahadur, Jaya Bahaddur
    - Revant
- Jayakrishna
  - Chandrabir=Ambikadevi Thapa
    - Balabhadra
    - Birabhadra

Children of Jang Bahadur:

Jagat Jang[1] =daughter of King Surendra | Jit Jang[1] =daughter of King Surendra | Tarakumari[1] =Prince Trailokya | Badan Kumari[1] =Gajraj Singh THAPA | Padma[2] | Lalit Kumari =Prince Trailokya | daughter[3] =Prince Trailokya

1. Children by Nanda Kumari Devi, sister of Sanak Singh Sripali Tandan Khatri, married in 1841.
2. Son by daughter of Ranasher Shah.
3. Daughter of Hiranyagarbha Kumari Shah.

Appendix 4

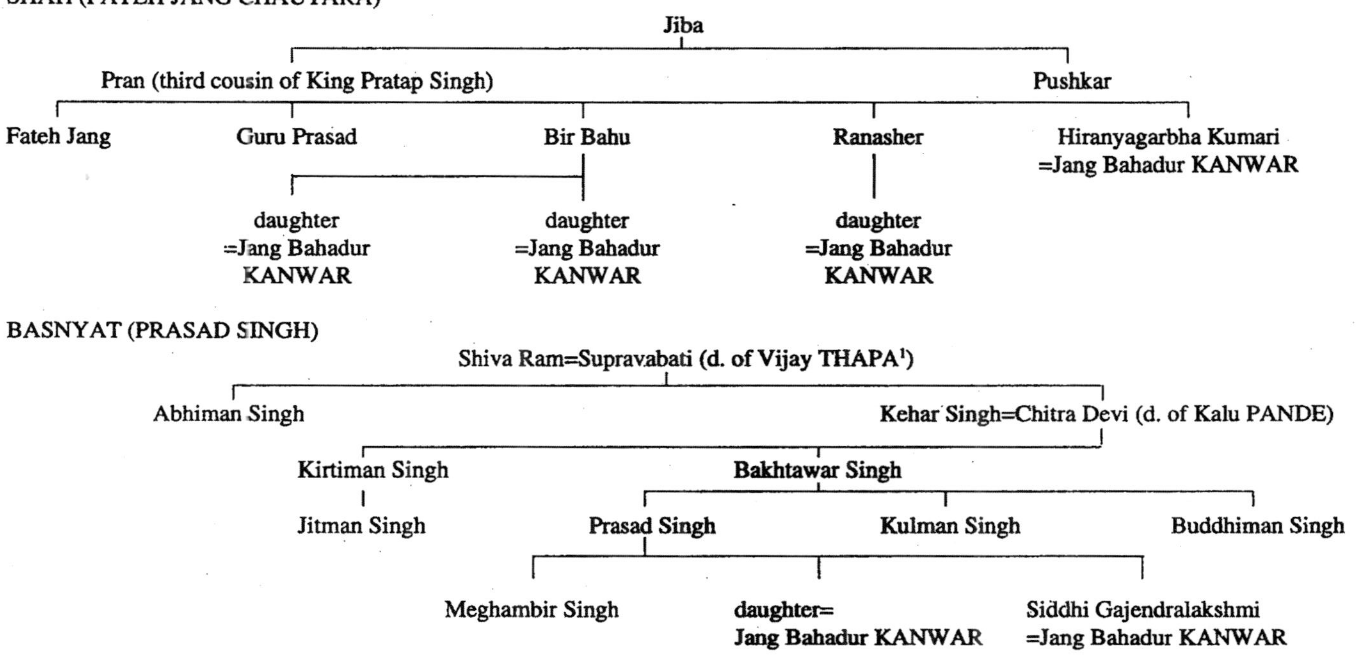

1. Great-great-grandfather of Bhimsen THAPA

Appendix 5

PANDE (KHAS/CHETRI)

(I) 'GORA' PANDE (DALABHANJAN)

- **Tularam**
  - Jagjit
    - Dalabhanjan
    - Singh Bir
  - **Ranjit**
    - Bir Keshar
      - Uday Bahadur =Lalit Kumari THAPA
      - Shamsher Bahadur =Janak Kumari THAPA
    - **Ranakumari= Nain Singh THAPA**
  - Bhotu
    - Garuda Dhoj
      - Dal Bahadur =Dirgha Kumari THAPA

(II) 'KALA' PANDE (RANJANG)

- **Kalu**
  - Bamsaraj
  - Ranasur
    - Shamsher Singh
      - **Kulraj**
  - **Damodar**
    - **Ran Keshar**
      - **Jagat Bam**
    - **Jang Keshar**
    - Karbir
    - Ranajang
    - Ranadal

Appendix 6

THAPA

(I) BHIMSEN

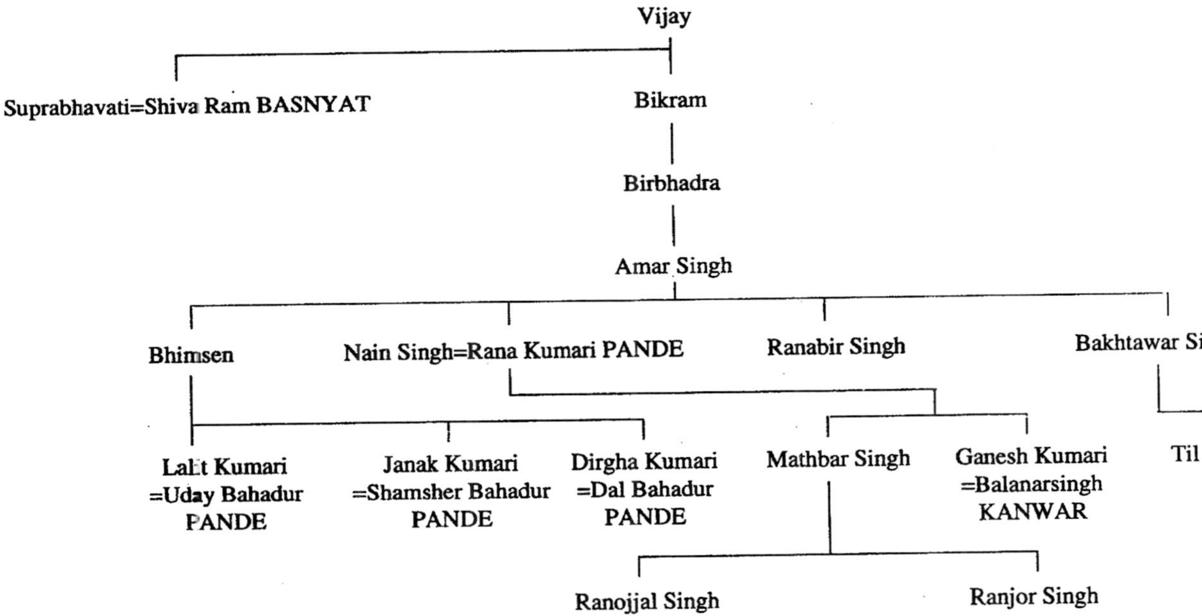

Appendix 7

(II) KAZI AMAR SINGH

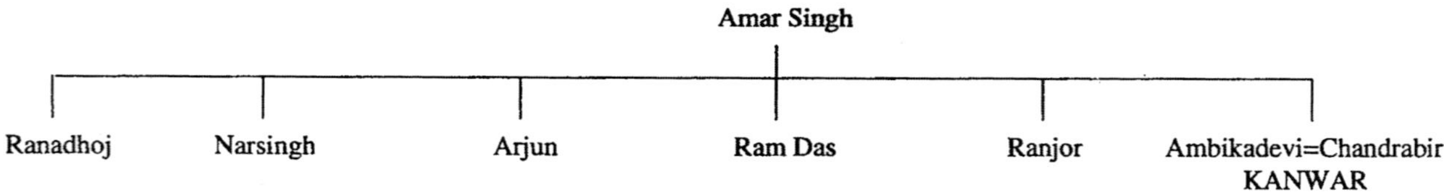

(III) HEMDAL SINGH

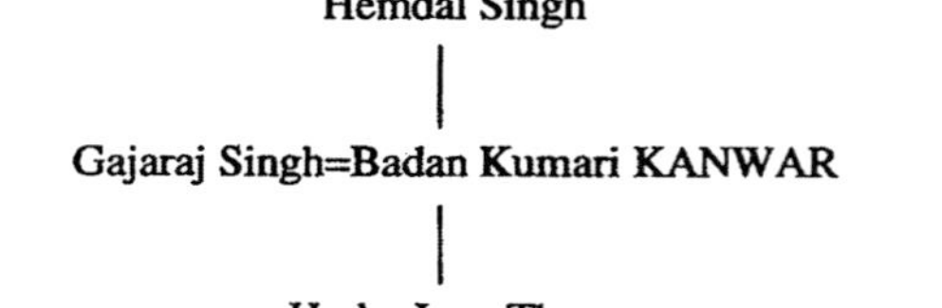

Appendix 8

THE GURU FAMILIES

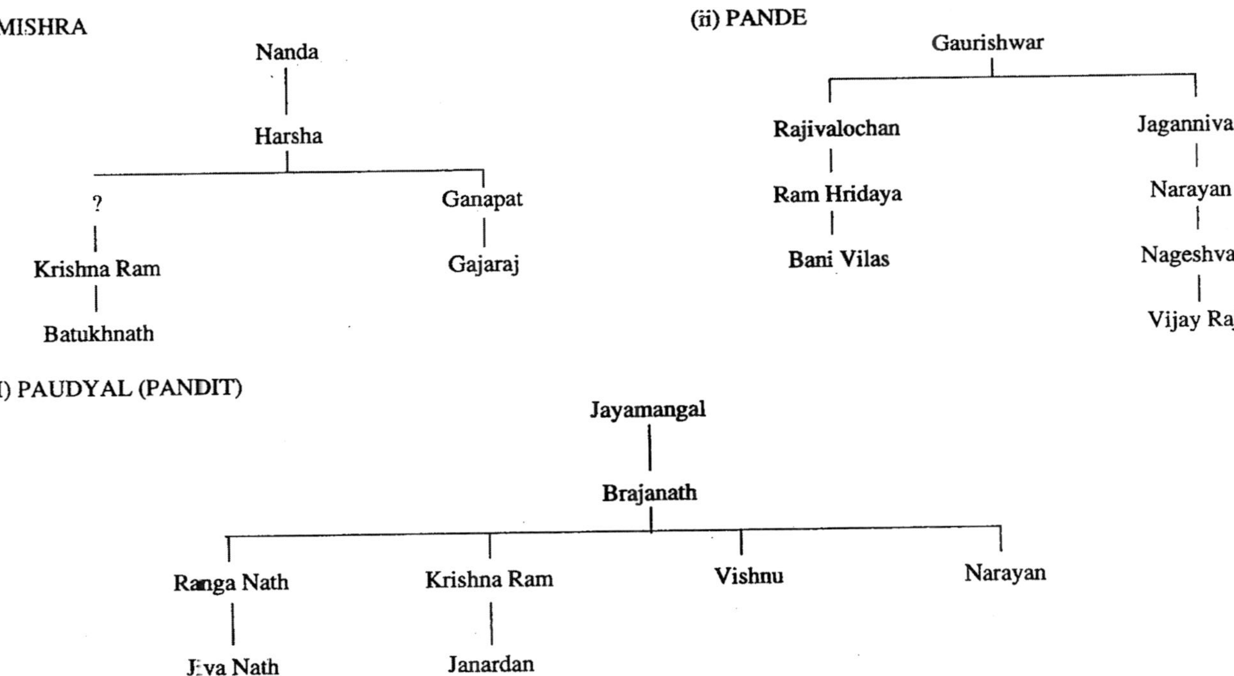

Bibliography

Western Languages

Adhikari, Krishna Kant. *Nepal under Jang Bahadur 1846-1877*, Vol. 1. Kathmandu: 'Buku', 1984.

Agarwal, Hem Narayan. *The Administrative System of Nepal. From Tradition to Modernity*. Delhi: Vikash, 1976.

Aitchison, C.U. *A Collection of Treaties, Engagements, and Sunnuds Relating to India and Neighbouring Countires*. Vols. I (1862), II (1863), V (1864) and XIV (1929), Calcutta.

Allen, Michael. *The Cult of Kumari–Virgin Worship in Nepal*. Kathmandu: University Press, 1975.

Ballantine, Henry. *On India's Frontier or Nepal. The Gurkhas' Mysterious Land*. London: Redway, 1896.

Berreman, Gerald. *Hindus of the Himalayas*. Berkeley: University of California Press, 1963.

Bhasin, A.S. *Documents on Nepal's Relations with India and China (1946-66)*. Bombay: Academic Books, 1970.

Bhattacharjee, G.P. *India and the Politics of Modern Nepal*. Calcutta: Minerva Associates, 1970.

Bista, Dor Bahadur. *The People of Nepal*. Kathmandu: Department of Publicity, 1967.

Cammann, Schuyler. *Trade Through the Himalayas: The Early British Attempts to Open Tibet*. Princeton, N.J.: Princeton University Press, 1951.

Caplan, Lionel, *Land and Social Change in East Nepal: A Study of Hindu Tribal Relations*. London: Routledge and Kegan Paul, 1970.

Chatterji, Bhola. *A Study of Recent Nepalese Politics*. Calcutta: World Press, 1967.

Chaudhuri, K.C. *Anglo-Nepalese Relations*. Calcutta: Modern Book Agency, 1960.

Chauhan, R.S. *Political Development in Nepal, 1950-70*. New Delhi: Associated Publishing House, 1970.

Davis, Hassoldt. *Nepal, Land of Mystery*. London: Robert Hale, 1942.

Digby, William, 1857. *A Friend in Need: 1887, Friendship Forgotten: An Episode in Indian Foreign Office Administration*. London: Indian Political Agency, 1890.

Edwardes, Sir Herbert Benjamin and Merivale, Herman. *Life of Sir Henry Lawrence*, Vols. I and II, London: Smith, Elder and Co. 1872.

Egerton, Francis. *Journal of a Winter's Tour in India: With a Visit to the Court of Nepal*. London: John Murray, 1852, 2 Vols.

Gaige, Frederick H. *Regionalism and National Unity in Nepal*. Berkeley, Los Angeles, London: University of California Press, 1975.

Furer-Haimendorf, Christoph von. *The Sherpas of Nepal: Buddhist Highlanders*. Berkeley: University of California Press, 1964.

———, *Himalayan Traders*. London: John Murray, 1976.

Goodall, Merill, R. 'Administrative Changes in Nepal', Chapter 10 in Braibanti (ed.), *Asian Bureaucratic Systems Emergent from the British Imperial Tradition*. Durban, N.C.: Duke University Press, 1966, pp. 605-42.

Goyal, Narendra. *The King and His Constitution: Observation and Commentary on the Constitution of the Kingdom of Nepal*. New Delhi: Nepal Trading Corporation, 1959.

———, *Political History of Himalayan States–India's Relations with Himalayan States Since 1947*. New Delhi: Cambridge Book and Stationery Stores, 1964. (2nd edition).

Gupta, A. *Politics in Nepal: A Study of Post-Rana Political Developments and Party Politics*. Bombay: Allied Publishers, 1964.

Hagen, Toni. *Nepal, the Kingdom in the Himalayas*. Berne: Kummerly and Frey, Geographical Publishers, 1961.

Hamilton, Francis (Buchanan). *An Account of the Kingdom of Nepal and of the Territories Annexed to this Dominion by the House of Gurkha*. Edinburgh: Archibald Constable and Co., 1819.

Harris, George L., *et al*. U.S. *Army Areas Handbook for Nepal (With Sikkim and Bhutan)*. Washington: Government Printing Offce, 1964.

Hasrat, Bikrama Jit, ed. *History of Nepal as Told by its Own and Contemporary Chroniclers*. Hoshiarpur: V.V. Research Institute Press, 1970.

Hitchcock, John T. *The Magars of Banyan Hill*, New York: Hold, Rinehart and Winston, 1966.

Hodgson, Brian Houghton. *Essays on the Languages, Litrature, and Religion of Nepal and Tibet, Together with Further Papers on the Geography, Ethnology, and Commerce of Those Countries*, London: Trubner, 1874.

Hunter, William Wilson. *Life of Brian Houghton Hodgson: British Resident at the Court of Nepal*. London: John Murray, 1896.

Husain, Asad. *British India's Relations with the Kingdom of Nepal*, London: George Allen and Unwin, 1970.

Jain, M.S. *Emergence of a New Aristocracy in Nepal (1837-58)*. Agra: Sri Ram Mehta and Co., 1972.

Joshi, Bhuwan Lal and Leo E. Rose. *Democratic Innovations in Nepal: A Case Study of Political Acculturation*. Berkeley: University of California Press, 1966.

Kirkpatrick, W. *An Account of the Kingdom of Nepal (being the substance of observations made during a mission to the country in the year 1793)*, London. William Miller, 1811.

Kramrisch, Stella. *The Art of Nepal*. New York: The Asia Society, Inc., 1964.

Krishnamurti, Y.G. *His Majesty King Mahendra Bir Bikram Shaha Deva: An Analytical Biography*. Bombay: The Nityanand Society, no date.

Kumar, Satish, *Rana Polity in Nepal: Origin and Growth*. Bombay: Asia Publishing House, 1967.

Landon, Perceval, *Nepal*. London: Constable and Co., 1928, 2 Vols.

Levi, Sylvain. *Le Nepal: Etude Historique d'un Royaume Hindion*. Paris: Ernest Leroux, 1905, 1908. Annales du Musee Guimet; Bibliotheque d'etudes, Tomes XVII, XVIII, and XIX.

Locke, John K., *Karunamaya – The Cult of Avalokitesvara – Matsyendranath in the Valley of Nepal*. Kathmandu: University Press, 1975.

——— *Buddhist Monasteries of Nepal*. Kathmandu, Sahayogi Press, 1985.

Manandhar, Tri Ratna. *Some Aspects of Rana Rule in Nepal*. Kathmandu: Purna Devi Manandhar, 1983.

Markham. Clements R. *Narratives of the Mission of George Bogle to Tibet and of the Journey of Thomas Manning to Lhasa*. London: Trubner, 1879.

Mihaly, Eugene Bramer. *Foreign Aid and Politics in Nepal: A Case Study*. London: Oxford University Press, 1965.

Mojumdar, Kanchanmoy. *Political Relations between India and Nepal (1877-1923)*. Delhi: Munshiram Manoharlal, 1973.

———. *Anglo-Napalese Relations in the Nineteenth Century*. Calcutta: Firma K.L. Mukhopadhyay, 1973.

———. *Nepal and the Indian Nationalist Movement*. Calcutta: Firma K.L . Mukhopadhyay, 1975.

Muni, S.D. *Foreign Policy of Nepal*. Delhi: National Publishing House, 1973.

Northey, W. Brook, and Morris, C.J. *The Gurkhas, their Manners, Customs and Country*. London: John Lane, 1928.

Oldfield, H.A. *Sketches from Nepal*. London: W.H. Allen and Co., 1880, 2 Vols.

Pemble, John. *The Invasion of Nepal: John Company at War*. Oxford: Clarendon Press 1971.

Petech, Luciano. *Medieval History of Nepal (c. 750-1490)*. Rome: Institute Italiano Per II Medio Estremo Oriente, 1958.

Prasad, Ishwari. *The Life and Times of Maharaja Juddha Shumsher Jung Bahadur Rana of Nepal*. New Delhi: Asia Publishing House, 1975.

Prinsep, Henry T. *A Narrative of the Political and Military Transactions of British India, Under the Administration of the Marquess of Hastings (1813-1818)*, Chapters II and V. London: John Murray, 1820.

Ramakant. *Indo-Napalese Relations 1868-1877*. Delhi: S. Chand and Co., 1968.

Rana, Pramode Shumshere. *Rana Nepal An Insider's View* (with a foreword by Professor M.R. Allen, University of Sydney, Australia). Kathmandu: Sahayogi Press, 1978.

Rana, Pudma Jung Bahadur (ed. A.C. Mukherji). *Life of Maharaja Sir Jung Bahadur of Nepal*. Allahabad: Pioneer Press, 1909.

Reed, Horace, B. and Marry I. Reed. *Nepal in Transition: Educational Innovation*. University of Pittsburgh Press, 1968.

Regmi, Dilli Raman. *A Century of Family Autocracy in Nepal*. Banaras: *Nepali National Congress*, 1950.

———. *Modern Nepal*. Calcutta:Firma K.L. Mukhopadhyay, 1961.

———. *Modern Nepal: Rise and Growth in the Eighteenth Century.* Vol. I, Calcutta: Firma K.L. Mukhopadhyay, 1975.

———. *Modern Nepal.* Vol. II, Calcutta : Firma K.L. Mukhopadhyay, 1975.

Regmi, Mahesh C. *Land Tenure and Taxation in Nepal.* Berkeley: Institute of International Studies, Univesity of California, 1963-68, 4 Vols.

———. *A Study in Nepali Economic History (1768-1846).* New Delhi: Manjusri Publishing House, 1971.

———. *Landownership in Nepal.* Berkeley, Los Angeles, London: University of California Press, 1976.

———. *Thatched Huts and Stucco Palaces: Peasant and Landlord in the Nineteenth Century Nepal.* New Delhi: Vikas, 1979.

Rose, Leo, E. 'Communism under High Atmospheric Conditions: The Party in Nepal', in Scalapino (ed.), *Comparative Communism in Asia.* New York: Prentice-Hall, 1965.

———. *Nepal—Strategy for Survival.* Berkeley: University of California Press, 1971.

———. *Nepal: Government and Politics.* New Haven: Human Relations Area Files, 1956.

Rose, Leo, E. and Margaret W. Fisher, *The Politics of Nepal: Persistence and Change in an Asian Monarchy.* Ithaca: Cornell University Press, 1970.

———. *England, India, Nepal, Tibet, China, 1765-1958.* Berkeley: University of California Press, June 1959.

Sanwal, B.D. *Nepal and the East India Company.* Bombay: Asia Publishing House, 1965.

Shaha, Rishikesh, *Nepal and the World*, 3rd edition. Kathmandu: Naya Nepal Prakashan, 1962.

———. *Heroes and Builders of Nepal*, 5th reprint. Calcutta: Oxford University Press, 1970.

———. *Nepali Politics: Retrospect and Prospect*, 2nd edition. Delhi: Oxford University Press, 1978.

———. *An Introduction to Nepal.* Kathmandu: Ratna Pustak Bhandar, 1975.

———. *Essays in the Practice of Government in Nepal.* Delhi: Manohar, 1982.

Slusser, Mary Shepherd. *Nepal Mandala – A Cultural Study of the Kathmandu Valley.* Princeton, N.J.: Princeton University Press, 1983.

Snellgrove, David. *Buddhist Himalaya: Travels and Studies in Quest of the Origins and Nature of Tibetan Religion*. New York: Philosophical Library, 1958.

———. *Indo-Tibetan Buddhism*, Indian Buddhists and their Tibetan Successors, 2 vols. Boston: Shambhala, 1987.

———. *Himalayan Pilgrimage: A Study of Tibetan Religion*. Oxford Bruno Cassirer, 1961.

Stiller, L.F. *Prithwinarayan Shah in the Light of Dibya Upadesh*. Ranchi: The Catholic Press, 1968.

———. *The Rise of the House of Gorkha: A Study in the Unification of Nepal*. New Delhi: Manjusri Publishing House, 1973.

———. *The Silent Cry: The People of Nepal (1816-1839)*. Kathmandu: Sahayogi Press, 1976.

———. (ed.) *Letters from Kathmandu: The Kot Massacre*. Kirtipur, Kathmandu: Research Centre for Nepal and Asian Studies, 1981.

Tucci, Giuseppe, *Nepal: The Discovery of the Malla*. London: George Allen and Unwin, 1962.

Tuker, Francis. *Gorkha, the Story of the Gurkhas of Nepal*. London: Constable and Co., 1957.

———. *While Memory Serves*, App. VIII, pp. 624-46. London, Cassel, 1950.

Uprety, Prem R. *Nepal: A Small Nation in the Vortex of International Conflicts, 1900-1950*. Kathmandu: Pugo Mi, no date.

Whelpton, John. *Jang Bahadur in Europe*. (with an introduction by Rishikesh Shaha), Kathmandu: Sahayogi Press, 1983.

Wright, Daniel, *History of Nepal*. Cambridge University Press, 1879.

Nepali Language: Unless Otherwise Specified

Acharya, Baburam. "Rana Sahi ra Shadyantra" (Rana Rule and Conspiracy), *Sharada*, XXI:5, V.E. 2013 (1957 A.D.), 1-8.

———. "Aitihasik Patra" (Historical Letter), *Purushartha*, I:1, Pous 2006 V.E. (December 1949-January 1950 A.D.), 11-13.

———. "Bhimsen Thapa ko Patan" (The Downfall of Bhimsen Thapa), *Pragati*, II:4 (1957), 115-123.

———. *China ra Tibet Sita Nepal ko Sambandha* (Nepal's Relations with China and Tibet). Kathmandu: Jorganesh Press, 1958. 35 pp.

———. "Sri Sri Jaya Prakash Malla", *Pragati*, 3, No. 1 (1958), 35-85.

———. "Bhimsen Thapa ko Utthan" (The Rise of Bhimsen Thapa), *Rup-Rekha*, V.E. 2017 (January-February, 1961), 5 pp.

———. "Janaral Bhim Sen Thapa ko Parakram ra Unle Samarjang Kampani lai Diyeko Danda" (Gen. Bhimsen Thapa's Prowess and the Punishment Meted Out by Him to the Samar Jang Company), *Arti*, Baisakh, (V.E.) 2024 (April 1967), 3-11.

———. *Nepal ko Samkshipta Vritanta* (A Brief Account of Nepal). Kathmandu: Pramod Shamsher and Nir Bikram Pyasi, 1964. 152 pp.

———. *Prithvinarayan Shah ko Sankshipta Jivani* (A short Biography of Prithvinarayan Shah), 4 Vols. Kathmandu: Royal Press Secretariat, 1967-1968. 843 pp.

———. *Baburam Acharya ra Uhanka Kirti.* Kathmandu: Institute of Nepal and Asian Studies, 1973. 148 pp.

Acharya Dixit. Keshar Mani. "Girvana Yuddha Bir Bikram Lai Bharat Bata Nepali Vakil ko Patra" (Letter from the Nepali Vakil in India to Girvana Yuddha Bir Bikram), *Sanskrit Sandesh*, I:9, 38-43.

Agrawal, Basudev Sharan. "Himalaya, Ganga ra Nepal" (Himalayas, the Ganges and Nepal), *Sanskritik Parishad Patra*, I:1 (1952), 17-20.

Bajracharya, Ḍhanabajra *et al.* (eds.). *Aitihasik Patra Sangraha* (A Collection of Historical Letters), Part I. Kathmandu: Nepal Samskritik Parishad, 1957. 110 pp.

———. "Girvan Yuddha Bir Bikram Shah Lai Amar Singh Thapa ko Patra" (Amar Singh Thapa's Letter to Girvana Yuddha Bir Bikram Shah) *Sanskrit Sandesh*, I:7, pp. 22-26, I:8, 35-38: and I:9, 31-34).

———. *Triratna Saundarya Gatha* (An Account of the Beauty of the Three Jewels). Kathmandu: Nepal Cultural Council, 1963. 317 pp.

Bhandari, Dhundiraj. *Nepal ko Aitihasik Vivechana* (Historical Analysis of Nepal), Banaras: Krishna Kumari, 1958. 368 pp.

Bisht, Som Dhwaj, *Shahi Sainik Itihas* (History of the Royal Army). Kathmandu: G.N.J. Shah and N.M.S. Basnyat, V.E. 2020 (1963 A.D.)

Dixit, Kamal (ed.). *Jang Bahadur ko Bilayet Yatra* (Jang Bahadur's Trip to England). Kathmandu: Madan Library, V.E. 2014 (1957 A.D.). 57 pp.

———. *Janga Gita* (Song of Jang). Lalitpur: Jagadamba Prakashan, 1983. 162 pp.

———. *Chandra Jyoti* (Light of Chandra), Lalitpur: Jagadamba Prakashan, 1984. 208 pp.

Giri, Tulsi. "Bharat-Birodhi Kaun, Nepal-Prem Kya" (who is Anti-India, What does Love for Nepal mean?) *Nepal Sandesh* (Hindi), Poush 17, 2023) (January 1, 1967)

Gorkha Vamsavali (The Chronicles of the Gorkha Kings). Banaras: Yoga Pracharini, V.E. 2009 (1952 A.D.). 144 pp.

Itihas Prakash (Lights on History). Kathmandu: Nepal Press, 1955-56, 4 Vols., paged separately.

Itihas-Samsodhan (History Corrections). A valuable series pamphlets published by various Nepali historians and Sanskrit Scholars. Contributors included Dhanabajra Bajracharya, Gautam Bajra Bajracharya, Akrur Kuwinkel, Babu Ram Nepal, Jnan Mani Nepal, Mahesh Raj Pant, Bhola Nath Poudel, Naya Nath Poudel, Mohan Nath Pandey, Shyam Raj Pokhrel, Laxman Satyal, Aishwarya Dhar Sharma, Kumar Dhar Sharma, Ghana Shyam Subedi and Maheshwar Raj Subedi, 1955-58.

Jnawali, Surya Bikram. *Amar Singh Thapa* (Hindi). Darjeeling: Ratnakar Press, 1951, 230 pp.

———. *Nepali Birharu* (Nepali Heroes). Darjeeling: Nepali Sahitya Sammelan, 1951. 87 pp.

———. *Rama Shah ko Jivan Charitra* (A Biography of Rama Shah). Darjeeling, 1933. 25 pp.

———. *Nepal Upatyakako Madhya Kalin Itihas* (Medieval History of the Nepal Valley). Kathmandu: Royal Nepal Academy, V.E. 2019 (1962 A.D.). 338 pp.

———. *Nepal Vijeta Shri Panch Prithvi Narayan Shah ko Jivani* (Life of King Prithvi Narayan Shah, the Conqueror of Nepal). Darjeeling. 1935.

Joshi, Satya Mohan. "Chini Nepali Samskritik Sambandha" (Sino-Napalese Cultural Relations), *Gorkhapatra*, September 23, 1960.

Lal, Manik. "Rana Haruko Nijamati Prashasan Pranali" (The Civil Administration System of the Ranas). Unpublished. Ms. 23 pp.

Lal, Shyam Bihari. "Nepal ko Baideshik Byapar ma Ek Adhyayan" (A Study in Nepal's Foreign Trade), *Byapar Patrika*, Vol. 2, No.7, Kartik, V.E. 2021 (October-November 1964).

Naraharinath, Yogi. *Gorkhaliharu ko Sainik Itihas* (Military History of the Gorkhas). Kathmandu: Annapurna Press, 1954. 24 pp.

———. *Itihas Prakash ma Sandhi Patra Sangraha* (A Collection of Treaties in the Illumination of History), Kathmandu, V.E. 2022 (1966). Published on the occasion of the Spiritual Conference convened at Dang. 786 pp.

———, and Baburam Acharya. *Sri Panch Bada Maharaj Prithvi Narayan Shah ko Divya Upadesh* (Divine Counsel of King Prithivi Narayan Shah the Great). Kathmandu: Shri Bagiswar Press, 1953. 38 pp.

Nepal-China Friendship Association. *Miteri Gantho* (Ties of Friendship). (A Collection of Articles on Nepal-China Friendship). Kathmandu, 1963. 41 pp.

Nepali, Chitta Ranjan. "Chautariya Bahadur Shah ko Nayabi Kal" (The Period of the Nayabship of Chautaria Bahadur Shah), *Sharada*, XXII:1, V.E. 2014 (1957 A.D.), 21-29.

———. *Janaral Bhimsen Thapa ra Tatkalin Nepal* (General Bhim Sen Thapa and the Nepal of His Day). Kathmandu: Jorganesh Press, 1957, 334 pp.

———. "Vartaman Nepal ko Nirmanma Sri Panch Prithvi Narayan Shah" (King Prithvi Narayan Shah's Role in the Building of Modern Nepal). *Pragati*, Year 3, Issue 2 (n.d.), 78-110.

———. "Nepal-Chin Yuddha", (Nepal-China War), *Sharada*, XXI:1, V.E. 2013 (1956 A.D.), 202-16.

———. "Nepal ra British Gorkha Rifles" (Nepal and the British Gorkha Rifles), *Rup-Rekha*, V:4, Bhadra, V.E. 2021 (August-September, 1964), 9-16.

———. "Nepal Ra British Samrajya" (Nepal and the British Empire), *Sharada*, XXI:3, V.E. 2013 (1956 A.D.), 11-12.

———. "Nepal ra Tibet ko Sambandha" (Nepal-Tibet Relations), *Pragati*, Year II, IV:10 (n.d.), 103-15.

———. *Shri Panch Rana Bahadur Shah*. Kathmandu: Shrimati Mary Rajbhandari, 1964. 154 pp.

———. "Trayi Shashan" (Triumvirate), *Sharada*, Year 24, Issue 3, Poush, V.E. 2016 (December 1959-January 1960), 1-14.

Pande, Totra Raj and Naya Raj Pant. *Nepal ko Sankshipta Itihas* (An Abridged History of Nepal). Banaras: V.E. 2004 (1947 A.D.).

Pant, Maheshraj, "Nepal-Angrej Yudda ko Tayari" (Preparations for Anglo-Nepali War), *Purnima*, I:2, Shravan Sankranti, V.E. 2021 (July 16, 1964).

———. "The Second Stage of Anglo-Nepal War", *Purnima*, 8, Magh 1, V.E. 2022 (January 14, 1966), 41-49.

Pant, Naya Raj. "Damodar Pande Lai Ran Bahadur ko Patra" (Letter from Ran Bahadur to Damodar Pande), *Sanskrit Sandesh*, I:5, 36-43.

———. "Shree Tin Maharaj Padma Shamsher ko kura" (An Account of the History of the Rana Period as Narrated by Shree Three Maharaj Padma Shamsher in Verse), *Purnima*, No. 40, Vol.10, No.4, no date, 123 pp.

———. *et al. Shree Panch Prithvinarayan Shah ko Upadesh* (Counsel of Shri Five Prithvinarayan Shah), 4 Vols. Lalitpur: Jagadamba Prakashan, no date. 800 pp.

Poudyal, Bholanath and Dhanabajra Bajracharya (eds.). *Galli ma Fyakiyeko Kasingar–Pandit Bhavani Datta Pande le Gare ko Mud-drarakshasa Haru ka Nepali Anubad* (Letters Thrown in the Street . . . Renderings in Nepali of the Mudrarakshasa Drama and other Sanskrit Works . . .). Kathmandu: Jagdamba Prakashan, 1961. 269 pp.

Sharma, Balchandra. *Nepalko Aitihasik Rup Rekha* (An Outline of the History of Nepal). Banaras: Madav Prasad Sharma, 1951. 440 pp.

Shrestha, Baburam. "Hamro Byapar Sthiti" (Our Commercial Situation), *Gorkhapatra*, Kartik 16, V.E. 2021 (November 1, 1964).

Shrestha, K.N. "Hamro Vyapar Bastusthiti ra Vikash Path" (Facts About Our Trade and Ways of its Development), *Gorkhapatra*, Poush 11, V.E. 2021 (December 25, 1964).

Singh, Iman. *Kirat Itihas* (Kirat History). Gangtok, Sikkim, 1952. 72 pp.

Tiwari, Ramji. *et al. (eds.). Abhilekh Sangraha* (A Collection of Inscriptions). Kathmandu: Samshodhan Mandal, 1961-63, Volumes 1-9, 11, paged separately.

———. *et al. (eds.). Aitihasik Patra Sangraha (Dosro Bhag)* (Collection of Historical Documents, Part II), Kathmandu: Nepal Samskritik Parishad, V.E. 2021 (A.D. 1964). 126 pp.

———, "Vikram Samvat 1843 ma Bhayeko Kehi Mukhya Ghatana" (Some Important Events of 1786), *Purnima*, 1:2, Shravan Sankranti, V.E. 2021 (July 16, 1964).

Upadhyaya, Ramji. *Nepal ko Itihas* (History of Nepal). Banaras: Subha Hom Nath Kedar Nath, 1950.

———. *Nepal Digdarshan* (A survey of Nepali History). Banaras: Gopal Press, 1950. 486 pp.

"Vyas", "Nepal-Bharat Vyapar Sambandha, Duwai Rashtra ko Arthik Hit ko Paripati" (Nepal-India Trade Relations, A Means for the Economic Benefit of Both Nations), *Gorkhapatra*, Jestha 30, V.E. 2024 (June 13, 1967), 4-5.

Index